Beyond
la
Frontera

Beyond *la* Frontera

The History of Mexico–U.S. Migration

Edited by

MARK OVERMYER-VELÁZQUEZ
University of Connecticut

New York   Oxford

OXFORD UNIVERSITY PRESS

Oxford University Press, Inc., publishes works that further Oxford University's
objective of excellence in research, scholarship, and education.

Oxford New York
Auckland   Cape Town   Dar es Salaam   Hong Kong   Karachi
Kuala Lumpur   Madrid   Melbourne   Mexico City   Nairobi
New Delhi   Shanghai   Taipei   Toronto

With offices in
Argentina   Austria   Brazil   Chile   Czech Republic   France   Greece
Guatemala   Hungary   Italy   Japan   Poland   Portugal   Singapore
South Korea   Switzerland   Thailand   Turkey   Ukraine   Vietnam

For titles covered by Section 112 of the US Higher Education Opportunity Act,
please visit www.oup.com/us/he for the latest information about pricing
and alternate formats.

Published by Oxford University Press, Inc.
198 Madison Avenue, New York, New York 10016
www.oup.com

Oxford is a registered trademark of Oxford University Press

Library of Congress Cataloging-in-Publication Data
Beyond la frontera : the history of Mexico-U.S. migration / edited by Mark Overmyer-Velázquez.
     p. cm.
   Includes bibliographical references and index.
   ISBN 978-0-19-538222-8
1. Mexico—Emigration and immigration—History—20th century. 2. Mexico—Emigration and
immigration—Government policy—History—20th century. 3. United States—Emigration and
immigration—History—20th century. 4. United States—Emigration and immigration—Government
policy—History—20th century. 5. Migrant labor—United States—History—20th century.
6. Mexicans—United States—History—20th century. I. Overmyer-Velázquez, Mark.
E184.M5B497 2011
304.873072—dc22   2010042949

Printed in the United States of America
on acid-free paper
Cover art by Favianna Rodriguez, Favianna.com

Para mi mamá,
su familia,
y todos los migrantes mexicanos que han cruzado y vivido
más allá de la frontera.

CONTENTS

Weaponized Fences and Novel Borderings
The Beginning of a New History?

Saskia Sassen
Columbia University

One of the outstanding features of this volume is the exceptional breadth of the spaces and the times through which it constructs the Mexico–U.S. history of migrations. A theme that is explicitly or implicitly present is the border—either as an actor or as an absence that makes itself felt as a specter. When I read these chapters I cannot help but see the many different worlds that are called forth by this particular border and indeed give "the border" an ever-shifting meaning.

Today, in most of the world, a national state border is a mix of regimes with variable contents and locations. Different flows—of capital, information, professionals, undocumented workers—each constitute bordering through a particular sequence of interventions, with diverse institutional and geographic locations. The actual geographic border is part of the cross-border flow of goods if they come by ground transport, but not of capital, except if actual cash is being transported. Each border-control intervention can be conceived of as one point in a chain of locations. In the case of traded goods the chain of locations might involve a preborder inspection or certification site. In the case of capital flows the chain will involve banks and stock markets located deep inside national territory and electronic networks that function above the level of national borders. In brief, institutional points of border control intervention can form long chains moving deep inside the country. The geographic borderline is but one point in that chain.

One image we might use to capture this notion of multiple locations is that the sites for the enforcement of border regimes range from banks to bodies. When a bank executes the most elementary money transfer to another country, the bank is one of the sites for border-regime enforcement. A certified good represents a case where the object itself crossing the border is one of the sites for enforcement: the emblematic case is a certified agricultural product. But it also encompasses the case of the tourist carrying a tourist visa and the immigrant carrying the requisite certification. Indeed, in the case of immigration, it is the body of the immigrant herself that is both the carrier of much of the regime and the crucial site for enforcement; and in the case of an unauthorized immigrant, it is, again, the body of the immigrant that is the carrier of the violation of the law and of the corresponding punishment (i.e., detention or expulsion).

And yet, notwithstanding this variety, today we are seeing a collapse of diversity and a starker bipolar differentiation than the older histories described in some of these chapters. A large segment of actors, from firms to professionals, move in protected transversal bordered spaces, constructed through the suspension of older border controls and new regulations granting global firms and transnational professionals cross-border rights and guarantees of contract. These bordered spaces are impenetrable from the outside. No coyote can take you across those novel borderings. At the other extreme are the less protected, those who need to demonstrate their claim to entry, whether tourists or migrant workers, and at its most extreme, a less protected, more persecuted mix of people for whom the crossing of the border has degraded into an operation marked by the violation of their most basic rights as human beings. The cross-border space of corporations and high-level professionals is marked by protections and opportunities. The cross-border space of migrants, whether documented or not, is marked by a shift from opportunity to confinements of all sorts, at its sharpest a space of capture and detention.

In its richness and complex histories, the Mexico–U.S. border is a heuristic space: it tells a story about interstate borders much larger than the conventional and formal account of such borders. It is a type of space that makes the migrants who cross that border historic agents whose moves signal a larger history in the making. I have long thought of certain migrations as vanguards that are telling us much more than their movement from misery to (hopefully) possibility. In my own research on intra-European migrations I have found that to capture this vanguard character of particular flows, it is necessary to detect the diversity of migrations even within a particular national and geographic flow. Here these chapters make an important contribution: they show us how beneath the overall seemingly never-ending Mexican flow to and from the United States lie multiple particular histories. There are endings and there are beginnings of new flows within the overall Mexican migration with diverse geographic and temporal frames and diverse activators of these flows.

Let me elaborate on this mix of themes.

A direct effect of globalization, especially corporate economic globalization, has been the creation of increasing divergence among different border regimes. Thus, the lifting of border controls on a growing variety of capital, services, and information flows has taken place even as other border regimes maintain closure. At one extreme, impediments to particular cross-border flows are now stronger than they were in the past, as is the case with the migration of low-wage workers. At the other extreme is the construction of specific "borderings" to contain, protect, and govern emerging, often strategic or specialized, flows that cut across traditional national borders. This is the case, for instance, with the new regimes in the North American Free Trade Agreement (NAFTA) and World Trade Organization (WTO) and especially the General Agreement on Tariffs and Trade for the cross-border circulation of high-level professionals. Where in the past these professionals may have been part of a country's general immigration regime, now we have an increasing divergence between the latter and the specialized global, rather than national, regime governing these professionals, including formal cross-border *portable* rights. This is a tighter border than the geographic border and even the weaponized fence. Mexicans who move through this regime are in a space that separates them radically from Mexicans who do not—there is no option for undocumented border crossing.

If there is one avant-garde historic agent in this shifting meaning of the territorial border today, it is the multinational corporation and global finance. The formalizing of their right to cross-border mobility is producing a large number of highly protected bordered spaces that cut across the conventional border. In that sense this is a type of global actor that operates not only in some electronic domain above borders, but also deep inside national territories. The effect is a partial but strategic denationalizing of national territory. There exists an interesting parallel with the specific protections and privileges granted to foreign firms through the regime informally referred to as the maquila.

The sharp shifts from geographic borders to transversally bordered spaces inside national territories are now far more common and formalized for major corporate economic actors than they are for citizens and migrants. Neoliberal policies, far from making this a borderless world, have actually multiplied the bordered spaces that allow firms and markets to move across conventional borders with the guarantee of multiple protections as they enter national territories. In contrast, citizens and migrants keep losing protections under neoliberal regimes.

This resonates with the other asymmetry: the international human rights regime is a weaker system of protections than the WTO provisions protecting the cross-border circulation of professionals. It is also weaker, although far broader, than the specialized visas for business people and the increasingly common visas for high-tech workers. In this process, particular legal protections get detached from their national territorial jurisdictions and become incorporated into a variety of often highly specialized or partial global regimes and thereby are often transformed into far more specialized rights and obligations.

The multiple regimes that constitute the border as an institution can be grouped on the one hand into a formalized apparatus that is part of the traditional interstate system and on the other hand into an as yet far less formalized array of novel types of borderings lying largely outside the traditional framing of the interstate system. The first has at its core the body of regulations covering a variety of international flows—flows of different types of commodities, capital, people, services, and information. No matter their variety, these multiple regimes tend to cohere around (a) the state's unilateral authority to define and enforce regulations in its territory and (b) the state's obligation to respect and uphold the regulations coming out of the international treaty system or out of bilateral arrangements. The second major component, the new type of bordering dynamics arising outside the traditional interstate system, does not necessarily entail a self-evident crossing of borders; it includes the formal portable rights referred to above, which come out of the new world-trading regime instituted in the 1990s, and it includes a range of dynamics arising out of specific contemporary developments, notably emergent global law systems and a growing range of globally networked digital interactive domains.

Global law systems are not centered in state law—that is, they are to be distinguished from both national and international law. And the global digital interactive domains are mostly informal and hence outside the existing treaty system; they are often basically ensconced in subnational localities that are part of diverse cross-border networks, ranging from financial networks articulated through specific financial centers to diverse global civil society networks. The formation of these distinct systems of global law or globally networked interactive domains entails a multiplication of bordered spaces. But the national notion of borders as delimiting two sovereign territorial states is not quite in play. The bordering operates at either a trans- or a supranational or subnational scale. And although these spaces may cross national borders, they are not necessarily part of the new open-border regimes that are state centered, such as those, for instance, of the global trading system or legal immigration. Insofar as these are global bordered domains that cut across national borders, they entail a novel instance of the notion of borders.

State sovereignty is usually conceived of as a monopoly of authority in a particular territory. Today it is becoming evident that state sovereignty both articulates its own borders and accommodates novel types of borderings. Sovereignty remains as a systemic property but its institutional insertion and its capacity to do the work of legitimating have become unstable. The politics of contemporary sovereignties are far more complex than notions of mutually exclusive territories can capture.

The question of a bounded, that is, bordered territory as a parameter for authority and rights has today entered a new phase. State exclusive authority over its territory remains the prevalent mode of final authority in the global political economy; in that sense, then, state-centered border regimes—whether open or closed—remain foundational elements in world geopolitics. But these regimes are today less absolute formally than they were once meant to be. An additional factor is that critical components of this territorial authority that may still have a national institutional form and location are actually no longer national in the historically constructed sense of that term; they are, I argue, denationalized components of state authority: they look national but they are actually geared toward global agendas, some good and some not so good.

In the case of the Mexico–U.S. border, it is becoming increasingly clear that it is a zone for the operations of a vast number of actors. We can see this in a number of conditions, including the seventy-plus nationalities present in the capital ownership of the northern Mexico border maquila, the hemispheric operations of drug cartels, and the significance of U.S.-made arms shipments for border operations linked to criminal trades of drugs and of people. In my reading, what dominates this border zone is a vast mix of processes that are actually mostly functioning within the law, notably the newly enabled flows through WTO and NAFTA. In that light, what stands out as a sharply delineated insertion of something new is the weaponized "protective" fence that began to be built in the 1990s, even as NAFTA was implemented. It is this that is the deviant presence: it stands out in a space that is marked by multiple and diverse cross-border transactions.

Insofar as the state has historically had the capability to encase its territory through administrative and legal instruments, it also has the capability to change that encasement—for instance, deregulate its borders and open up to foreign firms and investment or build a weaponized fence. The question that concerns me here is whether this signals that the capabilities entailed by territoriality, a form of exclusive and final authority, can be detached from geographic territory. Such detachment is conceivably partial and variable depending on what is to be subjected to authority. This in turn raises a question about how the issue of borderings functions *inside* the nation state. The "border function" is increasingly embedded in the product, the person, the instrument: a mobile agent that endogenizes critical features of the border. Further, there are multiple locations for the border, in some cases long transnational chains of locations that can move deep inside national territorial and institutional domains, such as the already mentioned facts that in financial flows, the actual border "moment" is often deep inside a country—a bank certifying the legitimacy of a money wire—and in certified agricultural products the first border "moment" is often deep inside the country of origin, notably Mexico.

The locations of bordering capabilities are today in a phase of sharp unsettlement that opens up a whole new research agenda. The chapters in this book help us see this larger transformation through the specifics and details of the diverse times and spaces of that construction we call the "Mexico–U.S. border." It is one of the most intense border zones in the world, which makes it particularly heuristic for the larger question of bordering.

The specialized types of reterritorializing of global actors briefly described here have contributed to the making of bordered spaces inside the exclusive territory of state authority. But they are not to be confused with state authority. In that sense they denationalize what has historically been constructed as national. This is a highly bordered event, but the nature of this border is foundationally different from that of the nation-state, that is, from interstate borders. In this context it is worth noting that extraterritoriality, a specific type of state territorial authority, is now largely used by Mexico in the United States to deal with the undocumented Mexican population.

Denationalized domains inside national territories create a whole new type of internal bordering. One question for research is whether these new types of internal borderings that have emerged over the past fifteen years increasingly weaken the geographic border. Could it be that the brutal weaponizing of the Mexico–U.S. border during that same period of fifteen years represents not a new phase but a last violent move on the part of a deeply unstable notion of the border?

PREFACE

A s with many studies of migration history, *Beyond la Frontera* is inspired in part by my own migratory past. Growing up a landed immigrant in Canada to Mexican- and U.S.-born parents, I experienced in small measure some of the historical questions this volume raises. Never really "at home" in any of those three countries, I have always sought to understand national migration experiences and narratives from a variety of cross-border perspectives. Of course, it is an immense privilege to be able to study and write about the often wrenching dislocations and arduous journeys as well as formida- ble successes of migrants. As many of us are, I am very fortunate to be the beneficiary of the migrations of my family's prior generations. Thanks to my infinitely patient and supportive partner, Jordanna Hertz, my immediate family has added Eastern European via New York City to the mix. Our three precious *hijitos*, Sarai Dov, Maceo Ilan, y Adan Amichai, are constant reminders of the intersecting paths of our combined past histories.

My first serious academic inquiry into the history and historiography of Mexican migration began in 2002 when, with the mentorship of Miguel Tinker Salas, I taught a historical survey of Chicana/o history at Pomona College. Trained predominantly as a modern *mexicanista* by Gil Joseph, my south-of-the-border approach to U.S. Chicana/o and American studies forced me to confront rigid notions of *mexicanidad* and facile assumptions about the national origins of Mexican migrants. Gil's superlative schol- arship and enduring support continue to shape my scholarship. Also at Yale, Patricia Pessar and Stephen Pitti deserve my sincere appreciation for reading earlier drafts of my work and writing letters of support.

Several fellowships supported the preparation of this volume. My inchoate under- standing of Mexico's migratory past began to take form thanks to an International Migration Institute Fellowship from the Social Science Research Council, directed by Roger Waldinger. Cesar Rodriguez, Jean Silk, and Nancy Rodriguez's assistance with a Yale University Council on Latin American and Iberian Studies Library Visiting Fellowship helped to advance my work. I completed the edits on the manuscript as the Peggy Rockefeller Visiting Scholar at the David Rockefeller Center for Latin American Studies (DRCLAS) at Harvard University. Merilee Grindle, Edwin Ortiz, June Erlick,

Hal Jones, and the other staff at DRCLAS provided an ideal environment for scholarly production. I am grateful for the lively discussions with the other fellows at the Center, in particular Jorge Duany and Robert Alvarez. My semester at DRCLAS was made possible and all the more enjoyable by the generous hospitality of the familia Holladay-Wolkoff. Joshua, Mara, Elana, and Peter housed, fed, and schlepped me with ineffable charm and *cariño*.

At the University of Connecticut I have had the good fortune to benefit from financial support and a long tradition of Mexican studies. Soon after arriving to UConn one of the pioneers of Mexican studies in the United States, Hugh Hamill, invited me to his home to review his library. Among the books Dr. Hamill generously offered me from his rich collection were those of his former student and colleague Lawrence Cardoso and Arthur Corwin, authors of two of the first long-range studies of Mexico–U.S. migration. I continue to learn from each of their research. A fellowship at UConn's Humanities Institute provided me with the time to read and write and, more importantly, the camaraderie and intellectual company of Dick Brown, Charles Mahoney, Jo-Ann Waide, Michelle Bigenho, Anke Finger, Robin Greeley, and Michael Lynch. In the history department Shirley Roe, with the assistance of Nancy Comarella, made it possible for me to put together leave time for this and future projects. I am indebted to all my colleagues in the department for fostering an engaging academic home. Several graduate students helped to energize this work with their own, including José Rodriguez and Andrés Pletch. I am particularly grateful for Andrés' diligent and creative assistance with the volume's bibliography and chronology. At UConn's Center for Latin American and Caribbean Studies, Elizabeth Mahan, Beth Summers, Carolyn Golden, Carrie Stevens, and the dynamic cohort of MA students have each helped to animate this project at various stages. Many thanks go to Adriana Vega por su ayuda con la traducción excelente del capítulo tres.

Other colleagues at UConn and elsewhere have been invaluable collaborators in the genesis and development of this project. Evelyn Hu De-Hart at Brown University's Center for the Study of Race and Ethnicity in America has become a treasured mentor and guide through the institutional labyrinths of ethnic and area studies. Thanks also to José Angel Hernández and *mis compadres* Enrique Sepúlveda, Ray Craib, Rick López and Guillermo Irizarry for their insights and comments on this project. I was thrilled that Favianna Rodriguez agreed to create an original piece of art for the book. It is an honor to have her beautiful and inspirational work on the cover.

This work started with an engaging and inviting conversation with Brian Wheel from Oxford University Press. I deeply appreciate his careful collaboration and encouragement with this volume. Danniel Schoonebeek guided me through challenges of formatting and submission. Marc Becker, Truman State University; Carlos A. Contreras, Grossmont College; Ellen Eisenberg, Willamette University; Terri Turigliatto-Fahrney, Ph.D., Saint Louis University; Claude Hargrove, Fayetteville State University; Monica Rankin, University of Texas; Fernando Fabio Sanchez, Portland State University and Dr. Christopher White, Marshall University helped to shape the initial manuscript and make Beyond la Frontera a better work altogether. Final thanks go to the volume's individual authors for their carefully researched and elegantly crafted original contributions. It has been a pleasure to put together this work with them over the past three years.

LIST OF FIGURES AND TABLES

Figures

Tables

INTRODUCTION

Histories and Historiographies of Greater Mexico

Mark Overmyer-Velázquez
University of Connecticut

> "México, país de emigración."
>
> —MOISÉS GONZÁLEZ NAVARRO (1960, 95)

Mexican migration to the United States has comprised the world's largest sustained movement of migratory workers in the twentieth and twenty-first centuries.[1] As part of the post World War II massive wave of migrants from across Asia, Latin America, and the Caribbean, in recent decades Mexicans have comprised by far the largest migrant group in the United States (Waters, Ueda, and Marrow 2007; Suárez and Páez 2009). Although frequently cast as peripheral to projects of nation-state formation and consolidation, over the past 160 years Mexican migrants and migration have played central roles in the economic and political development of both countries.[2] With roots in the nineteenth century, an increased migratory flow in the first decades of the twentieth century prompted the beginning of significant

---

1. Mexico's emigrant population is part of a global total of over 214 million emigrants (United Nations 2009).

2. In this chapter I am careful to distinguish between the sets of terms *migrant* and *migration* and *immigrant* and *immigration*. The latter set can imply a unidirectional path to the United States and, as such, has been linked to a historical privileging of assimilationist and melting-pot theories that ignore both the transnational movement of people back and forth across borders and their varied national and regional claims to identity and citizenship. Unless noted otherwise, I only employ the term *immigration* when referring to official government policies or legislative or organizational titles, as in *immigrant rights laws*.

Similarly, when possible, I avoid the term *America* as a substitute for the term *United States*. Because Mexicans are also of (Latin) American heritage and descent, it is inaccurate to believe that the term *America* refers uniquely to the United States. At times, authors in the larger volume use *North American* to mean a citizen or inhabitant of the United States, although that term can also include Mexicans and Canadians. Of course, the expression "Latin America" has its own problematic colonial history; see Walter Mignolo (2005).

immigration and emigration legislation that established enduring patterns in the binational relationship between Mexico and the United States. Throughout the twentieth century and to the present day, U.S. legislators have consistently and strategically constructed the Mexican migrant first as a temporary and then as an illegal, unassimilable racialized other, a permanent outsider used to fill the critical labor demands of an expanding industrialized economy (De Genova 2005; Ngai 2004; Noel 2006).[3] For its part, Mexico, always in an asymmetrical political and economic position vis-à-vis the United States, initially used a series of uncoordinated emigration policies to attempt to *prevent* the flight of its working citizens and then during and following World War II changed its broad legislative priorities to *facilitate* an out-migration that yielded economic gains through remittances and relief from unemployment and rapid population growth.

Given the current and persistent contentiousness surrounding the issues of legal and undocumented migration in Mexican and U.S. politics, it is time for an expansive, binational historical perspective that assesses the development and impact of migratory trends and practices as they developed in Mexico and the United States since the mid-nineteenth century. The interdisciplinary chapters in this volume provide that perspective. The chapters in *Beyond la Frontera: The History of Mexico–U.S. Migration* contribute original research and expand upon nation-bound historiographies using broad, transnational historical points of view to examine the impact of migratory trends as they developed in Mexico and the United States.[4] Social scientists have produced excellent studies of contemporary migration from Mexico. Chicana/o historians and historians of Mexico mostly have either scrutinized the arrival and adaptation of Mexican citizens to the United States (the only significant destination for Mexican migrants) or focused largely on the history of the people confined to Mexico's national territory. Yet, the migrants' departure from Mexico (up to 11 percent of its citizens have left) has been largely neglected and requires long-range historical studies.[5] Although some works analyze select periods and themes of this protracted binational relationship, none provides the critical synthesis necessary for understanding

---

3. For a study of comparative cases in Western Europe, see Lucassen (2005).

4. As Erika Lee (2003) has demonstrated, transnational frames help to explain national dynamics. Schiller et al. (1992) define transnationalism as a "social process in which migrants establish social fields that cross geographic, cultural, and political borders" (ix). In "Transmigrants and Nation-States," Nina Glick Schiller fine tunes the definition: "Even as migrants invest socially, economically, and politically in their new society, they continue to participate in the daily life of the society from which they emigrated but which they did not abandon" (1999, 94). For additional definitions of the term, see Portes (1996, 5–9), Gutiérrez and Hondagneu-Sotelo (2008), and Ong (1999). Some scholars such as Roger Waldinger (2008) critique scholars' ahistorical use of the term "transnational," arguing that there is nothing new about return migrant flows between countries of origin and destination. Although it would be hard to quarrel with Waldinger's historical analysis, I am reluctant to eschew the term entirely in favor of a critical and case-based usage.

5. To be sure, non-Mexicans have passed through Mexican territory on their way to the United States. Currently, Cubans and Central Americans are some of the largest migratory populations passing through Mexican space. Castillo, "Mexico–Guatemala Border." For a study of the early use of Mexico as a corridor to the United States, see McCullough (1992).

the development of migratory practices and discourses through the entire historical period to the present day.[6]

Whereas at the beginning of the twenty-first century the United States continues to be the country with the largest number of immigrants in the world, Mexico, by contrast, has emerged as the globe's leading country of emigration.[7] Experiencing a demographic explosion since the 1960s, people of Latin American and Caribbean origin and heritage in the United States in 2010 number over 50 million, or 16 percent of the country's total population.[8] One of every seven people in the nation identifies herself or himself as U.S. Latino (Hispanic), a group that has accounted for about half of the growth in the U.S. population since 1990.[9] At a record 12.7 million in 2008, Mexican migrants and their descendants make up nearly 65 percent of that Latino population and account for 32 percent of all immigrants in the United States, with growing populations in every state (Pew Hispanic Center 2009b; Zuñiga and Hernández-León 2005). More striking is the fact that almost 11 percent of everyone born in Mexico now lives in the United States, a percentage that has skyrocketed since 1970 when it equaled only 1.4 percent of the Mexican population.[10]

Yet it is impossible to know how Mexicans have become a dominant demographic presence and growing political and economic power in the contemporary United States without examining the multiple historical paths past generations chose to take on their way to *el Norte*. Furthermore, it is equally important to examine how scholars, politicians, and others have thought about and framed the historical narrative of Mexican migration: its inclusion and exclusion in national histories, periodization, and causation. This introduction examines the histories and historiographies of Mexican migration and the disciplinary and epistemological concerns in the study of this transnational phenomenon. By offering broad historical overviews of the subject,

---

6. For examples of studies examining periods in the nineteenth and twentieth centuries, see Cardoso (1980), González and Fernández (2003), Durand (1991), González Navarro (1994), Hart (1998), and Acuña (2008). The study by Escobar Latapí and Forbes Martin (2008) focuses intensely on the economic and legislative dynamics of contemporary Mexican migration, but lacks a larger historical context.

7. More migrant workers left Mexico between 2000 and 2005 than any other country in the world, according to a report released by the World Bank. The World Bank estimates that 2 million Mexicans migrated to the United States between 2000 and 2005, surpassing the 1.95 million Chinese who migrated to other countries, despite the fact that China's population is thirteen times as large as Mexico's. Worldwide migrant remittances reached US$180 billion in 2005, of which Mexicans accounted for US$23 billion. The World Bank credited increasing migration to a lack of economic growth, but ignored the impact of neoliberal policies, including NAFTA, while paying lip service to increasing debt in the global south. World Bank (2009).

8. This number includes Hispanics from Puerto Rico, the U.S. Virgin Islands, and other U.S. territories (U.S. Census Bureau 2010).

9. The demographic statistics outlined elide the fact that Latino/as can be simultaneously an extremely diverse and fluid assortment of self-conscious individuals and a unified ethnic community. The strategic definition as Latino/a—at once external and self-identifying—is inherently political, and it is complicated by several factors, including historical context, generation, language, gender, race, class, location, and country of origin. For a discussion of the historical origin of the terms Latino and Hispanic, see Overmyer-Velázquez, "Introduction." Also see Gutiérrez (2004), Oboler (1995), and Pew Hispanic Center (2009a).

10. CONAPO (National Population Council of Mexico); United Nations Population Division. A Pew Hispanic Center (2009e) report notes that "[n]o other country in the world has as many total immigrants from all countries as the United States has immigrants from Mexico alone. Other than the U.S., the country that hosts the largest number of immigrants is Russia, with 12 million foreign born, many of whom are natives of countries that were part of the former Soviet Union."

the chapters in *Beyond la Frontera* provide students, scholars, and general readers an important resource and points of departure for future in-depth translocal and transnational studies.

The Mexican American scholar Américo Paredes aptly named the space of this historical transnational relationship "Greater Mexico" (Paredes 1993). The longstanding demographic overlap and "intertwined notions of ethnic identity, political orientation, and national affiliation" are all fundamental elements of the mutually constitutive migratory histories of Greater Mexico (Gutiérrez 1999, 484). This book's chapters, outlined in detail below, engage this history in both a chronological and a thematic manner with reference to mutually influential periods in Mexican and Mexican American history. Taking into consideration these binational historical determinants and narrative constructions of Mexican migration, the concluding section points to some ways in which this volume might help us to better understand the persistent legislative debates in both countries around migrant rights and national sovereignty.

HISTORIES AND HISTORIOGRAPHIES OF GREATER MEXICO

Given the enduring migratory history between Mexico and the United States, it may seem a wonder that Mexican migration has not played a more prominent role in the historical study and narratives of both nations. Historians have produced studies of Mexican emigration and immigration (and its ethnic national correlate, Chicana/o history), but those perspectives privilege one national history (Overmyer-Velázquez 2007, 140). This may be because Mexican migrants are not accommodated by the racialized national mythologies of Mexico or the United States, invented traditions that have shaped the subject's scholarly inquiry, popular depictions, and political attentions.[11] José Moya points to the material reasons for this type of absence, arguing that "clearly, 'historical significance' forms an arbitrary concept defined less by the number of people affected than by economic power and academic resources" (Moya 1998, 2).

By crossing perceived static national borders, migrants disrupt the self-contained conceit of national unity; they rupture the imagined national community, causing an anxiety that is most often remedied through their elision and subordination in a jingoistic narrative of the nation (Overmyer-Velázquez, 2008b). Homi Bhabha examines this perception, arguing that there is "[an] attempt by nationalist discourses persistently to produce the idea of the nation as a continuous narrative of national progress, the narcissism of self-generation, the primeval present of the Volk" (Bhabha 1990). Similarly, in his discussion of transcultural encounters in Europe and Canada, historian Dirk Hoerder writes, "the powerful simplification or master narrative of 'national identity' and 'nation-state history,' in longue durée perspective, hides a complex interactive past, hides in particular the worlds the slaves made, the migrants built, the women created" (Hoerder, 2003, 16). Exploring the so-called "externalities of migration...," Arjun

---

11. In her work, *Migrant Imaginaries*, Alicia Schmidt Camacho relates and examines the history of Mexican migrant imaginaries—"symbolic field[s] in which people come to understand and describe their social being"—as formative elements of subaltern subjectivity in resistance to subordinating nationalist projects.

Appadurai further argues that there exists a "contradiction between the idea that each nation-state can truly represent only one ethnos and the reality that all nation-states historically involve the amalgamation of many identities. Even where long-standing identities have been forgotten or buried, the combination of migration and mass mediation assures their reconstruction on a new scale and at larger levels. Incidentally, this is why the politics of remembering and forgetting (and thus of history and historiography) is so central to the ethnicist battles tied up with nationalism" (Appadurai 1996, 156).[12] Reinscribing the too-often absent Mexican migrant into these national narratives helps us to understand the world in which they and we—or better, all of us—live (Rouse 1977; Craib and Overmyer-Velázquez forthcoming). Challenging static and bounded formulations of the "tyranny of the national in the discipline of history" (Gabaccia 1999), this volume explores the simultaneous development of two national histories from the perspective of the lives and state regulation of migrants crossing back and forth through a contested and porous border.[13] The chapters herein seek to uncover and retell those histories and historiographies to include Mexican migration as central to the historical and mutually constitutive narratives of both countries.

Furthermore, in addition to renarrating history from the perspective of the migrant, this volume also seeks to "reimagin[e] an American narrative with Latinos as meaningful actors" (Ruíz 2006, 656).[14] Although disciplinary divisions and institutional inertia have hindered the development of studies of Mexican migration history, a comprehensive history of Mexican migrants necessarily bridges the problematic divide between Latino/a and Latin American studies.[15] More importantly, these divisions have ultimately limited the scope and depth of researchers' inquiry and methodology.[16]

---

12. Herman Bennett (2009) refers to a similar historical amnesia with the study of Afro-Mexicans: "Herein is a story (or stories) that Mexico's nationalist historians have defined as a non-event (or a sequence of non-events) thereby confining it (or them) to historical invisibility" (11). See also Hernández's (2010b) use of Behad's (2005) notion of forgetting certain migrant pasts as fundamental to nation formation.

13. Of course, by attempting to "fill" the historiographic "gap," this volume is by no means immune to what Hayden White has called "the ineluctably interpretative aspect of historiography." See White (1973, 1984).

14. Henry Yu (2004) also compellingly asserts the importance of understanding national and regional spaces as "nodes" within a fluid trajectory of migratory movement. The space of the United States and the condition of "illegality" represent "only one of the ways that migration has been shaped in the last two centuries."

15. William Robinson (2007) forcefully argues the point: "To consider inquiry into the reality of U.S.-based Latino/a populations as 'Latino/a Studies' and inquiry into that reality south of the Rio Bravo as 'Latin American Studies' is patently absurd. But it is more than that: it is epistemologically bankrupt and politically disempowering. It renders invisible to 'Latin American Studies' the 40 million Latinos/as in the United States and cuts them off from the larger reality in which their lives are grounded at a time when our struggles and fates are more than ever shaped by our engagement with global-level processes and structures" (21).

16. Although not framed in this same way, Corwin's (1973) historiographical essay, "Mexican Emigration History, 1900–1970: Literature and Research," reviews the literature on Mexican migration from each of these three perspectives. Corwin begins his essay with the prescient lament of the "almost total...neglect by Latin Americanists both in the United States and Mexico" of the history of Mexican migration, especially in light of the burgeoning "ethnic study movement." As if in response, the late 1960s and early 1970s became a watershed era for Mexican migration studies by social scientists. Fueled in large part by a renewed interest and concern in Latin America as a result of the Cold War, increased

David Maciel and María Herrera-Sobek characterize the study of migration from three perspectives, arguing that Mexican, North American, and Chicana/o historians have each approached the subject from within their own historical and disciplinary contexts (Maciel and Herrera-Sobek 1998).

Histories of Mexico

Among historians of Mexico, both Mexican and non-Mexican based, the dominant national narrative has largely excluded the history of migrants leaving their patria for the north. Historical discussions have often taken a teleological view of historical development that narrates national history as bounded and progressing toward an increasingly "modern" end.

Despite the fact that at times during its modern history over one-tenth of Mexico's population has moved, temporarily or permanently, to the United States, Mexican academics have devoted relatively little attention to the historical study of Mexican emigration and its part in the making of modern Mexico. Studies during the first half of the twentieth century were often commissioned by the government and sought to guide the administration's policies (examples include Fábila (1929) and Loyo (1931)). The propagandistic trend of migration studies continued well into the post World War II era, when much attention was paid to the Bracero period (1942–1964), its economic impact, and the protection of emigrant laborers. One exception emerged in the 1960s with the scholarship of Moisés González Navarro, who proclaimed that Mexico was a "país de la emigración" (a country of emigration).[17]

The sociologist Jorge Bustamante argues that the indifference of Mexico's government and civil society toward Mexican migrants in the United States is deeply rooted in racism toward the country's indigenous population and is an "integral element" of Mexican culture. According to Bustamante, the long historical construction of racism and discrimination developed and nurtured since the colonial period has been refocused by Mexico's middle class and elites, who view migrants as "pochos" or second-class Mexicans. Proof of this indifference, he argues, can be seen in the glaring historical absence throughout the latter half of the twentieth century of large urban public demonstrations in support of migrant rights. This indifference has been further exemplified by a lack of support of his and others' scholarship of migration among colleagues in Mexican academia (Bustamante 2002).[18] Recent work by the prominent Mexican historian Enrique Florescano underscores this indifference. His recent book exemplifies the sparse treatment historians have given emigration in the national narrative construction of Mexico (Florescano 2002).

(undocumented) migration, and a militant and culturally nationalist Chicano/a movement, migration studies by social scientists began to flourish.

17. His works focus largely on Mexican immigration *to* Mexico. They include González Navarro (1954, 1960, 1994). For a critique of González Navarro's emphasis on a "failure" of Mexico's immigration history in the context of broader postindependence colonization and nationalization initiatives, see Hernández (2010a).

18. Jorge Bustamante is the founder and former president of the Colegio de la Frontera Norte (established in 1982), Mexico's premier research center for border and immigration studies. See also Durand, "From Traitors to Heroes."

Non-Mexican-based historians of Mexico are not immune to this trend. Recently published histories of Mexico lament the "lack [of] a sustained focus on the process of migration to and from the United States" (for example, see Joseph, Rubenstein, and Zolov 2001). The historiographic absence of migration can be seen as well in studies that examine the role of peasants—the dominant demographic among migrants—in Mexican nation formation and in broad histories of Mexico–U.S. relations.[19]

Histories of the United States

When U.S. historian Oscar Handlin declared that "immigrants *were* American history" (Handlin 1951, 3; emphasis in original), he neglected to include Mexican migrants in that history. North of the border, historians have also been reluctant to study Mexican migration per se. This is curious, especially because there exists a well-established literature of Borderlands study starting with the patrons Hubert Bancroft and Herbert Bolton, who wrote volumes on the history of Spanish, Mexican, and Anglo-American settlements (Bancroft 1886–1890; Bolton 1921). Most studies of migration to the United States have focused on groups from places other than Mexico and Latin America. Mexicans are given short shrift in the predominantly European-centric accounts of the North American demographic expansion, as in the work by Handlin. A handful of Mexican migration studies, however, did appear in the early part of the twentieth century. In the 1920s, the U.S. government, concerned about the potential negative impact of migrant Mexicans on U.S. society, encouraged and commissioned social scientists to produce the first studies of these "impoverished" migrants from a North American perspective. Sociologists and economists such as Victor Clark, Paul Taylor, and Emory Bogardus wrote lengthy studies of Mexican migrants primarily in the southwest (Clark 1974; Taylor 1928–1934; Bogardus 1934). Subsequent scholars have noted the pervasive racial stereotyping of Mexicans in much of this early literature (Vaca 1970). It was not until Carey McWilliams, a muckraking journalist and editor of *The Nation*, entered the scene in 1948 that Mexican migration received any concerted treatment. Historian Arthur Corwin points out that McWilliams' influential work, *North from Mexico*, is "one of the first debunkings of the 'fantasy heritage' promoted by chambers of commerce, western novelists, and Hollywood script writers who make much of fictional Spanish Dons and fiestas but look disdainfully at Mexican settlers and peons" (Corwin 1973, 5; McWilliams 1949). Mexican American historians have also touted McWilliams as a founder of Chicano/a studies and an inspiration for the production of ethnic and politically radical histories of the United States. Following McWilliams, studies by North Americans languished until the 1960s and 1970s when scholars such as Leo Grebler, Julian Somora, and others published research specifically about bracero

---

19. The chronological focus of Alan Knight's (1994b) nuanced examination of Mexican nation formation, "Peasants into Patriots," encompasses the nineteenth century through the years of President Lázaro Cárdenas (1934–1940). Although the flow of U.S.-bound migration in those years was relatively light, it is remarkable that the article, written in the early 1990s, does not consider Mexican emigration and its impact on Mexico's collective national identity formation. Similarly, the much revised work by Raat and Brescia (2010), *Mexico and the United States*, provides an excellent historical overview of Mexico–U.S. relations, but does not pay close attention to the dynamics of migration between the two countries. For a rare exception to this historiographic absence and a concise overview of the topic see Henderson, *Beyond Borders*.

labor (Grebler 1996; Samora 1971). Researchers from the fields of sociology, economics, political science, and anthropology continue to dominate the study of Mexican migration studies to the present day.[20]

Chicana/o Histories

With their roots in the work of Ernesto Galarza and the revived scholarship of McWilliams, the first generation of Chicano/a historians in the late 1960s and 1970s—many of them trained initially as historians of Mexico and Latin America— shaped their research and publications around an active political agenda. Although these scholars played a critical and important role in giving a voice to the history of Mexican Americans, they tended to oversimplify the complex experiences of this neglected group.[21] They positioned their subjects as victims of "internal colonialism," assigned little geographic and cultural differentiation to the experience of Chicanos/as from varied generational, gender, social, economic, and political backgrounds, and exaggerated the continuities between Mexican and Mexican American history and culture (Saragoza 1988–1990). Starting in the early 1980s several new works emerged that began to differentiate among the multiple historical realities of Mexican Americans. These new studies maintained the nationalistic stance of their predecessors, underscoring the "heroic" cultural maintenance of Chicano/a communities (Camarillo 1980; Griswold del Castillo 1990; Romo 1983; García 1981; De León 1982).

Through its first decades, Chicana/o scholars continued to neglect the history of migration, focusing instead on the history of immigrants *ya llegados* (already arrived). Critiquing this absence in the historiography, Alex Saragoza wrote, "[there is] a persistent flaw in Chicano scholarship: the tendency to underestimate the importance of continuing immigration, including the complexities of Chicano–*mexicano* relations in the formation of Chicano communities since World War II. And though the controversy over contemporary immigration has fueled prodigious amounts of research, it sustains a preoccupation with economic considerations and an aversion for understanding the Chicano–*mexicano* dimensions of Mexican immigration" (Saragoza 1988–1990, 36–37).

Saragoza furthermore maintained that the trend to characterize Mexican American migrants as transcendental and apolitical subjects reflected and contributed to the

---

20. Much of this literature and its methodology are summarized in articles authored and coauthored by one of the doyens of the field, Douglas Massey. For examples, see Durand and Massey (1992) and Massey (1987). Additionally, the Center for U.S.–Mexican Studies at the University of California, San Diego, has published many important studies on Mexico–U.S migration. Wayne Cornelius founded and directed the center, established in 1979.

There *are* some historical studies of the topic that bear mentioning. For example, studies by the authors in Hart's (1998) volume, *Border Crossings*, document the historical continuities between the Mexican and Mexican American working classes. Indeed, more work needs to be done in general on bi- and transnational labor ties among the Mexican, Mexican American, and U.S. working class and their relationship with migration. For a rare and earlier study of the topic, see Levenstein (1971). Also see Acuña (2008).

21. Acuña's (1972) pathbreaking work, *Occupied America*, is exemplary of this first generation of Chicano/a scholars. Acuña has since published a seventh and much altered edition (Acuña 2010).

ineffectual rallying attempts by Chicano political groups as they cast their constituents without differentiation. The "diversity among Chicanos," Saragoza continued, "must be the linchpin of any political strategy or project" (Saragoza 1988–1990, 37, 52). This homogenizing tendency has its historical south-of-the-border counterpart in Mexican writers like Octavio Paz, who years before simplistically portrayed the Chicano/a as a self-annihilating *pachuco* who "denies both the society from which he originated and that of North America" (Paz 1959).

More recently, studies of Chicano history have produced more inclusive and diverse frameworks of study that focus on the importance of migrants and migration and engage Mexico and the Mexican historical experience as more than perfunctory background material for Mexicans on U.S. soil.[22] New generations of Mexican American historians pay closer attention to regional and political differences and include analyses of gender and the integration of culture and politics (examples of this new literature include Zavella 1987; Ruíz 1978; Deutsch 1987; and Pitti 2003).

Despite these nation-centered articulations of the region's migratory history, it has been ultimately an intensely transnational social phenomenon.[23] In recent years a new set of epistemological and methodological approaches have taken shape that follow the lead of scholars such as Pedro Cabán and Frances Aparicio, who challenge the all-too-often insular, nationalist approaches of area and ethnic studies. This approach instead tends toward "contextualizing…research in relation to transnationalism, immigration, citizenship and globalization as a result of the demographic diversification of the Latino populations in the United States as well as of the hemispheric circulation of peoples, goods, capital, cultural texts, and labor" (Poblete 2003, xiv; see also Aparicio 2003). Examining Mexican migration with a different set of methodological and empirical lenses that take into consideration the transnational experience of migrants provokes a different set of questions that at once stake claim to the epistemological importance of utilizing binational source material and expand our understanding of Mexican–U.S. relations. Here scholars can reference the work of those such as Walter Mignolo and José Saldívar, who call for a "remapping" or reorientation of American studies through a discourse of "border thinking." Border thinking asks us "to re-imagine the nation as a site within many 'cognitive maps' in which the nation-state is not congruent with cultural identity." (Saldívar, 1997, ix). Viewed in this way, the Mexico–U.S. border and indeed Mexican and U.S. history become sites of "thinking from dichotomous concepts rather than ordering the world in dichotomies." Yet, far from ignoring national histories and the unique experiences of Mexicans and other Latinos/as in the United States, this approach builds upon older studies that examine

---

22. See, for example, Gutiérrez (1995), Gutiérrez (1996), and Sanchez (1993). As I elaborate below, however, these works rely primarily on U.S.-based sources and analyze the effect of immigration north of the border.

23. In their essay promoting an "Americas paradigm," a broadly transnational and hemispheric approach to the historical study of the western hemisphere, Shukla and Tinsman (2004) argue that scholars must consider nonnational social formations such as "indigenous settlement; European conquest and colonization; African slavery; Enlightenment-based independence movements and republic building; mass (im)migrations; populist welfare states; cold war political cultures" (5). See also their expanded edited volume (Shukla and Tinsman 2007).

the economic and social dimensions of Mexican migration from either side of the border (Mignolo 2000; Saldívar 1997).[24]

PERIODIZATION

Marcelo Suárez-Orozco writes that Mexican migrants to the United States "are at once among the 'oldest' and 'newest' Americans—in the provincial rather than hemispheric meaning of the term" (Suárez-Orozco 2001, 40). The temporal framing of Mexicans' historical departure from their homeland and arrival to the United States is an intimate and strategic aspect of the overall migration narrative. The scholarly periodization of this transborder phenomenon has always been guided by specific national and disciplinary perspectives. Defining the "origins" and various major stages of Mexican migration can be useful in organizing the complexities of the history, but it can also favor one set of national chronological progressions over another.

Some scholars mark the beginning of the Mexican presence in the borders of the contemporary United States with Fray Marcos de Niza's 1539 expedition into what is now the United States. Niza would be the first of thousands of Spaniards and later Mexicans to leave their patria and cross the borderlands for *el Norte*. Over the following three centuries, Spaniards in small numbers continued to settle in the present-day Southwest, as far east as Louisiana and north to Oregon and Colorado (Cardoso 1980, xiv). Most U.S. or Mexican American historians use the Mexican American War (known in Mexico as *la invasión norteamericana*) of 1846–1848 and the subsequent Treaty of Guadalupe Hidalgo that ceded the United States nearly half of Mexico's territory as an indication of the beginning of Mexican Americans/Chicanos as a discrete population in the United States.

Yet in his chapter in this volume, Juan Mora-Torres explains that although U.S. historians use 1848 as a national chronological milestone leading to the outbreak of the Civil War (1860–1865), historians of Mexico prefer to signal the change into a new era of liberal rule with the year 1854 and the beginning of the Ayutla rebellion. This example of differences in nineteenth century time frames sheds light on the issue of national periodizations. Given the predominance of U.S.-based interpretations of Mexico's migratory history, it is incumbent upon future studies to take this chronological inequity into account when framing their narratives.

Although for different reasons—as we will see below—both Douglas Massey and Gilbert González in this volume initiate their chronologies in the twentieth century. Massey's influential and oft-cited periodization is divided into five distinct eras (Enganche, Deportations, Bracero, Undocumented Migration, and Anti-immigrant Repression). Each period is largely determined by changes in U.S. immigration policy, which is in turn shaped by larger shifts in economic and foreign relations conditions. González constructs three "general time frames" (1900–1930, 1942–1964, and the 1980s to the present), which emphasize "industrial operations and/or economic policies emanating from the United States and implemented with the collaboration

---

24. Other scholars who seek to critically engage from a hemispheric perspective the institutional, methodological, disciplinary, and epistemological divides between ethnic and area studies include Nicholas De Genova (2005) and González (2004a).

of Mexico's elites." In an earlier work, González not only underscores the twentieth century parameters of his periodization, but also challenges scholars who originate the Mexican migration in the nineteenth century, arguing that the "dating of the beginning of Chicano history to the Treaty of Guadalupe Hidalgo in 1848 [is] without merit, as it avoid[s] the significant break between one historical event—the demise of the old Spanish and Mexican rule in the area—and the rise of a new, separate in time, migration-based population more than fifty years later" (González and Fernández 2003, 11–14). In his binational treatment of the historical development of emigration and immigration legislation in Mexico and the United States, David FitzGerald posits yet a different set of time frames following distinct legal milestones in each country.[25]

Yet other scholars eschew establishing "origins" and periodization all together, privileging the convergence of long-standing structural factors such as the nineteenth century trade routes that connected Mexican sojourners to the country's north and then to larger global capitalist circuits.[26] Migrant flows dating either from the mid-nineteenth or from the early twentieth century thus become historical moments marking the intensification of preestablished phenomena (like demographic shifts and intensification) rather than beginnings; hence, a "genealogy" of Mexican migration is, perhaps, more appropriate than that of "origins."[27]

Considering the vagaries of historical periodization, the authors of the volume's chronological chapters were provided with rough temporal frames within which to situate their arguments. Ultimately, they each, depending on their thematic focus, established binationally inflected timelines that overlapped one another. The annotated chronology in the volume's appendix can serve as a transnational source (here in the "beyond" nation-centered sense) to guide researchers to fashion a relatively unbiased temporal approach to the history of Mexican migration. The absence of any specific periodization allows for a variety of approaches to the study of the topic. The dates and events are culled from salient moments and economic and legal enactments in the two countries' histories.

CAUSALITY

Expressed differently, periodization is the temporal framing of historical shifts that cause migration to occur and endure. The volume's authors also differ on the historical etiology of Mexican migration. Some utilize variants of the "push–pull" theory of migration that examines independent causes of migration within the nation. Often

---

25. Further examples of varied thematic periodization can be found in the work of Jorge Durand (2004), "over the course of 100 years, Mexican policymaking has witnessed five phases: the early 20th century policies aimed at dissuading Mexicans from migrating; a policy of negotiation during and after World War II; the 'laissez-faire' approach of the 1970s and 1980s; the 'damage control' policy of the 1990s; and the current stage of proposals and talks that can be characterized as one of 'shared responsibility.'" Cano and Délano (2007) advance a five-stage periodization of Mexican state relations with migrant populations in the United States.

26. Here Moya's (1998) macro–micro and dialectical analytical framework serves as a guide. In his study of Spanish migrants to Argentina he identifies five "global revolutions" (demographic, agricultural, industrial, transportation, and political liberalization) that in combination served as the foundation for any one decision to migrate across the Atlantic.

27. E-mail correspondence with Dr. José Angel Hernández, University of Massachusetts–Amherst.

framed as conditions in dyadic opposition where, for example, Mexico's surplus of labor and scarcity of resources "push" migrants, whereas the U.S. demand for labor and superior economic resources "pull" migrants,[28] the elements are in turn conditioned by family and household economic arrangements, broader social and cultural networks and hierarchies, and historical alterations in U.S. immigration policy that have encouraged, dissuaded, or punished migrants depending on their perceived economic and social value and legal status.[29]

In their chapter, Luibhéid and Buffington argue against the more narrow forms of push–pull theories that posit a neoclassical economic model that privilege a male, heterosexual migrant *homo economicus* and view women and gender as externalities. Furthermore, they maintain that the broader historical political and economic structures that shape and condition migration are often ignored in favor of the choices of "rational" individuals. Gilbert Gonzalez in this volume and elsewhere puts a finer point on this critique, arguing that the economic dimensions of Mexican migration to the United States are intimately linked to a larger and long-standing asymmetrical imperial relationship between the two countries.[30] He maintains that most scholars have continued to ignore the U.S. causal role in the history of Mexican migration and use a mutually exclusive frame to explain the phenomenon as it developed through the twentieth century (see González and Fernández 2003, 61, for a detailed list of scholarship examining migration theory). "[I]f the forces of supply and demand work to eliminate economic disequilibria," Gonzalez queries, "why has there been an apparent permanent disequilibrium that no amount of migration from Mexico (or modernization therein) has been able to root out and that remains in effect after one hundred years?" (González and Fernández 2003, 34). Challenges to push–pull theories emerged in the 1970s, but even those such as world systems theory, which demonstrated the influence of global capitalism on disrupting and uprooting populations in the global south, continued to obscure the strategic and specific economic dominance of U.S. capital transmitted through government programs and private corporate networks.[31] All of these theories, Gonzalez posits, fail to account for the steadily increasing economic and political subordination of Mexico to the growing imperial ambitions of the United States.

---

28. The economic disparity between Mexico and the United States (often measured in gross national product per capita) is the world's largest with two countries sharing a land border. On the two countries' unequal economic relationship, see Weintraub (2010).

29. In *Beyond Smoke and Mirrors*, Massey, Durand, and Malone (2002) complicate this approach by asking (and answering) four interconnected questions: "What are the forces in sending societies that promote out-migration, and how do they operate? What are the forces in receiving societies that create a demand for immigrant workers, and how do they function? What are the motivations, goals, and aspirations of the people who respond to these forces by migrating internationally? And what are the social economic structures that arise in the course of migration to connect sending and receiving societies?" (7–23).

30. Much ink has been spilled concerning the hotly contested term "empire" in reference to the United States. Although often relegated to the dustbin of history, as in the "British" or "Roman" empires, until recently the term has either been ignored or substituted with convenient euphemisms such as "superpower." Some scholars such as Ferguson (2004) in *Colossus* not only utilize the term but also advocate a "better and stronger" U.S. empire as world policeman and democratic arbiter.

31. Anticipating this line of argument, Gómez-Quiñones (1983) asserted that "Mexican immigration has been closely tied to the economic dominance of Mexico by the United States, dominance which has helped maintain the Mexican economy in an underdeveloped state" (60; González and Fernández 2003, 32–35).

From the mid-nineteenth century westward expansion to the post North American Free Trade Agreement (NAFTA, 1994) era, the U.S. government has sought to position Mexico (and indeed all of Latin America) as the "material fountain of empire."[32] The push and the pull factors have been, in effect, part of the same process.

Yet some scholars argue that although macrolevel causal analyses that link U.S. empire and Mexican migration illuminate broader historical trends, they could further benefit from the incorporation of the variety of locally determined causes of emigration that, for example, Alanís Enciso painstakingly documents in his chapter in this volume.[33]

NATIONS AND BORDERS

Although the causes of migration and migration itself challenge nation-bound formulations, the nation-state historically has been and remains a critical arbiter in defining the movement, legal status, and identity of the migrant and hence of the nation itself. As recent scholarship on Mexico and the many bureaucratic mechanisms involved in Mexican migration has demonstrated, defining the historical formation of the nation and its borders is an elusive task (Joseph and Nugent 1994; Truett and Young 2004). Yet the governments of both Mexico and the United States strategically have acted in their own interest to regulate migration and mark the national boundary. For example, from the mid-nineteenth to the mid-twentieth centuries, and especially during the Bracero period, U.S. foreign policy played a formative role in shaping immigration policy toward Mexico. However, after 1965 a separation developed between foreign and immigration policies. By that time, both governments largely deemed Mexico-to-U.S. migration beneficial and the U.S. government in particular increasingly deferred to domestic agribusiness and industry labor demands to shape immigration policies (Rico 1992).

Although Mexico and the United States currently share a border, that dividing line was until relatively recently more of a social construction than a material barrier. Prior to the formation of the Border Patrol in 1924, and even several decades after that, the border was largely a symbolic space easily crossed by laborers, political refugees, and tourists (Massey, Durand, and Malone 2002, 24–26).[34] In recent decades, as Saskia Sassen illustrates in the Foreword, in the connections between flows of capital and people, the "geographic borderline is but one point in the chain; institutional points of border control intervention can form long chains moving deep inside the country." Given these long-standing relationships with the border and border crossing, current efforts to fortify and militarize the border have proven to be ineffective and, worse,

---

32. After a terse and cogent summary of these theories, Hoerder (2002) advocates a new paradigm of migration, a "mesolevel approach to migrant decision making" that examines the "holistic material-emotional dimensions of migrants in their everyday lives while taking into account broader structural factors" (1–21).

33. For an excellent collaborative study that integrates a multidisciplinary approach to examining detailed case studies of contemporary Mexican migration, see Massey et al. (1987).

34. On the performative and symbolic dimensions of the border, see Alvarez (1995), Lugo (2000), and Rosaldo (1997). Rosaldo (1997, 33) writes that "the U.S.–Mexico border has become theater, and border theater has become social violence. Actual violence has become inseparable from symbolic ritual on the border—crossings, invasions, lines of defense, high-tech surveillance, and more."

have not deterred undocumented migrants but instead forced them to cross through increasingly deadly terrain.[35]

Yet, although migration studies often depict the state as a monolithic entity, imposing its control from above, it is critical to disaggregate "the state" into its constituent elements—often at odds with one another—its local, regional, and national dimensions. Despite their seemingly unified structure, governments at all levels in Mexico and the United States have always suffered from highly fragmented emigrant and immigrant regulatory apparatuses (for examples from both sides of the border, see Calavita 1992; FitzGerald 2006a; and FitzGerald in this volume).

SUBJECTIVITIES AND STATUSES

Whereas Mexican and U.S. governments at various levels have worked to regulate and define migration and migrants, migrants historically have identified themselves within the context of their transnational experiences. As Kunal Parker (2004) argues, geopolitical spaces like the nation and their exclusive/inclusive characteristics are products of the historical "simultaneous creation of insiders and outsiders" (285), imagined and constructed by individuals and groups as either legal or illegal in mutual reference with one another over long periods of time. Similarly, a state's official representative, the citizen, is also a product of alterity, or otherness. As Linda Kerber (2005) writes, "The stateless are the citizen's other. The stateless serve the state by embodying its absence, by providing frightening models of the vulnerability of those who lack sufficient awe of the state. The stateless serve the state by signaling who will not be entitled to its protection, and throwing fear into the rest of us" (745). In other words, definitions of the migrant and the nation are mutually constitutive. As Jonathan Fox points out in his chapter in this volume, until the 1980s most Mexican migrants heralded from mestizo rural communities in the central-western states and identified with a ranchero culture. Upon arriving to the United States, first-generation Mexican migrants primarily identify with their national origin as Mexicans rather than with U.S.-based group identities as Latinos or Hispanics. In the past three decades, however, the growing number of indigenous migrants from Mexico has complicated this picture. The historical racialization of indigenous groups in Mexico combined with their experience of a U.S. racial hierarchy requires scholars such as Fox to utilize a cross-border perspective to understand the shifting endogenous and exogenous constructions of

---

35. In 2009 the U.S. Government Accountability Office discovered over three thousand breaches of a six-hundred-mile border wall, which has cost more than US$2.4 billion since 2005. According to the report, the government will have to spend US$6.5 billion over the next twenty years simply to maintain the wall. Wayne Cornelius (2009b) reports that "the existing border fortifications do not keep undocumented migrants out of the U.S. Not even half are being apprehended on any given trip to the border, and of those who are apprehended, the success rate on the second or third try is upwards of 95 percent." Still, many of those who do attempt to cross the border die trying. The *Associated Press* reported on October 3, 2009 that "the number of immigrants who died while sneaking across the Mexican border in the last 12 months is expected to surpass the previous year's total, even as fewer people are getting caught entering the country illegally. The Border Patrol says 378 people died near the border in the 11-month period that ended Aug. 31". See also Nevins (2002).

Mexican migrant subjectivities.[36] Furthermore, recent shifts in the origins and identities of Mexican migrants are just part of the country's larger history of racial and ethnic diversity. Mexico has a relationship with peoples from Africa and Asia that reaches back to colonial times and continues to play a formative role in the country's modern history.[37] Of course once in the United States, Mexican migrant identities are further transformed depending on the migrant's location, class, gender, sexuality, and generation (Portes and Rumbaut 2001).

CHAPTER SUMMARIES AS HISTORICAL OVERVIEW

Beyond la Frontera assembles a select number of distinguished scholars from a variety of disciplines to analyze critical themes in the historical experience of Mexican migration to the United States. The volume is divided into two sections. The first, *Chronological Histories*, examines the historical foundations of Mexican migration to the United States from the mid-nineteenth century to the present. The second section, *Comparative Themes*, analyzes and compares political, economic, social, and cultural themes that transcend regional and national boundaries and reveals some of the more salient sources of internal differentiation among Mexican migrants. I organized the volume and selected this range of topics to provide the reader with a broad historical and thematic introduction to the study of Mexico–U.S. migration. Although the comparative chapters offer in-depth examinations of topics including race formation, indigenous migration, law and legal practice, constructions of gender and sexuality, and migrant cultural representations, many more areas could have been added if space permitted.[38] The detailed and linked chapter summaries that follow provide a concise overview of the history of Mexican migration.

In Chapter One, Juan Mora-Torres explores the beginning of economic and social integration between the United States and Mexico as North American territorial expansion paved the way for the economic domination that would endure to the present day. The signing of the Treaty of Guadalupe Hidalgo at the conclusion of *la invasión norteamericana* of 1846–1848 and the Treaty of Guadalupe Hidalgo that ceded nearly half of Mexico's territory to the United States marked the beginning of the first waves of Mexican migrants coming to the United States.[39] The U.S. government's negotiation of the Hidalgo treaty and the subsequent Gadsden Purchase (1853) cut a border between

---

36. Lynn Stephen (2007) examines this dynamic of crossing multiple national, ethnic, and racial borders by employing the portmanteau term "transborder."

37. Although studies of Afro and Asian Mexican populations are few in number, they represent one of the most dynamic and growing fields of Mexican scholarship. Examples include Bennett (2009), Vaughn and Vinson (2007), Aguirre Beltrán (1989), Peña Delgado (2004), Hu-DeHart (1980), Chau Romero (2010), Gómez Izquierdo (1991), and Rénique (2003).

38. Examples of additional areas of inquiry could include studies of urban to urban migration; U.S. destinations such as Chicago, Los Angeles, and the U.S. northwest and northeast regions; and integration and assimilation from different generational perspectives. See Hernández-León (2008), Telles and Ortiz (2008), Gamboa (1990), Kasinitz et al. (2008), Portes and Rumbaut (2001), and Cornelius, FitzGerald, and Borger (2009).

39. The Spanish-speaking population in the territories acquired by the 1848 Treaty numbered approximately 100,000.

the two countries that for the most part remains in place today (Griswold del Castillo 1990).[40]

Mora-Torres demonstrates how the "official" international boundary was initially largely theoretical as Mexicans, arguing that "they did not cross the border, the boundary crossed them," continued to cross with little change from their pre-1848 life (McWilliams 1949, 110–11). That same year the discovery of gold in what would become the state of California and the initiation of industrialized agriculture provided the economic incentives to cross the newly drawn national boundary line. Depopulation of the northern states caused by the displacement of land and villages by encroaching railroad and other international, mainly U.S., corporations and continued Apache Indian raids on isolated villages caused the fragile and inchoate Mexican government to initiate repatriation programs to shore up the northern frontier with loyal citizens (De León 1982; De León and Stewart 1993; González Quiroga 1999, 115–81; Hernández, 2008). Just as had taken place in Texas in the previous decade, in those earlier years migrants arriving from Mexico to the United States also witnessed the rise of white supremacy and racially motivated violence against Mexicans, including lynching and expulsion.

Whereas Anglo American[41] farm owners weighed the costs of the economic and social integration of Mexicans in the U.S. labor market, Mexicans considered the limited option of the two paternalistic hacienda economies on either side of the border, with the U.S. version in places like Texas offering higher wages. U.S. agriculturalists complained that the presence of Mexican laborers undermined the stability of the slave trade. Mexican government officials lamented the hemorrhaging of their own workers to the north. Yet, as the economy grew in the U.S. Southwest, employers also viewed Mexican workers as critical and considered them a "reserve army of labor." The development of Mexico's increasingly prosperous north and the construction of a railroad network at the end of the century stimulated an internal migration from the country's southern and central provinces. The arrival of compatriots to the northern border also initiated the growth of border towns and a unique social and economic binational frontier zone.

During the "first age of migration" from 1820 to 1932, over 90 percent of the 50 million Europeans who migrated came to the Americas. In hopes of benefiting from this wave, Mora-Torres argues that Mexican elites in the nineteenth century developed a racist project to "civilize" Mexico's indigenous population—deemed an obstacle to economic and social modernization—by encouraging immigration by white Europeans. Despite passing of the Colonization Law of 1883, one of the hemisphere's most liberal immigration laws, the government of Porfirio Díaz (1876–1910) was unable to

---

40. For a study of frontier society leading up to the Mexican American war, see Reséndez (2005).

41. The racial terms "Anglo" and "white" are, of course, far from static and monolithic categories. As Neil Foley (1997) has explained in the case of 1930s Texas, "In reducing all whites of European descent into one category, the term *Anglo* thus fails completely to identify any single ethnic group." Texans used the terms "Anglo" and "Mexican" in opposition to one another. "Anglo," Foley continues, "denote[d], rather crudely, all non-Mexican whites, thereby conflating widely diverse cultural groups in Texas, such as Germans, Czechs, Irish, English, Polish, and French—to say nothing of Protestants, Catholics, and Jews" (8).

attract "redemptive" foreigners.[42] At the time of the Great Depression and the end of the century-long migratory wave from Europe, Mexico had become the only nation of net emigration in the Americas. As Mexican philosopher Antonio Caso wrote, "Los de fuera no vienen, los de casa se van" (those from afar do not come, those from home leave).

Although at the time of Mexico's independence in 1821 the geographic size, population, and economy of the United States did not far surpass that of Mexico, less than a century later the gap had irredeemably widened. By the end of the Mexican Revolution in 1910 the United States had increased its territory to five times that of its southern neighbor and grown its population to six times the size of Mexico's (15 million), and Mexico's economy had fallen to only 2 percent of the now Northern Colossus.

In Chapter Two, "Mexican Labor Migration, 1876–1924," Gilbert Gonzalez adopts the transnational approach of labor and civil rights leader Ernesto Galarza to examine the role of U.S. government, business, and literary production in promoting and sustaining Mexican migration. Galarza's oft ignored perspective emphasizes how, starting in the late nineteenth century, the U.S. development of a "virtual economic colony" in Mexico through enormous landownership and business production fostered the fundamental conditions for migration.

Simultaneous with mobilization of a Mexican migrant labor force both within Mexico and to the United States, Gonzalez argues that U.S. capitalists and journalists crafted a new body of literature that "orientalized" the Mexican worker as "The Mexican Problem": an infantilized peon in need of paternal care and redemption. This literature, published as travel accounts, novels, and academic studies, fashioned an "imperial mindset" that became "common knowledge" enabling and forming public attitudes and policy toward a growing Mexican migrant population.

Although some hawkish U.S. government representatives called for the complete annexation of Mexico, the dominant approach was one of "peaceful conquest" through economic expansion. In a scenario all too familiar in the history of U.S.–Latin American relations, U.S. government and business interests backed the overthrow of Mexico's democratically elected Sebastian Lerdo de Tejada (1872–1876) in favor of the pro-U.S. Porfirio Díaz. Thus, U.S. economic gains made earlier in the century were enhanced and solidified. Díaz opened Mexico to foreign investment and made land concessions to corporate bidders. By the end of the Porfiriato, primarily mining and railroad companies had ownership or control of 27 percent of Mexico's land.

The forced reallocation of land to businesses prompted a vast population displacement from the countryside that drove migrants into Mexico's cities and onto trains to the northern border; Mexicans had been transformed into "a surplus labor supply available to work on the expanding U.S. owned operations." As the U.S. Southwest economy grew at the turn of the century, U.S. labor recruiters drafted Mexicans for work in agriculture. Challenging the usual assessment that the Revolution prompted increased northbound migration, Gonzalez argues that migration in fact diminished and did not return to its previous levels until the violence subsided. Business interests manipulated U.S. immigration legislation in 1917 and 1924 to exempt Mexicans from

---

42. In "From Conquest to Colonization," Hernández (2010a) challenges the thesis of late nineteenth-century Mexican state whitening initiatives, arguing instead that European immigration was encouraged because of a broader Realpolitik stance by government officials.

entry restriction and successfully petitioned for the first bracero program for temporary Mexican contract labor from 1917 to 1921.

As the Mexican population expanded in the United States, women and families joined men to become part of new ethnically segregated communities (Wilson 2009). For youth in those communities, educators established "Americanization" curricula that sought to "remake" the Mexican into a civilized version of her former self. Yet segregation erected a barrier to integration into mainstream society and Mexican students were channeled into vocational schools "better suited to their needs."

By the 1920s the definition of "The Mexican Problem" had been recrafted to describe Mexican workers who, having developed working-class affiliations, began to organize in unions and protest labor conditions in a series of strikes. Meanwhile, Mexican elites depended on migration and, according to Galarza, viewed it as a "means to evade the necessary reforms required to resolve Mexico's underdevelopment and its subjection to the power of foreign capital."

A decade later during and following the Great Depression of 1929, officials and Mexicans on both sides of the border developed a very different relationship with migration. In what amounted to the largest deportation/repatriation movement in migratory history, over 350,000 people left the United States for Mexico in the 1930s. Over half of those migrants were minor children born in the United States but received by the Mexican government as nationals. As Fernando Alanis Enciso points out in Chapter Three, "The Repatriation of Mexicans from the United States and Mexican Nationalism, 1929–1940," Mexican migrants left the United States for a variety of reasons including forced deportation, family reunification, and personal economic convenience. The historiography on the subject, Alanis Enciso argues, elides this diversity of experience and also tends to focus on U.S. and Mexican government actions, ignoring the economic and cultural impact of the returnees on Mexican society. Although acknowledging the heightened xenophobia, racism, and repression during the period experienced by Mexican migrants in places like Los Angeles County, Alanis Enciso chooses to closely examine the repatriation of Mexicans to their patria as an element of the post-Revolutionary government's efforts to consolidate the nation-state.

Government officials drew on earlier federal initiatives that sought to construct a new Mexican identity by integrating the population through a system of patriotic education, the arts, and public rituals in the context of anti-imperialism and sinophobia. A series of short-term presidents in the early 1930s and then Lázaro Cárdenas (1934–1940) depicted return migrants as heroic figures and defenders of the patria and as either destitute and in need of care or filled with vital agricultural knowledge that could serve in the "self-colonization" and "Mexicanization" of the northern provinces.

Official programs to reincorporate migrants into Mexican society engendered mixed responses. Attempts to create a demographic bulwark against potential future U.S. expansionism by populating thinly settled areas and locations with a sizable non-Mexican community often failed for lack of funds and political support. Cárdenas hoped to rally popular support by raising funds in town and district committees throughout the country and develop a series of new colonies to house displaced migrants. Although the government sponsored Half a Million project raised a moderate amount of money and patriotic fervor around the country, the migrant colonies were less successful. With return migration greatly diminishing by the second half of the decade, the colonies lost support and, in some cases, politicians like Secretary of Labor Lombardo Toledano argued that the government should first aid "nationals that had remained in the country."

With the end of the Depression and the advent of World War II, the context for the departure and reception of Mexican migrants shifted yet again. Wartime mobilization in the United States resulted in labor shortages, predominantly in agriculture, and the subsequent drafting of an "emergency" contract immigration policy that would eventually last twenty-two years (1942–1964) and produce 4.6 million bracero (strong-armed men) contracts. For many Mexicans the Bracero period was a "source of shame, symbolic of a failed revolution and yet another reminder of Mexico's dependence on the United States."[43]

Most studies of the period document the labor and living conditions of the Mexican workers in the United States. However, in his chapter, "The Bracero Program, 1942–1964," Michael Snodgrass examines the impact of the bilateral agreement on Mexicans as most returned to their home communities and the diverse opinions of policy makers, antiemigration critics, and the migrants themselves.

To support their case, Mexican government officials drew on the anthropologist Manuel Gamio's sanguine analysis of migration that touted its nationalizing, civilizing, and technological benefits despite hardships and exploitation. Yet critics on the left and right of the political spectrum complained of the program's potential damage to Mexico's economy and sovereignty. At the local level the Catholic Church, condemnatory of the perceived proselytizing influence of U.S. Protestantism on their parishioners, offered blessings to migrants and lauded their donations to the sanctuaries and congregations. Emigrants themselves, young men heralding primarily from states in west-central Mexico, largely supported the program and its economic contributions to their communities.

Snodgrass challenges the dominant "safety valve" explanation for out-migration that holds that migrants—either forced or on their own accord—left Mexico, thus relieving impending pressures of unemployment or political unrest. By contrast, he argues, bracero migrants left for a host of reasons including land and labor shortage, neglect of agrarian initiatives, and short-term regional financial and environmental crises. Instead of strategically expelling political radicals, officials in the dominant Institutional Revolutionary Party (PRI) often used bracero contracts as part of a larger system of patronage and party rule.

Following the war and into the 1950s, migrants had established enduring social networks through generations of transnational movement: thousands obtained legal permanent residence, whereas others circumvented the tedious and often abusive contract system and crossed without documents to the North. In large part because of civil rights and union pressures in the United States, the Bracero Program was officially concluded in 1964. Mexico attempted to revive the bracero agreements, but by then undocumented Mexican laborers were easily fulfilling U.S. labor demands and thus obviating the need for further bilateral agreements.

---

43. For an extensive collection of oral history interviews, images, and secondary sources, see *The Bracero Archive*.

The increased flow of migrants through Mexico's north to the United States during the Bracero period helped to grow the population of the border region. Although it was meant to diminish emigration to the United States, the renewed development of the binational border zone through the massive Border Industrialization Program in Mexico ultimately helped to stimulate northward crossings. In Chapter Five, "Migration and the Border, 1965–1985," Oscar Martínez examines a transitional period in the history of Mexican migration to the United States when unbalanced binational cooperation between the two governments gave way to unilateral enforcement measures by the United States to stem the tide of a perceived "invasion of illegal aliens."

From the 1940s through the 1970s Mexico experienced an "economic miracle" that witnessed massive industrial and agricultural growth supported by soaring prices for oil exports. In this climate improved living standards aided a concomitant demographic surge in the country. Yet despite this economic expansion, there remained enormous wealth disparities in Mexico and, with increased demographic pressures and labor demands in the United States, the number of emigrants continued to grow unabated. The border region experienced this growth acutely as thousands of "green-card" workers commuted on a daily basis between Mexico and the United States. Mexico established incentives to lure multinational corporations to the region that in turn attracted an enormous supply of workers, mainly women, to new assembly plants. As Martínez points out, Mexican and U.S. cities along the two-thousand-mile border "functioned as a single economic entity linked to the world economy."

The end of the Bracero Program in 1964 foreshadowed the passage of the 1965 Hart–Cellar Act. An amendment of the 1952 Immigration and Nationalities Act, the 1965 legislation was celebrated as a civil rights era liberal reform of the racist and exclusionary national-origins quota system that had been in place without substantial mitigation since the 1882 Chinese Exclusion Act (De Genova 2005, 230). Despite its official reception as a progressive and radical departure from past restrictive migration legislation, the new law, which took effect in 1968, in fact deepened and solidified the temporary status of Mexican migrants and intensified the institutional framework that further enabled the codification of Mexicans as "illegals." Previously exempt from quantitative restrictions, Mexicans now faced a new numerical cap for migration far lower than the actual numbers that had continued to increase during the Bracero Program (Alba n.d.). As a result, Immigration and Naturalization Service apprehensions and deportations skyrocketed. The number of detained Mexican migrants in the United States rose from 151,000 in 1968 to 781,000 in 1976 when migration was further restricted.

Emigration increased yet again with the abrupt end of the Mexican "miracle" in 1982 when global oil prices, on which the economy depended, plummeted. Although a heated debate ensued over the exact number of undocumented migrants traveling on an annual basis to the "other side," public and political opinion in the United States grew increasingly anti-immigrant, resulting in a series of new punitive and restrictive immigration laws. President Carter (1976–1980) established yet another short-term plan to reduce the flow of undocumented immigrants through border and workplace enforcement and regulate their presence already in the United States. In what became a controversial and ultimately failed attempt at border control, the U.S. government erected a "Tortilla Curtain" along the border in El Paso, Texas, in 1978. Unsuccessful at reducing the crossing of undocumented migrants, the barbed wire–encrusted wall only served to ignite the anger of human rights and business organizations that, for different reasons, demanded its removal.

In Chapter Six, "Race and the New Southern Migration, 1986 to the Present," Helen Marrow initiates the volume's comparative thematic section. In the mid-1980s, for the first time in this century-long history, migrants in a sustained and growing manner began to travel to and settle in locations outside traditional U.S "gateway" states (Arizona, California, Illinois, New Mexico, and Texas). One of these new locations, the U.S. South (excluding Texas and Florida), a stranger to the historical settlement of Mexicans, witnessed a rapid rise in the arrival of migrants. Attracted to a burgeoning agricultural and industrial economy, Mexicans encountered a rigid and deeply entrenched binary racial boundary between blacks and whites that provided little cultural context for understanding and accepting the presence of Latino immigrants.

The most recent period of Mexican migration came with the passing of the Immigration Reform and Control Act, or the U.S. federal IRCA, in 1986. Thanks to IRCA, by 1990 a total of 2.3 million Mexicans acquired legal status in the United States. This fact and that of an increasingly militarized border fundamentally restructured the migration and settlement patterns of Mexicans through the present day. A securely guarded border dissuaded immigrants from returning to Mexico for fear of capture upon return to the United States. New legal status empowered migrants to move themselves and their families beyond historically established communities. California, with a declining economy and rising nativist, anti-immigrant activism, witnessed its first migrant population decline in decades while migrants journeyed to new locations in search of employment and cultural acceptance (Durand, Massey, and Charvet 2000). It is during this last, post-IRCA era that once-distant regions such as the U.S. South have received their largest influx of Mexican migrants.

A deepening economic crisis in Mexico and the related increased integration with and dependence on the U.S. economy following the passage of the General Agreement on Tariffs and Trade in 1986 and then NAFTA in 1994 further stimulated northbound migration.

Nonwhite/nonblack migrants arriving to the traditional U.S. South have begun to incorporate into and transform the region's racial hierarchies. Through ethnographic research and interviews Marrow examines how Mexican migrants and southern natives have shifted their understanding of ethnic and racial identities. Marrow finds that Mexican migrants perceive better social interactions with and treatment by white southerners than black. As such, Mexicans observe "that the boundaries separating themselves from whites, although existent, are somewhat more permeable than those separating either whites from themselves or whites from blacks." Structural conditions of access to and competition for employment symbolically and materially frame these perceptions, Marrow argues. In addition to suffering racial prejudice by both blacks and whites, Mexican respondents also cited discrimination along the lines of legal and citizenship status.

In Chapter Seven, "Indigenous Mexican Migrants," Jonathan Fox further complicates notions of race and ethnicity by examining the multiracial and multiethnic identities of indigenous Mexican migrants. Whereas most scholars, politicians, and community organizers employ conceptual frameworks that categorize Mexicans as ethnically homogenous, Fox points out that currently "more than one in ten Mexicans comes from a family in which an indigenous language is spoken." In recent years the percentage of indigenous migrants laboring in the U.S. agricultural industry has grow to 15 percent nationally, with a high of nearly 20 percent in California. Utilizing a comparative and binational approach, Fox demonstrates how the distinct yet intersecting categories of race, ethnicity, and national identity are transformed through the process of migration in specific local contexts.

Subordinated in Mexico and the United States as migrants and indigenous people, indigenous migrants work at the bottom of the labor pyramid and are denied full citizenship rights in both countries. Yet despite these disadvantages, indigenous migrants have been active leaders in community development and movements for social justice and political democratization.

Within the context of differing yet overlapping constructions of race and ethnicity in Mexico and the United States, Fox also focuses on how, in the face of repression and cultural and territorial dislocation, collective practices are emerging that redefine ethnic and racial group membership and "constitute a specifically indigenous Mexican migrant civil society." In recent years, as indigenous Mexican migrants reconstruct their relationships with their "home" communities in a transnational environment, they have forged pan-ethnic networks such as the Oaxacan Indigenous Binational Front. With members and locations in both countries simultaneously, Oaxacan Indigenous Binational Front members engage in multisited forms of social action and governance in places like Los Angeles and Baja California.

David FitzGerald examines the binational legal contexts of migration in Chapter Eight, "Mexican Migration and the Law." Although largely shaped by an asymmetrical dynamic that favored U.S. economic dominance, both countries' migration legislation also shifted course during the world wars, especially in the 1940s when for a brief time the United States was vulnerable because of an urgent need for agricultural workers. For the most part, however, the U.S. government has dictated the legal limits of migratory flow, often circumventing or directly contradicting Mexico's laws, preventing Mexico from enforcing its own laws meant to protect emigrants.

From a century-long historical perspective, FitzGerald argues that assumptions that Mexico's government has uniformly utilized emigration as a political and economic "escape valve" elide the fact that for the first half of the twentieth century Mexican elites viewed preventing emigration as central to the nation's economic and social health. At odds with a constitutional provision that guaranteed freedom of exit, federal, state, and local governments in Mexico imposed obstacles to emigration by requiring visas and developing antiemigration propaganda campaigns.

Following World War II and by the end of the Bracero Program in 1964, the rapid growth of Mexico's population and the increased labor demand in the United States led "both governments [to] tacitly accept massive illegal migration." In the past two decades Mexico has dramatically altered its policy toward its citizens north of the border. Indicative of this recent shift that sought to secure the economic and political resources of its migrants living abroad, President Ernesto Zedillo (1994–2000) declared that "the Mexican nation extends beyond the territory contained within its borders." Indeed, in 1998 Mexico permitted its citizens to obtain dual citizenship with the United States and, as of 2006, to vote in presidential elections. Mexican emigration policies also turned to protect migrants crossing the border and provide them with educational and legal assistance while in the United States.

FitzGerald takes the same care to examine the history of U.S. immigration policy toward Mexicans. He demonstrates how economic boom and bust cycles determined trends of promotion and rejection of Mexican migration to the United States. Invariably, attempts to deter migrants through border and domestic enforcement have failed. Instead, policies of deterrence have only forced migrants to find new and more dangerous locations to cross the border and remain for longer periods in the United States. FitzGerald argues that new laws must provide more space for legalized Mexican migration if further massive unauthorized migration is to be avoided.

The impact migration has upon the experience and regulation of Mexican identities is further explored in Chapter Nine, "Gender, Sexuality, and Mexican Migration." In the chapter, Eithne Luibhéid and Robert Buffington examine the "central role that gender and sexuality…play in the decision to migrate, the lives migrants lead, their work experiences, the government policies that seek to regulate them, and the anti-immigrant sentiments that shape those policies." As the authors point out, their focus on the gender and sexual identities of migrants also illuminates the broader political and economic contexts in which they are constructed and help form.

Many narratives of the Mexican diaspora generated from the United States cast migrants as racially and sexually primitive, vulnerable individuals that require supervision and control. These pathological descriptions of hyperfertile women and static, patriarchal families have guided heterosexist migrant research and legislation. Contrary to depictions of the United States as a panacea that purifies and liberates Mexicans of their deviant sexual proclivities and atavistic gender relations, Luibhéid and Buffington argue that lesbian, gay, bisexual, and transgender migrants often encounter increased discrimination in the United States.

The emergence of neoliberal economic policies in the 1980s and 1990s with programs such as NAFTA further disrupted normative notions of gender and sexuality. The combination of increased migration of women to el Norte and the erosion of barriers between public and private spheres forced migrants to reconsider their individual and communal identities. Immigration legislation that promoted the unification of heterosexual families further marked the difference between gay and straight migrants.

Although U.S. government attempts to regulate the gender and sexuality of immigrants have ultimately failed (for its part, Mexico does not attempt to police the sexuality of migrants), the enduring control and management of migrant identities has weighed heavily upon groups and individuals. Yet, despite facing multiple forms of repression and subordination, Mexican migrants have crafted ways of accommodating, resisting, and negotiating intrusion by the state.

In the volume's final thematic chapter, "Cultural Representation and Mexican Immigration," Alex Saragoza examines the depiction of Mexican migrants from the perspective of U.S. and Mexican media. He argues that although both countries have witnessed fundamental shifts toward more positive portrayals of Mexican sojourners, the mainstream television, radio, and film industries in the United States in particular continue to actively ignore migrants and their experiences. Nevertheless, immigration advocates and migrants themselves increasingly have found ways to challenge nativist representations and constructed new sites for the expression of *mexicanidad*, especially in local, community-based rituals and performances.

Focusing on popular media, Saragoza situates the bi- and transnational representations of migrants in their shifting historical contexts. The narrative arc in the United States has moved from racist, anticommunist-influenced depictions of "a siesta-loving, lazy, *peon* of the 1920s" to more moderate interpretations during the civil rights era, followed by renewed xenophobic representations during the Reagan era of the 1980s. Concomitant with the rise of neoconservatism in the 1980s was the onset of the so-called "Hispanic market" era that viewed a rapidly expanding Spanish-speaking immigrant population as a fertile market source. Influenced and funded by Mexican media conglomerates, Spanish-language media has continued to grow with the Latino population in the United States. The attacks of September 11, 2001, reanimated nativist sentiments and promoted anti-immigrant protests that conflated immigrants with terrorists.

Paralleling Mexico's legislative focus toward the country's emigrant population throughout the twentieth century, initial representations cast *mexicanos de afuera* as degenerate *pochos* and traitors to the patria. Yet, with the eventual political and economic embrace of migration following the Bracero era, media portrayals also became more positive and empathetic.

As media consumers, Mexicans on either side of the *frontera* and non-Mexicans in the United States have been influenced by film, television, and radio productions from both countries. Given the cross-border movement of both migrants and media, "what may have begun as a binational process became a transnational cultural phenomena as a consequence of the historical persistence of Mexican immigration and its attendant, circular cultural flows."

In the epilogue, "The Past and Future of Mexico–U.S. Migration," Douglas Massey concludes the volume with a sobering review of the history of Mexican migration to the United States and cautiously suggests some possible future directions.

After surveying the many cycles of economic change in both countries and the periods of U.S. recruitment, passive acceptance, and persecution of Mexican migrants, Massey concludes, "never before have so many immigrants been placed in such a vulnerable position and subject to such high levels of official exclusion and discrimination." The current stage of anti-immigrant repression emerged from the border militarization and domestic enforcement policies following IRCA in 1986 and then intensified in the wake of September 11, 2001 (Velasco Grajales 2008). This "new war on immigrants" has effectively stopped the flow of undocumented migration while forcing millions of unauthorized migrants to choose to remain in the United States and increasingly seek legalization and citizenship.

Although more than any other time in history Mexican migrants in the United States live without full legal protection and annual deportations have surged in number to over 350,000, the government's immigration administration is benefiting by leaps and bounds. The Border Patrol and the recently established Immigration and Customs Enforcement branch of the Department of Homeland Security have watched their budgets and staff grow multifold in the past two decades (see also Fernandes 2007). Massey points out that the current economic crisis has only further exacerbated these conditions, reducing, for example, the rate and amount of remittances sent back to families and communities in Mexico.

CONCLUSIONS

In his 2008 report on the status of human rights of migrants living in the United States, sociologist and UN Special Rapporteur Jorge Bustamante unleashed a scathing critique of the failure of U.S. government policies to adhere to their professed commitment to international laws, human rights norms, and protocols. In particular, he emphasized violations in immigrant deportation and detention actions, of migrant worker rights and the rights of women and children, and criticized the recurrence of racial profiling and the absence of habeas corpus and proper judicial review. Highlighting the experience of Mexican migrants, Bustamante's summary of recommendations for the government noted that "the United States lacks a clear, consistent, long-term strategy to improve respect for the human rights of migrants" (Bustamante 2008).

Given the historically inexorable flow of its compatriots over the northern border, the Mexican government has had little choice but to support migrants in the United States and their families at home. With remittances in recent years accounting for one of the main inputs to Mexico's gross domestic product, politicians have been reluctant to stem the flow of migradollars back to communities and state coffers. The Mexican government and civil organizations have found ways to support the political and cultural lives of Mexicans resident in the United States, including granting in absentia voting rights and financial and community support for the expression and maintenance of local village traditions.[44]

Although it continues to depend upon Mexican migrant labor to sustain various elements of its economy, the U.S. government has yet to secure an effective long-term solution to protect these hard-working people from arbitrary exploitation and conditions of vulnerability and deportability (Kanstroom 2007). If the contributions in this volume documenting the enduring transnational phenomenon of migration have taught us anything, it is that short-term, unilateral solutions for the sake of political expediency will continue to fail. Unfortunately, despite U.S. President Barack Obama's campaign promises and optimistic overtures to Mexican and other migrants, there seems to be little promise of comprehensive immigration reform.[45] Indeed, Homeland Security Secretary Janet Napolitano continues to promote ineffective and lopsided border and workplace enforcement measures. None of the new wave of immigration bills proposed in the 2010 congressional session addressed a true comprehensive approach to the problem that engages the participation of the Mexican government and Mexican migrants themselves in crafting long-term solutions. Rising nationalist and xenophobic

---

44. In the most recent display of official government support, Mexican president Felipe Calderón addressed a joint session of Congress about the plight of Mexican migrants during his May 2010 visit to Washington, D.C. Although acknowledging the U.S.'s sovereignty, Calderón forcefully condemned the U.S. government's treatment of migrants and urged legislators to legalize job-seeking immigrants (Birns 2010).

45. "Obama: Immigration Reform?" In 2010 the Obama administration deported a record number of Mexican and other immigrants back to their home countries, a 10 percent increase over similar efforts by the George W. Bush administration. On August 13, 2010, President Obama signed into law the Southwest Border Security Bill—supported by a bipartisan majority—that increased funds for the militarization of the U.S.–Mexico border by $600 million. The bill included funds to deploy 1,500 new Border Patrol agents as well as two aerial surveillance drones.

responses to immigration in the context of a global financial crisis have only further stymied the progress of reform. In the absence of federal legislation, state and municipal politicians have authored their own legislation that seeks to curtail the rights of migrant workers. Arizona's immigration law, Support Our Law Enforcement and Safe Neighborhood (SB 1070), which legalizes racial profiling in the guise of security, is but one example of thousands of new initiatives around the country.[46]

What is urgently required is an entirely new model that utilizes bilateral negotiations to remedy long-standing economic inequalities between the two countries; corrects historically based legislation at the national level that positions Mexican migrants as illegal, vulnerable, and racialized subjects; and promotes human and workplace rights at the local level.[47] As Susanne Jonas avers, what is needed are "an alternative set of policies—more in tune with current economic realities and stated U.S. political goals of promoting democracy and stability—[that] would be based on a cross-border reconceptualization of citizenship and would recognize the accountability of states to civil society across borders and at borders" (Jonas and Thomas 1999, xiii). Drawing on her work with migrant laborers, Jennifer Gordon goes a step further and advocates for a new framework of "transnational labor citizenship" that opens

> the fortress of labor and of the nation-state to a constant flow of new migrants, through a model that links permission to enter the country to membership in a network of cross-border worker organizations rather than to employment by a particular enterprise. In exchange for authorization to work, migrant worker members would commit to the core value of labor citizenship: solidarity with other workers in the United States, expressed as a commitment to refuse work under conditions that violate the law or labor agreements. (2007, 1)[48]

---

46. A federal judge blocked the most controversial elements of SB 1070 before it could take effect on July 29, 2010. Its legislation has prompted widespread protest in Arizona and around the country. Although most state legislation focuses on punitive and restrictive measures for migrants and their employers, some states have taken steps to support migrant rights and education. Resembling the still unapproved federal DREAM Act, ten states have passed laws granting in-state tuition rights that allow children of undocumented migrants to attend postsecondary institutions without paying prohibitive out-of-state fees.

47. Two decades ago Wayne Cornelius and Jorge Bustamante (1989) suggested a series of bilateral policy options to address the impoverished working and living conditions of Mexican migrants that are still very relevant today; they included the following: "Significantly expand opportunities for legal permanent immigration from Mexico"; "Develop mechanisms for harnessing the capital being generated through the labor of Mexican nationals in the United States, to promote broadly based economic and social development in migrants' places of origin"; "Press for an enforceable bilateral accord guaranteeing the labor and human rights of migrant workers"; and Mexico should "develop an explicit national policy on emigration...to spell out the specific interests of Mexico that are at stake." "Such a policy statement would help to combat widely held U.S. perceptions that Mexico has no interest in reducing the exportation of its "surplus" labor, and lacks realistic plans and programs that address the root causes of emigration to the United States" (14–18). Drawing on the work of Cornelius, Bustamante, and others, Jorge Castañeda (2007) forwards his own set of policy recommendations that, in addition to many of the aforementioned suggestions, includes securing Mexico's southern border to stem the flow of Central American migration through Mexico (168–94).

48. In *The Rights of Others* Benhabib (2004, 17) proposes a system that reconciles the "constitutive dilemma at the heart of liberal democracies: between sovereign self-determination claims on the one hand and adherence to universal human rights principles on the other." Rather than advocating for the end of

Equally important would be, following David Bacon, to listen to and act on the concerns and needs of migrants themselves and create avenues to political enfranchisement and a broader democratic process (Bacon 2008, esp. 250–61).

In the meantime, I hope that this volume contributes a much needed historical, transnational dimension to those discussions as we search and struggle for more just and equitable conditions for Mexican migrants.

---

states, Benhabib argues for additional "democratic attachments" to sub- and supranational spaces. In this system of cosmopolitan federalism, migrants would retain their national allegiances while establishing other claims and rights beyond the nation-state.

PART ONE

Chronological Histories

CHAPTER 1

"Los de casa se van, los de fuera no vienen"
The First Mexican Immigrants, 1848–1900

Juan Mora-Torres
DePaul University

INTRODUCTION

From Independence in 1821 to the end of the Porfiriato, Mexican elites fell under the spell of Alexander Von Humboldt's claim that Mexico was blessed with unmatched and bountiful wealth. For Mexico to fully harvest the fruits of its natural wealth, Humboldt prescribed a better government and a more "industrious" population. Regarding Humboldt's *Political Essay on the Kingdom of New Spain* (1803) as the authoritative study on Mexico, elites envisioned their country becoming one of the wealthiest nations in the world.

Mexican elites were convinced that they could do a better job in guiding Mexico into a prosperous future than the former Spanish colonial rulers. Taking into account that 80 percent of the population was made up of Indians and castas, they assumed that Mexico did not have the "industrious" population or a sizeable labor force that was needed to fully develop the country's vast resources. Not having the best labor in the world, however, did not blur their vision of Mexico's auspicious future. This was an obstacle that could be overcome by opening the doors to European immigrants and assimilating the native population into the nation.

In the euphoria of Independence, liberal elites believed that Mexico could follow the path that the United States was taking. As the nation that liberals sought to emulate, the United States was not that far ahead of Mexico in 1821. In terms of population, the United States had 3.6 million more people than Mexico, it was 100,0000 square miles larger (Mexico had 1.7 million square miles), and, as of 1800, it had an economy that was twice as large (Bender 2006, 200; Coatsworth 1978, 80–83). Having the advantage of its vast natural wealth and expecting the arrival of thousands of immigrants, it was just a matter of time before Mexico occupied its place among the leading nations of the world.

These discussions on bettering and enlarging Mexico's labor force coincided in time with Europe's demographic revolution (for a discussion of these revolutions, see Moya 1998, 13–44). One component of this revolution involved the migration of millions of people across oceans and within Europe. More than 50 million Europeans left for other continents between 1820 and 1932 and, in the words of historian José Moya, "nothing resembling this massive movement had ever happened before anywhere in the world" (Moya 2006, 2). Over 90 percent of the Europeans settled in the Americas, where they altered labor markets, economies, cities, cultures, and the politics of the main receiving nations (Department of Economic and Social Affairs 2004, v; Moya 1998, 46).

From the very begining of Independence Mexican elites were fully aware of the early immigration movements trickling across the Atlantic, especially to the United States. Lorenzo de Zavala, a liberal ideologue, noted in the early 1830s that Mexicans "could not help but envy" the increase in "population, wealth, and prosperity taking place in the United States of the North" (de Zavala 1831, 130). Convinced that the country's prosperity depended on large numbers of immigrants, the different Mexican governments expected thousands of Europeans to come to Mexico.

For instance, this desire for immigrants became an obsession and a national priority throughout the nineteenth century. Melchor Ocampo, one of the leaders of La Reforma, stressed that immigration "is without doubt one of the most urgent needs of the Republic" (Ocampo 1901, 136). A question was raised in a French pamphlet that outlined Napoleon III's intentions in Mexico, "(w)hen one runs over the catalogue of the riches of Mexico, its wealth in grain and gold—those two vital forces of nations— one is tempted to ask how it is that its inhabitants make no more of their advantages?" (Chevalier 1863, 8–9; see Hanna and Abbey Hanna 1947). As a failed state, the Mexican government had not provided the requisite conditions needed for developing the country's vast wealth. The French, on the other hand, would provide political stability and work at "bringing in immigrants" (Chevalier 1863, 8–9) who would teach skills to Mexicans and guide them into a properous future. During the early Porfiriato, elites were convinced that one of the requirements for making Mexico into a modern nation hinged on recruiting thousands of immigrants. To pave the way for the thousands that they expected, the Porfirian government passed one of the most liberal immigration laws in the Americas in 1883.

By the end of the nineteenth century reality began to set in with a small minority of the elites regarding the wealth of Mexico and the prospects of large-scale immigration. Justo Sierra disputed the "wealthy Mexico" claim, regarding it as nothing but a myth. "It is not true that we are the wealthiest nation in the world," he wrote, "the wonders that enchant the horizon, only enrich the imagination; we are very poor" (quoted in León Portilla 1964, 363; González Navarro 1994, 17). Mexico was very poor compared with the United States and the gap separating both nations had widened by the eve of the Mexican Revolution. The United States had six times more people than Mexico in 1910 and almost five times more territory, and the size of the Mexican economy had dwindled to 2 percent of its northern neighbor.

In the case of immigration, the United States counted 13.5 million immigrants in 1910 compared with Mexico's 115,972, a figure that included the unheralded Guatemalans and Chinese, who made up 36 percent of all immigrants. Six American countries surpassed Mexico in the number of immigrants, including Cuba (five times more) and Uruguay (two and half times more).[1] Whereas the four largest countries of the hemisphere (the United States, Canada, Brazil, and Argentina) became countries of immigration, Mexico, the fifth largest, fell on the other side of the migration equation, becoming, until the 1960s, the sole nation of emigration in the Latin Americas. One million Mexicans resided in the United States (not including Mexican Americans) in 1930 when the Great Depression brought an end to the first "Age of Global Migrations."

"Los de fuera no vienen," wrote Antonio Caso, the Mexican philospher and educator, and "los de casa se van" (González Navarro 1996, 254). In those ten words Caso captured one of the problems in Mexican history from Independence to the Mexican Revolution: Why did Mexico fail to recruit large numbers of immigrants? Why did Mexico become the only country in the Americas that exported labor in the first Age of Global Migrations? In this chapter I will examine the origins of Mexican migration to the United States from 1848 to 1900, the causes that propelled it, and the implications it had for Mexico becoming a nation of emigration.

"1848" AND THE ORIGINS OF MEXICAN MIGRATION

In the periodization of national histories, "1848" is more relevant to the United States than Mexico. Accordingly, a new chapter in U.S. history began in 1848 when the acquisition of Mexican territory upset the balance of political power between free and slave states. This ultimately led to the Civil War (1860–1865). Despite the recognition of the important role that the United States has had in shaping Mexico (as highlighted by two often cited quotes on U.S.–Mexican relations, Porfirio Díaz's "Poor Mexico! So far from God and so close to the United States!" and Sebastian Lerdo de Tejada's "Between the weak and the strong, the desert!"), historians prefer 1854 as the beginning of a new chapter when the Ayutla rebellion ushered a long era of liberal rule. My intention here is not to provoke a discussion on the periodization of national histories, but to discuss an important aspect that 1848 had on both nations: the origins of Mexican migration, the causes that kept it flowing from 1848 to 1880, and the implications it had for Mexico, especially for the border states.

Although the Mexican population was small in the ceded territories (less than 100,000), the back-and-forth movement of people within the vast Mexican frontier was well established decades before the creation of the boundary line, albeit at a small scale. The new boundary intensified the movement of people into two important migration flows. The first involved thousands of Sonorenses, who left for California during the Gold Rush. The second and largest was made up of *fronterizos* from Northeastern Mexico who migrated to Texas.

Matías Romero, a Mexican diplomat, wrote that the new boundary brought together two nations that offered a "striking contrast to each other" (Romero 1892, 460–61). As Romero indirectly pointed out, the United States and Mexico were on different roads of development throughout the nineteenth century. In the case of the

---

1. The United States received 32.5 million of the 56 million European immigrants that came to the Americas (58 percent of the total) between 1820 and 1932. On the other hand, Mexico received 1/200 of all immigrants. See Moya (1998, 46).

United States, the goal of "Manifest Destiny" of American continental expansion had been realized in 1848 and it had 18 million more people than Mexico. Between 1800 and 1845 the Mexican economy had fallen from 51 to 8.5 percent of the size of the U.S. economy. As the American economy expanded at mid-century, Mexico was in the middle of a prolonged economic crisis, a crisis in which it "lost" decades of economic development (Coatsworth 1978, 82). The "striking contrast" met at the boundary and it had the effect of destabilizing the northern Mexican states in various ways, from a dramatic increase in violence (banditry, filibuster, and Indian raids) to altering social relations, such as those involving landlords and servants. One of the effects of this destabilization was a significant migration of Mexicans to the United States.

Mexico's first "so far from God and so close to the United States" misfortunes happened just a few months after the signing of the Treaty of Guadalupe Hidalgo in 1848. The discovery of placer gold in the Sierra Nevada of Alta California attracted thousands of people from Mexico, the United States, South America (mainly Peru and Chile), Europe, and Asia (mainly Australia and China). Sonorenses formed an important component of this global migration to California. Having the advantage of traveling a shorter distance, Sonorense "forty-eighters" were among the first to arrive, months ahead of the "forty-niners." Five to six thousand Mexicans left for California between October 1848 and March 1849, mainly Sonorenses but also Sinaloenses, Chihuahuenses, Duranguenses, and Michoacanos. Those with financial resources sailed from Guaymas and Manzanillo to San Francisco, but most left from Tubac (Arizona) in Apachería. For purposes of protection from the Apaches, they left in caravans, crossing the Sonora–Arizona desert before arriving in Los Angeles. From there they traveled along the California coast, turning northeast to the Sierra Nevada.[2]

Many Sonorenses were *gambusinos*, experienced miners who worked with their own resources. Arriving months ahead of the thousands of fortune seekers (100,000 arrived in 1849), they staked their mining claims and created new settlements, such as Sonora. Their experience in panning and dry washing mining techniques in Sonora served them well, and they prospered not only in mining but also as *arrieros* (teamsters) and merchants who imported goods from Mexico. Around two thirds of the Sonorenses returned home in the fall of 1849 and the scant evidence suggests that they did well in Alta California. The 248 Sonorenses that landed at Guaymas between November 15 and December 1, 1849, returned with $426,000 pesos, an amount that averaged $1,718 per person (most of Mexico's labor force did not earn that much in their lifetime). Nine who returned on horseback brought $155,000 (an average of $17,227 per person). All together they brought back a reported $2,337,000 in 1849, a significant sum considering that Mexico received $15 million for the ceded territories (Quijada Hernández and Ruibal Covella 1985, 108; "Bonanzas en la Alta California" 1865, 111; Standart 1996; Guinn 1909–1911, 31–34; Pitt 1966, Chap. III; Uribe Salas and Ochoa 1990, 18–20).

Even the "less fortunate ones, who are very few," did well, returning with no less than $700 pesos ("Bonanzas en la Alta California" 1865, 111). This was probably the case of the people that Cotija, Michoacán, sent to California. Better known as *arrieros*

---

2. This was the second Sonorense migration to Alta California. A sizeable number of Sonorenses went to the San Fernando Mountains, where Francisco López had discovered placer gold in 1842. See Guinn (1909–1911, 41).

than miners, the Cotijeños had a long tradition of hauling goods throughout Mexico, from Tabasco to Durango and, in all likelihood, they practiced this occupation in California. Their brief experience in California transformed them, as a politician noted: "I know men who were born here and had never been anything else but lowly servants (*domesticos*). And having lived in Alta California for a short time, they began to dress [better] and learned a craft that allows them to have an independent and decent life" (García 1872, 557).

Most of the returnees had no "intention of returning to California," but within a short time, they "caught the gold fever" once more ("Bonanza en la Alta California" 1865, 111). This time, however, they took friends and family with them. Manuel Ainza, for instance, left for California in 1848 to "try his luck just like so many thousands of adventurers." He returned to Sonora in 1850, staying just long enough to sell his possessions and pick up his family, an indication that perhaps he had no intention of returning ("Jesus M. Ainza contra México" 1902, 334–35). Of the four people who left Bacoachi for California in 1849, three returned the following year. Shortly after, they returned to California with over forty people from Bacoachi (Acome 1850, 79).

The exact number of Sonorenses (and other Mexicans) who migrated to California during the Gold Rush is not known. Compared with the number of people who entered California during this time (300,000 by 1855), the Sonorense migration was small, numbering somewhere between 15,000 and 20,000 people. Yet this was the largest self-sustained migration of Mexicans to the United States until the early 1900s. Moreover, it was large enough that an attempt was made to open a U.S. custom house in Southern California in 1850 because "at least ten thousand Sonorans passed through Los Angeles on their way to the mines, generally returning in the autumn" (quoted in Guinn 1909–1911, 33).

The Sonoran migration was significant for two important reasons that came to have future ramifications. First, the large presence of Sonorenses contributed to the early form that race relations took in post-1848 California. With 300,000 people arriving by 1855, California had become a "settler" majority state. As settlers, the Sonorans replaced the Californios (around 10,000) as the largest group of Mexicans (and perhaps also in wealth), at least for a few years. Arriving ahead of most fortune seekers, the Sonorenses carved for themselves a sizeable share of the early Gold Rush economy. Their visibility in mining, transportation, and commerce brought upon them the wrath of "native" and foreign "white" miners who, as latecomers and inexperienced in placer gold mining, envied their success. In their view, these sectors of the economy belonged to the "white race." A Yankee traveler noted the typical attitude that white settlers had upon first contact with Mexicans: "[they] believe in the inalienable right of the white man to bully the inferior race" (Richardson 1869, 239).

Outnumbering the *gambusinos*, they formed vigilante groups to remove the "greaser" competition and enforce white supremacy in the mining camps (163 Mexicans were lynched in California between 1848 and 1860).[3] Although they defended themselves from vigilante violence, the California legislature ensured their mass expulsions when it passed the Foreign Miners' Tax Law in 1850, forcing 15,000 to 20,000

---

3. This figure includes Chileans and Peruvians. For a good study on the lynching of Mexicans in the southwest, see Carrigan and Webb (2003).

Mexicans (also Peruvians and Chileans) to abandon their mining claims either because they refused or could not afford to pay the $30 per month tax. The few Mexicans who remained in the mines did so under the protection of more powerful white miners who employed them as wage-earners and as contract workers who worked for a share of the placer gold (Standart 1996, 10–13; Almaguer 1994, 69–71).

The number of Mexicans who returned to Mexico after their expulsion from the mining camps is not known. Many returned home in the early 1850s, whereas others settled in San Francisco and Southern California, especially in Los Angeles, where they congregated in the *barrio* of Sonora Town. Others were stranded without the monies to return home. In their case and others of "Spanish origins," the Mexican government commissioned Jesús Islas, a Sonoran residing in California, to organize in 1856 the repatriation of "the Hispano-Americano population of Alta California who because of differences in language, customs and religion do not amalgamate with the Anglo-Saxon race" (see "Dispoción del 13 de Febrero de 1856" 1893, 607–612; Guinn 1909–1911, 14; Hernández, José, 2008, 205–21). The repatriation campaign was poorly funded and organized. Only a few returned to Sonora.

Second, this significant flow of people had negative effects on Sonora, a thinly populated state. "The next migration will be more numerous than the previous one because it will not only involve those that returned but also those that did not go the first time," a government official noted in 1849, who also mourned that "Sonora will be left with women and old people who are impeded from mounting a horse" ("Bonanzas en la Alta California" 1865, 111). Over one tenth of the state's population had left for California during the first three years of the Gold Rush and the state government did not have the means to put an end to it, leading the same official to ask what became the most pressing question facing Sonora, "What will be the destiny of the frontier and of the *pueblos* who face the greatest Apache attacks in view of such a horrendous depopulation?" ("Bonanzas en la Alta California" 1865, 111). The departure of around 15,000 people thus not only represented for Sonora a loss of human labor force, but also vastly undermined its ability to defend settlements from Apache incursions. Five Sonoran towns reported a loss of six thousand inhabitants, whereas all eleven *pueblos* that made up the district of Arizpe lost people, including four that were left completely deserted (Biso 1864, 79; Standart 1996, 5). Sonora needed these people to help "cultivate its vast deserts and defend it against the *barbaros*" ("Dispoción del 13 de Febrero de 1856" 1893, 14). The migration of thousands, coupled with the intensification of the post-1848 Apache raids, created a crisis like no other in Sonora's history.

The expulsion of Mexicans from the mining camps essentially closed the door for Sonoran migration to California. Although many migrants returned by the mid-1850s, the Apache raids, the "political revolutions," and the migration of Sonorenses to Arizona (although reduced compared to the Gold Rush era) prolonged the specter that "Sonora will become depopulated" (Mowry 1866, 50). The inability of the Mexican government to provide security, coupled with the bleak view of Sonora's future, were important factors that drove Sonorenses to Arizona. Life was slightly better in Arizona, but it came at a price. A migrant wrote on the condition of Sonorenses in Arizona, underlining that life was "very hard" for those "who love their nationality" for they were "obligated to vegetate in foreign lands" (Davíla 1894, 122).

The Sonoran migration to Alta California provides insights into the next phase of large migrations that began in the last years of the nineteenth century. First, Sonorans created a cyclical migration pattern in which the first migrants returned home much better off than when they left. Consequently, this encouraged others to follow them in their next sojourn (and the cycle was repeated). Second, after their removal from lucrative occupations (miners, merchants, and teamsters), they were reduced to common laborers. This *déclassé* also took place in Texas when Know Nothing Party members accused Mexican teamsters of the "fact" that they were "willing to carry goods at a lower price than American citizens." During the so-called "Cart-War" of 1857 (in which seventy-five Mexicans were killed), Mexicans cart drivers were removed from dominating key transportation routes that "amounted to millions of dollars" (Johnson 1914, 515) a year. Third, unlike every other immigrant group at that time, they returned to Mexico in large numbers (either by force or voluntarily).

Of the "striking contrasts" between nations, Romero pointed to two that directly contributed to *fronterizo* migration to Texas. Unlike Mexico, the United States did not have *alcabalas* (the internal taxes on the movement of goods) and had much lower import duties (Romero 1892, 460–61). These two "contrasts" came together at the Río Bravo and, in the words of a politician, it placed the *fronterizo* settlements "in a special situation in respect to the other *pueblos* of the Republic" (*Segunda parte del expediente formado en la Secretaría de Hacienda* 1869, 322–23). He meant that the Mexican settlements were locked in an unfavorable position vis-à-vis the American settlements that were located across the Río Bravo. Given that the prices of goods were two to four times cheaper in the United States than in Mexico, the Mexican border towns could not compete commercially with the new American towns that 1848 gave birth to (Brownsville, Roma, Eagle Pass, Rio Grande City, and Edinburg). Almost overnight, Matamoros lost its position as the commercial gateway into northeastern Mexico to Brownsville.

Located within the realm of two different economies, the U.S. side of the Río Bravo offered *fronterizos* much cheaper goods and slightly higher wages than in Mexico. This "special situation" forced *fronterizos* to choose between "abandon(ing) Mexico in order to enjoy cheaper goods" or remaining at home and becoming *contrabandistas* (smugglers), the only occupation that offered any real economic prospects. In this scenario, "thousands of individuals" chose "a more comfortable life," leaving "deserted" the Tamaulipas border towns. Not all *fronterizos* "who, for the love of Mexico, refused to abandon their country" became *contrabandistas*. In their case, they surrendered to "extreme poverty ['se morian de hambre']," the cost of staying put and not engaging in illicit activities.

Without any authorization from the Mexican government, Ramón Guerra, the governor of Tamaulipas, declared the *zona libre* (Free Zone) for his state in 1858, justifying it as a necessary measure aimed at curtailing the loss of people who "are constantly immigrating [sic] to the neighboring country" (*Segunda Parte del expediente* 1869, 324; Romero 1892, 462–63). This migration began in 1848 and it was large enough to create a "situation" that was "so untenable and disquieting" in the northeast (Romero 1892, 460–61). The *zona libre* permitted the entry of duty-free goods within a twelve-and-a-half-mile radius of the boundary and, thus, it provided *fronterizos* with "more opportunities to earn a living." Opponents of *zona libre*, on the other hand, condemned it for facilitating massive amounts of contraband into the interior. Guerra reminded them that *fronterizos* "see the American territory as offering more opportunities than in their homeland" and that the Free Zone provided them with the only secure means for survival in a region that was locked in an unfavorable position vis-à-vis Texas and the rest of Mexico (*Segunda parte del expediente* 1869, 329). As Guerra noted, the desire for "more opportunities" was the driving force behind *fronterizo* migration.

A Mexican government report divided the *fronterizos* who had settled in Texas into two categories. The "good Mexicans" made up the majority and they "are honest, hardworking people, fleeing the revolutions in their own country, and giving their labor, and not infrequently capital, to the state" (*Reports of the Committee of Investigations sent in 1873* 1875, 19). Criminals, army deserters, and runaway servants constituted the "bad Mexican" because upon fleeing Mexico they had violated Mexican laws. This report indicated that most *fronterizos* left for two reasons: the United States offered better economic opportunities (and security) and to escape from Mexican *peonismo* (and, to a lesser extent, the forced military drafts). This was not an "escape valve" migration of an excess population. In the sparsely populated North, their departure represented a significant loss of a labor force and this was most clearly highlighted by runaway servants.

In the poorly populated and isolated frontier, hacendados had kept their *sirvientes* in perpetual bondage. The "special situation" in which the Northeastern states were placed in 1848 had the effect of undermining the hold hacendados had over *sirvientes*. Almost overnight the new boundary provided *sirvientes* with the possibility of escaping from a life of servitude, an opportunity that did not exist prior to 1848. This possibility also opened up for African American slaves in Texas. For the slave, Mexico was "in his head," a subversive idea that kept alive the hope of freedom. Perhaps, for the *fronterizo sirviente* Texas was in his head, the hope that a better life was within their reach. The possibility of escape was not available to other *sirvientes* in the rest of Mexico or for most slaves outside of Texas (see Kelley 2004).

Closeness to the Río Bravo offered slaves in Texas "an opportunity to make their escape into Mexico; and it was supposed that the lower class of Mexicans aided them in their flight." Meanwhile, *sirvientes* "sought a home in Texas. Many of this class had been peons—indentured servants—at home, and readily associated with the servile population of Texas; some intermarrying with Negro women" (Thrall 1879, 372; Pennybacker 1912, 233). An American travel writer noted that escaped slaves "found sympathy" and "refuge" in Mexico, as did the runaway peon in Texas (Richardson 1869, 244). It might have been the case that many of first *sirvientes* who fled from Mexico settled as far away from the Río Bravo as possible such as in Matagorda County (near present-day Houston), where they "hang around the plantations, taking the likeliest Negro women for wives." In 1856 these so-called "vagabond peons" were expelled from Colorado County for supposedly plotting a slave insurrection (quoted in Montejano 1987, 28; on the expulsion of Mexicans from Texas, see Montejano 1987, 24–27; Johnson 1914, 515; Thompson 2007, 34–36; *Informe de la Comisión Pesquesidora* 1984, 130; González Quiroga 1999, 128–34; and Carrigan and Webb 2003). The expulsion of Mexicans expanded to other counties the following year. In San Antonio, "Mexican citizens by birth" were driven out of the city, arriving in Mexico "on foot and without any means, having been obligated to abandon all their property in order to save their lives" (*Informe de la Comisión Pesquesidora* 1984, 130). Given the 1856–1857 expulsions, it might had been the case that *sirviente* mobility was restricted to south Texas, where Mexicans constituted the majority of the population.

The history of slave and *sirvientes* runaways is calling for a historian. As a result, we do not have figures on the number of *sirviente* runaways. In the case of African American slaves, a historian has claimed that the number of fugitives who escaped to Mexico was "in the thousands" (see Kelley 2004).[4] The exodus of slaves and peons represented for Texan slaveholders and *fronterizo* landlords a loss not only of labor but also of property, creating an "irrepressible conflict between the Mexicans and their Texan neighbors" (Richardson 1869, 244). In an attempt to prevent this conflict from escalating into outright violence, representatives of Texan slave owners met with Santiago Vidaurri, the governor of Nuevo León-Coahuila, in 1855 to discuss an extradition agreement in which Mexican officials would return runaway slaves and the Texans fugitive *sirvientes*. Vidaurri endorsed an extradition agreement as long as it was made between the two state governments. Unable to reach an agreement with Vidaurri, the Texans organized a large raid into Mexican territory with the aim of recovering stolen horses and slaves. They were repelled by Vidaurri's forces but not before burning down Piedras Negras (*Reports of the Committee of Investigations* 1875, 191–94).

By crossing the Río Bravo, *sirvientes* escaped into a life that was slightly better than the one they were running away from. Most settled in the "Mexican region" of Texas, where they found employment in haciendas and ranchos. Restricted in mobility to south Texas, the new *patrones* often retained their services with individual debts amounting to as much as $400 (see Montejano 1987, 79). In this sense, Mexican *peonismo* extended its reach to south Texas. Toribio Lozano, an hacendado with properties on both sides of the Río Bravo, employed *sirvientes* from Agua Fria, Nuevo León, for his ranch in San Diego, Texas. When seven of his *sirvientes* were murdered by Anglo-American vigilantes in 1873, they owed Lozano $663 in advanced wages (individual debts ranged from $43 to $216; Guajardo 1875, 96).

All things considered, south Texas represented a "kinder" *peonismo* for the fugitive *sirvientes*. As the lesser of two evils, Texan hacendados and ranchers offered *sirvientes* slightly higher wages, more provisions, and better treatment. These incentives made a difference in motivating many *sirvientes* to seek refuge in Texas and, thus, they made possible the expansion of ranching in south Texas. An Eagle Pass *hacendada* wrote in 1852, "We have always paid more than twice [the average wage] of our permanent servants, but of late we have repeated proffers of good shepherds and field hands for six and seven dollars a month, with the addition of meat and coffee rations, which the Americans have made a custom, and therefore a social law at Eagle Pass" (Cazneau and Montgomery 1966, 103). By paying higher wages and providing more food rations, this *hacendada* had no problem recruiting, and, more importantly, retaining what she considered "our permanent servants." Richard King and Mifflin Kennedy became Mexicanized in their building of the King Ranch (a more polite term for a hacienda) into the largest "ranch" in the United States. They employed hundreds of Mexicans, who were known as the "Kiñenos," under a system of paternalism in which the *patron* took care of their peons' cradle-to-grave needs.

---

4. Even after Emancipation, African Americans continued to view Mexico as an alternative to racial oppression in the American south.

The integration of south Texas ranching into the expanding American economy provided Texan hacendados with more financial resources than their Mexican counterparts. In view of the "the scarcity of hands in Texas," wages for *vaqueros* (cowboys) doubled from $6 to $12 between 1858 and 1880. Better treatment, more food rations, and higher wages made Texas a better alternative to Mexico in the eyes of the *sirvientes*. With that being the case, the *ranchos* in Texas were "swarming with fugitive servants from Mexico" (*Reports of the Committee of Investigations* 1875, 19 and 401; Taylor 1934, 116–25). One study reported that 2,812 *sirvientes* (in addition to 2,572 family members) had fled to Texas just from Nuevo León and Coahuila between 1848 and 1873 (landlords lost close to $400,000 in unpaid debts). In all probability, the number of runaways was larger because half of the municipalities did not respond to the requested information and because Tamaulipas was not included in this report (*Reports of the Committee of Investigations* 1875, 401–403; Taylor, *An American Mexican Frontier*, 36).

While fugitive *sirvientes* labored to make south Texas an important ranching region, their absence in the Mexican Northeast thwarted the expansion of the hacienda in an age when landlords were reaching the zenith of their power in Mexico. The *"fuga de sirvientes* (runaway servants)" coupled with a shortage of *jornaleros*, the free laborers, forced landlords to depend more on debt peonage as the means for recruiting and retaining labor. Earning between 0.25 and 0.50 *centavos* a day in Nuevo León, *jornaleros* were paid more than *sirvientes* who earned 4 to 5 pesos a month, in addition to a small weekly ration of maize. Landlords would have preferred to employ *jornaleros* (and pay a little more), but they could not secure many of them. For the most part, labor in Nuevo León could only be secured by monetary advancements that often amounted to more than a year in wages. Montemorelos landlords advanced between 60 and 100 pesos in wages to servants. Those from Santa Catarina had to advance wages; "otherwise, it would be impossible to carry out agricultural work due to the shortages of *brazos*" (Bustos 1889, 154 and 162; *La voz de Nuevo León* 1889). According to a local official, the practice of wage advancements empowered *sirvientes* for the reason that many did "not comply with their obligations, some abandoning their work assignments, others moving or fleeing without paying back what they owe" (Bustos 1889, 142–43; Secretaría de Fomento 1886, 1680).

Proximity to Texas undermined Northeastern *peonismo* to the extent that "the institution of servants, once a specialty and considered necessary on the frontier, cannot today be sustained" (*Reports of the Committee of Investigation* 1875, 403). *Fronterizos* had the advantage of "*la fuga* (fleeing)," an alternative that did not exist for other *sirvientes* in Mexico. Thousands fled and for landlords this represented major losses in labor and money. "It is not so much the loss of money" that worried the Comisión Pesquesidora, a Mexican government commission, but the loss of people in northern Mexico, "where the population is sparse, the lack of men being a loss of capital to the country, considered as they are instruments of labor" (*Reports of the Committee of Investigation* 1875, 401–02).

Hoping to prevent the "fast disappearing" system of *sirvientes,* the Comisión Pesquesidora recommended to the Mexican government that it negotiate an extradition treaty with the United States. Accordingly, the extradition of fugitives "would close the door to the system of roaming, which is indulged in by the people of the state of

Nuevo Leon, Coahuila and Tamaulipas toward the frontier of Texas" (*Reports of the Committee of Investigation* 1875, 403). Closing the door into Texas was the only way to curve the erosion of debt peonage. Once this was done, "the tide of emigration will be diminished" because "it will be known to the fugitives that Texas is no longer a place of refuge where they can flee with impunity" (*Reports of the Committee of Investigation* 1875, 403–04). This recommendation did not go anywhere within the Mexican government. On the other hand, Texas was not going to close its doors to Mexican labor. South Texas' shift from ranching to large-scale agriculture after 1880 came to depend on the growth of Mexican labor.

Fronterizo migrants contributed to the rapid growth of the Mexican population in the United States. Growing at a much faster rate than in Mexico, the Mexican population in the United States more than tripled from 1850 to 1880, increasing from an estimated 81,508 to 290,642 (Gratton and Gutmann 2000, 143). Although the number of immigrants within the overall Mexican population is not known, we can assume that it was fairly large. For reasons of proximity to the United States, *fronterizos* composed the overwhelming majority of the Mexican immigrants. In a sample of Mexicans who applied for American citizenship in San Antonio, Miguel Angel González Quiroga estimated that 80 percent came from the four states bordering Texas (Nuevo León led the pack with 32 percent).[5]

In light of the migration of thousands of *fronterizos*, a congressman from Tamaulipas bluntly stated, "Mexico needs labor, not the United States" (*Segunda parte del expediente* 1869, 329). As the region with the most severe labor shortages in all of Mexico, the northern states suffered most from the consequences of this outflow of people. It had become much poorer. Antonio Moreno, a senator from Sonora, stated in 1878, "Nobody changes nationality to assume a worse condition, and it is very dangerous to see just beyond the conventional line prosperity and wealth, and on the other side destitution and poverty" (Moreno, 1879, 831–33).

Guillermo Prieto, the liberal intellectual, visited California and Texas in 1877. He wrote in *Viaje a los Estado Unidos* that "a multitude" of Sinaloenses, Sonorenses, and Baja Californianos had settled in California. He was surprised to learn that these migrants wanted to return to "our motherland" because they felt "uprooted in this country that has given so many refuge." According to Prieto (who was at this time a political enemy of Porfirio Díaz), the high taxes, extortions from military chiefs, "forced loans," and "*la leva* (the forced military drafts)" drove them out of Mexico. Their absence from Mexico made the country a poorer place because they represented a loss in "vigor, labor, and resources" (Prieto 1993, 59–60, 187–88). Prieto's education on the condition of Mexicans in the United States continued when he visited San Antonio. He wrote, "I learned that [Texas'] relations with Chihuahua had not been interrupted, but on the contrary, many peons emigrated, attracted by the higher wages. Oh! [Low] wages, on the one hand, and the *leva*, on the other, have brought many Mexicans here" (Prieto 1993, 323).

---

5. Of the 4,337 Mexicans who applied for U.S. citizenship in San Antonio from 1848 to 1880, only 57 were granted citizenship (around 1 percent) compared with 46.8 percent of Germans. See González Quiroga 1999, 168.

"LOS DE AFUERA NO VIENEN": IMMIGRATION AND MEXICAN "CHEAP LABOR," 1876–1900

During the early Porfiriato the liberal discourse on the "Indian problem" had shifted from one of assimilation (and redemption) to one of inherent racial inferiority. For example, Antonio García Cubas, Mexico's foremost statistician and geographer of the nineteenth century, considered Indians an impediment to the development of Mexico. In an 1880 lecture entitled "On the Decadence of the Indians," García Cubas argued that the ongoing "degeneration" of the Indians began with "the wars of conquest" and was conditioned by "the work in the mines, the former system of encomiendas and repartamiento, the plagues and civil conflicts, the rude labor." The end result was that Indians constituted a population that was unfit to be a column that could sustain the construction of the modern republic (quoted in Weyl 1902, 14). If anything, they were more of a hindrance in this project, an opinion echoed by a Michoacán official who divided Mexico's nonwhite population into "proletariats" and Indians. The proletariats, meaning mestizos, worked while Indians "vegetate like parasites in a diseased tree" (Bustos 1889, 134).

Historian Enrique Florescano wrote that "for the Porfirian 'Científicos,' like the liberals before them, the Indians were the main barrier that impeded the development of Mexico." The shift in elite discourse on the Indian problem, from one of assimilation to inherent racial inferiority, initiated what Florescano regarded as "a racist campaign without parallel in the history of the nation" (Florescano 1996, 320). A cleric of that time blamed this campaign on liberalism that had "infiltrated Mexican Catholics, and they have adopted, in regard to the Indians, the feelings of scorn and desires to exterminate them" (Planchet 1906, 283).

This anti-Indian campaign had various objectives, from justifying the dispossession of their communal lands to keeping large numbers of Indians in labor bondage. It also had an immigration dimension. The Porfirian obsession with recruiting immigrants was grounded on the long-standing premise that Mexico did not have the best of people to create a modern nation. Matías Romero summarized the dominant elite understanding on Mexican development: "Many people hold the belief that the solution to Mexico's economic and social problems consists in facilating European immigration, and as long they do not come to our country on a large scale, we cannot aim for a progress that is rapid and positive" (*Memoria de la Secretaría de Hacienda y Crédito Público* 1892, 21). Although no national census was taken until 1895, it was estimated that 80 percent of Mexico's population in 1880 was nonwhite, a percentage that had not changed much since Independence. Associating race with the status of nations, the elites who came to form the *Científicos* produced "studies" that confirmed that Mexico had an inferior racial stock. Romero, a proponent of "civilizing" the Indian (rather than replacing them entirely), reached the same conclusions as the *Científicos*: "We have a pure Indian population race which probably exceeds half of the population of the Republic…Indians have preserved, with slight modifications, the same customs that they had when Columbus discovered America four hundred years ago…they consume what they produce and produce little for exportation. From this point of view, the Indian represents no factor in our public wealth" (*Memoria de la Secretaría de Hacienda y Crédito Público* 1892, 21). Stated another way, Mexico had too many Indians and not enough people of European ancestry. It would remain a poor country until Mexico improved its population stock.

Taking into account the nation's racial handicaps, an intellectual calculated that Mexico would be thirty times wealthier if it could only substitute its 11 million inhabitants (majority Indian) for Europeans. Another intellectual asserted that 5 million Argentineans because of their increasing European "blood" were worth more than 11 million Mexicans. Another estimated that the value of "the work of 4 million *indias* who are tied to their *metates* (grinding stones)" was equivalent to the wages earned by 32,000 white women working in American farms (see González Navarro 1957, 150–57; Florescano 1996, 319–20; *Anuales del Ministerio de Fomento* 1881, 96–97, 107; Secretaría de Fomento 1886, 159).

Beside making the case for immigration, the Porfirian anti-Indian campaign served the purpose of rationalizing Mexico's low wage system by associating racial inferiority to their alleged low labor productivity. Without any evidence other than hearsay, Matías Romero calculated that an American bricklayer could lay 2,500 bricks in nine hours, whereas a Mexican could lay 500 in eleven hours. This made the American bricklayer six times more productive than the Mexican. Francisco Bulnes estimated that an Afro-Brazilian could take care of 3,868 coffee trees (*cafetos*) compared with 1,215 for a Mexican Indian, amounting to a three-to-one difference. An economist calculated that on a production scale of 100 (represented by the English worker), labor productivity in Europe ranged from 60 to 52 compared with 25 to 40 in Mexico (González Navarro 1957, 150–57; Florescano 1996, 319–20; *Anuales del Ministerio de Fomento* 1881, 96–97, 107). Percy Martin, an English travel and business writer, had a higher regard for the productive capacities of Mexican workers than the Porfirian intelligentsia. In the case of miners, he elevated their labor productivity to "one-half to three-fourths as efficient" as their American counterparts (Martin 1906, 61–62). With such low labor productivity, it was only logical that the Mexicans earn less.

The *Científicos* were convinced that the elevation of Mexico into a progressive nation hinged on recruiting thousands of immigrants. They were optimistic that thousands of immigrants would make Mexico their home as the Porfiriato created a new social order. To pave the way for the thousands of expected newcomers, the Mexican government passed the Colonization Law of 1883, one of the most ambitious and liberal immigration laws in the western hemisphere. Just like the many wonders that they anticipated from the arrival of railroads, Porfirians expected thousands of immigrants coming and transforming Mexico in many positive ways, including the upgrading of the population. Francisco Pimentel envisioned Europeans mixing with Indians and, in doing so, enlarging the mestizo population. This would have meant a major improvement in Mexico's racial stock because mestizos had a history of doing the "hardest of work such as that of the miner, cowboy, blacksmith and other work that the Indian does not do." Even if immigrants did not mix with Indians, the "laws of natural selection" dictated that the European population would grow, whereas the Indian population would decline over time without "resorting to violence or any form of suffering." (Pimentel 1903, 266) The Catholic newspaper *Voz de México* did not exaggerate when it associated the goverment's call for immigration with the desire to "gradually reduce the indigenous majority until they become a small minority" (Planchet 1906, 283).

The expected thousands of immigrants had not come to Mexico by the mid-Porfiriato, nor were there any forecasts of their coming in the near future. Various reasons were given that sought to explain Mexico's failure of becoming a land of immigrants. One of the most important dealt with Mexico's low wages. Of all the large countries in the Americas, Mexico paid the lowest wages. Antonio Hernández, who managed one of the largest textile mills in northern Mexico, stated that immigrants tended to be poor and unskilled, just like the majority of Mexicans. Consequently, they could not "compete with our workers of the proleteriat class who have few [basic] needs" (Bustos 1889, 322–23). Hernández pointed to an important marker that was defining the notion of "Mexican cheap labor": Mexico's low wages met the subsistence needs of its laboring population, an opinion shared by an American academic who asserted that Mexicans were satisfied "with the prevailing low standard of life" (Weyl 1902, 88).

Matías Romero, Mexico's ambassador (1882–1898) to the United States, shared Hernández' understanding of the relationship between low wages and immigration, stating that Mexico had "a surplus of labor and a deficit of capital, and we cannot have a large immigration until such conditions are changed" (Romero, 1898, 126). Romero continued, "the principle obstacle which has prevented us from having a large immigration is our low wages. Those who immigrate are generally poor wage earners, who want to better their condition, and they could not go to a country where wages are a great deal lower than in the United States, or even in Europe, as they could not compete with the native labor of our Indians" (126). On the issue of wages, the evidence supported Romero's contention. Latin American nations that paid higher wages succeeded in recruiting many more immigrants than Mexico. Wages in Argentina were higher than in the United States and eleven times more than in Mexico. Meanwhile, Cuba's wages rivaled those in the United States (Moya 2006, 17).

As one of the few realists within the Porfirian ruling class, Romero recognized that Mexico would not attract large numbers of immigrants until wages were substantially elevated, a scenario that he did not expect in the immediate future. Until then, any hope of large-scale immigration was nothing more than wishful thinking. Romero advised foreigners not to come to Mexico unless they had capital for investments or labor skills. Mexico offered capitalists a large, cheap labor pool, an incentive that ensured them a return on their "investments hardly to be equaled anywhere else." Skilled workers, on the other hand, could earn wages that were much higher than in their native lands (Romero 1898, 542). A British official seconded Romero's advice in presenting Mexico as "the country for the capitalist in search of investments; it is certainly the worst country for a young man to come in search of employment. Wages are low... these remarks do not apply to skilled labourers..." (Diplomatic and Consular Reports 1900, 25). Skilled workers made up a high percentage of Mexico's small immigrant population, concentrated in the administrative, supervision, skilled, and semiskilled positions in mining, smelting, railroads, manufacturing, and plantations. Few became Mexican citizens.

A. A. Robinson, the president of the *Ferrocarril Central Mexicano*, also agreed with Romero's assertion that cheap labor was one of the best benefits that Mexico offered capitalists. However, he disagreed with Romero and the *Científicos'* contentions that Mexico had an unproductive labor force. Robinson and other foreigners held Mexican laborers in a much higher regard than the *Científicos*, going as far as declaring them more desirable than American workers: they were cheaper, worked longer hours, and were less troublesome (most Mexican workers were not organized in unions and engaged in radical working-class politics). Considering their preoccupation with the growth of socialist, anarchist, and other radical working class movements in the United States and Europe, Mexico was a capitalist utopia when it came to the "labor question." On this issue, Robinson gave the example of a Mexican mine worker earning a peso for a twelve-hour a day in the early 1890s compared with their American counterparts who earned three dollars for the eight-hour day and "yet are striking whenever an opportunity affords and demand better remuneration" (*Chicago Daily Tribune* 1894, 6). This represented a six-to-one wage difference for the work day and much more if divided into hourly wages. A *Harper's* article presented the foreign investors view on Mexican labor:

> In spite of all that has been said to the contrary, labor in Mexico is relatively good, cheap and abundant. Experience has shown that three Mexicans will do as much as work as three Celts, and cost less. Labor there is subject to its caprices, as in the United States, but of a less vexatious and costly character. There is no country in the world, probably, where the construction of the railways is less complicated by the labor question than in Mexico. (*Harper's New Monthly Magazine* 1882, 756)

This article appeared in 1882 in the midst of a long era of intense labor troubles in the United States, highlighted by the Haymarket and Pullman strikes in the late 1870s.

Even foreigners who were not completely sold on Mexico conceded that cheap labor was one of its advantages. On this point, one of them compared American and Guanajuato miners. The former earned US$3.50, whereas the latter 0.75 *centavos*, for an almost a ten-to-one wage difference. In part, he justified the wage gap on the grounds that Mexicans were one half to three fourths as productive as Americans. Despite being less productive miners, Mexicans were "good and fairly reliable workers" and "such things as strikes and 'unions' are unusual, the Mexican being, as a rule, a perfectly tractable and fairly industrious worker, but requiring a careful overseer" (Martin 1906, 61–62). On a weighting scale, a Mexican worker was a much better bargain because he is "easily managed and does nearly all classes of work fairly well," whereas the "white worker demands higher wages, quite disproportionate to the character and the amount of work that he does, and is additionally much more difficult to manage" (Martin 1906, 62).

As noted, the Porfirian rulers and foreign capitalists held two contrasting views on Mexican workers. These opposing views were informed by contrasting Mexican workers with other workers in industrial nations. For the *Científicos*, the Mexican worker was inferior, unproductive, and, in the case of the Indian, a burden to national development. Foreign capitalists regarded Mexican common workers as just as good as any worker. They were the perfect working class vis-à-vis Americans: they were reliable, tractable, docile, and very cheap. This assessment of Mexican workers crossed the border in 1890s. By the turn of the twentieth century, the call coming from the owners of railroads, mines, and farms was, "we have to have the Mexican as cheap labor" (quoted in Taylor 1928–1934, 444).

The Porfirian state ensured a "good business climate" in Mexico by pegging the peso to silver (until 1905 when Mexico entered the gold standard), which gradually depreciated to the dollar (gold). "The foreign investor doubles his capital when he brings it to Mexico," Romero wrote, because "he gets advantage of cheap and docile labor for silver, and sells his exported goods for gold" (Romero 1898, 571). In pointing to two of the main benefits that Mexico offered investors, Romero trivialized the exploitation of Mexican workers. A Chicago journalist demonstrated how the Mexican silver system punished workers and rewarded capitalists (especially those in the export sectors of the economy).

> Being paid for with foreign money, this increase [in exports] naturally has added to the wealth of the country. That wealth has been divided between the owners of the land, the middlemen, the commission houses and the banks. The laborer has received none of it. It has made the rich richer, and the poor poorer by comparison, for there are only those two classes in Mexico, and the gulf that divides them is becoming wider every day. The capitalist pays the same wages to the laborer that he paid ten years ago, but he sells the results produced by the laborer for twice as much as he received them. (quoted in Pletcher 1958, 45)

Cheap labor paid in silver and exported goods paid in gold made Mexico attractive to foreign capitalists, especially Americans, who had the largest investment portfolio. These investments were converting Mexico into an extension of the American economy.

Mexican "cheap labor" was a central component of Mexico's good business climate. In this sense, the Porfirian state did its part in maintaining the low wage system by keeping labor unrest to a minimum. Consequently, Mexico did not develop a strong trade union movement that could advance the interests of the laboring populations during most of the Porfiriato. As the Porfiriato aged, workers used "voice" by forming unions (railroad workers, for example) and waging strikes (Río Blanco and Cananea), whereas others literally voted with their feet, as they "exited" to *el norte*, to borrow Albert O. Hirschman's terminology.

Capitalism and the Transformation of Mexico's Labor Markets, 1876–1900

On June 1, 1881, U.S. Secretary of State James Blaine wrote a letter to P. H. Morgan outlining the new American diplomacy to its southern neighbor. As the head of the American legation in Mexico, Morgan was instructed to first assure the heads of the Mexican government that the United States did not have the "faintest desire" of acquiring any territory "south of the Rio Grande," and second to propose a "new commercial" relationship that could benefit both countries. This meant, in other words, that the age of territorial expansion coming at Mexico's expense had come to an end and that the United States had a surplus of capital that it needed to be moved outside of its borders. Mexico was an excellent destination given that it lacked the capital to take advantage of its "wonderful and scarcely developed resources" (Blaine to Morgan 1881, 761–62).

Porfirio Díaz (1877–1880 and 1884–1911) and Manuel González (1880–1884) welcomed this gesture after a decade of many diplomatic troubles with the United States. They did not need any convincing about a new commercial relationship. Their strategy had targeted foreign investments as essential for the success of Mexican economic development. The strategy worked, because Mexico became the first country in the world where American capitalists invested large amounts of capital.

The new commercial relationship was not forged among equals but on profound and widening national differences. In 1880 the United States had 42 million more people than Mexico, it had grown to be almost five times larger in territory (with the recent purchase of Alaska), and the Mexican economy had declined to 3 percent of the size of the U.S. economy (Coatsworth 1978, 82). Railroad mileage, an important yardstick for measuring domestic economic development, highlighted this inequality. In 1900 the United States had 189,295 miles (not including over 60,000 miles in yards, sidings, and parallel tracks), a figure that amounted to over 40 percent of the world's railroad mileage. At this time, Mexico had 8,505 miles of tracks, which, for the most part, were "connected with the United States by four trunk railways built by United States companies, which are really extensions and feeders of the trunk lines of this country" (*The World Almanac and Book of Facts* 1902, 658; Bensel 2000, 295).

Despite being aware of the vast economic gap separating both nations, the Porfirians followed the aphorism that "a rising tide lifts all boats." They were convinced that Mexico's economic integration to the United States was the fastest route for Mexican modernization. Unlike the previous regimes, the Porfirian state had the political muscle to enforce the expansion of capitalism (and, when necessary, guide it in that direction). Their policies of "order (political centralization) and progress (capitalist development)" were reciprocal and reinforced each other, fostering in Mexico a good business climate. The regime opened the doors to large inflows of foreign capital, secured private property rights (Baldio laws and new mining codes, for example), and ended those obstacles that had prevented the expansion and unification of the domestic market (such as the *alcabalas* and, later, the *zona libre*). Moreover, it protected native industries with high tariffs and promoted the expansion of rural capitalism by endorsing *hacendado* accumulation of lands at the expense of the peasantry. In fomenting a good business climate, the dictatorship kept labor and political unrest to a minimum (at least until the early 1900s) and therefore helped maintain Mexico's low wage system.

More than anything, the arrival of railroads symbolized the ushering in of a new era for Mexico, one that was almost the mirror opposite of the previous ones: it established excellent relations with the great powers and, therefore, a better international image; it ensured high rates of economic and population growth; and it secured political stability and healthy government finances. Although much has been written on Porfirian modernization, the empirical research on the ways capitalism created emigration (and internal migration) has not yet been examined in a systematic fashion. With this in mind and limited by space, I will focus on how modernization created emigration by focusing on the impact railroads had on haciendas and on the geographic distribution of labor. The hacienda not only was the largest employer of people, but also dictated regional wage scales. Regarding labor distribution, one can generalize that the north and south suffered from labor shortages before the arrival of the railroad, a problem that central Mexico did not face.

Not all agree with Matías Romero's contention that Mexico's low wage system was the result of a surplus of labor, a relationship between supply and demand. Others argued that Mexico suffered from labor shortages. In 1887 a journalist sarcastically questioned these claims: "There are no laborers, there are no *brazos* in Mexico; and yet the wages are as low as in China! Is the absolute law of supply and demand false?" (Romero 1971, 340). Using *el ranchero* as his *nom de plume*, he argued that Mexico's labor problem was rooted in the hacienda, the largest employer of people in the country. Without many employment alternatives other than the hacienda, many desperate people sold themselves cheaply to *hacendados*, ending up not as "slaves in name," but as "slaves in fact" (Romero 1971, 342–44).

Other intellectuals shared *el ranchero's* understanding of how the hacienda kept large numbers of laborers under conditions of bondage. One noted that "a good Negro" slave (a reference to Brazil) could be purchased for a thousand pesos, whereas a "good Indian" in Mexico could be acquired by a wage advancement of one hundred pesos. This wage advancement (which was really a loan that was paid back in labor) carried an interest rate of 8 to 10 percent a month. The hacienda's low wages fortified *peonismo* because it was impossible for *sirviente* to work off the debt. Therefore, a growing debt ensured not only their attachment to the hacienda but also that of the following generation who inherited their parents' debt. In contrast to other modern societies where "the demand for labor raises wages," Mexican *peonismo* was slavery in disguise in that many families continued working on paying off a fifty-peso debt that had been acquired one hundred years earlier (Secretaría de Fomento 1886, 168).

A good segment of the Porfirian intelligentsia and elites singled out the hacienda as the main obstacle preventing the emergence of a modern labor system. As long as most laborers remained unfree, Mexico would have an uneven geographical distribution of labor in which some regions lacked workers, mainly in the north and south, and others had a plentiful supply, as in the case of most of central Mexico, where the majority of the population lived. In the late 1870s the local authorities in Michoacán, a state in central Mexico, were reporting that their municipalities had a steady supply of labor (in all likelihood caused by the ongoing dispossession of the Indian communal lands that was producing a large landless population). Responding to a survey that asked where their locatities needed immigrants, Bellavista de Achotan responded that there was no need for immigration because "Mexico does not yet have a shortage of labor," whereas Pátzcuaro stated that foreigners would only cause "misery to the *hijos del pueblo*, who can barely subsist from their wages" (Busto 1889, 131–34). Other parts of Mexico were not as fortunate as Michoacán. The "lack of *brazos*" in Nuevo León had caused a "great decadence" in ranching, whereas the collapse in mining was caused by "the absence of a population and capital." Campeche, in the south, had a dire need of "*brazos* for agriculture," and Durango could not develop a mining industry because "it needs *brazos* and capital." The Apache wars in Chihuahua, coupled with the "shortage in population," had "impeded the development of the sources of wealth" (Paz and Tornel 1882, 641, 644, 645, 657).

An employer from Coahuila recommended "*autocolonización*," a policy involving government action in facilitating "the transportation of those who lack work to places where there is a demand for *brazos*." He reported that three districts in Coahuila (La Laguna, Monclova, and Río Grande) suffered from a "shortage of *brazos*" and, "until now, the work that employers have done to bring families here from the interior has not produced the expected result" because of the "public troubles that have dispersed the families, some going to Texas and others returning to the interior" (Busto 1889, 323). The government entertained a policy of *autocolonización* but did not pursue it.

Just about the time that Blaine's letter to Morgan reached Mexico City, two railroad lines, the Santa Fe and the Southern Pacific, arrived in El Paso. The Texas and Pacific railroad arrived a few months later, while the Ferrocarril Central Mexicano had just started constructing the El Paso–Mexico City line. Looking north for a vision of what the future could entail, Porfirians expected railroads to produce in Mexico the same results as in the United States. They expected railroads to generate instant economic growth and bring in thousands of immigrants, as an American journalist noted in 1882, "reasoning from their experience of railways in the United States, they assume that emigration will follow the locomotives through the wilds of Mexico as promptly and copiously as it has done through the prairies of Iowa...In their imagination they see thriving villages springing up at every station...It is from conclusions such as these that dreams are made" (*Harper's New Monthly Magazine* 1882, 751). This vision was distorted upon contact with Mexican reality. A Monterrey newspaper highlighted the immediate impact that railroads had in Nuevo León upon their arrival in 1882, indicating that Monterrey lost population as "artisans fled to the United States or to the interior of the republic because they said they could not compete with the foreign goods that the trains brought." The newspaper also reported on the impact in other parts of the state: "*jornaleros*, attracted by good wages, deserted the haciendas to work in the construction of the iron horse, and, once left without employment they also migrated from the state. Due to the lack of productive employment many people migrated and, as a consequence, commerce languished. Sadly enough, the unemployed entered the ranks of banditry and vagrancy" (*La voz de Nuevo León* 1889). One can assume that the arrival of railroads produced similar "shocks" in other locations. As the Monterrey newspaper noted, the migration of people was one of the effects that railroads had in Nuevo León, a process that was repeated wherever the railroad passed.

The railroad simultaneously harmed and benefited *hacendados*. On the one hand, railroads raised wages to hire the thousands of people needed for railroad construction. This wage increase represented the first significant wage increase since Independence and an important employment alternative to the hacienda. Once in operation, railroads sparked the modernization of the economy, resulting in more employment alternatives. More employment opportunities forced landlords to raise wages to retain workers (Bancroft 1893, 281). On the other hand, railroads also increased property values, especially near railroad lines, leading landlords and surveyors to accumulate large concentrations of public lands (*terrenos baldios*), which included lands belonging to many peasant communities. "Foreseeing" the route of the railroad, the most astute land robbers engaged in what John Coatsworth called a "widespread assault on the property holdings of the Indian free villages" (see Coatsworth 1974, 49).

In 1881 surveyors arrived in Naranjo, Michoacán, shortly after a railroad construction company received a concession for the Patzcuaro–Uruapan line. The Indians of this *pueblo* lost most of their properties to the surveyors and nearby haciendas during the next couple of years. The anthropologist Paul Friedrich wrote that Naranjo "had become a village of hired men and migrant plantation hands, a sort of semi-proletariat" (Friedrich 1977, 46). What happened in Naranjo was replicated in other parts of Mexico. Backed by the growing power of the Porfirian state, landlords engaged in what the geographer David Harvey calls "accumulation by dispossession," the massive expropriation of peasant holdings (Harvey 2007, 159–60). Without land, the erstwhile peasantry either migrated to other locations in search of employment or attached them-selves to the hacienda as *jornaleros*, sharecroppers, tenants, or indentured servants. A few Naranjeños headed to the United States in the early 1900s, including Primo Tapia, who later became Michoacán's leading *agraristas*.

This mass displacement of peasants formed the basis of a demographic recomposi-tion of the type that Mexico had not experienced since the plagues of the sixteenth cen-tury that decimated much of the indigenous population. In addition to encouraging the massive land grab that directly led to demographic changes, the railroads routes also shaped Mexico's population recomposition. The railroad networks patterned migra-tion by facilitating the movement of people from one region to another. This mass movement of people transformed Mexico's labor markets, creating what could be called regional winners and losers.

In contrast to the immigrant-receiving countries in the Americas, Mexico's native population composed the overwhelming majority of the labor force.[6] It was the only large economy that did not depend on immigrants as an important source of labor. Not having the supply of hundreds of thousands of immigrants meant that the recruit-ment of labor in one region came at the expense of another. Within this scenario, the north and south, the two regions with chronic labor shortage, went in opposite direc-tions during the Porfiriato. By offering the highest wages in Mexico, employers in the north dealt with this problem by successfully recruiting thousands of migrants from central Mexico, creating in this process a labor market based on free labor. Unable to secure large numbers of laborers even at slightly higher wages than in central Mexico, southern employers fortified *peonismo* as a labor system (see U.S. Bureau of Foreign Commerce 1896, 115–21; Katz 1974).

In the early 1830s, Lorenzo de Zavala projected that the northern frontier had the greatest possibilities for development in all of Mexico. Far from the reach of Mexico City, which opposed progressive "change," the north was bound to be transformed by having direct contact with the westward-expanding American market economy and population. He predicted that "within half a century, it [Northern frontier] would be more powerful, rich, and proportionally populated than the Central states" (De Zavala 1831, 130–31). Although he did not foresee Mexico losing half of its territory to the United States (which he probably would had approved given his role in endorsing the Independence of Texas), the expansion of American capitalism into Mexico trans-formed the North from the most isolated, poorest, and "backward" region in Mexico into the wealthiest and most modern. The orbit of Mexican capitalism had shifted to the north by 1900. The massive infusion of foreign capital in the north, its integration into the American economy, and the great numbers of migrants from the interior who settled there made this "great divergence" possible.

Located between Coahuila and Durango, La Laguna serves as one of the best examples of the role migrants played in this "great divergence." A few years before the arrival of the railroad, La Laguna's higher wages were already attracting "a noticeable current of people from the interior." The railroad facilitated the transportation of thou-sands of migrants who came to La Laguna in search of "wages that were less miserable

6. When the Mexican Revolution erupted in 1910, Mexico had a population of 15 million, 1,500,000 more than the immigrant population of the United States.

than what they could obtain in the Center of the country" (*El Partido Liberal* 1887, 323). La Laguna's population increased from less than 20,000 in the 1870s to almost 200,000 by 1910, a figure that did not include the thousands of migrant farm workers who arrived every year to pick cotton. By 1910 out-of-state migrants made up over half of the population of Torreón and San Pedro de las Colonias, the two largest cities in Coahuila (Mora-Torres 2001, 131).

Hubert Bancroft, the historian and ethnologist, wrote that in Mexico, "wherever capital flows in, labor must follow, for the movements of both are and have been simultaneous" (1893, 285). There are plenty of examples in northern Mexico supporting Bancroft's observation, including the Sonora–Arizona copper belt, the Coahuila–Texas coal region, and Monterrey. In the case of Monterrey, the concentration of smelters, railroads, and other large enterprises transformed it from a low wage enclave to one of the highest paying cities in Mexico. When the smelters opened their doors in 1891, the average wages rose from $0.25 to $0.75 a day (for labor competition in Monterrey, see Mora-Torres 2001, 136–44). The news of this wage increase spread to other parts of Mexico, especially neighboring San Luis Potosí. By 1900 out-of-state migrants constituted 35 percent of Monterrey's 62,000 inhabitants (Potosinos founded their own neighborhood, San Luisito; Mora-Torres 2001, 134).

Macedonio Gómez, a politician and jurist, wrote that the economic development of Chihuahua was the result of "the *brazos* that are plucked from Michoacán" (Restauración 1894, 539). Although he did not expand on this point, Gómez made an important connection: the prosperity of a region depended, to a large degree, on its ability to recruit labor from another region. A growing economy, coupled with the absence of an additional supply of laborers that could have been obtained from immigration, meant that regions and employers had to compete for Mexican laborers. The battle for labor gave birth to a new occupation, the professional labor agent, better known as *enganchadores*. These labor brokers, who historians have not studied, operated throughout Mexico (and in the American southwest by way of labor agencies; for the case of the American Southwest, see Peck 2000, 40–46, 69–78). Paid according to the number of people they brought to employers, *enganchadores* traveled throughout Mexico recruiting *enganchados*, luring them with offers of free transportation, wage advancements, and the promise of higher salaries. They facilitated the transfer of workers from one place to another.

Just like any part of the country, northern Mexico served as fertile ground for the operations of the *enganchadores*. Monterrey, a major center of employment and transportation, had a large floating population of migrants. *Enganchadores* actively recruited these "floaters" with offers of higher wages and free transportation to such distant places as Yucatán, the plantations of southern Mexico, and the mines of Sonora. The presence of *enganchadores* in small and large localities in the North upset many employers. An employer went as far as urging the Chihuahua government to prohibit *enganchadores* from operating in the state. He had lost 80 percent of the workers who had been recently recruited in central Mexico (Mora-Torres 2001, 133–40, 153–56; Wasserman 1984, 121–22). In a competitive labor market foreign firms had the advantage of having the financial means to raise wages. To their resentment, Mexican employers were forced to raise wages to retain workers. A Mexican miner from Chihuahua complained that "wages have been raised by the entry of Colonel Greene to such an extent that I cannot hope to pay; in fact the miners...simply dictate what they should be paid, or they will not work" (quoted in Wasserman 1984, 123).

The wage gap between the north and the rest of Mexico widened within a relatively short period of time. In the early 1890s wages in the north ranged from a low of 0.52 *centavos* in Coahuila to a high of 0.86 in Sonora. On the other hand, workers earned from a high of 0.37 *centavos* in Jalisco, the highest paying state in the Bajío, to a low of 0.23 in Oaxaca (Obregón 1918, 342–343; Gónzalez Roa 1919, 165). The widening of the wage gap turned out to be the main force driving thousands of migrant to the north. This movement of people was large enough to produce major shifts in the distribution of Mexico's population, a conclusion that could be reached from census data. Between 1880 and 1910 the population of Mexico increased from approximately 9,500,000 to 15,160,407. During this time the share of the national population that belonged to Jalisco, Michoacán, and Guanajuato, the leading immigrant-sender states of the twentieth century, decreased from 24 to 22 percent. The share of Zacatecas and San Luis Potosí, two other immigrant-sender states, dropped from 10 to 7.5 percent. Meanwhile, the northern states of Sonora, Durango, Tamaulipas, Chihuahua, Coahuila, and Nuevo León gained 1,175,000 people, increasing their share from 10 to 14 percent.

In the early 1890s labor shortages were reported not only in the northern and southern states, but also in Michoacán and Veracruz, two states that had not faced such a problem in the past. Michoacán officials reported that labor shortages were beginning "to be felt" in the mines while *hacendados* "must seek the laborers, and cannot at times procure them, or if so, only at a considerable wage advance." Not too long ago when labor was more abundant, it was the *jornalero* who went to their *amos* (hacendado), pleading with them, "*señor*, I have five children and we have eaten the six *reales* (0.75 *centavos*, the weekly wage) that I have earned. What are we going to eat now?" (Bustos 1889, 131–34; Bancroft 1893, 277–79, 284). The days of complete *hacendado* domination over their lives were gradually coming to an end. At the turn of the twentieth century many Michoacanos, such as those from Naranjo, looked toward *el norte* and cities as the alternative to the state's starvation wages.

Higher wages in the north, however, did not mean that workers were enjoying life in paradise. One of the arguments that Porifirians used to justify the country's low wages emphasized that the cost of basic goods was much cheaper in Mexico than in the United States. Walter Weyl, an economist, summarized the substance of this claim: "it has been frequently stated that the cost of living in that country is very much cheaper than in the United States, and that the consequences of wages tend to equalize themselves to a certain point" (1902, 70). All things considered, everything evened out in the end. Weyl, however, inverted the logic of this argument: "[t]he conclusion to be deduced from this fact, however, is merely that Mexican labor consumes much less, and not, as has been too frequently assumed, that the individual article of consumption cost less." Maize, the main staple of the population, sold for two cents a kilo in Mexico and slightly less than a cent in the United States (Weyl 1902).

The north offered workers higher wages and, thus, a life slightly above subsistence. This small improvement was a decisive factor in the calculations people made to first head to northern Mexico and later to the United States, where the "American rate of wages is double that of the Mexican" (*Report of the Industrial Commission of Immigration* 1901, 759).

"Los de casa se van": Migration and the Geography of Mexican Wages, 1880–1900

H. P. Stabler, a fruit grower from California's Sacramento Valley, delivered a paper at the Twenty-seventh Fruit-Growers Convention in 1902. He told the growers that "labor is the problem of the twentieth century" (quoted in Daniel 1982, 51), meaning that the most urgent problem that growers faced was recruiting a large pool of seasonal workers. A year later, in 1903, an American official in Mexico City wrote that the "number of emigrants from Mexico to the United States is small and there is no possibility of any considerable increase therein in the future." He reached this conclusion on his estimates that only one fourth of the population could afford to travel and the "others are the poorer class, who could never acquire sufficient funds to make the trip to the United States unless living a few miles from the border" (Barlow, 1904, 175). He was right in suggesting that only a small percentage of the Mexicans could afford a train ticket to the United States and that most migrants were from the north. However, he did not perceive that the processes that were brewing large-scale migration were already at work. One of these processes involved the large presence of migrants from the interior who had settled in the north and were within reach of the United States. In 1904 a Laredo newspaper reported, "during all the months of this year we have noted that many Mexicans, in numbers that have averaged more than 500 souls, cross daily to the United States. They emigrate in groups of five, seven, and up to twelve people. The groups are made up of men, women, and children who are dressed in the clothing of rural workers from Mexico's interior and who carry on their backs the few possessions they had in their miserable homes" (*El Trueno,* October 23, 1904). These migrants who were coming by the thousands after 1900 solved "the problem of the 20th Century." Within a few years they would "Mexicanize" farm labor in California and in other parts of the United States.

In 1885 the government of Nuevo León made an important connection regarding how the price of goods in the United States gave rise to contraband in the northeast: "contraband will exist as long as there is a dividing line that is easy to cross and in which the price of goods on one side are higher than on the other. Thus, contraband will increase or decrease in mathematical proportions with the difference in prices between one side and the other" (Gobierno del Estado de Nuevo León, *Memorias de Gobierno 1885,* anexo 27). As a way of understanding the political economy of Mexican migration, we can alter this dictum by substituting immigration for contraband and wages for the price of goods. The "dividing line" widened the wage gap between Mexico and the United States at a moment when both economies were increasingly becoming more integrated. One dollar a day was, for the most part, the going "rate" for most Mexican laborers in the United States as of 1900 and half of that in northern Mexico (or one peso paid in silver). This wage difference is illustrated by Mexican railroad workers in Arizona and Sonora. The former earned $1 a day in 1893 and the latter $0.53 cents (*Chicago Daily Tribune,* August 20, 1896). Although $1 was the highest wage Mexicans could earn in either country, that wage was among the lowest for common laborers in the United States. On the other hand, the North's one peso a day for common workers was two to three times higher than in central Mexico. Briefly stated, the boundary shaped the geography of Mexican wages: northern Mexico was "best of the worst" and the American borderlands the "worst of the best."

The wages in smelting serve as a good example of how the best of the worst and the worst of the best came together at the boundary. The El Paso-based Kansas City Consolidated Smelting and Refining Company (later part of the ASARCO network) employed a large number of Mexicans, paying them $1 a day. Meanwhile ASARCO, one of the first American transnational corporations, paid smelter workers $2 (gold) in Pueblo, Colorado, one peso in Monterrey ($0.50 U.S. cents) and 0.62 *centavos* in Aguascalientes ($0.31 U.S. cents; Mora-Torres 2001, 132).

In the geography of Mexican wages, Chihuahua had the means to "pluck the *brazos*" from Michoacán. By the same token, the American Southwest had the means to do the same to Chihuahua. After "plucking" eight thousand workers from central Mexico with offers of higher wages, a Mexican miner claimed that he had lost 80 percent of his work force within less than a year. Most crossed the border to double their wages (Wasserman 1984, 122; Gordon 1999, 51). A Torreón newspaper insinuated that migrants quickly learned about this wage geography upon arrival in the north: "because of the close proximity to the United States, the recent arrivals hear about good salaries. They learn that instead of a silver peso that they could earn on this side [of the boundary], they could earn a gold peso on the other side. On the day least expected, they leave without paying the hacendado who contracted them, gave them wage advancements, and paid the transportation fare" (*El Nuevo Mundo*, October 10, 1907).

CONCLUSION

Almost by consensus the historical literature on Mexican migration makes the claim that Mexico had a labor surplus during the Porfiriato. This was the result of rapid population growth (from 9.5 to 15 million people) and the negative impact that capitalist modernization had on the lower classes (massive land displacements and high unemployment). Thus, Mexico's large landless and unemployed population composed the majority of those who migrated to the United States. Lawrence Cardoso, one of the first historians to write a book on Mexican migration, wrote, "labor was, therefore, just another commodity whose price was set by market laws of supply and demand. Why should employers pay in wages any more than the amount determined by the free market system? There were usually several people looking for any one job, and this allowed hacienda owners to depress or at least not raise wages" (Cardoso 1980, 10). Following the labor surplus argument, George Sanchez wrote that "wages fell because of the labor surplus created by both the land policy and the population boom of the late nineteenth century." Douglas Monroy argues that "the Porfirian political economy had the outcome of taking land from people and making them hungry. Wages went down and prices went up... and there were more people." Displaced artisans "competed in a job market crowded with hundreds of thousands of de-landed peasants" (Sanchez 1993, 20; Monroy 1999, 78, 82; see also Garcia 1981, 34–35; and Reisler 1976, 14).

One of the aims of this chapter is to challenge the common assumption that Mexico had a surplus population and therefore it could afford the emigration of laborers (the labor surplus claim becomes valid with the Mexican Revolution, but that is a different story). As the only large country in the Americas that failed to attract immigrants in the "Age of Global Migration," Mexico had to rely on its much unheralded native labor force for its economic development. The size of the Mexican labor force kept pace with the expanding economy until the last decade of the Porfiriato, when a sizeable number of workers began migrating to the United States. In the last decade of the Porfiriato the Mexican economy expanded more rapidly than in the earlier years. This expansion coincided with the dramatic increase in Mexican migration. This is indicated by the growth of the Mexican and Mexican American population in the United States, which increased from 400,000 to 640,000 between 1900 and 1910 (Gratton and Gutmann 2000, 143).

It was only then that the government and Mexican employers of all stripes became preoccupied with the specter of severe labor shortages that could be caused by growing emigration. The Mexican consul at Laredo reported in 1906 that the number of Mexicans crossing the border had increased, the migration "of our *braceros*" was leading to a "depopulation of our territory," and it was time to "put a dyke to this bloodletting before it is too late." The consul at Tucson reported the same ("Jesus M. Ainza contra México" 1902, 222). In 1907 Victor Clark, a U.S. Department of Labor economist, went to Mexico to study Mexican labor and the causes of emigration. He wrote that "labor is scarce in Mexico, that is, not adequate to the demand of the country's expanding industries" (Clark 1974, 513).

Although employers in Mexico feared the specter of labor shortages, the large employers of Mexican labor in the United States (railroads, mining, and agriculture) considered Mexico a large "cheap labor" reservoir. Mexico was emerging as the most important "reserve army of labor" for the American economy for the duration of the twentieth century and up to the present time.

CHAPTER 2

Mexican Labor Migration, 1876–1924

Gilbert G. Gonzalez
University of California–Irvine

The [the migrant] is forced to seek better conditions north of the border by the slow but relentless pressure of United States' agricultural, financial and oil corporate interests on the entire economic and social evolution of the Mexican nation....

Until Mexico can offer a far larger degree of economic security to its people, thousands of them will seek relief by migrating over the border, legally or illegally. Thus it becomes of primary importance to determine whether the economic policy of the United States is fostering or hampering the chances for creating a Mexico able to employ, feed, house, clothe, and educate its workers on a rising standard of living. To ignore this basic premise is to overlook the roots of the problem.

Ernesto Galarza
"Program for Action"
Common Ground (1949)

INTRODUCTION: EXPLAINING MEXICAN MIGRATION

Ernesto Galarza, a Mexican migrant and onetime farm worker, became one of the foremost agricultural labor and civil rights leaders of the twentieth century. Galarza knew well those forces that drove Mexicans northward within Mexico and eventually across the border. His explanation for Mexican migration has for too long fallen by the wayside, virtually unread and unheard. However, his approach to explaining Mexican migration is particularly valid to the period under review here. Indeed, it is as applicable today as it was when he first urged those interested in the Mexican migrant community to pay heed to the role of U.S. financial and industrial operations in Mexico in the uprooting of its citizens and sending them onto a migratory trail northward. Here I shall employ the transnational approach taken by Ernesto Galarza, who advised an examination of the role played by the United States in creating the economic conditions that fostered

Mexican migration to the United States. That approach emphasizes that Mexican labor migration begins in Mexico and proceeds northward into the United States, but the direct causes are not entirely rooted in conditions indigenous to Mexico.

In the late nineteenth century Mexico served as the first site of American economic empire, which paralleled European colonial interventions. Upon the advent of U.S. capital moving into Mexico, political figures, investors, bankers, and industrialists viewed Mexico as a vast investment opportunity but an opportunity founded upon a perception of Mexico as future territory under U.S. command (Hart 2002, 42–43).[1] The eventual outcome came close to the annexationists' objectives. The actions by U.S. investors and corporations in Mexico ultimately created a virtual economic colony through the construction and control of railroads, mining, oil operations, and vast land ownership while acknowledging a nominal Mexican sovereignty. These were the critical economic conditions referred to by Galarza that led to migration.[2]

However, more than just the migration of labor originated from the United States' economic expansion across the border. With the construction of railroads by U.S. corporations from the border southward, U.S. citizens began to travel into Mexico and launched the building of a body of literature on Mexico. Their widely published writings created a view of Mexican culture and Mexicans that corresponded with the transnational economic expansion then in progress. Mexicans had already been regarded as inferior social beings by investors and politicians and with increased travel, tourists, businessmen, journalists, missionaries, and academics joined in saddling Mexico and Mexicans with a spectrum of cultural and/or racial maladies, making them incapable of modernization without foreign assistance (i.e., U.S. investment and tutelage; Hart 2002, 42–43) That view, published widely in books and articles, followed Mexicans as they entered the United States and became "common knowledge," an informational source for defining Mexican migrants to the U.S. public. That information moved beyond the popular realm and became a key element shaping and validating public policy applied to the growing migrant population. An imperialist cultural construction composed initially by U.S. investors to justify their economic objectives and later written into a body of literature by travelers to Mexico ultimately defined Mexicans on both sides of the border. Upon crossing the border, that imperial mindset would significantly impact the lives of migrants as they found employment and settled into communities.

CONVENTIONAL APPROACHES TO EXPLAINING MEXICAN MIGRATION

Since the early twentieth century Mexican migration has been overwhelmingly a migration of labor. As such, Mexico has served as a valuable source of workers for

---

1. For studies that present the role of the United States in Mexico during this period as fundamentally positive and indicate that social and political conditions in Mexico prevented foreign capital from fully contributing to Mexico's economic development, see Haber (1989) and Coatsworth (1981).

2. While U.S. investors were busy moving into Mexico, the United States turned Puerto Rico, Cuba, the Philippines, and Hawaii into formal colonies. Shortly thereafter, the United States assisted in the creation of Panama to build the Canal and came to occupy the Dominican Republic for years to come. All the while, the United States supported dictators around Latin America.

U.S.-based industries operating in Mexico, as well as for industries north of the border. Men and women (and often children) either have migrated on their own account to seek work or have been recruited in one manner or another to work for a variety of economic branches. Without a doubt, since the early twentieth century, U.S. industrial corporations have been most pleased to have the privilege of an open door for securing Mexican labor when needed, but an open door for cheap, unskilled, semiskilled and, when necessary, disposable workers.

Mexican migration has arrived in three general time frames and comprising three legal statuses. The first significant migration occurred between 1900 and 1930 and was composed of documented, undocumented, and a short-lived contract labor program (1917–1921); the second flow encompassed the contract labor program known as the Bracero Program (1942–1964), as well as the documented and undocumented flows generated during and after the program; and finally, the third movement consists primarily of undocumented migrants stimulated by neoliberal policies, particularly free trade, beginning in the 1980s and continuing to the present. The third phase includes a standing contract labor program known as H2, which has served to bring workers on a temporary basis, numbering sixty-six thousand in some years. Each of these variations on migration has been inspired by conditions within Mexico originating in industrial operations and/or economic policies emanating from the United States and implemented with the collaboration of Mexico's elites.

Conversely, conventional approaches emphasize the "push–pull" model, regarding conditions originating in Mexico that lead to migration. In the first phase, the 1900 to 1930 period, the Mexican Revolution is said to have engendered the first push to migration; since that time a push to migration has originated from Mexico's poverty, unemployment, or a search for upward mobility not available in Mexico.

On the other hand, a pull, a continuous demand for labor in the United States, combines with the push to produce a push–pull effect. In that scenario, Mexico lacks something that the United States can provide (work) and Mexico has something that the United States has a need for (workers). Consequently, migration becomes a win-win situation, a preferred choice for Mexicans because it resolves their needs; simultaneously, migration resolves the need for labor in the United States. Mexico and the United States are, in this traditional explanatory model, equal, reciprocal neighboring countries; one needs labor, therefore providing a pull, and the other lacks employment opportunities and more and provides the push.

However, the record speaks otherwise. Galarza's words objectively emphasized that the push–pull model, which is repeated without question, fails to incorporate the critical role of U.S. imperial economic expansionism into Mexico and its far-reaching social consequences. Galarza understood that the United States simultaneously initiates the uprooting of Mexico's citizens, the push, and then recruits and/or opens the door to migrant workers, thereby constructing the pull, in essence a single, unbroken process.

PREPARING THE GROUNDWORK FOR MEXICAN MIGRATION

In the immediate post Civil War period, a widespread call across major U.S. cities demanded the total annexation of Mexico. The *New York Herald* urged that the United

States should "take all of Mexico" and create a "protectorate over Mexico." Such blunt imperialist calls were tempered by an alternative proposed by William Rosecrans, U.S. Minister to Mexico and investor in railroad construction in Mexico. Rosecrans replied that all benefits ensuing from annexation could be gained without the negatives through an emphasis on economic rather than territorial annexation. He defined the latter very clearly: "Pushing American enterprise up to, and within Mexico wherever it can profitably go...will give us advantages which force and money alone would hardly procure. It would give us the peaceful conquest of the country" (Pletcher 1958, 58). Rosecrans' admonition eventually became standard foreign policy toward Mexico and Latin America. Economic expansion by U.S. investors moved in unison with Rosecrans' proposal and supported those political figures willing to acquiesce to the "peaceful conquest" and collaborate with it. Fortunately for U.S. corporate investors, Porfirio Diaz filled that need.

Backing the overthrow of the democratically elected opponent of the open door to U.S. investors, Sebastian Lerdo de Tejada (1872-1876), and then recognizing the usurper Diaz were political measures connected to the pursuit of the economic conquest. Diaz emerged a staunch, if subservient U.S. ally and opened Mexico to U.S. capital from 1876 until he was ousted in 1910. By the late nineteenth century Mexico had come under the political and economic power of the U.S. investors. Centered in railroads, mining, oil, and agriculture, U.S. investments amounted to $1 billion by 1910. Americans in positions of political office described and often celebrated that relationship. In an article appearing in the *National Geographic* at the turn of the century, John Foster, former Minister to Mexico, noted Mexico's relationship with the United States quite candidly when he wrote that "Mexico is now bound to the United States by the iron ties of four railroads" (Gen. Foster, 1901). The U.S. consul in Nogales, Arizona, repeated the truth nearly twenty years later in reminding his readers in a *National Geographic* article that Mexico "is our market now linked with us by rail and sail and we must keep it" (Simpich 1919, 48). In the course of that economic tie anchoring Mexico to the United States, foreign ownership laid claim to half of the national wealth (Sheahan 1987, 297). The historian John Mason Hart summarized that transnational connection as one that "placed Mexico in a state of economic control of American capital" (interview with John Mason Hart, El Paso, TX, February 23, 2008).

Investors who welcomed Diaz included well-known figures such as William Randolph Hearst, Jay Gould, J. P. Morgan, Wells Fargo, the Guggenheim family, and major corporations such as Atchison, Topeka and Santa Fe, Union Pacific, Southern Pacific, New York Central, and Phelps Dodge. American capital developed and controlled Mexico's modern industrial operations, which were overwhelmingly intended to serve America's economic requisites. Rather than connecting Mexico internally as Presidents Lerdo and Benito Juarez anticipated, railroads extended American lines from the northern border to Mexico's interior to move goods into and out of the country. Designed, planned, and constructed by Americans, railroads connected Mexico with U.S. industrial production and moreover assumed power "over the infrastructure of the country." Telegraph lines, for example, were constructed by the railroad entities and accompanied the rails that placed Mexico in "immediate" contact with the United States (interview with John Mason Hart, El Paso, TX, February 23, 2008).

Shortly after completion, railroads then served to advance a rapid development of mining by allowing importation of modern machinery and the export of ores and metals. Spurs followed upon the completion of the initial lines and connected mining zones with the main branch lines. Railroads quickly became known as mining railroads, with at least 50 percent of cargo shipments related to mining at the turn of the century.

American mining operations supplied the United States with valuable copper, silver, and other materials to continue the industrial development of the United States. Precious metals exported to the United States amounted to $18 million in 1890 and two thirds passed through the railroad center of El Paso (Garcia 1981, 22). According to Hart, during the Diaz years "Americans had extracted what in modern day terms would be 100 billion dollars" but left the mining regions (and Mexico) impoverished (interview with John Mason Hart, El Paso, TX, February 23, 2008). The Batopilas mine in northern Mexico, one of nearly three hundred operated by Americans by the first decade of the twentieth century, served as a source of key materials for U.S. industrial production. The mine was run by the one-time architect for Washington, D.C., Alexander Shepherd. After receiving a concession measuring sixty-one square miles, Shepherd took over an existing undeveloped mine and ran the operation like a fiefdom. Known as *el jefe* (the boss) in the region, Shepherd counted the state's governor among his closest friends. Records showed the mine produced as much as $100,000 per month and it was said that Shepherd became a "millionaire many times over" (Parker 1979, 32–33). One visitor to the mine described "life at Batopilas as a perfect type of the old feudal days" (Marcosson 1916, 23).

As at Batopilas, the government concession to William Greene, who originally developed the Cananea mine (later taken over by Rockefeller interests) in the state of Sonora near the Arizona border, carried many privileges. The concession granted Greene the privilege of owning 440,000 acres of land surrounding the mining town. Josiah McC. Heyman writes of Cananea, "Cananea was owned by the Cananea Realty Co., whose 90 percent owner was William Greene, and which was chartered for virtually all functions, including land, transportation, water, factories and hotels. The Cananea Cattle Company controlled roads and permission to travel, as well as slaughterhouse and the meat supply; the bank was the Cananea Mercantile Bank; and the largest store was the Cananea Company store" (Heyman 1991, 29–30).

Complementing the mining operations, Phelps Dodge came to control half of all smelting in Mexico. Meanwhile, the semifeudal economic conditions under the control of the landed aristocracy remained protected and free from foreign intervention. Nonetheless, an astonishing 27 percent of the Mexico's land area came under American ownership or control. John Mason Hart described that landed pattern as a "colonial relationship if you look at the economics":

> in the economic relationship that came out of this we find Americans, a handful of American elites associated with industrial and finance capital controlling 92 million acres of Mexico's surface…Edward Marshall who was the former secretary of the Texas Oil Company…owned about two million acres in the state of Sinaloa and had property extending from Ciudad Juarez, El Paso to the Arizona line on the Sonora side. It was the largest fenced property, he liked to claim, in the world. (interview with John Mason Hart, El Paso, TX, February 23, 2008)

To activate these extensive industrial operations, Mexican labor became the primary source but only after the massive removal of peasants from traditional farming communities. That came in the wake of the construction of thousands of miles of railroads laid to a large extent over centuries-old communal farmlands.

Over 300,000 peasants were forcibly removed in the central plateau region (the most populous area of Mexico) as the Diaz administration granted generous concessions to railroads. Diaz meanwhile passed land laws that transferred peasant lands to landlords to take advantage of rails for export of agricultural products, which removed even more peasants from traditional villages. With no alternatives, peasants began a migratory trail to towns and cities, becoming a surplus population and an enormous labor pool. The historian Michael Johns noted that "railroads and the expanding haciendas [landed estates] threw so many off their lands in the 1880s and 1990s that nearly one-half of the [Mexico] city's five hundred thousand inhabitants...were peasants" (Johns 1997, 64; see also Haber 1989, 18; and Coatsworth 1981, 155–68). The historian Moises Gonzalez Navarro noted that the population removal, "a massive displacement from the countryside," was the most profound in Mexico's history (González Navarro 1957, 25). More than peasants were affected as the railroads impacted upon muleteers, carriage drivers, and teamsters, the primary method of passenger and cargo transport rendered unable to compete with railroads and thrown into the labor pool.

The uprooted were quickly and actively recruited to become the backbone of the work crews on American railroad, mining, and oil operations, most of which were located in the north. Victor Clark, writing for the U.S. Bureau of Labor in 1908, noted, "Like the railways, the mines have had to import labor from the south" and there was a "constant movement of labor northward inside of Mexico itself to supply the growing demands of the less developed states" (Clark 1974, 470). With the southern movement of American capital, hundreds of thousands of Mexicans migrated northward and radically altered the centuries-old demographic pattern of Mexico. However, it should be noted that the new population distribution originated in those projects engineered by American corporate investors. These projects uprooted Mexicans, sent them on a migratory trail, and ultimately transformed them into a surplus labor supply available to work on the expanding U.S.-owned operations.

MEXICAN MIGRANT LABOR IN MEXICO

Railroads were the first of the American operations to employ Mexican labor, which by 1900 numbered 140,000. By the 1890s mining began to enter in significant numbers and within a decade or so employed some 30,000 to 40,000 Mexican laborers. Oil operations centered in the Tampico area employed another 7,000. These industrial enterprises did not appear in populated areas and required the recruitment and transport of workers from the populated zones of the south to the depopulated rural north. In the state of Sonora the number of mine workers jumped from less than 6,000 in 1897 to over 17,000 ten years later and corresponded with the mining operations then opening up (Heyman 1991, 55). One American mining engineer's lament voiced in 1906 must have been repeated endlessly among superintendents in the expanding mining sites: "The increase in number of mining operations in recent years has been so great as to make the securing of adequate supply of labor a difficult problem" (Rogers 1908, 700).

However, not only Mexicans migrated into the mining camps; American business owners and managers, chemists, engineers, and highly skilled workers also accompanied the investments. Soon, new towns, binational company towns, and camps sprang up around the American-managed operations and new social relations surfaced. The Cananea mine located a few miles from the Arizona border, which eventually came to be owned by Rockefeller-controlled interests, provides an example found across the north. In 1906 a mining engineer wrote of the mine, "La Cananea presents a wonderful contrast to its earlier appearance...where eight years ago there were no persons other than a few warring prospectors...is now a camp of 25,000 persons with all the necessities and most of the comforts of civilization" (Woodbridge 1906, 623). Some five thousand to six thousand Mexicans labored in the Cananea mine and were housed in quarters separated from the Americans.

An editorial in *The Independent* summarized the economic tie binding the United States and Mexico and the consequent social relations in a few words: "practically all the capital invested in industrial enterprises in Mexico is foreign, while all the labor in these enterprises is Mexican" (Mexican Labor, 1924. Mexicans generally performed the unskilled work, paid half the wages of that paid to American workers for the same work (known as Mexican work and Mexican wage), and lived in segregated quarters apart from American management and other personnel associated with the venture (Heyman 1991, 58). One engineer employed at the Penoles mine described a common hierarchy within the mining zones: "at present the mine is producing 500 tons of ore per day...and approximately 1,200 men [are] underground. At the mine all the employees except superintendent, assistant master mechanic, electrician, head diamond setter, master mechanic...head pumpmen, head carpenter, foremen and cashier are Mexicans" (Rice 1908, 314).

Although the minority, Americans enjoyed substantial privileges in the form of golf courses, tennis courts, country clubs, and recreation halls built by the companies. In the Tampico oil zone, a country club with a swimming pool, tennis courts, and dance hall returned Americans to a familiar upper-class setting (National Archives, n.d.)[3] An entirely distinct experience befell Mexicans. Workers and their families lived in separate quarters in roughly hewn wooden or adobe housing or houses built from scrap, often one-room affairs. When traveling on railroads they sat in the third class, whereas Americans enjoyed the first class, which was serviced by English-speaking waiters.

Railroad maintenance workers, numbering thirty thousand or more, commonly lived in tents and boxcar camps, which one writer described as "strange little settlements" (Tweedie 1901, 87) stretched out along the thousands of miles of lines. Company stores generally supplied their daily needs at inflated prices. Men not only were employed as miners, railroad construction, and maintenance workers, but also they often served as *mozos*, servants in homes, and *cargadores*, baggage carriers for travelers and residents from the United States. In the first decade of the twentieth century some forty thousand Americans resided in Mexico and one mining engineer wrote, "I have finally decided that the only danger in thus traveling without a *mozo* lies in the possibility of meeting with some accident with no help.... Over the little used trails...it was easy to persuade

---

3. Film clips of Mexico including oil operations and housing for Americans and Mexicans.

me to use a *mozo*" (Lamb 1908, 160–62). Another mentioned that, "like the Turk, the Mexican is a great porter" (Martin 1906, 66). Seldom did Americans travel without a *mozo*; the wife of the Batopilas mine superintendent was said to travel regularly "borne by eight good men" (Shepherd 1938, 252).

The sexual division of labor found its way into the organization of labor across the spectrum of American-run enterprises. As men were brought into the mining camps, their wives and daughters were recruited to work as nannies, cooks, housekeepers, seamstresses, and washerwomen and tended to the American homes in the reserved sections found on the upper slopes of the company towns or in the American colony in Mexico City. Meanwhile, children of American families studied in their private schools and were taught by American teachers hired by the companies. Mexican families living in separate quarters marked by acute poverty seldom had a local school to send their children to. Although living separately, they labored for operations that connected directly to the heart of the American economy.

AMERICANS DEVELOP A COLONIZERS MENTALITY: ORIENTALISM

With the completion of railroads, Americans of various sorts beside those associated with business endeavors descended upon Mexico. Travelers included tourists, journalists, academics, novelists, missionaries, and diplomats who initiated a tradition that remained over the century. Visits to the pyramids of Teotihuacan, the floating gardens of Xochimilco, the temples in Oaxaca, Indian villages, and, for business people, the myriad mining operations, oil fields, and more became the order of the day. Protestant missionaries, on the other hand, pursued the conversion of Mexicans to Protestantism. But most travelers came to certain conclusions based on their experiences in Mexico regarding Mexico, Mexicans, and their culture.

Within a few years a substantial body of literature on Mexico appeared in the form of books and articles in professional and popular journals and newspapers. Mexico became a popular writer's subject, informing American readers about Mexico, its people, and its culture. But perhaps more importantly, writers told of the need to continue American economic expansionism into Mexico.

Those writings, in general, presented a view of Mexico that paralleled European literature regarding their colonial possessions, essentially an Americanized Orientalism. In fact, the term Oriental became for a time a favorite term among Americans for defining a "typical" Mexican for readers. One visitor's writing of his trip to Oaxaca became a common refrain: "I could not think of anything but Palestine. I gazed at this unceasing possession of donkeys, Egyptian carts, women in their shawls folded and worn on their heads in Eastern fashion; and in the background the white walls, red tiled roofs and domes of the churches of Oaxaca. For a moment I wondered if I were not mistaken, and had suddenly strayed into some corner of the Orient" (Winter 1907, 9).

A Protestant missionary informed his fellows back home, "now with regard to the character of the people, they are as Oriental in type, in thought, and in habits as the Orientals themselves. It is true they have a veneer of European civilization; but underneath this veneer…we find that they are genuine Asiatics" (Winton 1913, 9). Another writer noted other related distinctions: "Is it not an Oriental fact about them that they can be fed upon almost nothing, and are they not Oriental in the calm continuance of their own ways of dress and their own style of habitation?" (Blichfelt 1912, 45).

Not a few American writers noted the growing similarities with European colonial expansion. One wrote, "Mexico and the United States complement each other...Something of what India is to England, Mexico could and ought to be to the United States" (Griffen 1886, 48). Writing in 1912, a traveler applied the commonly held notion and counseled, "Protestant missions are as legitimate and almost as sorely needed in Mexico as in India" (Blichfelt 1912, 96). For others, that need was already being satisfied through the varied American industries. Well-read writers familiar with Kipling found that Americans in Mexico mirrored the English imperialists in India: "It is in the heart of the sugar-cane country. All the land, the sugar mills, the hotel, and most of the business firms are owned by Americans. The plantations are operated with modern American efficiency. The planters live a life that reminds one of Rudyard Kipling's stories of the life of the English in India. They have tennis clubs, polo fields, golf links, dances and bridge parties" (Carr 1931, 91). Along with American investments, the racialized social relations found in the United States were exported to the nominally sovereign Mexico. American social relations became transnational social relations and reflected a deep cultural parallel with European Orientalism.

AMERICAN ORIENTALISM: PEONISM

In the wake of the imperialist economic expansion and in support of it, Americans defined Mexicans as an entirely divergent form of human being living at the U.S. doorstep. In time, the use of the term Oriental was discarded in favor of an Americanized version. The Spanish term *peon*, word for common laborer or peasant, soon was Anglicized into peon to mean practically everything that the term Oriental encapsulated. One writer captured the mindset in his book published in 1907, which described a nation composed of the "little brown men": "It is almost unfair to the simpleminded, patient and docile peon of Mexico to speak of him as an Indian for he is at once confused with the bloodthirsty redskin of the north. He is a peaceful, if improvident, character, and is child in nature. He represents cheap labor and is one of the great attractions that brings wealth to Mexico" (Winter 1907, 192). Ralph Ingersoll, a retired mining engineer, surmised that "all Mexicans are children and have to be treated accordingly," (1924, 45) a view that meshed with the common knowledge regarding Mexicans. Like his compatriots, the leading American sociologist of the early twentieth century, Edward A. Ross, agreed that Mexicans as a people are "easily led as a child, and the master who understands him and means right generally has no difficulty in managing him" (1923, 14). In short, peon meant Mexican (the terms were interchangeable) and implied a person with an adult body but a child-like mind. Other aspects were also thrown in for good measure: Mexicans were alleged to be unambitious, oversexed, prone to violence and alcohol, and worst of all, likely to put off work till tomorrow (the mañana syndrome). Some claimed that Mexicans required religious training along the lines of European colonial subjects. For all of that, Mexicans contained acclaimed virtues; they were accessible, cheap, controlled, disposable, and abundant.

THE MEXICAN PROBLEM

Mexico, it was said with confidence, is incapable of modernization. The barrier, rooted in Mexico's cultural and/or biological makeup, was captured in a phrase known as "The Mexican Problem" and the solution to The Mexican Problem was the Americanization of Mexico. In short, Mexicans lacked all the qualities that Americans assumed were their defining characteristics and consequently the former could not hope to modernize like the United States. Across the United States, The Mexican Problem was discussed widely. In a book written as a paean to Porfirio Diaz, James Creelman (1911) followed popular thinking and titled a chapter "The Mexican Problem," explaining the need for American mentorship. Not to be outdone, Clarence Barron of the *Wall Street Journal* titled his book, *The Mexican Problem*. Like Creelman, Barron made clear the nature of the Problem: "At the present time the larger part of the good people of Mexico are children who want to be in debt and at the same time carefree.... He is simply in need of a strong helping hand" (1917, 12–13). In the minds of American writers, only a cultural transformation would solve The Mexican Problem and only the United States was capable of such an international mentorship.

The cultural transformation, according to most expressions, could only be achieved through continued if not increased American economic presence. Barron defined an Americanization that validated the billion dollars in American investments and sounded much like William Rosecrans' notion of peaceful conquest: "The redemption of Mexico must be the invasion of business, forcing upon the natives—the good people of Mexico—technical training, higher wages, bank accounts, financial independence and the rights of citizenship and accumulation" (Barron 1917, 14). In an article appropriately titled "The Americanization of Mexico," author Edward Conley summarized the cause and expected outcomes, saying that "Modernization and Americanization are almost synonymous terms," and predicted that "twenty years hence the Mexican family life will be on the American basis" (1907, 724). The former Consul General in Mexico City, G. A. Chamberlain, warned his compatriots shortly after the Mexican Revolution that "there is no middle ground. If we stop short of economic control we will travel again and again mere byroads of peace" (1920, 243). Theirs was the language of colonialism; the conceptualizations defining Mexicans for the American audience remained tied to Mexicans immigrants as they crossed the border. In the minds of many an American, The Mexican Problem in the form of multitudes of peons, a childlike people crowned with the mañana syndrome who served as cheap accessible labor, were entering the United States in alarming numbers.

MEXICAN LABOR AND THE MEXICAN PROBLEM COME TO THE UNITED STATES

By the early twentieth century Mexicans had not only become a huge labor supply for U.S. industrial operations within Mexico, but also soon became a major labor supply for agriculture, mining, railroads, construction, and services in the United States, particularly in the expanding Southwest. Many of the very operations that utilized Mexican labor within Mexico would soon recruit that labor northward. Phelps Dodge provides an example; the massive corporation controlled smeltering operations in Mexico and became one of the leading employers of Mexican labor housed in the company town barrio, Smeltertown, in El Paso. It soon became obvious that Mexico not only provided a rich supply of natural resources for U.S. industrial expansion, but also, above all else, had become a rich source of surplus labor utilized when the need arose within the United States. No other immigrant workers could be acquired so easily (nor could they be so easily disposed of).[4]

A study carried out in 1908 by Victor Clark of the U.S. Bureau of Labor noted the key role played by American operations in shunting labor northward. At times the recruits in a single mining zone numbered in the several thousands; one group of mining properties in the State of Chihuahua was reported to have imported eight thousand miners from southern mining areas. Not surprisingly, Clark found that "entire villages have migrated to other parts of Mexico, where employment has been found in the mines or on the railways" and that "along the northern portion of [railway] routes resident labor is so scarce that workers are brought from the south as section hands and for new construction." However, that migration was often under a "boss." Clark described the experience that must have been repeated endlessly (and similar to that experienced into the twenty-first century guided by *coyotes*): "recruited laborers whether destined for northern Mexico or for the United States, travel in parties, under a boss, or 'cabo' who holds the tickets. One is told of locked car doors and armed guards on the platforms of trains to prevent desertions on route." He concluded that migration, propelled by agencies working to satisfy the need for laborers in the mines, railways, and oil operations "has carried the central Mexican villager a thousand miles from his home and to within a few miles of the border, and American employers, with a gold wage have had little difficulty in attracting him across that not very formidable dividing line" (Clark 1974, 470). The Stanford University economist Samuel Bryan underscored the singularity of the migratory movement from the village or town in Mexico to the United States: "the movement from the more remote districts of Mexico to the newly developed industries of the North has become largely a stage in a more general movement to the United States. Entrance into this country is not difficult, for employment agencies in normal times have stood ready to advance board, lodging, and transportation to a place where work is to be had" (Bryan 1912, 726). Labor recruiting agencies operating in Mexico and at El Paso appeared nearly simultaneously with U.S. industrial operations to continue the ongoing transport of labor. At El Paso, at least fourteen independent labor recruiters surrounded immigrants as they came across the border to offer transportation to the work site and received fifty cents for every man recruited. Meanwhile, agents working for major employers of Mexican labor did their work to satisfy continuing labor needs. Five agencies working out of El Paso were reported to have transported 16,471 men "between July 1908 and February 1909" to labor on railroads (Garcia 1981, 54). Workers were transported to satisfy the continually expanding need for labor in American-controlled industries in Mexico but migration continued into the United States. Victor Clark and Samuel Bryan testified that Mexican migration to the United States was a single process originating in Mexico and that it was the social consequence of American capital expansion into Mexico.

---

4. Interview with Kitty Calavita, Irvine, CA, May 10, 2006. Professor Calavita makes the point that Mexican migration is distinctive and cannot be paralleled with European or Asian migration.

In either case, whether Mexican labor worked in the United States or in Mexico, it was integrated into the production of commodities for marketing in the United States. Upon crossing a virtual open border, Mexican workers were again housed in company towns, confined to "Mexican work," treated to dual wages, and segregated socially, in schools, restaurants, movie theaters, and recreation. As to be expected, the widely held notion of The Mexican Problem followed in their path. As soon as the migrant crossed the border, the workers' experiences in Mexico continued in the United States.

With the new century, the southwestern United States underwent substantial economic development requiring a constant growth in its labor force. That in turn required a relaxed administration of border vigilance. The historian Mario T. Garcia reported an observation written by an immigrant entering around 1900, who described the administrative measures applied to the applicant by the Immigration Service: "All you had to do coming from Mexico, if you were a Mexican citizen, was to report at the immigration office on the American side… give your name, the place of your birth, and where you were going to" (quoted in Garcia 1981, 37). With the assistance of an open border, Mexicans entered the United States in significant numbers as early as 1905, reaching nearly 18,000 in 1910, 20,000 by 1911, and 22,000 in 1912. The 1911 U.S. Immigration Commission Report testified that "immigration from Mexico has become an important factor" and that at least 50,000 more per year were entering without documentation (Senate Reports of the Immigration Commission, 682). This brought the entrants to 70,000 by the end of the first decade and in each of the first years of the second decade. The violence of the Revolution broke out in 1913 and rather than spur migration (as has been the general conclusion), migration was seriously curtailed, decreasing to 11,000 in 1913 and not resuming its former numbers until after the violence had subsided. Upon the end of the rebellion, migration continued on its previous path, reaching 17,000 in 1916 and rising to 87,648 by 1924. One should note that the Literacy Act passed in 1917 intended to lower the entrance of immigrants was suspended in June 1918 when railroads, agricultural, and mining corporations expressed great umbrage at no longer having an open border to satisfy their labor requirements (Garcia 1981, 47–48). The suspension, however, only applied to Mexican entrants.

Not satisfied with the availability of Mexican labor, cotton and sugar beet interests petitioned for a contract labor program to import temporary labor, which was initiated in 1917 and renewed annually until 1921. The program enabled importing approximately eighty-three thousand temporary workers. Contracted workers were eventually allowed to work in mining, railroads, construction work, and agriculture. However, the cotton industry in Arizona proved the primary beneficiary, hiring more than thirty thousand of the total and reported to have saved $24 million in production costs because of the labor program. Moreover, employers enjoyed a relatively free program, sans federal oversight that is, therefore, a relatively free hand in dealing with the contracted worker. In the end, some twenty-one thousand workers were said to have jumped their contracts and joined their compatriots in the *barrios* and *colonias* (Reisler 1976, 27–39; see also García y Griego 1983).

With the rising tide of Mexican migration, migrant worker settlements appeared as Mexicans moved into those regions where laborers were in short supply. The cultural baggage that American writers saddled Mexicans with attached to them as they crossed the border. Not a few noted that Mexicans brought with them all that had been attributed to Mexicans living in Mexico. The noted sociologist Emory Bogardus observed in his pioneering study *Essentials of Americanization*, "In the Southwestern states the Mexican Problem has developed rapidly since 1900" and, further, "Mexican immigrants represent the peon" (1919, 179). A Protestant minister with a long interest in Mexico advised his readers in his book appropriately titled *The Mexican as He Really Is North and South of the Rio Grande* to modify their thinking relating to Mexican immigration. He warned, "'That Mexican' [sic] no longer lives in Mexico, he lives in the United States...The "Mexican Problem"...reaches from Gopher Prairie to Guatemala" (McLean 1930, 34; for The Mexican Problem in the United States with an emphasis on Texas, see Montejano 1987, Chap. 8). His opinion caught on and spread across the United States. Carey McWilliams noted the increasing discussion of The Mexican Problem. Fifty-one articles on The Mexican Problem appeared in the *Reader's Guide* from 1920 to 1930, compared with "nineteen articles on the same subject in the previous decade" (McWilliams 1949, 206).

With the active recruitment of Mexican labor at the border and consequent immigration, The Mexican Problem and all that it entailed became a transnational Mexican Problem to be resolved by Americans north and south of the U.S.–Mexico border. The conceptualization of Mexican migrants as the nation's Mexican Problem touched upon every aspect of the Mexican migrant communities' experiences. Although Mexicans were defined as *the* problem, they satisfied the nation's hunger for cheap, controllable labor, until, that is, downturns in the economy slowed the need for labor, which is what happened in the post World War era beginning in 1921. In the Midwest thousands of one-time recruited workers victimized by the downturn were forced to accept transport to the border and repatriate. However, the downturn was short and, with the upturn, Mexican migration rose once again to reach new levels.

RAILROADS

Railroads were among the first to recruit and settle Mexicans along rail lines in New York, Chicago, Kansas, Illinois, Texas, Colorado, and California, among other states. Mexican labor migration was in full swing and orchestrated by recruiting within Mexico and along the border to meet the exigencies of the railroad corporations. The historian Mario Garcia reported that at El Paso in the late spring of 1911, "over 1,000 laborers arrived during the first days of June" and that "every train that arrived in Juarez during June brought 300 men to work on railroad section gangs in the Southwest" (1981, 43). Labor contracting agencies at El Paso worked day and night to fill orders for Mexican workers and in 1908, for example, "placed approximately two thousand Mexican track workers on American railroads every month" (Garcilazo 1995, 101). Writing for the U.S. Bureau of Labor, Victor Clark observed that "immigrants arrive at the border practically without funds...Here they are met by the representatives of large authorized labor contracting companies, who regularly supply an entire railway system, or many of its divisions, with all the labor needed, and by private agents looking for smaller bodies of men for some special section or simply speculating on labor" (1974, 475). From El Paso they were transported by rail, and in the words of one news reporter, "when ready for shipment, each is provided with a number and they are herded down to the Union Station not unlike cattle. It is needless to say that Pullman cars are not provided for their transportation" (quoted in Garcia 1981, 54). Cattle cars were the most common form of transportation to places like Los Angeles, which often took as many as nine days to complete.

In the Southwest Mexican laborers overtook previous ethnic groups in comprising the main of track workers. Between 1909 and the late 1920s Mexicans replaced Greek, Italian, Japanese, and Korean workers on the Southwest's six main railroads. In California 40 percent of all employed Mexicans worked for the railroads. A 1926 report by the Governor of California's office reported that on the six main southwestern railroads at least fifty thousand Mexicans were employed, comprising 75 percent of track workers (*Mexicans in California*, 1930, 91; see also Increase of Mexican Labor. 1933, 82). On the Santa Fe, the figure stood at 67 percent; the Southern Pacific reported an average of 84 percent. In tune with the Southwest, two thirds of the track labor force in the Central Plains and Midwest were Mexicans who came to dominate track labor across the nation (Garcilazo 1995, 59). Track work, the laying of tracks and the maintenance of existing tracks, the hardest labor, came to be known as Mexican work. Wages were attached to that definition and on average Mexicans earned less than white workers performing the same work.

In tandem with the massive increase in the employment of Mexican track labor, worker settlements appeared along the rail routes. In the early period, men were the main residents in the camps; some built their own housing or at least made their best efforts to construct a place to live, which were often overcrowded and ridden with unhealthy conditions. Companies frequently offered boxcar camps and bunkhouses, which were a step above the tent and shack camps but, nonetheless, were still overcrowded and unsanitary. In time, the employers came to believe that men with a family in tow made more reliable workers less willing to move on to a new employment, join a union, or strike and began to emphasize the hiring of men with families. As soon as a work gang was hired, they were transported with their families to the work site. There a foreman greeted them, and according to one who experienced a trip to Glamis, California, from Texas, he "pointed them [workers and family] to the only buildings in town, old boxcars on the siding." She recalled, "Inside the boxcar was like an oven" (Garcilazo 1995, 91). One agent working for the Northwestern Railway underscored the value of a family-tied workforce: "now the Mexicans have their families in section so they will stay" (Garcilazo 1995, 225).

In time, a transition to families led to the development of *barrios* or *colonias* with men, women, and children comprising the population. By the 1920s Mexican track worker settlements appeared across the United States in much the same fashion that track worker settlements in Mexico arose along the sides of the rails. One railroad agent speaking in El Paso noted that "groups of houses dot the desert from here to Los Angeles." Twenty-two boxcar settlements existed in four Southern California counties (Garcilazo 1995, 229). Conditions often replicated that of company town housing in Mexico; as one image of a Los Angeles, California, camp indicated, "Some cars contain as many as four families, packed together like cattle, and on hot days these ovens are unbearable forcing little ones with their mothers to turn and seek shelter underneath amidst the wheels" (Garcilazo 1995, 233). However, despite the emphasis on men with families, a third parallel with Mexico appeared. Rails allowed for the movement of workers into other lines of employment, most often agriculture, where labor scarcity seriously affected production and recruitment was the order of the day. Samuel Bryan would observe in 1912 that "[most] of the Mexican immigrants have at one time or another been employed as railroad laborers" (1912, 728). Mexican track workers in Saint Louis and Kansas City experienced their second round with recruiters who sought workers for the Midwestern sugar beet fields. Recruiters entered into the boxcar settlements and "announced job opportunities" and waited for the crowd of men to assemble and sign them on (Nodin Valdes 1991, 11).

With the widening employment of Mexican migrants, peonism made its debut. In concert with the spreading definition of the "average" Mexican, a Santa Fe Railroad official concluded in a 1911 article in relation to Mexican track workers that "a peon's mind is very much like that of a nine or ten year old child, with the difference that the child's mind matures and the Mexican never does" (Garcilazo 1995, 132). The American construction of a Mexican's defining characteristics accompanied immigrants northward and served to validate the corporations' treatment, working and housing conditions, and wages that workers experienced. A railroad engineer's writing that "the average Mexican laborer and family are satisfied with the most primitive arrangements so far as comfort goes" simply legitimized the housing conditions afforded Mexican track workers in Mexico and across the United States (Garcilazo 1995, 135).

AGRICULTURE

Agricultural employment followed the same recruitment pattern exhibited in the case of railroad workers. The construction and extension of railroads across the United States developed agriculture rapidly after 1900, particularly in the Southwest. Mexican workers followed the path established by the growth of large-scale corporate agriculture, described by contemporaries as factory farms. As southwestern agriculture expanded dramatically in the first decades of the twentieth century, the demand for workers increased at a pace captured in University of California, Berkeley, economist Paul Taylor's phrase, "Irrigation means Mexicans" (quoted in McWilliams 1949, 162). By the 1920s over a third of all employed Mexicans worked in agriculture. A 1922 study of agricultural workers in the Southwest reported that three fourths of fruit and vegetable workers and half of cotton workers were Mexicans.

In California, as in the Southwest, land came to be concentrated among a few large-scale producers who dominated the production of labor-intensive crops like citrus and other fruits, vegetables, and cotton. In the early 1920s, a total of 2.1 percent of all California farms produced nearly 30 percent of the nation's agricultural products and only 7 percent of the state's farms employed two thirds of the farm labor force. In keeping with the pattern across the Southwest, 10 percent of all California farming operations received over half of the state's farm income (Acuña 1981, 207–14). Citrus production, the second leading agricultural branch in the state, harvested 60 percent of the nation's crop and 20 percent of the world's supply. In the hands of large-scale corporate producers rather than the storied family farmer, labor-intensive crops required a ready supply of seasonal labor available for harvest and easily disposed of upon the end of the season.

Migrant and permanent resident labor became the social condition necessary for this productive system to function. Mexican labor in the form of families, women, and/

or men was quickly incorporated into the leading centers of the nation's crop production. The manager of the Los Angeles Chamber of Commerce summed the matter of Mexican labor in the state's economy: "We are totally dependent...upon Mexicans for agricultural and industrial common or casual labor. It is our only source of supply" (Weber 1994, 35–36).

Not surprisingly, The Mexican Problem was prone to modification and positive assessments of Mexicans as naturally endowed with agricultural worker skills were introduced to validate the widespread utilization of Mexican labor. A major figure in the citrus industry, Charles C. Teague, chairman of the powerful Southern California Fruit Growers Association, balanced the equation. Mexicans, the primary picker force on his 1,875-acre citrus ranch, were said to be "naturally adapted to agricultural work, particularly in the handling of fruits and vegetables...Many of them have a natural skill in the handling of tools and are resourceful in matters requiring manual ability" (1944, 141).

In the cotton fields of the San Joaquin Valley four cotton firms came to control production: Anderson Clayton, Pacific Cottonseed Products, J. G. Boswell, and Globe Grain and Milling Company held the upper hand. Spread out over six counties, cotton production was organized under the California Cotton Cooperative Association, "a preponderance of large growers, financiers and ginners" that determined much of the policies governing production. Cotton, the most labor intensive crop in the state, required an army of workers, which in turn required off-seasonal recruiting of workers in Los Angeles and other cities where Mexicans settled. By the mid-1920s no less than thirty-five thousand workers met the task. Eighty percent of the labor force was Mexican, largely in the form of family labor, which then led to the formation of rural labor camps. These in turn led to the formation of small communities of permanent workers. Some camps were company sponsored and others privately operated; in either case they provided nearby quarters for accessing the workforce (Weber 1973, 31–32, 36, 42–43).

The citrus industry is a second case requiring an army of workers. Approximately 75 percent of the citrus pickers were Mexican, primarily men with families, numbering over ten thousand in the mid-1920s. The citrus industry provides a clear example of company-sponsored housing to attract workers with families and to discourage workers from unionizing and striking. Three quarters of all citrus growers organized into the Southern California Fruit Grower's Exchange (later known as Sunkist) dominated industry policies. One policy it pioneered in 1915 was the construction of camp housing for Mexican workers and by the mid-1920s twenty-four worker camps were established throughout the four Southern California counties comprising the citrus belt. In addition to minimal rent, pickers were obligated to labor at any hour, any day of the week, and to work full-time during the six-month harvest season.

California's Imperial Valley is a third case. In 1900 the Valley was an empty desert expanse overrun by rattlesnakes, roadrunners, and jackrabbits; but with the diversion of the Colorado River to the Valley through a vast irrigation system, the land was reborn. By 1920, a total of 242,110 acres of irrigated farmland produced field crops, truck crops, citrus, and dairy products and pastured 83,000 head of livestock. The Valley rapidly developed into an agricultural center for the production of a variety of the nation's food supplies, expanding to a half a million acres of farming, dairy, and cattle ranching in the late 1920s. The region came to be celebrated as "America's Winter Garden" and the "Inland Empire." In keeping with the established pattern across the Southwest and emerging in the Midwest, the Imperial Valley depended on Mexican labor and as such became "one of the richest agricultural areas of the world" (Hodges 1933, 423). However, although workers were central to this success story, that success did not reach the masses of laborers imported to work the land. Concentration in the hands of a few giant enterprises characterized the system and composed the bulk of the Valley's beneficiaries. Workers, however, remained in the poorest of living conditions.

As the region developed, permanent and migrant farm worker settlements appeared; "Mexican quarters" in the language of the day, were developed in the towns that appeared with particular crops. The Mexican quarter in Brawley appeared with the expansion of vegetable, melon, and cantaloupe production, whereas the barrio in El Centro accompanied lettuce production. By the 1920s, of a total population of 54,500, Mexicans numbered 20,000 and occupied several communities established in tune with the Valley's development. On the other hand, seasonal production required migrant workers who generally arrived at each harvest from points north but also from across the border and occupied tents, huts, or cars, often in squalid camps along irrigation ditches. However, a Valley's crop was matured every month of the year and migrants and permanent settlers, who for the most part were Mexican migrants and children of the migrants, harvested the crops.

California's experience was far from novel. According to Rodolfo Acuña, "In 1922 Mexicans comprised 24 percent of sugar beet contract labor in Michigan, Ohio, Iowa, Kansas, and Minnesota" (1972, 209–10); this number increased to 50 percent in 1926. In Colorado, the nation's leading producer of sugar beets was dominated by the Great Western Sugar Company, which controlled 80 percent of production. In keeping with the pattern established by railroads and other areas of agricultural production, 15,000 Mexican beet workers (three fourths of the total labor force) harvested 110,000 acres. In the late 1920s that production, much of it based on family labor, would amount to $12 million (Vargas 2005, 28). That Mexicans immigrated to Colorado (and the other sugar beet–producing states) was no coincidence; the Great Western Company actively recruited Mexicans to the region and even transported them from the border. A report by the National Child Labor Committee found that "the general practice is for the sugar companies to send out in the spring of each year their labor recruiting agents, who will go into Texas, New Mexico and the Mexican border, where through employment agencies they recruit a sufficient number of families, especially those with large numbers of children" (Mautner and Abbot 1929, 29). Family was so much a part of the labor migration because of Great Western's requirement that "ninety percent of each [labor] shipment should consist of family labor." Consequently, in 1921 nearly 10,000 workers were shipped and the numbers increased over the years. In 1924, a total of 12,043 were shipped, followed by 14,538 in 1926 (Taylor 1928–1934, 115). In the towns not far from the fields, Mexicans settled and made their homes, or what could be called homes. According to Zaragoza Vargas, "living conditions for the families were inhumane. As one contemporary pointed out, there were no standards for the housing of sugar beet workers "equal to the standards fixed for the housing and care of cattle" (2005, 32).

Texas competed as well for securing harvest labor, particularly in cotton. Once the transition from farm tenancy to corporate agriculture was completed, seasonal labor became indispensable to production. A 1918 conference by Texas officials in cooperation with agricultural representatives reported that the south Texas area alone would require 40,000 Mexicans for the coming harvests (Garcia 1981, 50). Mexicans filled that bill. A few years later it was reported that three quarters of the 400,000 cotton pickers in Texas were Mexicans working primarily as family labor (McWilliams 1942, 230; see Barrera 1979, 77). In Nueces County, which led the nation in the cotton production by 1930, 97 percent of its laborers were Mexican. According to Neil Foley, Mexicans were fundamental to the dramatic development of cotton production, which increased from 6,000 bales in 1900 to 250,000 in 1930 (1997, 122–23). Again, wages were determined by ethnicity and notions of race. In 1908, west Texas farmers paid Mexican workers $1.00 to $1.25 per day, whereas American workers were paid $1.75 to $2.00 per day. The same distinction was found in the general area twenty years later.

Peonism visited upon Mexicans in Texas as well. In an article published in 1920 titled "The Mexican Peon in Texas," the author advised that "there are two classes of peons in Texas, those who intend to make the state their home and those who come only for the cotton picking season and return as soon as it is over" (Callcott 1920, 437). Victor Clark expressed a general conclusion regarding Mexicans and the labor for which they were recruited: "Cotton picking suits the Mexican for several reasons: It requires nimble fingers rather than physical strength... it employs his whole family; he can follow it from place to place... which seems to suit the half-subdued nomadic instinct of a part of the Mexican race" (1974, 482). This came from a federal employee, but his analysis could have been written by the head of any of the corporate enterprises utilizing Mexican labor. Clark added another aspect of Mexicans that would continue into the century: "the Mexicans are making their homes in the United States in increasing numbers and... are forming a civic substratum of our border states" (1974, 518).

One privilege taken advantage of by the surrounding American community was the availability of Mexican women to serve as nannies, housekeepers, cooks, and washerwomen. In El Paso, as in the rest of the Southwest, Mexican women were the primary source for domestic workers. Mario Garcia found that the U.S. Employment Bureau working with El Paso officials organized an employment office and, in November 1919, interviewed 1,740 Mexican women; of these, 1,326 were deemed worthy and sent to an employer. A resident of El Paso recalled that "almost every Anglo-American family had at least one, sometimes two or three servants: a maid, laundress, and perhaps a nurse-maid or yardman." Laundries too sought Mexican women and hired them to wash and iron. Mexican women in the city formed three-quarters of all domestic workers in 1920 and over 90 percent of the 1,528 laundry workers. In the largest laundry in El Paso, of a total of 166 employees, Mexican women comprised 134 (Garcia 1981, 60, 76).

In Los Angeles, a similar situation developed. Although roughly 10 percent of the residents were involved in migrant labor, the majority worked in urban industries. Mexican women provided a key source of workers in garment factories, laundries, and canneries. According to Douglas Monroy, three thousand women sewed garments in the 1920s and one quarter of all cannery workers were Mexicans (1999, 120–23). The number of domestic workers is unknown, but the Los Angeles School District trained young Mexican female students in the finer points of domestic work, which suggests that Mexican women provided a significant supply of housekeepers, nannies, seamstresses, washerwomen, and the like (see Kersey 1937, 45).

The Mexican integration into the developing Texas economy had its opponents, primarily from the smaller farmers who were in process of being subjected to the power of large farming enterprises. These were the restrictionists of the early 1920s led by Representative John Box, who argued that Mexicans undermined America's culture, and therefore America needed to limit Mexican immigration. On the other hand, antirestrictionists put forward several defenses arguing that Mexicans returned home at the end of the season, that they were the only people willing to do the work, or that whites can get better work outside of agriculture. In the end, the antirestrictionists won out and consequently the 1924 Immigration Act restricting Middle Eastern, Asian, African, and Eastern European immigration left the door open to unrestricted immigration from the western hemisphere, but most notably for Mexican migration. The Mexican Problem was not a sufficient reason to bar their entrance.

SEGREGATION

Segregation became the order of the day for Mexicans wherever they were settled and expanded to work, schooling, and recreation, into practically every aspect of their lives. However, rather than interpreting segregation as a means of keeping people out of the "mainstream" or of "marginalizing" them to the social and economic periphery, segregation was the method of integrating Mexican immigrants and their families into the heart of the American economy.

Indeed, Mexican laborers, women and men, were as integrated within the economy as were the board of directors of the huge corporations for which many of them labored. Residential segregation merely replicated the emphasis on Mexican migrants as the choice for a flexible labor supply. *Barrios* and *colonias* "across the tracks" served as a labor reserve where workers were easily pooled, accessed, and just as easily disposed of. Segregated settlements brought a variation of the border to the employers' doorsteps.

In like measure, with the passing of compulsory public education laws, segregated schooling in urban and rural areas provided a reproduction of labor from one generation to the next by emphasizing education adapted to the "special needs" of Mexican children. Volumes of studies repeated well-traveled ideas regarding Mexicans. A veteran school teacher writing a master's thesis titled "Methods of Teaching Mexicans" concluded that the "majority of Mexicans in our public schools are not representative of the better class of Mexicans. They represent, rather, the very lowest type, the day laborer, or the peon." Not surprisingly, she added that "the Mexican is naturally indolent" (Gould 1932, 3). As Mexicans arrived, opinions such as these entered into the halls of public policy bureaucracies. The curricular emphasis applied across the southwest to a large degree originated in the literature on Mexico by Americans and combined with the application of modern theories of intelligence and racial inheritance then in vogue. In his Master's thesis at the University of Southern California, an aspiring school administrator expressed a common theme among the public and boards of education: "The Mexican Problem...exists wherever there are Mexicans" (Treff 1934, 10). In a similar vein, the Assistant Supervisor for the Department of Compulsory Education advised his readers that "The Mexican Problem in the Los Angeles School System is principally the product of poverty...which, in turn, is largely the appendage of the immigrants from the Republic south of us" (Los Angeles School District Journal 1928, 154). The Los Angeles School Superintendent Susan B. Dorsey could not have agreed more. In a speech before a summer assembly of school administrators in 1923, she claimed, "it is unfortunate and unfair for Los Angeles, the third largest Mexican city in the world, to bear the burden of taking care educationally of this enormous group" (Los Angeles School District Journal 1923, 59).

Modern educational practices such as testing and counseling had an added impact on Mexican children. Intelligence research conducted upon Mexican children as early as 1915 found that the children scored well below the "norm." Academics and educators concluded that Mexican children were decidedly intellectually inferior to white children and schools must take that into consideration in educating Mexican children. Boards of education lost no time in creating Mexican schools as soon as enough Mexicans arrived in the district and reconstructed the curriculum to accommodate the nostrums applied to Mexicans. On the basis that Mexican children were culturally and intellectually inferior and that an injustice would befall them if forced to compete with Anglo American children, schools channeled children into industrial or vocational education. However, the ultimate resolution to The Mexican Problem required at least one added ingredient and that was Americanization, the remaking of the peon and his/her child into the "other Mexican." That reformation required school districts to direct Mexican children into compulsory Americanization coursework and a common policy in school districts was to title the first two years of elementary schools as "Americanization rooms." The successfully Americanized child, known across the southwest as the "other Mexican," spoke English exclusively and dressed and behaved according to the model placed before him/her, the American child. However, segregation constructed a formidable barrier to Americanizing the children. Instead, the schools promoted the idea that Mexicans were "different" and in a segregated environment Mexicans became conscious of themselves as separate peoples within the United States.

Although the reformed "other Mexican" was freed from cultural baggage said to be rooted in the Spanish language, she/he was still limited by intellectual ability and therefore highly suited to industrial or vocational education. In channeling children to a curriculum "suited to their needs," segregated schools operated as a form of controlled integration of Mexican children into the economy to fill the occupations held by their fathers and mothers. Although the policy may initially appear to be an obvious case of racism, upon further analysis it becomes clear that economic objectives played the key role in establishing the educational practice applied to the Mexican community.

School administrators were well aware of the kinds of work available to Mexicans, both women and men, and shaped the curriculum to that reality. In San Antonio, for example, the junior high school for Mexican students was simply called the Industrial School and offered special courses in "sewing, cooking and art work for girls; machine shop practice, auto repair, auto painting, top making, sheet metal work, plain bench and cabinet work in wood and a department in which type-setting and job printing are taught for boys" ("Vocational Education" 1924, 108). In Los Angeles, the Board of Education performed surveys of the jobs available to Mexicans and designed curricula accordingly (Los Angeles City Schools, 1926, 3). Those children deemed slow learners (scoring between 0.70 and 0.89 on the IQ test, with 1.00 being "normal") or "educationally mentally retarded" (below 0.70) were treated to a curriculum that emphasized agricultural labor, animal husbandry, domestic work, and other forms of handwork. At least half of the Los Angeles District's twenty-five thousand Mexican children were judged to fit within one of the two categories in the mid-1920s (McAnulty 1929, 6–7). Training for laundry work centered in the curriculum for the below-average female student. An official district publication pointed out that "several employers have told us that a dull girl makes a much better operator on a mangle than a normal girl" (Los Angeles School District Publication 1929, 89–90).

However, in agricultural areas where half of the Mexican immigrant population resided, schooling was organized to fit the labor needs of factory farms, which depended on permanent resident and migrant family labor. A common policy, particularly in Texas, was to deny Mexican children entrance to public schools or to reduce the school year in Mexican schools to correspond with harvest requirements (see Montejano 1987, 194–95). Paul Taylor reported that in Dimmit County, Texas, no more than 25 percent of Mexican children ages seven to seventeen attended school in the 1920s (1928–1934, 372). In the Colorado beet fields, Mexican school "attendance dropped by half in September, October and November, during the harvest season, and again during the part of June when the beet plants were thinned" (Vargas 2005, 30–31). In California, in Ventura County, a major agricultural area, schools placed signs on school entrances reading "No Migratory Children Wanted Here," meaning, of course, Mexican children (Cobb 1932, 103). No agricultural corporation would think of such a prohibition in the hiring of workers; ironically, the prohibition on school doors served their interests well and employers expressed no opposition to such measures. Undoubtedly they supported them.

MEXICAN MIGRANTS ENTER THE AMERICAN WORKING CLASS

The historical stage was set for the development of a working class consciousness, an opposition to oppressive and exploitative conditions that the Mexican community experienced leading to political and civic organizations, labor unions, protests, and strikes. In many ways, the methods used to correct exploitative conditions paralleled America's industrial workers' attempts to correct injustices. Mexican migrants were joined with the American working class. Smelter workers at the ASARCO plant in El Paso walked off their jobs in 1901 protesting a reduction in pay. Later that same year, Mexicans working for the El Paso Street Car Company struck in protest of low wages. In 1903, Mexican sugar beet workers in Oxnard, California, organized with fellow Japanese workers and carried out a month-long successful strike. In the same year, 3,500 Chicano miners in the Clifton–Morenci district launched a strike met by the violence of the Arizona Rangers. A few months later citrus workers in Ventura, California, went on strike. Later that year Los Angeles Mexican track workers employed by the Pacific Electric Railway organized into *La Union Federal Mexicano* and protested low wages. The Railway's refusal to accede led to an unsuccessful walkout by 700 men and active support from the women of the community. (Ten years later the same union struck again without success.) Los Angeles Gas Works employees launched a strike in

1910 and won a wage increase. In 1913 "one of the largest strikes in El Paso's early history" brought the smelter to a standstill as 650 workers walked off their jobs. In 1913 miners in Ludlow, Colorado, organized and launched a fifteen-month strike, left the company housing, and set up a tent colony. Strikers composed of Italian, Greek, Slav, and Mexican miners stood united until the National Guard was called and attacked the encampment in 1914 with machine guns and bombs. Eighteen people were killed, nine of them Mexicans; five were children (Acuña 1972, 202–03).

In 1915 Mexican and Anglo miners at Clifton–Morenci, Arizona, went out on a four and a half–month strike. In 1917 miners in the Bisbee and Jerome district went on strike, but this time officials' violence visited upon them. Police and vigilantes broke up the strike and over 1,800 strikers were summarily arrested, forced to board trains, and exiled in the New Mexican desert without basic provisions. In Colton, California, cement workers formed the *Trabajadores Unidos* and protested a planned lowering of wages; 150 men walked out and won a pay raise and union recognition. In Los Angeles 200 Mexican employees of the Pacific Sewer Pipe Company went on strike in 1918. El Paso garbage collectors and park workers left their jobs in 1919 demanding improved working conditions (Acuña 1972, 204). In that same year the *Pro Patria* club in Santa Ana, California, protested the decision of the Board of Education to establish a Mexican school. The Board consulted with the City Attorney, who ruled that if the purpose for segregating is to overcome problems stemming from language, attendance, or age, then segregation was legal (Santa Ana (California) Board of Education Minutes, 1919).

In the early twentieth century Mexican immigrants, the peons, were prized workers because they were readily available and allegedly controllable, loyal, childlike, and humble. Moreover, it was said that they were "naturally" adept at physical labor while willing to work for low wages and able to survive according to the peon's standards. That view of the Mexican sector of the U.S. working class would not endure and in the 1920s the corporate world came to know just what kind of workers they had recruited and welcomed with open arms. The meaning of the term The Mexican Problem was redefined to mean undependable, organized, and active workers. The redefinition would be further clarified during the Depression, particularly in California, when of the nation's 245 agricultural strikes, 170 were called in California involving 127,000 strikers, the majority of whom were Mexicans. Indeed, Mexican immigrants had become integrated within the center of the U.S. economy and politically active although socially segregated.

CONCLUSION

By the 1920s Mexican documented, undocumented, and contract labor had been incorporated into the heart of the American economy. Here we examined root causes leading to the late nineteenth and early twentieth century Mexican migration, a migration that begins in Mexico and leads to the United States. After having been uprooted as a consequence of the entrance of U.S. investors, bankers, and industrial corporations, Mexicans then became the primary labor supply in Mexico. An active recruitment campaign led workers to the U.S.-owned mining, oil, and railroad lines within Mexico; these same workers, documented or not, were then recruited to work on railroads, agriculture, mining, and construction across the border.

That migration resulted in a settlement pattern of permanent residents primarily across the southwest and to a lesser extent into the Midwest, which accompanied Mexicans' employment and integration into the center of the North American economy. Moreover, that migration proved the first steps in the formation of the modern Chicano community. For all practical purposes that experience, from migration to economic integration and incessant settlement and community formation, continues into the twenty-first century.

Galarza's explanation for Mexican migration rings true in the early twenty-first century as it did for the early twentieth century. Galarza considered Mexican migration a "palliative, a national narcotic" that postponed Mexico's coming to terms with its deeply rooted economic problems. Mexican elites depended on migration, observed Galarza, as a means to evade the necessary reforms required to resolve Mexico's underdevelopment and its subjection to the power of foreign capital (Anderson 1976b, 617). Consequently, the solution to Mexico's problems is postponed while the solution to North America's need for cheap, readily available, and disposable labor is realized. Galarza once said that Mexico serves as a huge, easily accessed pool of labor for U.S. corporations. One might add that the labor is disposable as well.

CHAPTER 3

The Repatriation of Mexicans from the United States and Mexican Nationalism, 1929–1940[1]

Fernando Saúl Alanís Enciso
Colegio de San Luis, A.C.

The Great Depression that hit the United States in 1929 made thousands of Mexicans leave that country. Between 1930 and 1934, unemployment, hunger, deportations, raids, and antiforeigner sentiment led to an unprecedented population movement of men and women from the United States to Mexico. It was the biggest repatriation in history and the largest known in the historiography of migration. The ways in which people moved varied widely, as well as the conditions in which they entered Mexico. Some came alone; others came with their families, they traveled by train, ship, carts, on foot, or in their cars; some would bring clothes, beds, heaters, wardrobes, sewing machines, phonographs, radios, and money. Many arrived without a cent and in deplorable conditions.

Given the intensive movement of people from north to south, as well as the difficult situation of the Mexican community in the United States, Mexican administrations—led by Presidents Emilio Portes Gil (1928–1930), Pascual Ortiz Rubio (1930–1932), and Abelardo L. Rodríguez (1932–1934)—took measures in the United States and at the border to help people return to their place of origin. They implemented a series of actions no other government ever had ever taken before. Consuls organized the repatriation of groups and negotiated discounts and aid with U.S.-based charity organizations to transfer their fellow Mexicans to the border. The Departments of the Interior, National Railroads, and Treasury coordinated their work to fund and transfer people from the border back to their home towns. Discounts were negotiated with U.S. railroad companies for those heading for Mexico.

---

1. Translation from the original, "La repatriación de mexicanos de Estados Unidos y el nacionalismo mexicano, 1929–1940," by Adriana Vega with Mark Overmyer-Velázquez.

Mexican administrations and the national press, representing both the government and the opposition, disseminated the image of a "generous Mother Land," which welcomed with open arms its sons and daughters returning from the United States. Also, they exalted repatriation as a "humanitarian act of true nationalism." Aid to destitute repatriates—those who reached an appalling state, who were moneyless after being detained and deported—was maximized and it acquired a patriotic connotation because it was sustained by an image emphasizing the return of Mexicans and their families.

During the same period, the repatriation of men with agricultural experience and know-how became the central focus of political discourse and irrigation policy of the era's governments. The promotion of the return of skilled laborers, according to some officials and intellectuals, would help to develop and modernize the country. This position was also endorsed by others who argued that such promotion would contribute to the colonization of the north of the Republic and would consolidate territorial sovereignty as it worked as a barrier to U.S. expansion, still openly supported by many people in the United States. Similarly, the support of certain return migrants would lead to the predominance of the national population over the foreign, present in some areas in the north such as Mexicali, Baja California.

A national campaign in favor of the return movement, called the Half-a-Million campaign, became the peak of all official actions; it was aimed at raising funds to "accommodate" those who were returning to Mexico. This enterprise was organized by private groups, civil society, and the Secretary of the Interior. From late 1932 to early 1933, the campaign fostered the creation of committees in almost every municipality in the Republic. These committees organized money-collecting projects, bullfights, dances, movie showings, plays, and festivals to raise money to support repatriation. The project reached many remote places within the country, thanks to government support and the collaboration and solidarity of many individuals and civil and labor organizations: politicians, merchants, teachers, employees (municipal, state, and federal), local and national political organizations, and other members of society. In the face of what was then considered an emergency and a national problem, a sense of solidarity in support of repatriation emerged from among a diverse range of groups in Mexican society from all over the country.

The government of General Lázaro Cárdenas (1934–1940) took a position similar to the one taken by those in power earlier in the 1930s. Even if it did not face return movements on a big scale—because social and economic conditions affecting the Mexican community in the United States changed and deportation declined—Cárdenas' government supported the return of the destitute and expressed itself in favor of utilizing the skills repatriates were supposed to have acquired abroad to colonize diverse parts of the country. The most outstanding element of the Cárdenas presidency was a highly nationalist repatriation project articulated through the foundation of a planned community called 18 de Marzo (eighteenth of March) in Tamaulipas (a name honoring the country's oil expropriation and one of the strongest symbols of revolutionary nationalism). Through this plan, in a moment of great polarization and discontent toward the regime, Cárdenas attempted to unite Mexican society around an official policy.

The most influential studies in the historiography of repatriation during the Great Depression have focused, on one hand, on exploring the actions of Mexican governments in the face of the mass return triggered by the depression and, on the other hand, on the measures that Los Angeles County, California, took to deport a large number of Mexicans. Such studies have also highlighted some of the tragic passages many Mexicans and their families endured when they were forced to abandon the United States (Hoffman 1974; Carreras de Velasco 1974; Balderrama and Rodríguez 1995; Guérin-Gonzales 1994; Walsh 2009). Abraham Hoffman, Mercedes Carreras de Velasco, Francisco Balderrama, and Raymond Rodríguez, the most influential scholars on the topic, have contributed significantly to the analysis of repatriation in the 1930s. However, these works do not examine the social, demographic, economic, cultural, and political impact that this movement had in Mexico. Unlike these studies, this chapter explores the impacts as they were experienced in Mexico.

This study analyzes repatriation as an element contributing to the consolidation of nationalism and, at the same time, to the construction of the postrevolutionary Mexican state. This work proposes that the return of destitute Mexicans coming from the United States turned into a national standard supported by the governments of Mexico from 1930 to 1940 and by some social sectors. Associated with a widely disseminated image of *paisanos* (countrymen or people of Mexican origin) who were returning from their plight, repatriation became a symbol of charity and nationalism that penetrated vast circles of society. In addition, in official discourse repatriation acquired an unprecedented relevance and level of circulation. Furthermore, the idealized and selective repatriation of men, supposedly qualified and with agricultural skills, unified several nationalist aspirations of the postrevolutionary political class: the colonization of the north with nationals, the reduction of foreign population, agricultural production in irrigated areas, and territorial sovereignty.

Similarly, the Half-a-Million campaign expressed an element of unity and identity for a great part of Mexican society and was experienced as a fundamental ingredient of nationalism. Through the call for cooperation and support of repatriation—and, above all, the positive response of a wide sector of society—loyalties and solidarities were consolidated; individuals and various groups cohered around the idea of belonging to the nation and promoted unity and collaboration. At an official level, repatriation reinforced the emerging notion of a "Mexican" identity. In a similar vein, it underscored mexicanness (mexicanidad) as a primary element of nationalism. All belonged to the same nation—even those who were part of the Mexican diaspora (México de afuera) in the United States.

The Cardenista period of repatriation was also used as a nationalist symbol, mainly when the president promoted the creation of a repatriates settlement (colonia). Cárdenas carried out this plan to appease the criticism he had received for supporting the arrival of Spanish refugees. The services the Cardenista regime provided to the Spanish Republic were considered the most salient element of Mexican foreign intervention. Cárdenas aided the legitimate government, overthrown by the rebellion led by Francisco Franco (1936), by providing nationally manufactured armaments and granting asylum to hundreds of Spaniards. Together with France, Mexico became the shelter of the republican *transterrados* (refugees). The exodus started in 1937 and ended in the first months of World War II. First, approximately five hundred children arrived, followed by an important group of Spanish intellectuals, and finally a mass of republican Spaniards, whose arrival was not well received by wide sectors of Mexican society (Fagen 1973, 29–30; Matesanz 1995, 119–70).

The Cardenista focus on repatriation paradoxically involved events that were not directly related to the United States but to Spain. That is, the position of the Cárdenas´ government was highly manipulative and demagogic, contrasting with positions taken by governments and society earlier in the decade. The differences between these two periods partly stemmed from the size of the return movement taking place in each of them. Early in the decade the repatriation was intensive and reached massive proportions (from 1930 to 1933), which led governments to tackle it urgently, connecting with society in an unprecedented way. However, in the second half of the decade, return movements declined considerably, so that the Cardenista government did not feel pressed to take hasty measures and Mexican society increasingly lost interest in the topic. Still, the president decided to use repatriation to promote unity and consensus in the country and thus counteract internal opposition to one of the axes of his foreign policies, the support to the Spanish Republic, and the provision of refuge to exiles.

This work rests on the idea that the manipulation of repatriation, at an official and nonofficial level, had components similar to two significant events in postrevolutionary nationalism: the educational project of the 1920s and xenophobia toward the Chinese community, which came to a head during the same period. In both cases, the formation of stereotypes had a national reach and brought cohesion to Mexican society. The educational project promoted "the Mexican" (lo mexicano) by means of images of the *china poblana* (traditional dress for Mexican women) and the *charro* (traditional Mexican horseman), among other symbols. Xenophobic policies and attitudes portrayed the *"chino"* as a dirty and degrading human being from an inferior race. In 1911 the anti-Chinese movement started with the slaughter of 303 Chinese people in Torreón, Coahuila. In the following years, Sinophobia played an important role in political mobilization in the northern border states (from Baja California to Tamaulipas) where Chinese communities preferred to settle since their arrival in Mexico in the nineteenth century. In the early 1930s, the hostility was at its highest when several anti-Chinese nationalist committees were formed in various parts of the country for the purpose of harassing and expelling the Chinese (Gómez Izquierdo 1991, 81–150).

Likewise, federal government institutions orchestrated and supported these educational and xenophobic policies, essentially institutionalizing these actions. The Secretary of Education supported the educational project, whereas the Secretary of the Interior and many state governments (Sonora, for example) encouraged hostility and the expulsion of the Chinese through legislation banning marriage between Mexican women and Chinese men, forcing companies to recruit Mexicans for at least 80 percent of their staff and preventing these companies from selling more than one type of merchandise. In the same way, the educational and xenophobic projects strongly resonated with Mexican society, fostering unity and identification among hundreds of people, allowing them to feel that they belonged to the same nation. The Secretary of Education disseminated its teaching plan to create a myth of common identity through libraries and fine arts (music, dance, theater, painting, and literature).

Similarly, Sinophobic attitudes and policies reinforced Mexican identity by conjuring an enemy and exalting the sense of membership in a superior group (the Mexican; see Pérez Montfort 1994, 7–11).

As with the educational and xenophobic projects, repatriation fostered the development of two stereotypes that became widely known throughout the country. The first stereotype portrayed Mexicans returning from the United States as poor, exhausted, sick, and grieving. References to this image were constant in the national and state press.[2] The other stereotype disseminated among political and popular classes was that of experienced repatriates who had acquired special skills during their stay in the United States and would supposedly return to support the development of the country and be incorporated into the national project. Several editorials appearing in the contemporary press underscored the belief that repatriates had special qualities acquired during their stay in the United States and that Mexicans should make the most of them for the "advancement and aggrandizement" of the country. The legislation and population projects of the time also echoed this opinion.[3]

In a similar manner, the process of return was institutionalized as it became a priority in the actions of the Departments of the Interior, Foreign Relations, Agriculture, and National Railroads, and it was integrated into the nationalist policy of the revolutionary elites in the 1933 *Plan Sexenal* (Six-Year Plan) and the 1936 Population Act. The Department of Demography and Repatriation also was founded that year. In the same way, the huge population movement managed to bring together large and diverse sectors of Mexican society, identifying them as Mexicans with the unified goal of repatriation. With the Half-a-Million campaign, solidarity around repatriation reached a national level and stimulated a strong relationship between the government and diverse groups in civil society. Later in the decade, President Cárdenas attempted something similar with his repatriation project, but it never achieved the same unifying results.

Stereotypes, institutionalization, and unification are three elements that were taken into account by government officials in their attempts to establish repatriation as a critical component of Mexican nationalism in the 1930s. The distinctive feature in this case lies in that repatriation represents a novel example of what the postrevolutionary elites promoted to carry out their project of unification and promotion of a national identity. Although the educational and cultural projects of the 1920s were planned and promoted "from above," repatriation, without any prearranged plans or programs (nobody would have thought that such a population movement would take place), became a symbol of internal unity and collective identification of Mexican society and its ruling class. Governing elites mobilized the repatriation movement to help consolidate the state still emerging from the violent years of the Revolution (1910–1920; Pérez, 1994b, 39–64; Vaughan 1991, 507–26).

---

2. *El intruso. Diario joco-serio netamente independiente,* Cananea, Sonora, January 15, 1931, and March 4, 1931. *El Universal ilustrado,* México, D.F., May 9, 1931. *El Nacional Revolucionario,* October 27, 1931. México, *Informe rendido por el C. gobernador constitucional del Estado,* Sebastián Allende, Archivo del Congreso del Estado, Guadalajara, Jalisco, 1933.

3. *El Pueblo. El periódico de todos,* Hermosillo, Sonora, March 28, 1931. Archivo General de la Nación, Fondo Presidentes, Alberlardo L. Rodríguez, exp. 017/19.

THE MOVEMENT OF MEXICANS FROM THE
UNITED STATES TO MEXICO, 1929–1940

During the 1930s a cycle unfolded in the history of Mexican emigration to the United States. This cycle initiated with the Great Depression that started in October 1929. The effects of the Depression were felt in the increasing unemployment rate emerging from a decline of labor force demand and the rise of pressure and a renewed hostility toward Mexican workers to leave the United States. Furthermore, U.S. immigration law, which had tended to be restrictive since the 1920s, was increasingly tightened to prevent the entrance of foreign workers (Hoffman 1974, 175).

The deportation policy was applied in many places in the United States and to all foreign groups to reduce unemployment and prioritize U.S. citizens for the available jobs. The deportation plan implemented by the Los Angeles County government was one of the most successful in the country. The Los Angeles County Public Health and Welfare Department deported hundreds of Mexicans and their U.S.-born descendants, paying for their transportation to the border. Immigration agents, led by William N. Doak, Secretary of Labor, also intensified actions in the large urban areas of the country (Texas, Illinois, Michigan, and Arizona). The final objetive of all of these operations was to deport migrants. (Balderrama and Rodríguez 1995, 68–77).

Many Mexicans were detained in their houses, work fields, streets, parks, and other public places and were automatically sent to the border with or without their families and without any money. Esteban Torres's father was arrested at the mine where he worked in Miami, Arizona, and put on a train bound for Mexico. His family never heard from him again.[4] Ezequiel Piña, his wife, and their six children born in the United States were also apprehended by the police in Montana and sent to the border; they had no opportunity to take their clothes and the goods they had in their homes.[5] Bernardo Moreno Grajeda's family, his wife, and his son, who were in Eagle Pass, Texas, were dispossessed of their belongings and deported by local authorities. They lost their land and the investment they had made when they arrived in the United States. They went back to San Luis Potosí "empty-handed."[6] The antiforeigner sentiment generated by the depression and the negative perception toward the Mexican community forced hardships upon many men, women, and children of Mexican origin as they were expelled, ipso facto, from the United States. These types of events have made this period one of the most tragic in the history of migrations.

Civil, welfare, and religious organizations in California, Texas, Michigan, and Illinois provided hundreds of unemployed people with clothes, food, and even transportation to Mexico. Some people were not directly forced to leave the country but news about harassment, local authorities' home visits requesting migration documentation, and the overall atmosphere of persecution led them to initiate their journey back to Mexico in their own vehicles and with their household items (furniture, heaters,

---

4. *La Opinión,* Los Ángeles, California, July 13, 2003. Interview with Esteban Torres (January 27, 1930), former (Democrat) Democrat Congress member to Congressional District 98, 1983–1999.

5. Interview with Ignacio Piña Osorno, son of Ezequiel Piña, who arrived in Mexico at the age of six. Ignacio was born in Utah in 1924; he currently lives in Bakersfield, California. October 9, 2003.

6. Interview with Bernardo Moreno Grajeda (June 27,1923). San Luis Potosí, December 24, 2002.

phonographs, radios, bicycles, sewing machines, washing machines). Simón Reyes's family who lived in Marinetti, Arizona, were having a hard time during the years after the work in the fields and the mines had ceased. Given the situation, Reyes decided to relocate his family to Bácum, Sonora, where the Mexican government gave them land.[7] In the face of lack of work, which worsened in San Antonio, Texas, and its surroundings, Apolonio Martínez Barcena and his family, including several children born in the United States, decided to leave San Antonio, Texas, for San Luis Potosí, Mexico.[8]

Personal motivations, unrelated to unemployment and the economic recession, also inspired some people to return to Mexico. In early 1931, Leocadio Ayala decided to return with all of his family to Mexico because his doctor suggested he should take his wife from Kansas City to a location where the weather would be restorative for her health.[9] Leocadio loaded his belongings onto a truck and set off on his journey to his native Surumuato, Michoacán. On the other hand, Marta Órnelas and her husband came back from Detroit, Michigan, because she wanted to see her mother. Even when there was no immediate need to leave, they seized the opportunity of the free trip on a train for repatriates, funded by the famous mural painter Diego Rivera. Like other people, they advantageously used discounts and special trips to go to Mexico to avoid paying otherwise expensive transportation fees.[10] Other families went back after having worked in Texan fields, as they did every year. This was the case of Román Castillo and his family, who came back from San Antonio, Texas, to Matehuala, San Luis de Potosí. His family was composed of Nieves Torres, his wife, and ten children, some of them born in the United States.[11]

A central characteristic of this population movement was the repatriation of hundreds of boys and girls who were U.S. citizens of Mexican origin, who entered Mexico with their parents because they had been expelled or deported or because they had decided to bring them in pursuit of a better life. Ezequiel Piña, Apolonio Martínez Barcena, and Román Castillo brought their U.S.-born children. Simón Reyes's family arrived at Bácum with three girls and one boy, all born in the United States.[12] In the list of repatriates the consuls made, there are records concerning the high number of minors born in the United States. Some scholars estimate that more than 50 percent of the people entering Mexico were minors (Oppenheimer 1932, 213–34; Gilbert 1934, 140).

According to official figures, between 1930 and 1934, more than 350,000 people moved from the United States to Mexico. Their motivations varied widely: violent expulsions, deportations, personal reasons, special repatriation programs, advantageous use of discounts made by railroad companies, termination of temporary jobs, or

---

7. Interview with Francisco Reyes (February 24, 1925), Bácum, Sonora, November 23, 2004.

8. Interview with Socorro Martínez de González, daughter of Apolonio Martínez. San Luis Potosí, S.L.P. April 17, 2003.

9. Interview with Alberto Ayala (1909), Pastor Ortiz, Michoacán, January 18, 2003.

10. Interview with Marta Órnelas Villalobos (July 29, 1912), León, Guanajuato, May 20, 2006.

11. Interview with Guadalupe Salinas Castillo, daughter of Lina Castillo Torres, migrant at the beginning of the twentieth century. Matehuala, San Luis Potosí, October 1, 2002.

12. Interview with Francisco Reyes (February 24, 1925), Bácum, Sonora, November 23, 2004.

simply parents returning with their children to Mexico.[13] The repatriates were of diverse composition: men, women, and, above all, U.S.-born boys and girls. Repatriation, understood as north-to-south movement of the population (from the United States to Mexico), was not tragic in all cases, as often indicated in the historiography. The entire decade did not bear witness to movements on a large scale either, as the majority of studies have documented.

The movement of people of Mexican origin from the United States to Mexico in the first years of the 1930s was of massive proportions that lasted a brief period of time and soon disappeared. According to data provided by the Department of Immigration of Mexico, from 1930 to 1931 return migration soared unprecedentedly in the history of migrations; it rose from 70,127 to 138,519 people, by far the largest year of return. After 1932, there was a significant decline in return migration from 138,519 in the previous year to 77,453, a decrease of nearly 44 percent. This trend continued during 1933, when 33,574 were repatriated, a decrease of 56.7 percent compared with the previous year; and in 1934, return migration decreased to 23,934 people (Alanís Enciso 2007b, 65–91). The downward trend continued in the second half of the decade as shown by statistics (from 1935 to 1940 a total of 75,489 repatriations), primary sources, and periodical accounts.[14] The movement of people caused by the Great Depression emerged in a spectacular manner and declined in the same way; it did not remain constant because of a series of economic and social factors that converged in 1934. Those factors included the New Deal effects in the Mexican community, the refusal of many people of Mexican origin to leave and their attachment to the United States, the negative perception of conditions in Mexico, the ease of pressure to expel foreigners, and the struggle for civil and labor rights in the Mexican communities in the United States (Alanís Enciso 2007a).

MEXICAN GOVERNMENTS: THE PATRIOTIC DUTY OF REPATRIATING THE INDIGENT

Central to the actions Mexican governments took in support of repatriation was the assistance to people requiring urgent help in the United States and on the border. This assistance focused on the transportation from the border to the towns of origin and on colonization studies for the settlement of repatriates in Mexico.

As soon as the large-scale return movements began, the Mexican government assumed as a patriotic duty the repatriation of nationals who were in the United States. The Secretary of the Interior immediately submitted to the President an agreement for the repatriation of all unemployed Mexicans. "Out of patriotism, then, as established

---

13. I consider 1930 a starting point because in that year a break in the migratory flow was recorded and the mass return caused by the recession was visible; also because repatriations in 1929, or before, are identified with normal repatriations within a period of high activity within the cycles of migration. Furthermore, I take 1934 as a finishing date because by that time the most critical moment of the return movement had passed and the positive effects of the U.S. recovery program (New Deal) were no longer felt among the population of Mexican origin.

14. 1935, 15,368; 1936, 11,599; 1937, 8,037; 1938, 12,024; 1939, 15,925; and 1940, 12,536, total: 75,489. *Seis años de gobierno*, 1940, 23; México, 1941, 20.

in the agreement [we should proceed to transport to Mexico] the population of our Republic that is out of work and is being treated most unfairly in the United States." According to this point of view, Mexicans in the United States were considered part of Mexico. Therefore, in a gesture of loyalty—or moral duty—toward them, the government supported the return to Mexico of citizens and their descents born in U.S. The Department of the Interior assumed the repatriation of Mexicans "without delay or restrictions [as] one of their basic duties towards Mexicans who, in their misfortune, had been abandoned among U.S. populations."[15]

Mexican governments during the *Maximato*[16] implemented several actions to aid their *paisanos*: those who were unemployed or starving; those who had been expelled or detained or had been requesting repatriation; and those who had reached the border and were living in utter squalor. Consulates supported repatriation from Texas, California, Illinois, Michigan, and other states. They organized the return, provided funds, and helped in obtaining free transportation to the border. From July 1930 to June 1931, Mexican government officials, committees organized by consulates, and Mexican individuals provided the financial capital for the repatriation of 60,207 men and 31,765 women, totaling 91,972, most coming from Texas and California (Carreras de Velasco 1974, 68–69). From July 1931 to June 1932, 124,894 Mexicans were repatriated and the government spent 73,404 pesos just in food aid (González Navarro, 1970, 539).

The fifty-two consulates established in the United States (mainly located in the Southwest, where the highest concentration of people of Mexican origin were found: California, Arizona, Texas, and New Mexico), apart from assisting in repatriation, continued to carry out various activities. As government agents, they were focused on the control of the community to conservative political ends rather than on the support of the independent actions of their *paisanos*. As studies of El Monte Berry (1933) and San Joaquín Valley (1934) agricultural strikes in California demonstrate, the consular intervention ordered from Mexico City complemented U.S. labor and immigration policies and ultimately reflected the American Federation of Labor's political conservatism. In other words, involvement of the Mexican government was at a significant distance from the interests of the Mexican community and more closely resembled an extension of labor policies imposed by a corporate state (González 2004b, 173–76; Balderrama, 1982, ix–xi).

Consulates also carried out a complex job that involved the protection of Mexicans against abuse committed by their employers and, at the same time, espionage to inform the central Mexican government about the movements of political exiles (above all those who supported the uprising of general José Gonzalo Escobar in March 1929) and religious exiles (those who had fled during the Cristero War, 1926–1929), who were looked upon as a potential threat to the stability of the regime (Smith 2002, 65; Alanís Enciso 2005). In sum, the relationship of consulates to the Mexican population in the United States was a mixture of complex and contradictory interests of the state

---

15. *La Voz de Chihuahua*, Chihuahua, Chihuahua, November 12 and December 28, 1930.

16. The term applied to the period from 1928 to 1934, during the reign of the *Jefe Máximo* (Supreme Chief or Plutarco Elías Calles) and of the Presidents he installed: Portes Gil, Ortiz Rubio, and Abelardo L. Rodríguez.

emerging from the Revolution, which went beyond the traditional interpretation of consuls as protectors of the Mexican diaspora.

National railroad companies established special quotes, donations, and free tickets for return migrants. The Secretary of the Interior provided free tickets from the border to their places of origin. General Luis Medina Barrón, the consul in El Paso, Texas, believed that it would be easy and "at the same time, patriotic" for railroads to transport Mexicans who had been deported to the main border cities (Smith 2002, 91). Thus, large contingents were mobilized from Ciudad Juárez, Chihuahua, Nogales, Sonora, Nuevo Laredo, and Tamaulipas to the center of the country. On certain occasions, trains were delayed and the paperwork was too slow to provide people with special tickets, which led to overcrowding. Nevertheless, the federal and municipal governments at the border tended to evict destitute repatriates quickly from border cities. This expedited action was meant to return migrants to their home towns so that they would not emigrate again and cause any social or economic trouble. Governments of the northern states took a similar position.

Dependent on the Treasury Department, the customs administration granted exemptions to facilitate transportation and entry of personal belongings into Mexico.[17] Accordingly, the Secretary of the Interior developed an assistance program through studies examining the possibility of granting land to migrants in certain places of the country. The Secretary designed a program establishing agricultural units first in the south and then in the north of the country. Moreover, the Secretary of the Interior conceived the repatriation program as a great work of state policy to recover workers who had been lost to migration. In a similar vein, the Department of Agriculture designed a plan to "re-populate" the Northern territory of Baja California with repatriates; it also conducted various studies to establish settlements in Guanajuato (Campo Saravia), San Luis de Potosí, Guerrero, Sonora, Sinaloa, Chihuahua, Baja California, Coahuila, Veracruz, Oaxaca, Chiapas, and Yucatán. Administrative officials, the press, and state governors made numerous and exaggerated references to the settlements alluding to the ease of accommodating large groups of repatriates. These studies were never put into practice and most of the people, nearly 80 percent, moved into the towns where their relatives and friends lived; 5 percent went to cities (Hoffman 1974, 80, 91, 148–51; McKay 1982, 133–36, 145). Only some settled in La Misa and Bácum, Sonora, or Mexicali, Ensenada, and Valle de las Palmas, Baja California, thanks to the support of federal and state governments.[18]

The Cárdenas government supported urgent cases of desperate migrants (paisanos) who had reached the border by giving them tickets to travel to their home towns. The Repatriation Section was created in late July 1936 within the Department of Demography of the Secretary of the Interior. It was created to reintegrate Mexicans into the country who were in a dire situation abroad, mainly in the United States and

---

17. *Excelsior*, México, D.F. February 8, 1934. México, *Diario de los Debates de la Cámara de Diputados*, September 1, 1934.

18. Archivo del Gobierno del Estado de Sonora (AGES), exp. 414.6 "32"/16 al 40; Interview with Francisco Reyes, Olimpia Reyes Flores, Consuelo Reyes Flores, and Susana Luna Flores. Bácum, Sonora, November 23, 2004. Interview with Rosario Vázquez Córdova, Guaymas, Sonora, July 26, 2003. *El Tucsonense*, Tucson, Arizona, December 19, 1929.

Canada.[19] Similarly, in the face of the dread the political class felt toward another possible mass repatriation like the one that took place from 1930 to 1933, the Mexican government promoted, on the one hand, studies to assess the situation and numbers of Mexicans in the United States, and on the other hand, studies to analyze the economic and geographical conditions of certain regions to establish the feasibility of settling a large number of return migrants at any given time.

Between 1935 and 1936, officials from the Department of Agriculture sent many of their representatives to study the conditions in Baja California to locate Mexicans coming from the United States.[20] In 1939, the Secretaries of Agriculture and Development as well as officials from the National Foreign Trade Bank conducted several studies indicating places where they considered repatriates could settle: Tamaulipas, Sonora, Chihuahua and Baja California; Nuevo León, Sinaloa, Northern Coahuila, and Veracruz, mainly in Los Tuxtlas and the Santa Ana Rodríguez region; San Luis de Potosí, Valle del Naranjo, and El Salto; Tambaca, Michoacán, Puebla, Guerrero, and Oaxaca coasts; and Jalisco.[21] The actions of the Mexican government centered on statements, some official tours, and, above all, studies to assess the possibility of relocating their citizens, but these actions had little effect because the government did not face any large-scale return movements. Furthermore, repatriates were neither a priority of the agrarian policy of the Cárdenas' government nor beneficiaries of government support; the government preferred to benefit those already in the national territory.

REPATRIATION: A NATIONAL STANDARD

In the early 1930s, the Mexican press and several municipal, state, and federal officials popularized the use of the terms *repatriation* and *repatriates*. These words were widely used from the northern border to the south as a way of defining the population movement that was taking place from the United States to Mexico, as well as a way of naming those who were entering the country. The concepts carried two connotations: (a) an image of tragedy because, according to this vision, repatriates were people who had been expelled from the United States and had been left in a deplorable condition after working and living there for many years and, therefore, (b) they required assistance from the Mexican government.

As Mercedes Carreras de Velasco points out, between 1930 and 1932 the word *repatriation* started to be used in Mexico to refer to returning Mexicans in all instances, even for cases of deportation. There was a pronounced tendency to refer to repatriation in all cases of Mexicans returning to Mexico, irrespective of whether they had been violently expelled, they were Mexicans or U.S. citizens, they were coming back voluntarily, or they had been coerced to do so. Hence, the entrance of hundreds of minors, U.S. citizens of Mexican parents, was not perceived as controversial or startling. In the eyes of Mexican officials they were just fellow Mexicans returning to their country. This view related to the fact that *repatriation* in Mexico, at an official level, meant returning to the

---

19. México, *Memoria de la Secretaría de Gobernación*, September 1936 to August 1937, 27.

20. *Excelsior*, (5 de marzo de 1935) March 5, 1935. Anguiano Téllez, *Agricultura y migración en el Valle de Mexicali*, 54.

21. *El Universal* y *Excelsior*, April 23, 1939.

patria. The Department of Foreign Relations and the Statistics Administration of the Autonomous Department of Press and Publicity established that the term *repatriate*, which had been accepted internationally and by Mexican Immigration Law, referred to Mexicans who returned to the country so that they would not be considered immigrants, that is, foreigners. Official sources do not help explain what Mexican officials understood as *repatriation* and its various shades of meaning. They simply refer to the *repatriates* or *repatriation* as the act of Mexicans and their children returning to patria, even if the children had been born abroad. The terms thus carried a nationalistic connotation, the origins of which possibly dated back to 1848 when Mexico lost Texas, New Mexico, Arizona, and Alta California territories and the government supported the repatriation of Mexicans who had remained in U.S. territory (Carreras de Velasco 1974, 57).[22]

The party line was that "the Mother Land would welcome with open arms [destitute] Mexicans coming from the United States." The patria welcomed their sons who had been abroad and, because of the economic depression, were living in a deplorable state. Given the situation, the government assumed a maternal attitude toward providing protection and shelter. An illustration entitled "The Return of the Argonauts" and published in the newspaper *El Nacional Revolucionario,* an official governmental periodical, exemplifies this image. The illustration shows a woman, the Mother Land, with outstretched arms on the Mexican side receiving thousands of people leaving the United States. These people "set out on a quest for the Golden Fleece and came back poor and sick. They only have the Mother Land left"[23] (Figure 3.1). This was a paternalistic vision of the state, which underscored the duty of repatriating the most unprotected nationals living abroad. The Secretary of the Interior favored an open-arms policy to receive "their sons." Officials constantly referred to repatriation as a "humanitarian act of true nationalism" and aid to destitute repatriates was charged with an element of charity and nationalism. The support of the repatriation of destitute Mexicans acquired a patriotic tone at an official level and many individuals made similar statements.

Antonio Pujol, delegate for the nationalist campaign in the state of Chihuahua, approached the Governor of Guanajuato for a donation to relieve the poor conditions of—many originally from that state—arriving to Ciudad Juárez.[24] Pujol appealed to the "recognized nationalism and patriotism" of the Governor, as well as to his "humanitarian sentiments" to help those destitute repatriates. He maintained that the donation would be a "sign of interest, commitment and nationalism of the governor of Guanajuato" and that it would be widely publicized in the press of Chihuahua's capital city. According to Pujol, the support of repatriation was equal to that of nationalism and generosity and something all should take pride in and acknowledge publicly.

Ignacio M. Monroy, a Mexican who disseminated a document throughout the country entitled *"Cédula de repatriación que será ejecutoria de civismo"* ("Repatriation

---

22. México, *Memoria de la Secretaría de Relaciones Exteriores de agosto de 1929 a julio de 1930,* 1714, vol. II. Archivos Económicos, Biblioteca Lerdo de Tejada, H03099–H03115, Estadísticas de Migración, *Revista de Estadística,* Dirección General de Estadística, D.A.P.P., México D.F., "Entrada y salida de nacionales y extranjeros, por calidades."

23. *El Nacional Revolucionario,* México, D.F. October 27, 1931.

24. Archivo del Estado de Guanajuato (AEG), exp. 1.03.1.19/1.

Figure 3.1   Return of the Argonauts, 1931.
"They went in search of the Golden Fleece and returned poor and sick.
They only have the Motherland left."

Source: El Nacional Revolucionario, October 27, 1931.

Notice for the Exercise of Civic Duties"), considered that supporting repatriation was a patriotic and civic gesture: patriotic because, through it, the Mother Land showed her material and emotional solidarity toward repatriates and civic because "it will translate the aspiration for aggrandizement, the homogeneous disposition for sacrifice."[25]

The nationalist standard of repatriation of destitute Mexicans raised by *Maximato* governments was, to a great extent, a stereotype because it generalized the characteristics of the return movement. Although a large number of Mexican migrants were forced—because of the circumstances in the United States—to enter Mexico and receive official support, the return cases were varied and the government's attitude was not terribly benevolent in some circumstances. Some migrants living in starvation in the United States presented several repatriation petitions that were rejected by

25. Archivo General del Gobierno del Estado de Nuevo León (AGGENL). Expediente relativo a la Campaña organizada por el gobierno del estado para reunir fondos a fin de ayudar a los repatriados. 1932. Cédula de Repatriación que será ejecutoria de civismo por Ignacio M. Monroy. Archivo Histórico de Morelia, Michoacán (AHM), caja 136, exp. 61.

the Department of Foreign Relations "due to the fact that in the current budget there is no item that would allow for such expenditure"[26] or because "the government is not available to accept your petition, given that the national budget is in very difficult circumstances."[27]

Cárdenas's government—free from any pressure of mass return movements—was also characterized as reluctant and distant regarding repatriation. It attended to the most urgent cases and openly stated that those Mexican citizens who were employed and were not urged to come back to Mexico should stay in the United States because the Mexican government was in no condition to grant them land or give them jobs. José Castrejón Pérez, Chief of the Population Service, agreed that those who could renew their rural partnership contract with Texan ranchers should do so. According to Castrejón, national economic problems and internal economic conditions prevailing in the country were the main obstacles to repatriation.[28] The fact that some Mexicans would stay beyond the Río Bravo, according to Castrejón, was not detrimental for Mexico. In a similar vein, Ramón Beteta, in July 1939, the subsecretary of Foreign Relations in California, volunteered to talk in person with groups of Mexicans who were eager for repatriation "to carry out the impossible task" of preventing them from being discouraged and, at the same time, convincing them not to try to go back to Mexico. Instead, Beteta continued, "they should wait for the government to be ready to receive them."[29]

Lombardo Toledano, General Secretary of the Mexican Worker Confederation, considered that even though his fellow Mexicans should not be abandoned in the United States, they could not be repatriated before their situation was studied or before federal authorities could approve a plan to determine the best procedure.[30] Toledano shared the position of an editorial in *El Universal* that pointed out that it would be wrong to attend the needs of those "fellow Mexicans away from their home" while workers and peasants in Mexico were suffering economic hardships. Hence, Toledano's was a call to apply the principles of a radical nationalism, which meant prioritizing those who had stayed in the country over those who had emigrated and were returning with children who were of another nationality.[31]

In general, however, repatriates were received with an official welcome speech. In the eyes of the political class and some individuals, to help, shelter, and receive repatriates in the country meant being nationalistic, patriotic, and humanitarian. Paradoxically, a reluctance to support the return movement prevailed under the guise of the country's poor economic conditions and the preference for attending to workers in the country. This tendency was reinforced as return movements declined in the second half of the 1930s.

---

26. Archivo General de la Nación México (AGNM), Fondo Presidentes (FP), Emilio Portes Gil (EPG), vol. 19, exp. 672/217, leg. 20.

27. Archivo Histórico de la Secretaría de Relaciones Exteriores (AHSRE), exp. IV-349–1; AGN, FP, ALR, exp. 244.1/67.

28. AGN, FO, Lázaro Cárdenas (LC), 503.11/3.

29. Archivo Particular de Ramón Beteta (APRB), exp. 312, leg. 6.

30. *El Nacional*, México, D.F. March 2, 1937

31. *El Universal*, México, D.F. July 29, 1937.

SELECTIVE REPATRIATION AND GREAT NATIONALIST PROJECTS

Another substantive part of official discourse and methods was directed toward attracting repatriates who had agricultural experience and knowledge. Ruling elites thought not only of assisting the needy but also of selecting "the best elements" to employ as specialized workers in irrigated areas and as colonizers of certain parts of northern Mexico (Aboites Aguilar 1995, 15). From the point of view of some officials, this plan would have significant implications for the country. Apart from contributing to the development of agriculture—a priority in the postrevolutionary project—repatriating skilled agricultural workers also would help consolidate territorial sovereignty and displace the foreign population. Specifically, selective and specialized repatriation was idealized as a great panacea, which would contribute to the resolution of the era's national problems.

The plan of agrarian transformation outlined by the Sonoran victors of the Revolution trusted agrarian transformation to a gradual evolution of the technical processes of farming, which above all could take effect in the heart of small land holdings. This perspective rested on the initiative of President Plutarco Elías Calles (1924–1928), who was determined to execute a far-reaching investment program. Irrigation would be a state tool to divide estates (latifundios), foster small-property building, and create a new agricultural middle class. Through this, the government intended to transform the agrarian panorama, weaken big landowners, and consolidate the new Mexican state (Aboites Aguilar 1997, 32–33). Successors to Calles, Portes Gil, Ortiz Rubio, and Abelardo L. Rodríguez, continued with this project.

The irrigation policy was directed toward the north of the country. The National Irrigation Commission (CNI) concentrated its efforts in Nuevo León, Coahuila, Chihuahua, Baja California, and Sinaloa. There was a political idea being nurtured that emphasized the phenomenon of population scarcity and the lack of development in territories neighboring the United States. State and federal governments felt they should support population in those regions and utilize hydraulic resources to develop agriculture and the generation of hydroelectricity, therefore preventing the precious liquid from reaching the border, where it would be used for U.S. projects. According to the historian Luis Aboites, a nationalist motivation toward territorial sovereignty was clearly behind irrigation and repatriates arriving from the United States played a central role within that project (Aboites Aguilar 1997, 34–35).

From the perspective of irrigation proponents, the development of a "scientific" agriculture, as General Calles liked to put it, had influenced Mexicans who had been driven to the United States because of the economic and political crisis. Javier Sánchez Mejorada, one of the first creators of the irrigation scheme, considered Mexicans who had emigrated to the United States the "most desirable" source of colonization (Sánchez Mejorada 1928). Likewise, they became seen as a reserve of skillful settlers, knowledgeable of modern agricultural techniques, exactly what the irrigation projects required. In a way, the nationalism and xenophobia that had been accentuated during those years ruled out the possibility of colonization through foreigners, an old obsession of liberals in the nineteenth century. Therefore, the idea of "autocolonization" by repatriates was adopted again by those who considered the migrants "useful elements" for the "education of the peasant masses," as described by the Secretary of Agriculture (Aboites Aguilar 1997, 37; Carreras de Velasco 1974, 114). The outlook of Sánchez Mejorada and his contemporaries was not new: since the beginning of the century numerous officials, consuls, and secretaries of state had favored an organized, small repatriation of agriculturists, "the best elements," to found agricultural colonies. The main purpose, ideally, was to support the development of the country and populate, produce, and educate local workers by means of the contact and knowledge repatriates would apparently bring. The novel feature of this movement was that in the early 1930s the number of people who left the United States led to an attempted enactment of what had been only previously imagined.

The proposal to establish repatriates with certain abilities in irrigated areas resonated with the idea(s) about improvement of the Mexican population through eugenics, a racist ideology in force in Mexico during the 1920s and 1930s. Eugenics applied medical–hygienic thinking that had been developed during the first half of the twentieth century and aimed to "keep or enhance the genetic potentialities of the human species." The eugenics project was also related to the racist concepts that had developed in the context of anthropological studies. The main concepts proposed included the following: (a) race was a deciding element of social life, (b) a standard of normality existed to which different human groups should adjust, and (c) there existed a conceptualization of social deviance in which inheritance played a deciding role. These orientations defined the course of social science in Mexico as well as demographic policy. Legislation and population projects followed the ideal of "improving the race" and promoting development; to this end it was proposed, among other things, to encourage the arrival of a white population, whose moral traits were considered superior and whose intellectual capacity was valued. Gilberto Loyo, a demographer who was close to Calles, thought that the population should be enlarged through selective migration of foreign technicians and agriculturists, as well as through the repatriation of skilled Mexicans for agricultural production (Urías Horcaditas 2001).

Manuel Gamio, a Mexican anthropologist who in the second half of the 1920s conducted research about Mexican migration to the United States, believed that the bodies, work habits, and knowledge of Mexicans who had migrated to the United States were more advanced than those of their fellow countrymen. Similarly, the repatriates were perceived as "technologically and culturally progressive"; hence, their return would make a positive impact on society and on the economy. From this point of view certain return migrants should be used advantageously by the state to promote development because repatriation could serve as a great educational system in which the returnees would be the "masters of life in general." According to this "integral" vision of development, repatriates would make the northern border a politically stable region, economically prosperous, more European, and whiter (Gamio 1930, 236–41).

The social engineering program of the CNI along Mexico's northern border rested upon a racialized concept of development. The colonization of CNI's irrigation systems by repatriates was supported by the belief of elites and commoners that northerners were culturally, economically, and racially more advanced than their fellow Mexicans living in the middle and south of the country. The state put forth an effort to develop the north of the country through the construction and colonization of hydraulic systems, which materialized in the aforementioned ideas about integral regional development, reinforcing the concept that the north was whiter and more progressive than the rest of the country. Thus, irrigation system planners such as Alejandro Brambila, Director of the Office of Agricultural and Economic Studies of the CNI, followed the evolutionary, environmentalist, and highly racialized perception of development and acculturation. Brambila, like Gamio, believed that repatriates would be protected from the negative influence of Indians and *mestizos* if they relocated in regions that were isolated and with a racially and culturally progressive population, that is, European. This type of regional development, based on irrigation, was thought to protect eugenic accultura- tion, achieved among repatriates during their exile in the United States, and to help the local population reach their progressive destiny, imminent because of their biology and Creole culture (Walsh 2005, 56, 67–68).

The CNI promoted the settlement of Mexican agriculturists coming from the United States in fully developed irrigation systems. In late 1931, groups were placed in the National Irrigation System "Presidente Calles" located in Aguascalientes (10 repatriated settlers); in Number 4, located in the municipality of Juárez, in the state of Coahuila, and the municipality of Lampazos, in the state of Nuevo León (105 repatri- ated settlers); and in Number 6, in the state of Coahuila (45 repatriated families).[32] The largest group settled in lands within the municipality of Juárez, in the state of Coahuila, where the Don Martín dam was located and was christened *Ciudad Anáhuac* (Anáhuac City). Unfortunately, the hopeful plan of establishing repatriates in irrigated regions fell short of expectations. In general, few people settled in these areas. According to a study carried out during that period, less than 5 percent of the total influx of repatriates was placed in irrigation projects. These figures were not a restraint for the official discourse, which continued to insist on the great qualities expected from specialized repatriates (Bogardus 1934, 140).

Proponents of the irrigation system did not focus only on exploiting the supposed skills and knowledge of the repatriates. They also thought the return migrants could contribute to the development and maintenance of a "Mexican identity." The aim was "full" incorporation into both the economic and the cultural sphere. In December 1935, the CNI authorities commissioned a movie by the filmmaker Agustín Jiménez entitled "Irrigation in Mexico," which featured the country's principal irrigation works. In one of the film's scenes, the narrator made an exaggerated claim that the government had shown special interest in those irrigation works, which in turn had benefited a "vast area of the territory" colonized by repatriates who the government wished to provide with sufficient means and work "to preserve the sense of nationality latent in them." From this perspective, the settlement of repatriates in irrigated areas would foster nationalism in those who had once left to the United States and now returned. The project was meant to bring about the consolidation of Mexican identity.[33]

The settlement of repatriates in northern Mexico also was considered a means to populate places that were thinly inhabited and, at the same time, to curb the expan- sionist drive among some U.S. citizens. In a study concerning the colonization of Valle Mexicali, Baja California, by A. G. Basich, Salvador Aguilar Chávez, and Antonio Garza

---

32. *Irrigación en México, Revista mensual*, Órgano oficial de la Comisión Nacional de Irrigación, vol. IV, número 3, (enero) January 1932, 203, 217, 222–24, 228.

33. *Irrigación en México, Revista mensual*, vol. XII, nos. 3 and 4, March/April 1936, 117.

Quintero, from the Colonizing Commission Number 1 of the Secretary of Agriculture and Development the authors stated that the expansionist intentions of some U.S. citizens should be blocked, intentions which were openly expressed regarding the incorporation of Baja California into U.S. territory. According to the authors of the study, the Mexican government should prevent the historical repetition of the "painful example of Texas and California" and Baja California because these territories were in similar positions to those in the mid-nineteenth century when the United States forcibly annexed nearly half of Mexico's territory. Given this situation, officials believed that actions should be taken promptly to "put a check on the greed and thwart the influence of the neighboring country." This would be achieved, according to Basich et al., by colonizing the region with Mexicans coming from the United States. The colonization would thus integrate Baja California into the national territory from a geographical, cultural, and economic standpoint.[34] Fostering colonization through repatriates would serve the purpose of preserving and consolidating territorial sovereignty and incorporate a region that had remained isolated from the country.

Participation by certain types of return migrants, apart from contributing to the population of the region and protecting territorial independence, would have a similar, or perhaps more significant, consequence: increase the national population in places where there was a preponderance of foreigners. This initiative was referred to as "Mexicanizing" (*mexicanizar*), or the promotion of the hegemony of Mexican nationals over foreigners in border areas they did not previously inhabit. This would be done through the settlement of Mexicans and the displacement, including expulsion, of foreigners, especially of Asian origin. This idea was strongly supported by official government policy, which had during the 1930s in the north exhibited a pronounced xenophobia against the Chinese community (Gómez Izquierdo 1991, 83–100).

Engineer Armando I. Santacruz, the commissioner of the Boundary and Water Commission of the Secretary of Foreign Relations, considered that the establishment of Mexicans coming from the United States to Valle Mexicali, Baja California—as Fernando España, a private businesman, had done—was a "laudable Mexicanization effort." Santacruz's remarks showed his support for the establishment of Mexicans in the valley because there had previously been a predominance of people of Asian origin, who controlled a great part of the region's economic life. Toward the middle of the decade, there were 1,221 Chinese, 454 Japanese, and 140 North Americans living in the region.[35] Santacruz believed that it was critical to urge Mexicans coming from the United States to settle there because only a few had moved from the interior to live in the region. This action, according to Santacruz, would help increase the national population, and foreigners would be then displaced from the area, resulting in an increasingly Mexicanized region.

---

34. AHSRE, Dirección General del Archivo Histórico Diplomático (DGAHD). Oficina de Límites y Aguas Internacionales (OLAI), exp. 1482.

35. There were also twenty-six Spanish, thirteen Germans, thirteen Italians, ten Yugoslavs, eight Greeks, five French, five Indians, four Poles, two Canadians, two Lithuanians, two Armenians, two Turks, two Syrian-Lebanese, two Cubans, one English, eleven Irish, one Hungarian, one Bulgarian, one Portuguese, one Chilean, and one Peruvian, a total of 1,918 foreigners. AHSRE, DGAHD, OLAI. exp. 1482.

The proposal to Mexicanize places where a foreign population predominated was in accordance with the nationalist ideas of the time. Ezequiel Padilla Peñaloza, Secretary of Public Education during the presidency of Emilio Portes Gil (December 1, 1928, to February 5, 1930), affirmed that "we need to nationalize, Mexicanize,...the press, the publication of books and magazines will be extraordinarily Mexican." Mexicanizing everything was the aspiration of the political class. Repatriation came to a head in 1931, which coincided with an intensive nationalist campaign in favor of "our race, our economy and our culture." Within this context repatriates were seen as elements that could contribute to development and identity. These positions reinforced two complementary aspects upon which revolutionary nationalism rested: on the one hand the impending defensive tone, working as a shield in the face of U.S. expansion and, on the other hand, the vindication of what was deemed national property to generate national reconciliation based on self-assertion (Pérez Monfort, 1994c, 39, 64).

The Population Act of 1936 reaffirmed the idea of a selective and idealized repatriation. It established that the task of the Secretary of the Interior was to accommodate nationals and immigrants in agricultural and industrial settlements that would themselves be founded to this end. The return movement would be carried out in a systematic fashion, only in justified cases and for certain individuals, especially agriculturalists in irrigated areas so that their abilities would be utilized to develop the land and colonize.[36] Based on this idea, and with a plan designed by Manuel Gamio, President Cárdenas, responding to criticism he received for supporting the arrival of Spanish refugees, decided to implement a repatriation project and established a settlement called 18 de Marzo in the Bravo River's lower valley in Tamaulipas.

Mexico's aid to Spanish refugees had two phases. In the first phase, efforts were made to provide accommodation for nearly twenty-five thousand asylum seekers who were in France; in the second phase, Narciso Bassols, Mexican Ambassador to France, negotiated with the French government and with representatives of the Spanish Republic, to return from France and give asylum to thousands of refugees of all ages and classes and arrange their accommodation in Mexico. From the beginnings of the Spanish Civil War until the years following the end of World War II, Mexico received nearly twenty thousand Spanish Republican refugees, an average of fifteen hundred per year. Refugees came from predominantly political, intellectual, technical, and urban backgrounds (Fagen 1973, 34–35; Pla Brugat 1994, 226–27; Lida, 1997, 75, 84, 92–93, 141).

Reactions in Mexico to the arrival of these exiles were varied and even contradictory. The government, headed by Cárdenas and his closest circle, as well as the Mexican intellectual elite, showed hospitality and support. But in the eyes of worker and peasant unions, the official welcome to exiles was questionable. They were of the opinion that in a decade of crisis and economic depression, in a poor Mexico with little material resources hardly able to escape from the instability produced by its own Revolution, Mexicans should not be competing for jobs and food with the newly arrived foreigners. The Revolutionary Unification Committee, the

---

36. *Diario Oficial*, p. 1. Artículo 7, cap. I. Título Segundo, Demografía, art. 29, Art. 36. (29 de agosto de 1936) August 29, 1936. Lombardo Toledano, *El Plan Sexenal de gobierno del Partido Nacional Revolucionario*. México, 1934, 10.

Constitutional Democratic Front, and the Mexican Social Democrat Center organized mass meetings in which leaders denounced the Spanish refugees as a threat to public peace and a burden to the economy. The National Synarchist Union and the Confederation of National Chambers of Commerce, both opposed to the government, also opposed the arrival of the Spanish exiles. Aquiles Elorduy, a member of the National Committee of the National Action Party, and Eduardo J. Correa presented themselves as "anti-refugees" because, according to them, the Spanish exile was an emigration of Communists or "Reds." Cárdenas' political adversaries, among them the two nationally important newspapers, *Excelsior* and *El Universal*, challenged this immigration and assumed a hostile attitude toward republican Spain (Lida, 1997, 117; Matesanz 1995, 363–435; Pérez Montfort 1992, 124, 148). In response to these criticisms, the Mexican government announced the repatriation of Mexicans from the United States.

Cárdenas gave Ignacio García Téllez very precise orders to carry out the repatriation project in two stages. The first stage should be done "before the first Spaniard arrived" in Mexico, without lengthy paperwork or careful scrutiny, simply confirming that repatriates were capable of working in agriculture and eager to return to Mexico. In the second stage settlers would be sent to the lower Bravo River valley, Tamaulipas, several miles away from Matamoros. Thus, it was completed. The first ships that arrived at Mexico with refugees, the *Sinaia*, the *Ipanema*, and the *Mexique*, docked in Veracruz on June 13, July 17, and July 27, 1939, respectively.[37] The repatriation process had been initiated in April of that year.

To execute the first stage of the plan, Ramón Beteta, Subsecretary of Foreign Relations, promoted repatriation from Texas with the intention of bringing preferably skilled agricultural workers. Likewise, Beteta helped to transfer those who were interested to the border: whole families, men, women, and children, many of them U.S. citizens. Eduardo Chávez, Director of Works in the lower Bravo River, Tamaulipas, was in charge of the second stage concerning the preparations to establish the colony and receive around 3,750 people who arrived in April and June 1939. The Cardenista project highlighted the United States in the history of Mexican emigration because the government managed to convince a large group to settle in Mexico at a moment when reluctance to leave the United States was notable. At first, consular reports on the reaction of the Mexican community in the campaign expressed fear, wariness, and opposition to official promises. At the same time, despite the many constraints they faced, the people in the settlements managed to stay. Living conditions for those who arrived were difficult: floods, lack of drinking water, bowel diseases, deficient food supply, semibuilt houses, and confrontation among local groups existed. Nevertheless, with just minimal aid from the federal government and the land they were granted, settlers managed to sustain themselves (Alanís Enciso 2007(a), 175–201, 241–300).

Mexican governments in the 1930s supported repatriation and constantly labored in favor of the return of destitute Mexicans and workers who supposedly had agricultural experience. At an official level, repatriation was viewed in two ways: first in terms

---

37. APRB, exp. 306. Leg. 5; Pla Brugat (1994, 219).

of destitute Mexicans and second in terms of skilled nationals with tools and agricultural background knowledge, which could theoretically be utilized for the benefit of the country. Actions and statements went both ways. One supported repatriation as a nationalist, humanitarian standard, heavily endowed with a patriotic fervor; the other aimed to consolidate the project of building a nation that should be agricultural, irrigated, colonized, "racially improved," Mexicanized, and sovereign.

THE NATIONAL REPATRIATION COMMITTEE

In late 1932, an organization that brought together various levels of the federal government (secretaries of state, governors, municipal presidents) and society groups (businessmen, politicians, military men, merchants, civilians, teachers, etc.) was created. The organization was formed to "accommodate and reincorporate" into Mexico repatriates coming from the United States. The commission showed a spirit of solidarity and good will toward the paisanos who were returning from abroad.

Toward the end of November of the same year, the Secretary of the Interior sought private-sector cooperation to resolve the difficulties brought about by the arrival of destitute people at the border and the transportation to their place of origin. To this end, several meetings were organized and headed by Jorge Ferretis and Alfonso Fábila as representatives of the Secretary of the Interior. Fábila was an expert in migration issues who wrote a text that had been widely disseminated in the country as propaganda against emigration (Fábila 1929). Andrés Landa y Piña, Chief of the Migration Department, Enrique Zúñiga, President of the National Chamber of Commerce, Alejandro Quijano, President of the Red Cross Association, José González Soto, from the Spanish Chamber, the General Secretary of Public Assistance, the General Secretary of the Confederation of Chambers of Industry, and the President of the U.S. Chamber of Commerce also attended those meetings. Likewise, representatives of the Chambers of Commerce of the Federal District were invited (Carreras de Velasco 1974, 92–93). These meetings led to the foundation of the National Committee of Repatriation, Accommodation and Reincorporation (CNR), whose main goal was to obtain funds through a national campaign to collect half a million pesos and attempt to relocate and reintegrate repatriates.

The CNR had set lofty goals for the campaign. Despite the fact that the country had not been hit by the economic crisis as others had been, the CNR sought to collect a considerable amount of money during a period in which many people led a life of bare subsistence. For its part, the goal of relocating some people in the national territory again showed the idealism that existed in large parts of the political class and society to "take advantage" of returnees to boost the country's development.

THE HALF-A-MILLION CAMPAIGN

On December 10, 1932, Eduardo Vasconcelos, Secretary of the Interior, announced that he was launching the Half-a-Million campaign, which the nation's President "enthusiastically supports and applauds." Vasconcelos determined that the project would last four weeks. To carry it out, he requested that the country's governors organize the campaign in their states as well as promote the creation of local committees and organize "fund-raising events, *jaripeos* (Mexican rodeos), charity fairs, and theater parties." In addition, state governments would request that municipal presidents create committees to raise funds to be sent to the Bank of Mexico. To reinforce this petition, the CNR sent municipal presidents a circular appealing "beyond any doubt, to their patriotic and humanitarian cooperation in this fundamental case, out of civility and racial solidarity."[38]

The Secretary of Interior's call to governors, municipal presidents, and society in general to participate in the fundraising events received a good reception throughout the country. During the last weeks of 1932 and the first weeks of 1933, committees were established in the capital cities of all states and in some municipalities. In Nuevo Laredo, Tamaulipas, the "Sub Committee for Repatriates" was established. The committee collected more than 508 pesos by selling beer during a bullfight, emblems for automobiles (50 pesos), and tickets for pedestrians crossing the international bridge (109 pesos).[39] In Ciudad Juárez, Chihuahua, the Committee for Repatriates had been working since early 1932, sponsored by the municipal president, and continued with its work upon the request of the CNR.[40]

In Guadalajara, Jalisco, the governor promoted the founding of the Local Committee for Repatriates to lead the fundraising project through festivals.[41] In Tecolotlán, the directors "of the schools for boys and girls" organized a theater performance to aid repatriates.[42] In Michoacán the executive branch of the state appointed the General Treasurer and the chief of the Department of Administration to work for the Municipal Committee for Repatriates in the state's capital city. Donato Guevara, Municipal President of Morelia, was asked to communicate with the municipal committees of the state to ensure that the project would be "as successful as possible.[43]

In Monterrey, Nuevo León, the local Chamber of Commerce, the City Council, and other institutions met to create a Repatriation Committee, which, in late January 1933, raised nearly five thousand pesos.[44] Likewise, Alfonso Garza, Municipal President of Villa de García, promoted the establishment of the Repatriation Committee of García to collect money in that district and share, "most gladly, his humble resources with their repatriate brothers, welcoming them to their Mother Land."[45] Garza emphasized fraternity with the people of Mexican origin coming from the United States and the welcome that the Mother Land gave them.

---

38. *El Nacional Revolucionario*, México, D.F. December 19, 1932.

39. *La Prensa*, San Antonio, Texas, January 25 and February 1, 1933.

40. Archivo Histórico de Ciudad Juárez, Chihuahua (AHCJC), Ramo Gobernación, circulares, exp. 2, no. 2012; AHCJC, Ramo Gobernación, circulares, exp. 2, no. 2155.

41. 41 México, *Informe rendido por el C. gobernador constitucional del Estado*, Sebastián Allende, Archivo del Congreso del Estado, Guadalajara, Jalisco, 1933.

42. *Las Noticias. Diario libre de la mañana*, Guadalajara, Jalisco, March 21, 1933.

43. AHM, c. 138, exp. 77, 1933.

44. AGGENL, documentos fuera de sección, Comité de Repatriación. Francisco A. Cárdenas, Monterrey, Nuevo León. México. January 19, 1933.

45. Archivo General del Estado de Nuevo León, documentos fuera de sección, Comité de Repatriación. Alfonso Garza a Federico T. de Lachica Villa de García, Nuevo León. March 24, 1933.

In Oaxaca, the expression of support for the Half-a-Million campaign and the nationalist exaltation fostered by the local government and social groups for this enterprise were remarkable. The state government created the State Committee for Repatriates, which organized movie showings in the Terán and Juárez theaters. The money raised through the sale of tickets was directed to assist repatriates. Furthermore, the authorities of the state's capital contributed with the equivalent of half a day's salary. The Confederation of Oaxacan Socialist Parties urged all its affiliate parties to cooperate in the project "to put into practice the human feeling of fraternity." The Confederation managed to raise 28 pesos through contributions from its members and the organization of a boxing match. The Oaxacan National Chamber of Commerce contributed 100 pesos and the Local Agrarian Commission sent 26.50 pesos. By February 1933 the state of Oaxaca had raised 433.31 pesos. *El Oaxaqueño*, a capital city newspaper, left records indicating the degree of commitment it had toward the campaign. Its motto was "Contribute to the aggrandizement of the nation by helping financially experienced and active elements that have returned to the country!"[46]

In Aguascalientes, the local government and civil society were very active participants. In the state's capital , the Local Repatriation Committee was created. The committee organized bullfights in San Marcos Square and festivals in Morelos Theater.[47] The office of the municipal president of Jesús María was one of the most committed bodies in the fundraising project. It organized a dance and a charity fair in its own building.[48] By mid June 1933, Felipe J. Valle, the General Treasurer of the state, reported that the amount raised by his office and the Municipal Treasury of Aguascalientes amounted to 2,242.83 pesos.[49]

In Guanajuato, the government founded the Central Committee for Repatriates of Guanajuato. The governor required all municipalities to create subcommittees to collect funds through *jaripeos,* charity fairs, theater festivals, etc. For the local executive branch, the project would be supported by the state because it was an "elemental patriotic duty."[50] Soon Committees for Repatriates were established in Uriangato, Apaseo, Álvaro Obregón, and Allende.[51] Governments also created committees in other states such as Campeche, Morelos, Tapachula, and Chiapas (Carreras de Velasco 1974, 95–97).

The Half-a-Million campaign was enthusiastically received in many parts of the country, from Ciudad Juárez to Oaxaca, from Nuevo Laredo to Campeche. State governments, municipalities, city councils, and even military groups cooperated to the extent they could. Reports of the activities carried out as well as the sums raised in different places of the country showed the sense of solidarity and unity toward repatriation,

46. *El Oaxaqueño*, Oaxaca de Juárez, January 9, 10, 12, 14, 24, and 31 and March 3, 1933.

47. *Alborada, un periódico revolucionario*, Aguascalientes, Ags. January 19, 1933.

48. AHEA, Secretaría de Gobierno, exp. 2, I-B.4, ramo Gobernación, 1932.

49. AHEA, Secretaría de Gobierno, exp. 2, I-B.4, ramo Gobernación, 1932.

50. AEG, exp. 1.03.85. Ramón V. Santoyo al presidente de la Junta de administración Civil. Guanajuato, Gto. December 12, 1932.

51. AEG, exp. 1.03.18., no. 403; AEG, exp. 1.03.18., no. 1474; AEG, exp. 1.03.18; AEG, exp. 1.03.18., no. 524.

which was attained among wide sectors of society. Despite this, on January 31, 1933, when the fundraising was programmed to conclude, the CNR's report showed that only something less than 200,000 pesos had been collected.[52] In early February, the Secretary of the Interior announced that the campaign would be extended "until the date authorities stipulate." But the impulse that had initially characterized the campaign dissipated, leaving the campaign in limbo.[53] Toward the end of June, after a quiet period during which the CNR did not report any significant activities and the actions of local committees and society's interest in general started to decline, the CNR tried to resume the campaign; however, it had by then lost the support of state governments and civil society. Both groups expressed themselves as reluctant to resume work on the project to which they had fully committed half a year before. The CNR then reported that the money raised amounted to $250,466.35 pesos.[54] From June to December, contributions declined considerably; during that period the CNR only managed to collect around 78,000 pesos. Fernando Sordo, Vice President of the Committee, reported that by December 31, the funds raised amounted to 318,221.65 pesos.[55] The amount was significant, although they did not meet the expected target.

"ACCOMMODATION AND REINCORPORATION"

The second goal of the CNR, to "accommodate and establish" the people in Mexico, was less successful. The CNR, together with the Secretary of the Interior, supported the establishment of two repatriate settlements. The first settlement, the Number 1, was set up in El Coloso, near Acapulco. In December 1932, twenty Mexicans arrived to Number 1 from Detroit, Michigan, having apparently received financial aid from Diego Rivera. Little is known about the establishment of this settlement, the role the CNR and the state government played, and the living conditions in which the group lived. However, what did become known is that most of the return migrants abandoned the settlement shortly after their arrival (Carreras de Velasco 1974, 121; Hoffman 1974, 139, 143). The second settlement, called Number 2, was founded in Pinotepa Nacional, Oaxaca. In April 1933, repatriates gathered in Mexico City and at the border. A total of 362 people were initially transferred to the Oaxacan settlement.[56]

At the beginning, the situation of settlement Number 2 seemed very promising. The Secretary of Agriculture provided it with agricultural machinery, financed its activity, and installed water pumps for irrigation. However, some problems of adaptation to the hostile environment arose: repatriates were not used to the climatic conditions in Oaxaca's coastal area, diseases broke out, an adverse atmosphere among the locals prevailed, and the authorities in charge of the project mistreated the settlers,

---

52. AGGENL, documentos fuera de sección, Comité de Repatriación, Circular general del Comité Nacional de Repatriación. México, D.F. June 26, 1933. AGGENL, documentos fuera de sección, Comité de Repatriación. Alfredo Levy al general Francisco A. Cárdenas, México, D.F. August 1, 1933.

53. AHEA, Secretaría de Gobierno, exp. 2, I-B.4, ramo Gobernación, 1932.

54. AHEA, Secretaría de Gobierno, exp. 2, I-B.4, ramo Gobernación, 1932.

55. *El Universal*, México, D.F., March 8, 1934.

56. AGN, FP, Abelardo L. Rodríguez (ALR), exp. 244/15.

forcing them to emigrate. In February 1934, the settlement was abandoned and settlers set off to Mexico City pursuing support from the government. Many of them emigrated to the United States once again, whereas others made a second attempt to settle in other parts of the country (Hoffman 1974, 140–41).

Between February and May 1934, the CNR fell apart. The failure of settlement Number 2 was widely spread in the national press and in the Mexican press in the United States. Some settlers who participated in the Pinotepa experiment brought charges against the CNR for the way in which they had been treated and for the lack of support. Given these denunciations, many thought that Mexico's Attorney General's Office should launch an investigation about the way the committee had used the funds obtained through the Half-a-Million campaign. Furthermore, a commission was assigned to investigate irregularities. The work done by the CNR turned out to be an example of corruption and the settlements it promoted failed, leading to its ultimate dissolution.[57]

Nevertheless, the foundation of the CNR and the fundraising projects that were carried out were greatly significant, not because of the money collected or the uneven attempts to found two repatriate settlements, but because the issue of "repatriation" reached every nook and cranny of the country. The campaign the CNR carried out had a nationwide circulation, from the border to the most isolated municipalities in the north and the south of the Republic. This was achieved thanks to coordinated government actions at various levels. State governments requested support from municipal presidents and summoned the population in their districts to support repatriation as an act of "humanity and true nationalism." There was authentic animation, euphoria, and communion among state and municipal governments, as well as among diverse social groups in Mexico in support of their compatriots arriving destitute from the United States.

The Half-a-Million campaign received a wide and important reception throughout the country. To this degree, it created a sense of unity and identification among various levels of society with the idealized purpose to "accommodate and reincorporate repatriates." For a time, in many parts of the country help was given to the indigent that had returned from the United States . A nationalist tone characterized the campaign as well as the government officials and citizens who supported it. According to Fábila and Landa y Piña, the campaign was a "patriotic and humanitarian" act, as well as an act of "elemental civility and racial solidarity."[58]

In April 1939, President Cárdenas carried out a repatriation project with results intended to reach those similar to the ones achieved in the Half-a-Million campaign: to unite the government with diverse groups in the country around the return of compatriots from the United States. The repatriation of Mexicans was widely publicized "from above" and presented by the government as a recognized and symbolic victory of Cardenista nationalism. The project had the goal of arousing among Mexicans a strong sense of patriotic pride and solidarity with the Mexican community in the United

57. AGN, Dirección General de Gobierno (DGG), Repatriados en Acapulco, exp. 2.096 (29) 55, caja 9, exp. 69. 1934; *El Universal*, México, D.F., February 9, 20, and 21, 1934.

58. AHM, exp. 43, C-118, Comité Nacional de Repatriación.

States, as well as rallying the general population around the government's initiatives at a moment during which the country was entering a serious crisis and society had become very polarized. Despite the absence of an urgent need for repatriation in large numbers, Cárdenas used repatriation as a symbol to demonstrate his support to the Mexican community in the United States. With this project, the government adopted an active role and claimed credit as the promoter of repatriation.

Given the restraint and decreases in labor, agrarian, and educational reforms, Cárdenas launched a project to divert national attention away from the serious economic and political situation impacting the country toward the end of the decade. Toward the end of the six-year presidential term, the government faced criticism and radical opposition to its reforms from a wide range of social and political actors. Groups affected by his policies reacted through protest, petitions for rectification, and even threats of violence. Additional reforms by the Cárdenas´ government included the economic reorganization of the country, massive support to large groups of workers and peasants, the removal of supporters of former President Calles from government offices, and broad alterations to the country's educational policy. The large land owner, the businessman, the average Catholic citizen, and many others attacked the new reforms (Knight 1994a, 48–49). The application of new social policies split Mexican society. On one side stood the beneficiaries and on the other the ones directly affected, including some groups of peasants and workers who, despite being part of the target group of official policies, had not benefited at all during the Six-Year Plan. Throughout 1939 and 1940 the divisive effect of these policies resulted in a politically explosive social situation and the backdrop against which the project of repatriation took place (Medina 1978, 13–14).

The Cardenista repatriation project and the Half-a-Million campaign both were supported by the federal government but with different results. One had an important penetration and was accepted nationwide; the other generated division and little interest. In his newspaper column entitled "Last Week," Salvador Novo, an intellectual who was remarkable for his fierce criticism of Cardenismo, showed his skepticism regarding the results of the Cárdenas´ plan. He considered it a task that would be carried out "as a provisional measure, while later, they would ultimately find a way to swim across the river which they [the migrants] preferred to call Grande instead of Bravo" (Novo 1964, 596–97).

Furthermore, the social and economic contexts in which the Cárdenas´ repatriation movement emerged were quite different from that of the earlier campaign. The Half-a-Million campaign took place at a time of mass deportations and returns. However Cárdenas's project was launched at a time when the return movement was not intensive and when the emigration of the Mexican community to the United States was strongly opposed. Toward the end of the decade, the repatriation was not a relevant issue for Mexican society, which was more interested in internal matters and criticism against the government, given the discontent generated by its social policies. In this sense, the Cárdenas' plan was artificially executed from above for political purposes and, as a result, it never penetrated wide sectors of Mexican society. Cárdenas never managed to establish the strong relationship between the government and civil society as had occurred with the Half-a-Million campaign.

CONCLUSION

Fernand Braudel points out that it is necessary to examine nationalism as an enduring trend in which myths, legends, customs, ideas, images, and symbols are spun according to rhythms that are not all subject to the back-and-forth of political and social struggles. The repatriation of Mexicans from the United States in the 1930s as an element of revolutionary nationalism fits this definition. During that decade—and even before—myths, ideas, images, and symbols were spun around repatriation. These elements were shaped not only directly by the political and social conflicts Mexico faced during the first decades of the twentieth century, but also by the idealizations and aspirations for the development of the country around migrants who went to the United States.

During the first half of the 1930s, the mass movement of population from the United States to Mexico attracted the attention of governments and society because of the number of people who returned to Mexico in deplorable conditions. The terms *repatriation* and *repatriates* were, as never before in history, used, spread, and repeated endlessly, both in Mexico and among the Mexican community in the United States.

Mexican governments supported those nationals who were most dispossessed and, at the same time, turned assistance into a symbol and a duty, which in turn served the purpose of legitimizing their policies before the masses. This attitude was not new. In 1908 Porfirio Díaz's government (1877–1911) had attended to citizens who had been deported from the United States because of the recession. President Álvaro Obregón also supported the repatriation of over fifty thousand nationals during the postwar depression (1921–1922; González Navarro 1954, 263–64, 278; Martínez 1972, 576–95). The moral duty and the state's obligation to repatriate the dispossessed was a tradition that reached a climax during the 1930s because of the number of people who entered the country from the United States. In this light, during that decade, repatriation became a great symbol of Mexican state nationalism, a resource to legitimize the government and its institutions, used to justify its role with the most dispossessed and with the Mexican diaspora in the United States. Unlike other instances where the construction of a national image prevailed over reality (as was the case with Mexico's educational reforms), repatriation was a determining factor in the construction of an image of Mexico as a nation of shelter and protection.

From the beginning of the twentieth century, the idea of utilizing repatriates in Mexico as skilled labor, "with useful knowledge" to support national development, had spread among journalists, the political class, and some intellectuals. In the second half of the 1920s, the idealism about "qualified repatriation" increased because it became related to the irrigation policies launched by President Calles. However, until 1930, little had been done to realize this ideal; in most cases, the government had only promoted studies to examine places that, in the future, supposedly would be colonized by repatriates. When the movement of Mexican population from the United States took place on a large scale, this idea acquired momentum because it was seen as a solution to various dilemmas faced by the country at that moment, some of which had been carried over from the nineteenth century (such as the colonization of the north of Mexico and territorial sovereignty vis-à-vis the United States) and others that appeared in the early twentieth century (expulsion of the Asian population). In the minds of many officials, repatriation would help to populate border regions, protect and consolidate national sovereignty, and "Mexicanize" places where foreign populations had been predominant. This way repatriation was linked to nationalism and acted as a force to preserve unity and defend sovereignty. The nation-state becomes the referent that makes the project meaningful, judicially, politically, and territorially sustaining it. Repatriation campaigns emerged during a time of cultural and geographical disaggregation and the need to build sovereignty and political and cultural unity, which would lead to the consolidation of the State rising out of the Revolution.

Postrevolutionary governments developed the formation of a Mexican identity through a series of symbols that would provide unity to a racially and culturally heterogeneous country. The actions implemented by the Secretary of Education were a key tool for the invention of identity. At the same time, other social and demographic notions and processes that developed, such as xenophobia and repatriation, helped to establish a special relationship between the government and civil society, one that exceeded the expectations of government officials. The Half-a-Million campaign was exemplary in this respect because it rallied various groups in the country around the goal to establish and assimilate repatriates. Given these achievements and the positive reception by wide sectors of society, repatriation was for a time a unifying element among large groups of people from different social strata and varying political backgrounds. The campaign managed to foster a sense of identity among Mexicans as members of a nation and to make them feel as if they were part of a national mission. Thus, repatriation was an issue that was approached both from above and from below; official sectors as well as significant parts of civil society supported and implemented repatriation as an act of patriotism, compassion, and solidarity toward "their brothers and sisters" who had emigrated to the United States.

The Cardenista project of repatriation was a symbol the government attempted to use to exalt nationality, build unity, and justify official decisions. In this case, material elements (the return plan) and sentimental and symbolic elements (repatriation) were integral parts of nationalism because they were utilized according to a predetermined plan of action that met the government's needs: appease the attacks against its reforms and the arrival of Spanish refugees. Fernando Vizcaíno states that the symbols that nationalism can appropriate can be diverse and numerous. Almost any element of reality, if the historical and intellectual conditions exist in addition to the political needs of a regime, can be the object of nationalist transformation: oil, railroads, a saint, a virgin, a war (Vizcaíno 2002, 270). During the era of Cárdenas it was also repatriation.

Finally, repatriation seen as a symbol, as an image and as an idealization (oversized given the movement of population unique in the history of both countries) fits three large groups of attitudes and postulates of revolutionary nationalism: (a) distrust toward the ruling powers, especially the United States, together with variable levels of xenophobia and anti-imperialism; there was an underlying resentment in Mexico because of the expulsion of thousands of people of Mexican origin, which was mitigated by a protectionist and patriotic stance; (b) assertion of national sovereignty through, among other things, the colonization and consolidation of the Northern border; and (c) the overestimation of Mexican identity (Bartra 1989, 199).

CHAPTER 4

The Bracero Program, 1942–1964

Michael Snodgrass
Indiana University–Purdue University Indianapolis

INTRODUCTION

In contrast to their northern neighbors, Mexicans did not experience—nor do they perceive—World War II as a watershed moment in their history. The war's indirect effects were certainly felt. Food shortages and inflation sparked protests in several cities. Manufacturing imports fell, which hastened Mexico's industrialization. News from the European and Asian fronts dominated headlines and the Germans even sank Mexican oil tankers off the Gulf Coast. Hence, Mexico joined the Allied cause shortly after the Americans declared war. But it sent few combat troops aside from Mexican immigrants who fought in the U.S. Army. Instead, Mexico's most celebrated contribution was a policy to export workers to the United States. Up north, the wartime mobilization had stoked fears of labor shortages, especially in agriculture. So Mexico's government agreed to an American proposal to contract guest workers to harvest the crops. They were called braceros, both at home and in the United States, which signifies "strong-armed men" but came to mean migrant farm laborers. By the war's end, more than 300,000 seasonal migrants labored as "soldiers of peace," as some veteran braceros still characterize their service.[1] It proved so popular—at least among the migrants and their employers—that what began as an "emergency" migration policy lasted twenty-two years (1942–1964). More than 4.6 million bracero contracts were issued, making it the largest importation of foreign labor in U.S. history. As a result, the Bracero Program became the most consequential and controversial policy enacted by Mexico's government during this era. Emigration reached unprecedented levels and the issue thus dominated the news and policy debates. The earnings sent home by braceros quickly

Funding to research this project came from a Fulbright Faculty Research Fellowship (2007) and a Research Support Funds Grant (2006) from the Office of Research and Sponsored Programs at Indiana University–Purdue University Indianapolis. I thank the editor, Danna Kostroun, and Myrna Santiago for their insightful comments on an earlier version of this chapter.

1. Interview with Francisco Javier González Núñez, Ameca, Jalisco, May 16, 2007. All interviews were conducted and translated by the author unless indicated otherwise.

surpassed oil as a source of foreign earnings. This policy, we see in retrospect, hastened Mexico's transition into a nation of emigrants. Thus, for some Mexicans the braceros became a source of shame, symbolic of a failed revolution and yet another reminder of Mexico's dependence on the United States.

The North American chapter of this transnational history is well documented. The braceros' labor helped transform southwestern agriculture, especially the fields of California, into the richest and most productive on the planet. Those who stayed on and raised families hastened the demographic and cultural transformation of the American Southwest (Garcia 2002; Montejano 1987; Pitti 2003). Today millions of Mexican Americans trace their families' roots in the United States to their father's or grandfather's arrival as a bracero. But these immigrants were the exception because the vast majority of braceros returned home, year after year, for more than two decades. Therefore, how and why they departed and what they experienced in *el Norte* is only part of the bracero story. Equally important—yet less understood—are the far-reaching effects that return migration had upon their communities. The Bracero Program fostered a generation of seasonal migrants who tied villages and neighborhoods of Mexico to fields and farm towns in California or Texas. The impact was greatest in a historic sending region that stretches from the border state of Chihuahua down through Durango and into the emigrant heartland of Zacatecas, Jalisco, Michoacán, and Guanajuato. Visit any town square in these contiguous states today and you are certain to encounter former braceros, the survivors who pioneered the region's famous culture of migration.

Despite its magnitude and consequences, the Bracero Program receives limited attention in textbook surveys of either U.S. or Mexican history. Americans rarely consider the workers who harvest our food. That might be why the braceros' story remained little known or forgotten until talk of a new guest worker program resurfaced in the early twenty-first century. Within the United States, students searching the Internet find the Bracero Program demonized as a system of "legalized slavery," as one of its American administrators later defined it. A renowned historian of immigration more accurately calls it "a form of imported colonialism."[2] Both depictions mirror views in Mexico, past and present, where critics disparaged the controversial program from the moment of its 1942 inception. For many, the state's proemigration policy was an affront to national dignity. Here was the Mexican government, after all, recruiting poor young country boys to go work for gringo farmers on lands that were once Mexican. Old-timers in rural Jalisco still joke, referring to the men who led Mexico in the 1840s and 1940s, that "Santa Anna sold them the land, and Avila Camacho rented the oxen."[3] The braceros were bribed by venal officials at home, shipped north in cattle cars, cheated by racist growers, and then sent back with little more than some new boots or a radio to show for their labor. Today, because of successful lawsuits by former braceros, Mexicans also know that corrupt bureaucrats in Mexico City made off with

---

2. Many American critics appropriated the slavery metaphor but it was the Department of Labor's Lee G. Williams who is quoted most frequently. Ngai (2004) borrows "imported colonialism" (13) from an American union official; see also González (2005)

3. Interview with Juan José Zepeda Santos and Andrés Dueñas Rodríguez, Ameca, Jalisco, May 15, 2007.

the compulsory savings that were deducted from their pay.[4] However, noted migration scholars like Jorge Durand now challenge these long-held, widespread, and distorted views. He emphasizes that for all its faults, the Bracero Program improved conditions for migrant workers, guaranteed their annual return, and offered access to economic resources unavailable to most rural Mexicans (Durand 2007, 16–26). Yet the strongest defenders of the program remain its alleged victims: the former braceros themselves. In their recollections, the very real hardships they confronted barely tarnished the benefits that seasonal migration offered: significantly higher pay, decent treatment, and the opportunity to improve their families' lives upon return.

This history of the Bracero Program examines it from three distinct perspectives: that of Mexican statesmen and policy makers, that of their antiemigration critics, and that of the migrants and their communities. The program endured far longer than envisioned for two principal reasons. On one hand, it satisfied the peculiar labor demands of politically influential growers in the southwestern United States. On the other hand, the opportunity to migrate north for a brief stint of hard field work was also embraced by working-class Mexican men of both rural and more urban backgrounds for whom no state policy in postwar Mexico proved more popular. That is because government-sanctioned emigration offered braceros the most viable means of realizing their individual and collective ambitions. Indeed, by the mid-1960s, no state policy would do more to transform the material conditions and cultural outlooks of Mexico's major emigrant-sending regions than the Bracero Program.

THE GROWERS GET THEIR WAY

Upon leaving home, the braceros' journey north across the border took them through a physical landscape that offered few abrupt changes to states with Spanish names and into farm towns or migrant *colonias* where their language was spoken, their music was heard, and familiar foods were consumed. But they came to the United States to work, and the system of industrialized agriculture that most migrants encountered was radically different from farm life back home, where labor relations were rooted in an older patron–client tradition rather than the more transitory and impersonal systems encountered in the Southwest. Some braceros labored on family farms in midwestern locales like Wisconsin or Nebraska, where few Latinos had yet to settle. However, the vast majority were hired out to politically influential grower associations in California or Texas. Those two states employed 80 percent of bracero labor at the program's peak. In the 1920s, banking and merchant capital had transformed southwestern agriculture from an economic system where small farmers and sharecroppers predominated to highly capitalized "factories in the fields."[5] In contrast to the mechanized grain belts of the Midwest, these labor-intensive cotton, fruit, and vegetable farms demanded strong

---

4. The claims are not wholly verified and are subject to distortion, because the mandatory deductions ended by 1949; but the scandal renewed attention to a forgotten history in both the United States and Mexico. Ken Ellwood, "Braceros Demand Lost Legacy," *Los Angeles Times*, Nov. 15, 1999; Ricardo Sandoval, "Braceros Want an Old Promise Met," *The Dallas Morning News*, January 27, 2002.

5. Arkansas, Arizona, and New Mexico received an additional 25 percent of braceros. Geographic distribution in Craig (1971, 177–78).

arms to pick their crops. Moreover, growers required a seasonal work force that they could mobilize—to follow the harvest cycle—yet also immobilize to prevent turnover and higher labor costs. They developed a stated preference for Mexican immigrant labor. Growers considered Mexicans more industrious, docile, courteous, and reliable than native-born or Asian alternatives. Some believed them racially suited for field labor. Others argued that life on the hacienda down in "Old Mexico" conditioned them to loyally serve a rural patron. Ironically, however, some growers hired armed overseers and housed these ostensibly pliable workers behind locked gates to prevent flight. Speaking candidly in 1917, one Californian explained that "We want Mexicans because we can treat them as we cannot treat any other living men" (Mitchell 1996, 88; see also Mapes 2004, 65–88).

But Mexican laborers proved no more malleable than the Filipino immigrants or white dust-bowl refugees who worked alongside them. The late 1920s and 1930s were punctuated by wildcat strikes, union drives, and considerable flight to higher-wage cities or northern states. In California, farmers struck back against militants in their fields with vigilante violence, housing evictions, and court injunctions against picketing. In Texas, state officials enacted vagrancy laws, blockaded county highways, and restricted "outside" labor contracting to prevent the northbound migration of labor (Montejano 1987, 197–219; Weber 1994). At the national level, the growers' political clout bought the exclusion of agricultural labor from New Deal legislation that guaranteed rights to union representation, collective bargaining, and a minimum wage. Farm workers had no labor rights. However, by the late 1930s, the effects of the dust bowl and Mexican repatriation transformed California's labor force into one that was whiter, more American, and more settled than ever before. Moreover, the well-documented plight of these migrant families struck a chord of sympathy with a public that made John Steinbeck's *Grapes of Wrath* a best-selling novel (1939) and film (1940). The progressive journalist Cary McWilliams optimistically concluded his seminal study of farm workers "that out of their struggle for a decent life in California may issue a new type of agricultural economy in the West." Much to the dismay of growers, McWilliams—who characterized their labor system as "farm fascism"—was named director of California's Immigration and Housing Commission (McWilliams 1939, 325; Mitchell 1996, 191–92; see also Majka and Majka 1982). But the looming war soon pushed the farm workers' plight out of the public consciousness, where it remained for a generation. Meanwhile, as the "Okies" abandoned field work for industrial jobs and military service, southwestern growers turned to Washington to resolve their apparent shortage of farm hands.

The cry of a labor shortage was by no means new, nor was the state's favorable response. During the First World War, the United States lifted entry requirements to permit the mass immigration of Mexican workers. By the late 1930s, southwestern growers began lobbying their congressmen for the right to contract foreign labor again. However, out in the field, Immigration and Naturalization Service investigators discovered why labor was scarce. One study found cotton wages in Texas were lower than those in Mexico. Another came across growers so insistent upon immigrant labor that they refused to hire unemployed workers from federal labor camps (Ngai 2004, 136–37). As a spokesman for California's largest growers association would later clarify, "We are asking for labor only at certain times of the year—at the peak of our harvest—and the class of labor we want is the kind we can send home when we get through with them" (Galarza 1964, 55). The specter of rotting crops led Congress to deliver. Five months after the United States declared war, the government lifted a prohibition against foreign contract labor that dated to 1885. The decision "was a momentous break with past policy and practice." Generations of Americans rejected contract labor as "the antithesis of free labor" because such workers were denied the right to choose employers or to quit. The United States had even terminated this colonial labor practice upon annexing Hawaii in 1898 (Ngai 2004, 137–38). Four decades later, Congress authorized its deployment on the U.S. mainland and what began as an Emergency Farm Labor Supply Program lasted another twenty-two years. During the war, seasonal migrants from Canada and the British West Indies harvested crops along the Atlantic seaboard. American railways contracted more than 100,000 Mexican laborers for maintenance-of-way crews (Hahamovitch 1997; Driscoll 1999). But the vast majority of guest workers labored in southwestern agriculture, harvesting lettuce, tomatoes, oranges, and cotton, and they all came north from Mexico. And they kept coming. There were in fact two legislatively enacted migratory labor agreements, the wartime accord and another (Public Law 78) that extended seasonal bracero contracting all the way through 1964. Historians find that such guest worker programs tend to last longer and grow larger than intended. They also generate parallel streams of undocumented migrants, foster migratory chains, and result in permanent settlement (Martin 2006, 89–101). What made the Bracero Program unique was that it built upon and reinforced a culture of migration dating to the late nineteenth century. What complicated its approval by the Mexican government were the well-known abuses that immigrants suffered in the past.

MAKING AND DEBATING THE BRACERO PROGRAM

Once approved by Congress, it fell upon hesitant officials at the American Embassy to negotiate a migratory labor accord with their Mexican counterparts. The diplomats feared that any mistreatment of migrants would undermine relations with a crucial wartime ally. Despite public ambivalence—and some outright hostility—Mexico had enlisted in the Allied struggle and signed a strategic military agreement in return for American pledges of economic assistance. But Mexican officials feigned reluctance when responding to the migration proposal. Their own growers also feared labor shortages. Economists warned of food scarcity if farmers abandoned the lands for jobs up north. Moreover, Mexican consular officials in the United States reported intense opposition from organized labor and three separate Mexican American civic organizations. These groups shared the consuls' own concerns that "past importations have provoked racial hatred, intolerance, and segregation" and "would worsen the farm worker's labor conditions." Migrants even wrote President Avila Camacho from California, warning that renewed immigration would undermine their own recent wage gains.[6] However, despite their apparent reservations, Mexican officials perceived

---

6. Messersmith, U.S. Embassy Mexico City to Washington, July 16, 1942, in Records of the Foreign Service Posts of the Department of State, Record Group 84, 850.4, United States National Archives and Records Administration (hereafter NARA: RG 84); Jesús Flores to President Manuel Avila Camacho, July 17, 1943, in *Boletín del Archivo General de la Nacion, México* 4:14 (October–December 1980), 10.

state-controlled migration as an effective antidote to a renewed and growing exodus of undocumented migrants. "It would be great if a country never faced the periodic need to permit its campesinos' departure," one diplomat wrote. "But it would be foolish not to guarantee adequate working—and living—conditions while they carry out their tasks" (Torres Bodet 1970, 508–09). So authorities seized the opportunity and marketed the Bracero Program as Mexico's commitment to wartime solidarity. The semiofficial press informed readers that Mexico was not "simply an exporter of human labor resources." Rather, the Bracero Program made it "a valuable ally of the democracies in the fight against the totalitarian powers...These workers must be considered not as immigrants but as Mexican citizens on a mission."[7]

Mexican officials astutely negotiated a migratory labor agreement with all the advantages that their strategic bargaining power then offered. Under the terms established, the U.S. government became the braceros' legal contractor. Contracts started at forty-five days, were renewable to six months, and guaranteed a minimum wage based on prevailing rates in the migrants' destination. A mandatory savings plan ensured that braceros returned home after each harvest with at least 10 percent of their earnings. Growers provided return transportation, housing, accident insurance, and subsidized food. Negotiators addressed public fears and concerns by insisting that braceros could "not be employed in military service...and will not suffer discriminatory acts of any kind." Most importantly, the agreement empowered Mexican inspectors to investigate working and housing conditions and permitted consuls to blacklist growers or regions that violated the accord. The Bracero Program thus enhanced the state's legal capacity to defend Mexicans abroad and challenge historic patterns of discrimination. In fact, Mexico's Labor Minister blacklisted Texas right at the start "because of the number of cases of extreme, intolerable discrimination" (McWilliams 1949, 270).[8] By 1948, consular officials had also sanctioned the state of Idaho and dozens of counties in the Mississippi Delta for unchecked cases of discrimination and contract violations (Gamboa, 112–14).[9] For policy makers, the Bracero Program offered an unprecedented opportunity to eradicate the hardships and abuses suffered by immigrants in the past. A decade later, Mexico's director of Migratory Labor Affairs optimistically confided to an American diplomat that "the problem of discrimination was gradually being resolved."[10]

These protective clauses and the mechanisms to enforce them convinced reluctant observers in both the United States and Mexico of the program's merits. Mexican policy makers argued correctly that the agreement's "collective contract for agricultural laborers" marked the first time that farm workers enjoyed federal labor rights in U.S. history. Moreover, the accord was enforced by Mexican labor inspectors ("who are constantly watching the farmers") and their vigilant counterparts in the U.S. Labor Department. That is why Americans sympathetic to migrant laborers initially endorsed it and why

---

7. *El Nacional*, Mexico City, Feb. 4, 1943.

8. Terms of agreement in Messersmith, Mexico City, July16, 1942, NARA: RG 84, 850.4, box 352.

9. Memphis Consul Cano de Castillo to Mexico, Trabajadores Migratorios, box 6/31 in Archivo Histórico "Genero Estrada" de la Secretaría de Relaciones Exteriores de México (hereafter Archivo SRE).

10. Miguel Calderón, Migratory Affairs, quoted in Messersmith to Washington, December 12, 1958, NARA: RG 84, 560 Braceros, box 6.

its greatest beneficiaries, the growers, remained its most shameful critics. A field officer for the Department of Labor, which had opposed it, confided to Mexico's Denver consul that the bracero agreement would enhance his agency's efforts to improve farm labor conditions. Writing in 1948, as the program neared expiration, Cary McWilliams endorsed "planned migration" as a "notable advance." He acknowledged its shortcomings but supported the program's renewal because he rightly assumed that migrants "will continue to follow the old, familiar path that leads them north from Mexico." These early supporters often witnessed, or read about, the arrival of bracero crews to small-town America where, during the war years, they received festive receptions, with flags waving, bands playing, and speeches of gratitude (McWilliams 1949, 267–69).[11] Perhaps that is why American foreign policy officials endorsed the Bracero Program, despite their lingering fears of a nativist backlash. Past studies by U.S. immigration commissions proved that migrants returned home with "a distinct affection for the United States" (Wyman 1996, 6).[12] The U.S. Ambassador arrived to the same upbeat conclusion about the braceros: "The knowledge they are receiving of our customs, habits and ways of living will bring a greater appreciation of our culture and our problems, which should add to a better understanding of our country. The effects of these programs will long outlive the war conditions that make them necessary."

Within Mexico itself, the agreement culminated in—and then escalated—a twenty-year debate about emigration policy. The issue posed a real dilemma for postrevolutionary governments. After all, in the years that preceded the 1910 revolution, the old regime's opponents blamed Porfirian economic policy for the "depopulation of Mexico" (Carreras de Velasco 1974, 44–45). The controversy intensified as the effects of revolution caused emigration to climb. Throughout the 1920s, the press published countless exposés about the hardships and discrimination faced by Mexicans abroad. Consular officials returned home to write scathing critiques meant to convince policy makers to curtail the exodus (Durón González 1925; Alfonso Fábila 1929; Santibáñez 1930). But as the decade progressed, more influential statesmen and social scientists theorized the potential rewards of emigration. An anonymous official at Mexico's Chicago consulate placed it in comparative perspective. His study of the city's Polish and Italian communities suggested that, with time and proper guidance, Mexican immigrants would enter industry, learn new skills, and save their earnings to send back home. The report favorably noted that Italian policy makers promoted emigration as a solution to regional underdevelopment. This position became common sense among Mexican diplomats like Jaime Torres Bodet, who favorably compared the braceros to the postwar migration of Spanish and Italian workers to more developed countries of western Europe.[13] It would be the beneficial effects of return migration that policy makers publicized to defend the Bracero Program from its domestic critics.

---

11. Denver Consul to Mexican Embassy, Washington, September 20, 1943, in Archivo SRE: Embamex, 1458–2; *Newsweek*, "Workers from Mexico," June 19, 1943.

12. Messersmith to Washington, August 11, 1943, NARA: RG 84, 850.4, box 352.

13. Torres served as Foreign Minister (1946–1948) and then Ambassador to France. Torres Bodet (1970, 508–09); consular report of June 1922 in Archivo General de la Nación (Mexico City), Ramo Obregón-Calles, 711-M-30, which cites Prime Minister Luzatti on emigration's positive effects on Italy's development.

Here is where the influence of the famed Mexican anthropologist Manuel Gamio became apparent. In 1926–1927, as emigration reached record levels, Gamio undertook a survey of Mexican immigrants in the United States. The relevance of the study rested on his focus—the migrants' ongoing connections to their homeland—and his conclusion: that the experience was beneficial for both Mexico and its migrants, despite the hardships they suffered (Gamio 1930). Gamio's study found evidence that emigration achieved the very ends sought by state policy makers at home. The "bitter humiliations" of racism, for example, fostered a greater sense of national identity (*mexicanidad*). Emigration also accomplished the state's goals of educating and uplifting the rural masses. Migrants learned "discipline and steady habits of work"; they were introduced to advanced agriculture and industry and "learned to handle machinery and modern tools"; they achieved a bit of social mobility and developed greater aspirations, both material and cultural. They improved their diets, hygiene, and housing standards (Gamio 1930, 128, 156–57, 178–84). Mexico benefitted from the money they sent back and because they brought their newfound skills, aspirations, and behavioral traits home. Not only did Gamio advise government officials on the Bracero Program, but also his research set the terms by which the state defended its controversial policy.

No federal policy provoked more sustained criticism in either wartime or postwar Mexico than the Bracero Program. Shortly after it began, the U.S. Embassy reported opposition "in practically every newspaper and magazine of importance in the capital."[14] The program's opponents came from across the political spectrum. Leftists decried a policy that deepened Mexico's economic dependency on the United States by exporting workers to perform demeaning tasks for gringo capitalists. Others feared their use as strikebreakers. The right perceived a "very vile but very effective" conspiracy to steal away Mexico's best workers, stifle development, and thereby maintain a market for American exports.[15] Muckraking journalists exposed the corrupt bureaucrats who bribed aspiring migrants at each stage of their journey to the border (Lázaro Salinas 1955). The conservative intellectual Salvador Novo penned an influential essay that lamented Mexico's "selective exportation of its finest resources." Like many, the avowed city slicker expressed sympathy toward his country cousins, whom he characterized as hapless victims of Mexico's own failed rural development policies. American diplomats recognized the bracero debate as a convenient forum "to criticize the whole Mexican Revolution." It became "so unfavorable and widespread that a real tribute must be paid to the Mexican Government for its adherence to the program in the face of such public criticism."[16]

The Catholic Church, whose political influence waned in postrevolutionary Mexico, had opposed emigration since the early 1920s. With its renewal, officials rightly feared the proselytizing influence of Protestant missionaries and decried the drinking, gambling, and prostitution that pervaded migrant camps. However, at the

---

14. Messersmith, Mexico City, May 11, 1943, NARA: RG 84, 850.4, box 352.

15. Messersmith, Mexico City, February 12, March 11, 1946, NARA: RG 84 850.4, box 730; *La Opinión*, Guadalajara, November 22, 1953.

16. Messersmith, Mexico City, May 18, 1944, NARA: RG84, 850.4, box 488; Salvador Novo, "Revolución y Braceros" (*Novedades*, 1948), in Perucho (2000, 63–65).

parish level, priests offered blessings to departing migrants. Some even secured bracero *permisos* on behalf of their impoverished parishioners (Hancock 1958, 39; Montoya 2001, 90). The influential Archdiocese of Guadalajara responded to the emigration dilemma with outreach programs of its own. Over the following years, it recruited priests from western Mexico to attend to braceros up north. Others visited the provincial recruitment centers "to warn the braceros of threats to their religion, against vices like drunkenness, and to neither waste their money nor forget their families." By the time the Bracero Program concluded, parishes in Jalisco were celebrating an annual Día del Emigrante with a special mass for "families of the absent ones." The parishes, in turn, grew dependent on the considerable donations bequeathed to their church by faithful migrants.[17]

Meanwhile, no development aroused greater controversy than the one American officials feared most: discrimination toward braceros in the United States. Throughout the program's history, Mexicans read hard-luck but real-life stories told by returning braceros about substandard wages, decrepit housing, lousy food, and abusive foremen. Critics blamed this lax enforcement on complacent Mexican consulates. But what most alarmed people back home were the well-documented cases of racial discrimination, ranging from physical violence by nativist gangs to the small-town merchants who refused service to Mexican customers, including several consular officials. This, one American official wrote, "is enough to make all Mexicans see red and it is practically the only subject on which Mexicans of all classes and all political persuasions seem to agree."[18] During the war, the press even compared discrimination against Mexicans to Nazi policy in Europe. Referring to a residential segregation ordinance adopted by a midwestern farm town, *Novedades* reminded its readers that "this measure ... was not taken in Germany against the Jews, but in Nebraska against Mexicans."[19]

American officials grew exasperated by the "sensationalist" press coverage. In confidential memos, some dismissed it as "unavoidable in the very nature of such programs." They also claimed, with some justification, that authorities "have gone to extraordinary lengths to protect [the braceros'] interests."[20] Others drew a distinction between "concrete cases of segregation"—those experienced by "cultured" Mexicans— and the class-based mistreatment of downtrodden braceros. Indeed, for at least some well-heeled Mexicans, the real concern was not discrimination but the character of the migrants themselves. The Ciudad Juarez Chamber of Commerce thus lamented the detrimental effects that "the departure of farm hands who generally are uneducated and uncultured people" would have on "the prestige and dignity of our country." As a result, Mexico "would continue to be considered as a place for conquest, a habitat of savages and a market where prices are quoted on men like beasts of burden." The idea that the immigrants' background brought shame to Mexico remained a common middle-class

17. Archivo Histórico Arquedíoces de Guadalajara (AHAG), Gobierno: Pastoral-Emigrantes, 1940–2001 (caja 1); AHAG, Comité Episcopal Mexicano, caja 1 (1947–1948), caja 2 (1960); AHAG, Parroquias, Tala, caja 5.

18. Guy Ray, Mexico City Embassy, October 6, 1943, NARA: RG 84, 840.1, box 330.

19. *Novedades*, Mexico City, November 11, 1941.

20. Messersmith, Mexico City, January 22, 1946, NARA: RG84, 850.4, Box 729.

refrain into the late twentieth century. But their American employers often lauded the braceros. "Their hard work and honesty," wrote a Wisconsin farmer of his twenty-five employees, "makes them a true credit to Mexico."[21]

NORTH FROM MEXICO

Despite the controversy, no policy implemented by Mexico's postrevolutionary government proved more popular with the rural poor than the Bracero Program. Its appeal was strongest in the traditional emigrant heartland of west-central Mexico, where state policies of anticlericalism and agrarian reform had violently divided communities just one generation before. When the state first announced the program, "the tremendous news caused something like a gold rush" (Simpson 1966, 347). It provoked a scandalous uproar in the nation's capital. Seemingly overnight, thousands of aspiring migrants from city neighborhoods and distant states converged on the National Stadium, awaiting recruitment. Some waited for weeks. Short on food and lacking shelter, they slept in parks and doorways, begged for food, and then queued up again in hopes of a bracero contract. It was a sad prelude to what awaited provincial recruitment centers in coming years. Meanwhile, warnings of imminent labor shortages soon arrived from those provinces. In Guanajuato, for example, the governor complained that "the exodus of our campesinos . . . is causing abandoned lands and declining [food] production." "The idea that Mexico is being denuded of its workers," the U.S. ambassador reported, "gets a lot of people worked up here."[22]

In its early years, the Bracero Program provoked protests from growers from throughout Mexico. But the extent of labor shortages depended on time and place and then on the state's own policy responses. Northern cotton districts fared the worst. So in the 1950s, authorities improvised a "pre-bracero" program by which aspiring migrants worked short cotton-picking stints in Sonora or Tamaulipas for low wages but a coveted bracero permit. Meanwhile, the flight of workers from Mexico's countryside was not only or primarily a consequence of the Bracero Program. The state's highly publicized industrialization policy accelerated rural–urban migration throughout the program's twenty-two-year history. During that time, ongoing gains in health care, diets, and mortality rates spurred a demographic revolution that doubled Mexico's population to more than 40 million. Those demographic pressures in rural Mexico partly explain why many returning braceros bypassed their villages for the lure of the city. They also explain why officials in states like Guanajuato overcame early fears of labor shortages. Instead they lamented the state's "excess population" and petitioned Mexico City for bracero permits for their unemployed farm workers and miners.[23]

---

21. *El Mexicano*, Ciudad Juárez, translated in Blocker, Ciudad Juárez, to Washington, NARA: RG 84, 850.4; Durand (2005); Praise for braceros in Consul Luis Duplan to Relaciones Exteriores, October 10, 1952, in Archivo SRE: Trabajadores Migratorios, Box 6, file 1.

22. Governor's report in *Guanajuato en la Voz de sus Gobernadores, Compilación de Informes de Gobierno, 1917–1991*, Tomo I (Guanajuato: Archivo General del Estado de Guanajuato, 1991), 639–40; Mexico City contracting in Messersmith, Mexico City, July 24, 1943, NARA: RG 84, 850.4, Box 352.

23. *Guanajuato en la Voz de sus Gobernadores*, Tomo II, 1033.

The system by which U.S. and Mexican officials recruited and contracted braceros underwent key changes but much continuity over the coming decades. The greatest change was in magnitude. The number of braceros climbed dramatically from an average of 50,000 per year during the 1940s to more than 400,000 by the mid-1950s. The greatest continuities were in the migrants' backgrounds. They were all men. Growers wanted seasonal, mobile workers who could be cheaply housed in barracks and Mexico expected braceros to return. The majority did, because they had family back home: 90 percent were twenty-one to forty-five years old, two thirds were married, and at least half were fathers. Many were sons and grandsons of migrants from regions with deep-rooted migratory traditions. During the program's history, roughly 45 percent of emigrants departed from Guanajuato, Jalisco, Michoacán, and Zacatecas. Another 20 percent hailed from Chihuahua and Durango. Six states thus supplied two of every three braceros, but they counted for only one quarter of Mexico's population. Why did the federal government assign so many quotas to these specific states? In 1946, Mexico's Labor Department developed a complex formula to calculate quotas based on regional labor needs, land tenancy patterns, and population density. Unfortunately, no records surface in the state or federal archives that prove the model's use by migration authorities. Perhaps the quotas reflected policy makers' knowledge of the region's history of migration. American growers certainly desired seasoned migrants. Moreover, the vast majority of aspirants who inundated Mexico City during the inaugural recruiting season arrived from west-central Mexico. And among the hundreds of individuals and groups who petitioned Mexican presidents for bracero *permisos* were a disproportionate number from farm towns, mining communities, and urban colonias in these sending states.[24] So did the quotas respond to socioeconomic calculations or to this popular demand? Or did it demonstrate the lobbying influence of the states' political leaders? Governors and mayors did request *permisos* for their districts, in response to local crises or to protests by their constituents.[25] Which—if any—of these factors account for the regionally selective recruitment of braceros remains a mystery, to which we return below. What is certain is that no region of Mexico experienced the Bracero Program's effects more than states like Jalisco or Durango.

Once an aspiring bracero acquired the *permiso*, he traveled to one of the internal recruitment centers administered by U.S. and Mexican authorities. After the initial debacle in Mexico City, the centers moved north, first to Irapuato and Guadalajara—deep in the emigrant-sending heartland—and then to the northern railway hubs of Monterrey and Empalme, a small-town junction near Sonora's Pacific coast. Those locations imposed real burdens on migrants, for whom securing a contract required both time and money. The time accrued as they waited days and often weeks, in the stifling heat of summer, in what observers described as a sad and humiliating human spectacle (Anderson 1976a). The money purchased their transport to the contracting stations and the food needed to endure the long wait. Some relied on charity, day jobs,

24. Messersmith, Mexico City, August 11, 1943, NARA: RG 84, 850.4, box 352; petitions to presidents in Archivo General de la Nación: Ramo Presidentes.

25. Eaton, Durango Consulate to Washington, January 31, 1945, NARA: RG 84, Durango General Records, 1936–1946, Box 72; Presidente Municipal Guanajuato to Governor, July 19, 1944, in AGEG: Gobierno box 1.19.83.

and the solidarity of fellow braceros to even survive. Many had already spent their savings or loans to acquire the bracero permit from a corrupt government official or on the black market. The *permiso* established the aspiring migrant's eligibility to be screened at the recruitment center. Once inside, the final processing took little time. A military official verified the completion of one's compulsory service. Hands were inspected for calluses to prove the bracero's experience as a working man. Then came the humiliating lineup, as men stood naked to await their medical screening for contagious disease. Once cleared, fingers were printed, credentials assigned, and trains were boarded for the final leg north. Upon crossing the U.S. border, braceros were fed, housed, deloused (by fumigation), and then contracted for work. Not until this point did a bracero learn his assignment: the regional destination, duration of contract, crops to be harvested, and piece rates to be earned. The journey from one's hardscrabble rancho to the modern American farm could consume an entire month and hundreds of pesos. But the return—in terms of dollars earned and contractual safeguards—apparently justified the sacrifice. There was never, in the program's twenty-two years, a shortage of aspiring braceros.

That so many men wished to migrate—and then repeat the experience—perplexed many of their contemporaries. Back home, literate Mexicans learned of the abuses suffered by their compatriots through muckraking journalism, scholarly investigations, literary depictions, and cinematic recreations of the emigrant experience. Most braceros knew what to expect. They heard stories from family and neighbors. They listened to late-night corridos, the folk ballads that wove tales of racism and deceit, and deep longings for loved ones and home (Fox 1999; Herrera-Sobek 1993). Once they arrived at the fields, the braceros would share grievances common to many workers. There were abusive foremen and toxic pesticides. They were underpaid and cheated out of piece rates. Bad weather caused idle days with no pay. They were hauled down back roads in deadly cargo trucks. Weather-beaten beds and lousy (sometimes rotten) food awaited them at camp. But as in the corridos, braceros learned to confront hardship with humor and to evoke a defiant pride in their hard-earned contributions to America's economic progress. Veteran migrants may have noticed significant improvements in labor camp housing since the 1930s. Fewer probably noted the extent to which farm wages stagnated in California, or fell in Texas, during the 1950s. That is because although wages varied widely—by region, crop, and season—they remained vastly higher than those earned in Mexico, especially when peso devaluations more than doubled the real value of dollars earned by braceros.[26] Most importantly, braceros were not the hapless victims that the program's opponents assumed. Recruits knew their rights before departing—or learned them in the labor camps—and proved adept at protesting. Mexico's Secretary of Foreign Affairs archived hundreds of files documenting not only the workers' protests but also successful efforts to redress their grievances. Consular officials recovered lost wages, fined employers, and blacklisted entire counties from Arkansas to Wyoming. Of course, as the program grew in magnitude during the 1950s, Mexico's capacity to defend the migrants effectively declined. But braceros continued to resist what they

---

26. Between 1948 and 1952, the exchange rate fell from 4.85/\$1 to 12.50/\$1, where it remained fixed until the 1970s. Average wages for farm workers in California climbed from \$0.85 to \$1.20 during the 1950s, meaning that hourly rates there surpassed daily salaries in rural Mexico.

perceived as contractual violations through formal protests, wildcat stoppages, or skipping out to return home or seek better jobs and pay elsewhere.[27]

Given the rumors and hardships associated with the Bracero Program—or because it required connections or money to secure a *permiso*—many young migrants did as their fathers and headed north on their own. By the 1950s, they could tap into migratory networks that tied rural villages in Mexico to farm towns or cities up north. Some migrated as braceros, saved a bit of money, and skipped out on their contracts. Others arrived *de alambre*, crossing the wire in Arizona, or entered as *mojados*, wading into what Mexicans call the Río Bravo and climbing out on the banks of the Rio Grande in South Texas. Whatever the means, these undocumented migrants chose to work without papers for their own good reasons. Some simply resisted the time, costs, hassles, and humiliations that a bracero contract required. Some, as women, were excluded from the program and went north for work or to unite with family. Still others, perhaps the majority, were the men who learned through word of mouth or personal experience that the bracero contract offered only hard labor in the fields, poor food and crowded barracks, and (most importantly) contractual limits on their occupational mobility. So they maintained their independence, took the risks of illegal migration, and found their way into industry or construction or jobs in the Midwest. Finally, some young migrants were recruited or assisted by the *coyotes* who turned human smuggling into a lucrative business during the years of the Bracero Program. They entered into a transnational black market in undocumented workers in which U.S.-based contractors, mostly of Mexican descent, hired them out to employers seeking low-cost and unprotected labor.

The U.S. and Mexican governments cooperated in the curtailment of illegal migration and then bargained hard on an effective solution. From the outset, Mexican officials had defended the Bracero Program as a favorable alternative to undocumented migration. They therefore supported a policy by which the United States deported hundreds of thousands of migrants into Mexico's interior by land, air, and sea, despite the significant burdens these return migrants imposed upon local authorities. In that way, the massive bilateral deportation policy became "the lesser-known companion of the Bracero Program" (Lytle Hernández 2006, 422; see also Ramón Garcia 1980). From the late 1940s, apprehensions escalated sharply, averaging nearly 700,000 from 1950 through 1954's Operation Wetback. That infamous campaign netted more than 1 million, including repeat offenders, as U.S. law enforcement and immigration officers launched a highly publicized military-style dragnet that apprehended "wetbacks" across the Southwest and into midwestern factory towns. Based on those figures, historians estimate that the number of undocumented migrants most likely equaled the number of legally contracted braceros. After 1954, deportations declined significantly, as enforcement slackened and bracero contracting escalated to peak levels. The number of migrants admitted as either permanent residents or with work visas ("green cards") also grew. Obtaining residency required little more than a letter verifying employment and a trip to a U.S. consulate. In the four years following Operation Wetback, an additional

---

27. See Archivo SRE: Trabajadores Migratorios files for extensive protests, follow-up reports by Mexican consuls, and names of farmers and farm cooperatives placed on blacklists; bracero resistance in Cohen (2006, 92–98).

150,000 such immigrants registered in California alone, and visas issued nationwide grew as the Bracero Program approached termination (Galarza 1964, 250).[28]

Meanwhile, the rising tide of undocumented migrants and the aggressive U.S. response pressured Mexican officials to renegotiate what formally became a second Migratory Labor Agreement (Public Law 78, 1951–1964). By 1950, when negotiations began, the war had passed and Mexico lost its strong hand at the negotiating table. Moreover, during the interregnum, the United States unilaterally adopted a policy by which Immigration authorities recontracted braceros at the border and hired them directly to growers. Determined to restore the old arrangement—with the U.S. government as the braceros' formal contractor—Mexican officials reluctantly acquiesced to a new accord. They forsook their long-time insistence that the United States penalize employers of illegal labor. American officials, exacerbated by the Mexican policy of "unilaterally blacklisting" counties and states, effectively watered down this exclusion clause. By then, Mexico had already lifted its prohibition against Texas growers, who had responded to their blacklisting through the mass importation of undocumented migrants. By the mid-1950s, Texas surpassed California as the largest employer of bracero labor, and the average number of contracts awarded annually grew *nine times* greater than during the "temporary" wartime program (Calavita 1992). But the abuses suffered by unprotected migrants—and reported by Mexican field inspectors—shaped Mexico's commitment to an institutionalized Bracero Program. Its endurance reflected the mutual dependence of both sending communities and their employer hosts on a guest worker system that proved of immense benefit to both.

PEACE THROUGH EMIGRATION?

As emigration escalated, Mexicans pondered its root causes. How did one explain the apparent desperation that led thousands of working-class men to leave their homes— and their homeland—to endure such hardships in a foreign land? Emigration was no longer a short-term effect of revolution or a question of "citizens on a mission." The so-called "Bracero Problem" had become a "National Shame."[29] According to the Mexico City press, it was symptomatic of "a shortage of work…[and] a lack of economic security." In Guadalajara, deep in sending country, editors outlined cultural and political causes: the pull of tradition and family ties, "foolish materialist propaganda…and the illusion of quick riches," the need to escape the clutches of oppressive union bosses and rural caciques.[30] Federal policy makers were more ambivalent. In a rare moment of public candor, Manuel Tello, the Subsecretary of Foreign Relations, explained to President Alemán that mounting emigration reflected the limits to agrarian reform: lands distributed to an earlier generation of peasants no longer sufficed for their sons. When speaking to reporters, however, Tello denied any "lack of opportunity in the countryside" and blamed the exodus on the braceros' "adventurous spirit."[31] Many former

---

28. *The New York Times*, October 11, 1965.

29. *Excélsior*, Mexico City, February 1, 1954; Craig (1971, 120–22).

30. *Excélsior*, Mexico City, January 22, 1954; *El Clarín*, February 10, 1951, *Nuevo Jalisco*, January 21, 1956; *El Informador*, July 27, 1951.

31. *El Informador*, July 13, 1951, July 25, 1952.

migrants agree that they were motivated, in part, by youthful curiosity and longings to know the United States.[32] They also concurred with Tello—and countless state and local officials—that demographic pressures were an underlying factor. What was the youngest son of a small farmer or ejidatario to do? What were his alternatives?

But the exodus of braceros out of west central Mexico owed to more complex factors than the individual quest for adventure or a collective land shortage, which predated the 1950s. On one hand, the Bracero Program built upon and reinforced a culture of migration that dated to the 1890s and intensified when these became battleground states of revolution, agrarian reform, and the Cristero War. Many braceros were in fact third-generation migrants. Pressures to emigrate grew stronger after the mid-1940s. In Guanajuato, mining went bust in a state where one in five families depended on the industry. So did the once-prosperous shoe and hat-weaving industries around the city of León. City officials pleaded for—and received—thousands of bracero contracts, hoping that migrant remittances would sustain families and revive local commerce. In the countryside, short-term crises compounded pressures to emigrate. The outbreak of foot-and-mouth disease (1946–1952) forced a mass livestock slaughter that devastated farm families in west-central Mexico. What Guanajuato's governor called the "worst drought in twenty-five years" persisted ten more, transforming lands in Mexico's traditional breadbasket into a "desert-like climate" better suited for cattle than crops.[33] Then came the long-term effects of agrarian reform: the decline in full-time hacienda jobs and the state's subsequent failure to deliver sufficient credit, water, or technical assistance to small farmers and land-grant recipients. Federal spending—on health, education, and infrastructure—went to the cities. Rather than address difficult agrarian issues, policy makers supported industrialization and a Green Revolution that largely bypassed the emigrant heartland to promote commercial agriculture in the north (Tutino 2007, 245–53). Feeding urban Mexico—and export markets—now took precedence over the land-grant communities established a generation earlier. One study thus concluded that "migration, not the ejido, proved to be Mexico's 'way out' of its development crisis" (Cross and Sandos 1981, 35).

Contemporaries assumed, like Manuel Gamio decades earlier, that "emigration acts as a real safety valve for men out of work." Keeping "would-be immigrants" home, Gamio suggested, would foster high unemployment and then "social struggle...disorder and conflict" (Gamio 1930, 178–84). The safety valve thesis of emigration dates back, at least, to early twentieth century studies of westward migration and European immigration to the United States. In Mexico's case emigration was said to alleviate social stresses left unresolved by state agricultural policies. "Politically and socially," Craig wrote in one landmark study, "the exodus of discontented, hungry campesinos served as a safety valve throughout the Bracero Program's history." For Luis González, migration "acted as a safety valve" in northern Michoacán by offering seasonal jobs to landless day laborers who increasingly resented the district's landowners. Indeed, writing in 1967, González blamed the program's recent termination on "the present state of discord, the contention between the young proletarians and the property owners."

32. Foster (1967) found that "the opportunity to see the world" (276) motivated Tarascan villagers to depart Michoacán.

33. *Guanajuato en la Voz de sus Gobernadores*, Tomo I, 808, 1014, 1058.

The one thing that mitigated this mounting class struggle was that former braceros came home and then headed on to Mexico City (Craig 1971, 60; González 1974, 306). Scholars have updated the safety valve thesis since the 1960s. Rather than interpret social peace as an inadvertent by-product of emigration, some suggest the state's explicit design to shape the Bracero Program to meet political ends. Cross and Sandos note that two thirds of braceros came from the west-central stronghold of antigovernment opposition, first the Cristero rebels and then the Sinarquista movement. Just as the state formally outlawed their Union Nacional Sinarquista party in 1944, it also "worked to destroy the movement's base by exporting its manpower." Thus did these pioneering migration scholars conclude that "for the government, encouraging migration meant rural peace through American agriculture" (Cross and Sandos 1981, 42–43).

Did state officials really utilize the Bracero Program to maintain rural peace through emigration? Interior Ministry records indicate genuine government concern about the militant, well-organized Sinarquista movement, which had a large and highly disciplined base among the rural "clases humildes."[34] Sinarquistas were among the first braceros. But no evidence links their departure to a targeted migration policy. When asked, old-timers from the regions where they operated scoff at the safety valve thesis because Sinarquismo had disappeared once large-scale contracting began in the early 1950s. Moreover, states like Jalisco received a disproportional share of bracero quotas into the 1960s, whereas Guerrero and Morelos were allotted a pittance, despite the postwar reemergence of agrarian radicalism in that region. Those states got military repression rather than bracero quotas. Meanwhile, Mexico's policy makers clearly studied European migration policy, so they likely knew of postwar Italy's promotion of emigration as both a means of rural development and an explicitly anticommunist safety valve.[35] The Bracero Program's American promoters certainly perceived Mexican labor migrations through a Cold War lens. The Council of California Growers marketed it as "one of our best counter measures against communism in Mexico" because the braceros returned home "imbued with democratic ideas and...our capitalistic wealth." Their opponents countered with their own Red Scare argument. Speaking before Congress, one union official cited a U.S. Immigration report "that Communist agents come across the border both in the guise of wetbacks and as legally contracted workers" (quoted in Gutiérrez 1995, 162). But although Americans updated their perennial immigration debate for the Cold War climate, neither U.S. nor Mexican officials discussed the Bracero Program in terms of anticommunism or an escape valve during its history. Although rural peace did prevail in the sending states, there is no persuasive evidence in support of the safety valve thesis. Neither suspicion nor outcome proves intentionality.

To the extent that the Bracero Program served political ends, it did so by awarding friends and members of the Institutional Revolutionary Party as it built its nationwide political machine. The bracero contract—a well-paid if short-term stint in the United States—served as one form of patronage that a ruling party boss could deliver

---

34. Gobernación intelligence reports on UNS activism in Jalisco and Guanajuato in AGN, Dirección General de Investigaciones Políticas y Sociales, boxes 771–73; see also Whetten (1948).

35. Christian Democrats employed this Red Scare strategy to pressure Western European and North American government to open their doors to Italian immigrants (Fanella 1999).

to his constituents or their sons, be they a family of local merchants or residents of a nearby ejido. Cronyism and self-enrichment grew endemic among a new generation of peasant leaders, union bosses, and government functionaries in postrevolutionary Mexico. The Bracero Program thus offered small-town municipal presidents, to whom governors doled out the quotas, the chance to reward loyalists and supplement salaries (FitzGerald 2006a). Yet they were also used to more beneficial ends. Honest mayors who did distribute *permisos* via lottery were known to hold some back to allocate to the needy. Trinidad Rodriguez, a former bracero from southern Jalisco, recalled that officials there reserved some permits for "the most destitute," usually small farmers who faced debts or lost a harvest.[36] It is also evident that the Institutional Revolutionary Party utilized the Bracero Program not to enrich its corrupt functionaries but to reward the working-class members of its "revolutionary family," meaning union workers and ejido members who benefited from the labor and land reforms of the 1930s. In Jalisco, for example, no counties received more *permisos* per capita than the sugar-growing regions south of Guadalajara. There they went to both local ejidatarios and union sugar mill workers, despite official prohibitions on the contracting of either land-grant recipients or industrial workers.[37] So although contemporary social scientists—and the state's critics—asserted the safety valve thesis frequently during the 1950s and 1960s, it seems that the Bracero Program sought to achieve distinct political ends: rewarding the state's allies rather than extending a prized bracero contract to potential dissidents.

RETURN MIGRATION

Since its 1964 termination, migration studies scholars have perceived the Bracero Program as a watershed because of the emigration patterns it established. Not only did it foster enduring ties between sending communities and host regions in the United States, but also it fostered a multigenerational culture of migration and consolidated the dependence of hundreds of villages and neighborhoods upon migrant remittances. Yet what were its immediate and long-term effects on the braceros, their families, and the communities that sent them north? We know that, in economic terms, their "migradolares" financed some land acquisition, much more home construction, and the purchase of tractors, tools, trucks, and sundry consumer goods otherwise unavailable to Mexico's rural poor. In contrast to migrants in the 1920s, braceros returning to west-central Mexico in the 1950s found the region more stable, prosperous, and suitable for investment (Durand 1992; see also Reichert 1982). But how many returnees invested their savings in productive enterprises? Or did bracero earnings simply provide family subsistence and thereby foster a self-perpetuating "syndrome of migration"? Furthermore, policy makers envisioned that emigration would not only bring material change but also produce a cultural transformation of the countryside. Did the

36. Interview with Trinidad Rodríguez Jiménez, Cofradía de la Luz (Cocula), Jalisco, June 27, 2007; Lottery reports in Archivo Histórico Jalisco (AHJ)-Gobernación, 1952, cajas 16, 17.

37. Based on author's interviews with former braceros from Ameca, Tala, and Villa Corona, Jalisco; quota records in AHJ-Gobernacion, 1951 (caja 3), 1952 (caja 17), 1958 (caja 7); details in Snodgrass 2011, 252–56.

migrants bring new skills, aspirations, and behavioral traits home and work to achieve a better life upon return? Evidence from social scientists who studied sending communities and more recent field research in the emigrant heartland indicate that braceros brought great change and benefits to postwar Mexico.

Statistical figures illustrate the program's magnitude. Over a twenty-two year period, the U.S. government issued more than 4.6 million contracts. One study estimates that, taking repeat braceros into account, at least 1 million individuals migrated legally during the program's history. Relatively few—less than 300,000—left during wartime. After that, an average of 211,000 braceros departed annually (1948–1964), with the median reaching 400,000 during the peak years (1954–1960). By then Mexico's estimated male population was 15 million and 40 percent of men were between the ages of fifteen and forty-five. (Ninety percent of braceros fell in this age range.) Thus, by the late 1950s about 7 percent of the country's working-age men labored as braceros each year. If we consider that some stayed on after their contracts expired and that an equal number migrated without papers, as conventional wisdom holds, then roughly 15 percent were absent each year. (Had the migratory pattern been reversed, 4.5 million American men would have been laboring in the fields of Mexico by 1955!) The impact was vastly magnified in the emigrant heartland states. In 1959, for example, more than 14 percent of the region's men departed as braceros. Assuming that an even greater percentage went north as undocumented workers—as anecdotal evidence and the states' deep-rooted culture of migration suggest—then at least 30 percent of working-age males labored in the United States each year.[38] These quantitative estimates are supported by village-level studies, in which field researchers estimated that 25 to 55 percent to "most able-bodied village men" to "just about everybody" went north by the later years of the Bracero Program (Foster 1967, 277; González 1974, 240; Reichert 1982, 417). If we consider that the majority were married with children, then the impact of their absence—and the money they earned and saved—becomes even greater.

A bracero's capacity to earn and save in the United States depended on chance, experience, and lifestyle. Upon arriving from Mexico to a U.S. reception center in El Paso, Texas, or Calexico, California, the braceros found their capacities to earn determined by the length of their contract and the bounty of their assigned harvest. The assignment was crucial, because a rich tomato crop offered far greater returns than a drought-stricken cotton field. Echoing many former braceros, Eustacio Casillas noted that "it always depended a lot on the luck of the draw."[39] Fifty years after they labored in the fields of California, former braceros recall with remarkable precision which crops they harvested and what piece rates they earned. Some braceros interviewed in Jalisco picked meager harvests for subsistence wages and saved nothing. Many never left home again after missing out on this commodity lottery. Those who persisted learned to cultivate ties with successful growers, whose own desire for experienced and reliable hands ensured yearly stints on their farms, a practice condoned and facilitated by

---

38. Calculations based on figures compiled by Oficina Central de Trabajadores Emigrantes, Secretaría de Gobernación, in Vargas y Campos (1964, 82–85); Dirección General de Estadística, *Anuaria Estadístico de los Estados Unidos Mexicanos,* 31; Ngai (2004, 157); estimates on undocumented migration in Cross and Sandos (1981, 43).

39. Interview with Eustacio Casillas Franco, Valle de Guadalupe, Jalisco, May 24, 2007.

U.S. immigration authorities. Many braceros earned their legal residency—attainable in those days with an employer's letter—by cultivating such relations. On the other hand, former braceros readily acknowledge that a migrant's fondness for drink, cards, or the brothels shaped his willingness and capacity to save. Such diversions were readily available around the labor camps.

During interviews, the wives or widows of former braceros are typically the first to admit that a family's ability to benefit reflected a migrant's lifestyle up north. Guadalupe González's husband, for example, took a liking to cards and left some of his earnings at the gambling tables that flourished in bracero housing camps. Back home, women tended to their families' lands and fed their children by cleaning homes, vending food, and (when possible) moving back to their parents' home. "All that time he was struggling up there," Maria Rodríguez recalled, "we were battling down here as well."[40] Some migrants, one study found "seemed to forget their families, and there were cases in which mothers and children suffered because of this neglect." One wonders how many women experienced their husbands' absence as a moment of liberation. "I was much happier when he was gone," one Oaxacan woman told an American anthropologist, because his migration brought a temporary respite from domestic violence (Foster 1967, 276; Stephen 2007, 181–82). The experiences of women and children left behind remain one of the least-explored aspects of the Bracero Program. But most of those interviewed in Jalisco and Guanajuato recall their husbands and fathers as hardworking, responsible migrants who sacrificed themselves up north to make life better back home.

The savings earned by braceros indeed became a major source of income for the migrants' families and for Mexico during the period. Contemporary estimates on remittances ranged widely—from $25 to $100 million annually by the early 1960s—and only accounted for savings wired back home through official channels. Braceros also sent cash back with acquaintances and nearly all returned with lump sums despite the criminal gangs and bandits who preyed upon migrants. Regardless of the precise quantity of remittances, the effect was substantial. Nationally, migrant earnings became second only to tourism (and in some estimates mining) as a source of foreign earnings. They helped offset Mexico's balance of payments deficit and were regularly credited with this effect by Mexican presidents in their state-of-the-nation addresses (Creagan 1965, 546; Durand 1992, 58). Unlike the foreign exchange generated by tourism or mineral exports, these migradolares went directly to the braceros and their families and then into local economies. Reports by both Mexican authorities and U.S. consular officers indicated that remittances profoundly benefited regional market towns, and local merchants were certainly among the Bracero Program's greatest beneficiaries. This is why contemporary researchers came to consider "the export of labor services to the Unites States" a basic economic activity in the key sending states.[41]

---

40. Interviews with Aurora Medina Sánchez, Ameca, Jalisco, May 15, 2007; Guadalupe González Gómez, Ameca, May 16, 2007; María Rodríguez Bautista, Ameca, May 16, 2007; and Viviana Gómez Vásquez, San Francisco del Rincón, Guanajuato, June 13, 2007.

41. One study of ten counties in Zacatecas estimated that migrants remitted nearly $500,000 in the first seven months of 1944. Dr. Salvador Castro Rivera, Zacatecas, August 3, 1944, to Marte Gamez, Secretario de Agricultura, in Boletin del AGN, Mexico, 4:14 (1980); Lentnek (1969, 78, quoted).

The majority of braceros were members of Mexico's first postrevolutionary generation. Born in the 1920s or 1930s, they came of age in a time of peace, when change came not through radical reform but in more gradual and less perceptible fashion. Ethnographers who observed migrant sending communities therefore differed on the extent of change taking place. The Bracero Program's material effects were most obvious because migrants spent their earnings. They returned with new boots, blue jeans, "loud sports jackets," and cowboy hats for themselves. They brought clothes, perfume, and kitchenware for their wives and toys for their children. Some outsiders—and local elites—dismissed the triviality of this new consumerism and pretentiously scolded return migrants for their "prolonged binges" and "meaty contributions to the cantinas." Many did develop a new taste for beer up north. But they also capitalized on their work and sacrifices to acquire consumer goods that were otherwise unavailable to the rural poor: radios, tools, sewing machines, generators, and "mechanical gadgets" like blenders, irons, and even televisions. In a few towns, such appliances preceded the arrival of electric power. Everywhere, the new gadgets made life easier for their owners, who were distinguished as migrant households (Whetten 1948; May Diaz 1966, 37). Indeed, no change proved more conspicuous than the new or improved houses that bracero savings purchased. "A better home," one anthropologist heard, "is all we think about around here." Another found that all but one of forty-two "new or significantly improved houses" in the Michoacán village of Tzintzuntzan "had been paid for out of bracero earnings" (Belshaw 1967, 335; Foster 1967, 286). Their new dwellings distinguished these Norteños just as they had the "Yanks" who returned to Ireland or the "Americani" who went back to Italy. And in all cases the return migrants—at least those who put their relative prosperity on display—could generate community resentment. The novelist Augustín Yañez, who served as Jalisco's governor during the Bracero Program, captured the mix of envy, fear, and resentment expressed toward these "Northerners" as they returned home with their flashy new clothes, uppity airs, and upwardly mobile intentions. However, a contemporaneous study found that, in rural Michoacán, locals considered the migrants' hard-earned prosperity as "safe wealth" in that "it was recognized as not having been acquired at the expense of others" (Yañez 1971, 153–57; Foster 1967, 315).

First-hand observers also disagreed on whether migrant earnings contributed to the rural economy, as proponents of emigration had hoped. Some highlighted the "superficiality" of material change. Foster found that "bracero earnings have contributed little or nothing to the long-term good of the community." His colleagues interviewed braceros who did return with "new ideas about agriculture." But few skills learned on the industrialized farms up north applied to their smallholding agrarian lifestyles. That is why "some are restless and reluctant to settle down again in the same isolated villages from which they migrated, and some of those are moving into Mexico City." Three quarters of the braceros from San José de Grácia came home and made their way to the capital. González thus concluded of his hometown that "when everything is added up, it turns out that the Bracero Program took more than it gave" (Foster 1967, 316–17; Whetten 1948, 272–75; Belshaw 1967, 130–31; González 1974, 243).

The pessimists are balanced by studies finding that even short bracero stints produced beneficial results. Bracero earnings kept families on their land. More importantly, return migration marked one of the few times when farmers possessed thousands of pesos in a single moment, "investment funds" that purchased farm implements, oxen, irrigation pumps, cattle, or additional land. In one case, return migrants developed and sustained a community's small-scale dairy industry for twenty years (Lentnek 1969, 78–79). Several braceros from Tepatitlán, in the highlands of Jalisco, planted the area's first peach and apple orchards. Those who capitalized most were the second- or third-generation migrants from that region who built on the lessons of their forefathers. Astute braceros knew to skip out on poor harvests and head for the cities in search of trusted labor contractors from their hometowns. During ten years of bracero and undocumented labor, Eustacio Franco saved an average of US$1,800 annually, either in the fields or on construction crews in Los Angeles. The one-time sharecropper saved money for family maintenance, then invested in dairy cows, and eventually purchased his own small ranch. Manuel and Rogelio Rodríguez, sons of an entrepreneurial farmer, traveled to the United States throughout the 1950s, working as braceros or without papers in the railroad and restaurant industries. Pooling their money, they returned home to run a cargo-hauling service with the trucks they purchased.[42] Throughout west- and north-central Mexico, other return migrants established new lives for themselves as carpenters, barbers, tailors, or shopkeepers. These were the exceptional cases that inspired others to migrate. But not all young men from rural Mexico came from villages with an established culture of migration. Even less had the level of education, ambition, and know-how to capitalize on the opportunities offered by bracero work.

Rather than embark on new careers or trades, most braceros departed with modest goals and built upon their accomplishments as the seasons passed. Landless farm workers and sharecroppers' sons dreamed of buying a parcel of land and some did. Others simply paid off debts, purchased basic necessities, and set aside for next year's journey. The Bracero Program thus built on a rural Mexican tradition by which seasonal labor migrations were a means of economic survival. But it is easy to underestimate the profound effects of even limited remittances. In the hardscrabble towns of western Guanajuato, the decline of the local hat-weaving industry left no employment options other than seasonal farm labor. The wife of one former migrant therefore associates the Bracero Program with the moment "when hunger disappeared from this place." Communities of smallholding farmers and ejidatarios benefited even more. They retired their mules for "smarter, more peaceful and durable" teams of oxen. They could then purchase steel plows to better turn their poor soils. By the 1950s, Jalisco's ejidatarios were investing their savings in hybrid seeds and newly available fertilizers, just as state agriculture officials had envisioned. Moreover, they modernized without recourse to the government's agricultural credit bank, which few trusted. Progress thus came to the countryside not as a Green Revolution but in piecemeal fashion. It nonetheless resulted in greater agricultural productivity and easier working lives on the small farms and ejidos of west-central Mexico. Here, then, we might interpret the Bracero Program

---

42. Interviews with Casillas Franco and Manuel y Rogelio Rodríguez Pulido, San José de Gracia, Michoacán, June 26, 2008.

as less a reflection of a failed agrarian reform policy than a means by which it could succeed.[43]

Its proponents also marketed the program as a means of uplifting the rural poor. Manuel Gamio, after all, devoted his research more to the cultural than economic consequences of emigration. And here is where the findings of contemporary social scientists coincide most with the braceros' own recollections. Belshaw found that migrants returned as "new men": "They acquired a new dignity and self respect... and began to realize it was in their power to change things." Some argued that braceros, upon returning, had become more self-reliant and less deferential toward "the political leader or the rural patron," a development also found among migrants returning to nineteenth century Europe. But these ostensible effects of migration—the newfound ambition, confidence, or defiance—may have predated and therefore shaped young men's desire to escape the economic or political constraints of rural life, as González argued (Belshaw 1967, 346–48; Hancock 1958, 122–23; González 1974, 225–26; Wyman 1996, 141–42, 170–71). Whatever the case, former braceros certainly regard emigration as an educational experience. "We started to open our eyes a bit more," one recalled when reminiscing upon his weekends spent exploring the cities of California's central valley. Many understood that the purpose of the Bracero Program was to improve life at home. "The idea was to progress," another recalled, "to buy a little parcel of land, some cows, and to make oneself a capitalist." "We brought great ideas back from there," Javier Salazar remembered, noting his own introduction to commercial seeds, fertilizers, and planting techniques. Others adopted new crops. Braceros from western Guanajuato returned from Michigan to plant potatoes and onions, not to market but to improve their own diets. Despite earlier promises from revolutionary reformers, Mexico's campesinos never benefited from agricultural extension services like those delivered to American farmers by state agencies or local universities. In that regard, the Bracero Program did serve as the vocational school that Gamio had envisioned.

Meanwhile, migrants from more urban backgrounds, like Jalisco's sugar mill workers, returned to invest their savings in home renovations based upon their American experience. "That is what cultura is," recalled Francisco González, "having a bathroom, a real roof, and a tile floor." "We all wanted concrete houses after we saw how they lived up there, and now it was possible thanks to the money from up north." "This place," he concluded of his hometown, "escaped from its stagnation."[44] Former braceros attribute these cultural changes to emigration and return migration. But their sending communities were subjected to external influences that may have arrived even if the Bracero Program ended with the war. During the 1950s, once isolated townships in northern and west-central Mexico saw the arrival of paved highways, electricity, secondary schools, radio, and even the mobile cinemas that the U.S. Consulate sent out to teach locals about modern agriculture, hygiene, and housing.[45] So the winds of change came from many directions. But the braceros' experience abroad left them, and

---

43. Interview with Pedro Domínguez Arrellano, San Francisco, Guanajuato, June 13, 2007; Javier Salazar Areola, Ameca, May 14, 2007, and Jose Manuel Zavala Salazar, Tala, Jalisco, June 28, 2007.

44. Interviews with Gómez Vásquez and Benjamín Rosas López, San Francisco del Rincón, Guanajuato, June 13, 2007; Zavala Salazar; and Francisco Javier González Núñez, Ameca, Jalisco, May 16, 2007.

45. U.S. Consulate program in Archivo Municipal de Arandas (Jalisco), December 1951, box 2.

perhaps their communities, more open to new ideas and with greater expectations than ever before. As has been shown for comparative cases from Asia or southern Europe, the return migrants' ability to capitalize upon their savings or their educational experience depended less on what they learned than upon regional economic dynamics. In a few cases braceros indeed came home to promote new forms of economic development that were otherwise not possible in rural Mexico. But for the most part, they employed their innovative ideas and hard-earned savings to accelerate the modernization of their sending communities through new patterns of consumption, commerce, housing, and agriculture (Brettell 2003, 72–77).

U.S. State Department officials who negotiated the Bracero Program were pleased to learn of another consequence: the positive attitude that guest workers developed toward their host society. One striking feature of oral history interviews is the extent to which the hardships that braceros suffered "are usually looked upon as part of the game" (Foster 1967, 276). Luis González found braceros content with their treatment because many of their contractual rights were enforced and "always to a greater degree than were most provisions of labor legislation in Mexico." The American historian Leslie Byrd Simpson recalled "the obvious pride" expressed by former migrants as they told their stories, offering "nothing but praise for the treatment they received." Reporting from the far north, Hancock credited migration for a "lessening of the 'damned gringo' attitude among much of the Chihuahuan population." Belshaw drew similar conclusions and therefore felt that, with the Bracero Program's conclusion at the time of his research, "the U.S. will be denying itself a badly needed device to stem the tide of anti-American sentiment" in Latin America. In fact many field researchers expected far more serious consequences as the U.S. Congress debated the Bracero Program's fate in the early 1960s. Writing from the emigrant heartland, George Foster concluded that its termination "is almost certain to cause a major economic (and perhaps social) crisis…in the thousands of Mexican villages which have grown accustomed to this outside source of aid…[T]he consequences will be serious until the Mexican government and Mexican industry can take up the slack" (González 1974, 241; Belshaw 1967, 132–33; Hancock 1958, 123–24; Simpson 1966, 349–50; Foster 1967, 287–88).

CONCLUSION: CLOSING THE DOOR

The Bracero Program ended where it began, in the halls of the U.S. Congress. Growers protested its termination with their customary warnings of "entire crops being lost, the price of food doubling…family farming ruined and communism erupting in Mexico." But the mechanization of harvesting had already weakened demand for field hands (Galarza 1964, 16 (quoted); Calavita 1992, 143–44). More importantly, public debate shifted perceptibly in the civil rights era. At a time when national TV viewers chose among four stations, CBS broadcast a prime-time documentary that illustrated how little the lives of farm workers had changed since Americans first read *The Grapes of Wrath*. "Harvest of Shame" prompted viewers to flood congressional offices with letters of opposition, whereas its opponents now demonized the Bracero Program with metaphors alluding to slave labor. In this more liberal political climate an opposition alliance of church, labor, and Mexican American activists swayed liberal Democrats to vote against renewal. However, despite the shift in legislative power to urban America, the Bracero Program nearly survived. The bill to terminate it unilaterally—Mexico had no say in the matter—passed by only seventeen votes (Ngai 2004, 158–66; Hawley 1966).[46]

The last braceros returned to Mexico when the 1964 harvest concluded. More than twenty years had passed since thousands of eager young men departed the Mexico City train station as "citizens on a mission." A generation later, migrants returned to a nation living through a "Mexican Miracle" of economic dynamism and political stability. The International Olympic Committee had just awarded the 1968 Summer Games to Mexico City, illustrating Mexico's status as a model of Third World development. The capital grew into the largest metropolis in the Americas and the dominant industrial center of Mexico, with 40 percent of its factory jobs. Urban Mexico therefore exerted a greater pull on rural migrants than the fields or cities of *el Norte*. But the end of bracero contracting alarmed officials concerned about population growth rates—Mexico's was among the world's highest—and the 200,000 men forced to stay home in 1965. It was no coincidence that Mexico initiated the Border Industrialization Program that very year. The binational agreement gave birth to the sprawling assembly plants near the U.S.-Mexican border known as maquiladoras. Today they employ almost 20 percent of industrial workers. But they developed slowly and, contrary to their planners' vision, they preferred to hire young women rather than the men who once migrated. So when Mexico's miracle of growth ended abruptly, in 1982, communities whose ties to the migrant trail dated to the Bracero Program headed north from Mexico once again. The former guest workers now invited themselves. But their renewed exodus built on a migratory culture that twenty-two years of bilateral, state-sanctioned emigration had institutionalized in Mexico's traditional sending states.

---

46. Congressional vote against program's renewal in *The New York Times*, May 30, 1963.

CHAPTER 5

Migration and the Border, 1965–1985

Oscar J. Martínez

University of Arizona

INTRODUCTION

During the period covered in this chapter, Mexican immigration to the United States increased significantly as a consequence of unfavorable economic conditions in Mexico, rising labor demand in the United States, watershed developments along the U.S.–Mexico border, and historic policy changes that altered the requirements for gaining legal permanent entry into the United States. Undocumented migration reemerged as a contentious issue in the United States as the country struggled to find a solution to the problem. An intense public debate spawned new initiatives at the highest levels of the U.S. government for dealing with employers who hired undocumented workers, for legalizing the status of the undocumented population living in the United States, and for stopping the flow of illegal immigrants at the border. Years of work in the U.S. Congress would eventually lead to the passage of a comprehensive immigration law in 1986, a subject covered in the next chapter. The Mexican government of course followed closely the discussions in Washington and monitored the treatment of its citizens in the United States and along the border. Inevitably, the vitriolic tone of the debate and episodes such as the 1978–1979 "Tortilla Curtain" incident produced friction in the U.S.–Mexico relationship. This chapter examines general trends in Mexican immigration to the United States between 1965 and 1985, with an emphasis on the major developments as mentioned above.

ECONOMIC CONDITIONS IN MEXICO
DURING THE PERIOD

In the mid-1960s, Mexico was in the midst of an "economic miracle," meaning the achievement of high productivity rates and a notable rise in the overall standard of living. The miracle began during World War II and continued into the 1970s. Between 1940 and 1970 the national product expanded more than fivefold, with annual rates of growth exceeding over 6 percent most years. On average, manufacturing grew by almost 8 percent annually and agriculture by about 6 percent. By the late 1960s industry made up about a quarter of the national product and employed over 16 percent of all workers. Both agriculture and industry became sources of savings and earners of foreign exchange (Alba and Potter 1986, 56). Significantly, despite having a very high population growth rate, by 1970 Mexico had developed the ability to meet most of its food needs and to export increasing amounts of agricultural products such as cotton, coffee, fruits, vegetables, and livestock. Food production benefited enormously from the Green Revolution, which, through cross-breeding and use of pesticides, greatly expanded yields of wheat, corn, and other crops (Cline 1962, 233–34).

Dazzled North American academic writers marveled at the post World War II transformation of the country. For example, Howard F. Cline wrote in 1962 that Mexico showed signs of losing "the appearance of a 'semi-colonial' area," adding,

> For much of its recent history the [Mexican] Republic was primarily a supplier of raw materials to industrialized areas of the world. Its fibres, minerals, and petroleum, developed by a small group of local and foreign capitalists, went abroad, and in return it received manufactured articles, even foodstuffs. For local consumption, its own industrial plant provided a few products: beer, glass, soap, and other homely items not worth the shipping costs to foreign exporters. A few merchants and agencies sufficed to handle the trade, and often the small amounts of capital required for commercial and industrial transactions. As security against loss and inflation, local capital normally went abroad or poured into real estate, either urban holdings or plantation enterprises. Most of these elements have now been transformed. Mexico has been in the throes of an industrial revolution. (Cline 1962, 270)

Foreign trade, especially with the United States, drove much of the Mexican economy. In the 1960s and early 1970s, as Mexico became more industrialized, metals and other raw materials declined as a percentage of all exports, manufactured goods went up, and agricultural products stayed about the same. In the mid-1970s, however, with the discovery of new oil deposits, petroleum exports rose substantially, and by the end of the decade raw materials comprised about 68 percent of all exports. Overall, the value of Mexican exports to the United States rose from $1.7 billion to $10 billion between 1975 and 1980, whereas imports went up from $5.1 billion to $15.1 billion (Cline 1962, 292–94; Cline, 1971, 389–90; Weintraub 1990, 67–68; Pastor and Castañeda 1988, 205). The Mexican miracle, already on shaky ground by the late 1970s, came to a screeching halt in 1982 when demand for Mexican exports dropped as a result of an international recession. Worst of all, the price of oil tumbled following years of upward movement. With drastically reduced foreign oil revenues on which the country had become dependent, economic activity came to a near standstill. Investment capital dried up, the value of the Mexican peso took a steep dive, businesses collapsed, overall productivity plummeted, unemployment skyrocketed, and the government was forced to borrow money to pay its huge debts. Policy mistakes on the part of Mexican leaders undoubtedly contributed to the severity of the debacle, but overreliance on such an unstable commodity as oil to drive the economy and to provide a large share of government revenues lies at the heart of the crisis.

The petroleum industry in Mexico spawned problems familiar to countries whose economies have been negatively affected by the volatility of international oil markets.

When demand and prices are high, the infusion of sizable amounts of oil revenues from abroad distorts normal economic activity as disproportionate emphasis is placed on the oil industry, whereas other sectors are neglected. In addition, fervent oil economies encourage overborrowing, generate inflation, and breed corruption. When oil demand and prices plunge, which occurs frequently and often abruptly, oil-dependent economies must then cope with large drops in revenues and the burdensome task of repaying high-interest loans incurred during the "good times." All of these problems beset Mexico during the crisis of the 1980s when an oil glut wreaked havoc on oil-dependent economies around the world. Thus, Mexico's national product grew feebly by an average of less than 2 percent after 1980, dropping below zero in 1982, 1983, and 1986 (figures from Werner, Barros, and Ursúa 2006, 82).

The severe downturn of the 1980s forced Mexico to reassess national economic policies. At the same time, the United States, through institutions like the World Bank and the International Monetary Fund, pressured the Mexican government to abandon its traditional role as manager of economic affairs. The Miguel de la Madrid administration (1982–1988) determined that the time had indeed come for Mexico to greatly diminish government involvement in the economy, instead letting free-market mechanisms more fully determine economic activity. Subsequent reforms included reducing government expenditures, cutting social programs, selling public enterprises to private companies, encouraging more foreign investment, and promoting external trade by lowering tariffs. It would take years for Mexico to recover from the devastating crisis of the 1980s.

During the decades of the economic miracle, Mexico made impressive gains, but a large percentage of the population remained impoverished and the number of people migrating to the United States actually increased in the 1960s and 1970s. Even in good times Mexico's economy could not keep up with the demand for well-paying jobs among laborers and blue collar workers. Statistics revealed great inequalities in society. In 1968, for example, the richest 10 percent of the population possessed 42 percent of the national income, whereas the poorest 50 percent possessed only 17 percent of the income. By 1984 some improvement had taken place, but the richest 10 percent still controlled 37 percent of the income, whereas the poorest 50 percent controlled 25 percent of the income. As suggested by those figures, poverty impacted much of the population. In effect, in 1980, 46 percent of all households in Mexico lived below the poverty line, with one third lacking enough resources to cover minimum food requirements (Rudolph 1985, 380; Graizbord and Aguilar 2006, 92–94). High population growth rates, which stood on average at 3.4 percent annually in the 1960s and 3.3 percent in the 1970s, compounded the enormous social problems faced by the Mexican people (Rudolph 1985, 378–79). The elevated population growth rates produced an excess labor force, many of whose members sought relief outside Mexico. And, with the collapse of the Mexican economy in the early 1980s, the pressures on the masses mounted and cross-border migration intensified.

Meanwhile, in the United States, beginning in World War II and lasting for decades, a great need for cheap labor developed precisely in those sectors of the economy where Mexican workers could be most useful. The demand for agricultural and urban low-skilled workers throughout the United States, including border rural communities and cities along the border, would result in the influx of millions of Mexicans into the country.

BORDER COMMUTERS, BRACEROS, MAQUILADORAS, AND MIGRATION

By the early 1960s, the Mexican border region had become one of the fastest-growing areas of Mexico as a result of an expanding economy based on ties with the United States and consequent migration from the interior of the country to the northern frontier. A significant percentage of the Mexican border population derived its livelihood from American-driven tourism and from employment in agriculture, manufacturing, and services on the U.S. side of the border. According to surveys conducted by the U.S. Immigration and Naturalization Service, there were about thirty-four thousand legal commuting workers along the border in 1963, forty-four thousand in 1966, forty-eight thousand in 1969, and forty thousand in 1973 (Table 5.1). These workers were popularly known as "green-carders," meaning that they possessed documents (green cards that later became blue cards) to reside permanently in the United States but chose to live in Mexico and make the daily trek to their jobs north of the border. Simultaneously an unknown number of U.S. citizens who resided in Mexico, as well as thousands of undocumented workers, also made their way to jobs in the United States every day. Because of leniency on the part of U.S. authorities at the time, undocumented commuters found it rather easy to cross the border.

A border-wide survey conducted in 1969 revealed that green-card commuters received an average of $1.55 an hour, $0.05 below the U.S. legal minimum wage at that time. Significantly, 27 percent of the male commuters and 42 percent of the female commuters earned below $1.46 an hour. Wages were generally higher in the western border areas than in the eastern regions. For example, the area east of El Paso reported an average green-card hourly wage of $1.33, whereas El Paso–Nogales–Douglas reported $1.53, San Luis–Calexico $1.51, and San Diego $2.34 (North 1970, 114–15).

Table 5.1. Number of Mexican Green-Card Commuters, 1963–1973

	1963	1966	1969	1973
All ports	34,223	43,687	47,876	39,813
Major ports				
Brownsville	1,796	2,032	2,306	1,635
Laredo	2,490	2,581	3,312	2,225
Eagle Pass	1,586	1,604	1,968	1,616
El Paso	13,492	11,772	13,140	13,223
Nogales	1,464	1,614	1,371	822
San Luis	1,239	4,234	3,616	4,337
Calexico	4,692	7,616	8,788	4,750
San Ysidro	5,855	9,281	10,481	9,063
All others	1,609	2,953	2,534	2,142

SOURCE: Surveys conducted by the U.S. Immigration and Naturalization Service, cited in U.S. Select Commission on Western Hemisphere Immigration, 1970; El Paso Area Fact Book, 7–9; North (1970, 27).

The border commuting system generated considerable debate in the United States, often occasioning bitter controversy. Leading the fight against the green-carders were the U.S. unions, whose leaders argued that commuters depressed the local wage scale, increased unemployment among U.S. citizens, and often worked as strikebreakers, making union organizing more difficult.[1] Critics persuasively correlated high-unemployment and low-income data and the low degree of unionization along the U.S. side of the border with green-card worker statistics to substantiate their claims (North 1970, chap. 5). U.S. proponents of the program, led by border business owners and industrialists, marshaled arguments in favor of the green-carders. The business community insisted that the commuters attracted industry to the area, spent much of their money in the United States, and held jobs that U.S. residents did not want. Defenders further warned that if thousands of commuters were forced to move across the border, their sudden influx would greatly aggravate extant social problems. Aside from citing economic arguments, green-card advocates pointed out that it would be inhuman to deny employment to persons who just happened to live "across the border" and unjust to disrupt a long-standing tradition in the region.[2]

The debate reached its high point in the 1960s and early 1970s. In 1961, labor leaders in El Paso struggled for months and came close to having the U.S. Department of Labor declare a ban against the green-carders. Only strong diplomatic protests in Washington on the part of the Mexican government prevented such action.[3] The controversy continued and reached the halls of the U.S. Congress, resulting in extensive hearings by the Select Commission on Western Hemisphere Immigration in 1968.[4] Legislation introduced included a bill cosponsored by Senator Edward Kennedy that sought to curb the influx of commuters. Yet opposition forces, including the U.S. State Department, delayed action on the matter. Frustrated by the lack of success in obtaining favorable legislation, U.S. labor unions sought legal recourse, arguing that green cards violated immigration laws. The case reached the U.S. Supreme Court and, on November 25, 1974, this body upheld the legality of the alien commuting system.[5] Commuters continued to live in Mexico and work in the United States, but as time passed the task of crossing the border on a daily basis became more time-consuming because of increasing congestion in the ports of entry and periodic shut downs of the crossing points as a consequence of political demonstrations. To avoid such problems, eventually an unknown—but probably a large percentage—of the commuting population moved permanently to the United States.

Although opponents of border commuters failed in their efforts to abolish the daily flow of green-carders to work sites in the United States, in 1964 an ideologically similar coalition of critics succeeded in ending the Bracero Program, the biggest bilateral guest worker arrangement between the two countries. The Bracero Program was a contract labor agreement enacted in 1942 in response to a World War II–created labor emergency

1. *El Paso Economic Review* 8 (April 1971), 1.

2. *El Paso Economic Review* (U.T. El Paso, April 1971), 1.

3. *El Paso Herald Post*, 1961: 4/21, 1; 6/22, 1; 6/23, 1; 6/24, 1; 7/11, 1; 7/12, 13.

4. U.S. Select Commission on Western Hemisphere Immigration, *The Impact of Commuter Aliens along the Mexican and Canadian Borders: Hearings* (1968), Parts I–IV.

5. *New York Times*, May 4, 1969, 78; *Saxbe v. Bustos*, 419 U.S. 65 (1974).

in the United States (for details see chapter 4). Mexico agreed to help its neighbor, and the Mexican economy as well, by facilitating the participation of its workers in the program. Although scheduled to end after the war, post-1945 renewals prolonged the agreement until 1964. The Bracero Program constituted a major catalyst in promoting immigration to the United States from the time it started to the time it ended and even beyond. From 1942 to 1964, Mexican workers signed almost 5 million contracts to work in U.S. agriculture, food processing, railroad maintenance, and other sectors. All along an undetermined but likely large number of braceros, accustomed to earning dollars, sought and received legal permanent residency in the United States. Others became freelance undocumented workers. When the program ended, a large percentage of the ex-braceros still living in Mexico immigrated to the United States either legally or illegally.

The Bracero program generated heated debate in both countries. Many Mexican growers constantly complained of labor shortages in Mexico, whereas human rights activists demanded that the program be suspended until exploitation and discrimination against Mexicans ceased in the United States. The Mexican government, although cognizant of the exploitation and abuse of migrants in the United States, considered that the remittances sent home by braceros and the alleviation of unemployment problems in Mexico justified participation in the program. In the United States, employers strongly supported the program, as did the federal government. But U.S. labor unions complained bitterly that braceros lowered wages and harmed unionization efforts. By the early 1960s the anti-Bracero Program forces in the United States became increasingly influential as the Democratic Party, which favored U.S. organized labor, took control of the government. Pressure grew and in December 1964 the U.S. Congress terminated the agreement with Mexico. In the face of the elimination of job opportunities abroad on which for many years literally millions of its workers had depended, Mexico now had to confront the formidable challenge of creating new employment alternatives at home.

Mexico's answer to the crisis was to stimulate industrialization along the border with the United States, given that large number of unemployed ex-braceros had settled in the Mexican border region. Foreign corporations, as well as domestic investors, were invited to set up assembly plants in the border cities. Although the industrialization initiative got off to a slow start in 1965, within a few years border factories mushroomed, and employment opportunities proliferated. Multinational corporations from the United States, Asia, and Europe found the abundant cheap-labor pools in centers like Ciudad Juárez and Tijuana, and the proximity of these cities to the lucrative U.S. market, ideal factors in addressing the problems of rising production costs and international competition. By the 1970s a who's who of leading global companies operated border plants engaged in a wide variety of assembly operations. In time, some high-tech industries made their appearance on the border as well. Routinely, these companies established infrastructure on the U.S. side of the border to support the work in Mexico, including administrative, transportation, and warehousing centers. In that way both Mexican and U.S. border cities functioned as a single economic entity firmly linked to the world economy (Fernández-Kelly 1983; Sklair 1993; Stoddard, Martínez, and Martínez Lasso 1987; Wilson 1992).

Between 1970 and 1984, the number of border maquiladoras grew from 120 to 585, whereas the number of employees rose from 20,327 to 184,400 (Martínez, 1988, 119).

Most of the plants were heavily concentrated in Ciudad Juárez and Tijuana, whereas Matamoros, Reynosa, and Mexicali emerged as second-tier centers of maquiladoras and Nuevo Laredo, Piedras Negras, Ciudad Acuña, and Nogales as third-tier centers. Select cities in Mexico's interior also embraced maquiladoras (Martínez 1978, 133).[6]

The significance of the Border Industrialization Program in relation to migration is that it did not diminish the flow of workers to the United States as anticipated. On the contrary, the program encouraged international human movement. In the 1960s and 1970s, critics of the maquiladoras rightly pointed out that the original purpose of the program, to alleviate the pronounced male unemployment at the border, had not been accomplished. Indeed, at the time the program began, women who had only recently joined the work force and who were paid lower wages than men made up well over 80 percent of the maquiladora labor force. That percentage dropped very slowly in subsequent years. Even by 1975 women still comprised over 78 percent of the maquiladora line workers and still about 70 percent a decade later (Sklair 1993, 167).

Just like the Bracero Program, the maquiladoras primed both legal and illegal immigration to the United States because new generations of workers from the interior of Mexico were lured to the border region in search of factory jobs. Large numbers of workers, especially men, found the low-paying, tedious assembly work highly unattractive. Many of those who did become factory workers, including women, quickly familiarized themselves with the higher wages and better employment opportunities north of the border and left their maquiladora jobs in search of employment in the United States. Because most ordinary people did not qualify for legal immigration because of U.S. policy changes that took effect after 1965, the only alternative for determined workers became illegal immigration.[7]

U.S. IMMIGRATION POLICIES

After World War II, Americans became increasingly uneasy about the favoritism in U.S. immigration law that privileged western and northern Europe, and pressures mounted to eliminate the quotas that, since the 1920s, had discriminated against Third World countries outside the western hemisphere. A debate in the U.S. Congress eventually led to the passage of the landmark Immigration and Nationality Act of 1965, which took effect in 1968. This law dramatically altered immigration patterns to the United States, opening the door widely for Asian countries. It also affected the flow of Mexican immigration in a significant way.

Most importantly, apart from eliminating immigration preferences based on national origin, the 1965 Act introduced a new method for allocating immigrant visas based on family ties and occupational skills. In practical terms such provisions restricted legal immigration to individuals who had relatives in the United States and workers whose training, skills, or expertise was in demand among U.S. employers. The Act also set numerical limits of 170,000 for the eastern hemisphere and 120,000 for the western hemisphere, as well as a 20,000 per-country requirement for foreign relatives

---

6. *Twin Plant News* (September 2002).

7. The link between maquiladoras and migration has been debated by scholars. See Williams and Seligson 1981.

of resident aliens. The 20,000 per country quota, which excluded spouses, children, and parents of U.S. citizens, did not take effect until 1976 for the western hemisphere. Although many Mexicans met the new family requirements and could obtain permanent residency in the United States, the masses of poor, uneducated, and unskilled would-be immigrants who lacked kin connections north of the border could no longer qualify for visas. Unlike groups such as Asians and Cubans, whose immigrant ranks included large numbers of highly educated, professional people, Mexican entrants overwhelmingly originated in the most marginalized sector of society.

As Table 5.2 shows, after 1965 the number of Mexicans who immigrated to the United States legally gradually increased, but the number who entered without documentation skyrocketed. In 1967, the year before the new law took effect, the U.S.

Table 5.2. Mexican Immigrants Admitted to the United States and Deportable Aliens Located, 1961–1985

	MEXICAN IMMIGRANTS ADMITTED	DEPORTABLE ALIENS LOCATED
1961	41,632	88,823
1962	55,291	92,758
1963	55,253	88,712
1964	32,967	86,597
1965	37,969	110,371
1966	45,163	138,520
1967	42,371	161,608
1968	43,563	212,057
1969	44,623	283,557
1970	44,469	345,353
1971	50,103	420,126
1972	64,040	505,949
1973	70,141	655,968
1974	71,586	788,145
1975	62,205	766,600
1976	57,863	875,915
1976 (Jul–Sept 1976)	16,001	221,824
1977 (Oct 1976–Sept 1977)	44,079	1,042,215
1978	92,367	1,057,977
1979	52,096	1,076,418
1980	56,680	910,361
1981	101,268	975,780
1982	56,106	970,246
1983	59,079	1,251,357
1984	57,557	1,246,981
1985	61,077	1,348,749

SOURCE: *Statistical Yearbooks of the Immigration and Naturalization Service*; Moore, 1976, 41.

Immigration and Naturalization Service (INS) apprehended 161,608 undocumented immigrants. That number rose dramatically in subsequent years, more than tripling by 1972 and slightly surpassing 1 million illegal entrants in 1977, 1978, and 1979. In each of the next three years the number dropped below 1 million, but then it surpassed 1 million again in 1983 and 1984, reaching an all-time high of 1,348,749 in 1985. U.S. officials estimated that between 60 and 75 percent of all apprehended immigrants during those years were Mexicans (Corwin 1982, 227, 282).

The high apprehension numbers fueled alarm and speculation regarding the size of the undocumented population permanently residing in the United States. Some public officials spoke of an ongoing "illegal alien invasion" of the country. In 1974, U.S. Attorney General William Saxbe proclaimed that as many as 7 million undocumented people lived in the United States, whereas U.S. Commissioner of Immigration Leonard F. Chapman Jr. stated that the number could actually be as high as 12 million. Chapman's pronouncement led the media to routinely use the 12 million figure in sensationalist stories about immigration, triggering public fear and a renewed demand for enhanced border enforcement. Subsequent U.S. government–commissioned and academic studies, however, yielded estimates of the undocumented population that undermined Commissioner Chapman's exaggerated assertions. None of those serious estimates would exceed 8 million undocumented immigrants. Further downsizing of the inflated number promoted by Commissioner Chapman took place in 1980 when, after examining data from the U.S. Census, government demographers reported that the undocumented population likely did not exceed 6 million (Corwin 1982, 279–84).

Meanwhile, in Mexico, government-sponsored studies undertaken by the Centro Nacional de Información y Estadística del Trabajo (CENIET) rejected the U.S. numbers as highly exaggerated and emphasized the seasonal, temporary, and circular nature of cross-border migration. Acknowledging that the number of deportable Mexicans in the United States had indeed increased from 1972 to 1977, in the view of CENIET's researchers the permanent undocumented Mexican population could not possibly have reached more than 436,000 in 1972, 606,000 in 1974, and 1.2 million in 1977 (Corwin 1982, passim; discussion of the CENIET studies appears on pp. 267–73).

The "numbers game" peaked in 1980–1981, at which time historian Arthur F. Corwin traveled throughout the United States collecting statistics and opinions from a variety of sources. Corwin put his own interpretation on the gathered data and summarized it as shown in Table 5.3. In his opinion, between 8 and 10 million undocumented people lived in the United States, with Mexicans making up well over half of that population. The great disparities in the calculations resulting from the numerous studies conducted both in Mexico and in the United States are not surprising in light of the difficulties of gathering data from undocumented immigrants. In retrospect, the lower estimates proved to be more accurate, given that just 3 million immigrants would take advantage of the opportunity to legalize their status under the landmark amnesty provision of the Immigration and Reform Act of 1986.

Unquestionably the popularization of the highest estimates by U.S. politicians and the media intensified the debate about immigration policy, driving anti-immigrant forces to accelerate the pressure on the White House and the U.S. Congress to take forceful action against the undocumented population. The argument that the only way to

Table 5.3. Speculative Estimates of Undocumented People in the United States, 1981

PLACE OF ORIGIN	LOW	HIGH
Mexico	5,400,000	6,790,000
Caribbean	400,000	530,000
Central America	390,000	500,000
South America	270,000	380,000
Asia	440,000	540,000
Philippines	250,000	300.000
Middle Eastern and East Indian	320,000	350,000
Other (Canada, Europe, etc.)	500,000	600,000
Total	7,970,000	9,990,000

SOURCE: Summary calculations by Arthur F. Corwin based on data and estimates by government officials, academics, newspapers, ethnic leaders, and others. Corwin (1982, 248–50).

stop illegal immigration was to penalize employers gained popularity in Congressional hearings, and in 1972 and 1973 the House of Representatives passed bills that called for fines and jail sentences for those who hired undocumented workers. The U.S. Senate, however, rejected both bills as a result of pressure from business groups and Hispanic organizations. The debate raged through the presidential election of 1976, which Jimmy Carter won. In an effort to shore up support from the Hispanic community, the new president appointed Lionel Castillo Commissioner of Immigration. Castillo traveled throughout the country and met with many groups with the intent of assuring them of the administration's support for improving the broken immigration system. On August 4, 1977, Carter presented a new proposal for addressing immigration issues, especially the thorny problem of undocumented migration.

THE CARTER PLAN

Citing the groundwork on immigration performed over the previous seven years in the U.S. Congress and the results of a comprehensive study by his administration, Carter called for "a set of actions to help markedly reduce the increasing flow of undocumented aliens in this country and to regulate the presence of the millions of undocumented aliens already here."[8] The major "actions" proposed by Carter were designed to: (1) "Make unlawful the hiring of undocumented aliens," with "injunctions and fines of $1,000 per undocumented alien hired" and court-imposed criminal penalties for injunction violators and repeat offenders. Employers would be held responsible for properly checking documents of job applicants. Social security cards would be designed to make them more difficult to forge, but "no steps would be taken to make the social security card a national identification

---

8. Jimmy Carter's Immigration Proposal, presented at a briefing at the White House on August 4, 1977, 1. Manuscript copy, author's files.

document." Labor contractors and job brokers would be subject to penalties as well. Discrimination by employers against U.S. minority workers would be minimized by stepped-up enforcement of civil rights laws by federal agencies. (2) "Increase significantly the enforcement of the Fair Labor Standards Act and the Federal Farm Labor Contractor Registration Act, targeted to areas where heavy undocumented alien hirings occur." (3) "Adjust the immigration status of undocumented aliens who have resided in the U.S. continuously from before January 1, 1970 to the present" by granting them "permanent resident alien status; create a new immigration category of temporary resident alien for undocumented aliens who have resided in the U.S. continuously prior to January 1, 1977; make no status change and enforce the immigration law against those undocumented aliens entering the U.S. after January 1, 1977." (4) "Substantially increase resources available to control the Southern border, and other entry points, in order to prevent illegal immigration." At least two thousand new Border Patrol agents would be sent to the border, a large number of current agents would be shifted to the busiest cross points, and an "anti-smuggling Task Force" would be created to disrupt and destroy alien smuggling organizations. (5) "Promote continued cooperation with the governments [of countries] which are major sources of undocumented aliens, in an effort to improve their economies and their controls over alien smuggling rings." Possible economic assistance would be provided to the source countries, including trade preferential treatment, technical help, and "population programs." (6) Support "pending legislation to increase the annual limitation on legal Mexican and Canadian immigration to a total of 50,000, allocated between them according to demand."

Carter's initiative immediately drew fire from various interest groups who objected to different parts of the plan. The business sector assailed the proposed employer sanctions as unreasonable, whereas Hispanic organizations expressed concern that such penalties would trigger widespread job discrimination, especially against Mexican Americans. But the amnesty provision generated the most controversy because many conservatives in the U.S. Congress and in the public arena as well considered that idea far too radical. Ultimately, Carter's plan got nowhere in the Congress. Yet it is noteworthy that many of the "actions" proposed by Carter, including employer sanctions and amnesty, would eventually be incorporated into U.S. immigration law almost a decade later with the passage of the Immigration Reform and Control Act of 1986.

Mexico closely monitored the immigration debate in the United States and grew increasingly uneasy with the anti-Mexican rhetoric in the media and in Washington, leading to frictions between the two countries. In addition to tensions over the immigration stalemate in the U.S. Congress, disagreements over trade disrupted the normally business-like and reasonably cooperative bilateral relationship. The high point in the international quarrel specifically regarding immigration took place in late 1978 when a plan became public that the United States would build military-like fences along the border to keep unlawful immigrants and smugglers from entering the country. The fences controversy merits detailed discussion in view of the heat that it generated at the time and the significance that border blockades and barriers would assume in later years.

THE "TORTILLA CURTAIN" EPISODE

Before the 1970s, fences on U.S. soil could be found along stretches of the border in both rural and urban areas. Ranchers, for example, fenced their properties to stop human trespassing and to prevent livestock from running loose. Beginning in the early twentieth century, the U.S. government on various occasions financed the construction of fences in urban areas such as El Paso, Nogales, and San Ysidro to enforce the official hours when ports of entry remained closed and to make it more difficult for undocumented immigrants and drug smugglers to cross the border.

In El Paso, by the 1970s various fences were in evidence in the vicinity of the border. But, apart from obvious, aging INS fencing directly on the north bank of the Río Grande, it was impossible to know which of the other barriers had been erected to deter illegal immigrants or smugglers and which had been built to keep people out of irrigation canals and away from the railroad yards and to prevent accidents along the new border highway. Federal agencies like the INS and the International Boundary and Water Commission, as well as the state of Texas, the city of El Paso, and private railroad companies, had all participated in building fences in the vicinity of the border. Unfortunately, a lack of historical research regarding the actual construction of border fences makes it impossible to provide a comprehensive listing of all the extant fences in the 1970s and when they were erected.

It is difficult as well to know how effective the fences and observation towers were in stopping undesirable people, diseased animals, and smuggled merchandise from penetrating the border. These structures certainly slowed down the surreptitious traffic, but in reality the impact was minimal. The flow of undocumented migration continued at high levels from the 1940s to the 1970s, and so did the smuggling of narcotics and many other products.

Another important dimension of the story that has not received due attention from historians is the public reaction to the presence of man-made barriers in border communities. On the U.S. side, more than likely each border fence episode before the 1970s elicited a mixed response, just as occurred during the Tortilla Curtain incident and in the most recent debates about the latest border wall proposal. On the Mexican side, it is a good bet that all along there has been overwhelming opposition to barriers and observation towers installed by the U.S. government. One indication of the level of opposition in Mexico to fences and watchtowers comes from the actions of former Ciudad Juárez Mayor René Mascareñas Miranda, who revealed in a 1976 oral history interview his involvement in convincing U.S. authorities to remove the towers in El Paso in the late 1950s.

> During my term as mayor, my good friend Ambassador Robert Hill [U.S. ambassador to Mexico] paid us a visit. It must have been in the fall of 1958. At that time we were working to open the Cordova Bridge, and I took him to Cordova Island.[9] We came directly to one of the observation towers. I had taken the road that led to that tower purposely so he could see it. He did and without my saying a word he asked, "What is that, a water tower?" "No sir," I replied, "It is an observation tower.

---

9. Cordova Island was essentially a patch of land belonging to Mexico left isolated by the shifting Río Grande and consequently widely used by border crossers and smugglers.

Pretend we are in a concentration camp, and we are under observation. Surely they are looking at you with eyeglasses, and they must be asking themselves, 'What the devil is the U.S. ambassador doing on that dusty road with the mayor of Juárez?'" The ambassador said, "This is an insult to Mexico." I replied, "It is good that you consider it an insult, because I do too. Why don't you bring up the matter with your State Department so those towers will disappear?" Three months later there were no more towers. (Martínez 1976, 287–88)

With some obvious satisfaction, Mascareñas Miranda also related that the following year he, along with the governor of Chihuahua and the County Judge of El Paso County, personally cut the barbed wire fence that surrounded Cordova Island when the announcement was made that a proposed new international bridge at that spot would become a reality. Mascareñas Miranda expounded further on his feelings toward border fences.

I don't like the idea of fences. We don't live between East and West Germany. The communist wall that is there is a slap in the face to any nation that boasts of being democratic. We want greater fluidity and communication between us. We don't want barriers; we don't want barbed wire fences. We brag that we are two neighborly countries, two friendly nations, and that this is the longest border in the world where one does not see a single soldier, a single rifle, a single bayonet, or a single affronting or discriminatory sign. (Martínez 1976., 287, 289)

By the early 1960s, the disappearance of the observation towers and elimination of barbed wire fencing in El Paso–Ciudad Juárez, along with the settlement of the century-old Chamizal land dispute that altered the boundary line (in favor of Mexico) in that area as well, improved the relationship between the two countries (on the Chamizal dispute, see Liss 1965). However, after 1965, with rising undocumented migration, the difficult immigration issue surfaced anew to once again take center stage in U.S.–Mexico diplomatic interaction. The perception that a foreign "invasion" was underway led many immigration restrictionists in the United States to concentrate their attacks on Mexico, which they identified as the country most responsible for threatening U.S. sovereignty. Thus, the eruption of the Tortilla Curtain incident in 1978–1979 followed years of frustration in the United States over the persistence of the border problem. What made it worse was that in Washington, D.C., attempts to find a comprehensive solution to immigration issues failed repeatedly.

In the absence of a legislative response to border concerns, the U.S. Congress responded affirmatively to an INS appropriation request and approved funding in 1977 and 1978 for the building of fences in El Paso, San Ysidro (on the boundary line south of San Diego), and San Luis, Arizona (on the line south of Yuma). The new structures in El Paso and San Ysidro had two purposes: (1) to replace dilapidated fences that were full of holes, some big enough to allow cars through, and (2) to force undocumented immigrants away from the urban areas and into the open desert where they could be caught more easily. Thus, in late October 1978, the INS made a routine announcement that new twelve-foot-high fences topped with barbed wire would be built in El Paso and San Ysidro. Fencing with barbed wire was not new on the border, but what attracted attention was a remark by the boastful contractor in Houston that the new fences would "sever the toes of anyone trying to scale [them]." The U.S. press quickly sensationalized the story by referring to the fences as the Tortilla Curtain and highlighting the feature in the builder's design that called for the inclusion of sharp razors and wires capable of cutting off fingers and toes of climbers.[10]

Objections to the fences quickly surfaced. In Mexico, government officials and other leaders assailed the INS, charging that the fences were a slap in the face to Mexico and that border crossers would face added dangers. Loud protests erupted as well among Mexican American organizations in the United States. Many Hispanic leaders denounced the INS for its inhumane approach to dealing with undocumented immigrants and for not consulting in advance with the border community. In Texas, Governor William Clemens spoke strongly against the Tortilla Curtain, saying, "I don't believe that we and Mexico should have any sort of Berlin Wall on our borders."[11] U.S national leaders issued statements as well. President Jimmy Carter, Attorney General Griffen Bell, and Ambassador to Mexico Patrick J. Lucey publicly opposed the design of the fences, expressing surprise that barriers that included features that might injure immigrants were even under consideration. Lucey characterized the builder's comments referring to the "toe-cutting" capability of the fences as "outrageous."[12]

On the defensive, INS officials denied the allegation that armed troops would be sent to patrol the border and declared their intent to make the proposed fences safer by removing the objectionable razors that might cause physical harm to immigrants.[13] Commissioner Castillo held meetings with leaders of Mexican American organizations to explain the alterations in the design. Chicano activists, however, were not satisfied with the changes in the proposed barriers. They demanded that no new border fences be constructed. In El Paso, the Coalition against the Fence held a demonstration in December 1978 protesting the Tortilla Curtain as well as the possible militarization of the border.

In February 1979, U.S. President Jimmy Carter and Mexican President José López Portillo discussed the fence controversy as part of a broader bilateral agenda in a meeting in Mexico. The discussions were held in an atmosphere of tension and achieved little on either the immigration controversy or the oil and natural gas trade negotiations, the other issue that troubled the U.S.–Mexico relationship at the time. An incident in El Paso–Ciudad Juárez the following month increased the friction. Angry Mexican women whose crossing cards had been taken by U.S. Immigration inspectors held a protest that turned into a near riot at one of the international bridges. Militant protestors arrived to support the women, blocked traffic, tore down a U.S. flag, and threw it into the Río Grande (Martínez et al., 1979, 20–21).

The final outcome of the Tortilla Curtain debate, demonstrations, and official meetings was the scaling back of the original menacing design of the Tortilla Curtain. By the time construction began in the summer of 1979, the infamous barbed wire and razors feature had disappeared and the length of the fences had been reduced in both

10. *Washington Post*, October 24, 1978, p. A6; *El Paso Herald Post*, October 25, 1978, p. A1; *New York Times*, November 7, 1978, p. 22.; *Washington Post*, December 24, 1978, p. A3.

11. *New York Times*, November 7, 1978, p. 22.

12. *Washington Post*, December 24, 1978, p. A3.

13. *El Paso Herald Post*, October 25, 1978, p. A1; Ibid., pp. 20–22.

El Paso and San Ysidro (Martínez, et al., 1979, 20–22). As borderlanders grew accustomed to the new barriers, the INS in subsequent years added more fencing in those two communities and in other parts of the border as well. But the post-1979 construction structures lacked the dangerous designs that had brought notoriety to the Tortilla Curtain, and the work proceeded with little controversy on either side of the border.

In the midst of the Tortilla Curtain episode, border scholars conducted several opinion surveys in El Paso–Ciudad Juárez and San Diego. One survey undertaken by Professor Ellwyn R. Stoddard that focused on leaders revealed that 70 percent of El Paso influentials opposed the construction of the fence, and an even higher 86 percent of important people in Ciudad Juárez objected to the project. "El Pasoans who opposed the fence gave reasons for their attitudes quite similar to those expressed by Ciudad Juárez leaders who also opposed it," wrote Stoddard. "Most of them saw the barrier as unnecessary, ineffective and of short duration for the expense involved. Many were disturbed by its design…, but mostly critical of the insensitivity of federal officials in commencing such a project unilaterally without some input from Mexican officials" (Martínez, et al, 1979, 27–28).

I decided to conduct my own surveys after reading in the El Paso press and hearing claims from U.S. immigration officials and others that most El Pasoans, particularly Mexican Americans, strongly supported the building of the Tortilla Curtain. Such support allegedly stemmed from firm opposition to undocumented immigration and from the desire to keep out Mexicans from Ciudad Juárez, especially juveniles, who were said to be committing many crimes in El Paso. I found it disturbing that the *El Paso Herald Post* had concluded that overwhelming backing for the INS proposal existed in the city based on a few interviews with residents in a predominantly middle class neighborhood called Sunset Heights (near the border) and especially from responses in returned questionnaires published in the *Herald Post* that had solicited reader opinions about the fence. Of the 807 persons who returned questionnaires, 86 percent supported the fence and only 7 percent opposed it. Some supporters added comments, including the following: "Build it 2,000 miles long." "But we'd prefer a cheaper way, a minefield." "Also, electrify the fence with 2,000 volts of electricity." And from opponents: "The fence will be full of holes, just wait and see…waste of taxpayer monies." "Travel 1,000 miles and be stopped by a six-mile fence? Nuts!" "Use the money to develop jobs in Mexico."[14]

In the unpublished reports that summarized the results of my surveys, I pointed out that the newspaper had failed to indicate that its interviews and "polls" were not scientific, and therefore the results should be considered at most suggestive and certainly not conclusive. I also wrote that persons who responded to such requests from the media tended to be senior citizens, conservative, affluent, and predominantly Anglo American. I added that it was a safe bet that many were retirees who habitually passed their free time writing letters "to the editor" or participating in sundry opinion polls. Further, few from the working class sector of the Mexican American community in El Paso read the *Herald Post*, let alone engage in filling out and mailing newspaper questionnaires.

---

14. *El Paso Herald Post*, December 6, 1978, A1–A2.

Table 5.4. Results of the "Tortilla Curtain" Survey Conducted in February 1979 with Fifty Residents of South El Paso and Fifty Merchants with Businesses in South El Paso

Are you in agreement that the fence should be built?

	Yes	No	Neutral
Residents	17 (34%)	17 (34%)	16 (32%)
Merchants	14 (28%)	31 (62%)	5 (10%)

If built, do you think the fence will stop undocumented persons from crossing the river?

	Yes	No	Not sure
Residents	6 (12%)	40 (80%)	4 (8%)
Merchants	8 (16%)	40 (80%)	2 (4%)

Problems with undocumented persons:

	Yes	No	Not sure
Residents	13 (26%)	35 (70%)	2 (4%)
Merchants	13 (26%)	35 (70%)	2 (4%)

Problems experienced by those who answered previous question affirmatively (number of times):

	Residents	Merchants
Theft	7	10
Theft and vandalism	—	1
Vandalism	—	1
Break-in/entered home	4	—
Nuisance	2	1

SOURCE: Unpublished data in author's files. Surveys conducted by author and Mario Galdós.

Assisted by a graduate student, we set out in February 1979 to determine the viewpoints of fifty randomly selected Mexican American residents of South El Paso, a poor neighborhood adjacent to the border, and of fifty randomly selected business persons of different ethnicities who serviced that part of the city. At the time (and now), South El Paso served as a prominent and immediate pathway for hundreds of undocumented immigrants who crossed the international boundary on a daily basis.

The results of our door-to-door surveys showed that the assumed "strong support" for the Tortilla Curtain among South El Paso's Mexican Americans and businessmen was in fact not there[15] (Table 5.4). Among the community residents, 34 percent opposed the fence, 34 percent supported it, and 32 percent were neutral. Eighty percent felt the fence would not stop people from crossing the border, 12 percent said it would, and 8 percent were not sure. When asked whether they had experienced problems with undocumented persons, 70 percent answered no, 26 percent said yes, and 4 percent were not sure. Those who reported problems mentioned break-ins, attempted break-ins, and theft as their main grievances. When asked whether they knew for sure if the intruders were undocumented people, they expressed uncertainty, revealing awareness that many incidents of petty crime invariably involved individuals indigenous to the

---

15. Complete results of the surveys are in author's files.

community. At the time (and now), South El Paso had serious social problems stemming from poverty and widespread unemployment, especially among the youth.

The merchants were even less enthusiastic about the INS fence. Sixty-two percent opposed it, 28 percent favored it, and 10 percent were neutral. Eighty percent believed that the fence would not stop people from crossing the border, whereas 16 percent felt it would and 4 percent were not sure. Despite the stories that had appeared in the media regarding widespread theft and vandalism in the southside stores allegedly caused by undocumented juveniles, only 26 percent of the merchants had experienced such problems, and the national identity of the perpetrators was unclear. Seventy percent had not encountered problems and the remainder were uncertain. The most common complaint among those who reported problems was theft. Coincidentally, the percentage of merchants reporting problems was the same as that of the residents.

Interestingly, the viewpoints concerning the Tortilla Curtain in El Paso differed significantly from those found in San Diego. In that California city, two surveys suggested very strong support for the fence. One mail-out from a congressman found that 64 percent of his constituents endorsed it, whereas only 29 percent dissented. A more formal survey of opinion throughout the city yielded similar results: 68 percent supported the fence, 26 percent did not, and 6 percent gave no opinion (Martínez, et al., 1979, 30, 67).

Two major factors must be considered in attempting to understand the variance in the opinions in El Paso versus those in San Diego. First, El Paso is directly adjacent to the border and its economy was (and remains) highly integrated with Mexico, whereas San Diego is about twenty miles from the border and its economy was only minimally dependent on Mexico at the time of the Tortilla Curtain incident. Since the late 1970s, the degree of cross-border integration between San Diego and Baja California has increased significantly. The real border community in the San Diego area was (is) San Ysidro, but the opinions of its residents were not sought because its small size made it rather inconsequential in international affairs. Second, at the time of the controversy Mexican Americans comprised about 63 percent of El Paso's population but only 15 percent of San Diego's population. Thus, El Pasoans were more directly linked with Mexico and tended to be more sensitive to the negative impact that a dangerous fence could have on cross-border relations. By contrast, most San Diegoans did not feel strong links to Mexico and saw undocumented immigrants largely as a menace to the United States.

FINDINGS OF THE SELECT COMMISSION AND CONGRESSIONAL STALEMATE

While the Tortilla Curtain drama played out, the larger debate over the need for immigration reform continued in the Executive and Congressional branches of the U.S. government. Upon seeing that his plan would not make it into legislation, President Carter joined the Congress in 1978 in creating the Select Commission on Immigration and Refugee Policy. This body was charged with evaluating existing laws, policies, and practices pertaining to immigration matters and with making recommendations for new legislation. The Commission, which included Cabinet secretaries, members of Congress, and other citizens appointed by the President, issued its final report on March 1, 1981. In general, the Commissioners recommended that the United States (1) work closely with other countries and with international organizations to promote better understanding of the issues and to enhance cooperation to improve the handling of international migration flows; (2) strengthen enforcement against illegal immigration on the border and in the interior, including deterrents in the workplace; (3) legalize undocumented immigrants already living in the country; and (4) increase the overall extant annual legal immigration quota from 270,000 to 350,000.[16]

The Commission's recommendations formed the basis for more immigration proposals that surfaced in the Congress. In 1982, the Senate passed a new bill, but it was killed in the House by a coalition of business and Hispanic groups. That bill included employer sanctions, and even some labor organizations came out against it because some of their membership included undocumented workers. In 1984, both the House and the Senate passed separate bills. However, the two chambers could not reconcile differences that existed in the two bills. After that the proponents of legislative reform gained the upper hand by successfully addressing many of the concerns expressed previously by diverse interest groups. The new momentum would lead to the passage of the Immigration and Reform Act of 1986 during the second term of the Ronald Reagan administration. The law was also called the Simpson–Mazzoli Act, in recognition of the years of work in the U.S. Congress that Senator Alan K. Simpson and Representative Romano L. Mazzoli had done to fashion many disparate bills and amendments to bills into a document that had sufficient support to become the law of the land.

CONCLUSION

The two decades from 1965 to 1985 constitute a transitional period in the history of Mexican immigration to the United States. Before 1965 the United States and Mexico worked together to manage a significant part of the flow of workers across the border through the guest worker agreement known as the Bracero Program. After 1965 the bilateral cooperation ceased and the relationship between the two neighbors deteriorated as the flow of undocumented migrants increased substantially. The United States unilaterally passed a law that year that would make legal immigration practically impossible for ordinary Mexicans without U.S. family connections, strong job qualifications, or advanced education. The law strongly affected Mexico because, with some exceptions, it was mostly poor, uneducated, and low-skilled Mexicans who migrated to the United States. Given the push factors that prevailed in Mexico for the masses and the pull factors that attracted foreign workers to the United States, Mexicans inevitably turned to illegal immigration. Mexico sought to alleviate unemployment among ex-braceros and other job seekers by creating the Border Industrialization Program; this initiative not only did not solve the problem, but also encouraged even more migration to the United States.

The rising number of apprehensions of undocumented immigrants in the 1960s and 1970s put the national spotlight in the United States once again on that thorny

---

16. Select Commission on Immigration and Refugee Policy, *U.S. Immigration Policy and the National Interest* (Washington, D.C.: Government Printing Office, 1981).

problem, triggering an emotional debate familiar to historians. Similar controversies had broken out during the 1920s over immigration quotas, during the depression of the 1930s over economic and social concerns, and during the 1950s over Cold War–triggered anxiety related to unauthorized foreigners living in the United States. The debate in the 1970s over undocumented migration led to legislative proposals in the U.S. Congress and to a new plan submitted by President Jimmy Carter. Although unsuccessful, both the congressional and the presidential initiatives contained two novel provisions, sanctions for employers and amnesty for undocumented migrants. These ideas would eventually be incorporated into the landmark U.S. Immigration and Reform Act passed in 1986. The immigration debate also stirred up demands for new border fences and triggered the Tortilla Curtain incident of 1978–1979. The barriers that were built following that episode served as a prelude for the implementation of border blockades and the construction of walls in the 1990s.

The United States and Mexico understood abundantly well that economic need prompted Mexicans en masse to cross the border and that the U.S. economy needed and benefited from their labor. It was clear then that only a binational comprehensive approach would have any chance of effectively managing the migration flow. But the political climate in the United States did not allow for devising and implementing such a holistic framework or for having Mexican government officials participate in negotiations that would lead to effective legislation. The immigration issue then was simply too "hot" in the U.S. political system. So the focus in the United States remained on border enforcement rather than on finding lasting solutions to the problem.

PART TWO

Comparative Themes

CHAPTER 6

Race and the New Southern Migration, 1986 to the Present

Helen B. Marrow[1]
Tufts University

INTRODUCTION

The mid-1980s marked a decisive turning point in U.S. immigration history, particularly for two groups: U.S. southerners and Mexican migrants. Before then U.S. southerners were relatively isolated from foreign-born immigrants, who preferred settling in other regions of the country instead. Likewise, before then Mexicans tended to migrate primarily to the U.S. Southwest, where their presence dates back to at least 1848, when various states in this region were still part of Mexico. However, beginning in the 1970s increasing numbers of people began migrating into the U.S. South, attracted by its rapidly developing economy. And beginning in the mid-1980s Mexican migrants began moving away from their traditional states and cities of settlement into other parts of the country, including into the South. These two trends—the changing economy and demography of the U.S. South and the changing demography of Mexican migration—have continued to accelerate and converge into the twenty-first century. Today, Mexicans are the largest and most visible "Hispanic/Latino" and "immigrant" group in a wide array of cities, towns, and rural areas throughout the U.S. South—a region known historically for *not* having large populations of Hispanics/Latinos or foreign-born immigrants and also for creating and policing one of the world's most stringent racial boundaries between "whites" and "blacks."

This chapter provides a brief overview of the reasons why Hispanics/Latinos, including Mexican migrants, have settled in the traditional U.S. South over the past few decades, followed by a discussion of the ways in which their growing presence intersects with and challenges southern understandings of race, race relations, and discrimination. I begin by focusing on the phenomenal transformation of the southern economy since the mid-twentieth century, a development that has *pulled* Mexicans, alongside

1. Support for this chapter was provided by a grant from the Robert Wood Johnson Foundation.

migrants from many other countries as well as other parts of the United States, into the region. I then detail the ways in which key economic and political developments in Mexico and other parts of the United States have *pushed* Mexican migrants away from their traditional southwestern settlement states into new ones, including in the U.S. South. Finally, I speculate on how Hispanic/Latino newcomers, including Mexican migrants, may ultimately become incorporated into, and potentially transform, the U.S. South's heretofore binary racial hierarchy.

THE U.S. SOUTH IN THE LATE TWENTIETH CENTURY

For most of U.S. history, the region known as the "South" attracted relatively few foreign-born immigrants compared with the rest of the United States. In every decade from 1850 to 1970 the South was home to a smaller percentage of immigrants than any other region of the country (Bankston 2007), a distinction it strongly maintained even during mass immigration from Europe and Asia at the turn of the twentieth century. For instance, whereas the proportion of the total nonsouthern population that was foreign born in 1860 was 14 percent, the corresponding figure in the South was only 5 percent. In 1910, following mass immigration from Europe and Asia, these figures widened to nearly 15 and 2 percent, respectively (Reimers 2005), and even as late as 1950 only 1.6 percent of the South's population was foreign born, compared with 6.9 percent nationally and 13.4 percent in the immigrant-heavy Northeast (Eckes 2005). The foreign-born presence in the "traditional South,"[2] defined here as the former eleven confederate states minus Florida and Texas, which have greater experience with "Hispanics/Latinos" (Bankston 2007; Mohl 2002; Saenz 2000), has historically been even lower than that in the total South. In 1910 only 0.3 percent of North Carolina's population was "foreign-born white," and Alabama, Georgia, Mississippi, North Carolina, and South Carolina together contained less than 1 percent of the country's total foreign-born population (Schmid 2003). As late as 1950, each of the traditional southern states still exhibited foreign-born percentages of less than 1 percent (Eckes 2005).

These low numbers have led scholars to characterize the traditional South as "relatively untouched" by nineteenth century European and Asian immigration (Schmid 2003), despite the fact that the region's social and cultural isolation is frequently overdramatized and a variety of immigrant groups did settle throughout it (Bailey 2005; Bankston 2007; Berthoff 1951; Greenbaum 1998; Loewen 1988; Quan 1982; Reimers 2005; Weise 2008). Simply put, scholars agree that the historical proportions of immigrants in the South, and particularly in the nine states comprising the traditional South, were small in comparison to those elsewhere in the country. This was primarily because of the South's plantation agricultural economy before World War II (which offered few attractive job opportunities to immigrants, especially in comparison to expanding industrial opportunities in the Northeast); to the South's relatively undeveloped transportation, communication, and education infrastructures before World War II; and to the South's hostile racial and political climate before the Civil Rights Movement (Bankston 2007; Eckes 2005; Reimers 2005). Between 1864 and 1914, as

---

2. Thus, my definition of the "traditional South" includes Alabama, Arkansas, Georgia, Louisiana, Mississippi, North Carolina, South Carolina, Tennessee, and Virginia.

Berthoff (1951) writes, "immigration hardly affected southern society in any meaningful sense.... Despite exceptions ... the practical problem of amalgamating alien cultures weighed lightly on the South" (345).

However, migration into the U.S. South began increasing in the 1970s, and by 1990, the Midwest had moved down to replace the South as the least common region of foreign-born immigrant settlement (Bankston 2007). Several factors lie behind this dramatic demographic shift, including a much improved southern racial and political climate since the Civil Rights Movement. Yet the main factor is the region's phenomenal economic transformation from a predominantly plantation agricultural into a commercial and industrial economy as it has become increasingly globally integrated since World War II (Cobb 1982; Cobb and Stueck 2005; Eckes 2005; Himes 1991; Kasarda, Hughes, and Irwin 1991; Peacock, Watson, and Matthews 2005; Wright 1986). As Eckes (2005) writes, the South of the 1950s was relatively disadvantaged and economically depressed. Its residents' per capita income hovered around 60 percent of the national average, and its economic landscape was rural and agricultural, heavily dependent on commodities (like tobacco, cotton, and peanuts), and lacking in a strong manufacturing base. But during the next half century, the region soared economically. Its residents' per capita income increased to 87 percent of the national average by 2001; it added 81 percent of the nation's growth in manufacturing employment between 1950 and 1975; it accounted for 28 percent of manufacturing value added by 2000; and it created 35 percent of new service jobs between 1992 and 2002 (a period when all regions of the country were diversifying their employment bases as manufacturing declined relative to high-and low-end services). Massive improvements in information and communications infrastructures facilitated the flow of goods and information throughout the South, whereas improvements in transportation (including interstate highways and jet travel), air conditioning, and education facilitated economic development and made life in the region more hospitable. By the turn of the twenty-first century large corporations (especially those in retailing, petroleum, and commercial banking) had increased their presence in the South dramatically, whereas foreign corporations (such as German and Japanese automakers) had established a permanent presence in the U.S. market by making foreign direct investments in a variety of southern manufacturing facilities. By 1998 the South obtained 31.3 percent of the nation's foreign direct investments and was home to 30.5 percent of the employment it generated—approximately equal to the region's current (and growing) share of the national population.

This "dramatic economic metamorphosis," as Kasarda, Hughes, and Irwin (1991, 40) term it, has reversed much of the South's image as an economic and political backwater, catapulting many southern states—especially Texas and Florida, but even other traditional ones, such as North Carolina—up the "economic momentum" index:

> [North Carolina's] Gross State Product increased 4.6 times from $59,750 million in 1980 to $272,934 million in 2000.... At the same time, educational levels, although still relatively low, rose in the state.... Because of these trends, per capita income reached 90% of the national level in 1996, up from about 80% in 1980. By the end of the 1990s, North Carolina ranked sixth in the nation on an economic momentum index that combines shifts in employment personal income and population with growth above the national average. (Torres, Popke, and Hapke 2006, 45)

In so doing, it has also produced an important demographic shift—turning the South from a predominantly labor-exporting to a labor-importing region. Although an estimated 10 million southerners left for other regions of the country between 1910 and 1950, between 1970 and 1978 approximately 3.5 million migrants entered the region instead (Eckes 2005), and in-migration trends continued through the 1980s, 1990s, and 2000s.

Despite all of the recent media attention given to Hispanic/Latino and foreign-born immigrant population growth in the region, most migrants to the South are actually whites and blacks from other parts of the United States. For example, between 1990 and 2000 the total population of six traditional southern states (Alabama, Arkansas, Georgia, North Carolina, South Carolina, and Tennessee) grew by 5.2 million people, including 2.3 million whites (who accounted for 45 percent of the growth), 1.3 million blacks (26 percent), and 900,000 Hispanics (17 percent; Kochhar, Suro, and Tafoya 2005). In the South as a whole, the African American population increased by 1.7 million people in the 1970s, another 1.9 million in the 1980s, and still another 3.6 million in the 1990s (Frey 2001). Such high growth rates distinguish southern states from traditional nonsouthern Hispanic settlement states such as California, New York, New Jersey, and Illinois, where white populations declined and black populations grew more slowly over the 1990s (Kochhar, Suro, and Tafoya 2005). Many white and black internal migrants are taking up employment in high-end service and professional jobs in expanding metropolitan centers such as Atlanta, Charlotte, and Raleigh–Durham, attracted by the improved economies, low-density residential lifestyles, and warm climates of these southern "New Sunbelt" cities (Frey 2001). And many of the African Americans among them are "returning home" from earlier ventures that either they or their ancestors made north, now that the South offers an improved economic and less hostile political and racial climate than it used to (Eckes 2005; Frey 2001, 2004; Stack 1996).

But indeed, the South's economic transformation has also attracted substantial numbers of nonwhite/nonblack migrants, including native-born Hispanic and Asian American internal migrants from other parts of the United States as well as foreign-born immigrants, who come predominantly from Mexico although they hail from a wide variety of countries (Ansley and Shefner 2009; Capps et al. 2007; Smith and Furuseth 2006; Greenbaum 1998; Kasarda and Johnson 2006; Kochhar, Suro, and Tafoya 2005; Lippard and Gallagher 2011; Mohl 2002; Odem and Lacy 2009; Schmid 2003; B. E. Smith 2003; Saenz et al. 2003; Vásquez, Seales, and Marquardt 2008). Many Hispanic migrants,[3] primarily those who are foreign born, work in rural southern agriculture, which has shifted toward a predominantly foreign-born labor force since the 1980s (Barcus 2006; Dale, Andreatta, and Freeman 2001; Emery, Ginger, and

---

3. Although I recognize that the term Hispanic is controversial, especially in other parts of the United States, I employ it in this chapter for two reasons. First, it provides a convenient way to refer to both foreign- and U.S.-born individuals who fit the U.S. Census' official definition of Hispanics/Latinos, thereby maintaining relative consistency with the dominant understanding of who this racialized ethnic category includes at the turn of the twenty-first century, as defined by major U.S. public institutions. Second, and more importantly, it reflects how the terms Hispanic and Latino were used on the ground in the rural South during the time of my field research in 2003–2004—largely interchangeably and referring to both foreign- and U.S.-born individuals—while maintaining consistency by using only one term as much as possible.

Chamberlain 2006; Gozdziak and Bump 2004; Griffith 1993, 2006; Griffith et al. 1995; McDaniel and Casanova 2003; Smith-Nonini 2005, 2009; Studstill and Neito-Studstill 2001; Torres, Popke, and Hapke 2006; Torres et al. 2003). Others are employed in urban and rural southern manufacturing and textiles sectors, which have undergone dramatic economic restructuring and downsizing in recent years (Engstrom 2001; Donato, Bankston, and Robinson 2001; Donato, Stainback, and Bankston 2005; Hernández-León and Zúñiga 2000; Willis 2005) or work in rural southern food processing plants, where the demand for low-skilled labor has increased dramatically since the 1970s, as food processing companies have decentralized and deskilled production into rural areas of the South and Midwest that have lower wage rates and unionization levels, in response to greater international competition and declining profit margins (Cravey 1997; Donato et al. 2008; Dunn, Aragonés, and Shivers 2005; Fink 2003; Gozdziak and Bump 2004; Griffith 1993, 1995a, 1995b; Guthey 2001; Hirschman and Massey 2008; Kandel and Parrado 2004; Parrado and Kandel 2008; Schoenholtz 2005; Striffler 2005, 2009; Stuesse 2009; Stull and Broadway 2004). In urban areas, Hispanic migrants are employed in construction and various high- and low-end services sectors, including landscaping, tourism, restaurants, and janitorial services, all of which have been expanding to meet the needs of the region's economic and demographic boom (Bailey 2005; Bump 2005; Smith and Furuseth 2008; Johnson-Webb 2003; Odem 2008; Parrado and Kandel 2008; Rich and Miranda 2005; Smith, Mendoza, and Ciscel 2005; Winders 2008). Although Hispanics' rates of professional/managerial and self-employment in the South are relatively smaller in comparison, they are growing. For example, Hispanics' self-employment rate rose 425 percent in North Carolina between 1995 and 2005, primarily in professional and business services and construction (Kasarda and Johnson 2006).

Overall, the three dominant patterns of Hispanic settlement and occupational concentration, according to Barbara Ellen Smith (2003), illustrate the strong *pull* of the massive economic restructuring and development processes that have transformed the South into "the nation's most racially integrated and economically dynamic region" (Cobb and Stueck 2005, xi) since World War II. The first is agricultural employment in nonmetro areas of the South witnessing low Hispanic population growth. The second is employment in labor-intensive industries (such as furniture and poultry processing) in predominantly white, nonmetro areas of the upper South witnessing high Hispanic population growth. And the third is employment in a combination of industries (including construction, services, and manufacturing) in mixed-economy, metro areas of the South witnessing high Hispanic population growth. The economic pull of these various employment sectors is largely responsible for the emergence of both southern Hispanic "hypergrowth" metropolitan areas (Fischer and Tienda 2006; Suro and Singer 2002) and nonmetropolitan ones (Kandel and Cromartie 2004). To fulfill an expanding demand for labor, many urban and rural southern employers have recruited Hispanic migrants from other parts of the country and from abroad, both directly (often utilizing formalized government contracting programs) and indirectly (often shifting toward a reliance on Hispanic migrants' own social networks; Cravey 1997; Fink 2003; Griffith 1993, 2005a, 2005b, 2006; Griffith et al. 1995; Johnson-Webb 2003; Parrado and Kandel 2008; Smith-Nonini 2005, 2009; Stull and Broadway 2004; Zúñiga and Hernández-León 2005).

Nevertheless, other political and economic *push* factors are also at play behind the rising presence of Hispanics, especially Mexican migrants, in the traditional South.

MEXICAN MIGRATION IN THE LATE
TWENTIETH CENTURY

For most of the twentieth century, foreign-born Mexican immigration to the United States has been highly concentrated, primarily in the five "Mexican gateway states" of Arizona, California, Illinois, New Mexico, and Texas. Between 1910 and 1960, for example, roughly 85 percent of all Mexican immigrants migrated to Texas, California, and Arizona, whereas only 11 percent migrated to other states (Durand, Massey, and Capoferro 2005). During the "bracero era of migration" (1942–1964), Mexican immigration increasingly shifted away from Texas and toward California, a trend that continued into the "undocumented era of migration" (1964–1985), when California consolidated its position as the premier destination for Mexican immigrants, capturing a full 53 percent of foreign-born Mexican immigrants in 1970 and an even higher 57 percent in 1980. Mexican immigrant concentration in California peaked at 58 percent in 1990, whereas its counterpart in Texas bottomed out at 22 percent, completing the shift from Texas to California; meanwhile, Mexican immigration into the other forty-five "nongateway" states fell from 11.2 percent in 1910 to 8.5 percent in 1980 (Durand, Massey, and Capoferro 2005).

Yet in 1986, the United States passed a crucial piece of legislation that fundamentally altered the geography of Mexican migration: the Immigration Reform and Control Act (IRCA). The IRCA involved a tripartite strategy with the goal of eliminating illegal immigration: first, two legalization programs, one for long-term undocumented immigrants and another for temporary Seasonal Agricultural Workers (SAWs); second, a new system of employer sanctions that prohibited the hiring of illegal immigrants; and third, stepped-up enforcement activity at the U.S.–Mexico border. As a result of IRCA's legalization programs, approximately 2.3 million Mexican immigrants (and another approximately 700,000 non-Mexican immigrants) gained legal status between 1987 and 1990. Approximately 55 percent of them lived in California, with approximately 40 percent in the southern portion of the state alone (Massey, Durand, and Malone 2002).

Such a massive legalization not only saturated local labor markets in southern California but also gave these newly legalized Mexican immigrants the political freedom to move elsewhere in search of better job opportunities. Meanwhile, the new system of employer sanctions encouraged employers to shift to labor subcontracting in the hopes of avoiding stiff penalties for hiring undocumented immigrants directly, and the costs that they assumed for hiring new intermediary subcontractors were passed down to workers in the form of lower wages. Finally, the downward pressure on wages caused by IRCA's legalization and employer sanctions strategies occurred against a backdrop of deteriorating economic conditions and growing anti-immigrant sentiment in California during the early 1990s. As the state entered a severe economic recession resulting from cutbacks in the defense industry, unemployment rose, wages stagnated, and public sentiment began to turn against immigrants. In 1994, California voters passed Proposition

187, which sought to bar undocumented immigrants from receiving publicly provided health, education, and welfare services. Although it was declared unconstitutional by the California courts three years later, Proposition 187 sent a strong symbolic message to Mexican immigrants that they were no longer welcome there (Massey and Capoferro 2008; Massey, Durand, and Malone 2002).

Thus, as Durand, Massey, and Capoferro (2005) write, the early 1990s witnessed "an unusual coincidence of conditions in California: an IRCA-induced restructuring of immigrant employment toward subcontracting, declining net wages for immigrants, a severe recession and high unemployment, growing native hostility, and greater wage competition triggered by a flood of newly legalized immigrants entering local labor markets" (12). The expansion of freedom and mobility among newly legalized Mexican immigrants (who were also now eligible to sponsor family members of their own for legal immigration) took place within a larger context of increasing regional economic integration among the United States, Canada, and Mexico following passage of the General Agreement on Tariffs and Trade in 1986 and the North American Free Trade Agreement in 1994 and alongside a deepening economic crisis in Mexico following a huge peso devaluation in December 1994 (Massey, Durand, and Malone 2002). Like other profound economic dislocations associated with the process of economic development in Latin America, which have uprooted various segments of the lower and middle classes and given them greater incentives to migrate northward in search of better wages and socioeconomic stability, the economic crisis in Mexico generated new needs for capital, credit, and security among lower- and middle-class Mexicans in both traditional and new sending states of Mexico, encouraging additional migration northward (Durand, Massey, and Capoferro 2005). Together, these political and economic *push* factors not only encouraged Mexican immigrants already in California in the late 1980s and early 1990s to migrate elsewhere in the country for better job opportunities, but also encouraged new and aspiring Mexican immigrants to avoid California entirely.

Adding fuel to the fire, in the mid-1990s new and aspiring *undocumented* Mexican immigrants were further channeled away from California by the selective militarization of the U.S.–Mexico border, particularly in the forms of Operation Blockade, launched in El Paso, Texas, in September 1993 and Operation Gatekeeper, launched in San Diego, California, in October 1994. These border control efforts were intended to stop the flow of illegal Mexican immigration into the United States at its two most popular points of entry through a strategy called "prevention by deterrence." Yet they had the unanticipated effects of shifting illegal Mexican immigration through new, less densely populated entry points (like the deserts of Arizona and the wilder parts of the lower Río Grande Valley in Texas) and later into new final destination states. They also had the unanticipated effects of transforming a once temporary and circular illegal Mexican migration stream into a more permanently settled one because border militarization raised the costs not only of crossing the border *into* the United States, but also of crossing back out again and thus having to contemplate a difficult repeat entry (Cornelius and Lewis 2007; Durand, Massey, and Capoferro 2005; Massey and Capoferro 2008; Massey, Durand, and Malone 2002).

The end result of these *push* factors, combined with the *pull* factors of increased job growth and labor demand in many southern, midwestern, and mountain nongateway states, was a massive redistribution of Mexican migrants away from traditional border crossing points as well as their five traditional gateway settlement states. This pattern emerges most visibly in U.S. Census data after 1990. Between 1990 and 2000, the percentage of foreign-born Mexican immigrants located in California dropped 10 percentage points, from 58 to 48 percent and continued to decline to an all-time low of 19 percent in Texas. In contrast, the share going to the forty-five nongateway sates more than doubled, reaching the highest percentage in the history of U.S.–Mexico migration (21 percent) in 2000 (Durand, Massey, and Capoferro 2005). Geographic dispersion is even more visible among *recently arrived* Mexican immigrants. Whereas 63 percent of Mexican immigrants who arrived between 1985 and 1990 went to California, only 35 percent of those who arrived between 1995 and 2000 did. In contrast, whereas only 13 percent of Mexican immigrants who arrived between 1985 and 1990 went to nongateway states, 35 percent of those who arrived between 1995 and 2000 did. Therefore, after three decades of declining diversity in Mexican immigrants' destinations between 1960 and 1990, their variety increased dramatically in the 1990s. As Figure 6.1 illustrates, by 2000 new centers of reception had emerged in Florida, Idaho, Nevada, New York/New Jersey, and North Carolina, and others were emerging in Georgia, Iowa, Oregon, and Minnesota (Durand, Massey, and Capoferro 2005).

Massey and Capoferro (2008) show that geographic dispersion is evident among foreign-born immigrant groups other than Mexicans, but not in as concentrated a fashion. The geographic settlement patterns of other Latin American immigrant groups were much more diverse in 1990 to begin with and did not change radically by 2000. Similarly, those of Asian immigrant groups were even more diverse than those of other Latin American immigrants in 1990 and exhibited little change by 2000, whereas those of non-Asian/non-Latino immigrants also exhibited relatively high diversity by 1980 and increased slightly by 2000 before stabilizing thereafter. The geographic settlement patterns of Mexican immigrants, by contrast, had transformed radically from a homogeneous baseline in 1990, when approximately two thirds of recently arrived Mexican immigrants went to California alone. Massey and Capoferro (2008) argue that although these differential patterns of dispersion provide some positive support for the roles of IRCA, Proposition 187 in California, and surging labor demand in nongateway states in shifting all immigrant groups' settlement patterns from gateway to nongateway states, they also signal the crucial role of U.S. border enforcement policies in shifting those of *Mexican immigrants* most markedly.

AN EMPIRICAL OVERVIEW OF HISPANIC AND IMMIGRANT PRESENCE IN THE TRADITIONAL SOUTH

These two trends—the changing economy and demography of the U.S. South and the changing demography of Mexican migration—accelerated and converged into the twenty-first century. Tables 6.1 and 6.2 document the increasing numbers of people of "Hispanic/Latino origin ethnicity" living in traditional southern states from 1980 to 2007, comparing them with figures at the national level and in both "traditional immigrant" and "traditional Mexican immigrant" gateway states. Data come from 5 percent Integrated Public Use Microdata Samples of the 1980, 1990, and 2000 U.S. Censuses and

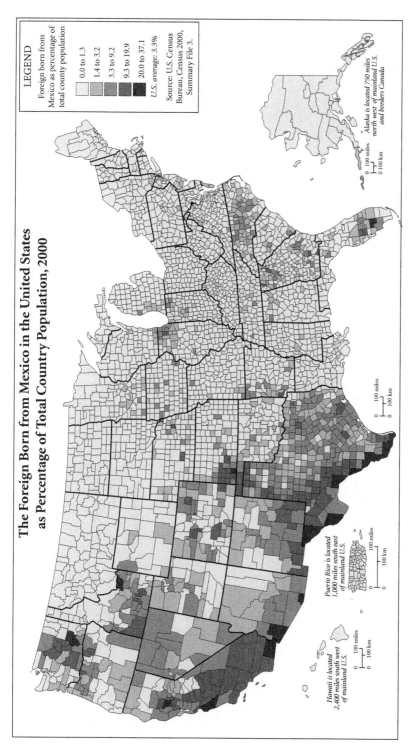

Figure 6.1 Percentage of Population, Foreign-born from Mexico, 2000 U.S. Census.

Source: Originally published on the Migration Policy Institute Data Hub (http://www.migrationinformation.org/DataHub), a project of the Washington, D.C.-based Migration Policy Institute, an independent, nonpartisan, nonprofit think tank dedicated to the study of movement of people worldwide. Reprinted with permission.

The Foreign Born from Mexico in the United States as Percentage of Total Country Population, 2000

LEGEND

Foreign born from Mexico as percentage of total county population

0.0 to 1.3
1.4 to 3.2
3.3 to 9.2
9.3 to 19.9
20.0 to 37.1

U.S. average: 3.3%

Source: U.S. Census Bureau, Census 2000, Summary File 3.

Alaska is located 750 miles north west of mainland U.S. and borders Canada

Puerto Rico is located 1,000 miles south east of mainland U.S.

Hawaii is located 2,400 miles south west of mainland U.S.

Table 6.1. Hispanic Origin Ethnicity Population by U.S. State of Residence, 1980–2007[a], Traditional Immigrant and Mexican Immigrant Gateway States[b]

	1980	1990[c]	2000	2007	CHANGE 1980–1990	CHANGE 1990–2000	CHANGE 2000–2007
ARIZONA	**448,660**	**686,742**	**1,293,036**	**1,739,157**	**53%**	**88%**	**35%**
% Hispanic of state's population	**(16.5)**	**(18.8)**	**(25.2)**	**(29.7)**			
Native born Hispanic origin population	*364,360*	*502,354*	*819,575*	*1,094,039*			
% Native born of state's Hispanics	*(81.2)*	*(73.2)*	*(63.4)*	*(48.8)*			
Mexican origin population	*403,600*	*625,885*	*1,080,251*	*108,376*			
% Mexican origin of state's Hispanics	*(90.0)*	*(91.1)*	*(83.5)*	*(88.5)*			
NEW MEXICO	**480,980**	**572,655**	**761,252**	**832,817**	**19%**	**33%**	**9%**
% Hispanic of state's population	**(36.7)**	**(38.0)**	**(44.7)**	**(44.9)**			
Native born Hispanic origin population	*451,000*	*512,955*	*643,387*	*691,900*			
% Native born of state's Hispanics	*(93.8)*	*(89.6)*	*(84.5)*	*(83.1)*			
Mexican origin population	*231,480*	*330,612*	*340,258*	*431,084*			
% Mexican origin of state's Hispanics	*(48.1)*	*(57.7)*	*(41.8)*	*(51.8)*			
CALIFORNIA	**4,575,860**	**7,563,270**	**10,904,256**	**12,383,283**	**65%**	**44%**	**14%**
% Hispanic of state's population	**(19.3)**	**(25.5)**	**(32.3)**	**(35.9)**			
Native-born Hispanic origin population	*2,871,300*	*4,095,784*	*6,075,101*	*7,258,340*			
% Native born of state's Hispanics	*(62.7)*	*(54.2)*	*(55.7)*	*(58.6)*			
Mexican origin population	*3,633,000*	*6,074,368*	*8,541,966*	*10,293,693*			
% Mexican origin of state's Hispanics	*(79.4)*	*(80.3)*	*(78.3)*	*(83.1)*			

ILLINOIS	648,440	882,240	1,518,401	1,870,074	36%	72%	23%
% Hispanic of state's population	(5.7)	(7.7)	(12.2)	(14.9)			
Native-born Hispanic origin population	404,480	511,374	810,535	1,083,128			
% Native born of state's Hispanics	(62.4)	(58.0)	(53.4)	(57.9)			
Mexican origin population	413,900	616,995	1,144,681	1,464,711			
% Mexican origin of state's Hispanics	(63.8)	(69.9)	(75.4)	(78.3)			
TEXAS	3,015,100	4,304,325	6,637,415	8,223,008	43%	54%	24%
% Hispanic of state's population	(21.1)	(25.4)	(31.9)	(36.3)			
Native-born Hispanic origin population	2,419,060	3,159,077	4,479,755	5,506,326			
% Native born of state's Hispanics	(80.2)	(73.4)	(67.5)	(67.0)			
Mexican origin population	2,777,680	3,912,159	5,148,230	6,993,057			
% Mexican origin of state's Hispanics	(92.1)	(90.9)	(77.6)	(85.0)			
FLORIDA	871,640	1,557,635	2,658,878	3,630,578	79%	71%	37%
% Hispanic of state's population	(8.9)	(12.1)	(16.7)	(20.9)			
Native-born Hispanic origin population	341,680	618,401	1,169,727	1,730,796			
% Native born of state's Hispanics	(39.2)	(39.7)	(44.0)	(47.7)			
Mexican origin population	77,140	157,484	362,099	576,880			
% Mexican origin of state's Hispanics	(8.8)	(10.1)	(13.6)	(15.9)			

(Continued)

135

Table 6.1. Hispanic Origin Ethnicity Population by U.S. State of Residence, 1980–2007[a], Traditional Immigrant and Mexican Immigrant Gateway States[b] (Continued)

	1980	1990[c]	2000	2007	CHANGE 1980–1990	CHANGE 1990–2000	CHANGE 2000–2007
NEW YORK	1,688,180	2,155,499	2,835,875	2,956,552	28%	32%	4%
% Hispanic of state's population	(9.6)	(12.0)	(15.0)	(16.0)			
Native-born Hispanic origin population	1,218,240	1,380,027	1,685,544	1,760,263			
% Native born of state's Hispanics	(72.2)	(64.0)	(59.4)	(59.5)			
Mexican origin population	40,820	89,291	257,301	369,339			
% Mexican origin of state's Hispanics	(2.4)	(4.1)	(9.1)	(12.5)			
UNITED STATES	14,775,080	21,938,225	35,084,271	43,355,316	48%	60%	24%
% Hispanic of country's population	(6.5)	(8.8)	(12.5)	(14.9)			
Native-born Hispanic origin population	10,483,980	13,809,367	20,802,366	26,089,346			
% Native born of country's Hispanics	(71.0)	(62.9)	(59.3)	(60.2)			
Mexican origin population	8,771,800	13,440,061	20,829,881	27,856,034			
% Mexican origin of country's Hispanics	(59.4)	(61.3)	(59.4)	(64.3)			

SOURCES: Five percent Integrated Public Use Microdata Samples (IPUMS) of the 1980–2000 U.S. Decennial Censuses and 2007 American Community Survey (Ruggles et al. 2004), author's analyses, household weighted data.

[a]Hispanic origin is defined as anyone declaring some Hispanic-origin ethnicity as defined by the U.S. Census, regardless of place of birth (i.e., Hispanic, Latino, Spanish, Mexican, Mexican American, Chicano, Puerto Rican, Cuban, Central American, South American, etc.). Mexican origin is defined as anyone declaring some Mexican-origin ethnicity, regardless of place of birth (i.e., Mexican, Mexican American, Chicano, etc.). Native-born is defined as anyone born inside U.S. territory or U.S. possessions or abroad or at sea with U.S. citizenship.

[b]The "big five" traditional total immigrant gateway states are California, New York, Texas, Florida, and Illinois (Massey and Capoferro 2008). The "big five" traditional Mexican immigrant gateway states are Arizona, California, Illinois, New Mexico, and Texas (Durand, Massey, and Capoferro 2005).

[c]Percentages of Mexicans among total foreign-born populations in 1990 may appear small because of large numbers of foreign-born respondents recorded as being "Abroad, not specified" in that year (compared with in 2000–2007 data).

136

Table 6.2. Hispanic Origin Ethnicity Population by U.S. State of Residence, 1980–2007[a], Traditional Southern States[b]

	1980	1990[c]	2000	2007	CHANGE 1980–1990	CHANGE 1990–2000	CHANGE 2000–2007
ALABAMA	34,940	22,336	71,340	121,538	-36%	219%	70%
% Hispanic of state's population	**(0.9)**	**(0.6)**	**(1.6)**	**(2.7)**			
Native-born Hispanic origin population	*31,360*	*17,603*	*39,164*	*58,831*			
% Native born of state's Hispanics	*(89.8)*	*(78.8)*	*(59.4)*	*(48.4)*			
Mexican origin population	*20,100*	*8,534*	*40,926*	*84,459*			
% Mexican origin of state's Hispanics	*(57.5)*	*(38.2)*	*(57.4)*	*(69.5)*			
ARKANSAS	17,120	20,885	84,081	143,652	22%	303%	71%
% Hispanic of state's population	**(0.7)**	**(0.9)**	**(3.2)**	**(5.2)**			
Native-born Hispanic origin population	*15,180*	*15,206*	*44,363*	*68,886*			
% Native born of state's Hispanics	*(88.7)*	*(72.8)*	*(52.8)*	*(48.0)*			
Mexican origin population	*10,620*	*13,119*	*58,838*	*108,376*			
% Mexican origin of state's Hispanics	*(62.0)*	*(62.8)*	*(70.0)*	*(75.4)*			
GEORGIA	62,860	99,059	431,008	665,891	58%	335%	54%
% Hispanic of state's population	**(1.2)**	**(1.5)**	**(5.3)**	**(7.4)**			
Native-born Hispanic origin population	*50,020*	*56,050*	*166,185*	*295,950*			
% Native born of state's Hispanics	*(79.6)*	*(56.6)*	*(38.6)*	*(44.4)*			
Mexican origin population	*27,620*	*45,477*	*274,472*	*414,327*			
% Mexican origin of state's Hispanics	*(43.9)*	*(45.9)*	*(63.7)*	*(62.2)*			

(Continued)

137

Table 6.2. Hispanic Origin Ethnicity Population by U.S. State of Residence, 1980–2007[a], Traditional Southern States[b]   *(Continued)*

	1980	1990[c]	2000	2007	CHANGE 1980–1990	CHANGE 1990–2000	CHANGE 2000–2007
LOUISIANA	102,020	90,303	111,488	129,005	-11%	23%	16%
% Hispanic of state's population	**(2.4)**	**(2.2)**	**(2.5)**	**(3.1)**			
Native-born Hispanic origin population	*78,080*	*57,204*	*68,679*	*67,271*			
% Native born of state's Hispanics	*(76.5)*	*(63.3)*	*(61.6)*	*(52.1)*			
Mexican origin population	*26,500*	*22,920*	*34,586*	*43,155*			
% Mexican origin of state's Hispanics	*(25.4)*	*(25.4)*	*(31.0)*	*(35.3)*			
MISSISSIPPI	23,500	15,801	36,718	50,141	-33%	132%	37%
% Hispanic of state's population	**(0.9)**	**(0.6)**	**(1.3)**	**(1.8)**			
Native-born Hispanic origin population	*21,060*	*12,684*	*23,504*	*24,814*			
% Native born of state's Hispanics	*(89.6)*	*(80.3)*	*(64.0)*	*(49.5)*			
Mexican origin population	*13,860*	*7,455*	*20,108*	*35,016*			
% Mexican origin of state's Hispanics	*(59.0)*	*(47.2)*	*(54.8)*	*(69.8)*			
NORTH CAROLINA	58,220	67,128	374,316	648,245	15%	458%	73%
% Hispanic of state's population	**(1.0)**	**(1.0)**	**(4.7)**	**(7.3)**			
Native-born Hispanic origin population	*49,160*	*45,435*	*145,441*	*285,453*			
% Native born of state's Hispanics	*(84.4)*	*(67.7)*	*(38.9)*	*(44.4)*			
Mexican origin population	*28,320*	*29,016*	*239,222*	*425,334*			
% Mexican origin of state's Hispanics	*(48.6)*	*(43.2)*	*(63.9)*	*(65.6)*			
SOUTH CAROLINA	33,960	27,114	91,210	172,910	-20%	236%	90%
% Hispanic of state's population	**(1.1)**	**(0.8)**	**(2.3)**	**(4.1)**			
Native-born Hispanic origin population	*4,000*	*19,761*	*45,207*	*79,005*			
% Native born of state's Hispanics	*(86.2)*	*(72.9)*	*(49.6)*	*(45.7)*			
Mexican origin population	*2,680*	*8,895*	*50,697*	*108,201*			
% Mexican origin of state's Hispanics	*(56.0)*	*(32.8)*	*(55.6)*	*(62.6)*			

TENNESSEE	34,980	31,275	115,577	189,583	-11%	270%	64%
% Hispanic of state's population	**(0.8)**	**(0.6)**	**(2.0)**	**(3.2)**			
Native-born Hispanic origin population	*30,940*	*24,441*	*57,352*	*85,499*			
% Native born of state's Hispanics	*(88.5)*	*(78.1)*	*(49.6)*	*(45.1)*			
Mexican origin population	*19,760*	*13,860*	*73,532*	*124,125*			
% Mexican origin of state's Hispanics	*(56.5)*	*(44.3)*	*(63.6)*	*(65.5)*			
VIRGINIA	82,280	154,401	332,772	466,295	88%	116%	40%
% Hispanic of state's population	**(1.5)**	**(2.5)**	**(4.7)**	**(6.2)**			
Native-born Hispanic origin population	*54,620*	*75,738*	*155,212*	*226,075*			
% Native born of state's Hispanics	*(66.4)*	*(49.1)*	*(46.6)*	*(48.5)*			
Mexican origin population	*23,900*	*32,589*	*77,766*	*121,122*			
% Mexican origin of state's Hispanics	*(29.0)*	*(21.1)*	*(23.4)*	*(26.0)*			
UNITED STATES	14,775,080	21,938,225	35,084,271	43,355,316	48%	60%	24%
% Hispanic of country's population	**(6.5)**	**(8.8)**	**(12.5)**	**(14.9)**			
Native-born Hispanic origin population	*10,483,980*	*13,809,367*	*20,802,366*	*26,089,346*			
% Native born of country's Hispanics	*(71.0)*	*(62.9)*	*(59.3)*	*(60.2)*			
Mexican origin population	*8,771,800*	*13,440,061*	*20,829,881*	*27,856,034*			
% Mexican origin of country's Hispanics	*(59.4)*	*(61.3)*	*(59.4)*	*(64.3)*			

SOURCE: Five percent Integrated Public Use Microdata Samples (IPUMS) of the 1980–2000 U.S. Decennial Censuses and 2007 American Community Survey (Ruggles et al. 2004), author's analyses, household weighted data.

[a]Hispanic origin is defined as anyone declaring some Hispanic-origin ethnicity as defined by the U.S. Census, regardless of place of birth (i.e., Hispanic, Latino, Spanish, Mexican, Mexican American, Chicano, Puerto Rican, Cuban, Central American, South American, etc.). Mexican origin is defined as anyone declaring some Mexican-origin ethnicity, regardless of place of birth (i.e., Mexican, Mexican American, Chicano, etc.). Native-born is defined as anyone born inside U.S. territory or U.S. possessions or abroad or at sea with U.S. citizenship.

[b]Traditional southern states are defined as the eleven former confederate states minus Florida and Texas.

[c]Percentages of Mexicans among total foreign-born populations in 1990 may appear small because of large numbers of foreign-born respondents recorded as being "Abroad, not specified" in that year (compared with 2000–2007 data).

the 2007 American Community Survey and capture representative population trends within a 5 percent margin of error (Ruggles et al. 2004). Hispanics/Latinos include all persons declaring some Hispanic origin ethnicity as defined by the U.S. Census (i.e., Hispanic, Latino, Spanish, Mexican, Mexican American, Chicano, Puerto Rican, Cuban, Central American, South American, etc.), regardless of whether they are native born or foreign born.

Table 6.1 shows that Texas and Florida—the South's two contemporary immigrant "access" states (Bankston 2007)—have long had a much larger population of Hispanics/Latinos than any of the nine traditional southern states. Texas' Hispanic population increased from 3,015,100 in 1980 to 8,223,008 in 2007, whereas Florida's increased from 871,640 in 1980 to 3,630,578 in 2007. In contrast, Table 6.2 shows that the nine traditional southern states started out with much smaller Hispanic populations in 1980, ranging from just 17,120 in Arkansas and 23,500 in Mississippi to 82,280 in Virginia and a peak of 102,020 in Louisiana. Despite these lower absolute numbers of Hispanics/Latinos, their relative proportions began to grow slowly in selected traditional southern states during the 1980s, surged during the 1990s, and then continued growing at above-average rates into the mid-2000s.

For instance, the Hispanic populations of Virginia, Georgia, Arkansas, and North Carolina—which Bankston (2007) refers to as new southern economic "opportunity" states—posted positive Hispanic growth rates as early as the 1980s (at 88, 58, 22, and 15 percent, respectively). In some cases these growth rates even rivaled those in traditional immigrant and traditional Mexican immigrant gateway states during the 1980s. By contrast, the Hispanic populations of Alabama, Mississippi, South Carolina, Louisiana, and Tennessee—which Bankston (2007) refers to as southern "limited migration" states—declined during the 1980s (by 36, 33, 20, 11, and 11 percent, respectively). These declining rates reflect the relative lack of economic industrialization and globalization in the lower South compared with the upper South during this decade, particularly in the three "Deep South Triad" states of Alabama, Mississippi, and Louisiana, which constitute one of the nation's oldest peripheral regions, with stagnant economies and slow-growing metropolitan areas (Elliott and Ionescu 2003). In 1980, the large majority of Hispanics in all of these traditional southern states were native born, ranging from a low of 66.4 percent in Virginia to a high of 89.8 percent in Alabama. Roughly half also reported some kind of Mexican-origin ethnicity (such as Mexican, Mexican American, or Chicano), with notable exceptions in Louisiana and Virginia, where Hispanics were more likely to report Central or South American origin ethnicities instead.

Over the 1990s, however, Hispanic population growth rates in the traditional southern states surged. They surpassed the national average rate of 60 percent, as well as rates in traditional immigrant and traditional Mexican immigrant gateway states (which ranged from a low of 32 percent in New York to a high of 88 percent in Arizona) by very large margins. The upper South opportunity states continued to lead the way. During the 1990s, North Carolina's Hispanic population grew by 458 percent, Georgia's by 335 percent, and Arkansas' by 303 percent (Virginia's slowed down in relative comparison, to 116 percent). But in this decade, compared with the 1980s, southern opportunity states were also joined by another upper South state (Tennessee) and several lower South previously "limited migration" states (South Carolina, Alabama, and Mississippi) that were beginning to undergo more rapid economic development. The three Deep South Triad states continued to post the lowest absolute numbers of Hispanics in 2000, as well as the lowest relative Hispanic growth rates over the 1990s. Nonetheless, in this decade only Louisiana posted a Hispanic growth rate (23 percent) below the national average or below that in traditional immigrant and traditional Mexican immigrant gateway states.

Thus, the 1990s were truly remarkable in the U.S. South. The proportions of Hispanics among southern states' total populations rose notably in the course of these ten years, for example, from 1.2 to 5.3 percent in Georgia, 1.0 to 4.7 percent in North Carolina, and 0.9 to 3.2 percent in Arkansas. *Native-born* Hispanics contributed significantly to these rising numbers, signaling that population growth in the 1990s was spurred in part by the internal migration of Hispanics born in other U.S. states, as well as by some "natural increase" of Hispanics born in these southern states themselves. For example, Alabama's native-born Hispanic population rose from 17,603 in 1990 to 39,164 in 2000; likewise, Georgia's rose from 56,050 to 166,185, Louisiana's from 57,204, to 68,679, North Carolina's from 45,435 to 145,441, Tennessee's from 24,441 to 57,352, and Virginia's from 75,738 to 155,212.

Nonetheless, the proportions of native-born to foreign-born Hispanics in traditional southern states actually *decreased* during the 1990s, signaling that a significant proportion of Hispanic population growth during this decade was fueled by *foreign-born Hispanic immigrants* (Saenz et al. 2003; Vásquez, Seales, and Marquardt 2008). To illustrate, whereas Georgia's native-born Hispanic population rose from 56,050 in 1990 to 166,185 in 2000 (for a total addition of 110,135 native-born Hispanics), its foreign-born Hispanic population rose from 43,009 in 1990 to 264,823 in 2000 (for a total addition of 221,814 foreign-born Hispanics), reducing the percentage of native-born Hispanics among Georgia's total Hispanic population from 56.6 percent in 1990 to 38.6 percent in 2000. Across the traditional southern states, a similar trend emerged in the 1990s: the number of native-born and foreign-born Hispanics grew rapidly, although the number of foreign-born Hispanics grew most rapidly. By 2000, the Hispanic populations of traditional southern states, although still smaller in absolute numbers than those in traditional immigrant and traditional Mexican immigrant gateway states (see Table 6.1), had grown extremely rapidly, had become more heavily populated by foreign-born Hispanic immigrants as opposed to native-born Hispanics, and had become more heavily Mexican in ethnic origin (see Table 6.2).

Between 2000 and 2007, the Hispanic populations of traditional southern states continued to increase, although their growth rates tapered in comparison to the high levels posted during the 1990s. During the first seven years of this decade, most traditional southern states registered Hispanic growth rates between 50 and 90 percent, although Virginia's grew only by 40 percent and Mississippi's by only 37 percent. Only Louisiana posted a Hispanic growth rate (16 percent) below the national average rate of 24 percent or below rates in traditional immigrant and traditional Mexican immigrant gateway states (which ranged from a low of 4 percent in New York to a high of 37 percent in Florida). Also, the declines in the proportions of native-born to foreign-born Hispanics witnessed in traditional southern states between 1980 and 2000 began to stabilize and in some cases even reverse between 2000 and 2007 (with the exceptions of Mississippi and Louisiana). This signals that the Hispanic populations in many of these states had begun to mature by the mid-2000s, likely through some relative decrease in foreign-born immigration as well as through the additional natural increase of Hispanics born in these states themselves. By 2007, most traditional southern states' Hispanic populations had also become more heavily Mexican in ethnic origin as well, continuing a trend in effect since 1980, which is also evident in data on the foreign-born immigrant population, to which I now turn.

Tables 6.3 and 6.4 document the increasing numbers of foreign-born immigrants living in traditional southern states from 1980 to 2007, comparing them with figures at the national level and in both traditional immigrant and traditional Mexican immigrant gateway states. Foreign-born immigrants include all persons born outside U.S. territory or U.S. possessions or abroad or at sea without U.S. citizenship. Table 6.3 shows that, again, Texas and Florida, the South's two contemporary immigrant "access" states, have long had much larger population of foreign-born immigrants than any of the nine traditional southern states. Texas' foreign-born population increased from 956,660 in 1980 to 3,819,090 in 2007, whereas Florida's increased from 1,117,980 in 1980 to 3,436,074 in 2007. In contrast, Table 6.4 shows that the nine traditional southern states started out with much smaller foreign-born populations in 1980, ranging from just 29,080 in Arkansas and 30,520 in Mississippi to 118,280 in Georgia and a peak of 222,700 in Virginia. Despite these lower absolute numbers of foreign-born immigrants, their relative proportions began to grow in most of the traditional southern states during the 1980s, increased even faster during the 1990s, and then continued to grow at above-average rates into the mid-2000s. In each of these decades, the growth of Mexican immigrants outpaced that of other nonMexican immigrants, often by large margins.

For instance, all of the traditional southern states witnessed some foreign-born population growth during the 1980s. As we saw in data on the Hispanic/Latino population, the new southern economic "opportunity" states of Georgia, Virginia, and North Carolina led the way in foreign-born population growth, although here they were joined by Louisiana (whose foreign-born population expanded by 94 percent) instead of Arkansas, and the southern "limited migration" states of Alabama, South Carolina, and Tennessee followed suit with slower foreign-born growth rates (Mississippi registered zero foreign-born growth during the 1980s). In most states the foreign-born Mexican population rose much faster than the total foreign-born population, surpassing the national average foreign-born growth rate of 43 percent as well as foreign-born rates in traditional Mexican immigrant gateway states (which ranged from 18 percent in Illinois to 80 percent in California). For example, the Mexican foreign-born population grew by an astounding 1,130 percent in Georgia, 926 percent in North Carolina, 410 percent in Virginia, 300 percent in Arkansas, 298 percent in South Carolina, and 227 percent in Alabama. Nonetheless, in 1990 Mexicans still comprised relatively small proportions of traditional southern states' total foreign-born populations; whereas Mexicans constituted 20.6 percent of all immigrants in the United States in 1990 and upward of 28 percent of those in traditional Mexican immigrant gateway states, they constituted just 1.8 to 9.4 percent of immigrants in the traditional South.

Over the 1990s, similar to what we saw in data on the Hispanic/Latino population, foreign-born population growth rates in traditional southern states increased notably. They surpassed the national average foreign-born growth rate of 52 percent and often also rates in traditional immigrant and traditional Mexican immigrant gateway

Table 6.3. Foreign-born Population by U.S. State of Residence, 1980–2007[a], Traditional Immigrant and Mexican Immigrant Gateway States[b]

	1980	1990[c]	2000	2007	CHANGE 1980–1990	CHANGE 1980–1990	CHANGE 1990–2000
ARIZONA	186,940	320,259	705,419	950,365	71%	120%	35%
% Foreign-born of state's population	**(6.9)**	**(8.8)**	**(13.8)**	**(16.2)**			
Foreign-born Mexican population	*74,420*	*163,271*	*444,369*	*597,390.00*	*119%*	*172%*	*34%*
% Mexican of state's foreign-born population	*(39.8)*	*(51.0)*	*(63.0)*	*(62.9)*			
NEW MEXICO	60,380	95,838	166,203	192,771	59%	73%	16%
% Foreign-born of state's population	**(4.6)**	**(6.4)**	**(9.1)**	**(10.4)**			
Foreign-born Mexican population	*23,800*	*52,452*	*108,791*	*132,357*	*120%*	*107%*	*22%*
% Mexican of state's foreign-born population	*(39.4)*	*(54.7)*	*(65.5)*	*(68.7)*			
CALIFORNIA	3,746,880	6,752,123	9,100,384	9,579,063	80%	35%	5%
% Foreign-born of state's population	**(15.8)**	**(22.8)**	**(26.9)**	**(27.8)**			
Foreign-born Mexican population	*1,283,900*	*2,514,639*	*3,926,474*	*4,157,559*	*96%*	*56%*	*6%*
% Mexican of state's foreign-born population	*(34.3)*	*(37.2)*	*(43.1)*	*(43.4)*			
ILLINOIS	857,440	1,008,957	1,582,803	1,746,947	18%	57%	10%
% Foreign-born of state's population	**(7.5)**	**(8.9)**	**(12.8)**	**(14.0)**			
Foreign-born Mexican population	*174,180*	*288,507*	*616,455*	*675,298*	*66%*	*114%*	*10%*
% Mexican of state's foreign-born population	*(20.3)*	*(28.6)*	*(38.9)*	*(38.7)*			
TEXAS	956,660	1,703,381	3,059,835	3,819,090	78%	80%	25%
% Foreign-born of state's population	**(6.7)**	**(10.1)**	**(14.7)**	**(16.9)**			
Foreign-born Mexican population	*516,260*	*961,727*	*1,900,132*	*2,343,626*	*86%*	*98%*	*23%*
% Mexican of state's foreign-born population	*(54.0)*	*(56.5)*	*(62.1)*	*(61.4)*			

(Continued)

143

Table 6.3. Foreign-born Population by U.S. State of Residence, 1980–2007[a], Traditional Immigrant and Mexican Immigrant Gateway States[b] (Continued)

	1980	1990[c]	2000	2007	CHANGE 1980–1990	CHANGE 1990–2000	CHANGE 2000–2007
FLORIDA	1,117,980	1,776,468	2,785,053	3,436,074	59%	57%	23%
% Foreign-born of state's population	**(11.4)**	**(13.8)**	**(17.5)**	**(19.8)**			
Foreign-born Mexican population	*14,220*	*58,406*	*192,935*	*312,460*	*311%*	*230%*	*62%*
% Mexican of state's foreign-born population	*(1.3)*	*(3.3)*	*(6.9)*	*(9.1)*			
NEW YORK	2,457,440	2,993,123	3,957,066	4,037,575	22%	32%	2%
% Foreign-born of state's population	**(14.0)**	**(16.7)**	**(20.9)**	**(21.8)**			
Foreign-born Mexican population	*11,060*	*48,711*	*165,089*	*211,392*	*340%*	*239%*	*28%*
% Mexican of state's foreign-born population	*(0.5)*	*(1.6)*	*(4.2)*	*(5.2)*			
UNITED STATES	15,142,700	21,586,277	32,866,997	38,044,370	43%	52%	16%
% Foreign-born of country's Population	**(6.7)**	**(8.7)**	**(11.7)**	**(13.1)**			
Foreign-born Mexican population	*2,242,100*	*4,447,867*	*9,247,556*	*11,200,178*	*98%*	*108%*	*21%*
% Mexican of country's foreign-born population	*(14.8)*	*(20.6)*	*(28.1)*	*(29.4)*			

SOURCES: Five percent Integrated Public Use Microdata Samples (IPUMS) of the 1980–2000 U.S. Decennial Censuses and 2007 American Community Survey (Ruggles et al. 2004), author's analyses, household weighted data.

[a]Foreign-born is defined as anyone born outside U.S. territory or U.S. possessions or abroad or at sea without U.S. citizenship. Mexican-born is defined as anyone declaring place of birth in Mexico.

[b]The "big five" traditional total immigrant gateway states are California, New York, Texas, Florida, and Illinois (Massey and Capoferro 2008). The "big five" traditional Mexican immigrant gateway states are Arizona, California, Illinois, New Mexico, and Texas (Durand, Massey, and Capoferro 2005).

[c]Percentages of Mexicans among total foreign-born populations in 1990 may appear small because of large numbers of foreign-born respondents recorded as being "Abroad, not specified" in that year (compared with 2000–2007 data).

Table 6.4. Foreign-born Population by U.S. State of Residence, 1980–2007[a], Traditional Southern States[b]

	1980	1990[c]	2000	2007	CHANGE 1980–1990	CHANGE 1990–2000	CHANGE 2000–2007
ALABAMA	53,580	64,101	115,432	161,381	20%	80%	40%
% Foreign-born of state's population	**(1.4)**	**(1.6)**	**(2.6)**	**(3.6)**			
Foreign-born Mexican population	*360*	*1,176*	*23,285*	*48,921*	*227%*	*1880%*	*110%*
% Mexican of state's foreign-born population	*(0.7)*	*(1.8)*	*(20.2)*	*(30.3)*			
ARKANSAS	29,080	35,629	85,250	126,963	23%	139%	49%
% Foreign-born of state's population	**(1.3)**	**(1.5)**	**(3.2)**	**(4.6)**			
Foreign-born Mexican population	*840*	*3,356*	*31,918*	*58,212*	*300%*	*851%*	*82%*
% Mexican of state's foreign-born population	*(2.9)*	*(9.4)*	*(37.4)*	*(45.8)*			
GEORGIA	118,280	223,663	641,761	864,947	89%	187%	35%
% Foreign-born of state's population	**(2.2)**	**(3.5)**	**(7.9)**	**(9.7)**			
Foreign-born Mexican population	*1,640*	*20,177*	*194,778*	*243,971*	*1130%*	*865%*	*25%*
% Mexican of state's foreign-born population	*(1.4)*	*(9.0)*	*(30.4)*	*(28.2)*			
LOUISIANA	54,240	105,228	138,320	154,985	94%	31%	12%
% Foreign-born of state's population	**(1.9)**	**(2.5)**	**(3.1)**	**(3.8)**			
Foreign-born Mexican population	*3,200*	*3,888*	*10,577*	*13,561*	*22%*	*172%*	*28%*
% Mexican of state's foreign-born population	*(5.9)*	*(3.7)*	*(7.6)*	*(8.7)*			

(Continued)

Table 6.4. Foreign-born Population by U.S. State of Residence, 1980–2007[a], Traditional Southern States[b] (Continued)

	1980	1990[c]	2000	2007	CHANGE 1980–1990	CHANGE 1990–2000	CHANGE 2000–2007
MISSISSIPPI	30,520	30,585	49,586	61,674	0%	62%	24%
% Foreign-born of state's population	**(1.2)**	**(1.2)**	**(1.7)**	**(2.2)**			
Foreign-born Mexican population	*560*	*855*	*8,984*	*19,278*	53%	951%	115%
% Mexican of state's foreign-born population	*(1.8)*	*(2.8)*	*(18.1)*	*(31.3)*			
NORTH CAROLINA	99,380	156,288	482,215	698,039	57%	209%	45%
% Foreign-born of state's population	**(1.7)**	**(2.4)**	**(6.0)**	**(7.9)**			
Foreign-born Mexican population	*980*	*10,056*	*169,543*	*259,347*	926%	1586%	53%
% Mexican of state's foreign-born population	*(1.0)*	*(6.4)*	*(35.2)*	*(37.2)*			
SOUTH CAROLINA	61,620	71,457	142,963	222,209	16%	100%	55%
% Foreign-born of state's population	**(2.0)**	**(2.1)**	**(3.6)**	**(5.3)**			
Foreign-born Mexican population	*460*	*1,833*	*31,108*	*64,221*	298%	1597%	106%
% Mexican of state's foreign-born population	*(0.7)*	*(2.6)*	*(21.8)*	*(28.9)*			
TENNESSEE	64,200	79,890	189,617	274,505	24%	137%	45%
% Foreign-born of state's population	**(1.4)**	**(1.6)**	**(3.3)**	**(4.6)**			
Foreign-born Mexican population	*940*	*2,382*	*43,513*	*72,016*	153%	1727%	66%
% Mexican of state's foreign-born population	*(1.5)*	*(3.0)*	*(22.9)*	*(26.2)*			

VIRGINIA	222,700	385,023	650,385	827,101	73%	69%	27%
% Foreign-born of state's population	**(4.2)**	**(6.2)**	**(9.2)**	**(11.0)**			
Foreign-born Mexican population	*1,860*	*9,489*	*36,422*	*57,398*	*410%*	*284%*	*58%*
% Mexican of state's foreign-born population	*(0.8)*	*(2.5)*	*(5.6)*	*(6.9)*			
UNITED STATES	15,142,700	21,586,277	32,866,997	38,044,370	43%	52%	16%
% Foreign-born of country's population	**(6.7)**	**(8.7)**	**(11.7)**	**(13.1)**			
Foreign-born Mexican population	*2,242,100*	*4,447,867*	*9,247,556*	*11,200,178*	*98%*	*108%*	*21%*
% Mexican of country's foreign-born population	*(14.8)*	*(20.6)*	*(28.1)*	*(29.4)*			

SOURCES: Five percent Integrated Public Use Microdata Samples (IPUMS) of the 1980–2000 U.S. Decennial Censuses and 2007 American Community Survey (Ruggles et al. 2004), author's analyses, household weighted data.

[a] Foreign-born is defined as anyone born outside U.S. territory or U.S. possessions or abroad or at sea without U.S. citizenship. Mexican-born is defined as anyone declaring place of birth in Mexico.

[b] Traditional southern states are defined as the eleven former confederate states minus Florida and Texas.

[c] Percentages of Mexicans among total foreign-born populations in 1990 may appear small because of large numbers of foreign-born respondents recorded as being "Abroad, not specified" in that year (compared with 2000–2007 data).

states (which ranged from a low of 32 percent in New York to a high of 120 percent in Arizona). The upper South "opportunity" states continued to lead the way. During the 1990s, North Carolina's foreign-born population grew by 209 percent, Georgia's by 187 percent, and Arkansas' by 139 percent (Virginia's and Louisiana's slowed down in relative comparison, to 69 and 31 percent), and were further joined by several lower South previously "limited migration" states (Tennessee at 137 percent, South Carolina at 100 percent, and Alabama at 80 percent). Again, the three Deep South Triad states continued to post some of the lowest absolute numbers of foreign-born immigrants in 2000, as well as the lowest relative foreign-born growth rates over the 1990s of all southern states, yet their growth rates still exceeded many of those in traditional immigrant and traditional Mexican immigrant gateway states during this decade.

Even more importantly, the *Mexican* foreign-born populations of these traditional southern states jumped dramatically during the 1990s, far surpassing the average Mexican foreign-born national average rate of 108 percent as well as Mexican foreign-born rates in traditional Mexican immigrant gateway states (which ranged from 56 percent in California to 172 percent in Arizona). And not only did Mexican foreign-born growth rates rise in several of the upper South "opportunity" states (to 1,586 percent in North Carolina, 865 percent in Georgia, and 851 percent in Arkansas), they rose even more impressively in many of the lower South previously "limited migration" states (to 1,880 percent in Alabama, 1,727 percent in Tennessee, 1,597 percent in South Carolina, and 951 percent in Mississippi). Even Louisiana, the low-growth outlier among traditional southern states, witnessed a 172 percent increase in its Mexican foreign-born population during the 1990s, equal to the highest rate of increase in a traditional Mexican immigrant gateway state.

Thus, whereas in 2000 the foreign-born populations of traditional southern states remained much smaller in absolute numbers than those in traditional immigrant and traditional Mexican immigrant gateway states (see Table 6.3), they had grown much more rapidly since 1980, and their Mexican foreign-born populations had increased particularly dramatically. Overall, the proportions of foreign-born immigrants among southern states' total populations had risen notably in the course of these ten years, for example, from 6.2 to 9.2 percent in Virginia, 3.5 to 7.9 percent in Georgia, 2.4 to 6.0 percent in North Carolina, 2.1 to 3.6 percent in South Carolina, and 1.6 to 3.3 percent in Tennessee. And whereas Mexicans constituted just 0.7 to 5.9 percent of all foreign-born immigrants in the traditional South in 1980 and only 1.8 to 9.4 percent in 1990, by 2000 they constituted a full one to two fifths of all foreign-born immigrants in many traditional southern states! Consistent with the literature documenting the significant geographic dispersion of immigrants, particularly *Mexican* ones, after IRCA was implemented in 1986 and selective border militarization began in 1993, foreign-born Mexican immigration into the traditional South picked up substantially in the late 1980s and reached full force in the 1990s.

Between 2000 and 2007, the foreign-born populations of traditional southern states continued to increase, although again at tapered rates compared with the high levels posted during the 1990s. During the first seven years of this decade, most traditional southern states registered foreign-born growth rates between 25 and 55 percent and foreign-born Mexican growth rates between 55 and 115 percent (again, only Louisiana posted a foreign-born growth rate below the national average of 16 percent). By 2007, the percentage of Mexicans among southern states' total foreign-born populations had continued to increase, reaching an impressive one third to one half of all foreign-born immigrants in every state except Virginia and Louisiana.

Various case studies in the traditional South confirm the significance of the 1990s to Hispanic population growth, particularly that driven by foreign-born Mexican immigrants. In Dalton, Georgia, for example, Hernández-León and Zúñiga (2000) find that although some "trailblazing" Mexican pioneer migrants did arrive during the pre-IRCA era, the majority arrived after 1992. Furthermore, although many of these Mexican migrants were "secondary migrants" who had first come from Mexico to a traditional immigrant-receiving state (such as California, Texas, Florida, and Illinois), those who were more recently arrived were also more likely to be direct migrants from Mexico. Hernández-León and Zúñiga (2000) argue that these patterns highlight the importance of IRCA in shifting many Mexican immigrants' settlement preferences away from traditional destination states into new southern ones. Before 1986, Mexican migrants in Dalton, Georgia, had clearly preferred California and Texas as gateway states, whereas increasingly after 1987, Georgia had become the single most important destination for migrants undertaking their initial move to the United States. This pattern fits with an overall picture of Mexican migration into the South that was led by the arrival of native-born Mexican Americans and foreign-born Mexican secondary migrants coming from traditional gateway states in the late 1980s and early 1990s, gradually shifting to include more direct migrants from Mexico by the late 1990s and early 2000s, as migration streams matured (Leach 2004; see also Bump, Lowell, and Pettersen 2005; Donato et al. 2008; Guthey 2001; Lacy 2007; Torres et al. 2003).

Although there is impressive heterogeneity among Hispanics/Latinos in the traditional South, overall statistics show that they are younger, more heavily male, more heavily foreign born, more heavily Mexican, and more disadvantaged in terms of human capital (education and English language ability) compared with those in traditional-immigrant receiving states, especially during the initial years of migration and settlement (Kochhar, Suro, and Tafoya 2005). Additionally, foreign-born Hispanics/Latinos in the traditional South tend to be more recently arrived and are more likely to lack legal status compared with those in traditional immigrant-receiving states (Passel and Cohn 2009; Marrow 2011; Saenz et al. 2003; Vásquez, Seales, and Marquardt 2008), two factors that contribute to low income levels and high poverty rates (Lacy 2007; Torres, Popke, and Hapke 2006).

FITTING INTO AND TRANSFORMING THE SOUTHERN RACIAL BINARY

The recent and rapid entry of substantial numbers of nonwhite/nonblack migrants into the traditional South is intriguing for many reasons. One is that southerners, especially those living in rural areas and small towns,[4] are less familiar with post-1965 immigrants

---

4. Immigrants to the traditional South have settled disproportionately in metropolitan areas, preserving rural southerners' relative isolation from contemporary immigration even compared with their urban southern counterparts (see Bankston 2007; Eckes 2005; Elliott and Ionescu 2003; Kasarda and Johnson 2006; Neal and Bohon 2003).

and have lower levels of identification with immigrant histories of their own compared with their counterparts living in other parts of the country, especially those in historical immigrant gateways such as New York and Chicago. Second, the traditional South is the physical and symbolic homeland of African Americans, continuing to host the country's highest absolute and relative numbers of blacks (see Figure 6.2).[5] Third, the traditional South is the region where the U.S. racial "binary," which has long served to divide superordinate whites from subordinate nonwhites, remains the strongest even today (McClain et al. 2006, 2007). Together, these features magnify the boundaries separating the region's two dominant groups—whites and blacks—both from each other and from newcomers, throwing into sharp relief the major questions scholars are asking about how contemporary nonwhite/nonblack migrants will become incorporated into, and potentially transform, the U.S. racial hierarchy.

One way to see how Hispanic newcomers, including Mexican migrants, are fitting into as well as challenging the South's strong racial binary is to examine how they are self-identifying themselves racially and ethnically, as well as how southern natives are externally identifying them. Another way is to examine how Hispanic newcomers, including Mexican migrants, interpret their social relations with whites and blacks, including the ways in which they perceive discrimination from either group. In this section I touch briefly on each pattern, drawing on 129 individual semistructured interviews and additional ethnographic research that I conducted between June 2003 and June 2004 in Bedford and Wilcox counties, pseudonyms for two nonmetropolitan new immigrant destination counties in eastern North Carolina, a subregion of the traditional rural South where poverty is acute and the black–white binary is extremely sharp (see Marrow 2008, 2009, 2011; Torres, Popke, and Hapke 2006). Seventy of the 129 interviews were conducted with Latin American immigrants of varying nationalities, in Spanish and English. Most were conducted with Mexicans ($N = 39$), but others were conducted with South Americans ($N = 16$), Central Americans ($N = 14$), and 1 Cuban ($N = 1$). Eighteen of the interviews were conducted with U.S.-born Hispanics, mostly Mexican and Puerto Rican Americans, in Spanish and English. Finally, 41 of the interviews were conducted with white ($N = 27$) and black ($N = 14$) "key native informants," in English, triangulating findings among the Hispanic respondents.

Hispanic Newcomers' Racial/Ethnic Identifications

In 2003–2004, Hispanic respondents in eastern North Carolina both self-identified and reported external identification by southern natives most strongly as something other than whites or blacks, particularly as Hispanics, Latinos, or people of some "other race" (see Table 6.5). This includes respondents who were not asked how they identify but who nonetheless used the terms Hispanic, *hispano*, or Latino frequently in their interviews (25.0 percent). It also includes respondents who self-identified as part of this group secondarily even when their primary identifications were by national origin (9.1 percent).

---

5. Figure 6.2 illustrates the southern "black belt," a region that stretches in an arc from Virginia to eastern Texas and that was originally named for its dark soils and position as the center of plantation cotton agriculture, but is now known for its predominant African American population, persistent poverty, high unemployment, low education, poor health, and high infant mortality (Wimberley and Morris 2002).

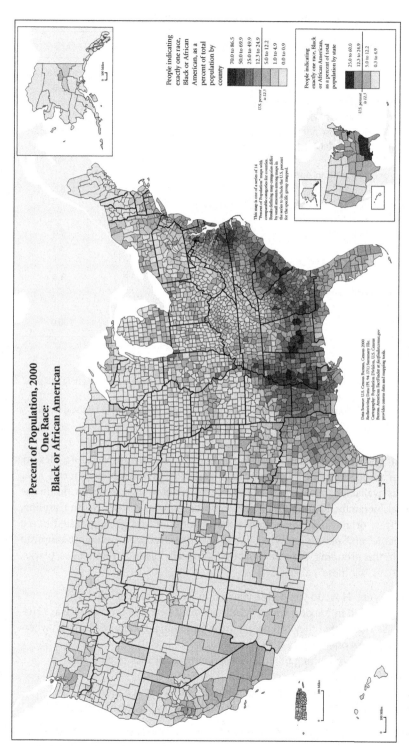

Figure 6.2 Percentage of Population, Black or African American (One Race), 2000 U.S. Census.

Source: Brewer, Cynthia A. and Trudy A. Suchan. 2001. "Mapping Census 2000: The Geography of U.S. Diversity." Census 2000 Special Reports (CENSR/01-1). Washington, DC: U.S. Department of Commerce, Economics and Statistics Administration, U.S. Census Bureau (June). http://www.census. gov/population/www/cen2000/atlas/pdf/censr01-1.pdf (last accessed December 17, 2009). Available in the public domain.

Table 6.5.   Racial and Ethnic Self-Identifications of Hispanic Respondents, 2003–2004[a]

PRIMARY SELF-IDENTIFICATION	N	%
Hispanic or Latino	26	29.5
Question not asked (but respondent uses the terms Hispanic, *hispano*, or Latino throughout interview)	22	25.0
Question not asked or response not specified (or respondent did not understand the question)	12	13.6
National Origin (six Mexican, one Puerto Rican, one Argentine)	8	9.1
Hispanic or Latino (but respondent thought he/she was white before migration or is perceived as white by U.S. natives)	· 7	8.0
Mestizo, Spanish, or Indian	6	6.8
White or Caucasian (and/or does not think Hispanic/Latino is a race)	3	3.4
Other (American, "a string of things," "it doesn't matter")	3	3.4
Black	1	1.1
Total	88	100.0

SOURCE: Author's interviews.

[a]Questions asked to gauge respondents' racial/ethnic self-identifications:

(1) How do you define yourself in terms of race or ethnicity? Like when you receive any forms here or if people ask you "What is your race or ethnicity?," how do you respond?

(2) What do other people think you are? If people think you are Hispanic, do you ever do anything to tell them that you are [ETHNIC GROUP]?

As illustrated by Ricardo and Noélia, an immigrant couple from Veracruz, Mexico, foreign-born respondents in this group have generally picked up such terms after migration, as available language to make sense of their new place as minorities in the South's racial hierarchy. Ricardo and Noélia reported how in eastern North Carolina, Latin American–origin newcomers from a variety of countries get aggregated into a larger "Hispanic" or "Spanish" grouping that is sometimes reduced even more simply to "Mexican." In this grouping, they are portrayed as racially distinct from whites, blacks, and Asians (e.g., "Chinese") alike:

INTERVIEWER: How do you define yourself in terms of race or ethnicity?
RICARDO: Well, in Mexico, we are Mexicans. And here, for everyone we are Hispanics. That's what they call people from Colombia, Paraguay, Uruguay, wherever . . . every one of them the same.
NOÉLIA: It's the only thing that they have on forms for race or ethnicity.
RICARDO: "Hispanic."
NOÉLIA: Hispanic, black, white, and sometimes they say "Chinese."
RICARDO: Or sometimes to play with us, and they say "Spanish" instead.

Yet some Hispanic respondents either self-identified or reported external identification by southern natives as whites. A few (approximately 3 percent) self-identified as whites, adamantly resisting both the Hispanic/Latino and the black labels even when natives see them as such. Others (approximately 8 percent) either self-identified ethnically as Hispanics/Latinos and racially as whites (as did Davíd, an immigrant from Medellín, Colombia) or thought that natives perceive them to be whites because of their light skin or hair color (as did Isabel García, a naturalized citizen from Buenos Aires, Argentina):

> DAVÍD: I consider myself white. I don't think Hispanic is a race. That just indicates where we come from.
>
> ISABEL GARCÍA: Until I open my mouth, people here think I'm American. Sometimes. And then when I open my mouth, many times they ask me if I'm German or Italian. But they don't think I'm Latin. Because I don't look like the stereotype of the Latin person.

Importantly, white racial identification emerged most strongly among light-skinned and more middle-class respondents from countries in South America and the Caribbean, whereas Hispanic and other racial identification emerged most strongly among dark-skinned and lower-class respondents from Mexico and Central America.[6]

By contrast, very few respondents identified or reported external identification by southern natives as blacks.[7] Only one self-identified as black (Carmen, a dark-skinned Hispanic American of Puerto Rican, Panamanian, and African American ancestry), and only two others reported ever being identified by natives as black, with both varying over time. Lourdes, a Cuban American originally from Miami, said that whereas she was identified as white in majority-white Minneapolis and later as black in a majority-black locale in Tennessee, she is now identified as Mexican (and even referred to by the generic name "María") in eastern North Carolina, because "there are so many Mexicans here." Lidia, a legal permanent resident from Oaxaca, Mexico, reported being discriminated against by whites and called "black" when she first migrated to North Carolina in 1980, especially by lower-class natives. But Lidia said that this is something that has changed since because immigration into the area has increased and natives have become more familiar with and willing to acknowledge Hispanics as a distinct group.

Therefore, respondents' strongest internal and external identifications as Hispanics, Latinos, or people of some other race denote an early pattern of incorporation that exhibits some collective social distance from both whiteness and blackness, resisting full categorization into either of the traditional South's dominant binary racial categories. Yet respondents' stronger internal and external identifications as others and whites than as blacks also denote an early pattern of incorporation that exhibits greater collective social distance from blackness than whiteness. Although class and skin color did influence respondents' racial identifications, they generally

---

6. The former also identify more strongly as whites in U.S. Census data than the latter, at the national and North Carolina state levels (Ruggles et al. 2004, weighted data, author's analysis).

7. In the 2000 Census members of *all* Latin American immigrant groups in North Carolina identified more strongly as whites and "other race" than blacks, and the only two groups with high rates of black racial identification (Panamanians at 19.0 percent and Dominicans at 10.5 percent) make up a small portion of North Carolina's Hispanic population (Ruggles et al. 2004, weighted data, author's analysis).

did so within a "nonblack" zone. Even dark-skinned, poor, and unauthorized Mexican and Central Americans tended neither to self-identify nor perceive external identification as blacks (Marrow 2009).

Hispanic Newcomers' Social Interactions with Whites and Blacks

Hispanic respondents' patterns of nonblack identification are based on several factors, including their social interactions with whites and blacks in their places of destination, through which they develop a sense of how they are viewed and of where the strongest boundaries between groups lie. Within the complex range of intergroup relations that I documented between members of these three groups in 2003–2004, intriguing patterns emerged. Overall, Hispanic respondents perceived better interpersonal relations with whites than with blacks; they perceived that whites treat Hispanics better than whites treat blacks, and many also perceived that Hispanics are "discriminated" against more by blacks than by whites (a pattern I discuss in more detail below). Together these patterns show that through their social interactions many Hispanic newcomers had come to perceive that the boundaries separating themselves from whites, although existent, are somewhat more permeable than those separating either blacks from Hispanics or whites from blacks. These patterns also highlight how the contours of discrimination in the traditional South, historically employed to separate whites from blacks based on racial differences in skin color, have now expanded to separate both whites and blacks from newcomers, drawing on differences more intimately related to citizenship and civic and cultural belonging.

To illustrate, many (although certainly not all[8]) Hispanic respondents perceived that Hispanics are discriminated against more by blacks than whites (see also Griffith 2005; Rich and Miranda 2005). Delmira, a formerly undocumented immigrant from Mexico City who is now a legal permanent resident, and Ricky, a Mexican American from McAllen, Texas, expressed this sentiment:

> DELMIRA: Blacks still have that "For years we've been discriminated and discriminated" [mentality]. And sometimes it's the opposite sometimes. They discriminate against Hispanics.
> RICKY: Blacks feel threatened. They think that Hispanics are going to take something away from them, and they have tendency to treat Hispanics a little bit wrong.

To be sure, Hispanic respondents acknowledged some discrimination from some rural southern whites. Yet in many cases what they had expected to encounter from these whites, based on their knowledge of U.S. immigration policy or their interpersonal relations with whites elsewhere in the United States, was worse than what has actually transpired in eastern North Carolina. Furthermore, Hispanic respondents tended to report a balance in their interactions with whites in eastern North Carolina, noting that although some displayed acts of prejudice and discrimination, others did not, and still others displayed friendliness, acceptance, and a surprising degree

---

8. Some Hispanic respondents reported that blacks do *not* discriminate against Hispanics as strongly as whites do, usually saying that blacks understand what discrimination feels like or harbor their greatest resentment toward whites rather than Hispanics (Marrow 2011).

of cultural cosmopolitanism that helped to counter other whites' negative responses. Alvaro, a formerly undocumented immigrant from Coahuila, Mexico, who is now a legal permanent resident, described this bifurcated response many Hispanic newcomers perceived from whites:

> ALVARO: I would say that fifty percent of whites, they have a good attitude to the Hispanics. But the other fifty percent, that's where I would say that it's a bad attitude to the Hispanics. It's like everybody says, there are bad apples and good apples. But at least to me, it's a kind of half and half.

By contrast, Hispanic respondents like Alvaro perceived less variation in blacks' responses:

> ALVARO: I see more white people, Caucasians, doing or trying to do, positive things to the Hispanic community versus the African American people. With a better attitude, with a better approach. Whites are being more kind. I can't say [the relationship between Hispanics and blacks] is good. Because my opinion is that a big part of the African American population, they really doesn't accept the Hispanic community. We are intruders. Just a small part, one probably quarter of the population, they are the ones who realize or can see us as allies.

Why Hispanics perceived more negative treatment—which they often interpreted as discrimination—from rural southern blacks than whites may seem counterintuitive, given the legacy of white-on-nonwhite discrimination in the traditional South, the larger gap separating the material positions of Hispanic newcomers from whites than from blacks in the region, and the relative lack of resources with which rural black southerners can truly discriminate against other groups. Yet Hispanic newcomers were interpreting discrimination from blacks in two key ways. First, they perceived that education and class strongly structure natives' responses to their presence, with better-educated and higher-class natives responding more positively than less-educated and lower-class ones (Fennelly 2008; Hernández-León and Zúñiga 2005; Marrow 2008; Mindiola, Niemann, and Rodríguez 2002; Vallas and Zimmerman 2007). By this class-based logic, because blacks in eastern North Carolina are poorer than whites, at both the group and the individual levels, Hispanics likewise perceived that blacks' reactions to newcomers are more negative because African Americans respond to greater fears of being displaced or "leapfrogged" by Hispanics, not only economically in low-wage workplaces but also socially in lower-class neighborhoods and public schools (Marrow 2008, 2011). As expressed by Alicia, an immigrant from Chile who was in the process of naturalization through her white American husband, discrimination comes mostly from black Americans "and the white people that here you call 'rednecks.' It's social class that accounts for it."

In this way, the structural conditions affecting Hispanic newcomers and blacks in the rural South create a context in which Hispanics' interpersonal relations with blacks are more heavily shaped by symbolic—if not actual—economic competition than are their relations with whites (Dunn, Aragones, and Shivers 2005; McClain et al. 2007; Rich and Miranda 2005; Stuesse 2009). Concording with Hernández-León and Zúñiga's (2005) argument that interethnic interactions in the U.S. South do not develop separately from class relations, Hispanic and white respondents alike singled out African Americans' lower class status relative to that of whites as a primary reason why blacks are responding more poorly to Hispanics:

> NINA: There is a lot of black–Hispanic tension, and I've heard a lot about it. You know, really a lot of it comes from the fact that in the African American culture here you don't have a lot of students getting really high grades. It's not a part of the culture. There's some bad feelings on the part of African American students when Hispanic students start doing very well, which a lot of them already are.
>
> INTERVIEWER: Jealousy, you mean?
>
> NINA: Yes. Like I know one little [Hispanic] girl who was doing really well in school. She was getting 3s and 4s in everything [on her end-of-grade tests]. And she was beaten up by a black student in school. I really do think there is some jealousy. Of African American students feeling that these people are not even from here, they are only recently arrived, they don't even speak the language. And here they are, and doing better only after a little bit of time. They are doing well. And that's hard on African Americans. And I kind of see the same tension with the adults. You know, a lot of adults say that Hispanics are here to take their jobs and work for less. They say they're taking all of our jobs. And it's not really like that, but that's the feeling. The feeling of jealousy of having these people be new, being undocumented, not being from this country, and having their jobs. And so I do see conflict between Hispanics and African Americans.

In such competitive situations, negative tensions between minority groups carry great potential for misinterpretation as group rejection (Rockquemore 2002) or even discrimination (Kasinitz et al. 2008), such as when a college-educated undocumented Colombian respondent working in a textile mill in Bedford county said, "I feel the blacks don't like us. And that it is worse than with the whites," or when a poor undocumented Guatemalan respondent working in a food processing plant in Wilcox county said that "the black race does not like Hispanics very much because they think that we are taking away their jobs," reporting that this thing "you could even call racism, right?" makes him feel "humiliated" and "made fun of" by some blacks. In turn, these perceptions of competition-induced rejection and discrimination can foster resentment, stereotyping, and distancing against blacks.

Second, Hispanic newcomers reported experiencing discrimination and exclusion not just because of class-based competition or along a *vertical skin color axis* along which white natives can mark them as racially inferior, but also along other dimensions that, when viewed together, comprise a separate *horizontal (non)citizenship axis* along which both white and black natives can mark and ostracize them as undeserving civic and cultural "outsiders" (Kim 1999; see also De Genova 2006). That is, in 2003–2004, when Hispanic respondents spoke of prejudice and discrimination, they did so in terms of civic and cultural belonging (i.e., nonracial exclusion along lines such as English language ability, class status, personal appearance, nativity, real or presumed legal status, and so forth) as well as race and skin color (i.e., racial exclusion). In fact, in many instances Hispanic respondents only implicated their physical features or skin colors as factors in how they experience discrimination insofar as such traits serve to denote or signal civic and cultural "outsiderness" instead.

For example, many Hispanic respondents reported being stopped by law enforcement officials for "driving while Mexican" or "driving while Hispanic." Although they understood that these officials often identify them as Hispanic according to their physical appearances, they thought that this is primarily because their Hispanic features are associated with probable lack of legal status, which is something that ultimately serves to ostracize them along civic and cultural lines as undeserving foreigners instead. As Jiménez (2008, 2010) argues, in the contemporary era of unprecedented Mexican immigration, race has become so tightly conflated with nativity and citizenship that having dark skin, indigenous features, or Spanish surnames often serves the purpose of implying that Hispanics are foreign born and likely also undocumented, even if they are U.S.-born citizens. By this logic, Hispanic newcomers in eastern North Carolina are undergoing a complex process of racialization, yet it is one in which they perceived that "nonracial" discrimination (particularly along the lines of noncitizenship) is most important, with "racial" discrimination playing a compounding role.

Furthermore, Hispanic respondents often perceived blacks to be the worst perpetrators of this horizontal civic and cultural exclusion. Merced and Octavio, an undocumented immigrant couple from Sinaloa, Mexico, expressed great frustration with local blacks who "ignore them" when they attempt to communicate in English, whereas they noted that whites "try to help" them more:

MERCED: Even though some blacks do understand you, they say they don't.

OCTAVIO: Right. They say, "I don't understand what you are saying. What do you mean?" And if there is someone around who speaks a little Spanish, they'll say, "Wait a moment." But if there isn't, the bad thing is that they will just ignore you. They'll say, "I don't understand you."

MERCED: Exactly! It's even happened to me! Sometimes I go up to our English teacher, and I'll ask him, "How do you say X thing?" And he says, "You say it like this." And then I say it back to him like he said it to me, and he tells me, "Yes, you've got it!" So I ask him, "How come some black people tell me they don't understand what I am saying to them?"

OCTAVIO: Almost the majority of *gringos* ask me to talk, and they will try to understand me. And they help me. I will say it, and they will try to understand and if there is a problem, they will correct it and say, "No, say it this way." However, there are other people who make fun of you. There is some difference [between whites and blacks] there.

Like Merced and Octavio, other Hispanic respondents perceived that whites are more "open-minded" toward them and their "foreign" cultures than blacks, whom they perceived as "staying more separate" and attempting to exclude Hispanics more strongly. Raquel, a 1.5-generation undocumented youth, originally from Honduras, who dropped out of her high school in Tennessee after the tenth grade, recalled severe rejection by black schoolmates who ostracized her according to her foreign dress and personal appearance, compared with whites, who came to form her close circle of friends. Laura, an immigrant from Chihuahua, Mexico, thought that there is "more communication and common interests" between Hispanic newcomers and whites than between Hispanic newcomers and blacks, perhaps because "whites try to strike up more conversation with Hispanics" to get to know more about them and their backgrounds, whereas "blacks, well, not as much." Likewise, Stephanie, a legal permanent resident from Guanajuato, Mexico, thought that "Hispanics and the white Americans get along better" than Hispanics and blacks do "because the blacks put up a barrier that you can't get across. Maybe because of their color. Because they feel like they are another race. And they just want to preserve their group."

Even when Hispanics did not perceive whites as open-minded, they did not necessarily see blacks as more so. Eugenio, a 1.5-generation undocumented youth from Oaxaca, Mexico, thought that although whites ostracize Hispanics as "dirty" and undeserving foreigners, blacks do so even more strongly. Here Eugenio tapped not only into the acute threat of socioeconomic disenfranchisement that lower-class African Americans feel in the face of rising immigration, but also into their sense that they, like whites, are the kind of "real Americans" that Hispanics are not:

EUGENIO: They always look at you and they say, "Well, you know, he doesn't speak English." Because I've been in restaurants and I've had black people sitting next to me, or white people. And they're just talking fast. They just keep on yapping, yapping, yapping…"Look at that. He's dirty. And all these Hispanics come and steal our jobs." And this and that. Well, one time I turned around, I said, "Excuse me, what did you say? Because I couldn't hear you exactly. And I would like to hear what you said again." Those people just stood up and left. Because that's what I like doing. I like sitting down. I don't say a word, and I want to hear what people say about us. That's how I know what problems Hispanics have in this country. They'll sit there and, man, they'll just keep on talking trash about you.

INTERVIEWER: This negative treatment, this talking trash—do you think Hispanics get it mostly from white Americans or black Americans?

EUGENIO: They get it mostly from blacks.

INTERVIEWER: And why?

EUGENIO: Honestly, I don't know. Like one time, during Hurricane Floyd, all the lights went out. And the Salvation Army, or the soldiers would come over here to Bedford Mobile Home Park with dump trucks. And they would drop clothes off here, or water, or canned foods. In the center of the Mobile Home Park. And I overheard a conversation that a black lady had. She said, "You know, look at 'em. They come over here to our country, to our land, steal our jobs, steal our money. And now they even want to steal our needs [i.e, donated relief items]. Those needs are for us, the Americans." You know, I was just listening to that. They were saying this and that about us.

Just why these Hispanic respondents perceived greater horizontal civic and cultural exclusion, which they interpreted as discrimination, from blacks than whites is still unclear. Opinion data show that lifelong southern blacks support *less* restrictive immigration policies and *less* exclusionary policies toward unauthorized immigrants than do lifelong southern whites; however, data also show lifelong southern blacks espousing more particularistic ideas about what it takes to be American than lifelong southern whites (Griffin and McFarland 2007) and blacks exhibiting greater concern about undocumented immigrants than whites in Virginia (Vallas and Zimmerman 2007). Opinion data from Durham, North Carolina, also show that blacks exhibit *fewer* negative stereotypes toward Hispanics than Hispanics exhibit toward them (McClain et al. 2006), which may be consistent with my observation that blacks in eastern North Carolina were not aware of how exclusively Hispanics perceived them to be acting. Perhaps blacks in eastern North Carolina were simply unaware of how poorly they were treating Hispanics—particularly if the characteristics associated with noncitizenship, rather than aligning Hispanics and blacks together as "collective blacks" at the bottom of the regional racial hierarchy, exacerbate feelings of competition instead. Or perhaps Hispanics' antiblack stereotypes or observations of whites' stigmatization of blacks were also flavoring their interpretations of whites and blacks' behaviors, leading them to judge those of blacks as more harsh.

Regardless, Hispanic newcomers perceived negative treatment from blacks and described it as "unexpected," in contrast to perceiving more "surprisingly" pleasant interpersonal relations with whites, especially when they harbored initial expectations of encountering significant discrimination from whites rather than blacks. For instance, one of the things that most surprised Inés, an undocumented immigrant from Medellín, Colombia, was encountering discrimination by blacks against Hispanic newcomers, not by whites against either blacks or Hispanics. And despite having heard about the Ku Klux Klan and anti-immigrant vigilante activity on the U.S.–Mexico border before migrating to the United States, Mauro, an undocumented immigrant from Guatemala City, Guatemala, reported being surprised to encounter interpersonal discrimination not from whites, but from a black coworker who refused to return his smiles and greetings each morning at work. By contrast, "From what I have gotten to know of white Americans, they have always been very friendly. I have never felt any discrimination from them." These perceptions of horizontal exclusion by African Americans can, like those arising from economically induced competition, foster resentment, stereotyping, and distancing in return.

CONCLUSION

In this chapter, I have provided an overview of the reasons why Hispanics/Latinos, including Mexican migrants, have settled in the traditional U.S. South over the past few decades. After centuries of lagging economically and demographically behind other regions of the country, the U.S. South has become increasingly economically integrated within the national and global economies since World War II, and new patterns of both internal and international migration reflect the region's flourishing dynamism and opportunity. Key economic and political developments in Mexico and other parts of the United States have further shaped migration patterns among Hispanics/Latinos, especially Mexicans, by providing them with incentives to leave (or avoid) traditional settlement states and cities and also by making traditional southern states look more appealing as destinations. Together these trends have dramatically expanded the Hispanic/Latino and immigrant populations of traditional southern states, fundamentally changing the face of what was arguably once the most culturally and racially "settled" region of the United States.

I have also provided a brief overview of Hispanic newcomers' racial/ethnic identifications and patterns of intergroup relations in eastern North Carolina in 2003–2004, with the purpose of illuminating a few key points about how Hispanic newcomers might become incorporated into, and potentially transform, the heretofore binary southern racial hierarchy. First, there are some early signs that Hispanic newcomers are self-identifying and being externally identified by natives in ways that elude the U.S. South's two dominant racial categories of "white" and "black." As Vásquez, Seales, and Marquardt (2008) note, these are potential signs of a "subversion of a long-standing biracial order" in the traditional South (29). Nonetheless, there are also early signs that Hispanic newcomers are self-identifying and being externally identified by natives in ways that might simply reconstitute the southern binary racial order over time—yet this time according to a new "black/nonblack" divide in which most Hispanics may come to be included as nonblacks (Gans 1999; Kasinitz et al. 2008; Lee and Bean 2007; Marrow 2009, 2011; Yancey 2003).

Second, some very real and disturbing tensions have emerged between blacks and Hispanics in both urban and rural areas of African Americans' regional homeland (LeDuff 2000; Marrow 2011; Mohl 2002; McClain 2006, 2007; Schmid 2003; Swarns 2006a, 2006b; Stuesse 2009; Torres, Popke, and Hapke 2006), although, of course, not all black–Hispanic relations are conflict ridden nor are all white–Hispanic relations smooth. Here I have chosen to focus on Hispanics' perceptions of discrimination by blacks because they illustrate how immigration has altered the contours of discrimination in this symbolic region, expanding them outward from a historical orientation around racial differences in skin color that have served to separate whites from blacks to include new differences around citizenship and civic and cultural belonging that now serve to separate both whites and blacks from newcomers, too (De Genova 2006; Kim 1999). In the contemporary multiracial South, discrimination takes on multiple meanings and dimensions, and it is not something that Hispanic newcomers in eastern North Carolina felt is solely racial or originates solely from whites.

Nonetheless, anti-immigrant sentiment has increased throughout the South since 2003–2004 (Ansley and Shefner 2009; Lippard and Gallagher 2011; Marrow 2011; Odem and Lacy 2009), and new efforts to build coalitions among blacks, Hispanics, immigrants, and progressive whites have emerged in response—both to combat rising nativism and racism among whites and to temper simmering conflict between blacks and Hispanics. Perhaps these trends will lead Hispanics, including Mexican migrants, to perceive greater discrimination from whites in the future, particularly if they also perceive blacks to begin exhibiting more solidarity and empathy rather than exclusion in the context of their everyday interactions (and not just in elite coalition-building projects) than they did in 2003–2004.

CHAPTER 7

Indigenous Mexican Migrants

Jonathan Fox

University of California, Santa Cruz

INTRODUCTION[1]

In the United States, when the terms "multiethnic," "multicultural," and "multiracial" are used to refer to Mexican migrants, they usually refer exclusively to relationships between Mexicans and *other* national origin groups. Yet Mexican society is itself multiethnic and multiracial. From an indigenous rights perspective, the Mexican nation includes many distinct *peoples*. To take the least ambiguous indicator of ethnic difference, more than one in ten Mexicans comes from a family in which an indigenous language is spoken (Serrano Carreto et al., 2003). Increasingly, indigenous Mexican community activists in the United States are now *trilingual*. For some who immigrated as children or teenagers, Spanish is neither their first nor their second language. Yet in the United States, most scholars, health clinics, civil rights groups, cultural workers, labor organizers, and funding agencies treat Mexicans as ethnically homogeneous. This unspoken assumption provokes both invisibility and visibility; whereas many indigenous migrants submerge their cultures and identities, others "come out" in defense of respect for racial equality and cultural difference.

The Mexican migrant population in the United States increasingly reflects the ethnic diversity of Mexican society, but our conceptual frameworks have yet to catch up. This essay explores a series of puzzles about collective identity formation that emerge once one recognizes ethnic difference among Mexican migrants. The first issue is that both Mexican migrant and Mexican indigenous collective identities complicate widely

1. This chapter is a substantially revised and updated version of Fox (2006). Some sections draw from Fox and Rivera-Salgado (2004) and Fox (2004). This work was inspired by long-term conversations with Gaspar Rivera-Salgado, Rufino Domínguez Santos, Romualdo Juan Gutiérrez Cortés, Odilia Romero, and Leoncio Vásquez of the Binational Front of Indigenous Organizations (FIOB, formerly known as the Oaxacan Indigenous Binational Front). For discussions of the FIOB, see, among others, Bacon (2006), Domínguez Santos (2004a, 2004b), Hernández Díaz (2002), Martínez Saldaña (2004), Ramírez Romero (2003), Rivera-Salgado (1999, 2002), and Velasco (2002, 2005a, 2005b), as well as http://www.fiob.org (including *El Tequio* magazine). Thanks also for conversations with Xóchitl Chavez, Sylvia Escárcega, Martha García Ortega, María Dolores París Pombo, and Lynn Stephen.

held ideas about race, ethnicity, and national identity. Although these three concepts are often used interchangeably when discussing Mexicans in the United States, race, ethnicity, and national identity are not synonyms. Yet if these three concepts are analytically distinct, then where and when does one leave off and the other begin? Second, when migrant and indigenous identities *overlap*, as in the case of indigenous Mexican migrants, then the conceptual puzzles about how to distinguish among racial, ethnic, and national identities are sharpened. A comparative and binational approach suggests that it is useful to look at the specific experiences and identities of indigenous Mexican migrants in the United States through lenses that draw both from frameworks that focus on processes of racialization and from those that emphasize the social construction of collective identities based on ethnicity, region, or religion. In other words, this approach unfolds at the intersection of ethnic and area studies frameworks.

The point of departure for analyzing collective identity formation here is that both in the United States and in Mexico, indigenous migrants are subordinated both as migrants and as indigenous people. Economically, they work in the bottom rungs of ethnically segmented labor markets. In the social sphere, they also face entrenched racist attitudes and discrimination from other Mexicans in both countries, as well as from the dominant U.S. society. Systematic language discrimination by public authorities aggravates human rights violations in both countries (e.g., Padgett and Mascarenas 2009). Like many other Mexican migrants, in the civic–political arena, most indigenous migrants are excluded from full citizenship rights in both countries. At the same time, also like other migrants, indigenous Mexicans bring with them a wide range of experiences with collective action for community development, social justice, and political democratization, and these repertoires influence their decisions about who to work with and how to build their own organizations in the United States.

HISTORICAL CONTEXT

Until the 1980s, most Mexican migrants did share a common social and cultural heritage, coming primarily from *mestizo* rural communities in the central-western states. Many identified with a *ranchero* culture, located in an intermediate position in Mexico's social hierarchy, in between urban and indigenous societies (Farr 2006). This "historic" sending region has profoundly shaped both scholarly and popular understandings of Mexican migration in the United States. Yet over the past two decades, the Mexican migrant population has diversified dramatically—ethnically, socially and geographically—in terms of both where they come from and where they settle in the United States.

Most of the first indigenous Mexican migrants to the United States were from the central-western state of Michoacán, of Purhépecha origin, as well as Mixtecs and Zapotecs from Oaxaca in the south. Indigenous Mexican migration to the United States dates back at least to the early twentieth century. Indeed, the father of Oaxacan-born cross-border revolutionary and later political exile Ricardo Flores Magón was indigenous. In the 1920s, pioneering scholar of Mexicans in the United States Manuel Gamio documented migrants of "Mesoamerican" origin, although without further ethnic specification (1971, cited in García Leyva, 2003). Weber also recalls the role of Primo Tapia and other Purhépechas who joined the Industrial Workers of the World while in the United States before returning to lead *agrarista* struggles in the 1920s (2008). Indeed, Weber reassesses her own research to take into account the previously "unseen" Purhépecha identities embedded in her oral histories with immigrants who came to the United States in the 1920s (2008). Subsequently, as in the case of Mexican migration to the United States more generally, the bracero contract worker program (1942–1964) played a key role in launching the indigenous community social networks that sustained later migration (e.g., Cohen 2004). Although southern Mexico accounted for a small proportion of bracero recruitment, testimonial evidence indicates that the first Mixteco migrants to the United States were recruited after having migrated to northern Mexico (Domínguez Santos 2008; Gil Martínez de Escobar 2006, 66).

Until recently, however, most indigenous migrants worked in large cities or as farm workers *within* Mexico, as in the case of the longstanding seasonal migration from the Chiapas highlands to work in plantation agriculture.[2] The massive rural out-migration process that drove Mexico's urbanization in the mid-twentieth century was substantially indigenous in origin and generated a rich anthropological literature in the 1970s and 1980s (Sánchez Gómez 2005, 2007). In the 1960s, for example, Zapotecs from Oaxaca' northern Sierra began moving to Mexico City in large numbers, where they formed hometown associations and developed mutual aid practices and shared broader collective identities based on region of origin that are remarkably reminiscent of contemporary migrants to the United States (Hirabayashi 1993, 1997).

In Oaxaca, Mixtecos began leaving their villages to become seasonal plantation laborers early in the twentieth century, with substantial numbers migrating on foot within Oaxaca and to Veracruz in the 1930s, with others going as far as Chiapas (e.g., Guidi 1999). Mixteco farmworkers began migrating to the Valley of Culiacan in Sinaloa in the 1940s. Mixteco participation in Sinaloa's farmworker unionization campaigns was widespread, first under the banner of the left-wing Central Independiente de Obreros Agrícolas y Campesinos (López Monjardin 1991; Posadas Segura 2005). These struggles included the hometown-based *Organización del Pueblo Explotado y Oprimido*, a group whose activists later brought that organizing tradition to California's Central Valley and became a founding member of one of the first binational indigenous migrant organizations.[3] Other Mixtecos migrated to Mexico City, beginning as early as the 1930s. In 1981, subway workers from San Miguel Tlacotepec launched one of their first hometown associations, *Comité Cívico Popular*.[4]

Oaxacan migration to Baja California began with the first generation of Mixteco seasonal migrants in the 1950s and 1960s. There they were able to make contacts with mestizo migrants from central Mexico who were more familiar with how to reach the United States. Indeed, indigenous migrants to Baja then referred to those who helped them across the border as *"camaradas"* rather than *"coyotes,"* implying a perception of interethnic solidarity. By the 1980s, Baja's agroexport economy grew significantly

---

2. In 2000, Mexico's farmworker population was estimated at more than 3 million, approximately two thirds of whom were landless and one third were subsubsistence smallholders (Salinas Alvarez 2006, 49).

3. This entire paragraph draws from Domínguez Santos (2004b), who was among the founders of the Organización del Pueblo Explotado y Oprimido.

4. The recent study by Cornelius et al. (2009) focuses exclusively on migration from the same municipality.

and entire families from Oaxaca began settling down, leading to a wave of land occupations for housing rights. During this period a new cohort of Oaxacan-identified migrants were born in Baja: as some put it, "Nací aquí en la colonia, pero soy de Oaxaca!" [I was born here in the neighborhood, but I'm from Oaxaca!] (Camargo Martínez 2004, 84).

Moving north from Baja California, indigenous migrants began to increase their share of the overall cross-border migrant population in the early 1980s, following what is sometimes known as the *Ruta Mixteca*.[5] In the 1990s, both circular and settled migration grew most notably in both urban and rural California and increasingly in Texas, New York, New Jersey, Florida, North Carolina, Georgia, Oregon, and Washington. Although migrants often settle together with their *paisanos*, that does not mean that all or most migrants from a given village end up in the same place or that members of the same ethnic group settle in the same region. For example, Purhépecha migrants have settled in North Carolina, the Midwest, and California (Anderson 2004; Leco Tomás 2009; Martínez 2002). At the "translocal" level, many communities of origin form satellite, or "daughter" communities that are widely dispersed through the United States (e.g., Stephen 2007). For example, in the case of San Juan Mixpetec, Oaxaca, Besserer documented remittances from 151 distinct locations in 7 Mexican and 15 U.S. states (2004).

Estimates of the overall size of the indigenous migrant population vary widely. One research strategy takes advantage of the U.S. Census' distinction between racial and ethnic self-identification. Those who choose to self-identify as both American Indian in terms of race *and* Hispanic/Latino in terms of their ethnicity can be considered Latin American indigenous migrants—primarily Mexican, but also Guatemalan. If one combines these two categories in the case of the 2000 Census, the population of indigenous migrants in the United States totals 407,000 (Huizar and Cerda 2004). Greater precision regarding self-identified peoplehood is not possible because the official Census follow-up question asks about "tribe"—not a meaningful concept for Latin American–origin indigenous peoples. More than half of these self-reported indigenous migrants are in the west, with California reporting 154,000, followed by 22,000 in Arizona, 15,000 in Colorado, and 12,000 in New Mexico. Moving eastward, Texas reported almost 50,000, followed by New York with 30,000, Illinois with almost 13,000, and Florida with 11,000. In California, organized indigenous migrants had campaigned to encourage their communities to self-identify on the 2000 Census. Although governmental and civil society efforts in the 1990s did reduce the undercount, the 2000 Census still missed substantial numbers of indigenous migrants (Kissam and Jacobs 2004). Nevertheless, the 2000 findings serve as a clear-cut "floor" that documents both the growing numbers and the relative geographic distribution of indigenous migrants

---

5. The first wave of research on Oaxacan migration to California includes Kearney (1988, 1995, 2000), Nagengast and Kearney (1990), Edinger (1985), Guidi (1992), Zabin et al. (1993), Zabin (1992a, 1992b, 1997), Wright (2005), Besserer (1999a, 1999b), and Escárcega and Varese (2004). Although the early research focused specifically on Mixtecos in rural California, Zapotecs migrated to urban areas, both in Mexico and in California. On Zapotec migration, see Aquino Morechi (2010), Cohen (2004), Gutiérrez Nájera (2007), López and Runsten (2004), Hirabayashi (1993, 1997), Hulshof (1991), Klaver (1997), Melero Malpica (2008), Robles (2004), and Stephen (2007).

(Huizar and Cerda 2004). Census outreach in collaboration with indigenous migrant community leaders continued in 2010.

In addition to the increased dispersal of indigenous migrants throughout the United States, they also now come from an increasingly diverse array of Mexico's indigenous ethnic groups, now even including Mayans. Indeed, whereas the scholarly literature on indigenous migration has long been focused primarily on Oaxaca, in recent years the ethnographic research on Mayan migration from the Yucatan has expanded significantly.[6] More recently, young Mayans from Chiapas have also been increasing their migration to the United States.[7] Indeed, researchers in Chiapas have pointed out that migration has grown sharply despite the substantial land redistribution that followed the Zapatista uprising—apparently too little, too late (Villafuerte Solís and García Aguilar 2006).

One of the most significant efforts to document patterns of indigenous migration to the United States involves the Department of Labor's National Agricultural Worker Survey (Gabbard et al. 2008). They represent a growing share of the farm labor force across the country, although many indigenous migrants also go straight to urban service jobs, as in the case of Zapotecs in Los Angeles (Lopez and Runsten 2004).

The authors of the National Agricultural Worker Survey explored different ways of asking language and race questions to improve accuracy given the ambiguities inherent in indigenous self-identification. The survey found that the proportion of Mexican-origin farm workers from southern Mexico grew from 9 percent of in 1990–2002 to 27 percent in 2005–2007, most notably in the San Joaquin Valley and Central Coast of California, San Diego (Martínez, Runsten, and Ricardez 2005), south Florida (Schmidt and Crummett 2004), and the Willamette Valley of Oregon (Stephen 2007), later reaching the state of Washington (Holmes 2006), North Carolina, and the Delmarva peninsula (Kissam et al. 2001). For the years 2005–2007, 8 percent of farm workers reported that they grew up in homes where adults spoke indigenous languages, and half of them report that their primary language was indigenous. Questions about racial identification showed an increase from 3 percent in 1990–1992 to 13 percent in 2005–2007. Combining the language and race indicators increased the reported indigenous share of U.S. farm workers to 15 percent in 2005–2007 (Gabbard et al. 2008, 18–20).

An innovative, large-scale survey of indigenous village migrant networks among California farmworkers reveals patterns of geographic distribution of communities of both origin and settlement (Mines, Nichols, and Runsten 2010). The primary sending regions are western and southern Oaxaca, as well as the adjoining eastern region of Guerrero. Overall, 73 percent of the sending communities are Oaxacan, 15 percent are in Guerrero, and the remaining 12 percent come from Puebla, Chiapas, Veracruz, and Michoacán. More than 80 percent of the sending communities are small villages of under three thousand inhabitants. This study also documented ethnic segmentation of labor markets, with a major presence of indigenous farm workers in the

---

6. See Adler (2004), Burke (2004), Cornelius, FitzGerald, and Lewin (2006), Pérez Rendon (2005), and Whiteside (2006).

7. See Rus and Rus (2008), Williams, Steigenga, and Vásquez (2009), and Aquino Moreschi (2009).

most arduous farm labor tasks (e.g., picking raisins and strawberries). The study also included research in sending regions, which found that although youth in communities with more established networks were thinking twice about crossing the border because of the cost and the danger, "in some of the poorer, newer networks the people continue to feel obligated to go north due to a lack of options."[8]

COMPARATIVE AND BINATIONAL APPROACHES TO RACIAL, ETHNIC, AND NATIONAL IDENTITIES

The concepts of race, ethnicity, and national identity all refer to ways of understanding and expressing collective identity and all refer in some way to shared ancestry, yet each one highlights a different dimension of the identity that is shared. For migrants to the United States, Mexicanness is simultaneously national, racial, and ethnic, but which is which, when, and why? These three concepts clearly overlap, but are also presumably somehow distinct—the challenge is to identify those distinctions with greater precision. Bringing together intellectual frameworks and lessons from practice from both the United States and Latin America can help to address this conceptual challenge.

In the arena of Mexico's dominant national political culture, both indigenous peoples and cross-border migrants have long been seen as less than full citizens, especially by political elites. This powerful historical legacy only began to change substantially within Mexico in the mid-1990s. For migrants, Mexico's President Vicente Fox dramatically changed the official discourse, describing them as "heroes" rather than as traitors or *pochos*. He even claimed all U.S. citizens of Mexican descent as members of the national diaspora, blurring longstanding distinctions between Mexicans and Mexican Americans (Durand 2004).

In practice, full democratic political rights in Mexico are still widely denied both to migrants and to indigenous peoples. Although indigenous Mexicans can access "full Mexicanness" to the degree that they give up their languages and commitments to ethnic autonomy, migrants are still widely seen by many as watering down their *Mexicanidad* through exposure to U.S. and to Mexican American culture. This is one reason why the long-promised right to vote abroad for migrants was stuck in political limbo until 2005—Mexican citizens in the United States are still seen by influential elite political actors as too vulnerable to manipulation by U.S. interests to be trusted with the right to vote (Castañeda 2006; Martínez Saldaña and Ross Pineda 2002). For both migrants and indigenous peoples, less than full command of the Spanish language is another powerful mechanism for exclusion from equal membership in Mexico's national polity and imaginary. Consider the common analogous phrases: those Mexicans who "don't even speak English" (in the United States) and those Indians who "*ni siquiera hablan español*" ("they don't even speak Spanish"—a common Mexican reference to "monolingual" indigenous people). In other words, both ethnic difference and cross-border mobility remain in tension with the dominant approach to Mexican national identity.

---

8. Personal e-mail communication with Rick Mines, coordinator of the Indigenous Farmworker Survey, February 17, 2009. See www.indigenousfarmworkers.org.

In the 1990s, for most first-generation Mexican migrants, national origin persisted as a primary collective identity, more than U.S.-based constructs of *Latinidad* or *Hispanidad*.[9] Especially in regions with a large critical mass of first-generation migrants, it is possible for Mexican migrants to reject, modify, or postpone acceptance of more nationally rooted U.S. ethnic identities, such as Chicano or Mexican American. Despite the pull of national identity, Mexicans migrants also find themselves inserted into a U.S. social hierarchy that assigns them to a racial category. In other words, migrants' subjectively *national* Mexicanness is widely treated as a *racial* identity in the United States. The concept of racialization is increasingly being applied to understand Latino experiences in the United States. A fuller understanding of the dynamics through which racialization processes affect Mexicans would require more systematic cross-regional comparison within the United States.[10] A cross-border perspective deepens our understanding of the process because for many indigenous migrants, racialization begins in Mexico and among other Mexicans in the United States.

In the case of Mexican migrants, the racialization is closely linked to their locations in the labor market, which in turn are linked to labor process and language use and only loosely connected to phenotype. "Mexican work" has long been widely understood in U.S. popular discourse as the kind that even low-income Americans won't do, at least for the wages offered.[11] In addition, however, racial and ethnic difference *among* Mexican migrant workers also interacts closely with the changing division of labor. In the California fields, after approximately 1 million undocumented farm workers regularized their status following the 1986 amnesty, they gained the labor mobility and the bottom rungs in the labor market opened up, repeating long-term cycles of "ethnic succession." At the same time, some employers and contractors pursued recruitment strategies that encouraged ethnic differences in their labor force (Krissman 1996, 2002).

Holmes' detailed ethnographic study of Triqui strawberry pickers in Washington state finds a close correlation among the division of labor, ethnicity, and the level of danger, strain, stress, and humiliation involved in their specific jobs (2006, 2007). In the process, they are frequently reprimanded and subjected to racial slurs: *"perros* [dogs], *burros* (burros), *Oaxacos* (a derogatory term for 'Oaxacan'), or *indios estúpidos* [stupid Indians]" (Holmes 2006, 1782).

One of the clearest indicators of the racialization of the division of labor is that it is understood as somehow natural that indigenous workers should be limited to the most strenuous jobs. As Holmes found,

---

9. Among foreign-born Latinos in the United States, 68 percent identify primarily with their country of origin, rather than as Latinos or Hispanics (Pew Hispanic Center 2002, 7), although this pattern is likely to have changed following the wave of mass mobilization for immigrant rights in 2006 (Fox and Bada 2009).

10. See notable recent work on Mexicans in Chicago, including De Genova (2005), De Genova and Ramos-Zayas (2003), and Arredondo's analysis of the relationship between national and racial identities among Mexicans in the 1930s (2008). On the historical processes of racialization of Mexicans in California, see Almaguer (1994), Menchaca (2001), and Pitti (2003), among others. On the distinctive contemporary dynamics of racialization of Mexican migrants in New York City, see Smith (2006). See also Glenn's cross-regional comparative approach (2002).

11. The use of the term "Mexican work" dates back at least to the 1920s (Arredondo 2008). See also Striffler's ethnographic study of "Mexican work" in an Arkansas poultry plant (2002, 312).

when asked why very few Triqui people were harvesting apples, the field job known to pay the most, the Tanaka Farm's apple crop supervisor explained in detail that "they are too short to reach the apples, and, besides, they don't like ladders anyway." He continued that Triqui people are perfect for picking berries because they are "lower to the ground." When asked why Triqui people have only berry-picking jobs, a mestiza Mexican social worker in Washington state explained that "*a los Oaxaqueños les gusta trabajar agachado* [Oaxacans like to work bent over]," whereas, she told me, "*Mexicanos* [mestizo Mexicans] get too many pains if they work in the fields." (2006, 1787)

Imposed racialized economic and social hierarchies can be counterposed with collective identities that migrants themselves generate.[12] When one looks at the interaction among race, ethnicity, and national identity among those Mexican migrants who engage in sustained collective action as Mexicans, it turns out that most emphasize their primary identification with *other* collective identities. For example, in the case of New York's Asociación Tepeyac, this identity is strongly faith-based (e.g., Galvez 2009). Most often, however, these additional identities are *territorial* and *subnational*, based on their communities, regions, or states of origin in Mexico, as can be seen in the widely observed growth of migrant hometown associations and their home state federations. In other words, migrants' shared Mexicanness, whether understood primarily in national, ethnic, or racial terms, is necessary but not sufficient to explain how and why they turn collective identities into collective action. The shared identities that inspire collective action show that they pursue a wide range of ways of *being* Mexican (just like Mexicans in Mexico). One could go further and argue that these widespread patterns of Mexican migrant collective identity formation and collective action, based on cross-border, translocal, regional, and ethnic identities, constitute a form of *resistance* to racialization, reminiscent of the mutual aid societies in the early twentieth century. Before further exploration of the specific forms that indigenous migrant identities and actions take, however, it is worth reflecting on how different intellectual and political traditions in the Americas frame indigenousness.

Indigenous peoples are usually conceptualized in the United States as constituting a race, whereas in Latin America they tend to be seen as ethnic groups.[13] This poses a puzzle, raising questions about how the concepts of race and ethnicity are defined and applied. Where does ethnicity leave off and race begin? Given that they often overlap, both conceptually and in practice, can they be disentangled? Are indigenous peoples distinct from other Mexicans racially, ethnically, or both? To ask the question a different way, is Mexican society multiracial, multiethnic, or both? The answer to both is both.

Few indigenous peoples in Mexico identify as *nationalities*—in contrast to some other Latin American countries (e.g., Ecuador)—and in contrast to the United States. Although U.S.-style reservations are widely viewed as anathema in Mexico, they do

---

12. Analysts of collective identity formation among indigenous migrants in Baja California differ over the degree to which this process is induced externally or generated internally (Martinez Novo, 2006 and Velasco Ortiz 2004a, 2004b, 2007).

13. For example, the Mexican Census does not collect data on race and defines indigenousness primarily in terms of language use. See Serrano Carreto et al. (2003). An Afro-Mexican organization, *Mexico Negro*, has called for the census to take race into account (Graves 2004).

rest on a limited degree of territorial sovereignty, self-governance, and at least nominal legal recognition of peoplehood that does not currently exist in Mexico. As of a constitutional reform in 1991, the Mexican government officially recognized that indigenous peoples are ethnically distinct and that Mexico is a multi*cultural* society. In 2001, following the Zapatistas' remarkable address to Congress, Article 2 of the Constitution was further reformed to recognize modest expressions of autonomy (although indigenous rights advocates did not consider this a step forward). At the same time, for native peoples in both countries, patriotism has long been a powerful force. In Mexico, across the political spectrum, indigenous peoples' organizations claim the national flag and the nationalist legacy of the Mexican revolution as their own, as highlighted by the Ejército Zapatista de Liberación Nacional's (EZLN's) official reverence for both sets of symbols, not to mention the names of the EZLN and the National Indigenous Congress.

In Mexico, the concept of race is widely associated with the postrevolutionary state's revindication of *mestizo* identity, embodied in the idea of the *Raza Cósmica*. This powerful discursive strategy challenged the Europhilic white skin privilege associated with the prerevolutionary regime, but at the same time promoted an ethnically homogenized view of Mexican collective identity. In this view, Mexicanness required full cultural assimilation for indigenous peoples, and total Spanish immersion was required for anyone who wanted access to formal education, at least until the late 1970s—including boarding schools not so different from those infamous in North America. In other words, this view promoted racial equality in theory while denying ethnic equality in practice. The regime's proposed bargain was class-based "inclusion" as Mexican peasants in exchange for giving up their autonomy, both in terms of their rights to sustain indigenous identities and in terms of freedom of association more generally.[14]

In Latin America, indigenous identity is less strictly bound to lineage and perceived phenotype than in the United States, not unlike the more flexible way in which blackness is understood in the region. In Latin America, indigenous peoples have long been defined primarily by such criteria as community membership, language use, and what are presented as ancestral collective traditions. Some of these traditions may, upon closer inspection, turn out be colonial and neocolonial mechanisms of authoritarian control by local elite brokers, backed up by the government, as Rus showed in the case of ritualized alcohol consumption in highland Chiapas (1994). In contrast to the United States, indigeneity in Latin America is rarely defined in tribal terms—except, for example, by outsiders to refer to some lowland Amazonian populations that have had little Western contact and to refer to some Mexican indigenous groups close to the U.S. border.[15] Yet as Wade's work implies, the processes of the social construction of race in Latin America are not *so* contingent as to elide all differences between racial and ethnic identity (1997).

Shifting back to U.S.-based intellectual traditions, classic approaches to Chicano identity also have difficulty with the concept of a multiethnic Mexico. Those that recognize the indigenous side of *mestizaje* tend to homogenize indigenous identity

---

14. On the relationship between national and ethnic identities in Mexico, see Gutiérrez (1999).

15. In Mexico the Yaqui, for example, or the O'Odham peoples, who live on both sides of the border, use the term tribe.

through the implicitly nationalist lens of Aztec/Nahua/Mexica ethnoracial roots. For many other Mexican indigenous peoples, however, the Aztecs were foreigners and often oppressors. Even today, Nahuas—although numerically the largest single ethno-linguistic group among Mexico's indigenous peoples—represent at most one quarter of the one in ten Mexicans who meet the government's linguistically based definition of ethnic identity. For reasons not well understood, Nahuas represent a substantially smaller fraction of the indigenous migrant population in the United States, which is still disproportionately composed of Zapotecs, Mixtecs, and Purhépechas.

In the dominant U.S. view, in contrast to Mexico, even partial indigenous heritage is enough to confer minority racial status, although formal (and state-structured) tribal membership is contingent on narrower definitions of lineage (often highly gendered). Most tribes use a definition of blood quantum for determining membership, some-times with different rules for men and women members who marry nonmembers. When tribal membership is contested, race can trump shared culture and history—as in the debate about excluding mixed indigenous/black peoples from tribal member-ship in Oklahoma.[16] More recently, narrow economic interests can also divide tribes. In California, the official leaders of some "gaming tribes" expelled numerous tradition-alist members to increase the income from gambling for those who remain (in official discourse they are "disenrolled").[17]

Historically, U.S.-born Native Americans were denied U.S. citizenship until 1924, ostensibly because of their tribal membership (Hull 1985, 13). This marked the first time that they could vote in national elections. Indigenous migrants were treated differently, however. As part of the more general policy that excluded nonwhite immigrants from the right to become naturalized U.S. citizens, this racial political exclusion was extended to Mexican migrants who appeared to be indigenous. Indigenous Mexicans were only allowed to become U.S. citizens after the 1940 Nationality Act allowed nonwhite immi-grants to naturalize (Hull 1985 and Padilla 1973, cited in Menchaca 2001, 282–85).

In contrast to the "blood quantum" approach in the United States, Latin American indigenous identity has long been seen in Latin America as socially and culturally con-tingent. For decades, indigenous people who move to the cities and appear to leave behind collective cultural practices, language use, and community membership have long been seen as having changed their ethnic identity. Nevertheless, they are often still openly racialized by dominant systems of oppression, although the processes and mechanisms vary greatly from country to country, ranging from *cholos* in Andean cit-ies to urban Indians in Mexico City.[18] Indeed, many urban Indians in Mexico—like indigenous migrants in the United States—continue to maintain ties with their com-munities of origin. Hirabayashi documents patterns of migrant hometown organiza-tion and socially constructed, politicized regional identities that are remarkably similar to experiences of indigenous migrants to the United States (1993). Gil Martínez de

---

16. See Glaberson (2001). For broader context, see Garroutte (2003), among others.

17. See De Armond (2003). Because of the official structures of tribal governance created by the U.S. federal government, these disenrolled members have little legal recourse (interview, Prof. Renya Ramirez, UC Santa Cruz, Fresno, CA, July 10, 2004).

18. On urban Indians in Mexico, see Yanes, Molina, and González (2004). On urban indigenous migrants in Latin America more generally, see Altamirano and Hirabayashi (1997).

Escobar documents migrants' construction of multisited forms of governance through which local civic power and representation are shared between the community of origin and communities of residence that are located both in the United States and in Mexican cities (2006). Yet although migrants in the United States often make more money than migrants who work elsewhere in Mexico and are therefore able to make larger financial contributions to community development investments back home, it is more difficult for them to visit home personally and to provide community service when called upon, even for those with immigration documents. Consider, for example, the experience of Leoncio Vásquez, trilingual interpreter and senior staffer of the Fresno-based Binational Center for the Development of Oaxacan Indigenous Communities. When called upon to provide service to his community of origin, as secretary to the municipal agent, he took a leave of absence from his job and relocated for his one-year term.[19] Shortly after beginning his service in Oaxaca, however, he was recalled back to Fresno for two weeks of jury duty—an unusually clear case of the challenges involved in the construction of practices of "civic binationality"—the process of becoming a full participant in the civic life of both societies."[20]

COLLECTIVE IDENTITY FORMATION AMONG INDIGENOUS MEXICAN MIGRANTS

Until relatively recently, the primary basis of indigenous collective identity in Mexico was highly localized. Most Mexican indigenous people identified primarily with their home community, to varying degrees with their home region, and only rarely with their broader ethnolinguistic group. Membership has long been internally regulated by each community's traditional norms, and the rights of membership are usually contingent on compliance with high levels of mandatory material contributions and public service (*tequio*). In response to migration, some communities are making membership requirements more flexible, whereas others hold firm and literally expel those who do not comply through a process that some members call "civic death" (Mutersbaugh 2002; Robles 2004; Gil Martinez de Escobar 2006).

The longstanding central role of community in defining ethnicity is summed up in the ambiguity inherent in the dual meaning of the term "*pueblo*," which in Mexico is used to refer both to community (as in village) and to (a) people. This dual meaning of pueblo was crucial to allowing both the government and the indigenous movement negotiators to agree on the text of the Mexico's 1996 San Andrés Accords on Indigenous Rights and Culture, which remains a key reference point for the ongoing political struggle for full recognition of Mexico's indigenous peoples. The government was willing to accept the possibility of indigenous autonomy if it was limited to the community level, but not if "pueblo" referred to an ethnic group that claimed rights as a people.

The process of the social construction of broader ethnic and pan-ethnic Mexican indigenous identity is where the racialization approach, emphasizing shared experiences of racially based oppression, is most clearly relevant. Nagengast and Kearney

---

19. Personal e-mail communication, April 1, 2009.

20. For further discussion of civic binationality, see Fox (2007) and Fox and Bada (2008, 2009).

(1990) pioneered the analysis of how the shared Oaxacan migrant experience of ethno-racial discrimination, both in northwestern Mexico and in California, drove the process of "scaling up" previously localized to broader Mixtec, Zapotec, and pan-ethnic Oaxacan indigenous identities. These experiences of racialization bring class and culturally based oppression together in forms that some would consider classically subaltern. This shared experience helps to overcome perceived conflicts of interest inherited from longstanding intervillage rivalries back home (these widespread conflicts were and are very convenient for regional and state elites). For indigenous farm workers, language and cultural differences with their bosses are key bases of ethnic discrimination, but they are also oppressed based on physical characteristics associated with specifically racial differences. For example, height became a widespread basis for contemptuous treatment, as summed up in the widespread derogatory diminuitive "*oaxaquito.*" This specific term, by homogenizing Oaxaca's ethnic differences, also racializes. As a result, in the indigenous migrant context, the term "Oaxacan" takes on a meaning beyond its territorial significance, coming to serve as shorthand for a pan-ethnic indigenous identity.

The relevance of this approach to identity formation, which associates the transition from localized to broader indigenous identities with migration, racial oppression, and resistance, is confirmed by the actual trajectory of the Indigenous Front of Binational Organizations (FIOB). The organization was first called the "Mixteco–Zapoteco Binational Front" and then changed its name to "Oaxacan Indigenous Binational Front" to reflect the inclusion of other Oaxacan ethnic groups. This inclusionary approach eventually attracted non-Oaxacan indigenous migrants to the organization, especially in Baja California and California, provoking an internal debate over whether to drop the regional term "Oaxacan" from its name. The FIOB's Baja members are migrants as well, although they did not cross the border. In March 2005, delegates representing several thousand FIOB members in Oaxaca, California, and Baja California agreed to change the name, while keeping the acronym, to the "Indigenous Front of Binational Organizations" (still FIOB). Their newly elected Binational Commission included members of four distinct Mexican indigenous groups, including a Purhépecha transportation engineer from the Baja-based contingent (Cano 2005). To rephrase this in the spirit of this essay's effort to reframe Mexican migration as a multiethnic process, these representatives included speakers of *five different Mexican languages.*

It is not only national rural-to-urban and transborder migrations that have raised questions about the degree to which indigenousness depends on once-rigid notions of localized community membership, shared language, and ancestral territory. The most well-known case of indigenous mobilization in Mexico emerged from a process of *rural-to-rural* migration. The original core region of the Zapatista rebellion—the *Cañadas*—is inhabited primarily by migrants from other Chiapas regions and their families, going back at most two generations (Leyva Solano and Ascencio Franco 1996). Liberation theology ideas that drew heavily on the Exodus are central to their cultural and political history. Before leaving the highlands to settle in the Cañadas and the lowland forest, these communities also had extensive prior experience with seasonal migration for wage labor, where they joined an ethnic mix as plantation farm workers. It is not a coincidence that their sense of indigenous identity is profoundly multiethnic, with ethnically distinct base organizations united under a multiethnic indigenous political leadership (primarily Tzetzal, Tzotzil, Chol, and Tojolobal). More recently, they adopted an explicitly racial solidarity discourse, in which leaders speak of the shared interests, despite differing ideologies, of people who are the *"color de la tierra"* ["the color of the soil"] (EZLN 2001). This definition of shared interests is made more complex by their other shared identities, as when Zapatista Comandante Felipe also appealed to Mexican factory workers as *"hermanos de nosotros"* ["our brothers"] (García Leyva, 2003, 15).

In this sense the EZLN and FIOB can both be seen as multiethnic organizations that first emerged in communities of settled migrants. In the first case the original migration had gone south and in the second case the migration went north, but in both cases their experiences and understandings of indigenousness can only be explained with reference to their (albeit very different) migration processes. In addition to both emerging from migrant communities, in both cases, early on a small number of political activists also played key roles by encouraging the scaling up of previously localized collective identities with rights-based ideologies.

The political trajectories of the two organizations came together briefly in the late 1990s, most notably when the FIOB organized polling stations in the U.S., as part of the Mexican national civic referendum that called both for recognition of indigenous rights in Mexico and for the right for migrants to vote in Mexican elections (Rivera-Salgado 2002; Martínez Saldaña 2004). Although they share the goal of self-determination and autonomy, their strategies differ dramatically. Whereas the EZLN does not participate in elections, the FIOB actively participates in local and state-level electoral politics, in coalition with the Party of the Democratic Revolution. Whereas the EZLN has created its own dual-power municipal governance structure, the FIOB works within Oaxaca's unusual system of customary law to encourage broader participation and accountability within existing municipalities. In Calforina, the FIOB also actively encourages voter participation and campaigns for immigration reform.

In summary, the FIOB works to create autonomous spaces and representation "within the system," both in the United States and in Mexico, whereas the EZLN remains firmly planted outside the system, conditioning their incorporation on more radical institutional change. Their political relationship with the diaspora is also sharply different. For the FIOB, sustaining balance in the binational relationship has been a challenge. Yet whereas the FIOB emerges from the cross-border migration process and has generated a worldview and structures of representation that take migration into account, the EZLN has yet to construct a broad political strategy for engaging Zapatista migrant youth from afar. Their approach varies by region, depending on the presence of prior traditions of internal migration (as in the cases of Los Altos and the Northern Zone). According to the most in-depth study of this process,

> The migration of Zapatista rank and file has been addressed exclusively within their communities, not by the EZLN as a movement. Zapatista communities have had total autonomy to create their own agreements...to cope with the departure of their young people. According to one of the members of the Junta "Hacia la Esperanza" [Zapatista local governing council]..."Each community has its agreements, and we can't get involved." The Junta is aware that it would be difficult to try to apply a uniform approach to deal with emigration, since each Zapatista community has their own way of organizing and solving their problems, as well as because in many

communities, Zapatistas live together with non-Zapatistas. The Zapatista governing councils are interested in communities coming to their own agreements, to avoid "breaking the community spirit." (Aquino Moreschi 2010: 192). The diversity of stances taken by organized sending communities Chiapas and Oaxaca underscores the local, family-based intimacy of migration decisions, as well as the difficulty of developing a broader, more politicized approach to encouraging "long-distance militancy" in unfamiliar terrain.

INDIGENOUS MIGRANTS, PEOPLEHOOD, AND TERRITORY

In Latin America, as in other regions of the world, classic definitions of indigenous rights, especially those involving demands for autonomy and self-determination, are closely linked to the concept of *territory*, which includes but is broader than (agrarian) land rights. Land rights are limited to individuals, families, groups, or communities, whereas *territories* are associated with the broader concept of peoplehood—and therefore are a foundation of ethnic identity.[21] The ethnohistorical basis for claims to both land and territory is clearly distinct from demands for rights that are based on, for example, redressing *racial* injustice, which are not as dependent on proving that specific territories are ancestral homelands. In most of Latin America, ethnohistorically based land claims have proven more "winnable," perhaps because of their more limited spillover effects.[22]

In this context, the extensive spread of longer-term, longer-distance out-migration throughout Mexico's indigenous regions raises serious questions about the nature of the link between ethnic identity and the territorial basis of peoplehood because many of the *pueblo* in question no longer live in their homeland, sometimes for generations. Indeed, neither the FIOB nor much of the EZLN base their claims to rights on territorially based ancestral domain. Instead, both use broader multi- and pan-ethnic discourses to make claims based on racial discrimination, class oppression, and human rights.

In their redefinition of the relationship between peoplehood and territory, Oaxacan indigenous migrants have gone further and have socially constructed the cross-border public space known as "Oaxacalifornia." This transnationalized sphere emerged from the Mixtec and Zapotec migration processes of the 1980s, from Oaxaca to Baja California, and then to California (later reaching Oregon and Washington as well; see Stephen 2007). In Oaxacalifornia, migrants bring together their lives in the United States with their communities of origin, sustaining deterritorialized communities from which new forms of social, civic, and cultural engagement emerged.[23]

---

21. For a theoretical discussion of "peoplehood," see R. Smith (2003).

22. On "multicultural citizenship reforms" in the region, which differentially affect peoples of African and indigenous descent, see Hooker (2005).

23. "Oaxacalifornia" itself is an unusual example of a term coined by a scholar, Michael Kearney, and widely appropriated by the communities themselves, as indicated by even a casual review of the pages of the binational *El Oaxaqueño* newspaper.

In this context, Oaxacan migrants deploy the term *paisano* in what could be called a kind of "situational territorial identity" with a distinctively indigenous character. As the FIOB's former Oaxaca coordinator put it,

> the word *paisano* can be interpreted on different levels...it depends on the context in which it is used. If we are in a specific community, you say *paisano* to mean being part of that community...it's a mark of distinction for the person, showing their honorability...This term has been part of the peoples' culture...With the need to migrate to other places, we find ourselves meeting people who, after talking a bit, we find out are from the some region, in a place filled with people from other states. There the concept is used to distinguish ourselves, and to bring us together more. Then the word reflects our identity as brothers.[24]

Here we see how collective identity "scales up" from home community to shared region of origin in the course of the migration process. At the same time, its territorial meaning turns out to be inseparable from its pan-ethnic character, serving both to bring indigenous Oaxacans together and to distinguish them from Mexicans from other states. Regional identity melds with pan-ethnic identity.

In this context, one analytical puzzle that emerges is why, despite the challenges posed by migration, some communities within some ethnic groups create their own membership organizations and public spaces more than others. Consider the Nahua migrant experience. Although they are Mexico's largest single group of indigenous language speakers—and some have been migrating for perhaps a century—Nahua migrants have not sustained visible membership organizations in the United States. Yet this does not mean that they are not organized or capable of cross-border collective action. On the contrary, it turns out that Nahua migrants supported a pioneering and successful 1991 campaign in defense of their communities of origin against a hydro-electric dam planned for the Alto Balsas region of northern Guerrero (García Ortega 2002; Good 1992). Coinciding with the Quincentenary, their sense of peoplehood as Nahuas was defined by this sense of shared *regional* identity, which was itself forged by the shared threat of inundation and dispossession. At the time, migrant supporters of the resistance to the dam demonstrated their full sense of shared ethnic and regional identity. This experience shares with the Chiapas rebellion and the creation of Oaxacalifornia the close link between collective (pan)-ethnic identity and socially constructed regional identities.

To frame this process of redefining the territorial basis of identity and membership, it is worth exploring some of the concepts that anthropologists and sociologists have used to describe cross-border migrant identities that become the basis for collective action. The nascent process through which migrants are creating their own public spaces and cross-border membership organizations is built on the foundation of what are increasingly referred to as "transnational communities," a concept that refers to groups of migrants whose daily lives, work, and social relationships extend across national borders. Transnational communities are grounded by the combination of their sustained cross-border relationships with the sustained reproduction of their cultural legacy in the United States. Some generate their own public spheres, as in the notable

---

24. Interview, Romualdo Juan Gutiérrez Cortés, Huajapan de León, Oaxaca, May 2000.

example of at least ten different annual Oaxacan Guelaguetza dance and music festivals held in the United States, each one organized by a different set of membership organizations. The Zapotec term Guelaguetza refers to the courtesy of mutual exchange. This festival, originally in honor of the corn god, was partly appropriated by the church and then by the state government. In the process, it became a *pan-ethnic* celebration and a major point of Oaxacan pride, both at home and in the diaspora.

These California festivals are the embodiment of *Oaxacalifornia* as an autonomous, pan-ethnic public sphere that is both uniquely Mexican and differently Mexican. They are held in parks, high school auditoriums, and college campuses, and the largest has been held in the Los Angeles Sports Arena, the former home of the Los Angeles Lakers basketball team. In each festival, hundreds volunteer their time so that thousands can come together, and parents can share their culture with their children. Indeed, few had had the opportunity to see such a festival when they were living in Oaxaca. With so much activity, California's multigenerational Oaxacan migrant dance groups are in high demand, and they represent yet another network of membership organizations. Each of the annual festivals reveals an x-ray of the social networks and organizational styles of different strands of the web of Oaxacan civil society in California. For example, some are strictly cultural, others work with local Latino politicians and organizations, some collaborate with the PRI-controlled Oaxacan state government, and others, such as the FIOB, fiercely guard their political independence.

To describe cases where migrant collective action has transformed the public sphere in the United States, some analysts use the concept of "cultural citizenship." This term "names a range of social practices which, taken together, claim and establish a distinct social space for Latinos in this country" [the United States] and serves as "a vehicle to better understand community formation . . . It involves the right to retain difference, while also attaining membership in society."[25] This process may or may not be linked to membership in a territorially based community, either in the home country or in the United States. Instead, it may be driven by other kinds of shared collective identities, such as racialized and gendered class identities as Latina or Latino workers. The idea of cultural citizenship is complementary to but quite distinct from the notion of transnational community, which both focuses on a specific kind of collective identity and emphasizes sustained cross-border community membership.

A third way of conceptualizing migrants as social actors sees them as constructing a *de facto* form of what one could call "*translocal community citizenship.*" This term refers to the process through which indigenous migrants are becoming active members both of their communities of settlement and of their communities of origin. Besserer's work has detailed indigenous migrants' construction of multisited forms of participation, representation, and governance (1999a, 1999b, 2004). Like the idea of transnational community, translocal community citizenship refers to the cross-border extension of the boundaries of an existing social sphere. The idea of translocal community citizenship therefore involves much more explicit boundaries of membership in the public affairs of a community that is geographically dispersed, or "deterritorialized." Yet when indigenous village governance is reconfigured to incorporate the

---

25. See Flores with Benmayor (1997, 1). See also Rocco (2004).

representation of the community in diaspora, membership becomes reterritorialized (Gil Martínez de Escobar 2006). Besserer also points out that these emerging forms of multisited shared community governance are quite distinct from hometown associations. Whereas membership in hometown associations is voluntary, often constituting a form of cross-border grassroots philanthropy, transnational citizenship involves the obligatory duties that sustain the right to community membership.[26] The challenges inherent in sustaining this process of long-distance membership have produced a wide range of community responses and proposals (Kearney and Besserer 2004).

Like cultural citizenship, the term "community citizenship" refers to a socially constructed sense of membership, often built through collective action, but it differs in at least three ways. First, community citizenship incorporates the term *that is actually used by the social actors themselves* to name their own experience of membership. In indigenous communities throughout rural Mexico, a member in good standing—one who fulfills specific obligations and therefore can exercise specific rights—is called a "citizen" of that community (often but not always male).[27] Note that this use of the term citizen for full membership in local indigenous communities appears to *predate* the widespread usage of the term by national and international civil society organizations. In contrast, it is not clear whether the idea of cultural citizenship has been appropriated by those it refers to. Second, the idea of translocal community specifies the public space within which membership is exercised, whereas cultural citizenship is deliberately open-ended as to the *arena* of inclusion (local, regional, or national? territorial or sectoral?). Third, the concept of cultural citizenship focuses, quite appropriately given its goals, on the contested process of negotiating new terms of incorporation *into U.S. society*, in contrast to the emphasis embedded in the idea of translocal community citizenship on the challenge of sustaining binational membership in a cross-border community.

The concept of translocal community citizenship has its own limits as well. It does not capture the broader, rights-based perspective that transcends membership in specific territorially based (or reterritorialized) communities, such as the migrant movement for Mexican voting rights abroad or the FIOB's emphasis on indigenous and human rights. These collective identities are shared beyond specific communities. The idea of translocal is also limited insofar as it does not capture the frequently *multilevel* process of engagement between migrant membership organizations and the Mexican state at national and state as well as local levels.

These different concepts for describing migrants as social actors are all complementary and reflect important dimensions of that process; each one refers to social processes of migrant identity and organization that may overlap but are distinct, both in theory and in practice. At the same time, they do not capture the full range of migrant collective identities. The broader idea of *"migrant civil society"* provides

---

26. For discussion of the strengths and limitations of the related concept of "transnational citizenship," see Fox (2005). On hometown associations; cross-border power relations, see Fox and Bada (2008).

27. On gender and Oaxaca indigenous community membership, both in migration and in communities of origin, see Maldonado and Artía (2004), Stephen (2007), Velasco (2002, 2004), and Velásquez (2004). For one of the few studies of masculinity among indigenous migrants, see Hernández Sánchez (2006).

an umbrella concept for describing diverse patterns of collective action (Fox 2007). Migrant civil society refers to *migrant-led membership organizations and public institutions*, which includes four very tangible arenas of collective action—membership organizations, nongovernmental organizations, communications media, and autonomous public spaces. Some elements of migrant civil society could be seen as representing a U.S. "branch" of Mexican civil society, others reflect the Mexican branch of U.S. civil society, and still others embody arenas of overlap between the two, as in the case of the FIOB itself. Although Mexican migrant organizations are increasingly engaged both with U.S. civic and political life and with Mexico, the FIOB is still one of the very few mass organizations that represent members both in the United States and in Mexico.

CONCLUSIONS

The collective practices that are beginning to constitute a specifically indigenous arena within Mexican migrant civil society show us a new side of what otherwise is an unrelentingly devastating process for Mexico's indigenous communities—their abrupt insertion into globalized capitalism through international migration in search of wage labor. Their migratory experience has both broadened and transformed previously localized identities into ethnic, pan-ethnic, and racial identities, while also questioning widely held homogenous understandings of Mexican national identity. At the same time, "long-distance membership" in their home communities, as well as the construction of new kinds of organizations not based on ties to the land, raises unanswered questions about the classic close association among land, territory, and indigenous identity. The Mexican indigenous migrant experience also raises questions about how to think about the racialization process, which has been largely seen through U.S. lenses. The now substantial literature on Oaxacan migrants shows that, for many indigenous Mexicans, "racialization begins at home"—that is, in Mexico and among other Mexicans in the United States.

Mexican migrants and indigenous peoples both pursue self-representation through multiple strategies, coalitions, and repertoires. They also share the experience of having long been widely perceived by others as faceless masses—both in Mexico and in the United States. Until recently, they have been recognized as either victims or threats, but not as collective actors. Both migrants and indigenous Mexicans are now in the midst of a long-term process of building their capacities for self-representation in their respective domains. Indigenous Mexican migrants are no exception. Do their organizations represent the indigenous wing of a broader cross-border migrant movement that would otherwise leave them out? Do they represent the migrant wing of the broader national indigenous movement that would otherwise leave them out? Yes, and yes, but most of all they represent themselves, both indigenous and migrants.

CHAPTER 8

Mexican Migration and the Law

David FitzGerald

University of California, San Diego

M ore people of Mexican birth lived in the United States in 2008 than the total
number of immigrants in any other country in the world. Equally striking, more
than half are living in the United States illegally (Pew Hispanic Center 2009b, 1). How
have U.S. and Mexican law shaped and reacted to this massive migration?

One misconception about immigration from the United States to Mexico is that
the Mexican government has always encouraged its citizens to leave as an economic
and political escape valve. The following pages uncover the largely forgotten efforts of
the Mexican government to manage emigration and migrants over the past century.
Mexican policy has been regularly undermined by much more consequential U.S. policies. Ineffective early attempts by the Mexican government to control emigration flows
have given way to new forms of institutionalized ties between the Mexican government
and Mexicans abroad.

I then show how U.S. law regulates immigration from Mexico. American commentators and politicians frequently ask why Mexicans don't simply "get into line" to
immigrate through official channels.[1] In practice, many Mexicans do get into line. The
5.7 million Mexicans legally living in the United States in 2008 represented 21 percent
of all legal immigrants, far outnumbering any other immigrant nationality of origin
(Pew Hispanic Center 2009b, 2). Yet for the many Mexicans who lack specialized skills
or ties to close family members in the United States, the supply of immigrant visas
is dramatically lower than the high U.S. demand for their labor. For them, the line
to become a legal immigrant never moves forward. Efforts to prevent unauthorized
Mexicans from entering and working in the United States have proved largely ineffective, although those efforts have unleashed a set of unintended and often harmful
social consequences. I conclude by outlining the bilateral challenges of a comprehensive immigration reform.

---

1. See, for example, http://blog.thehill.com/2007/05/21/illegal-immigrants-need-to-get-in-line-with-
everyone-else-rep-john-culberson.

AN UNSTOPPABLE EXODUS

From the onset of mass emigration to the United States at the turn of the twentieth century to the beginning of the bracero temporary worker program in World War II, Mexican officials and intellectuals were generally critical of the demographic, economic, and ideological effects of emigration. They believed that Mexico's population was insufficient to achieve its full economic potential, particularly in the vast northern provinces. The 1848 loss of the northern half of Mexico to the United States was blamed on the weak Mexican population base in Texas and California prior to the war. Preventing further emigration of Mexicans to the United States thus became central to elite understandings of national demographic health (Loyo 1935). Ideological objections to emigration complemented economic and demographic calculations. The government sought to unify a populace splintered by ethnicity and class around the common foreign menace of the United States, a country that had intervened militarily in Mexico as recently as 1919. Nationalists objected that emigration to the northern nemesis stripped many Mexicans of their cultural and legal nationality (González Navarro 1994, 253.)

A Campaign of Dissuasion, 1900–1942

Attempts to dissuade emigration began as early as 1904, when Mexican federal and state authorities ordered county governments to stop issuing travel documents used by U.S.-bound workers. Governors of states with high levels of emigration repeatedly asked the Secretariat to restrict or prohibit emigration, but federal officials usually argued that although they wished to discourage emigration, they could not constitutionally prevent it. The constitution leaves room for situational interpretations, however. Article 11 of the 1857 constitution, in effect until 1917, established freedom of exit and travel within the country subject to administrative restrictions in criminal and civil matters. Exit in the 1917 constitution was restricted further by reference to a separate body of migration law and Article 123, specifying that county authorities must ensure that workers emigrating abroad have signed contracts detailing wages, hours, and repatriation costs borne by the employer.[2]

Officials rarely applied the constitutional measures restricting labor emigration. The United States contracted seventy thousand Mexican workers from 1917 to 1921 as a unilateral wartime emergency measure. In violation of Mexican law, the contracts were not visaed by U.S. consuls. Yet the Mexican government did not try to block the exit of contracted workers with anything other than a propaganda campaign, largely because the presidency and Secretariat of Foreign Relations (SRE) did not want to antagonize the United States during the vulnerability of revolutionary turmoil (Aguila 2000).

Subnational governments promulgated many of the most vigorous antiemigration policies. The governments of sparsely populated northern states like Sonora and Chihuahua prohibited the exit of scarce workers by instructing the migration offices in Ciudad Juárez and Nogales to deny workers exit permits and to prevent the operation of *enganchadores* (labor recruiters from U.S. companies). In 1918, Tamaulipas raised

---

2. *Constitución Federal de los Estados Unidos Mexicanos*, 1857; *Constitución Federal de los Estados Unidos Mexicanos*, 1917. See Fitzgerald (2009).

its international bridge fees to discourage emigration, which was pulling labor away from its industries. The following year, the government of Jalisco restricted the issuance of passports to appease local industrialists and farmers complaining of worker shortages and asked municipal presidents to select poor emigrants most in need of repatriation aid from the state government. Given Jalisco's dense population, ostensible fears of labor shortages were more about reduced labor supplies driving up wages than the absolute shortages that sometimes occurred in northern states (Fitzgerald 2009).

Following the end of World War I, the Carranza government feared the prospect of massive deportations of Mexican workers and selectively financed repatriations as a preemptive measure to avoid national humiliation. Simply the potential for restrictive U.S. policies shaped Mexican policy even before the U.S. government acted. The Mexican government sponsored fifty thousand repatriations at a cost of $1 million during the 1921–1922 U.S. depression. The expense of repatriation prompted the federal government to suspend its program in 1923 and once again rely on periodic public warnings not to emigrate and a 1925 ban on selling railway tickets in the interior to laborers heading to the United States (Reisler 1976; Alanís Enciso 1999).

A 1926 migration law gave authority to the Secretariat of the Interior to prevent workers from leaving Mexico without contracts approved by the municipal president in the place of origin. To enforce this law and fine violators, emigration control officers were deployed along the border, in trains, and in major cities of the interior (Landa y Piña 1930). The 1917 Mexican prohibition of leaving without a contract, combined with the 1885–1952 U.S. prohibition on entering with a contract, meant that Mexican labor migration to the United States was illegal according to the laws of at least one of the countries. Although the United States made exceptions for Mexicans to the ban on contracted workers during the "wartime emergencies" of 1917–1921 and beginning in the 1942 Bracero Program (Reisler 1976), from 1921 to 1942, the anticontract provision in U.S. law meant Mexico could not enforce its own contract laws aimed at protecting emigrants.

Encouraging repatriation of emigrants in the United States had been Mexican federal policy since the Porfirian era (1877–1911; Aguila 2000), but the state's ability to control the flow of repatriates and design effective reintegration programs was sharply limited by Mexico's asymmetric interdependence with the United States. With the onset of the Great Depression, U.S. officials at all levels of government began using multiple forms of persuasion and even deportation to repatriate an estimated 400,000 Mexicans. Trying to make the best of a difficult situation by framing repatriation as the calling home of the nation's sons by a state dedicated to protecting all of its workers, the Mexican government cooperated with U.S. authorities and paid for thousands of repatriates' transportation home from the border (Alanís Enciso 2003a). The Mexican government attempted to avoid social and political unrest by encouraging the repatriates to disperse across Mexico's territory. It initiated agricultural colonies with modern farming methods, mostly in sparsely populated northern states. To the government's disappointment, most repatriates returned to their heavily populated states of origin in the central west, where they did little to transform local agriculture. Authorities rarely backed repatriate agricultural colonies with sufficient planning or resources (González Navarro 1994; Alanís Enciso 2007a). Since its onset, migration patterns had largely been determined by U.S. policies and labor demand despite the attempts of Mexican federal, state, and county governments to protect their interests.

The Bracero Program, 1942–1964

Mexican federal policy shifted dramatically in 1942 when the U.S. and Mexican governments negotiated a series of agreements that ended in 1964, providing for 4.6 million bracero contracts for temporary agricultural work in the United States. There were a further 5 million apprehensions of illegal immigrants by U.S. authorities during the same period (García y Griego 1983; Durand and Massey 1992). The immediate cause for the shift in Mexican policy was a sudden increase in its bargaining power with the United States, brought on by the historical conjuncture of a wartime alliance with the Allied powers and increased U.S. demand for agricultural workers. These circumstances allowed the Mexican government to negotiate a favorable bilateral agreement that hypothetically would exchange a pool of unemployed laborers for a source of remittances and modernizing influences (García y Griego 1983; Cohen 2001).

Long-standing disagreements between Washington, D.C., and Mexico City over government supervision of contracts, wages, and working conditions erupted in October 1948. Mexican officials pressured the U.S. government to make concessions by refusing to allow workers to cross into the United States. Under pressure from employers, U.S. immigration officials opened the border at El Paso, allowing an estimated four thousand illegal entrants across in three days. Mexico responded by abrogating the agreement, which was not renegotiated until August 1949 (Craig 1971; Cohen 2001). Similarly, when the U.S. government adopted a policy of unilateral contracts in January 1954, Mexican troops clashed with thousands of rioting workers attempting to cross the border illegally. Successful crossers were welcomed by American immigration officials and shipped to the fields (Calavita 1992; Cohen 2001).

The practical application of U.S. immigration policy, even when it contravened U.S. law, once again undercut Mexico City's stance on emigration. Mexico City attempted to restrict illegal migration, whereas important elements of the U.S. government encouraged it. Throughout the mid-1950s, a similar cycle in which the Mexican government promoted bracero emigration and then suddenly tried to stop all emigration continued with the vicissitudes of the guest worker negotiations. Unfortunately for Mexico, the United States had the option of replacing Mexicans with workers from other areas like the Caribbean, whereas Mexican labor emigration was exclusively dependent on the United States (Craig 1971). Given the asymmetries in their relationship and a proven inability to stop emigrants from leaving, the Mexican government had few means of forcing U.S. concessions.

Laissez-Faire, 1965–1989

Through the early 1970s, the Mexican government unsuccessfully attempted to revive the bracero agreements that ended in 1964. The U.S. government saw little reason to resume the program so long as undocumented immigrants met U.S. labor demand. Both governments tacitly accepted massive illegal migration. From the experience of the Mexican government, emigration appeared practically impossible to regulate. The rapidly increasing Mexican population, which rose from 19.7 million in 1940 to 48.2 million in 1970, meant serious emigration restriction was no longer needed in any case. The demographic deficit had been resolved so well that population growth was becoming a new problem. Whereas the 1947 Law of Population outlined the government's attempt to increase population through natural growth, immigration, and repatriation, its 1974 reform noted that population increases were a growing strain on the economy and state services, and the government began to successfully reduce the national fertility rate (Fitzgerald 2009).

As part of this effort to slow demographic growth, official policy shifted from taking "measures to prevent and avoid emigration" and fining workers who emigrated without a contract in 1947 to "restrict[ing] the emigration of nationals when the national interest demands it" and removing the penalties for leaving without a contract in 1974. In October 1974, President Echeverría told President Ford that Mexico no longer sought a renewal of the Bracero Program (Secretaría de Gobernación 1996; de la Garza and Szekely 1997). The policy of laissez-faire continued through the 1980s, when a series of economic crises sent growing numbers of mostly unauthorized migrants north. Without enough jobs being created each year for adolescents entering the labor force, Mexican authorities had little incentive to stem the flow. Emigration became an economic escape valve at a national level that had the added benefit of relieving pressure on the political system.

Embracing Emigrants Abroad, 1990–2009

Mexico's policies toward emigrants already abroad changed dramatically in the early 1990s. Underlying migration patterns had changed, in large part because of the U.S. 1986 Immigration Reform and Control Act (IRCA), which accelerated a trend toward permanent settlement by legalizing 2.3 million Mexicans. The newly legalized then sponsored the immigration of their family members. A pattern of circular, mostly male migration gave way to permanent migration of whole families (Massey, Durand, and Malone 2002). Emigrants and their resources became less accessible within Mexico, prompting the Mexican government to try to embrace them better abroad.

Mexican partisan politics spilling over into the Mexican population in the United States was the proximate cause of the policy reorientation. For the first time since the 1920s, the ruling party and competitive opposition parties vied for the favor of the Mexican population in the United States. Cuauhtémoc Cárdenas, the center-left opposition candidate for president in 1988 who later founded the Party of the Democratic Revolution (PRD), drew large crowds of Mexican migrants while campaigning in California and Chicago. Cárdenas appealed to Mexican citizens to influence the vote of their family members in Mexico and promised emigrants dual nationality and the right to vote from abroad. Emigrant rights groups, many of which were affiliated with the PRD, formed to demand a voice in Mexican politics.

The ruling Institutional Revolutionary Party (PRI) responded quickly to counter the PRD's overtures toward migrants. Most points of the Mexican political spectrum now agree, at least publicly, that Mexicans outside the country should be included somehow in Mexican political life. In his 1995–2000 National Development Plan, PRI President Ernesto Zedillo declared that "the Mexican nation extends beyond the territory contained within its borders." These were not irredentist claims, but rather discursive moves seeking the political and economic resources of Mexicans in the United States.

The creation of a Mexican lobby in the United States became one of Mexico's primary foreign policy goals beginning with the 1993 campaign to pass the North American Free Trade Agreement in the U.S. Congress. The Mexican consulates also worked with Mexican American political organizations to try to defeat California's 1994 Proposition 187, which would have sharply restricted unauthorized immigrants' access to social services had the proposition not been struck down in federal court after it passed. In general, there has been little to show for the lobbying effort, in part because Mexicans in the United States tend to be quite suspicious of the Mexican government (de la Garza et al. 2000; Suro and Escobar 2006).

Remittances have proved to be a much richer resource. Mexico received US$25 billion in remittances in 2008, notwithstanding a fall-off during the global economic crisis.[3] Remittances tend to be private, household-level transfers that can only be taxed when they circulate in the local economy. Many government agencies have tried to channel remittances toward collective projects. The Mexican government has institutionalized ties with emigrants through the SRE's Program for Mexican Communities Abroad (PCME) since 1990. The PCME creates formal ties between hometown associations (formed by migrants from the same community of origin) and the Mexican government at the federal, state, and county levels. These relationships are the basis for matching funds programs like *Tres por Uno* (3×1), in which migrants and Mexican government agencies jointly develop infrastructure projects in migrants' places of origin. By 2008, the program was spending roughly US$125 million a year on nearly twenty-five hundred community projects, with a quarter of the funding coming directly from migrants.[4] Levels of collective remittances are modest overall, although they can improve the quality of life in impoverished rural areas. Most importantly, collective remittances strengthen the more diffuse hometown ties that channel the massive volume of household remittances.

Matching fund programs and other emigrant initiatives survived the change in administration from the PRI to the center-right National Action Party in 2000. One of President Fox's first official acts in 2000 was to inaugurate a Presidential Office for Communities Abroad directed by Juan Hernández, a dual national literature professor born in Texas. The cabinet-level position was abolished in 2002 after conflicts with Secretary of Foreign Relations Jorge Castañeda over how to manage two cabinet agencies simultaneously conducting foreign policy. In 2003, the PCME and the presidential office were folded into the new Institute for Mexicans Abroad, which includes an advisory council composed of 105 Mexican community leaders and 10 Latino organizations in the United States, 10 special advisors, and representatives of each of the 32 state governments in Mexico. In 2009, the advisory council of the Institute for Mexicans Abroad called for the creation of a new cabinet-level position that would coordinate Mexico's emigration policy.[5]

---

3. Banco de México. http://www.banxico.org.mx/documents/%7BB7CBCFAF-AB7D-BE65-F78F-6827D524C418%7D.pdf

4. Secretaría de Desarollo Social. http://www.sedesol.gob.mx/archivos/8015/File/4totrim08/penccg/03_3x1_para_Migrantes.pdf

5. On emigration policy since 1989, see Fitzgerald (2004) and Godoy's (1998) analysis of Mexican congressional debates.

Homeland Politics and Dual Nationality

One of the principal novelties in the relationship between the Mexican government and its emigrants is the former's promotion of dual nationality. Naturalizing abroad has been grounds for losing Mexican citizenship or nationality since 1857. Since the adoption in 1886 of a mixed system of attributing nationality based both on descent (*jus sanguinis*) and on birth in the territory (*jus soli*), many children born to Mexican nationals in *jus soli* countries like the United States or born in Mexico to foreigners from *jus sanguinis* countries were *de facto* dual nationals. "Voluntary" foreign naturalization was grounds for denationalization beginning in 1934, but the interpretation of voluntary narrowed in 1939 and 1993, so that emigrants who adopted a foreign nationality as a requirement of employment were considered to have involuntarily naturalized and thus were able to maintain their Mexican nationality. They became *de facto* dual nationals as well. Although 1993 nationality legislation adopted the principle that nationality should be singular and required *de facto* dual nationals to choose a single nationality at the age of majority, just five years later, the "nonforfeiture" (*no pérdida*) of nationality law taking effect in 1998 protected native Mexicans from mandatory denationalization, although they may still voluntarily expatriate. In effect, the nonforfeiture legislation was a dual nationality law. The term "dual nationality" was likely not adopted in official documents to avoid raising the hackles of those who discursively associate dual nationality with "dual loyalty" and to maintain a semblance of continuity in Mexican law (Fitzgerald 2005).

The substantive prerogatives of dual nationals remain contested and ambiguous. On its face, the Mexican constitution prohibits dual nationals from holding public offices, including those of federal deputy, federal senator, president, and state governor. The 1917 Constitution still in effect specifies that these positions are reserved for "Mexicans by birth," and Article 32 specifies that positions for which one is required to be Mexican by birth "are reserved for those who have this quality and do not acquire another nationality." The question of whether dual nationals can serve as federal deputies has not been resolved conclusively, however. Manuel de la Cruz, a dual U.S. and Mexican national and long-time California resident, was believed to have won election to the Mexican Congress's Chamber of Deputies based on his position on the PRD's party list in 2003. Despite the controversy over whether a dual national was legally eligible for the office, none of the Mexican political parties formally challenged de la Cruz's election with election authorities, likely because they wanted to avoid antagonizing emigrants. At the last moment, after de la Cruz had already been issued a key to his new congressional office, the Federal Electoral Tribunal ruled that to rectify a technical miscalculation, it would reapportion to another party the PRD's seat that de la Cruz thought he had won (Fitzgerald 2006b).

De la Cruz never took federal office, but the question of the political rights of dual nationals will likely resurface as it becomes increasingly common for Mexicans residing in the United States to run for office in Mexico. Andrés Bermúdez, a successful farmer known as the "Tomato King" living in the Sacramento area, was elected mayor of his native town of Jerez, Zacatecas, in 2001, but was denied his office by the state electoral commission because he was not a local resident. In response, his allies in the Zacatecas state conference passed a law in 2003 that allows binational Zacatecano residents to run for state and local office. Bermúdez was subsequently elected again and served his term. The same law established an extraterritorial election district for Zacatecanos in the United States who now elect two senators to the state congress (Smith and Bakker 2007). Demands by the PRD for a national extraterritorial district have not been successful, although there is precedent for such districts in countries as diverse as Italy, Colombia, and Poland (Ellis 2007).

Mexico allowed expatriate voting for the first time in its 2006 presidential election. Roughly 3 of 10 million Mexicans in the United States were eligible to vote. Yet only 57,000 tried to register, and fewer than 33,000 cast a valid ballot. Part of the reason for the low turnout is that emigrant interest in Mexican politics is widespread but shallow. Moreover, Mexican authorities did not carry out voter registration abroad. Voting was only allowed by mail, in the first instance to deliberately suppress turnout, but also to avoid provoking a potential nativist backlash in the United States. A new ban was put on Mexican presidential campaigning abroad under the logic that the Mexican electoral authorities would not be able to supervise campaigning if it were done in another country (Smith and Bakker 2007; Waldinger, Porzecanski, and Soehl 2009). The introduction of subnational external suffrage in the major migrant sending state of Michoacán's 2007 gubernatorial election yielded equally meager results. Only 997 Michoacanos abroad tried to register to vote, of which 691 fulfilled the requirements and 349 mailed in valid votes.[6] Future voting is likely to yield higher rates of participation as emigrants become accustomed to the procedures, which might also be streamlined under emigrant pressure, but it appears that the emigrant vote will only affect the tightest elections.

Emigration Policy

Although emigrant activists, Mexican political parties, and the Mexican government have created new ways for emigrants to engage in Mexican politics, the fundamental story of emigration policy since the end of the Bracero Program is one of continuity in accepting both legal and illegal labor emigration as inevitable. Emigration control is implemented now by the Grupo Beta police force, which first formed in Tijuana in 1990 and later expanded across the northern and southern borders. In 2000, the 75 Grupo Beta agents stationed on the two thousand-mile U.S. border arrested around one hundred *coyotes* a month for violating the ban on human smuggling in the 1996 amendments to the General Law of Population. A debate within the Mexican government arose in June 2001 over whether Grupo Beta could forcibly prevent emigrants from crossing in the most dangerous areas. The government ultimately decided that migrants could not constitutionally be prevented from leaving, and in August 2001, Grupo Beta gave up its control functions altogether to focus on protecting undocumented migrants from bandits, conducting rescue operations, and supplying information about how to cross safely. The Secretariat of the Interior's National Migration Institute has a multimedia campaign asking citizens to report *coyotes* to a toll-free telephone number and to avoid crossing into the United States in dangerous wilderness areas in which hundreds of migrants die every year (Fitzgerald 2009). In 2005, the National Migration Institute began distributing over a million copies of an educational comic booklet for undocumented migrants with detailed tips on how to avoid the

---

6. *Cambio de Michoacán* (2007); Instituto Electoral de Michoacán, http://www.prep.com.mx.

major risks of undocumented crossings by carrying water, following power lines north, and always keeping the *coyote* in sight.

A disclaimer on the back of the booklet summarizes the federal government's current stance toward illegal migration: "This consular protection guide does not promote the crossing of the border by Mexicans without the legal documentation required by the government of the United States. Its objective is to publicize the risks that [such crossings] imply, and to inform about the rights of migrants regardless of their legal residence."[7] The right to exit in the Mexican constitution has always been subject to situational interpretations and tempered by qualifications, however, including the authorization to use coercion in the 1926 migration law. The 1974 General Law of Population still in effect requires departing labor migrants to present themselves to Mexican migration authorities, show a work contract authorized by the destination country consulate, and provide proof that they met the entry requirements of the destination country (Secretaría de Gobernación 1996). Clearly, undocumented migrants hiking across the Arizona desert do not meet these criteria. There are no longer penalties for violating this article in the General Law of Population. The argument for a constitutional right of exit is a convenient way of legitimating the federal government's minimal efforts to restrict unauthorized emigration.

Temporary Migrant Programs

Although there are no bilateral guest worker programs between the United States and Mexico, individual Mexican states effectively help to administer the U.S. government's H2B program for temporary, unskilled, nonagricultural workers. For example, since 2001, the government of Jalisco has recruited workers and helped them to apply through the U.S. consulates to fill positions mostly as golf course landscapers. In 2004, 136 H2B visas were issued with the office's assistance. The alternative is to leave the program to what one state official called "a mafia" of H2B veterans who arrange the paperwork for newcomers for an exorbitant fee. In response to a new breed of *enganchador* charging $1,500 to $4,000 in recruitment fees, the government of Zacatecas went a step further in 2001 by negotiating a pilot program with the U.S. consulate in Monterrey that recruits temporary workers under the direction of the Zacatecas government. Although these guest worker programs operate independently of the Mexican federal government, they are a window into the sort of large-scale, truly bilateral programs that are the federal government's goal (Fitzgerald 2009).

Mexican President Vicente Fox (2000–2006) made a migration accord with the United States a pillar of his foreign policy. A fundamental philosophical shift has taken place in the SRE away from the "policy of no policy," in which Mexican authorities long turned a blind eye to massive unauthorized migration across its northern border, to a more active stance. Mexican officials do not want to repeat their lack of involvement in U.S. legislation like IRCA, whose debate they did not participate in based on the premise that Mexican intervention in sovereign U.S. policy making would legitimate U.S. interventions in Mexican politics. High-level bilateral meetings in 2001, including a presidential meeting in Washington, D.C., on September 7, 2001, centered on the design of a new temporary-worker program, an increase in the number of visas issued

---

7. Instituto Nacional de Migración, http://www.inami.gob.mx.

to Mexicans, and regularization of unauthorized migrants in the United States. Four days later, the 9/11 attacks derailed the bilateral talks (Rosenblum 2004). President Felipe Calderón (2006–present) downplayed his predecessor's vocal expectations of a bilateral migration accord but was clearly interested in the same goal of legalized flows.

U.S. IMMIGRATION LAW

Immigration law in the United States has sometimes treated Mexicans differently than other nationals, but even where the law is universal, it affects Mexico with particular intensity given the Mexican dominance of contemporary U.S. immigration stocks and flows. The following sections describe the legal line to get into the United States and efforts to control unauthorized migration at the border, in the U.S. interior, and at U.S. workplaces. Like the Mexican government, the U.S. government has struggled to control migration flows, but U.S. policy has been far more consequential in shaping migration outcomes, even when those outcomes are not intended. Local and state governments in the United States are attempting to address the perceived failures of federal policy within the sharp constraints of constitutional interpretation, giving control over immigration to the federal government. A restrictive turn at all levels has increased the value of U.S. citizenship and prompted a wave of naturalizations by Mexicans in the United States. At the same time, the issue of illegality continues to loom large, prompting renewed efforts at a comprehensive immigration reform.

Contemporary Legal Migration

Most people who enter the United States legally come on various kinds of nonimmigrant visas meant to allow temporary stays for tourism, business, or work. In 2007, a total of 7.4 million entries were made by Mexicans—more than the nationals of any other country—under the "I-94" nonimmigrant category for long-term stays in the United States or for entry at airports. These figures do not include the millions of entries by holders of border crossing cards, which permit travel within twenty-five miles of the border for as long as a month. From 1998 to 2002, the U.S. State Department issued over 5.8 million border crossing cards to residents of Mexican border cities (DHS 2008b, Table 26; GAO 2008).

The line to work in the United States begins with several temporary worker programs. Of the 462,000 H-1B visas issued to highly skilled workers in 2007, a total of 3.9 percent were issued to Mexicans, putting Mexico in fourth place ahead of China. Mexicans were issued 91 percent of the more than 87,000 H-2A temporary agricultural visas and 68 percent of the 155,000 H-2B and H-2R seasonal nonagricultural worker visas (DHS 2008b). Congress sets visa caps on the programs, with the exception of the H-2A agricultural visas, which do not have a cap but remain unpopular among farmers because of their onerous requirements and the ready supply of unauthorized labor (Martin 2005).

The line to immigrate for permanent settlement is governed by a separate set of regulations. Immigrant visas, or "green cards," authorize a legal permanent resident (LPR) status that is renewable every ten years. In 2007, nearly 150,000 Mexicans comprised 14 percent of all new LPRs, almost twice as many as any other national-origin group. In most years, more than half of "new" LPRs were already living in the United States when they gained LPR status. In 2007, a total of 59 percent of new LPRs of all nationalities adjusted their status rather than entering for the first time (DHS 2008c, 1).

A preference system regulates the number of green cards issued every year. In 2007, a total of 226,000 annual visas were available for family preferences, broken down into subcategories for different kinds of family relationships (see Figure 8.1). The employment preference system allots 147,148 visas, the vast majority of which are for skilled workers. In a putative attempt to maintain the diversity of new immigrants and in an effort to keep any one country from dominating flows, each country in the world is limited to receiving 7 percent of the total number of family-sponsored and employment preferences, meaning a cap of 26,120 visas per country under the preference system in 2007. Spouses and children of U.S. citizens and parents of adult citizens are exempt from the caps in the family preference system. Exempt immediate family members comprised 46 percent of all LPRs in 2006 (DHS 2008c).

How do Mexicans benefit or suffer discrimination under the current system? Informal discrimination, whether practiced by Border Patrol agents (Heyman 1995), immigration officers at points of entry (Gilboy 1991), or immigration courts (Coutin 1998), is difficult to assess systematically, although scholars have made important contributions in this area. Within the formal sphere, the same policies can be considered discriminatory or universalistic depending on whether the unit of analysis is the *source country* or the *individual citizen* of the source country. During the national origins quota system from 1921 to 1965 that differentially assigned immigration quotas to different countries based on their ethnic desirability, Mexico and the rest of the countries in the western hemisphere were exempt from the quotas. Most policy makers preferred Mexican immigrant workers because they were thought to have an extremely circular immigration pattern and reluctance to settle permanently. A limit was first set on immigrants from the western hemisphere in 1968. Seven years later, the State Department dropped its opposition to country limits on Mexico and Canada, which

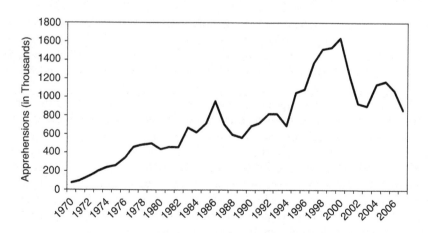

Figure 8.1 Apprehensions along the Southwest Border, 1980-2007.

Source: INS/DHS Annual Yearbooks

it had historically rejected based on the logic that they were neighboring countries. When country limits within the western hemisphere were introduced in 1976, legal immigration from Mexico immediately fell by 40 percent. Presidents Ford and Carter unsuccessfully urged a reform that would provide more visas for Mexicans (Massey, Durand, and Malone 2002, 43; Zolberg 2006, 343–44).

All independent countries now receive the same maximum number of immigrant visas under the employment and family preferences (DHS 2008c). The country quotas are nondiscriminatory where the source country is the unit of analysis. At the same time, provisions for the reunification of the closest family members outside of the country caps have favored Mexico as a country, given its long, sustained, massive migration to the United States. There were 150,000 new Mexican LPRs in 2007 despite the country quota of 26,120 because of the prevalence of strong family ties.

Where the individual is the unit of analysis, the limit of 26,120 visas per country discriminates against individuals from countries where there is a high level of demand to immigrate to the United States. Under the current system, Mexico is treated the same as small countries such as Monaco or countries with little history of migration to the United States such as Djibouti. Consequently, the waiting period to process an immigrant visa through family preference categories under the country limits varies widely among national origin groups. For example, in 2006 unmarried adult daughters and sons of U.S. citizens waited twelve years if they were Mexican, fifteen years if they were Filipino, and "only" five years on average if they were nationals of other countries (see Table 8.1).

Policies vary in the extent to which their discriminatory effects are intended or unintended. Where national origin is not an explicit criterion for selection, discriminatory effects may still be intended in the degree to which policy makers are aware that social attributes are differentially distributed among national populations. A preference for highly skilled migrants will thus favor Britons as a group, for example, and disfavor Mexicans as a group, even if highly skilled Mexicans are treated the same as highly skilled Britons. On the other hand, the large Mexican presence in U.S. agriculture gives Mexicans an advantage relative to other potential agricultural migrants in Central American and the Caribbean. For instance, the 1986 IRCA was universalistic in form, but Mexicans comprised three quarters of the immigrants that it legalized, and the percentage was even higher in the Special Agricultural Worker program under which legalization requirements were looser (Massey, Durand, and Malone 2002, 90).

Notwithstanding the large numbers of Mexicans who do benefit from the current U.S. immigration system, it is practically impossible for those who are low skilled to obtain an immigrant visa under the employment preferences. Even for those who have an immediate family member who is a U.S. citizen, financial requirements for sponsors create a class barrier to legal entry. Since 1996, family sponsors have been legally responsible for economically supporting an immigrant until he or she works ten years, naturalizes, or leaves the United States. Sponsors must be able to financially support their own household as well as sponsored immigrants at 125 percent of the federal poverty guidelines ($26,500 for a family of four in 2008).

Given the insatiable U.S. demand for Mexican labor and the persistent wage gap between the two countries in a context of massive migration sustained for a century,

Table 8.1. Years to Process Immigrant Visas for Mexicans, Filipinos, and All Other Nationals, 2006

PREFERENCE CATEGORY	MEXICANS	FILIPINOS	OTHER NATIONALS
1st (unmarried adult sons & daughters of US citizens)	12	15	5
2A (spouses & children of legal permanent residents)	7	4	4
2B (unmarried sons & daughters of legal permanent residents	14	10	9
3rd (married sons & daughters of US citizens)	12	15	8
4th (brothers & sisters of adult US citizens)	13	22	11

SOURCE: Department of Homeland Security. www.dhs.gov.

the current system guarantees that many Mexicans will continue to enter legally when they can under family sponsorships. When they cannot, many will choose to enter illegally.

Illegality[8]

The Department of Homeland Security (DHS) estimates that there were 7 million unauthorized immigrants from Mexico in the United States in 2008, representing 61 percent of the total unauthorized population (DHS 2009a). Just over half of all Mexicans living in the United States are unauthorized, and among Mexicans who have been in the country for less than five years, 85 percent are unauthorized (Passel 2005a, 16).[9] Nearly 89 percent of the 961,000 foreign nationals apprehended by the DHS in 2007 were Mexican (DHS 2008a).

There are several principal modes of illegality. The most obvious is what the U.S. government terms "entry without inspection"—clandestine entry or entry through an official crossing point with fraudulent documents. Most migrants apprehended when entering clandestinely forgo their right to an immigration hearing and are quickly returned to Mexico with little further consequence through the "voluntary removal" process (Cornelius, Fitzgerald, and Borger 2009). In 2007, more than 891,000 migrants were detained and agreed to return without a removal order. About 83 percent involved Mexicans (and a handful of Canadians) who were apprehended by the Border Patrol.

---

8. Most terms used to refer to the legal status of migrants are heavily freighted with political baggage. Restrictionists typically use the term "illegal aliens." Sympathizers typically prefer terms like "undocumented migrants." Here I generally follow Bean et al.'s (2001) less-charged usage of "unauthorized migrants" to describe persons living and/or working in the United States without the authorization of the U.S. government.

9. Because of its illegal nature, precise figures on the unauthorized population are impossible to obtain, but demographers have created estimates that most scholars believe to be reliable using the "residual method" calculated by subtracting the number of known legal immigrants from the total foreign population known through census and government survey data. Statistical adjustments are made for deaths, emigration, and other factors. The "residue" is the estimated unauthorized population (Passel 2005a).

An estimated 25 to 40 percent of all unauthorized immigrants entered the United States legally and then overstayed their visas, a figure that is probably lower for Mexicans than for other unauthorized immigrants (Passel 2005a, 3). Other foreigners are living in the country legally as tourists or students, but are violating the terms of their visa by working. An unknown number temporarily fall out of status because of long bureaucratic delays while adjusting their visas.

Building on the legal fact that Mexicans are disproportionately represented among the unauthorized population, restrictionist politicians have been effective in discursively presenting illegal immigration as a "Mexican" problem (De Genova 2004). For example, in former California Governor Pete Wilson's 1994 reelection campaign, television advertisements showed surveillance video of scores of migrants running up the freeway past a U.S. border entry point as an announcer ominously intoned, "They keep coming." Wilson's campaign used the advertisements to present an image of Mexicans pouring across a border out of control. He won reelection and helped support the passage of Proposition 187, which stripped unauthorized migrants of the right to a wide range of social services, although most of the proposition was subsequently declared unconstitutional in federal court (Barkan 2003).

Around the same time as Wilson's reelection campaign, the Clinton administration began an intensive buildup of agents and control infrastructure along the border with Operation "Hold the Line" in El Paso in 1993 and "Gatekeeper" in San Diego in 1994. Similar programs were eventually extended along urbanized sections of the entire border. The number of Border Patrol agents between 1996 and 2008 grew from 5,878 to 17,819. The proposed 2009 DHS budget soared to $10.94 billion for Customs and Border Protection and $5.68 billion for Immigration and Customs Enforcement (DHS 2009b).[10] New fencing and sophisticated surveillance systems have been added amid enthusiasm for increased enforcement from both Republicans and Democrats in Congress.

Apprehensions by the Border Patrol along the southwest border increased from roughly 80,000 in 1970 to just shy of 1 million in 1986, when the economic crisis in Mexico and the prospect of legalization under IRCA sent unprecedented numbers of citizens north. At the beginning of concentrated border enforcement in 1993, annual apprehensions were running around 820,000. They increased to 1.6 million in 2000 and have since declined to 858,000 in 2007 (see Figure 8.1).[11]

Although the Department of Homeland Security claims that the decline in apprehensions since 2000 is attributable to its increased enforcement efforts, there are reasons to be skeptical that enforcement alone is responsible for the downturn. The most notable declines were in 2007 and 2008—likely the result of job losses in U.S. sectors like construction, in which Mexican immigrants are overrepresented (Pew Hispanic Center 2009a), at least as much as because of increased border enforcement. The greatest paradox is that the border policy has bottled up unauthorized migrants in the United States once they have crossed. The DHS estimates that between 2000 and 2008,

---

10. Department of Homeland Security, http://www.dhs.gov. The "Minutemen" vigilante group has also conducted widely publicized efforts on small stretches of the border since 2005 to make a symbolic stance against illegal migration by reporting unauthorized crossers to the Border Patrol.

11. These data measure apprehension events, not the number of persons caught.

the number of unauthorized Mexican immigrants living in the United States *grew* from 4.7 to 7 million (DHS 2009a). Unauthorized migrants are increasingly likely to stay in the United States for long periods to avoid the physical risks and high costs of multiple clandestine crossings. The probability that unauthorized migrants would return to Mexico fell from 0.25 to 0.30 per year before IRCA in 1986 to 0.10 by 1998, with most of the decline following the onset of concentrated border enforcement in 1993 (Massey, Durand, and Malone 2002, 131–32).

Annual studies between 2005 and 2010 conducted in three small Mexican towns of large-scale emigration in the states of Jalisco, Oaxaca, and Yucatan, and the U.S. destinations of their migrants, tell the same story of limited deterrence. There are two ways to measure the effectiveness of border deterrence strategies. The first is to measure the extent of *remote deterrence*—that is, whether border enforcement policy inhibits potential migrants from deciding to migrate in the first place (Zolberg 2003) by making people in the Mexican interior aware of illegal migration's high price and physical dangers. The second measure is the extent of *immediate deterrence*—whether border enforcement policy prevents unauthorized migrants who do attempt to cross the border from successfully entering the United States.

The evidence for *remote deterrence* is mixed. In the 2010 study of every adult from Tlacuitapa, Jalisco, a series of logistic regression models measured the effects of knowledge and perceptions of border enforcement on the intent to migrate to the United States among individuals in the prime migration age cohort (15–45) who had never received any legal permission to enter the United States. Having previous migration experience, being male, not having children, and having more family members in the United States proved to be robust predictors of a Tlacuitapense's intent to migrate to the United States in the coming year. In some of the models, a perception that crossing the border without papers was very dangerous predicted that a Tlacuitapense would be less likely to self-report an intention to migrate in the next year. However, the primary danger at the border was not seen to be the Border Patrol per se, but rather gang violence and the bandits who prey on migrants. It appears that Tlacuitapenses associated border gangs with the escalation in drug violence along Mexico's northern border following Felipe Calderón's election to the presidency, a wave of violence that resulted in 28,000 deaths between 2006 and mid-2010 (Duran-Martinez, Hazard, and Rios 2010).

There is little evidence that U.S. policy has an immediate deterrent effect on attempted crossers. Among unauthorized migrants interviewed in the three communities, between 24 and 47 percent were apprehended on their most recent attempt to cross the U.S. border. Between 92 and 97 percent were able to successfully cross eventually, almost all on their first or second try (see Figure 8.2) (Cornelius, Fitzgerald, and Lewin Fischer 2007; Cornelius, Fitzgerald, and Borger 2009; Cornelius et al. 2010; FitzGerald, Alarcón, and Muse-Orlinoff, forthcoming). Among Tlacuitapenses, the probability of being apprehended at least once in his or her attempt to enter the United States trended upward, from 27 percent before implementation of the 1986 Immigration Reform and Control Act to 44 percent between 2002 and 2009. The *eventual* success rate, however, remained steady at 95 percent or higher (FitzGerald, Alarcón, and Muse-Orlinoff, forthcoming).

There is strong evidence that the major effect of enforcement efforts has not been to deter unauthorized migrants, but rather to unleash a series of unintended

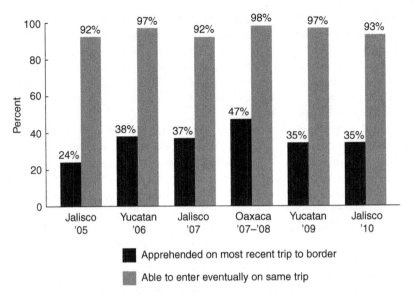

Figure 8.2 Percent of Unauthorized Migrants from Three Mexican Communities Apprehended at Least Once and Border Crossing Success Rates, 2005-2010.

Source: Mexican Migration Field Research Project surveys. N = 1289.

consequences. Usage of coyotes has soared. The same surveys show that more than nine of ten migrants now use coyotes, most of whom are contracted in the sending community to provide guaranteed door-to-door service for a set fee. Coyote fees have increased from several hundred dollars in the early 1990s to about $2,500 in 2008. In a 2009 survey of unauthorized migrants from a new migrant sending community in Yucatán, migrants reported working an average of five months after migration to pay off their coyote debt. Mom-and-pop coyote operations have become sophisticated networks of operatives on both sides of the border using safe houses, tunnels, falsified papers, and other expensive ways to move clients.[12] Broadly speaking, coyotes are providing efficient services.

Border enforcement in urban areas has channeled unauthorized migrants toward wilderness areas and shifted clandestine entry strategies at official ports of entry (Massey, Durand, and Malone 2002). The fee charged by coyotes to enter illegally through an official border crossing point is roughly similar to the fee for crossing clandestinely, but in 1996, the consequences of falsely claiming to be a U.S. citizen became severe—a lifetime ban on legal immigration to the United States. Consequently, unauthorized migrants surveyed in 2007 reported a drop in crossings through official ports

---

12. Mexican Migration Field Research Project surveys by the Center for Comparative Immigration Studies at the University of California, San Diego, in Tlacuitapa, Jalisco (2005); Tunkás, Yucatán (2006); Tlacuitapa (2007); San Miguel Tlacotepec, Oaxaca (2007–2008); Tunkás (2009); Tlacuitapa (2010); and their satellite communities in the United States.

of entry from 37 percent prior to 1993 to 22 percent between 2000 and 2006 ($N = 196$). Of those crossing through a port of entry, 82 percent hid in vehicles between 2000 and 2006, up from 39 percent prior to 1993 ($N = 51$). Showing false, "rented," or borrowed documents has become a less popular strategy given the 1996 law, falling from 57 percent before 1993 to 12 percent from 2000 to 2006.[13]

Most importantly, the rechanneling of unauthorized migration has indirectly caused the deaths of thousands of clandestine migrants who seek to circumvent border fortifications by crossing in wilderness areas and rivers and canals with an elevated risk of dying from exposure or drowning. From 1998 to 2008, a total of 4,331 bodies of Mexican nationals who died trying to enter the United States illegally were recovered—an average of more than one migrant a day (Cornelius 2001; Secretaría de Relaciones Exteriores 2010). An unknown number of bodies remain lost in remote regions.

To the extent that border control policy channels illegal migrants into remote corridors where their lives are at risk, and the poor state of the U.S. economy makes it more difficult to find family in the United States who can finance the coyote's fee, border control has some weak remote deterrent effect. The lack of jobs in the United States is probably even more consequential in reducing apprehensions, because the U.S. labor market is the primary pull factor for labor migrants. In any case, almost all of those who do try to circumvent border controls eventually succeed.

Enforcement of immigration laws has been concentrated at the border since the mid-1990s even as changes in the law have resulted in increasing numbers of Mexicans detained in the interior. The 1996 Antiterrorism and Effective Death Penalty Act and 1996 Illegal Immigration Reform and Alien Responsibility Act, which were enacted in the wake of the bombing of the Oklahoma City federal building, made it easier to deport noncitizen criminals and mandate their detention until they are deported. Most importantly, these laws subjected noncitizens to mandatory deportation for an expanded list of "aggravated felonies," applied the harsher new standard retroactively to crimes for which punishment had already been served, and sharply restricted judicial discretion over how the law is applied. Immigrants brought to the United States as children have increasingly been deported to Mexico and other countries with which they have no substantive social ties. The 1996 laws tripled the number of immigrant detentions in the 1990s (Hernández 2008).

Most unauthorized Mexican immigrants who are detained are returned to Mexico without passing through a formal legal proceeding. Of migrants who went through a formal removal process in 2007, 65 percent, or 209,000 migrants, were Mexicans. Formal deportation carries serious legal and social consequences, including a permanent bar to legal reentry for aggravated felons and up to twenty years for certain other kinds of deportees and imprisonment for subsequent illegal reentry to the United States (DHS 2008a).

An estimated half-million unauthorized migrants have standing deportation orders. Since 2003, the National Fugitive Operations Program has sought increased funding from Congress by emphasizing its focus on arresting dangerous illegal aliens

---

13. Mexican Migration Field Research Project surveys.

with serious criminal backgrounds. (Entry without inspection by itself is a minor violation).[14] Yet through fiscal 2007, nearly three quarters of the 96,000 migrants the program detained at a cost of $625 million did not have any criminal convictions. By 2007, only 9 percent of the migrants arrested by the program's teams had a criminal record, and 40 percent of the detainees were nonfugitives without a deportation order whom agents picked up as "collateral damage" during raids looking for someone else (Mendelson, Strom, and Wishnie 2009).

Historically, most attempts to punish U.S. employers for hiring workers without legal authorization have failed because employers have asserted their preferences for cheap, flexible labor. Perhaps most famously, the "Texas Proviso" inserted by the farm lobby in the 1952 immigration act explicitly excluded employment as a form of "harboring" illegal immigrants. A 1986 IRCA provision for the first time made knowingly hiring or continuing to employ unauthorized immigrants a federal crime (Brownell 2005).

Employer sanctions dropped sharply in the immediate aftermath of IRCA. The number of Immigration and Naturalization Service (INS) audits of employers per fiscal year dropped 77 percent from almost 10,000 in 1990 to less than 2,200 in 2003. Warnings to employers declined from 1,300 to 500 over the same period. The number of fines assessed for illegal hiring dropped 82 percent from nearly 1,000 in 1991 to 124 in 2003 (Brownell 2005). Changes in government record-keeping make direct comparisons between years difficult, but despite a recent uptick, the chances of an employer being investigated, much less fined, remain extremely small. In 2008, Immigrations and Customs Enforcement carried out workplace raids resulting in 1,103 criminal arrests, mostly for harboring or knowingly hiring illegal immigrants. The raids yielded 5,184 administrative arrests of immigrants, mostly for immigration violations.[15] Given that there are 8.3 million unauthorized immigrants among the 154 million workers in the United States (Passel and Cohn 2009, 3), the chances of being caught in such a raid are extremely slim.

The number of unauthorized workers continued to soar after the employer sanctions in IRCA were put into place, but the sanctions did have serious and damaging consequences on the labor force. Businesses in sectors with a large presence of unauthorized workers shifted to more subcontracting to protect themselves from employer sanctions. For example, rather than directly hiring janitors, a business might hire a janitorial contracting company. If immigration authorities determined that a janitor was working illegally, the janitorial subcontractor would be legally liable, not the business where the cleaning took place. A second effect of employer sanctions was to lower the wages of Mexican workers of all legal statuses as employers in effect insured themselves against the costs of a government fine for hiring unauthorized workers by lowering all of their workers' wages (Massey, Durand, and Malone2002). Wages fell for unauthorized Mexican workers even more than for authorized Mexican workers. After controlling for different levels of human capital, unauthorized Mexican men earned an average of 12 percent less than authorized Mexican men following the advent of employer sanctions in 1986 (Brownell 2008).

14. U.S. Code: Title 8, Section 1325.

15. DHS. http://www.ice.gov/pi/news/factsheets/worksite.htm

Although the requirement that employers examine workers' legal documents was deliberately written so loosely that it is almost impossible to prosecute employers who make cursory checks, employers can still get a sense from the documents about which workers are unauthorized and thus more easily subject to retaliation (Brownell 2008). A study of union organizing campaigns from 1998 to 1999 found that more than half of the campaigns involving unauthorized workers included employers' threats to call the INS on their own workers (Bronfenbrenner 2000). Another study of workplace raids by the New York district office of the INS from 1997 to 1999 found that more than half of the workplaces were subject to federal or state labor agency proceedings (Wishnie 2004). From the standpoint of immigration authorities, raiding workplaces whose owners ask to be raided has the advantage of avoiding a political backlash from businesses (Brownell 2008).

The Supreme Court's 2002 decision in *Hoffman Plastic Compounds v. NLRB (National Labor Relations Board)* underlines how the law post-IRCA is not deterring unauthorized immigration, but rather is making the increasing number of unauthorized workers more vulnerable to exploitation. The court ruled 5–4 that an employer who unlawfully fires a worker for union organizing activities is immune from ordinary labor law liability for back pay if the employee is an illegal immigrant whose unauthorized status was only learned by the employer after the firing. In effect, the decision limits the labor rights of unauthorized immigrants and arbitrarily rules that immigration law trumps labor law (Martin and Schuck 2005).

IRCA also established pilot employee verification systems in which employers voluntarily check the eligibility of potential employees with a government database to make sure they are eligible to work legally. The pilots evolved into the electronic employment eligibility verification program known as E-Verify in 2007. As of February 2009, a total of 113,000 employers had registered for E-Verify, representing only 2 percent of businesses nationwide. Even if participation were made mandatory at a national level, the development and maintenance of a database would be enormously expensive both for the U.S. Citizenship and Immigration Services and the Social Security Administration. The databases are also riddled with errors (GAO 2007; Sacchetti 2009).

Subnational Law

The U.S. federal system opens up opportunities for an extremely wide variety of responses to immigration at different levels of government. Contradictions develop within jurisdictions and across jurisdictions as different policy makers attempt to liberalize or restrict immigration. A series of Supreme Court cases settled in the 1880s around the exclusion of Chinese laborers established the "plenary power" of the federal government to have sole authority within the U.S. federal system to control immigration (Zolberg 2006). Nevertheless, there is significant variation among states, counties, and municipalities in the way that immigrants are treated under certain kinds of law. In 2007, a total of 1,059 immigration-related bills were proposed in subnational jurisdictions, 16 percent of which passed. Of the 167 bills passed, 60 expanded the rights of immigrants, 26 contracted their rights, 24 regulated their employment, 30 regulated law enforcement and criminal justice, and 64 served other functions. The top five states that passed immigration-related legislation were Hawaii,

Texas, Arizona, California, and Colorado (Laglagaron et al. 2008; Varsanyi 2006). As at the national level, subnational measures are often as much about symbolic politics as practical efforts.

Many parts of the United States have a long tradition of offering some form of noncitizen voting, or "alien suffrage." Between 1776 and 1926, noncitizens intending to naturalize in the United States who lived in twenty-two states and territories could vote in local, state, and even federal elections. In 1996, however, during a period of backlash against immigrants, Congress made it a federal crime for noncitizens to vote in federal elections. States are still able to determine qualifications for voting at the local and state levels. Contemporary examples of municipal governments allowing noncitizen voting are typically confined to small liberal cities in the Northeast, like Cambridge and Amherst, Massachusetts, and Takoma Park, Maryland. School boards have been much more open to noncitizen voting, including Chicago since 1988 and New York City from 1970 to 2003 (Hayduk 2006).

Many cities have created "sanctuary" policies that aim to prevent municipal employees from enforcing federal immigration law. For example, San Francisco's City of Refugee Ordinance mandates that that "no department, agency, commission, officer or employee...shall use any city funds or resources to assist in the enforcement of federal immigration law...unless such assistance is required by federal or state statute, regulation, or court decision" (Hendricks 2008). Narrower policies against local law enforcement agencies routinely enforcing federal immigration laws are more common. The most influential of these policies is Los Angeles's 1979 "Special Order 40," still in effect. Similar policies have been adopted in New York, Chicago, San Diego, Houston, Miami, Phoenix, Atlanta, Denver, and Seattle.

On the other hand, mostly smaller police agencies have sometimes deliberately sought out unauthorized immigrants to arrest and turn over to federal authorities. Police in Chandler, Arizona, rounded up 432 unauthorized migrants over five days in 1997. In the aftermath of the 9/11 terrorist attacks, Attorney General John Ashcroft asked state and local police to volunteer to enforce immigration laws. Some police have informally adopted such a policy, whereas others have entered into formal "287(g) agreements" (named after Section 287(g) of the Immigration and Nationality Act) to turn over unauthorized immigrants to federal authorities. As of October 2008, Immigration and Customs Enforcement had signed 287(g) agreements with sixty-seven law enforcement agencies, which detained 43,000 immigrants in fiscal 2008 (GAO 2009; Pham 2004, 2008).

Proponents of 287(g) agreements argue that the only way to effectively enforce immigration law is to draw on the greater resources of subnational police agencies and that for local police to turn a blind eye to immigration status tacitly accepts law-breaking. Opponents of routine local enforcement of federal immigration law, including many police chiefs in large metropolitan areas, argue on practical grounds that such enforcement undermines the willingness of unauthorized migrants to cooperate with the authorities, which makes policing more difficult in cities with large unauthorized populations. Searching out the unauthorized to punish them for the civil infraction of entry without inspection would also divert police resources from dealing with criminal violations, a disadvantage that would be compounded if a federal mandate to enforce immigration laws were unfunded. Civil rights activists argue that police lack training in immigration law and would inevitably fall back on racial profiling to search out the unauthorized (Pham 2004, 2008).

Unauthorized minors have had a de facto right to public primary and secondary education since the Supreme Court invoked the Fourteenth Amendment's equal protection clause in its 1982 *Plyler v. Doe* ruling against the Tyler, Texas, school board, which had attempted to charge unauthorized minors $1,000 each to attend public school (Martin and Schuck 2005). Of the estimated 2 million unauthorized immigrant children, about 70,000 graduate from U.S. high schools each year. Their eligibility to attend public universities and colleges and pay in-state tuition emerged as a hot political issue in the late 1990s. Some states have tried to restrict unauthorized students from higher education outright. The Alabama State Board of Education passed a policy effective in 2009 mandating that prospective students at Alabama's two-year colleges prove their legal residence in the United States to gain college admission (Chishti and Bergeron 2008b).

Congress attempted to prevent states from charging in-state tuition to unauthorized immigrants in 1996. Section 505 of the 1996 Illegal Immigration Reform and Immigrant Responsibility Act mandates that unauthorized immigrants "shall not be eligible on the basis of residence within a State for any postsecondary education benefit unless a citizen or national of the United States is eligible for such a benefit without regard to whether the citizen or national is such a resident." Nevertheless, ten states, including the major immigrant gateways of California, New York, Texas, and Illinois, offer in-state tuition to unauthorized immigrant students who have graduated from their high schools, subject to conditions that vary by state. In-state tuition policies for the unauthorized are associated with a 2.5 percentage point increase in the college enrollment of noncitizen Mexican young adults (Kaushal 2008; Konet 2007).

Supporters of excluding the unauthorized argue that taxpayers should not subsidize the education of people who are in the country illegally and that out-of-state citizens should certainly not pay more than unauthorized foreigners for the same education. The average cost for in-state tuition and fees at a four-year public university is $5,836 compared with $9,947 for out-of-state residents. Unauthorized students are not eligible for federal loans and grants, and they cannot legally work to support themselves, so efforts to prevent unauthorized immigrants from eligibility for in-state tuition all but cuts off access to higher education. Supporters argue that children should not be penalized for their parents' decision to bring them to the United States illegally, that years of residence confer the right to a higher education, and that restrictionist policies will retard the unauthorized population's social mobility and depress performance for unauthorized high school students who will lose the incentive to study hard to get into college. A second set of arguments against restriction claims that the 1996 act infringes on legitimate state rights, university personnel should not be required to enforce federal immigration law, and universities should be able to set their own in-state tuition criteria (Konet 2007).

Congressional attempts to create another avenue for some unauthorized immigrant minors to gain legal status and go to college have been unsuccessful as of this writing. In 2007, a Senate vote to end a filibuster on the Development, Relief, and Education for Alien Minors (DREAM Act) failed by eight votes. The measure would have granted provisional legal residency to unauthorized immigrants who entered the United States as children and graduated from a U.S. high school, subject to various conditions. The students would then be required to complete a college associate's degree or serve in the military as a condition of remaining in the United States (Passel 2003; Konet 2007).

The mayor of Hazleton, Pennsylvania, a small town in the Rust Belt experiencing a sudden influx of Latino immigrants, opened a new front in local municipal efforts to target unauthorized immigrants through a 2006 city ordinance that prohibited landlords from leasing to unauthorized immigrants and that penalized businesses employing unauthorized immigrants. Several small cities across the country, including Farmer's Branch, Texas; Valley Park, Missouri; Riverside, New Jersey; and Escondido, California, adopted similar policies. The model was short-lived. A federal judge struck down the Hazleton ordinance as a violation of the plenary power rule the following year and the California legislature passed a bill prohibiting cities from requiring landlords to check whether their tenants are legal residents (Pham 2008).

However, subnational efforts to restrict the hiring of unauthorized workers have been given a boost by an Arizona law effective in 2008 that requires all employers in Arizona to use the federal E-Verify system to check the employment eligibility of future hires. Employers with unauthorized workers can have their business licenses suspended for up to ten days and be put on probation; a second offense leads to revocation of their license. Supporters of the bill argued that IRCA allows states to impose employer sanctions through "licensing and similar laws," whereas opponents invoke the federal government's plenary power over immigration (Chishti and Bergeron 2008a; Pham 2008).

Nine states issue driver's licenses regardless of the bearer's immigration status (National Immigration Law Center 2008). Proponents argue that issuing driver's licenses even to unauthorized immigrants recognizes the fact of their integration into U.S. society, helps track that population by bringing it within the government's documentary controls, and reduces uninsured motoring. Opponents marshal the same arguments used against other forms of accommodation of unauthorized immigrants, with the additional argument that issuing driver's licenses to the unauthorized is a security threat in light of the 9/11 attacks in which eighteen of the nineteen terrorists used driver's licenses to pass airport security checkpoints. In 2005, Congress passed the REAL ID Act stipulating that by May 2008, federal government agencies would only accept licenses from states that excluded unauthorized immigrants and fulfilled expensive technical requirements (*Migration News* 2008).

Citizenship

The restrictive turn in many immigration laws since the mid-1990s has underlined the increasing value of holding U.S. citizenship. Like most countries, the United States offers birth citizenship through a mixed regime of *jus sanguinis*, passing U.S. citizenship to children born anywhere of a U.S. parent, and *jus soli*, giving U.S. citizenship to children born in U.S. territory (Weil 2001). Where the United States stands out from most other liberal countries of immigration is an unusually strong form of *jus soli* that affords U.S. citizenship even to children born in the United States to unauthorized parents. This expansive view of *jus soli* is rooted in the Supreme Court's 1898 interpretation of the Fourteenth Amendment in *U.S. v. Wong Kim Ark*, which has created a significant constitutional hurdle for those who have periodically attempted to remove birthright citizenship for children of unauthorized immigrants (Schuck and Smith 1985).

Naturalization is the third path to citizenship. In most cases, the requirements for naturalization include legal permanent resident status, five years of U.S. residence, and the completion of an English language, civics, and history test. Historically, Mexicans have been among the immigrant groups least likely to naturalize, given high levels of temporary migration and a political culture in Mexico that long viewed U.S. naturalization as a quasi-traitorous act. In an effort to boost the naturalizations of Mexicans in the United States so they would become more politically powerful, the Mexican government began to allow dual nationality in 1998 (Fitzgerald 2005).

In 1995, 19 percent of eligible Mexican immigrants naturalized compared with 66 percent of Europeans and 56 percent of Asians. By 2001, more than one third of eligible Mexican immigrants were naturalizing. The increase in Mexican naturalization rates is probably a reaction to the anti-immigrant U.S. political climate in the mid-1990s, which yielded California's 1994 Proposition 187, the 1996 Illegal Immigration Reform and Alien Responsibility Act easing deportations of legal residents, and the 1996 Personal Responsibility and Work Opportunity Reconciliation Act limiting welfare benefits for noncitizens. In 2007, Mexicans were 18.5 percent of the more than 660,000 naturalizations that year, far more than the nationals of any other country in absolute terms. Mexicans have naturalized to protect themselves from the growing practical distinction between being a legal resident and citizen (Passel 2005b; but see Balistreri and Van Hook 2004).

CONCLUSION: A NEW IMMIGRATION REFORM?

President George W. Bush announced a unilateral plan for reforming U.S. immigration policy in 2004. Although the plan was not meant to establish an accord with Mexico, any changes in U.S. law would disproportionately affect Mexicans. The Bush proposal eventually evolved into the Comprehensive Immigration Reform Act of 2007, which failed to pass a Senate filibuster in June 2007. The bill would have provided a path to legalization for most of the unauthorized already living in the United States, increased spending on border enforcement, made the electronic employee eligibility verification system mandatory, increased the financial penalties on employers who hire unauthorized workers, established a new temporary-worker program, and created a Canadian-style "point system" for selecting immigrants in a way that would favor occupational skills, higher education, and English fluency (*Migration News* 2007).

As efforts to achieve immigration reform have continued to be discussed under the administration of President Obama, policy makers have considered several major questions to be resolved in a comprehensive reform:

- Should unauthorized migrants living in the United States have a path to become legal residents and/or citizens? If so, what should be the required period of residence, English-speaking ability, and fines, and should there be a requirement to leave the United States before legalizing?

- What kinds of employer sanctions for hiring unauthorized workers, databases for identifying eligible workers, and enforcement strategies should be developed without seriously elevating the risk of discrimination against Latinos or foreigners legally eligible to work?
- Should there be a new temporary-worker program or simply a revision of existing temporary-worker programs? How many times should temporary-worker visas be renewable, and should they offer the holders the possibility of eventually becoming a citizen? Should the visas be portable among different employers, what should be the incentives for migrants to return to their home country, what labor rights should temporary workers have, and what provisions should be made for family reunification?
- What border enforcement measures should be in place, and should further elements in a comprehensive reform be contingent on first reducing unauthorized crossings?

Perhaps the most fundamental issue is whether Mexico should be given special consideration in U.S. immigration policy. The 1921–1965 national origins quota system has long been discredited as racist, yet the vestiges of a nationality-specific system remain in the per-country limits for employer and family preferences. Through the 1970s, U.S. presidents supported a continuation of special consideration for Mexico and Canada given their status as friendly neighbors with long migratory and economic ties to the United States. The massive demand for immigrant visas in Mexico makes it stand out as a special case. At the same time, Mexico is not alone as a country with some kind of "special relationship" with the United States or a much higher demand for immigrant visas than the current supply. If special consideration were given to Mexico, might it not also be due to former U.S. colonies like the Philippines and Cuba, which are also the source of hundreds of thousands of immigrants and many more who would like to come? If it seems egregious that Mexico, with its 100 million citizens, is treated the same as Djibouti, is it not stranger still that China and India, with their hundreds of millions, have the same per-country limit of 26,120? The most liberal solution may be to end the country-of-origin criterion altogether for purposes of new immigrant admissions and replace it with a worldwide ceiling in which any foreigner could compete for slots divided along universalistic grounds of family reunification and a diverse range of skill sets for which there is demand in the U.S. economy.

On the Mexican side, even in the unlikely scenario that a bilateral immigration agreement were reached, it is unclear whether the political will exists in Mexico to regulate unauthorized migration in return for a larger share of legal flows. The right to exit that is enshrined in the 1948 Universal Declaration of Human Rights and the 1917 Mexican constitution is routinely invoked in Mexican policy circles, although that right has never been absolute in international law (Aleinikoff 2002), Mexican law, or Mexican administrative practice.

Given the high U.S. demand for Mexican labor, the maturity of the social networks linking particular Mexican communities of origin and U.S. destination and a culture of emigration and dependence on remittances in many parts of Mexico, a legal immigration system that does not make significantly more room for Mexican immigrants is almost guaranteed to result in massive, unauthorized migration. Many migrants would prefer to come as temporary workers, and a well-designed program could channel much of that demand into legal temporary migration, even as scholars recognize that much of that temporary migration would inevitably become permanent and require some regular means of status adjustment to avoid creating a large permanent underclass of noncitizens. What is certain is that without a legal queue to admission that moves forward, large numbers of Mexicans will continue to jump across the border line in the desert sands of the Southwest.

CHAPTER 9

Gender, Sexuality, and Mexican Migration

Eithne Luibhéid
University of Arizona

Robert Buffington
University of Colorado at Boulder

INTRODUCTION

Public policy debates in Mexico and the United States (and the scholarship that informs them) focus almost exclusively on the role of economic forces—higher wages and demand for migrant labor in the U.S. coupled with lower wages and chronic under/unemployment in Mexico—in initiating and sustaining Mexican immigration. Although this emphasis on labor supply and demand addresses one important aspect of migration, it is nonetheless insufficient. One of the most glaring insufficiencies is its failure to appreciate the central role that gender and sexuality—in conjunction with economic and political forces—play in the decision to migrate, the lives migrants lead, their work experiences, the government policies that seek to regulate them, and the anti-immigrant sentiments that shape those policies.

The importance of gender and sexuality has become especially apparent in recent years as more and more Mexican women have migrated to the United States to work. From the beginning, many scholars of Mexican–U.S. immigration have acknowledged gender (but seldom sexuality) as a significant variable. Studying gender, however, has typically meant studying women. But recent work makes it clear that gender—understood as involving women, men, and other gendered identities—shapes all aspects of migration. For example, men experience migration *as men* rather than simply as workers, women experience migration *as women* whether they migrate to work or stay at home, employers seek out *male* workers and *female* workers, and immigration policies and the periodic anti-immigrant panics that help shape them target *male* migrants and *female* migrants. Scholars working in queer, transgender, and feminist of color theory have further complicated matters by calling into question this fundamental gender binary. Precisely because it is so deeply implicated in migration processes (and in the asymmetrical power relations that these processes reflect, construct, and maintain), gender is not an independent variable that scholars can factor in or factor out at their discretion. Any credible account of Mexican migration, then, must deal centrally with gender.

Sexuality too plays an important and unavoidable role in migration. This is true in no small part because it is so often the focus of migrant anxieties and desires, public fears, workplace discipline, and state regulation. This focus on migrant sexualities emerges most clearly in Mexican nationalist fears about lost masculine vigor and feminine chastity, nativist U.S. diatribes against hyperfertile Mexican women and hypermasculine Mexican men, and homophobic U.S. immigration policies that favor heterosexual family reunification, at least for the economically advantaged. At a more fundamental level, people in most societies make sense to themselves and to others only through being sexed and gendered as male or female in particular ways—a process that subjects them to prevailing social norms that are promoted, maintained, and policed by society's cultural, economic, and political institutions. The migration experience is exceptional in this regard because it intensifies these subject-making processes and exposes their many contradictory effects as migrants struggle to make sense of their lives in the face of often radically different cultural norms, labor market demands, and state policies. In sum, failure to take into account the centrality of both gender and sexuality to migration seriously impoverishes our understanding of the lived experiences of migrants, the discourses that circulate around them and shape those experiences, the disciplinary regimes that structure their work, and the binational state policies and practices that seek to categorize and regulate their lives.

Because the best ethnographic data on gender and sexuality come from the past two decades of Mexican migration scholarship, this chapter is heavily weighted in favor of recent developments. At the same time, we will argue that many of the processes analyzed by contemporary ethnographers shed considerable light on earlier migrant self-fashioning and the disciplinary regimes that shaped and sought to control it. The chapter has three sections. The first section describes how scholars have come to understand the ways in which gender and sexuality structure migration. It also describes how application of these insights to Mexican migration has been complicated by the fact that in the United States, Mexican migration has been typically framed in colonialist, racist terms that work through logics of gender and sexuality. The second section critically examines neoliberalism as a hegemonic ideology and practice that has conditioned migration between Mexico and the United States in gender and sexual terms. This is reflected in recent changes in U.S. immigration laws that further extend and intensify neoliberal processes. The third section focuses on how migrants variously inhabit, negotiate, and transform restrictive immigration laws and, by extension, the immigrant experience itself through a reconfiguration of gender and sexual norms.

PART 1: GENDER AND SEXUALITY IN MEXICAN MIGRATION STUDIES

Migration studies have been framed historically in narrow neoclassical economic terms—supply and demand, cost/benefit rations, rational choice, etc.—that ignore, marginalize, or trivialize the role of gender and sexuality. Yet, presumptions about gender and sexuality saturate the neoclassical migration model. At its conceptual center is a pioneering male migrant—a head of household accompanied or followed by a dependent wife and children—who makes the "rational" decision to migrate for a better life, defined primarily in terms of material well-being. Thus, whatever his motivations might be, this migrant *homo economicus* is nonetheless gendered (as male), sexualized (as heterosexual), and individualized (as a rational actor) in particular ways. Many scholars, especially in recent years, have critiqued the application of neoclassical economic theories to migration, noting that they ignore the structural factors that generate and condition migration (Sassen in this volume), disregard state policies that constrain it (Fitzgerald in this volume), and fail to predict actual migration flows with any consistency (Castles and Miller 2009, 21–23).

In addition, feminist scholars have long criticized neoclassical migration theorists for their refusal to acknowledge the centrality of gender. According to the sociologist Pierrette Hondagneu-Sotelo, the 1970s and 1980s witnessed efforts to "counter the exclusion of women subjects from immigration research and to counter sexist as well as androcentric biases... [by] actually taking women into account" (1999, 5). Subsequent research moved beyond "adding women" to exploring how gender analysis demanded a reconceptualization of migration histories, theories, and methodologies. This meant among other things that gender became "not simply a variable to be measured, but a set of social relations that organize immigration patterns" (1994, 3). Hondagneu-Sotelo notes that "we have witnessed a shift away from the premise of a unitary notion of 'women' or 'men' to an increasingly accepted perspective that acknowledges how multiplicities of masculinities and femininities are interconnected, relational, and most important, enmeshed in relations of class, race, and nation" (1999, 4). Thus, migration scholars like Hondagneu-Sotelo have increasingly understood gender, not only as ascribed, but also as fluid, multiscalar, power laden, and subjective (Donato et al. 2006, 13).

Sexuality has also emerged as an important category of analysis in migration scholarship. Despite its growing sophistication, gender analysis with its focus on heterosexual reproduction and family life often privileges binary gender categories (men and women) and heterosexual relations (Warner 1993, xxi; Manalansan 2006, 224). As Eithne Luibhéid explains, "part of the problem is that sexuality continues to be viewed by many immigration scholars as 'natural' or 'private.' Sexuality scholars, of course, have convincingly established that sexuality is neither an unmediated natural drive nor a private matter; on the contrary, the state and powerful social groups intervene into and deploy sexuality in normative ways" (2004, 227). These deployments work to maintain and reinforce hierarchies of race, gender, class, and nation. Moreover, sexual regimes affect not only those defined as "minorities" or "deviants," but also everyone subjected to their disciplinary power. As a category of analysis, sexuality, like gender, is best seen as fluid, multiscalar, power laden, and subjective.

Using these increasingly sophisticated theoretical tools, migration scholars have begun to expose the complex ways in which gender and sexuality shape migration on one hand and in which migration shapes gender and sexuality on the other. Yet, establishing how this works in the context of Mexican migration has been fraught with difficulties. One major problem is that, in the United States, nationalist and neocolonialist logics have framed the gender and sexuality of Mexican migrants. Modern forms of nationalism typically depend on and deploy the logic of heterosexual family to inscribe and naturalize social hierarchies including male control of female sexuality and labor, notions of racial and class supremacy, and a civilizational scale that places societies supposed to be "advanced" at its apex (McClintock 1993). In the late nineteenth and early twentieth century United States, policy makers, scholars, and the general public alike constructed racial differences through gender and sexuality. "Proper" heterosexual relations grounded in "natural" differences between men and women were considered part and parcel of a developmental process that had rewarded the accumulated virtues of white, Protestant, Anglo-American society with demonstrable political, economic, social, and perhaps even moral advantages (Somerville 2000, 25). When it came to non-Anglos, deviations from normative heterosexual standards, whether in gendered or sexual terms, were understood to reflect not only racial difference but also a lesser stage of cultural development—and in the case of immigrants in particular a possible degenerative effect on the more "advanced" host country.

These constructions had a tremendous impact on everything from the actual treatment of migrants to academic studies of migration. For example, in the early twentieth century United States, the seemingly insatiable desire of employers for Mexican labor was accompanied by a "racialized construction of the Mexican immigrant as primitive in terms of sexuality and premodern in terms of conjugal rites and domestic habits" (Ferguson 2004, 13). This racialized construction worked through normative claims about gender and sexuality and legitimized the treatment of Mexican workers as inherently subordinate and thus disposable.

Most Mexican laborers were men whose families remained on the other side of the border and who could be sent back to Mexico when their labor was no longer needed. Yet, steady numbers of migrant families also settled in the United States. In these cases, racist and racializing constructions of Mexican gender and sexuality coalesced around the tropes of the macho Mexican American man and the deferential family-oriented Mexican American woman, tropes that have shaped generations of research, policy making, and human struggle. Social science research, in particular, constructed the Mexicano/Chicano family as "an outmoded patriarchal institution" whose cultural difference represented backwardness and, by extension, pathology within universalizing and evolutionary models of modernization and acculturation (Baca Zinn 1979, 59–61).

With regard to the racializing and colonizing effects of these long-standing discourses on Mexican genders and sexualities, anthropologist Matthew Gutmann notes that "in the United States, the term *machismo* has a rather explicitly racist history... [it] has been associated with negative character traits not among men in general, but specifically among Mexican, Mexican American, and Latin American men. Contemporary popular usage of the term *machismo* in the United States often serves to rank men according to their presumably inherent national and racial characters. Such analysis utilizes nonsexist pretensions to make denigrating generalizations about fictitious Mexican male culture traits" (Gutmann 1996, 227).

Similarly, researchers in the United States have devoted considerable attention to the alleged hyperfertility of Mexican and Mexican American women as an important indicator of abnormal gender and sexual "pathologies"—a serious concern for a diverse constituency ranging from racists to politicians, nativists, and family-planning advocates. According to historian George Sanchez, in the early decades of the twentieth century, "both nativists and Americanists shared a common concern: the nativists wanted to control Mexican population growth for fear of a 'greaser' invasion," while Americanists viewed unrestricted population growth as a vestige of old world ways that would have to be abandoned in a modern industrial world" (Sanchez 1990, 258). Americanists thus targeted Mexican women in an attempt to reduce birthrates at the same time as they developed theories about "the presumed inability of Mexican women to control reproduction" (Sanchez 1990, 258) and chastised them in an attempt to alter their mothering and childrearing patterns. This characterization of Mexican and Mexican American women as irresponsible "breeders" and inadequate mothers continues to incite anti-immigrant passions and shape immigration policy to the present day (Chavez 2001, 2007, 2008).

As these examples illustrate, mainstream attitudes in the United States—shared to some extent by Mexican policy makers—have been shaped by racial and national hierarchies, a colonialist teleology of progress and modernization, and the conviction that either Mexican gender and sexual norms could be changed through the inculcation of modern ideas (the preferred view in Mexico) or else they were static, unchangeable, everywhere the same, symptomatic of racial difference and cultural backwardness, and dangerous to the well-being of the United States (Gutiérrez 2008).

These frameworks have informed generations of research into Mexican migration, gender, and sexuality. In her groundbreaking study of gender and Mexican migration, Hondagneu-Sotelo points out that "when looking at Mexican and Chicano families, Anglo observers have often confused an ideal type family, which resembles a caricature of submissive, self-sacrificing women and dominant, aggressive, tyrannical men, with what is a more varied social reality. Buttressed more by negative and ethnocentric stereotypes than by research, the Anglo gaze casts the Chicano family—and by extrapolation, the Mexican family—as a static, homogenous entity where patriarchy and pathology reign" (1994, 9). In contrast, she insists on the varied and changing nature of gender norms and social relations among Mexicans within and outside Mexico and resists the perception, common in Mexico and the United States, that migration produces gender "liberation" for women.

Although Hondagneu-Sotelo rightly acknowledges the power of patriarchal ideas and institutions in Mexico and among Mexican migrants, she refuses to treat this as exceptional or buy into the assumption that U.S. society is not patriarchal. Instead, she finds that "patriarchal relations do not automatically disintegrate or break down once immigrants adapt to new ways of life in the United States, yet neither does patriarchy remain preserved intact...Patriarchal gender relations undergo continual renegotiation as women and men rebuild their families in the United States" (Hondagneu-Sotelo, 1994, 193). At the same time, her findings refute the assumption that changes in gender relations among Mexican migrants result from exposure to mainstream U.S. gender norms. "Changes in Mexican immigrant families' gender relations," she argues, "do not result from any 'modernizing' Anglo influence or acculturation process. Most Mexican immigrants live their lives in the United States encapsulated in relatively segregated jobs and well-defined immigrant communities" (195). Residential and labor markets segregated by race, class, gender, and sexuality mean that Mexican migrants often have limited interactions with Anglo society and culture. In addition, community pressure to maintain their Mexicanness can inhibit migrants from embracing U.S. culture in any obvious way.

Structural factors like "racism, insecure and low-paying jobs, and (often) illegal status" (Hondagneu-Sotelo, 1994, 195–6) rather than ideological exposure provide a more likely explanation for changes in gender relations. As the men in Hondagneu-Sotelo's study suffered the social effects of diminished status, women enhanced their social position through paid employment, their primary role in consolidating settlement and building social networks, and their experience utilizing public and private forms of support (185). Patriarchy was not abolished in this instance, but it was not left unchanged either. This suggests that most migrant men still have more status and freedom than most women but no longer enjoy the same spatial mobility, power, and prestige as before, whereas many migrant women gain more "autonomy, resources and leverage than they previously [had] in Mexico" (196). Hondagneu-Sotelo's findings are consistent with a growing body of scholarship that exposes the mixed, often contradictory effects on gender status produced by migration and with other studies of Mexican migration that resist the modernization and acculturation frameworks that remain covertly tied to white, middle-class, heterosexual norms and neocolonial notions of social evolution derived from an idealized U.S. model.

In a similar vein, extensive research by Mexican scholars has greatly expanded our understanding of migration's mixed and contradictory effects on gender status and gender relations in sending communities in Mexico.[1] A recent overview of that research notes that "the social norms that determine the proper spaces for men and women, the type of activities that they should or shouldn't undertake, and the control of female sexuality, along with the particularities of their place in family systems characterized by reciprocal obligations and structures of authority, affect the possibilities of female migration in ways not experienced by men" (Szasz 1999, 171). The complexity of these gender differences makes it impossible to generalize about women's migration experiences or community responses to women who stay at home while their partners migrate. This is especially true with the dramatic increase in women's migration in recent years. Under these "accelerated" conditions, ethnographer Rosío Córdova Plaza explains, "when a community is confronted with internal contradictions to its cultural biases... the result has been unprecedented, paradoxical environments in which female sexuality—the locus par excellence of social control—is subjected to forces that oscillate between heightened vigilance over women's fidelity and greater permissiveness toward the seeking of feminine erotic pleasure" (Córdova Plaza 2007a, 37).

Studies of how sexuality shapes and is shaped by migration have faced similar challenges and reached similar conclusions to those of gender and migration scholars. In his analysis of the migration experiences of Mexican migrant men who have sex with men (MSMs), Lionel Cantú shows how sexuality "shapes and organizes processes of migration and modes of incorporation" not just for MSMs but for all migrants

---

1. See for example, the essays by Fagetti, D'Aubeterre Buznego, da Gloria Marroni, and Zárate Vidal in Barrera Bassols and Oehmichen Bazán (2000) and essays by Córdova Plaza and da Gloria Marroni in Córdova Plaza et al. (2007b).

(Cantú 2009, 21).[2] He argues further that, in its refusal to adequately consider the connection between culture and political economy, migration research has generated models of Mexican sexualities as static, unchanging, and inherently different from Euro-American sexualities. These ahistorical sexual archetypes work to "other" Latinos, constructing them as culturally backward and erasing internal differences (77–79). Moreover, they ignore the role of global capitalist expansion in the transformation of sexualities—including through the asymmetrical circuits of information, commodities, and tourism that connect Mexico and the United States (164). Within this essentializing framework, migration by MSMs becomes little more than a search for "liberation" in the supposedly more open (i.e., modern), less homophobic (i.e., less traditional) North.

In response, Cantú shows that sexuality and political economics are thoroughly intertwined in Mexico and variously shape MSM migration. Indeed, all of the men he interviewed mentioned financial considerations, including discrimination in the workplace, among their reasons for migrating to the United States (2009, 132). As one interviewee explained, in Mexico, even business networks depend on maintaining the right image, "which means a wife, children, and social events tied to church and school" (132). Although many gay men in Mexico suffer discrimination at work and elsewhere, Cantú shows that gender, class, and cultural factors play a decisive role in shaping migration possibilities and desires among his informants: for example, well-to-do Mexican men who can maintain a gay or bisexual lifestyle with minimal costs may be less likely to migrate, whereas at the other end of the spectrum, some gay or bisexual men might want to migrate but lack the economic resources and social networks to make migration possible (165).

By focusing on the connections between cultural factors and political economy, Cantú is able to challenge mainstream assumptions that migration automatically results in "liberation" for MSMs in the United States or that "liberation occurs as a result of exposure to Anglo ways and institutions. Although many of Cantú's informants expected to experience new opportunities for self-expression and self-fashioning in the United States, they frequently faced racism, heterosexism, cultural and language barriers, and anxieties around their undocumented status instead. Changes in their self-identities, practices, and ways of living resulted from negotiation of these obstacles, rather than from modernization or acculturation. And these changes were complex. For example, for some interviewees, "discovering the virulence of racism in the United States seemed to counterbalance any feelings of sexual liberation.…in their attempts to escape from one form of bigotry, most…discovered that not only had they not entirely escaped it but they now faced another. As [one of Cantú's informants] said, 'it wasn't true that homosexuals are free, that they can hold hands or that Americans like Mexicans.'" (138–9). To deal with this situation, some created alternative families and households, assisting "one another through the trials and tribulations of being queer immigrant Mexican men" (141). And, in some cases, physical separation from their

---

2. Cantú acknowledges that sexual categories are burdened by histories, cultures, and power relations that do not translate well across languages and contexts. Thus, he employs gay, homosexual, MSM, and queer as contingent terms of analysis.

families, combined with their ability to send home small sums of money, transformed men's relationships with family members and resulted in acceptance (137).

Other researchers similarly warn against simplified models that reduce gay, bisexual, or MSM migration to a search for opportunities for "sexual liberation" in the United States, while ignoring the complex links between sexual, social, and economic motivations. For example, Héctor Carrillo et al. observe that many men see leaving Mexico as providing both economic opportunity and the chance to live a more openly gay or bisexual life in a place where that openness does not affect their families. Thus, even family members who clearly accept their sexual orientation often encourage them to leave, in part to protect them from stigma and in part to protect the family name. Sexual migration among Mexican gay and bisexual men may also encompass other, related motivations, such as the desire to get away from an ex-lover or pursue a relationship with a U.S.-born man, including a tourist or visitor who might provide companionship, acceptance, or financial support (Carrillo et al. 2008, 7).

Scholarly confusion about sexuality is not confined to the study of gays, lesbians, transgender individuals, or queers. According to sociologist Gloria González-López, most investigators who study the sexuality of heterosexual Mexican migrants use an acculturation model that "perceives the sexuality of Latinas and Latinos as a unidimensional entity that is transformed along a continuum between both a Hispanic, or Latin American, sexuality (traditional and conservative) and a North American sexuality (modern and liberal)" (2005, 25). As a result, they tend to miss or misrepresent the "complex, nonlinear, and diverse" nature of Mexican migrant sexualities (25–26). In contrast, González-López argues that migrant women and men experience "erotic journeys…shaped by social networks, women's paid employment, demanding schedules, and a fast-paced routine, among other social factors" (5) along with new sexual risks including HIV exposure, gang violence, drug and alcohol abuse, and child sexual abuse. It is through these complicated individual journeys, rather than simply through exposure to mainstream U.S. cultural values, that they come to attach new meanings to love, sex, intimacy, and relationships. "Migration does not necessarily mean sexual liberation or sexual modernity" (253), she concludes, but instead results in a complex formation produced by intersecting inequalities, social conditions, and migrant agency. The shift from simplistic acculturation models to those that stress the complex nature of heterosexual identities, practices, and ideologies has greatly expanded our understanding of the links between migration and changing sexual mores.

Recent scholarship on HIV/AIDS and migration has also prompted necessary revisions in dominant theoretical frameworks, although in some instances it too has tended to ignore or downplay the complex realities of Mexican and Mexican American cultures, identities, and sexualities. Once researchers realized the global nature of the HIV/AIDS epidemic, its links to migration (including sex tourism) became a central concern. Although preliminary studies focused on physical transmission of the disease between bodies and across borders, its cultural dimensions quickly surfaced. Among other things, scholars discovered that different cultures understood human sexuality in different ways, especially with regard to the complicated question of sexual identifications and identity categories (Manalansan 2006, 228). In Mexican and Mexican American working-class cultures, for example, sexual orientation is most often linked to gender performance rather than same-sex desire. Men who act like men—aggressive, masculine, penetrating—and women who act like women—passive, feminine, penetrated—are generally seen as "normal" even when they engage in same-sex relations, whereas men who act like women and women who act like men are seen as "queer" even if they have sexual relations with the opposite sex. Although this active/passive construction grossly oversimplifies Mexican and Mexican American sexual identities and appears to be losing ground to "modern" notion of sexual identity in Mexico and among Mexicans in the United States, it does alert us to major cultural differences with important implications for efforts to deal with the transmission of HIV/AIDS across the U.S.–Mexico border and in Mexican and Mexican American communities in the United States.

Social science scholarship on HIV/AIDS and Mexican migration has mushroomed since the 1980s. Much of this research has focused on men: men as vectors of transmission to their wives, MSMs, and men in occupations identified as particularly at risk of infection such as migrant farmworkers and day laborers. In many cases, however, it has failed to take into account critical structural factors like women's experiences and the sexual orientation of the men involved (Organista, Carrillo, and Ayala 2004, S230).[3] A review by González-López and Salvador Vidal Ortiz raised other concerns, noting that early research on HIV/AIDS and migration focused on "the psychological needs of those perceived to be most 'at risk,' or those infected with HIV, instead of on the structural circumstances that place them in such risky positions," whereas the next wave of research "established a psycho-cultural model as a central aspect of how to deal with HIV prevention" that often essentialized cultural differences between Latino and Anglo gay men (González-López and Vidal Ortiz 2008, 314).

Despite these problems, González-López and Vidal Ortiz observe that the search for culturally appropriate responses to HIV/AIDS "began a process that has allowed for Latino gay identity formation in the United States and, given the current trends of globalization, all over Latin America" (314). Similarly, Cantú's editors note that he "argues that it has been through HIV/AIDS prevention efforts that "gay Latino" organizing has taken place... [and] shows not only the impact these nonprofits have had in the development of a 'gay Latino' men's culture, but also, more importantly, the culturally specific (and negative) readings of Latino homosexualities as risk factors for HIV infection" (Cantú 2009, 2). They add, however, that under President George W. Bush significant amounts of HIV funding was redirected to faith-based organizations, which meant that the "queer of color organizations conducting HIV prevention work, to which Cantu refers, have disappeared in the last decade" (7).

As this whirlwind tour of recent advances in gender, sexuality, and Mexican migration studies reveals, scholars have effectively challenged the omission of gender and sexuality from migration studies; contested racist, heterosexist, nationalist, and neocolonialist discourses on migration; and analyzed the way in which gender and sexuality structure migration processes. The section that follows, then, explores the ways in which migration processes work to "produce" the gender and sexuality of migrants.

---

3. There are important exceptions. For example, see Castañeda and Zavella (2007).

PART 2: GENDER, SEXUALITY, AND
THE NEOLIBERAL PROJECT

Early on, scholars recognized that the ascendancy of neoliberal economic polices in Mexico and the United States beginning in the early 1980s and culminating in the 1994 North American Free Trade Agreement was profoundly altering migration patterns, processes, and experiences. Over time these policies have deepened integration on one hand and exacerbated differences on the other. Both countries have experienced the erosion of traditional forms of subsistence, expansion of service and informal sectors, decline in manufacturing, reductions in public sector employment, and the explosive growth of global cities. Moreover, through the globalization of production, workers in Mexico have increasingly found themselves employed by multinational corporations, producing goods for export under the supervision of non-Mexican managers. Alongside tremendous changes in the economy, cutbacks in family support and public services have pushed increasing numbers of women into the labor market, particularly into its underpaid and unregulated sectors. All of these changes have helped fuel migration from Mexico and create a strong demand for migrant labor in the United States (Massey, Durand, and Malone, 2002, 50). Yet, although capital, goods, and information move more freely between the two countries, human movement into the United States from Mexico has become increasingly restricted.

Along with greater restrictions on immigration, neoliberal economic policies have changed migration in other important ways. For one thing, more Mexicans than ever, especially women, have chosen to immigrate to the United States despite assurances that "free trade" would develop Mexico's economy and keep undocumented workers at home. For another, much of the newest and best ethnographic work points to major "structural adjustments" in gender and sexual practices and ideologies as a result of migration, globalization, and transformations within Mexico.

Although most analysts stress the importance of neoliberal economic doctrine for Mexican migration, they often neglect its implications for human subjectivity—the way people see themselves and others see them (Buffington 2007). In addition to its well-known economic prescriptions, neoliberalism promotes a major shift in people's sense of themselves and their relationships with others by casting all relations—including self-understanding and interpersonal relationships—in economic terms. To become a good neoliberal subject is to become what the sociologist Nikolas Rose calls an "entrepreneur of the self," an efficient self-manager who calculates costs and benefits, learns from mistakes, assesses risks, minimizes losses, and maximizes gains in all aspects of personal and public life. Classic nineteenth century liberalism—the dominant ideology of nation-state formation in Mexico and the United States—allowed for a private sphere (maintained mostly by women), free from the demands and logics of the marketplace, in which people (almost always men) could develop their character and talents in preparation for entry into a ruthlessly competitive public sphere. In contrast, neoliberalism seeks to impose market logic on all aspects of human life to ensure that each individual realizes his or her full potential as a producer and consumer. As part of this process, the proper neoliberal subject must turn his or her back on the alleged inefficiencies and inertia of traditional culture, especially the "unreasonable" demands of community, kin, and family.

On the surface, neoliberalism with its emphasis on self-management and individual choice appears neutral on gender and sexuality. In practice, it relies heavily on normative notions of gender and sexuality to determine an individual's advantage or disadvantage with regard to everything from family status to occupational suitability to political positioning in a fashion akin to the classic liberal doctrine of comparative advantage that enjoins each country to do what it does best in the global economy (i.e., provide surplus labor, supply raw materials, export manufactures, control trade). In most cases, emphasis on individual comparative advantage typically works to reinforce, even naturalize, conventional gender and sex roles. But for many people, especially working-class migrants from rural areas, neoliberalism's stress on self-management and individual choice, along with its incitement of individual desires (whether for consumer goods or new forms of interpersonal relationships), is often narrated as personal liberation from traditional oppressions, as an end to female subordination, patriarchal families, community scrutiny, religious constraints, and homophobia. Some ethnographers have unquestioningly accepted their informants' accounts, insisting that despite its drawbacks immigration has empowered migrants, especially women and queers (LGBT), to take charge of their lives, rethink their relationships, and embrace the modern world. This interpretation disregards the many ways in which neoliberalism reproduces female subordination, supports patriarchy, privileges heterosexual relations, and so on—even when its subjects narrate the shift from traditional to neoliberal modes of subjugation as increased freedom rather than new forms of constraint. Moreover, it supports the troublesome conclusion that Mexico's chronic social problems result from its failure (and by extension the failure of its people) to become sufficiently modern. In response, Decena et al. (2006) stress the need to differentiate immigrants' narratives from their lived experiences where gender and sexuality remain complex and contradictory. Understanding the powerful linkage between neoliberalism and the formation of Mexican migrants as gendered and sexed subjects, then, helps us get at the heart of recent changes in the migration experience.

Although we insist in this section and the next on the need to explore the subject-making dimension of neoliberalism and its impact on recent migrants, work regimens, and immigration policy, we also note that neoliberalism intensifies processes of migrant self-fashioning, labor discipline, and state regulation that have long been characteristic of immigration from Mexico to the United States. Close examination of twentieth century U.S. immigration policies reveals important continuities and shifts in the ongoing regulation of the gender and sexuality of Mexican migrants. On the surface, immigration control would seem to be about deciding who gets to enter and who doesn't. Alongside this superficially straightforward gate-keeping function, however, immigration policy works to govern populations in more complex ways. According to the social theorist Michel Foucault, the governance of human populations or "governmentality" has two interlinked aims, the production of desired outcomes and the avoidance of undesired ones, and it pursues these aims through the regulation of gender and sexuality (Foucault 1991). Although U.S. immigration control seeks to realize these aims, its efforts—as with most manifestations of governmentality—are messy, open-ended, and contested. Nonetheless, it remains the central site for the regulation of migrant subjects.

The roots of the current immigration control system lie in the 1965 Immigration and Nationality Act (INA). The INA established two major routes to legal permanent residence in the United States, through immediate family ties or specified U.S. labor needs, and capped annual admissions for each country. In 1976, the INA was extended to Mexico (and Canada) and significant numbers of Mexicans, many of whom had participated in social networks and labor migration circuits for decades, suddenly found themselves classified as undocumented workers or "illegal aliens." Their labor remained in high demand but they found it impossible to attain legal entry, either as temporary workers or permanent residents. Although the lack of documents failed to deter migration in most cases, undocumented status has rendered migrants more vulnerable and exploitable than before. Yet, because policy debates tend to address migration in individual rather than structural terms, migrants often take the blame for their own exploitation and deaths, whereas the government (which regulates and criminalizes them) and employers (who demand and exploit their labor) are absolved of responsibility. For complex reasons, the criminalization of large numbers of Mexican migrants has proven good for business and mainstream politics and the process has steadily expanded in recent decades (Nevins 2002; Inda 2006; De Genova 2002).

For most Mexicans (and others) who seek legal permanent residency in the United States, family ties are the only realistic option.[4] Although analysts and policy makers typically distinguish family reunification from labor migration, family migrants are often workers or future workers. And some scholars suggest that family reunification policies benefit the state in several ways, allowing it to position itself as "a benevolent actor reuniting broken families," displacing the responsibility for recruiting low-wage workers onto those families and then making them responsible for social costs that arise in the process (Reddy 2005, 109). Family reunification policies have produced complex forms of exclusion and subordinate inclusion. This is so, in large part, because they are organized around patriarchal, heterosexist, middle class, and culturally specific norms of biological reproduction and legal recognition. Because queer kin, extended family members, and "fictive" kin are not recognized as family under the law, they have no legal basis for immigration.

For those eligible for legal migration based on recognized family ties, immigration law has historically insisted on patriarchal, heterosexual, immediate family relations. Prior to World War II, most U.S. employers (supported by local officials and immigration policy) expressed a strong preference for family migration because they felt that the presence of wives and children kept male workers in line—less likely to leave, organize, strike, fight, drink, visit prostitutes, seduce local women, etc.—and provided a supplemental workforce willing to work for even less money than adult men. As part of the negotiations for the 1942 Bracero Program, however, Mexican government officials insisted that it include only men, preferably male heads of household who would return home to their families in rural Mexico once their work contracts ended, bringing with them much-needed job skills, modern attitudes, consumer goods, and

---

4. Routes to legal permanent residency through employment remain limited because only certain skills provide a basis for labor migration. The so-called "diversity visa" lottery provides a small window of possible entry for migrants, yet Mexicans are never eligible because the lottery is reserved for citizens of countries that send relatively few migrants to the United States each year.

investment capital (Cohen 2006). Although the program ended in 1964, its exclusive reliance on temporary male workers coupled with U.S. immigration's family preference meant that Mexican men were better positioned than women to gain legal status. Thus, when the "amnesty" provisions of the 1986 Immigration Control and Reform Act (IRCA) legalized some 2.3 million previously undocumented Mexican workers, men with documented work histories in the United States were the principal beneficiaries, receiving 58 percent of Legally Authorized Worker and 85 percent of Special Agricultural Workers visas. As Donato et al. (2008) explain, "fewer women had the U.S. experience making them eligible to apply. Women were also less likely to have the evidence necessary to document their case, such as rent receipts, paycheck stubs, and utility bills, because they were often in the name of their partners or, because women worked in the informal sector, such documentation did not exist" (465).[5]

IRCA has had other gender-specific consequences as well. When men apply for wives to join them, these women enter as legal dependents. For those accustomed to managing family and work responsibilities in Mexico while their husbands work in the north, this represents a significant loss of status. As one woman, whose husband had been in the United States for three years, explained to an ethnographer, "[here in Mexico] I take care of the fields, our animals... I'm currently painting our house. I have to do all the work my husband used to do. And I'm still responsible for everything I did before—cooking, cleaning, caring for the children... Now I am a man *and* a woman!" (Boehm 2008, 16).

The 1996 Illegal Immigration Reform and Immigrant Responsibility Act (IIRIRA) further strengthened new migrants' dependence on sponsoring relatives. As the act's title indicates, immigration policy typically encourages migrant dependency through the use of neoliberal constructs like privatization and personal responsibility that invariably take gendered and sexualized forms (Duggan 2003, Luibhéid 2005). Under the IIRIRA, those seeking to sponsor a relative for migration must first sign a legally binding affidavit of support and demonstrate that their income or assets reach at least 125 percent of the federal poverty level for a household that includes the migrant, the sponsor, and any other dependents. These affidavits remain in effect until the migrant has naturalized, accrued forty qualifying quarters of work, permanently departed the United States, or died. They are not voided by divorce, although they may be temporarily waived in cases of abuse or battery. Sponsors may be required to reimburse the federal government for any benefits the migrant receives and migrants may in theory sue their sponsors for inadequate support (Luibhéid 2005, 80). These regulations have further institutionalized forms of dependency that are gendered, generational, and heterosexist (the system doesn't recognize same-sex families) to privatize the costs associated with family migration and make those involved more "responsible."

The IIRIRA's implementation of sponsorship requirements went hand in hand with a major overhaul of welfare that same year. The Personal Responsibility and Work

---

5. According to Donato et al. (2008), after IRCA all migrants tended to earn lower hourly wages, and there was a shift "toward more hours worked, the informalization of work, and tax payments" (476). At the same time, "men's and women's employment conditions became more differentiated" (473). Thus, IRCA negatively affected both men and women, "but for many conditions of work, the impacts were larger (and worse) for women than men" (483).

Opportunity Reconciliation Act targeted immigrants and the U.S. poor (especially women of color), making it more difficult for undocumented migrants to receive even emergency public assistance and reducing the eligibility of legal immigrants (Smith 2007).[6] Retrenched welfare, combined with the affidavit of support system, meant that low-income migrants had "to absorb the social costs of poverty and a 'healthy' unemployment rate" (Reddy 2005, 110).

In addition, many migrants became afraid to seek benefits for which their citizen children were entitled, fearing this might affect their ability to become citizens themselves. They also feared being arrested and deported as a result of other legal changes. For example, the Anti-Terrorism and Effective Death Penalty Act, also passed in 1996, had expanded the list of "aggravated felonies" that mandated deportation and barred migrants from ever reentering the United States. IIRIRA further expanded the aggravated felonies list and significantly reduced judges' discretion in cases where migrants sought relief from deportation, including recognition of a migrant's ties to U.S. citizens or legal permanent residents (LPRs; including parents, heterosexual spouses, or minor children who depended on them). As a result, migrants who engaged in even relatively minor crimes such as shoplifting (whether or not they were convicted) became vulnerable to detention and deportation. Making the situation worse, the law was retroactive, so that migrants whose convictions had occurred years before (including when they were children) and who had already served any required prison time were suddenly deportable, even when it was to countries where they did not speak the language and no longer had ties (Coonan 1998, 612). Thus, many migrants admitted through family ties began to find that changing immigration laws (derived from neoliberal notions of privatization and personal responsibility) were disassembling and dividing their families.

The expanded criminalization and policing of immigrants who are legal permanent residents have intersected with the growth of immigrant detention more generally. The case of Victoria Arellano, a twenty-three-year-old transgender HIV-positive Mexican migrant who died in 2007 while in Immigration and Customs Enforcement custody, drew attention to the harsh detention conditions and the ways in which gender and sex discrimination often work to make a bad situation worse. Arellano had lived in the United States since she was a child. She worked in a West Hollywood supermarket and volunteered at a Hollywood drug and alcohol abuse treatment facility. After being arrested on a traffic charge, she was sent to a detention facility in San Pedro, California, on the grounds that she had entered the country without authorization. Although she presented as a transgender woman, Arellano was held in a male detention facility. There, she was denied access to necessary HIV medications. When she fell seriously ill, fellow inmates repeatedly tried to assist her, but in vain. She was finally taken to a local hospital, where she died shackled to a bed with two immigration agents standing guard.

---

6. Legal immigrants became ineligible for supplemental security income, which is cash assistance for the poor, disabled, or elderly, and for food stamps—although the latter provision was repealed in 1998. The new law also barred new immigrants from federal means tested benefits for five years and gave states the option of barring current immigrants from these benefits, which include TANF and Medicaid (Fix and Zimmerman. 2001, 410–11).

More restrictive and punitive immigration policies have frozen increasing numbers of families into mixed status (i.e., families that include combinations of citizens, legal immigrants, and undocumented immigrants).[7] Mixed-status families tend to have lower than average incomes and face a range of other struggles including differential treatment of family members, spillover effects from discrimination against noncitizen family members (i.e., the inability to access social services or insurance), the legal separation of families (i.e., when they cannot meet income requirements or as a result of stepped up deportation), and the de facto treatment of citizen children as noncitizens (Fix and Zimmerman 2001). To make matters worse, some policy makers have proposed even more stringent anti-immigrant measures like denying birthright citizenship to children born in the United States to undocumented parents (Chavez 2008, 88–90). As the example of mixed families demonstrates, recent changes to immigration policy have further entrenched normative family models and female dependency as a requirement for migration, created webs of surveillance that operate through these family relationships, restricted many migrants' capacities to legalize even through recognized family ties, made reunification increasingly unavailable for families who cannot meet income and asset requirements (thus reserving "family" as a privilege for the more economically advantaged), and begun to actively disassemble families by criminalizing minor status violations and deporting violators. Even these changes have not been enough for some critics who have repeatedly proposed significant reductions in family-based immigration slots and the implementation of a point-system that would allocate the bulk of LPR slots based on criteria that include language, age, education, skills (particularly in high-skill or high-growth areas), and work experience. Such a shift—although fully in line with flexible, neoliberal logics—would further reduce opportunities for legal migration by working-class people from Mexico—without, however, reducing the demand for their labor.[8]

Under the current system, migrants in same-sex relationships are denied access to immigration visas through their intimate relationships with U.S. citizens and legal residents. As a result, same-sex couples must negotiate a maze of bureaucratic obstacles to obtain visas on other grounds. Yet, visas are difficult and expensive to acquire, expire relatively quickly with no guarantee of renewal, and often tie migrants to exploitative employers. Binational same-sex couples thus live with the constant threat of being separated, while being unable to plan for a future. When visa strategies fail, law-abiding couples break up, engage in long-distance relationships, or have the U.S. partner migrate. Other couples engage in sham heterosexual marriages or lapse into undocumented status, risky strategies that impose high costs on individuals and relationships (Immigration Equality and Human Rights Watch 2006; Luibhéid 2008). The Uniting American Families Act, first introduced in 2005, seeks to remedy discrimination against

---

7. For example, the Anti-Terrorism and Effective Death Penalty Act toughened the penalties for undocumented immigrants who sought to reenter the United States legally at a later date. Thus, migrants who were eligible for legal admission through family ties but who had previously spent time in the United States undocumented suddenly found that they could not legally join their families in the United States.

8. See "How Changes to Family Immigration Could Affect Source Countries' Sending Patterns."

same-sex binational couples, yet it would subject them to the same requirements as those facing heterosexual couples, requirements that mostly benefit the well-to-do.[9]

Some gay, lesbian, or transgender migrants have sought admission through the asylum system. In theory, anyone who can prove either past persecution or a well-founded fear of future persecution on account of race, religion, nationality, membership in a particular social group, or political opinion is eligible for asylum. In practice, asylum decisions are influenced by an applicant's country of origin. Widespread, media-fueled U.S. fears of opening the "flood gates" to large numbers of potential applicants from countries like Mexico (or China) have politicized the asylum process and made it more difficult for Mexicans (and others) to access.

For queer migrants, the asylum route is particularly fraught. Until 1990, U.S. immigration law barred admission of lesbians and gay migrants. In 1994, however, Attorney General Janet Reno ruled that homosexuals could be considered "a particular social group" for purposes of seeking asylum, thus making characteristics previously considered grounds for exclusion or deportation a basis for seeking legal entry through the asylum system. Further entrenching the contradictions, HIV-positive migrants, technically barred from entering the United States after 1993, were made eligible for asylum if they could prove persecution because of their HIV status.[10] Despite frequent discrimination at the hands of immigration officials, transgender migrants were nonetheless eligible to apply for asylum if they could prove persecution in their countries of origin on account of their gender identities.[11]

The asylum system has opened the door for small numbers of Mexican men (and smaller numbers of women) persecuted in Mexico through rape, beating, imprisonment, attempted murder, and continual intimidation. Yet, asylum politics remain

---

9. The Uniting American Families Act has gained broad bipartisan support, but has not been enacted. More than thirty-five thousand binational same-sex couples would potentially be eligible to seek relief if it were to pass.

10. In 1993, Congress added HIV to the list of "communicable diseases of public health significance," making HIV-positive status a basis for refusing admission to the United States. As a result, even HIV-positive temporary visitors were barred from entering the country. All migrants seeking LPR status were to be tested and those found to be HIV positive were rejected unless they could meet stringent waiver requirements. Lesbians and gay men, however, were not eligible for the waiver based on a same-sex relationship with a U.S. partner. In January 2010, HIV was finally removed from the list of communicable diseases of public health significance. People no longer have to disclose their HIV status to legally enter the United States, and the HIV testing requirement to become an LPR has been ended. See Immigration Equality, "HIV issues.".

11. Transgender migrants experience a myriad of difficulties with the immigration process, beginning with the basic problem that official documents may not accurately reflect their gender identity, which results in numerous bureaucratic difficulties. Immigration officials often consider transgender migrants deviant, lacking good moral character, and/or liable to become public charges, all of which preclude legal admission. Moreover, transgender individuals frequently suffer discriminatory arrests, which are also grounds for exclusion. Legally married couples that include transgender partners have experienced difficulties entering on the basis of their relationship, even if it is a male–female relationship. In 2004, the Department of Homeland Security, U.S. Citizenship and Immigration Service (USCIS) instructed officers to deny spousal or fiancée petitions filed on behalf of transgender migrants. In 2005, the Board of Immigration Appeals reversed this policy, holding that a marriage involving a transsexual spouse is valid for immigration purposes, so long as the marriage was valid in the country where it was contracted. Despite this ruling, some USCIS officials continue to misapply the law.

deeply entangled in nationalist and colonialist logics. For example, courts and the media often position the United States as the "savior" of Mexican asylum seekers, without acknowledging that queers, women, people of color, and the poor often experience severe violence in the United States and that migrant status (perceived or actual) further compounds their risk of violence including through encounters with the immigration, asylum, and criminal justice systems.

U.S. immigration officials often depend on essentialized notions of Mexican gender and sexuality to arrive at asylum decisions. For instance, when gay men seek asylum, courts often assume that the "passive," presumably effeminate partner in a male same-sex relationship is at risk of persecution but that the "active," presumably manly partner is not. As noted earlier in this chapter, these sorts of assumptions fail to grasp the range, complexity, and fluidity of sexual and gender identities in Mexico.[12] They also ensure that "the boundaries of sexual identities...become entrenched in nationalist discourse even while the borders of sexual politics between the two nations converge" (Cantú 2009, 56).

Judicial confusion around sexual identities plays out in various ways. For example, in *Soto-Vega v. Ashcroft*, the judge found that Soto-Vega had indeed suffered past persecution at the hands of Mexican police and the public—but he did not believe that Soto-Vega was likely to suffer future persecution because, in the judge's opinion, he did not "appear gay."[13] As Soto-Vega's attorney argued, the judge's "non-evidence based" (48) opinion relied on stereotype, improperly assumed that people in Mexico shared this stereotype, and ignored the evidence that "Mr. Soto-Vega *had been* identified as gay—and *was* persecuted on that basis" (49).[14] More troubling still, the judge argued that Soto-Vega could avoid future persecution in Mexico by keeping "his appearance and conduct from making it 'obvious' that he is gay" (39). As Soto-Vega's attorney explained, such a judgment "impose[s] restrictions on...speech and conduct not demanded of those who seek asylum on the basis of other characteristics such as religious or political beliefs" (12–13). Indeed, such standards "undermine completely the very reasons for granting asylum based on sexual orientation" (13). The judge's ruling was overturned on appeal. Soto-Vega and other such cases reveal the complex ways in which sexuality and Mexican origin interweave in the asylum process.

---

12. For discussion of research that has emerged in response to the active/passive paradigm, see González-López and Vidal Ortiz (2008, 311).

13. These kinds of decisions reflect not only culturalist or essentialist notions of Mexican genders and sexualities, but also judges' own limited understandings of same-sex sexualities. In asylum cases, applicants must prove they are "really" gay or lesbian; yet proving this requires understanding and addressing judges' own sometimes limited understandings of homosexuality. Information that challenges judges' assumptions about homosexuality (e.g., applicants who claim to be lesbians but are married to men) must be carefully explained and contextualized (e.g., the marriage occurred under coercion or as a way to escape violence) for the case to succeed. Moreover, applicants face hurdles in proving that persecution they suffered was on account of their sexuality, rather than something else. For further information about the difficulties of queer asylum cases, see Sridharan (2008).

14. United States Court of Appeals For the Ninth Circuit, No. 04–70868, Jorge Soto Vega, Petitioner, v. John Ashcroft, Attorney General, Respondent, On Appeal from the United States Board of Immigration Appeals, Opening Brief of the Petitioner, by Jon W. Davidson, Lambda Legal Defense and Education Fund, Inc.

Gender-based asylum claims often present similar difficulties. For example, successful claims by Mexican lesbians are rare, in large part because the system does not adequately address how gender intersects with sexual orientation in distinctive ways that can result in a "well-founded fear of persecution," especially for racialized, working-class women.[15] The recent L.R. case, involving a working-class Mexican woman who sought asylum from severe and prolonged abuse at the hands of her common-law husband, was denied in part because of difficulties in defining her "particular social group." A Department of Homeland Security brief on the case argued that attempts to classify L.R. as a member of a social group composed of "Mexican women in abusive domestic relationships who are unable to leave" were untenable because a "particular social group cannot be significantly defined by the persecution suffered or feared" because such a definition is "impermissibly circular" (Preston 2009b).

Asylum remains extremely difficult to win. Asylum seekers from "friendly" countries seldom succeed and poor or working-class asylum seekers are generally suspected of being "mere economic migrants" rather than people needing protection. Asylum possibilities for LGBT people are "closely linked with the domestic political, social, and legal climate surrounding gays and lesbians. Although the climate has become more accepting of gays and lesbians, some states and localities still ban homosexual conduct. This situation, combined with the difficulties in proving LGBT identity and other factors, makes sexual orientation claims especially challenging."[16] Opportunities for asylum were further reduced under IIRIRA, which instituted a requirement that migrants must file for asylum within one year of entering the United States or else forfeit their opportunity. Immigration Equality explains that this rule "has created unique hardships for LGBT/H asylum seekers because they are often unaware that their sexual orientation, gender identity, or HIV status can form the basis of an asylum claim, and are often afraid to disclose these intimate aspects of their identity to a government official given the persecution they faced in their own country."[17] Asylum seekers who have criminal convictions also face difficulties. The Real ID Act of 2005 further reduced asylum opportunities by heightening the burden of proof on asylum seekers, demanding corroborating evidence (which is often unavailable) and making it easier to find that an applicant lacks credibility.

Border policing is another important site where U.S. immigration policies, practices, and personnel seek to regulate the gender and sexuality of Mexican migrants. Ongoing efforts at "prevention through deterrence" have concentrated manpower, military technology, and other resources at major crossing points for undocumented migrants to "raise the difficulty, financial cost, and physical risk of illegal entry to such a

---

15. See National Center for Lesbian Rights, The Challenges of Successful Lesbian Asylum Claims. Essentializing and negative constructions of women assumed to be lesbians by immigration officials predates the asylum system. In 1960, an immigration agent in El Paso, Texas, denied entry to Sara Harb Quiroz (a legal permanent resident) because in his eyes—at least according to Quiroz's lawyer—she looked like a lesbian. But as Eithne Luibhéid points out, in the context of "the long U.S. history of viewing and treating the bodies of women of color as sexually other," it is not at all clear which trait or combination of traits triggered his response (2007, 112). Several appeals and a (possibly) sham marriage failed to prevent her deportation (122).

16. Sridharan (2008).

17. LGBT/HIV Asylum Manual, 1. Asylum Law Basics, Immigration Equality.

level that deterrence would be achieved at points of origin in Mexico" (Cornelius 2004). Rather than deter illegal immigration, the strategy has increased migrants' reliance on *coyotes* (people smugglers), resulted in growing numbers of deaths as migrants attempt to cross the border at more deserted and less hospitable locations, and contributed to an upsurge in vigilante activities by nativist groups in the United States. As more and more women join the migration stream north despite these worsening conditions, they become especially vulnerable to rape, sexual abuse, and sex trafficking.[18] Indeed, rape and sexual abuse are so common "that women heading north start using birth control pills" in anticipation of being assaulted (Falcón 2007, 206). And there is considerable evidence that the militarization of the border has encouraged an institutional culture that normalizes the sexual abuse and rape of women by U.S. officials, crimes for which "accountability [is] difficult and often impossible to secure" (Falcón 2007, 203, 214).

Beefed up border enforcement has not prevented migration but it has encouraged increasing numbers of undocumented migrants to stay longer or settle in the United States to avoid the tremendous costs and risks of clandestine crossings. Under these circumstances, transnational parenting, which requires active involvement in caring for children who are left in Mexico while their parents work in the United States, presents even greater challenges (Dreby 2010; Hondagneu-Sotelo and Avila 1999; Stephen 2007, 200–6). In the United States, migrants' possibilities are shaped not only by legal constraints, but also by the ways in which states and local municipalities have teamed up with Immigration and Customs Enforcement to extend surveillance into everyday activities like walking down a street, "driving while Mexican," seeking health care, reporting a crime, or sending a child to school. As the anthropologist Lynn Stephen describes, the border painfully "permeates [migrant] memories and self-identities regardless of their location or actual immigration status" because others constantly "read" and treat them as illegal, based on their appearance and regardless of their status (2007, 144).

The border functions as more than a site for U.S. immigration enforcement. It is also a liminal zone in which images and discourses of gender and sexuality circulate in complicated, sometimes disturbing ways that implicate the Mexican migrants who live in it or pass through it. Scholarship about the disappearance and murder of hundreds of young women in the border city of Ciudad Juárez has exposed how global capitalism and patriarchal states "create conditions of possibility" for gendered, sexualized, racialized violence that particularly targets the poor with impunity (Fregoso 2007, 53; Fregoso and Bejarano 2010). At the same time, widely disseminated representations of the Juárez murders extend long-standing discourses in both Mexico and the United States that portray the border as a site of "excess, prostitution, drugs and contraband" (Fregoso 2007, 45). Historian Ramón Gutiérrez notes, for example, that for Anglo residents of San Diego, California, "the international boundary between Mexico and the United States has long been imagined as a border that separates a pure from an impure body, a virtuous body from a sinful one, a monogamous conjugal body regulated by the law of marriage from a criminal body given to fornication, adultery, prostitution, bestiality and sodomy" (1996, 255–6). The vice attributed to border cities like Tijuana and Juárez, which dates back as least as far as U.S. prohibition, is seen as "constantly

---

18. Although women are especially vulnerable to sexual assaults and sex traffickers, children and men are victimized as well.

threaten[ing] to spill across the border to corrupt the American body politic" despite the fact that "Tijuana first developed as an escape valve for the sexually repressed and regulated American Protestant social body of San Diego" (Gutiérrez 1996, 255, 257). These negative images associated with the border in the popular mind—in both Mexico and the United States—are transposed metaphorically onto Mexican immigrants whose imagined exposure to this zone of gender deviance and sexual violence is seen as a contaminating influence.

Regulating a zone constructed by cross-national relations of power, domination, and violence is certainly no easy matter. At the same time, U.S. immigration policies, practices, and personnel charged with fostering the "free" flow of capital, goods, and information while inhibiting human movement—including through the regulation of migrant genders and sexualities—have worked instead to put migrants in harm's way. But, as we will see in the next section, Mexican migrants have responded to the challenges posed by immigration to the United States in various ways (most of them unforeseen by policy makers), many of which have greatly influenced their understanding of gender and sexuality.

PART 3: MIGRANT RENEGOTIATIONS

In the previous section, we saw how U.S. immigration policies, practices, and personnel have attempted to categorize, regulate, and police the gender and sexuality of migrants. Although these attempts to "make sense" of migrants have invariably failed to meet their stated objectives (rationalization, management, control, etc.), they have had serious repercussions for those subjected to their attention. These effects are compounded by the radical cultural shift involved in migration from Mexico to the United States with its own complex, contradictory, and fluid notions of gender and sexuality.

As we will see in this section, the growing scholarship on transnational migration provides rich insights into the different ways that Mexican migrants have accommodated, resisted, and negotiated these regimes of institutional and cultural power. In recent years, migration scholars have begun to pay greater attention to the transnational aspects of the migrant experience, especially the need to "develop and maintain multiple relations—familial, economic, social, organizational, religious, and political—that span borders" (Glick Schiller et al. 1992, ix). Since the 1970s, neoliberalism (along with related phenomena like flexible accumulation and corporate globalization) has destabilized economies, especially in the "developing" world, funneling more and more people into migration flows. At the same time, increased restrictions on migration into the "developed" world have encouraged migrants to develop the flexible transnational strategies they need to survive in a neoliberal world.

Linkages between gender and sexuality on one hand and neoliberalism and transnational survival strategies on the other are readily apparent in some cases and harder to untangle in others. For example, a study by Howe et al. (2008) involving working-class transgender sex workers who migrate between Guadalajara and San Francisco clearly demonstrates these intersections. In this case, economic and gender/sexual factors are thoroughly intertwined, producing "a clear combination of dynamics...that include economic migration (crossing the border to earn dollars) but also more subtle sexual migration that involves the pursuit of gender-transformative treatment, capital to start a small business, and a place of relative tolerance" (Howe et al. 2008, 33). Their lower-class status—reinforced by the fact that transgender people face very limited employment possibilities—combined with their engagement in sex work renders them undesirable on criminal and moral grounds under U.S. law (Howe et al. 2008, 36). These disadvantages force them to cross the border without authorization, sometimes paying *coyotes* up to $2,500 a trip (Howe et al. 2008, 38). To obtain logistical and financial help with crossing, many transgender migrants develop networks of other transgender sex workers, a transnational networking strategy long associated with Mexican migrants but organized in this case around a shared identity forged through a specific kind of adversity (Howe et al. 2008, 39).

Although crossing the border is costly and dangerous, it is also a metaphorical site "of shifting identities, conflict, cooperation, and creative responses to a hierarchically organized world" (Howe et al. 2008, 38) that fuels their desire to refashion their gender and class identities and to have new experiences. Once transgender migrants reach San Francisco, however, their economic and social possibilities are constrained by the "illegal" combination of undocumented status and sex work. As undocumented migrants without an established credit history, their rental options are limited; all of the migrants interviewed resided in a run-down, single-occupancy hotel in a poor neighborhood, where they paid exorbitant monthly rent for a room and shared bathroom. Moreover, every client who entered was charged a $10 fee by the front desk, which the landlord kept. As Howe et al. (2008) explain,

> the relatively isolated lives led by transgender sex workers in San Francisco involved many vectors of vulnerability: undocumented status, language barriers, heterosexism, gender role expectations, and perhaps most significantly, participation in an illicit economy of prostitution. Their marginalization as undocumented, Spanish-speaking migrants, in combination with being gender 'transgressive' in their gender and sexual presentation and practices, appeared to limit the possibility of their engaging more fully with transgender or gay communities in San Francisco; it also limited their participation in Mexican migrant communities in the city. (45)

Gender, sexuality, and neoliberal immigration policies intertwined in very different ways for the middle-class heterosexual Mexican women studied by Felicity Schaeffer-Grabiel (2007). Most women were highly educated and many held tourist visas that enabled them to cross legally into the United States. At the same time, they used internet matchmaking services to find U.S. marriage partners. According to Schaeffer-Grabiel, "these women were not interested in merely migrating to the United States to work; they repeatedly described wanting to find a good, hardworking, and compatible partner with whom they could share their ideas and feelings. And most were not interested in migrating at a lower class level, so they sought marriages that could protect and hopefully augment their way of life in Mexico and the United States" (507–8). Imagining U.S. men as "the kind of men who respect strong and successful women" (508), transnational marriage offered them a strategy for achieving their desired identities as consumers in a global marketplace capable of successfully negotiating the limits imposed by middle-class salaries in Mexico. Moreover, neoliberal U.S. immigration laws have increasingly privileged middle-class heterosexuality and entrepreneurial self-fashioning, self-supporting subjects—and these preferences facilitate precisely these kinds of relationships. Despite their advantages, the women also experienced the contradictory aspects of transnational strategizing. As Schaeffer-Grabiel explains, "what women want and the types of men these services attract are almost always at odds. Many US men are looking for the traditional wife and family relationship they believe existed during the 1950s" (512) and turn to Mexican women, who they expect to fulfill these expectations.

Other transnational migration studies reveal even more ways in which gender, sexuality, and neoliberal immigration laws shape migrant strategies and outcomes. These include Lionel Cantú's research into Mexican migration by MSM, Héctor Carrillo et al.'s study of the binational construction of HIV risk factors among Mexican migrant gay and bisexual men, and Jennifer Hirsh's analysis of changing notions of heterosexual marriage (as ideology and practice) among Mexican women and men on a transnational circuit that runs between Atlanta, Georgia, and small towns in Michoacán.

Related research on Mexican migration—focused on its transborder rather than transnational aspects—also offers rich resources for understanding how migrants renegotiate gender and sexuality in the context of neoliberal immigration laws, economic structural adjustments, and changing social conditions. This research is especially concerned with new family forms that emerge in the migration process. In *Borderlands/La frontera*, Chicana feminist poet Gloria Anzaldúa famously theorized the U.S.-Mexico borderlands as a gendered, sexualized, "queer" space where the first world rubs up against the third, producing vibrant cultures, fierce oppressions, and innovative resistance strategies. Building on Anzaldúa and subsequent borderlands theorists, Denise Segura and Patricia Zavella have published an important edited volume, *Women and Migration in the U.S.-Mexico Borderlands*, that advocates a binational approach to thinking about the multiple structural inequalities faced by women in the U.S.-Mexico borderlands and their creative responses to those inequalities. As they explain, "when women become the center of analysis, questions change and previously held assumptions become subjects of inquiry" (Segura and Zavella 2007, 19). In a special issue of *Gender and Society*, Segura and Zavella further propose a "feminist borderlands project" that "interrogates the multiple meanings of borders and borderlands," including but not limited to the U.S.-Mexico borderlands (2008, 539). For example, Lynn Stephen argues that Mixtec and Zapotec migrants who move between communities in Oaxaca, California, and Oregon experience "transborder lives." Through the term "transborder," Stephen highlights that "the borders they have crossed and continue to cross are much more than national ... [they] are ethnic, cultural, colonial, and state borders within Mexico as well as the U.S.-Mexico border ... [and] ethnic, cultural, and regional borders within the United States. For these reasons it makes more sense to speak of transborder migration ... rather than simply transnational" (2007, 23). Stephen's luminous ethnography "highlights [migrants'] creative responses" (31) to these many borders within their multi-sited lives, including in gendered terms as it becomes accepted for both men and women to work outside the home. Creative or not, Stephen notes the high price women often pay for transborder mothering:

> If women come to join their husbands in the United States they may initially leave children behind and give birth to others in the United States, who automatically become citizens. In this case, women must worry about children in two distinct

contexts. In the United States they hope their children will be able to take advantages of the opportunities they have, particularly in terms of education. They feel additional pressure to send sufficient funds to support their children in Mexico as well as provide the best lifestyle possible for their children in the United States. (205)

In a similar transborder vein, Emma Pérez (2003) has proposed the use of decolonial imaginaries and strategies of disidentification (in which subjects define themselves against the dominant cultures) to uncover and honor queer histories of the U.S.–Mexico borderlands that are otherwise lost under the lens of white, heteronormative viewpoints. Growing scholarship on the phenomenology of the undocumented subject living in the borderlands also richly contributes to our understanding of the connections among gender, sexuality, and Mexican migration. For example, Sarah Willen (2007) praises the development of scholarship that has theorized illegality as a juridical status and a sociopolitical condition, but argues that "a third, crucial dimension remains palpably missing from this model: the impact of illegality on migrants' everyday, embodied experiences of being-in-the world" (10) including attention to the ways that illegality shapes migrants' "subjective experiences of time, space, embodiment, sociality, and self" (10).

CONCLUSION

As several decades of scholarship have solidly established, gender and sexuality shape and are shaped by migration processes. Yet, gender and sexuality are never already constituted attributes; rather, they are produced through specific regimes. Neoliberalism, which significantly fuels contemporary migration, operates in and through gender and sexual regimes. As we have seen, it proposes specific forms of regulation and inequality that are gendered and sexualized—and to which migrants respond and negotiate in varied ways, based on their circumstances. Consequently, gender and sexuality are being produced in new ways and deployed to new (and not so new) ends. What remains constant, however, is that contemporary regimes of gender and sexuality continue to produce and naturalize inequalities. In the case of Mexican migration, these inequalities are inseparable from a long history of racist, nationalist, and (neo)colonialist relations vis-à-vis the United States. For that reason, paying special attention to the subaltern migrant populations caught in the interstices of those relations—poor and working-class women and men (typically racialized as "Mexican"), queers, undocumented migrants, etc.—offers a means to understand not just their lives, which are often rendered invisible, but also how the larger system works, for whom it works, and what is at stake in challenging it.

CHAPTER 10

Cultural Representation and Mexican Immigration

Alex M. Saragoza[1]

University of California, Berkeley

He came from the sky, but not in an airplane
He came in his ship all the way from Krypton
And it appears that he is not an American
Rather, he is just like me, undocumented

From the song, *Superman es illegal*, by KINKY

This emergent multi-bit reality does not fit neatly under transnationalism nor under post-nationalism. And even in cases where it might fit, we lose something when we explain it in those terms.

SASKIA SASSEN

INTRODUCTION

In the 1948 Mexican-made film, *Ustedes los ricos*, an early scene involves a conversation between the main character, Pepe, and his sidekick, nicknamed *el bracero*, about the upcoming birthday of Pepe's wife, Celia. Using mangled English, *el bracero* explains that in the United States the event is called "happy birthday." In a subsequent scene, Pepe's friends sing the traditional *mañanitas* song to Celia, at the conclusion of which *el bracero* breaks out with a heavy-accented rendition of the happy birthday song, only to be shouted down by the rest of the group. Sixty years later, in the U.S.-produced movie, *Under the Same Moon* (2008), a young Mexican American female visits the "office" of a woman who arranges the border crossing of undocumented workers. The Mexican American woman explains in "Spanglish" that she is willing to cross over a child for

1. I am indebted to Lily Castillo-Speed, Marisol Zapater, and the staff of the Ethnic Studies Library at UC Berkeley for their assistance.

money. With ill-disguised scorn, the female *coyote* spurns the offer.[2] Made more than half a century apart, these two films bear testimony to the extensive process of cultural representation generated by the persistence and magnitude of Mexican immigration to the United States. This cultural realm holds an enormously broad spectrum of cross-border forms without idiomatic boundaries, encompassing popular expression as well as novels, plays, poetry and works of art.[3]

This essay delves primarily into the popular imaging of Mexican immigrants and its historical formations. Toward this end, the English-language media plays a central role, but the Spanish-language media also commands consideration. A bifocal lens to this history allows for a more complete understanding of the cultural representation created by Mexican immigration. Indeed, the emergence and development of the Spanish-language media complicates a story that is at once binational and transnational—binational in the sense, for example, that *Ustedes los ricos* was produced by a Mexican motion picture company and was basically intended for audiences in Mexico. The *el bracero* character in the film reflected the imaging of returning immigrants, evident cinematic acknowledgement of migration *al norte* as a consequence of the so-called Bracero Program. On the other hand, the showing of *Ustedes* at a "Mexican" moviehouse like the Million Dollar Theater of Los Angeles added a transnational dimension for the Mexican-made movie, given an audience composed presumably in part if not largely by Mexican immigrants.

This process would be essentially inversed in the making of *Under the Same Moon*, where the main actors and director were of Mexican origin, in a film using a screenplay by a U.S.-born Latina, for a motion picture distributed by a major U.S.-based studio. Yet, a prominent morning television talk show in Mexico had a lengthy segment on the film and interviewed two of its cast members on the eve of the film's premiere in Mexico City. In a similar fashion, Mexican-born musical artists living north of the border, for instance, have also sold their recordings in their native country and have them played on radio stations south of the border. As several scholars have noted, this process of exchange has punctuated the culture of migration between the two countries; what may have begun as a binational process became a transnational cultural phenomenon as a consequence of continuing Mexican immigration and its attendant, circular cultural flows. And more recently, developments on both sides of the border suggest an emergent, complicated transition, as suggested in the epigram to this essay by Saskia Sassen.

The cultural representation of Mexican immigrants, however, must be understood in light of their generally negative depiction by the English-language media, given its influence and ascendant position. It is beyond the scope of this essay to detail the

---

2. *Ustedes los ricos* was a sequel to the hugely popular *Nosotros los pobres* (1947); the main star attraction in both films was Pedro Infante, arguably the most popular entertainer of his time, rivaled perhaps only by the comedian Mario "Cantinflas" Moreno. Infante's following crossed the border, and both films played to large audiences in the United States; later, via television, the films would be repeatedly shown on both sides of the border.

3. This essay does not cover the representation of immigrants in the fine arts, such as literature, art, and drama, given the space constraints for this volume, as well as the question of access and circulation. For much of the public, regardless of language preference, the imaging of Mexican immigrants comes primarily from the popular media (i.e., films, television, radio).

long history of the racialized representation of Mexican immigrants for a non-Latino public, where the distinction between the foreign-born and the native-born has too often been conflated. In this arc of time, the biased imaging of Mexican immigrants has flared periodically to the national level (e.g., at the onset of the Great Depression). Moreover, much of the negative portrayal of Mexican newcomers has been sustained by subnational sources, such as local newspapers, radio, and television stations. This historical process also holds an enduring international dimension. The penetration of the American media overseas has meant the widespread dissemination of stereotypes of Mexicans and Mexican immigrants, from the silent movie era through the contemporary period; space constraints disallow a full discussion of this latter issue (see de Grazia 2005, esp. 297–303). Furthermore, the discursive practices associated with anti-Mexican immigrant representations have been reformulated over time. The Mexican immigrant as a siesta-loving, lazy *peon* of the 1920s, for instance, has given way to additional stereotypes in subsequent decades. In brief, anti-Mexican nativism in the print media, film, radio, and television has witnessed variations in expression and intensity over time and place.

On the other hand, for decades the view from Mexico of their *paisanos en el norte* was at best ambivalent if not disdainful. This imagery seeped across the border into theaters that showed movies from Mexico or into the lyrics of recordings played on Spanish-language radio programs.[4] But this perception in Mexico of *mexicanos de afuera* has changed in the more contemporary period, with corresponding consequences for the depiction of Mexican immigrants on both sides of the border.

Nonetheless, the fundamental asymmetries in the relationship between the United States and Mexico have basically paralleled the means to portray Mexican immigrants. There are several historical aspects to the capacity of U.S.-based sources of cultural production to represent Mexican newcomers. First, Hollywood—film and television production—has exercised a foundational influence in the formation of the basic stereotypes of people of Mexican origin. As numerous scholars have shown, the record of the American entertainment industry has been less than salutary in its treatment of Mexicans in general. Hollywood has shown a willingness in recent years to rectify the crude stereotypes of the past, although often as a means to satirize or to criticize mainstream society. Second, access to information via the media has become much more available since the 1970s, such as 24/7 news programs and their capacity for selective coverage of "immigrant issues." The well-known then commentator on CNN, Lou Dobbs, for instance, earned a dubious reputation for his jaundiced reports on the "immigrant invasion."[5] Such programming has been usually echoed by conservative talk radio, another contemporary development in the U.S. media (where the notorious Rush Limbaugh is just one of many pundits with nativist propensities). Third, local print and broadcast media have an underappreciated impact, in which "hometown" journalists have frequently served to nurture anti-immigrant sentiment through their biased attention to "immigration" (Branton and Dunaway 2009). A fourth source of

---

4. Maciel and Herrera-Sobek have written several essays on this aspect of the history of the representation of Mexican immigration. For representative examples of their work, see Maciel (1992) and Herrera-Sobek (1993).

5. On this point, see Hollar (2006).

this imbalance has come from the proliferation of so-called "think tanks" that promote an implicit if not explicit nativist agenda.[6] The Internet constitutes a fifth arena for the imaging of immigrants, as a multitude of websites have appeared that pander to racially charged perceptions of Mexican immigrants in general, "illegals" in particular (see Sohoni 2006). Finally, it should be emphasized that the prejudicial representations of immigrants must also take into account what is not reported, pictured, or heard.

The sum of these diverse sources of nativist imagery has renewed old stereo-types (e.g., Mexican immigrants as health menace; the swine flu pandemic of 2009 was deployed for such purpose by nativists). Meanwhile, reconfigured discursive forms have reinforced embedded negative cultural assumptions (e.g., the association of immi-grants with criminality has been rehashed in the link of *recien llegados* with drug traf-ficking and illicit drug use; See "Paranoia Pandemic" 2009). And although these freshly minted discourses usually aim at "illegal" immigration, the distinction between legal and unauthorized immigrants has been generally lost in the coded language of the new nativism toward Mexican immigrants.

For immigrant communities and their supporters, the capacity to counter nativist views has been generally much less than their adversaries, past or present. As a recent study has observed, for example, liberal pundits have addressed the question of immigra-tion sparingly as opposed to their conservative counterparts (see Brookings Institution 2008, 42). Moreover, unlike many right-wing groups and think tanks, proimmigrant organizations have not commanded comparable financial backing from well-endowed foundations and/or wealthy patrons. The digital divide (i.e., access to the Web) adds but another factor in the imbalance between immigrants' rights activists, in contrast to their nativist opponents, in the contest over the representation of immigrants. And the so-called use of contemporary "attack journalism" or "shock jocks" has been an approach largely eschewed by media outlets in defense of immigrants and their representation.

To dwell on the asymmetries over the cultural representation of Mexican immi-grants, however, threatens to underestimate the ability of Mexican-origin communities and their advocates to deflect if not counter their racialization. Immigrants have not been hapless victims of nativist rhetoric and media. As this essay will discuss below, the proimmigrant demonstrations of 2006 in various cities in the United States tes-tified to the capability of immigrants and their allies to respond forcefully to their ill treatment, including their negative cultural depiction. The protests of 2006—presaged by the demonstrations of 1994—revealed a capacious immigrant-inflected cultural space, derived from the conjunction of historical developments, in which the Spanish-language media had become a key element. To be sure, the commercialization of cul-tural production afforded by large-scale Mexican immigration also played a role in that process (see Davila 2001, 153–80). Nevertheless, the portrayal of Mexican migration cannot be reduced merely to a chronicle of racist imagery, a romanticized narrative of resistance, or a product of slick capitalist ethnic merchandising. Rather, the cultural representation of Mexican immigrants points to a complicated history that traverses the border and destabilizes the facile binaries that have been employed to depict the experience of newcomers from Mexico.

---

6. On the enormous information generated by right-wing think tanks, see Dolny (1998).

FRAMING THE REPRESENTATION OF
MEXICAN IMMIGRATION

Three factors frame this essay's discussion of the historical portrayal of Mexican new-comers. First, the English-language media fundamentally shapes the cultural represen-tation of Mexican immigrants. Second, despite the dominance of U.S.-based film, radio, and television, the presence of the Spanish-language media and its transborder circuits must also be taken into account. Third, the characteristics of immigrant networks (such as the size, composition, and destination points of the migrant flows from Mexico to the United States) also deserve comment, but because of space limitations for this essay, the latter aspect will receive less direct attention. Each of these primary factors in the representation of Mexican immigration must be historicized because the correlations among them shift over time and place in light of political, economic, and cultural con-ditions. For example, the relatively recent movement of immigrants into the southeast of the United States, a nontraditional receiving site for Mexican newcomers, has led not only to a rise in nativist rhetoric in that region, but also to the emergence of a cultural rejoinder (e.g., the appearance of Spanish-language radio stations in places where few if any had existed before). Along this vein, the English-language media witnessed a cru-cial change after the 1960s, when the three major networks gradually lost their grip on the televised scape of the United States: the appearance of cable channels, Fox News for instance, multiplied the means for coverage of topics, such as immigration by nativist pundits. Given the significance of the latter point, this essay will give particular atten-tion to the background of this contemporary aspect of the English-language media. In brief, the historical interplay of the three factors noted above reflects a multivalent and complex story, but for heuristic reasons, they will be discussed separately.

THE ENGLISH-LANGUAGE MEDIA

In the history of the racialized representation of Mexican immigrants in the United States, certain periods have been especially important. The first phase, from about the 1920s through the 1950s, played a fundamental role; it reflected the cumulative racist-inflected views toward Mexicans rooted in the distant past, from the colonial rivalry between Spain and England to the U.S.–Mexican War (see the excellent essay by Mariscal 2006, 61–80, esp. 61–64). This initial phase was marked by the formative era of mass entertainment, notably film, radio, and sound recording, where the large-scale circulation of newspapers, comic books, and magazines provided yet another source of popular imagery. A decisive outcome of this period was the tendency of the media to conflate Mexican immigrants into the established repertoire of Mexican stereotypes. In effect, the difference between U.S.-born people of Mexican origin and Mexican immi-grants became generally indistinguishable by the American media: to be of Mexican origin in the United States was to be an immigrant, an inherent foreigner.

    The images of this era thrived on the accumulated stereotypes associated with Mexicans: sleepy, fatalistic, apathetic peasants, although capable of sudden bouts of murderous rage or tearful sentimentality, usually spurred by their alleged love of liquor. Mexican immigrant women fared badly if not worse because they were basically reduced to the binary of stoic rural Indian-like female or smoldering harlot of easy virtue; but in both images, the rampant fertility of Mexican immigrant women was established and proved to be a tenacious trope. Radio added sound effects to this imagery that became ubiquitous: the heavy-accented female Chihuahua dog in Disney's *Lady and the Tramp* (1955) echoed a tradition that easily made its way into television, such as the character "Pepino" in the television series *Beverly Hillbillys* (1957–1963). Immigrants invariably found themselves slotted into images of "mexicannness" that became standardized: sombreros, serapes, sandals, mustaches, braided women in colorful "Mexican" blouses and skirts, all of which appeared in various guises, from travel posters and commercial advertisements to the décor of restaurants and the visual landscapes of films and televised programming and even into textbooks. Immigrants became simply newcomer additions to this inventory of images (see Davila 2008, 73).

As Charles Ramirez Berg has summarized for cinema, this foundational imaginary of Mexicans included several stock stereotypes: the *bandido*, the harlot, the buffoon, the Latin lover, and the dark lady. Each of these archetypes held an immigrant-related dimension. The *bandido*/bandit imagery associated criminality with Mexicans in general, regardless of place of birth. The harlot and dark lady presumably represented the two sides of the inherent sexual nature of Mexican women. The harlot suggested an intrinsic fiery sexuality, whereas the detached demeanor of the "lady" veiled a smoldering desire awaiting the hand of the appropriate male to unleash it. The Latin lover image offered a masculine version of the hypersexuality of Mexicans, leading to a favorite nativist trope: Mexicans have large families as a result of their inability to control their sexual instincts. The buffoon stereotype (which can be of either gender) relied on humor derived from stereotypic behavior, where the use of "Spanglish," for example, directly ties this archetype to immigrants (Ramirez Berg 2002, 66–86). In one way or another, these stereotypes became the basis for the images that were projected onto Mexican newcomers.

These foundational images held a malevolent dimension, as evidenced, for instance, in the consequences of the government's "crackdown" on unauthorized immigration in the mid-1950s, named Operation Wetback. Laced with Cold War overtones, the media's alarmist coverage of the issue reinforced the representation of Mexican immigrants as sources of various dangers to the American public (see Astor 2009). Major newspapers gave play to the notion that communist spies and saboteurs could enter under the cover of the unchecked entry of "illegal aliens." This distorted coverage deepened with the nascent entry of televised news into American homes by the early 1950s. A much larger audience for this coupling of nativism with anticommunist fervor was made available by the newsreel segments that usually appeared at movie houses, when television sets were still a novelty in most family living rooms and motion picture attendance remained high.[7] Whatever persisted of the benign attitudes created by Mexican men who provided their labor to the wartime effort, those sentiments shrank before the nativism spurred by the government's Operation Wetback and its racist underpinnings. In short, this formative stage in the media possessed few redeeming exceptions to the generalized demeaning depiction of Mexican immigrant women and men.

---

7. See for example, American Path News, "Border Crisis Comes as Mexicans Seek U.S. Jobs," vol. 25, no. 55, February 16, 1954; Hearst News of the Day, "Mexico 'Wetbacks' Keep U.S. Border Patrol Busy," vol. 25, no. 250, February 18, 1954; Universal News, "Wetback Roundup [in] California," vol. 27, no. 584, July 5, 1954.

FROM THE 1960s TO THE 1980s

A second stage of the English-media's attention to immigrants developed in the 1960s and lapped over into the 1980s, punctuated by the implications of the Latino civil rights movement for the imaging of Mexicans in general. The scholarly assault on the racist rendering of Mexicans (and other racialized groups), combined with legal remedies, had an enduring albeit incomplete effect. The crude racism of the past receded, but it was too often accompanied by the lack of any consistently positive media representation of Mexicans at all, regardless of which side of border they were born on.[8] Nativist extremism lurked in the background, flashed occasionally, but infrequently penetrated into mainstream motion pictures, television programs, or related forms of popular culture. Strident anti-immigrant agitation failed to find much public support or media attention at that time.

Rather, the cultural corollaries of the civil rights movement opened a space in which immigrants found a measure of succor and affirmation. The growth of bilingual education, the expansion of community-based programs, the push by activists for greater attention to Mexican culture by public institutions, and similar efforts legitimated and multiplied the sites for the expression of *mexicanidad* that inevitably encompassed Mexican immigrant communities. Understandably, this process had its greatest impact in areas with a large resident Mexican population. From San Antonio and Chicago to Los Angeles and Denver, cultural activities, often sponsored by municipal or county agencies and/or supported by public funds, touted the presence of Mexicans specifically and "Hispanics" more generally. From museums to county fairs, Mexican culture was performed, displayed, lauded, or acclaimed, allowing immigrants a representational capital that partially eclipsed the glare of a racialized past symbolized by ignorant *peones* and their sundry guises.

The cultural project generated by Latino activism established a brake on the crass stereotypic depictions of those of Mexican descent in general, including immigrants by extension. In response to Latino critics, for instance, the Frito-Lay company gave up its "frito-bandido" character in its advertising; and NBC withdrew Bill Dana's "Jose Jimenez" television show that was steeped in stereotypic humor. Similarly, Mexican-origin writers, artists, and dramatists, some of whom were of immigrant backgrounds, found a much more receptive climate as publishers, art galleries, and playhouses made way for works that often touched on themes of Mexican immigration. Significantly, much of this work celebrated the connection between Mexico and those of Mexican origin in the United States and marked the so-called Chicano renaissance (see Maciel, Ortiz, and Herrera-Sobek 2000, introduction). This recognition of Mexican heritage had limited accessibility among many Mexican immigrants, as such activities took place beyond their reach. Nonetheless, the synergies created by the Chicano-based cultural movement held dividends for the representation of immigrants of Mexican origin. Granted, much of this outpouring of attention to Mexican culture was invested in essentializing forms without politically progressive content, but this burst of public acknowledgement of Mexico and its cultural patrimony, however idealized and stylized, contributed to a cultural space inclusive of the presence of Mexican immigrants.

---

8. See National Council of La Raza (1997). For a similar conclusion, see Pachon et al. (2000).

At more local and quotidian levels, the surge in migration after 1960 meant an expansion of the cultural circuits generated by an increasing Mexican-born population in the United States, such as the tours by Mexico-based musical artists, the multiplication of community-based "Mexican" dances, and the public observance of Mexican civic holidays, like the sixteenth of September. The commercial implications of these trends were not lost on English-speaking businessmen in the major destination points of Mexican immigration. Slowly and then with greater frequency, there began to appear on storefronts, radio spots, and televised advertisements slogans, for instance, that read, "*se habla espanol.*" Moreover, immigrants began to organize sports leagues and tournaments, and in countless communities Mexican-immigrant oriented businesses sprouted and/or expanded, providing the means for public cultural displays, from video and record stores to *panaderias* and *tortillerias*. Schools with large numbers of Mexican immigrant children (particularly those with bilingual and/or migrant education programs) began to have *piñatas* and food sales and related activities that frequently led to the celebratory performance of "Mexican" cultural forms (albeit stylized), from the formation of "folklorico" dance troupes to the staging of *posadas, dia de los muertos,* and fundraisers featuring traditional dishes.

These localized displays of *mexicanidad* gained a large measure of their visibility from the pressure on the media industry by minority groups and their supporters. Latino activists, using the fairness doctrine of Federal Communications Commission as leverage, for example, pressed local media in many cities to establish community-based advisory groups as a means of pushing local stations to give more and positive attention to minority group-related stories. As a result, English-language television stations, for instance, began to cover locally sponsored "5 de mayo" festivities and similar activities. (Media outlets also began to hire Latino media professionals, in which concerns over affirmative action also played a role.) In short, the 1960s and 1970s witnessed the growth of a palpable, publicly sanctioned, immigrant-inflected cultural space that impinged upon the English-language world in a distinctively different ways. The *mexicanidad* of newcomer communities was no longer as confined as it had been in the era of de facto and de jure segregation; immigrants had breached in effect the English-only wall of the media. Still, uninformed reporting persisted; film studios generally avoided positive portrayals of immigration or immigrants, and television nourished previously established stereotypes by recycling movies and cartoons from the past. In this sense, much of the effort of Latino cultural activists focused on efforts to rehabilitate the image of Mexican-origin communities. Nonetheless, an incremental change in the cultural representation of Mexican immigrants developed as a consequence of Latino activism in general and that of the Chicano movement more specifically. Meanwhile, restive nativists encountered relatively fewer opportunities to vent their views, but their time came soon enough.

REAGANISM AND NATIVISM

The neoconservative surge from the 1980s through the 1990s created a highly polarized political period in which Mexican immigration became a hotly contested issue. Yet, the Reagan era possessed a basic inconsistency when it came to Mexico and Mexicans in the United States. On the one hand, it was Reagan who signed landmark immigration legislation in 1986 that eventually regularized the status of about 2.7 million former unauthorized residents (of whom the majority were from Mexico, through the Immigration Reform and Control Act, or IRCA). Moreover, during his presidency, the recognition of "Hispanics" in the United States became literally official. Reagan himself made the proclamation in 1988 changing National Hispanic Week (coinciding with the dates of Mexico's Independence Day observance) to "National Hispanic Month." On the other hand, in the midst of Mexico's debt crisis, the Reagan administration pushed Mexican policy makers toward neoliberal reforms, exacerbating the conditions conducive to migration. In addition, American officials engaged in "bashing" Mexico, such as for its drug trafficking, among other allegedly Mexican-borne ills inimical to the welfare of American society. More so than in the previous decade, Mexico became an object of White House criticism through the Reagan administration's posture toward its neighbor to the south. According to nativists, Reagan committed a major mistake regarding IRCA, but the neo-Cold War foreign policy stance of his presidency, its manifest retreat from civil rights, and its "America first" mentality produced an ideological context ripe for xenophobia; nativism came out from the shadows in the neoconservative climate engendered by reaganism.[9]

Armed with large amounts of cash, favorable political conditions, and a context of imperial jingoism, anti-immigrant groups found themselves in a position to oppose much more openly and aggressively the entry of Mexicans into the United States. The advances made by the civil rights groups of the 1960s and 1970s refused, however, to concede any ground, making for a battle of epic proportions. From the National Endowment for the Humanities and the Smithsonian Institution to state and local political skirmishes, the so-called cultural wars summoned nativists and their opponents alike. The battles raged over a wide range of issues, large and small, as the imaging of immigrants as cultural threats to the fabric of American society resurfaced with renewed vigor, from the politics of arts funding to the writing of U.S. history texts.

In this charged environment, nativists generally rearticulated their claims into a discourse that was presented in distinctly new ways (see Nevins 2002, 112–19). For example, Reagan era rhetoric on the need to cut taxes and social spending was translated into an effective mantra: Mexican immigrants meant a heavy toll on the wallets of "American" taxpayers' wallets. Thinly veiled Malthusian arguments also resurfaced in "reports" from right-wing organizations over the numbers of Mexicans immigrants that were swamping the "lifeboat" of America's capacity to bear the load. The emphasis on the numbers of immigrants clearly turned on the archetype of an earlier era's racialized view on the hypersexuality of Mexican females. The two arguments fused when hardcore nativists and their conservative allies promoted the notion that immigrant mothers wanted to have their children in the United States, not only to exploit America's generous welfare system, but also for the children to become citizens of the United States and thus have easy entrée to the country's benefits.[10]

---

9. On Reagan's foreign policy and neo-Cold War thinking, see Grandin (2007).

10. The term "anchor babies" has been used by xenophobes to refer to the alleged practice of undocumented mothers having their children in the United States to benefit from citizenship, welfare laws, etc. For a typical example of this type of nativist rhetoric, see Federation for American Immigration Reform (2008).

More importantly, the media's coverage of the "immigrant" issue, as Joseph Nevins has emphasized, centered on the "illegal" immigrant, that is, the criminality of the act of the undocumented crossing of the border (Nevins 2002, 62–65). This argument in the nativists' rhetorical arsenal reformulated the association of immigrants with criminality into a loss of control of "America's border," where lawless entrants trampled with impunity on the sovereignty of the United States. From this nativist perspective, crossing the border without authorization not only became an affront to law-abiding Americans, but also introduced people into the country without any respect for rules and regulations. The neoconservative movement's concern for "law and order" was redeployed against illegals with special vehemence by nativists, reaffirming the image of Mexicans as foreigners unfit to become good Americans. Thus, the terms immigrant and Mexican became entrenched code words for illegal in the discursive practices nurtured by reaganite conservatism.

Of decisive significance, reaganism fostered two interrelated strands within the so-called new nativism: one composed of a hodge-podge of xenophobic extremist groups with a white supremacist tinge and a second current that presented itself as centrist, responsible organizations—often funded in part if not primarily by right-wing donors—which sponsored research, conferences, and information that increasingly reached into mainstream media channels. The more extremist groups basically focused their attacks on immigrants toward like-minded audiences in the recesses of the right-wing fringe of American politics.[11] More insidiously, nativist think tanks sought widespread public recognition and mainstream media attention for their professed reasonable concerns over immigration. The two anti-immigrant currents essentially worked in tandem; xenophobic claims were given credence by the statistics, data, press releases, and "experts" marshaled by neoconservative "research centers" and their attendant venues. In this sense, the Reagan era produced a fundamentally important outcome: an unremitting polarization in the debate over immigration, where neoconservative think tanks abetted extremist nativist representations of Mexican immigrants.

The touchstone of the new nativism was the passage of the infamous Proposition 187 in California in November 1994. In the midst of a recession and concerns over public finances, the promoters of the referendum conducted a xenophobic campaign, playing not only to the discursive practices afforded by reaganism (immigrants as a drain on the state's resources, especially its schools and social services), but also on more extremist imagery, including that of "illegal hordes" invading California. The early stereotypes of Mexican immigrants as ignorant, indolent peasants paled in comparison to those used by fear-mongering nativists in support of Proposition 187. The anti-immigrant campaign prepared the way for a subsequent move, Proposition 227 in June 1998, which outlawed bilingual education in the state. Well-practiced English-only sloganeering was coupled with the arguments constructed for the voters' approval of Proposition 187, including the climbing numbers of immigrants in the state and the professed costs of bilingual education. Nativists also played to the cultural dangers over the alleged unwillingness of Spanish-speaking immigrants to learn English. For others, immigrants spelled an irreparable fracturing of American society into balkanized

---

11. See the website http://www.rightwingwatch.org for a partial listing of extremist organizations. See chapter appendix for list of right-wing and nativist organizations.

groups. And, in the more fevered minds of xenophobes, immigrants comprised the storm troopers of a Mexican attempt to retake the territory ceded to the United States following the War of 1846.[12]

The passage of Proposition 187 and Proposition 227 within a four-year span in a pivotal electoral state gave the new nativism an enormous boost of media attention and political visibility. Influenced by the calls for greater enforcement of border controls (and perhaps the polling on the issue of immigration), President Bill Clinton put into action Operation Gatekeeper in September 1994; two years later, he signed the Illegal Immigration Reform and Responsibility Act—the title of the legislation bore the unmistakable imprints of the California referendum. Not surprisingly, nativists exploited the moment as a bevy of publications appeared with ominous warnings of the dire consequences of unrestrained Mexican immigration regardless of legal status: Peter Brimelow's *Alien Nation* of 1996 was emblematic of a tide of books and articles that publicized the alleged dangers of immigrants, most specifically those from Mexico.[13]

The public reach of these arguments took place in a decidedly different media scape from a previous era because changes in mass communications in the United States contributed crucially to the potency of nativist claims and imagery. The full emergence of 24/7 televised news programming, the proliferation of right-wing talk radio, and the reaganite-inspired visibility of conservative organizations gave the new nativism a broad platform from which to promote its views. The appearance of CNN, Fox News, MSNBC, Headline News, and similar cable outlets paralleled the maturation and spread of conservative media and its nativist character. At the same time, The American Enterprise Institute, The Heritage Foundation, Federation for American Immigration Reform, and the Center for Immigration Studies, among other neoconservative organizations, offered ostensibly responsible, scholarly reports and publications over immigration, illegals in particular, which provided fodder for xenophobic groups, such as American Cause and NumbersUSA, to name but two of a slew of similar groups.[14] Extreme, xenophobic claims tended to capture the bulk of the attention and ire of proimmigrant advocates, but the artfulness of the new nativism was perhaps best served by the credence given to the so-called "experts" who appeared on op-ed pages of newspapers, on sound-bites in newscasts, as interviewees in published articles, and on conservative-leaning talk shows broadcast as "news magazines." In short, the limited spectrum of the television news of an earlier era had been replaced by the 1990s with a media field of enormous proportions, providing unprecedented opportunities for well-heeled nativist groups to present the "Latino threat" to a like-minded public.[15]

---

12. For an overview of these developments, see Chavez (2008).

13. It is important to emphasize that the spike of publications of this sort took place in the backwash of Proposition 187, indicative of the significance of that California referendum for the nativist movement in the 1990s. For examples of that surge in publications, see Chavez (2008, 31–34).

14. See the website of the People for the American Way, http://www.pfma.org, for other examples of these types of organizations.

15. The Project for Excellence in Journalism tracked the talk radio shows and their attention to the issue of immigration during a twenty-six-day period in 2007 and noted the preponderance of right-wing

In this widening media scape, the end of the Fairness Doctrine further constrained the ability of proimmigrant groups to counter the xenophobic framing of migration to the American public. The Reagan-appointed head of the Federal Communications Commission pledged once in office to do away with the concept of balance and fairness in the media as undue government meddling. A majority of the Supreme Court subsequently agreed, and in 1987 the fairness doctrine was declared unconstitutional. Congress attempted to resurrect the fairness provision through legislation, but Reagan vetoed the measure and a congressional override failed to materialize. As a consequence, many local television and radio stations dissolved their community advisory boards, networks lessened their attention to balance in reporting and coverage, and well-endowed neoconservative causes and their xenophobic allies had yet greater access to an expansive mainstream media. In the absence of the fairness doctrine, conservative broadcasting thrived unencumbered by regulatory restraint.

Spawned in large measure by Reagan era neoconservatism, the nativist lobby therefore held a powerful, multifaceted means to represent immigrants in a negative light.[16] The neoconservative political drift on immigration became bipartisan, when the Clinton administration proved vulnerable to the nativist pull, as evidenced by its authorization of Operation Gatekeeper, among other measures. In short, the reshaping of the media scape of the Reagan era and its aftermath held few redeeming qualities when it came to the representation of immigrants. As a report on the media and immigration noted, "traditional journalism presented a distorted portrayal of immigration; when the new forms of media supercharged that portrayal, the search for policy compromises became more difficult" (Brookings Institution 2008, 3). And, the representation of Mexican immigrants in other forms of the English-language media held scant remedy to this dismal record of American reporting.

9/11 AND ITS AFTERMATH

Taking advantage of the cumulative impact of previous efforts, nativists exploited the terrorist attacks of 9/11 to promote their criticism of Mexican immigrants. The anxieties generated by the threat of terrorism offered the extremist nativist fringe a semblance of credibility, best captured in the spasm of coverage to groups along the U.S.–Mexico border allegedly guarding a vulnerable America from the sum of all dangers represented by Mexican illegal immigrants. The daily media attention to the war on terror in its various forms, amplified by neoconservative pundits on television and radio, served to heighten public concerns over foreigners in the United States. The imagery of Operation Wetback in the midst of McCarthyism was refashioned into the threat represented by immigrants entering a porous border and providing "cover" to would-be terrorists. Once again, the border became a matter of national defense. If this were not enough, the slide in the U.S. economy that followed 9/11 served to further another nativist claim that immigrants were taking jobs from American workers (as opposed to the benefits of immigrant labor). In this post-9/11 atmosphere, the two

---

commentary, as opposed to proimmigrant pundits. The end of the fairness doctrine in 1987 clearly contributed to the use of radio for political purpose. On this latter point, see Chinni, 2007.

16. For an overview of these connections, see Zeskind, 2005.

currents within the new nativism thrived. Reports from right-wing think tanks nourished xenophobic commentary on radio and television on a range of topics, such as drivers' licenses and public college admissions for illegals. Not surprisingly, the nativists' calls for immigration reform were inevitably demands for the greater militarization of the border, for more restrictive admissions criteria, and for increased punitive measures against immigrant "lawbreakers."

The negative representation of Mexican newcomers after 9/11 intensified the polarization of the debate over immigration in general, that from Mexico most specifically. In a sprawling, detailed study, the Brookings Institution highlighted the negative consequences of the mainstream media's inadequate, flawed, and selective coverage of the issue of immigration. The study noted that the lack of informed attention by the mainstream media on immigration greatly facilitated the capacity of nativists to advance their views (Brookings Institution 2008, 23–31). Thus, the belated effort by the Bush administration to pass new immigration legislation in 2006–2007 provided nativists with a broad stage to mount their views on Mexican immigrants among a public made wary by the war on terror and its attendant imagery. Significantly, the anti-immigrant campaign tended to maintain a key racialized feature of the past (i.e., the conflation of Mexicans, legal or undocumented, into the coded rhetoric of nativism). To make matters worse for the representation of immigrants, the major networks and their print counterparts often played into the hands of xenophobes. As one report put it, "the cumulative portrait drawn by nearly 30 years of American journalism emphasizes illegal or uncontrolled migration rather than the much larger movement of people that has been legal and orderly." The same report went on to state that the "emphasis on illegality applies not only to the means by which people enter the country but also to their activities once here…and when those lawbreakers are identifiable as members of a group by virtue of national origin, race or nativity or all three, stereotyping is equally inevitable" (Brookings Institution 2008, 24).

In this setting, the representation of Mexican immigrants in the English-language media invariably suffered. As Leo Chavez has aptly summarized, nativists conjured a "Latino threat" based largely on the presence of Mexican immigrants, where the tropes of the past had been reconfigured into a far more menacing specter to the American public. For Chavez, three nativist images were of particular importance, those of "invasion, reconquest and the Quebec model" (2008, 26–40). The "invasion" concept renewed Malthusian arguments, whereas the "reconquest" allegation turned on separatist paranoia. The "Quebec model" fears relied on the stock assimilationist, melting pot view of U.S. immigration history—Mexicans simply had refused to become good American citizens and to embrace this country's cultural norms, unlike previous immigrants (i.e., those of European origin). Meanwhile, the mainstream media maintained its distorted, inconsistent coverage of the topic (Brooking Institution 2008, 19). Pushed into a defensive mode, proimmigrant supporters parried a multiplicity of xenophobic charges and contended with the nativists' ample resources and allies.[17] In this surge of anti-immigrant sentiment, newcomer communities and their defenders gave little ground, unwilling to bow to the multipronged nativist onslaught that characterized the

17. See for an example of this sort, Chomsky (2007).

waning years of the administration of George W. Bush. In this process, the shortcomings of the coverage of immigration by the English-language media served the interests of an alternative source of news and entertainment long overlooked by the dominant media corporations of the United States.

THE SPANISH-LANGUAGE MEDIA

For decades, the American media basically marginalized the presence of the Mexican-origin population. Communication laws, racist assumptions, nativist thinking, and/or indifference conspired to push non-English-language programming to the periphery of the mainstream mass communications in the United States. The iconic early-morning radio programs in Spanish (e.g., *horas rancheras* type shows dating since the late 1920s)—despite their evident popularity—failed to receive concerted attention from the major radio networks and later from television executives and their motion picture counterparts.

This generalized neglect by the American entertainment industry facilitated the opportunities of Mexican-based Spanish-language media to reach *paisanos* in the United States. So-called "border stations" reached audiences in the United States since the onset of commercial radio broadcasting in Mexico. As a consequence, by the 1930s Mexican recording stars (ironically on the labels of U.S.-based companies, such as RCA Victor) had legions of listeners north of the Mexican border. By the eve of World War II, Mexican-based films, radio programs, and recordings allowed for sources of *mexicanidad* in *el norte*. Composed in part if not largely by immigrants, sundry organizations, social clubs, and mutual aid societies emerged in the initial wave of large-scale Mexican migration of the early 1900s, expanding the cultural space that implicitly competed with that of the dominant society (see Monroy 1999). Thus, in scores of cities immigrant-based civic groups observed traditional Mexican holidays, such as Independence Day festivities (sixteenth of September). Moreover, the popularity of Mexican movies by the 1930s, for instance, meant a counter to the racist imagery of U.S.-made films. And radio personalities, such as the famed Pedro Gonzalez, offered yet another means to challenge the overriding prevalence of negative images generated in that era by the English-language media.[18] And Gonzalez, like other Mexicans performers living in the United States, recorded songs and entertained on live broadcasts that sustained a notion of Mexican identity *afuera de la patria*.

This transnational cultural space, however, held crosscurrents that complicated any easy definition of "Mexican." Regional variations, generational differentiation, class-inflected distinctions, and urban/rural permutations played out in the elastic meanings of *lo mexicano* north of the border. The Mexican public early on developed a prejudicial view toward their compatriots in the United States, accentuated by the nationalist essentialism of the postrevolutionary cultural project of the Mexican state. The resultant perception in Mexico (which usually collapsed Mexican Americans with

---

18. The role of DJs on Mexican radio has traditionally been more than just an announcer. Rather, *locutores* have usually played other roles as well, including everything from marital counselor to political commentator.

Mexican immigrants) became the symbolic image of the *pocho*, with its negative connotation if not outright scorn for "anglicized" compatriots in the United States. The "Americanized" Mexican character "Frank" in the film, *Ni sangre ni arena* (1938), starring the hugely popular comedian, Mario Moreno "Cantinflas," embodied this pejorative view that appeared in Mexican movies of that era. Notions of "Americanized" Mexicans (*agringados*) as traitors to *patria* (nation) generally characterized the representation of *mexicanos de afuera* (i.e., as contaminated or culturally corrupted by their exposure to the United States).[19] The acculturation of Mexicans to American mainstream culture was real enough and widespread, especially among the children of Mexican immigrants, but it was a process subject to variation and nuance that was usually lost in the simplistic binary that emerged in the discourse over *pochismo* as opposed *lo mexicano*. For decades, within the Mexican media the representation of Mexican immigrants too often fell victim to this facile dichotomy through the post-World War II era.

Furthermore, the Mexican binary between *pochos* and *mexicanos* had its parallels on the other side of the border, where Mexican Americans made distinctions between *los recien llegados* as opposed to those who had acclimated to American social and cultural norms; feelings of disassociation toward Mexican newcomers among U.S.-born residents of Mexican-origin were not uncommon (see Foley 1997, 8). Such attitudes by Mexican Americans were informed by class differences, job competition, levels of fluency in English, and familiarity with American ways, as well as the negative imagery projected onto Mexican immigrants by the English-language media. Still, the social distancing between these two broad groupings was subject to variations that defied clearly marked cultural boundaries.

By the end of the 1950s, these two broadly defined groups within Mexican-origin communities in the United States—one native, the other Mexican born—overlapped in a complex cultural interplay north of the border. Spanish-language radio stations arose in various parts of the United States, such as KCOR in San Antonio (1943) and KGST in Fresno (1949), to name two examples (where the owners were of Mexican origin). In large measure because of the impact of the Bracero Program, the post-World War II era witnessed the growing numbers and settlement of Mexican-born newcomers, fueling the expansion of outlets of the Spanish-language media. Through the Cold War years, and despite the persistence of evident public prejudice, Mexican communities continued to stage festivities tied to Mexican cultural referents. Although usually stylized, such events offered representations of Mexico and Mexicans that harbored a positive affirmation of *lo mexicano*. (Mexican Americans were not immune to these nostalgic displays punctuated with nationalist sentiment; an untold number of weddings, christenings, and birthday fests featured "Mexican" music and related cultural elements that sustained a social realm distinct from mainstream American norms, regardless of the level of acculturation among its participants or their attitudes toward Mexico.)

---

19. The Mexican comic German "Tin Tan" Valdes made his career from his parody of the pocho-like pachuco character, beginning in 1942 on XEJ radio station in Cd. Juarez, across from El Paso, Texas. His popularity quickly took him to the pinnacle of the media at that time, XEW in Mexico City, where he became a regular on the "El Patio" show and starred in various films. "Tin Tan" became in effect the caricature in Mexico that was associated for years with Mexican Americans.

This fluid, at times aloof relationship between immigrants and U.S.-born Mexicans began to change as immigrants were gradually folded into the larger scheme of Latino activism. The pan-ethnic nature of Latino reformism of the 1960s and 1970s eased this transition, where immigrants began to assume a place in the notion of Latino civil rights. Events in Mexico, as will be noted below, contributed to an inadvertent and then instrumental convergence between Latino civil rights organizations and a shift in Mexican views toward *mexicanos de afuera*.

Meanwhile, the presence of the Spanish-language media in the United States expanded notably between the 1960s and 1980s, underscored by the spread of a television network linked to the huge Mexican media conglomerate known as Televisa. Initially named the Spanish International Network and later Univision, the Mexican-based corporation underwrote the extension of the network and provided the bulk of its programming for more than twenty years. (This connection would eventually be reduced drastically by the Federal Communications Commission, given that Televisa's interest in Univision violated U.S. communications laws.) The maturation of the Univision network coincided with a distinct aspect of the 1980s' Reagan years, that is, the onset of the so-called "Hispanic market" era, as Arlene Davila has admirably shown (2001, esp. 88–125). While nativist discourse multiplied under reaganism, the Spanish-language media spearheaded the construction of the Latino population as an enormous market for American enterprise. This commercialized move, fueled by the desire of the Spanish-language media for more advertising revenues, came with near official government sanction of "Hispanic heritage."[20] In this process, the Spanish-language media championed greater attention to Hispanics, which in most parts of the country meant a Mexican-inflected definition. The outcomes of IRCA added another ingredient to this scenario. Through the provisions of the 1986 legislation, a large number of Latino immigrants, overwhelmingly of Mexican origin, were granted legal residency. Subsequently, a large proportion of immigrants legally brought family members from Mexico and settled in the United States. Thus, the audience for the Spanish-language media increased substantially in important media markets and augmented the claims of Univision and its counterparts in radio broadcasting about the growth and importance of the so-called Hispanic market. This process extended the cultural space for immigrants because media conglomerates, such as Clear Channel, began to convert their radio holdings in selected areas into Spanish-language formats.[21]

The confluence of Spanish-language radio and television with the demographic increase of the Mexican immigrant population led to attendant commercial media effects, such as the rise in the selling of recordings by Mexican artists, the staging of musical concerts by Mexican musical groups at major venues, and the promotion of sporting events that depended substantially on the participation of Mexican immigrants. Thus, in American cities with large Mexican immigrant populations, soccer

---

20. National Hispanic Heritage Week was initially declared by Congress in 1968. It became National Hispanic Heritage Month by Congressional approval in 1988 and was endorsed by Ronald Reagan on September 13, 1988.

21. Among many examples of this trend, on September 16, 2004, the large media company, Clear Channel, announced more than a doubling of its Spanish language radio stations, from eighteen to another twenty to twenty-five stations. http://www.clearchannel.com/PressRoom.

matches between the U.S. and Mexican national teams, for instance, often played before sold-out crowds that were invariably dominated by raucous fans chanting "Mexico, Mexico, Mexico" and waving the *tricolor*. As the historian David Gutierrez has noted, the accretion of these trends, however commercialized, also meant the formation of a cultural space at odds with the nativist-infused imagery reflected in much of English-language media programming.[22]

For the Spanish-language media, this period was also marked by a transition in the relationship between Mexico and its citizens in the United States, where the 1988 Mexican presidential campaign played a significant role. In that electoral contest, the dominant party of the country, the *Partido Revolucionario Institucional*, or the Revolutionary Institutional Party, won the hotly disputed election as a result of evident voting fraud. Prior to the election, the left-of-center opposition candidate, Cuauhtemoc Cárdenas, had visited several Mexican immigrant communities in the United States; large audiences composed mainly by immigrants turned out wherever he made stops on his thinly disguised political tour (Cárdenas hailed from Michoacán, a major immigrant sending state in Mexico). The enthusiasm expressed at these gatherings was not lost on his opponent, Carlos Salinas de Gortari. Soon after assuming the presidency, Salinas quickly moved to form an agency to connect the Mexican state with immigrants in the United States through the establishment of the *Programa para las comunidades mexicanas en el extranjero* (Program for Mexican Communities Abroad); this program would be continued by subsequent presidential administrations (although the names of the agencies changed to disassociate them from Salinas' initiative; see Boruchoff 1999).

Two additional elements contributed to this turn in Mexican policies and attitudes, although space constraints prohibit a more detailed discussion. First, anti-U.S. sentiment flared at the conclusion of the Salinas presidency in 1994. When the country entered a steep recession in that year, the crisis discredited the economic promise of the North American Free Trade Agreement specifically and the neoliberal ideology of reaganism more generally. A devastating devaluation of the peso followed, necessitating a bailout loan by the United States and international lending institutions. The wrath of the Mexican public toward Salinas' policies invariably implicated the United States and its promotion of neoliberal dogma. Second, in this context, the California electorate passed Proposition 187, where the racially charged attacks on Mexican immigrants further inflamed anti-U.S. attitudes in Mexico. The Mexican press, public intellectuals, and talk show commentators generally perceived support for the measure as an indication of anti-Mexican views on the part of ungrateful Americans, who were quick to exploit Mexican workers but were just as willing to discard them when expedient. The consequent large-scale marches by immigrants and their supporters in protest of Proposition 187 received substantial sympathetic coverage by the Mexican media. Thus, the mounting critique in Mexico of U.S. policies increasingly incorporated the plight of Mexican immigrants and summoned their defense. For much of the Mexican media, *paisanos* had become victims of failed neoliberal policies, of exploitative employers, and of callous *yanqui* politicians willing to pander to nativist fear mongering and anti-Mexican sentiment.

---

22. See the essay by Gutiérrez (1999).

As a result, the representation of immigrants in Mexico moved decidedly away from the pejorative *pochismo* of the past. The importance of remittances, particularly in areas of large-scale out-migration to the United States, also contributed toward a more empathetic view of *mexicanos de afuera*. At the same time, Mexican media coverage on the abuses of immigrants resonated with the neoliberal-inspired policies attributed to the now vilified Salinas regime. In this light, the move by the Clinton administration to appease nativist pressures added more fuel to the heated criticism in Mexico over the depiction and treatment of immigrant *paisanos*. If the success of Proposition 187 fired the aims of nativists, its passage also facilitated a discernible shift in the Spanish-language media on both sides of border on the question of immigration.

In 2001, President George W. Bush held a much publicized meeting with his Mexican counterpart, Vicente Fox; both men appeared to be intent on mending the disrepair in the relations between the two countries, including the ripple effects generated by Proposition 187 and similar efforts in other parts of the United States. But the positive aura created by that celebrated partly evaporated with the attacks on 9/11. Mexico slipped far down on the list of foreign policy priorities of the United States, including any concern for immigration reform. Worse, to the dismay of Mexican observers, nativists turned the "war on terror" into a new venue of anti-immigrant discourse with inherently negative implications for the imaging of Mexico and Mexicans. Not surprisingly, the media in Mexico generally questioned Americans' concerns over border security and immigration as a ruse to promote xenophobia, stirring further support for *paisanos* in the United States from the Spanish-language media. The Secure Fence Act of 2006, which militarized the border to new heights, met with near unanimous disapproval by the Mexican media. This view marked much of the Spanish-language media in the United States, especially through radio programs and newscasts in areas with large concentrations of Mexican immigrants. Moreover, at that time, Spanish-language broadcasts gave favorable coverage toward the Mexican workers involved in labor actions in Houston, Texas, for example, which stoked further the smoldering anger among newcomers toward their treatment in the United States.

In sum, a historic turn had taken place in the representation of Mexican immigrants in official and public discourse south of the border. The Spanish-language media had become a voice for the concerns of immigrants because its shift in tone and coverage was magnified exponentially by the lack of similar positive attention from the English-language media.[23] This evident move by the Spanish-language media on both sides of border converged with the significance and visibility of immigrants' rights to the agenda of Latino civil rights activism. Thus, the new nativism had contributed decisively to the formation of a widespread political front encompassing immigrants, Latino civil rights advocates and their supporters, labor groups, academics, Latino students, and community-based organizations into a cross-border groundswell in defense of the rights of Mexican newcomers.

---

23. For an example of the differences between Spanish-language versus English-language media and politics, see Constantakis-Valdes, 2008, 152.

IMMIGRATION PROTESTS OF 2006

Space constraints do not allow for a full accounting of the massive proimmigrant demonstrations in the year of the passage of the Secure Fence Act in the midst of congressional discussions toward immigration reform legislation (see Gonzales 2009). For our purposes, the antinativist marches testified to the important role of the Spanish-language media in the magnitude of the turnout and its representational implications. Clearly, the marches and their meanings blunted the message of anti-immigrant groups. Spanish-language media outlets spent long segments on the protests, where radio hosts, television news editors, and the Mexican press generally portrayed the protesters in positive if not heroic terms. Equally important, the impact of the marches carried over into the proposed reforms to immigration policy the following year. In this regard, the Project for Excellence in Journalism analyzed the Senate debate on the immigration bill in late June 2007. The conclusions of that report showed the distinct position of the Spanish-language media in the immigration debate. The Project's study found that the major English-language networks "covered the issue substantially less [where] there were eight stories during this period... By comparison, Telemundo and Univision aired a total of 18 stories focusing on the immigration bill during the same period" (Brookings Institution 2008, 56). This difference possessed pivotal political repercussions.

Through 2006–2007, nativists celebrated their ability to block immigration reform and to promote a huge increase in the militarization of the border; their glee, however, was short lived. The declining approval ratings of George W. Bush, the disastrous course of the war on terror, and the economic troubles during Bush's last year in office tarnished the Republican Party, the nativists' main avenue to elected officials. The Bush administration's failed attempt at immigration reform in fact served to widen the rifts within the GOP because immigration had become a wedge issue among Republicans themselves. The presidential nomination of Senator John McCain, who had incurred the wrath of nativists in the past with his immigration reform efforts, deprived xenophobes within the GOP to place the issue prominently on the platform for the presidential campaign. Rather, the political fallout from immigrant bashing since the 1990s had damaging consequences for the Republican Party in key electoral states. The racialization of immigration for political purpose had come back to haunt conservative purveyors of the new nativism. As the *New York Times* subsequently editorialized in February 2009, the "Republican campaign against immigration has always hidden a streak of racialist extremism. Now after several high-water years, the Republican tide has gone out, leaving exposed the nativism of right-wingers clinging to what they hope will be a wedge issue."[24] The willingness of Republican politicians in particular to pander to xenophobes held an inescapable consequence: with their manifest anti-Mexican rhetoric, nativists spurred U.S.-born and naturalized residents of Mexican origin toward the Democratic Party with even greater effect. By polarizing the question of immigration reform with a racialized tinge since the 1994 passage of Proposition 187, neoconservatives had created a political battle with virtually no room for compromise. The association between Republicans and racist anti-immigrant groups contributed

---

24. "The Nativists Are Restless," *The New York Times*, February 1, 2009; see also Dickinson, 2008.

significantly to Latinos overwhelmingly supporting the Democratic Party's presidential candidate in the 2008 elections, Senator Barack Obama.

In 2004, Samuel Huntington, the venerable Harvard professor of strategic studies, wrote an essay in the magazine *Foreign Policy* entitled "The Hispanic Challenge." The nativist aspects of the controversial article (along with Huntington's other writings of a similar sort) set off a wave of criticism from Latinos and non-Latinos alike. For all of the heated comment about Huntington's arguments, his anti-Mexican immigrant tract failed to elicit concerted political support except among die-hard nativists and their political allies. Rather, the Hispanic challenge as posed by Huntington and his adherents became best understood as counterproductive by the conclusion of the 2008 presidential campaign. In their clash with Huntington and his cabal, Mexican immigrants and their supporters had made an emphatic point through the ballot box, but the casualties in the bitter war of words, images, and headlines were only too real. The increase in hate crimes against Mexican immigrants, the dead bodies of would-be border crossers, and the often devastating results of Immigration and Customs Enforcement raids for immigrant families bore testimony to the grim consequences of the new nativism.

Throughout the United States, the new nativism plies its work in various forms, using biased images and information in the promotion, for example, of local and state legislative measures with manifest anti-immigrant provisions.[25] Nativists deploy now well-worn discursive practices, and they move with alacrity to take advantage of current events to mint fresh arguments. The drug trade–related violence along the border of 2008–2009 offered another opportunity to paint immigrants in a negative light, using the sensationalized coverage by the media as yet another variation on the theme of the immigrant as criminal. Anti-immigrant pundits continue their rants, whereas the extremist current of the new nativism embraces notions of white supremacy; and the Internet bristles with strident rightist screeds against immigrants. In the midst of this vitriol, death continues to stalk the border (see Nevins 2005). The impact of the new nativism cannot be underestimated in its capacity to engender anti-Mexican attitudes and to sustain images of immigrants framed by racism, prejudice, and fear (see Sanchez 1997).

If further proof was needed, the passage of tough, manifestly anti-immigrant legislation in Arizona in April 2010 signaled the utility of illegals as a weapon in a ripe political context: electoral campaigning, recessionary pressures, and a party hungry to regain its former power. Signed into law by a GOP governor up for reelection, the measure (SB 1070) met a fate similar to that of California's Proposition 187 of 1994, when a federal court barred its implementation in late July 2010, pending further appeal. Yet, the popularity of the legislation with Arizona voters was not lost in the heated political environment as the November electoral season drew near. Mexican government officials immediately chastised the law, whereas previously mobilized proimmigrant groups quickly mounted more protests to the measure. In a rejoinder to the criticism of his administration's alleged failure to secure the border and in tacit response to the Arizona vote, President Obama made a speech in early July on the need to fix the

---

25. The National Conference of State Legislatures has maintained a record of nativist legislative efforts that reflects the extent of state-level anti-immigrant laws that have been proposed and/or passed by state legislative bodies since 2005. See the website of the organization for its reports at http://www.ncsl.org.

immigration system. To add more drama to the issue, on the heels of the judicial stay of the legislation a prominent Republican senator poured more fuel onto the political firestorm by proposing a change in the constitution to disallow birthright citizenship to children born in the United States of undocumented mothers; other legislators soon lent their support to the idea and called for hearings on the matter. With SB 1070 and its political fallout gaining momentum and media attention, Democrats reacted with legislation in August 2010 that provided another $600 million to strengthen border security, including the hiring of an additional one thousand Border Patrol agents. Not surprisingly, on both sides of the border the Spanish-language media gave concerted attention to SB 1070 and subsequent related events, as well as Mexican newspapers, magazines and television newscasts. In short, Spanish-language media coverage was decidedly critical of the Arizona measure and of the ensuing nativist clamor.

Yet, shards of hope exist in the highly contentious battle over the representation of Mexican immigrants. In the primetime television series, "Ugly Betty," for instance, over several episodes in the 2008–2009 season, a subplot dealt sympathetically with the issue of undocumented migration that involved a main character, Betty's father. In cinema, recent vehicles have addressed the question of immigration that clearly reject nativist views, such as the *Three Burials of Melquiades Estrada* (2005) and the more celebrated film *Babel* (2006). The involvement of Mexican artists in these three examples is perhaps not insignificant: Salma Hayek (producer of "Ugly Betty"), Guillermo Arriaga (screenwriter of *Three Burials*), and Alejandro Gonzalez Iñárritu (director of *Babel*). In general, Hollywood has rebuffed explicitly anti-immigrant themes. Whereas in the past, for instance, science fiction "alien" films may have reflected nativist fears, as Charles Ramirez Berg has persuasively argued, the more current movies of this genre have often served to reveal the shortcomings of American society, rather than veiled anti-immigrant imagery.[26] Moreover, op-ed pages of the mainstream press have been less than kind to the new nativism. And even in nontraditional receiving areas, newspapers have been willing to brave nativist ire with their stands. The *Tennessean* of Nashville, for example, opposed an anti-immigrant inspired English-only initiative, which was subsequently defeated by the city's voters in January 2009.

CONCLUSION

In the film *Under the Same Moon (La misma luna)*, the sound track includes the song by the musical group Kinky, "*Superman es illegal*," and there is also a scene involving a traveling band, played by the musical group Los Tigres del Norte, the iconic voice of immigrants in the United States. In its debut, the film made $2.6 million, "the highest opening weekend ever for a Spanish-language film in the U.S.," according to *Time* magazine (Keegan 2008). The soundtrack of the movie also features the voice of "El Cucuy," one of Los Angeles' most popular Spanish radio DJs, in which he sprinkles his morning talk show in the film with antinativist barbs. In the backdrop of the marches of 2006, the evident popularity of the motion picture reflected the oppositional space forged by immigrants and their supporters. The demonstrations of 2006 marked a critical

---

26. See Ramirez Berg (2002, 153–82) for his discussion of science fiction "alien" films of the 1980s and 1990s as metaphors for nativism.

moment, where immigrants exercised their rights as citizens of a denationalized social reality, to use the terms of Saskia Sassen.

As Leo Chavez has argued, perhaps the most disheartening outcome of this contemporary surge in nativism in the United States has been the trenchant divisiveness bred by the purveyors of xenophobia. In this regard, it important to take into account the multitude of local means by which nativism sows its seeds. Proimmigrant groups have tended to focus their criticism of the media at the national plane, where network commentators have attracted singular attention for their "immigrant bashing." Much of the insidious effect of the new nativism and their nationally known pundits, however, comes from "a massive echo chamber of right-wing radio gladiators and small-town newspaper columnists [who] have become the main sources of information for millions of Americans about the causes and effects of Hispanic immigration."[27]

In response, immigrant communities and their allies have constructed a countercurrent to the new nativism, where the Spanish-language media has played a contributing role, however cautious. Indeed, critics of the Spanish-language media have lamented its aversion to an aggressive approach against nativist discursive practices.[28] Yet, as a report by the Brookings Institution made clear, the English-language media "differs significantly in coverage of immigration from the Spanish-language media" (Brookings Institution 2008, 83). In brief, the shortcomings of the English-language media have made by comparison its Spanish-language counterparts an oppositional force against xenophobia.

In sum, the contemporary breadth of that cultural space shaped by Mexican immigrants has developed a hardened resilience and evident capability to contest the new nativism. This representational "third space" has facilitated the sustainability of popular means of expression against xenophobes in innumerable community-based organizations, groups, and venues, including bilingual and Spanish-language media. As Josh Kun has noted, this distinctive space encompasses a broad and diverse spectrum of expression, where musical compositions provide a revealing lens regardless of the style of music. These lyrics point to the emergence of a politicized identity among immigrants indicative of a "surrendering of older models of nationalism and national identity as static entities permanently tied to fixed places on maps" (Kun 2004; see also Kun 2006).[29] In this sense, the immigrants' attachment to Mexican symbols—such as the waving of Mexican flags at proimmigrant demonstrations—may be less an expression of allegiance to Mexico or nationalist nostalgia and more an indication of a cultural arena that opposes nativists on the one hand and on the other implicates a criticism of the inequities engendered by a neoliberal Mexican state.

In the classic Mexican film of 1953, *Espaldas Mojadas* (Wetbacks), the main protagonist decides in the end to return to his *patria*, accompanied by a Mexican woman who had lived and worked for a time in the United States; a fellow *paisano*, initially

---

27. See the editorial "The New Nativism," 2006.

28. See the criticism of Baker-Cristales (2009). On the issue of empowerment and the media, see Rivera-Salgado and Wilson (2009, 9–13); also see Ayon (2009).

29. In another piece, Kun notes the use of cell phones and other technologies that enlarge the immigrant-inflected space of communication and expression; see Kun (2009).

reluctant to join them, at the last moment crosses the border for their redemptive journey back to Mexico. Over fifty years later, in *Under the Same Moon*, the plot centers on a young boy's trek to find his undocumented immigrant mother in Los Angeles, his ties to "home" sundered by the death of his grandmother. After a series of misadventures, he finally locates his mother, but tellingly at the film's ending, there is no indication of a redemptive return to their Mexican homeland. Instead, mother and son must make their way in the gritty immigrant space of a globalized city, cast into a life of uncertainty and ambivalence. In this less than welcoming environment, they are not without friends or resources, as the film makes apparent in various scenes. As the soundtrack suggests, such as the lyrics of the song "*Superman es ilegal,*" or the commentary of a Spanish-language radio DJ, Mexican immigrants have shaped a resistive field, shorn of idealized nationalist nostalgia or romanticized notions of assimilation into life in America.

In this light, the cultural representation of Mexican immigration has made a historic turn, although the mainstream American media offers small comfort to immigrants or their allies. Although Hollywood has moved away from the crass racialization of newcomers, the entertainment industry has shown a reluctance to address the question of immigration in a consistent, progressive manner. Instead, television programs and films on immigrants remain exceptions to the general rule of avoidance rather than engagement with the issue.[30] Nevertheless, immigrants have developed the means to counter nativist imagery, where the contest between immigrants and their detractors is no longer as one-sided as it was in the past. But the battle against nativist representations of Mexican immigrants is far from over.[31] The racialized residual stereotypes of the past and their influence, it appears, will erode slowly, unevenly, if at all. The TV Land channel, for example, continues to make available old programs with immigrant stereotypes; and the Cartoon Network in 2002 finally ended the long-running "Speedy Gonzales" character from its repertoire in the United States.[32]

In light of the past, the marches of 2006 marked a watershed in the representation of Mexican immigrants, on both sides of the border (Felix, Gonzalez, and Ramirez 2008). To a large extent, this shift has been the work of immigrants themselves. Along with their supporters, immigrants have created a potent rejoinder to the new nativism across a multivalent, denationalized terrain. As a consequence, the history of the cultural representation of Mexican immigrants in the United States has turned to a new chapter, with its conclusion yet to be written.

---

30. See the report by the Project on Excellence in Journalism, 2007.

31. See the report by Beirich (2009).

32. Although Speedy Gonzales was taken off the Cartoon Network, owned by Fox Corporation, it was still available overseas, including Latin America. See Park, 2002.

Appendix
Right-Wing and Nativist Organizations
(selected list)

American Cause
American Coalition for Immigration Reform
American Conservative Union
American Immigration Control Foundation
American Enterprise Institute
Americans for Tax Reform
American Renaissance
Cato Institute
Castle Rock Foundation
Center for American Unity
Center for Immigration Studies
Center for Study of Popular Culture
Coalition for a Fair Judiciary
Eagle Forum
Federation for American Immigration Reform
Free Congress Foundation
Heritage Foundation
Landmark Legal Foundation
Lynde and Harry Bradley Foundation
National Association of Scholars
New Century Foundation
NumbersUSA
John M. Olin Foundation
Pacific Legal Foundation
Pioneer Fund
Rockford Institute
Scaife Foundation
United to Secure America
U.S. Border Patrol
U.S. English
U.S. Inc.

Epilogue
The Past and Future of Mexico–U.S. Migration

Douglas S. Massey
Princeton University

INTRODUCTION

As the foregoing chapters have shown, Mexico–U.S. migration is a complex historical process more than a century in the making, one that is now firmly established and fully institutionalized on both sides of the border. Although economic problems in Mexico and persistent labor demand in the United States represent the ultimate causes of the cross-border movement, the historical development of Mexican immigration has been driven primarily by policies enacted north of the border. Periods of active recruitment from the United States have been followed by eras of passive acceptance, which in turn have given way to periods of persecution and discrimination. The first such cycle began with labor recruitment in the early 1900s and ended in the 1930s with a wave of extra-legal police actions and mass deportations that halved the Mexican immigrant population and ended cross-border traffic for a decade.

We are now at the end of another such cycle, one that began in 1942 with the reinstatement of Mexican labor recruitment and has now reached the stage of xenophobia and repression. Although anti-immigrant hysteria is hardly new in American history, the current situation is unusual in its breadth and scale. Never before have so many immigrants been placed in such a vulnerable position and subject to such high levels of official exclusion and discrimination. What the future holds is unclear and depends on policy decisions yet to be made. Before speculating about the future, however, we must come to terms with the past to understand just how we became entangled in the current immigration quagmire.

MEXICO–U.S. MIGRATION IN HISTORICAL PERSPECTIVE

The origins of mass Mexican migration lie in the early twentieth century and at least since the 1950s what has changed over time is not so much the size of the inflow as the legal status in which the migrants have entered. Figure E.1 illustrates this fact by showing trends in Mexican migration to the United States in three categories: documented,

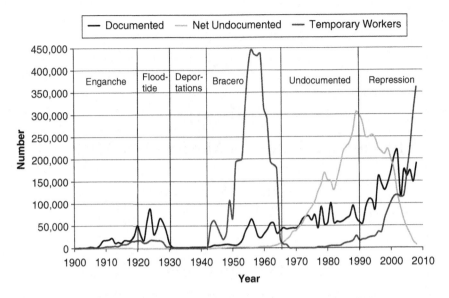

Figure E.1 Mexican Migration to the United States in Three Categories.

undocumented, and temporary legal workers. The data on documented migrants and temporary workers come from official U.S. immigration statistics, whereas the net flow of undocumented migrants was estimated using data from the Mexican Migration Project (MMP; Massey et al. 2009). In the data series on documented migrants, former undocumented migrants who legalized under the 1986 Immigration Reform and Control Act (IRCA) are excluded from the figures because they are already included in the estimated flow of undocumented migrants.

The history of Mexico–U.S. migration can be divided roughly into five periods based on how migrants entered the United States. The first era has been called *The Era of the Enganche* (Spanish for "hook"; Durand and Arias 2000). Early in the twentieth century, recruiters from the United States followed rail lines deep into Mexico to find workers to replace the Japanese, whose immigration had been prohibited in 1907 by a "Gentleman's Agreement" in which Japan agreed to stop its citizens from emigrating to the United States in return for an American promise not to ban them from doing so (Zolberg 2006). Throughout the West, labor shortages immediately ensued in agriculture, mining, and the railroads themselves, and U.S. employers quickly dispatched recruiters southward to find replacement workers.

Convincing peasant farmers to undertake a long journey for unknown work in foreign land was not easy and recruiters overcame this reluctance with promises of high wages, lodging, transport, and a signing bonus. When migrants finally arrived at the job, however, they often found that travel costs, lodging, and bonuses were to be deducted from their wages, which turned out to be considerably less generous than originally promised, leaving the recruited workers feeling "hooked."

The U.S. demand for Mexican labor increased with the outbreak of the First World War, which cut off the flow of immigrants from Europe while stimulating industrial production at home; and when the United States entered the war in 1917 the government itself joined the recruitment effort by establishing a temporary worker program. The era of the enganche drew to a close after the war, by which time migrant networks had become sufficiently well established to make cross-border migration a self-sustaining system. As the U.S. economy entered the Roaring Twenties, moreover, Congress passed a series of quota laws designed to prevent immigration from Europe. Because the quotas did not apply to the western hemisphere, and given that the Mexican economy was still suffering the aftereffects of the 1910 Revolution, rising labor demand in the United States was paired with a ready supply of workers to produce a remarkable surge in migration that historians have labeled the *Era of the Flood Tide* (Cardoso 1980). According to official statistics, from 1920 to 1929 some 488,000 Mexicans arrived legally and another 148,000 came as contract workers. By 1929, the Mexican-born population of the United States stood at 740,000 compared with just 100,000 in 1900.

Despite the fact that Mexican immigration was instigated by U.S. recruitment efforts and that the surge of the 1920s was officially welcomed as a solution to domestic labor shortages, the collapse of the U.S. stock market in late 1929 ushered in the Great Depression and instantly rendered Mexican immigrants unwelcome, leading to the *Era of Deportations* (Hoffman 1974). From 1929 to 1939, a total of 469,000 Mexican citizens were forcibly expelled from the United States and by 1940 the Mexican-born population of the United States stood at only 377,000, less than in 1920.

As quickly as the welcome mat for Mexicans was withdrawn with the onset of the Great Depression, however, it was put out again once the United States entered the Second World War. A few months after Pearl Harbor, the U.S. government approached Mexico to negotiate a bilateral treaty known as the Bracero Accord, which granted Mexicans access to temporary work visas and inaugurated the *Bracero Era* (Calavita 1992). As shown in Figure E.1, the period from 1950 to 1965 was dominated by the rise and fall of this temporary worker program. The era started small with just 4,200 migrant workers in 1942, but by 1945 the program had expanded to nearly 50,000 per year. After a brief lull in 1946, the program resumed steady growth and peaked in 1956 at 445,000 workers.

During the latter half of the 1950s the number of braceros averaged 433,000 per year and then declined to a yearly average of 233,000 during the early 1960s. Because Mexico was not under quota limitations, legal Mexican immigration also grew during the Bracero Era, increasing from around 2,200 per year in 1942 to more than 55,000 in 1963. With ample opportunities for legal entry through the early 1960s, undocumented migration was virtually nonexistent, and border apprehensions averaged just 30,000 per year.

The year 1965, however, marked yet another transition between eras as a result of a U.S. policy shift. In that year the United States unilaterally canceled the Bracero Program and passed amendments to the Immigration and Nationality Act that imposed the first numerical limits on legal immigration from Mexico, restrictions that grew increasingly stringent with amendments passed in 1976 and 1978. Whereas in 1959 Mexicans had access to 438,000 temporary work visas and an unlimited number of residence visas, by 1979 just 1,725 work visas were issued and the annual quota for Mexican immigrants who were not immediate relatives of U.S. citizens stood at just 20,000 (Massey 2009).

As the demand for Mexican workers continued to grow and the supply of legal workers dried up, the gap was filled by unauthorized workers, launching the *Era of*

Undocumented Migration (Massey, Durand, and Malone 2002). From 1965 to 1986, the United States ran a de facto temporary labor program based on the circulation of undocumented workers and the number of border apprehensions steadily rose, increasing from 55,000 in the former year to 1.7 million in the latter. Although U.S. border enforcement efforts rose year by year, until 1986 they roughly kept pace with increases in the underlying migratory traffic to yield a constant probability of apprehension that averaged 33 percent (Massey and Singer 1995). With a 33 percent likelihood of arrest on any given attempt, the likelihood of successful entry over a series of attempts approached certainty, especially for a migrant contracted for the services of a paid border-crossing guide, or coyote (Singer and Massey 1997).

Although millions of Mexicans entered the country each year during the undocumented era, millions also returned. From 1965 to 1986, an estimated 85 percent of undocumented entries were offset by departures, yielding a modest increment to the undocumented population each year, which grew to around 3 million by 1986 (Massey and Singer 1995). As shown in Figure E.1, net undocumented migration rose from zero in the early 1960s to 150,000 in the late 1970s and then climbed to around 300,000 in the late 1980s. During this time legal immigration fluctuated between 50,000 and 100,000 persons per year.

The era of undocumented migration came to an end around 1990. Thereafter, rising border enforcement and the implementation of ever harsher anti-immigrant policies steadily cut the undocumented inflow. The new era of anti-immigrant repression reached full flower in the wake of September 11, 2001, but its roots go back even earlier. The stage was set by IRCA, which in 1986 began a border militarization that has continued and accelerated to the present day. Then in 1993 and 1994 a series of border blockades—Operation Hold the Line in El Paso and Operation Gatekeeper in San Diego—were launched in an all-out effort to curtail undocumented traffic through the two busiest sectors of the Mexico–U.S. border (Massey, Durand, and Malone 2002).

In1996 the rising pressure on immigrants at the border was augmented by legislation that banned legal permanent residents, not just undocumented migrants, from eligibility for certain public entitlements. In the same year, the Antiterrorism and Effective Death Penalty Act was passed to give federal authorities broad new powers for the "expedited exclusion" of *any* foreigner, legal or illegal, who had *ever* entered without authorization or committed a crime, no matter how long ago (Massey 2007). Given that an estimated two thirds of legal Mexican immigrants originally entered the United States without documents (Massey and Malone 2003), this legislation placed the vast majority at risk of arbitrary deportation, whether currently in legal status or not.

The September 11 attacks thus occurred against a backdrop of rising exclusionary policies directed toward immigrants, and in the wake of the attacks on the twin towers Congress quickly passed, without significant debate, the USA Patriot Act. Ostensibly directed at terrorists, in practice it unleashed a new war on immigrants, dramatically escalating enforcement actions within the interior of the United States by authorizing the immediate deportation, without hearings or evidence, of any alien—legal or illegal—that the Attorney General had "reason to believe" might commit, further, or facilitate acts of terrorism (Massey 2007).

These anti-immigrant policies took a growing toll on undocumented migrants, and the net inflow fell from around 300,000 persons per year in 1990 to 200,000 in 2000 and then plummeted after September 11 to reach near zero by 2008. It was not only enforcement actions that caused the decline in undocumented migration, however, for just as U.S. policies were closing one door to the country, they quietly and without fanfare opened another. Temporary worker migration began to increase in response to farm labor shortages in the late 1990s, but after 2001, as undocumented migrants found it increasingly difficult to get to the fields, the number of temporary work visas issued to Mexican farm workers surged. Whereas in 1990 only 17,000 temporary workers entered from Mexico, by 2008 the number exceeded 360,000, a figure not seen since the heyday of the Bracero Program. As of 2008 workers who would have entered the United States as undocumented migrants in 1988 were coming in as legal temporary workers.

After 1990 the number of legal immigrants entering the United States continued to rise, despite numerical restrictions. Ironically, the rising tide of legal immigration from Mexico was itself an unintended consequence of the increasing pressure put on permanent residents by U.S. legislation. With noncitizens barred from key entitlement programs, at risk of expulsion for earlier immigration violations, and denied access to due process in immigration proceedings, Mexican resident aliens increasingly sought protection by acquiring U.S. citizenship. Whereas Mexicans historically displayed the lowest rate of naturalization of any major immigrant group, as pressure on noncitizens mounted, naturalizations surged.

A rising rate of naturalization carries important implications for immigration because each new citizen acquires the right to bring in parents, spouses, and minor children without numerical limitation while also gaining the right to petition for the entry of brothers and sisters under quotas. In short, each new citizen creates more legal immigrants down the road. This process is illustrated in Figure E.2, which graphs trends in Mexican naturalizations and the legal entry of U.S. citizen relatives, drawn from official statistics. Prior to 1980, naturalizations were uncommon among Mexicans, never exceeding 10,000 per year. The passage of IRCA in 1986, however, began to shift the calculus of migrant decision making firmly in the direction of citizenship, for as a condition of receiving permanent resident status, legalizing immigrants were required to take courses in English and U.S. civics, two requirements of citizenship. Beginning in 1992 millions of former undocumented migrants began to reach their fifth year in permanent resident status, instantly rendering them eligible for U.S. citizenship (Massey, Durand, and Malone 2002).

This surge in the number of Mexicans eligible for citizenship occurred just as a wave of anti-immigrant sentiment swept through the country, cresting with the passage of Proposition 187 in California, where more than half of all the newly legalized immigrants lived. This proposition, which sought to involve state and local officials in immigration enforcement and ban undocumented migrants from receiving public services, triggered a countermobilization that yielded an unprecedented surge in naturalization and voter registration during 1995 and 1996. Whereas just 23,000 naturalizations occurred in 1993, the year before Proposition 187's passage, by 1996 the figure had reached 255,000, a tenfold increase in just three years.

Just as this wave of naturalizations crested, Congress acted to limit the eligibility of legal immigrants to entitlements and declare them deportable for prior immigration violations, prompting another surge in naturalizations that crested at 208,000 in 1999; then, just as this latest surge was receding, Congress passed the Patriot Act to bring

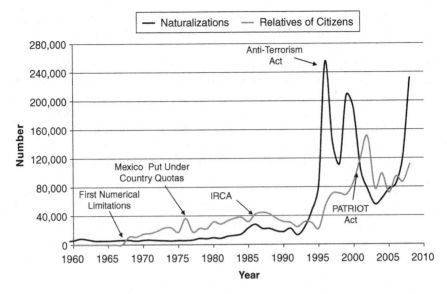

Figure E.2 Mexican Naturalizations and Entries of Citizen Relatives.

about yet another surge to 232,000 naturalizations in 2008, yielding another wave of new citizens that has not yet crested.

This pattern of rising and falling naturalizations is mirrored with a lag by a corresponding set of peaks and valleys in the entry of citizen relatives. Whereas before 1996 the entry of citizen relatives fluctuated around 40,000 per year, thereafter it shot upward to reach 150,000 in 2002, with successive surges to 99,000 and 94,000 in 2004 and 2006, respectively. As of 2008, the figure was climbing toward 120,000 and, given the sharp increase in naturalizations from 2004 to 2008, this upward trend will no doubt continue. Thus, by seeking to increase the pressure on legal immigrants, congress inadvertently increased the volume of legal immigration for years to come.

As the first decade of the twenty-first century draws to a close, therefore, Mexican immigrants find themselves in a very strange and precarious position in the United States. On the one hand, those who can avail themselves of U.S. citizenship are doing so in large numbers, whereas a combination of harsh enforcement, expanding guest worker migration, and economic turmoil has reduced undocumented migration to near zero. On the other hand, seven million undocumented Mexicans already live in the United States and constitute 55 percent of those currently present, and the number of temporary workers is pushing toward 400,000 per year. Given the increasing pressure put on legal immigrants, the limited rights of temporary workers, and the lack of rights accorded to undocumented migrants, it is safe to say that never before have so many Mexicans lived in the United States without full protection of the law.

THE NEW ERA OF REPRESSION

In the wake of 9/11, Americans apparently need concrete symbols on which to project their fears and insecurities, and illegal migrants and the Mexico–U.S. border have been

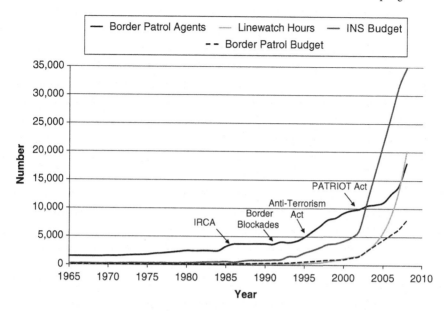

Figure E.3 Indicators of U.S. Immigration Enforcement Effort.

appropriated for the purpose. The War on Terror has become a War on Immigrants although none of the 9/11 hijackers entered from Mexico, that country has no terrorist cells, and it contains no significant Islamic population. After 9/11 U.S. enforcement efforts have risen exponentially both along the border and within the United States, despite the fact that the volume of undocumented migration has been declining steadily since 1990. The unprecedented scale of the new war on immigrants is indicated in Figure E.3, which shows trends in the budgets (in thousands of dollars) of the Border Patrol and Immigration and Naturalization Service (now the Department of Homeland Security), as well as the total number of Border Patrol Agents and the total number of "linewatch hours" spent patrolling the border (the latter expressed in tens of thousands of hours).

From 1965 to 1986, each series changed very little, but afterward the lines begin to rise, slowly at first, but accelerating after the launching of the border blockades in 1993–1994 and then increasing exponentially after the passage of the Patriot Act in 2001. Between 1986 and 2008, the number of Border Patrol Officers went from 3,700 to 18,000, the number of linewatch hours increased from 2.4 million to 201 million, the Border Patrol Budget increased from $151 million to $7.9 billion, and the INS budget went from $4.7 billion to $35 billion. In addition, the newly created Immigration and Customs Enforcement branch of Homeland Security quickly grew after its founding in 2002 to encompass 17,000 workers with an annual budget of $59 billion.

The primary purpose of these agencies is to arrest and deport immigrants, and that is what they are doing. Figure E.4 demonstrates this fact by showing trends in apprehensions and deportations from 1965 to the present. Since the passage of IRCA in 1986, arrests of undocumented migrants at the border have fluctuated between 800,0000 and 1.6 million per year, although the number of undocumented migrants

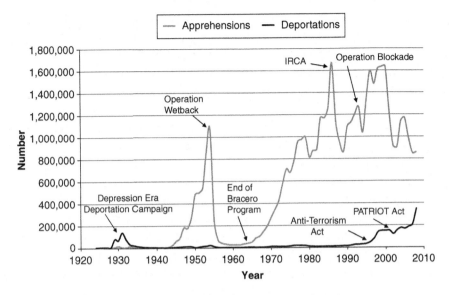

Figure E.4 Border Apprehensions and Internal Deportations from the United States.

has declined, but what is truly remarkable is the surge in deportations, which climbed from just 11,000 in 1986 to a record level of 350,000 during 2008. Even at the height of the 1930's deportation campaign, only 139,000 persons per year were expelled from the United States. Under current conditions, it is as if Operation Wetback of the 1950s has been made permanent and the 1930's deportation campaign institutionalized at three times its earlier size. In a very real way, therefore, the United States increasingly looks like a police state to Mexican immigrants, irrespective of their documentation. The population of detained aliens has increased by 50 percent since 2001, averaging 31,345 persons on any given day, up from just 6,259 per day in 1992. In the most recent fiscal year, some 320,000 immigrants were incarcerated, awaiting trial or deportation (Tumlin, Joaquin, and Natarajan 2009).

This rising tide of immigrant arrests, deportations, and incarcerations has been accompanied by a rise in anti-immigrant rhetoric, which increasingly frames Mexicans as a threat to America's security, workers, culture, and way of life, a trope that Leo Chavez has labeled the "Latino threat narrative" (Chavez 2008). Among U.S. magazine covers that he examined from 1965 through 1999, two thirds portrayed immigration as threatening; the frequency of this theme rose steadily over time (Chavez 2001). Within the media, martial language is increasingly used to portray the border as a "battleground" that is "under attack" from "alien invaders." Immigrants have been labeled a "time bomb" that will "explode" to destroy American society. Border Patrol Officers are "defenders" who, although "outgunned," seek to "hold the line" against attacking "hoards" that launched "Banzai charges" along a beleaguered frontier (Andreas 2000; Dunn 1996). In its coverage from 1992 to 1994, the *LA Times* made use of war metaphors in 23 percent of the stories about immigration and in 20 percent of the stories about immigrants (Santa Ana 2002).

The Latino threat narrative gained particular momentum in the 1980s when Ronald Regan framed immigration as a question of "national security," stating that terrorists and subversives were just two days driving time from the nearest border crossing and referring to foreigners as a "fifth column" of subversives who would "feed on the anger and frustration of recent Central and South American immigrants" (Massey, Durand, and Malone 2002). The attacks of September 11 confirmed the supposed link between immigration and national security and made the border a central front in the war on terror. According to Renato Rosaldo, "the U.S.-Mexico border has become theater, and border theater has become social violence. Actual violence has become inseparable from symbolic ritual on the border—crossings, invasions, lines of defense, high-tech surveillance, and more" (Rosaldo 1997, 27–38).

War metaphors have now become a standard trope among pundits to describe immigration from Mexico. Referring to undocumented migration explicitly as "an invasion of illegal aliens," Lou Dobbs sees it as part of a broader "war on the middle class" (Dobbs 2006). Conservative pundit Patrick Buchanan, meanwhile, portrays immigration as part of an "Aztlán Plot" hatched by Mexicans seeking to recapture lands lost in the Mexican–American war (Buchanan 2006). In an interview with *Time* magazine, he said that immigration constituted a "state of emergency" and warned, "If we do not get control of our borders and stop this greatest invasion in history, I see the dissolution of the U.S. and the loss of the American southwest—culturally and linguistically, if not politically—to Mexico" (Chu 2008).

In 2004 Chris Simcox founded the Minutemen Civil Defense Corps to "do the job the government won't do...defend the U.S. border" by deploying vigilante border agents to prevent the entry of "drug dealers, gang bangers and way too many criminal foreign nationals [who] are creating havoc in our communities and threatening our public safety" (Massey 2007). The project quickly became a media sensation, with 1,725 articles on the Minutemen appearing in 2005 and 1,182 in 2006 (Chavez 2008). In this environment, it is hardly surprising that a 2006 survey revealed that almost half of all Americans (48 percent) came to believe that "newcomers from other countries threaten traditional American values and customs," 54 percent said that Americans needed to be "protected against foreign influence," and 60 percent of those who had heard of the Minutemen approved of their activities (Kohut and Suro 2006).

These increases in exclusionary attitudes have been accompanied by parallel shifts in public behavior. According to U.S. Justice Department Statistics, the number of anti-Hispanic hate crimes increased 24 percent in the years after 9/11 and the number of victims rose by 30 percent (Federal Bureau of Investigation 2009). Moreover, although immigration policy historically has been the preserve of the federal government, since 9/11 state and local authorities have increasingly implemented anti-immigrant laws and policies. According to the National Council of State Legislatures, state laws related to immigration increased dramatically after 9/11. Some 200 bills on immigration had been introduced and 38 laws enacted by 2005, but this proved to be just the beginning: by 2007 immigration-related legislative activity had tripled to 1,562 bills and 240 laws (National Council of State Legislatures 2009). In addition, 23 states have now signed cooperative agreements with federal authorities to assist in arresting and detaining undocumented migrants under the 287(g) provision of the Patriot Act (Tumlin, Joaquin, and Natarajan 2009).

LIFE IN THE ERA OF REPRESSION

U.S. immigration policies and public attitudes have thus undergone a steady evolution toward greater repression, moving from official acceptance and legal accommodation before 1965 to grudging tolerance through 1986 to rising hostility during the 1990s and culminating in an outright war on immigrants after September 11. As might be expected, the shift to stringent internal policing and heightened border enforcement has had profound effects on the behavior of Mexican immigrants. One of the most important changes has been a pronounced shift in the geography of Mexican migration. Although the buildup of enforcement resources along the border began in 1986, full-scale militarization matured only with the launching of Operation Hold the Line in El Paso–Juarez during 1993 and Operation Gatekeeper in San Diego–Tijuana in 1994.

Prior to the 1990s, the overwhelming majority of undocumented migrants had entered the United States through Tijuana on their way to destinations in California, so the effect of Operation Gatekeeper was especially pronounced, as shown in Figure E.5, which draws upon MMP data to show the annual percentage of undocumented migrants entering through Baja California and going to Californian destinations. Whereas in the early 1980s two thirds of all undocumented migrants entered through Baja California, after IRCA's passage this percentage began to fall, bottoming out at 26 percent and then rising slightly in recent years. Most of the undocumented flow was displaced to a new corridor through Sonora into Arizona, which in 1980 accounted for just 6 percent of all border crossings but reached 58 percent by 2003 (not shown).

Within the United States, the effect of this shift in crossing behavior was to divert flows decisively away from Californian destinations, yielding a new geography of Mexican settlement. As seen in Figure E.5, the percentage of migrants going to a

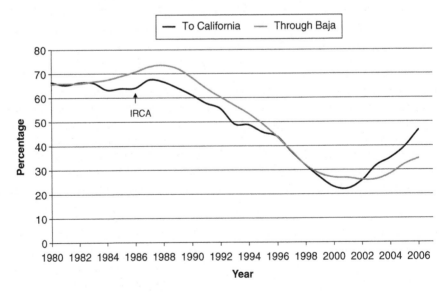

Figure E.5 Percentage of Undocumented Migrants Crossing Through
Baja California and Going to California.

Californian destination fell from 66 percent in 1980 to bottom out at 22 percent in 2002. This same trend is indicated by data from the U.S. Census and American Community Survey, which reveal that two thirds of Mexican immigrants who arrived between 1985 and 1990 settled in California compared with just one third among those who arrived between 1995 and 2000 and during 2000–2005 (Massey and Capoferro 2008).

As already noted, in addition to changing the geography of Mexican migration, the militarization of the border also contributed to a reduction in undocumented migration. This reduction is explored in Figure E.6 in greater detail by showing the probability of taking a first and subsequent undocumented trip to the United States. The probability that a Mexican aged fifteen or older would undertake a first undocumented trip rose from around 7 percent in 1980 to peak at around 11 percent in 1989, whereupon it moved slowly downward to reach 6 percent in 1998. Over the same period, however, the likelihood that a U.S.-bound migrant would take an additional trip steadily increased, from around 17 percent to around 28 percent. Until the end of the 1990s, therefore, the principal effect of the huge increase in border enforcement was to reduce slightly the entry of new immigrants but actually to increase reentry by people with prior migratory experience.

After 1998, however, the likelihood of both initial and repeat migration began to fall quite rapidly as the massive increase in enforcement, combined with the collapse of the U.S. economy and the opening of new avenues for legal entry, finally acted to reduce the odds of undocumented migration to low levels. As of 2007, the likelihood of new entries was virtually nil and the probability of repeat migration had fallen below 5 percent.

In addition to finally deterring undocumented migrants from heading north, the militarization of the border also had the paradoxical effect of reducing the rate of return

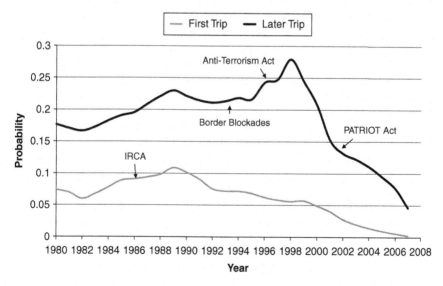

Figure E.6 Probability of Taking a First and Later Undocumented Trip to the United States.

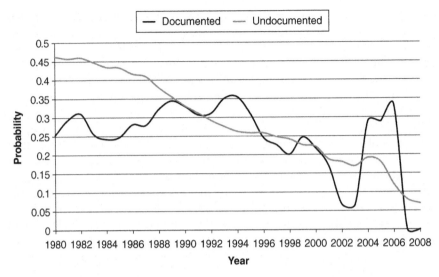

Figure E.7 Probability of Returning to Mexico within 12 months of Entering the United States.

among those already present north of the border. In the years following IRCA, the costs and risks of undocumented border crossing rose substantially, with the death rate tripling and smuggling fees increasing by a factor of nearly six, going from an average of $500 per crossing in the late 1980s to around $2,900 in 2008 (Massey et al. 2009). As the costs and risks of undocumented border crossing rose, migrants responded quite logically by minimizing border crossing, not by remaining in Mexico as U.S. authorities intended, but by hunkering down in the United States once they had made it across.

Figure E.7 shows the probability of returning to Mexico within twelve months of entering the United States for both documented and undocumented migrants, again computed from MMP data. In 1980 the likelihood of returning within a year was about 46 percent for undocumented migrants; but after IRCA's implementation the probability fell steadily to reach a record low of just 7 percent in 2007. Although legal immigrants, in theory, have the freedom to enter and exit the United States as they please, in reality many live in families that include undocumented migrants and the fates of the two groups are therefore closely intertwined. Historically documented migrants had lower probabilities of return than undocumented migrants, but after 1989 the likelihoods converged and proceeded downward at the same rate. Once the events of 9/11 occurred and the Patriot Act took effect, rates of return migration by documented migrants plummeted before rallying in 2003–2005 and then dropping to zero in 2007.

CONCLUSION: THE FUTURE OF MEXICO–U.S. MIGRATION

The current situation with respect to Mexican migration to the United States is historically unprecedented. The number of people involved is daunting. Some 12.7 million

Mexicans currently live in the United States, constituting around 10 percent of Mexico's total population and 4 percent of the U.S. population. Mexicans currently represent 37 percent of all immigrants in the United States. Not only is the number of Mexicans living north of the border unprecedented, but also the share who lack documents is at a record level. Of the nearly 13 million Mexicans present in the United States, 7 million are present without authorization, meaning that a majority of all Mexican immigrants, some 55 percent, have no effective rights and are thus exceedingly vulnerable both socially and economically. On top of these remarkable statistics, Mexican migration has shifted from being a regional phenomenon mainly affecting California, Texas, and Illinois to being a national issue that touches all fifty states and the District of Columbia, with rapidly growing Mexican populations in places that have not experienced significant immigration in living memory (Massey 2008).

As the number of people in exploitable circumstances has risen through undocumented migration, the expansion of temporary labor migration, and legislative restrictions on the rights and privileges of legal resident aliens, the pressure on Mexican immigrants has increased to new heights. As a matter of deliberate public policy, authorities in the United States have massively militarized the Mexico–U.S. border, increased the intensity of police actions against immigrants within the United States, and implemented xenophobic laws and policies at the state and local level. The most recent of these is Arizona's SB 1070, which was passed by the state legislature and signed by the governor on April 23, 2010. SB 1070 made the failure to carry immigration documents a crime and gave the police broad power to detain anyone suspected of being in the country without authorization, making it by far the toughest state immigration law in the nation.

These official actions have unfolded within a broader social climate of rising anti-immigrant sentiment and a growing number of hate crimes. In this context, legal as well as illegal migrants have come under attack with the passage of new laws to strip them of eligibility for certain entitlements, limit their access to the courts, and render them deportable for past violations of immigration law, no matter how long ago they occurred.

Despite the rising pressure and growing climate of hostility, however, immigrants show no inclination to return to Mexico. Indeed, although the volume of undocumented migration has now slowed to a trickle, the volume of return migration has fallen even further and faster among both documented and undocumented migrants. Mexican immigrants thus find themselves in the difficult situation of being cut off from their homeland by a militarized border while being increasingly marginalized in the United States by rising hostility and official exclusion. In the absence of a shift in U.S. policies, the only possible outcome is the creation of a large underclass that is permanently divorced from American society and disenfranchised from its resources, with little hope of upward mobility.

That the formation of such an economic underclass is already well advanced is suggested by Figure E.8, which shows trends in real hourly wages earned by Mexican immigrants, native-born Mexican Americans, and native-born non-Hispanic whites from 1950 to 2007, computed from U.S. Census and American Community Survey data. During the years of the postwar economic boom from 1950 to 1970, the wages of all three groups rose dramatically. From 1970 to 1990 wage growth slowed for Mexican

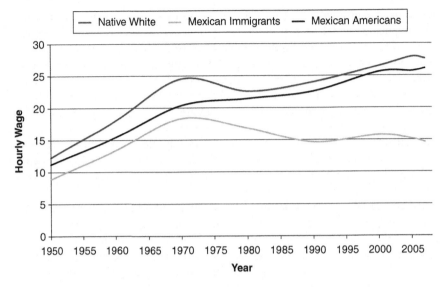

Figure E.8 Trends in Real Hourly Wages Earned by Mexican Immigrants, Mexican Americans, and Non-Hispanic Whites.

Americans and native whites, but fell in absolute terms for Mexican immigrants. After 1990 wage growth picked up for native whites and Mexican Americans but immigrant wages continued to stagnate. In 2007, Mexican immigrants earned roughly the same wage they earned in 1965, when the Bracero Program ended and quotas were placed on legal Mexican immigration. In other words, as the share of people without labor rights has grown and official discrimination against them has increased, Mexican immigrant wages have increasingly fallen behind those of other U.S. workers.

The effect of the Mexican immigrants' growing estrangement from their homeland is also evident in financial data, most notably in the flow of "migradollars," money entering Mexico from migrants in the United States (Durand 1988). The flow of migradollars into Mexico at any point in time depends on the number of migrants present in the United States, of course, but also on their propensity to send money home and the amounts they are inclined to send, both of which tend to decline with time spent in the United States (Durand et al. 1996). The flow also depends on the degree to which migrants return home regularly and bring savings with them when they do, both of which also decline with time spent in the United States; and we know from results already presented that return migration has dropped to record low levels.

Thus, we expect to see a drop in the volume of migradollars, which during the 1990s had become a large contributor to Mexico's balance of payments and international liquidity. Figure E.9 shows the trend in the average amount returned to Mexico each year through migrant remittances and savings, computed in 2007 dollars using MMP data. The average amount repatriated by migrants fluctuated around $5,000 per year through the mid 1980s and then dipped to a nadir of about $2,500 in 1993, but then increased dramatically during the economic boom of the 1990s as migrants stayed

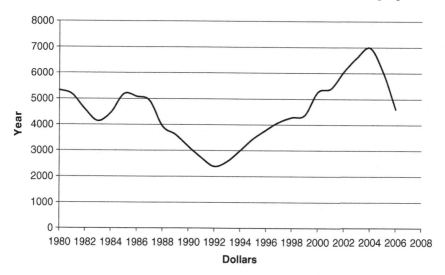

Figure E.9 Average Amount of "Migradollars" Sent and Brought Back by Mexican Migrants.

longer to work more hours and earn more money. This increase came to a halt, however, after 2003 when the volume of migradollars took a sharp downturn. As migrants accumulate more time in the north and remain separated from Mexico by a militarized border while earning low wages under increasingly precarious conditions in the United States, the inflow of money from the north can be expected to continue to decline, with serious economic implications for Mexico, especially during a period of economic dislocation and recession in North America.

In sum, the status quo of escalating border enforcement, more intense internal policing, and formal exclusion by government agencies predicts a bleak future for Mexican immigration, both for the population of increasingly marginalized migrants living in the United States and for the friends and relatives in sending communities that came to depend on their savings and remittances for consumption and investment. For the foreseeable future, the only real hope lies in immigration reform initiatives now being formulated in Congress, proposals that would regularize the status of undocumented migrants and ease the restrictions on the legal entry of Mexican immigrants moving forward. If such reforms are not enacted, the problem of Mexican immigration will be resolved over time as the undocumented migrants age and die off, whereas those with documents naturalize in growing numbers and more and more of their U.S.-born children reach voting age. If an ending to the war on immigrants has to wait until this time, however, much human suffering will ensue in the interim and in the end there will be hell to pay for the United States socially, economically, and politically.

Appendix
Chronology of Mexican Migration

This chronological overview provides the researcher with a longue durée view of migration between Mexico and the United States. The absence of any externally imposed periodization allows for a variety of approaches to the study of the topic. The dates and events were culled from salient historical moments and economic and legal enactments appearing throughout the volume's chapters. Additional material was added by the editor.[1] An attempt was made to include a balance of relevant chronological markers from both countries, as well as other formative milestones in both countries' history of migration.

1539
Franciscan friar Marcos de Niza embarks on an expedition that takes him north of Sonora into the present day United States.

1790
The United States passes the Naturalization Act, for the first time legislating citizenship and limiting naturalization to "free white persons."

1836
The state of Texas declares independence and initiates a war against Mexico's central government.

1846
The Invasión norteamericana/Mexican–American War begins following the annexation of Texas by the United States.

---

1. Additional sources used include Chomsky, *"They Are Taking Our Jobs!"*; FitzGerald, "Inside the Sending State"; and Durand and Massey, "The Costs of Contradiction."

1848

Concluding the war between Mexico and the United States, the Treaty of Guadalupe Hidalgo ceded to the U.S. territories making up the present-day states of Arizona, New Mexico, Nevada, Colorado, Wyoming, Utah, and California. Additionally, Mexican residents of ceded territories are given several options with regard to their legal status: (1) they can choose to leave their homes and relocate south of the newly established border; (2) they can remain in their homes, now in the United States, but elect to maintain their Mexican citizenship; (3) they can formally elect to become U.S. citizens; or (4) if the former Mexican citizens remain in their homes and do not formally elect to retain Mexican citizenship, they will be presumed U.S. citizens after one year.

1849

With the Passenger Cases, the Supreme Court of the United States asserts federal jurisdiction concerning matters of foreign commerce. Additionally, the Court asserts that the imposition of taxes on noncitizens by states is unconstitutional.

1853

Authorizing the purchase of land from Mexico in present-day Arizona and New Mexico for $10 million, the Gadsden Purchase is signed by President Franklin Pierce and then ratified by the U.S. Senate in 1854. The purchase is motivated by the desire to build a southern railroad route to the Pacific. Mexican president Santa Anna reluctantly agrees to the purchase for lack of funds in the Mexican treasury, but is generally considered to have ceded too much land and then to have squandered funds received.

1854

Ayutla Rebellion launched on March 1. Seen by many in Mexico as the initiation of a new era of liberal rule in Mexico.

1856

In *Dred Scott v. Sandford*, the Supreme Court of the United States denies the slave Dred Scott and his wife freedom by asserting that being born in the United States does not necessarily imply citizenship and that peoples of African descent cannot claim citizenship. The decision is seemingly in contradiction with the Missouri Compromise and further strains relations between the North and the South.

1857

A new constitution is drafted in Mexico. Article 11 asserts the freedom to exit from and travel within the country, with exceptions in cases of criminal and civil matters.

1868

The Fourteenth Amendment to the United States Constitution is ratified, asserting that "all persons born or naturalized in the United States and subject to the jurisdiction thereof" are citizens and are to be accorded "equal protection."

1870

The U.S. Naturalization Act of 1870 is passed, allowing "white persons and persons of African descent" to be naturalized.

1876

Porfirio Díaz becomes President of Mexico until 1880 and then again from 1884 until 1911 for a period known as the Porfiriato.

1882

The Chinese Exclusion Act is passed in the United States, placing a moratorium on Chinese immigration for ten years and marking the first major piece of legislation restricting immigration into the United States. In another act of legislation, the Immigration Act of 1882 levies a fifty-cent head tax on all immigrants landing at U.S. ports. Because of an urgent need for increased migrant labor in the United States following the ban on Chinese immigration and the fact that Mexicans are not subject to the new head tax because they enter the United States through land routes rather than ports, Mexican migration to the United States increases.

1883

The government of Mexican President Porfirio Díaz passes the Colonization Act with the hopes that a liberalized immigration policy will attract "redemptive" foreigners and thus help "civilize" the nation.

1885

The Contract Labor Law is passed in the United States, prohibiting the importation of workers by sea. The recruitment of Mexican workers is still allowed as they enter the United States through land routes.

1891

The Immigration Act of 1891 establishes the Bureau of Immigration under the auspices of the Treasury Department for the purposes of oversight and enforcement of immigration laws.

1892

Ellis Island opens as a main point of entry for immigrants entering the United States and remains in operation until 1954.

1897

In the case of Rodriguez, a federal judge in Texas designates Mexicans as being "white enough" and thus eligible to become naturalized U.S. citizens.

1898

In the case *U.S. v. Wong Kim*, the U.S. Supreme Court interprets the Fourteenth Amendment validating the citizenship of children born in the United States to parents in the United States illegally.

Following the Spanish–American War, the United States assumes territorial control of Puerto Rico, Guam, the Philippines, and Hawaii. Although not granted citizenship, residents are considered "nationals" and can thus enter the United States.

1900

Railroad companies in the United States employ approximately 140,000 Mexicans.

1901

At the ASARCO steel plant in El Paso, Texas, Mexican, and American workers walk off the job in protest to a pay reduction.

1902

The Newlands Reclamation Act is passed in the United States, allocating federal funds toward agricultural development in the U.S. Southwest. The expansion of railroad networks as well as general increase in wages results.

The United States renews the Chinese Exclusion Act of 1882 indefinitely.

1903

Mexican and Japanese workers in Oxnard, California, organize a successful month-long strike. Citrus workers in Ventura, California, also go on strike. In Los Angeles, Mexicans working for the Pacific Electric Railway organize La Union Federal Mexicano protest of low wages.

Control over the Bureau of Immigration is transferred from the Treasury Department to the Department of Commerce and Labor.

1904

Attempting to undermine Article 11 of the 1857 Mexican constitution allowing freedom of travel within and exit from Mexico, the Mexican government orders municipalities to stop issuing travel documents to workers bound for the United States.

1906

The U.S. Naturalization Act of 1906 requires immigrants to learn and speak English as a requirement for naturalization.

The U.S. Bureau of Immigration is renamed the Bureau of Immigration and Naturalization. It is subdivided in 1913, only to be reunited in 1933 as the Immigration and Naturalization Service under the auspices of the Department of Labor.

The United States first places inspectors at the border with Mexico. They are primarily concerned with Chinese illegally entering the country through Mexico.

1907

A "Gentlemen's Agreement" between the United States and Japan stipulates that Japan will prevent its citizens from migrating to the United States in exchange for the United States not to ban them from doing so. In response to the subsequent reduction in cheap foreign labor, recruiters from the United States start penetrating into Mexico in search of pools of cheap labor.

1910

Beginning of the Mexican Revolution; end of thirty-three-year rule of Porfirio Díaz.

Mining and railroad companies have ownership or control of 27 percent of Mexico's land.

Gas Works employees in Los Angeles, including Mexican immigrants, launch a strike and win a wage increase.

1911

Anti-Chinese sentiments contribute to the murders of 303 individuals of Chinese descent in Torreon, Coahuila.

A report by the U.S. Immigration Commission claims that "immigration from Mexico has become an important factor" and estimates that approximately fifty-thousand new immigrants are entering the United States without documentation per year.

1913

In El Paso, Texas, 650 Mexican smelter workers walk off their jobs and bring a halt to production. They demand a reduction in hours from twelve to eight hours a day and a $0.35 increase in their daily wages.

1915

Miners at Clifton-Morenci, Arizona, including Mexican immigrants, go on a four-and-a-half month long strike. Southern California Fruit Grower's Exchange (Sunkist) begins a policy of constructing camp housing for Mexican workers.

1917

Against the veto of U.S. President Woodrow Wilson, the Immigration Act of 1917, also known as the Asiatic Barred Zone Act, is passed, prohibiting all immigration from Asia. Additionally, the Literacy Act of 1917 is also passed, restricting the immigration of illiterate migrants. In 1918, however, reacting to protests from railroad, agricultural, and mining interests, application of the Literacy Act to Mexican migrants is suspended.

Cement workers in Colton, California, including Mexican immigrants, form the Trabajadores Unidos to protest a planned lowering of wages. A total of 150 workers walk out, winning a pay raise and union recognition. Miners in the Bisbee and Jerome districts of Arizona, including Mexican immigrants, go on strike. A total of 1,800 strikers are arrested.

A precursor to the 1942–1964 Bracero Program, cotton and beat sugar lobbies in the United States unilaterally push for a temporary labor program that is renewed until 1921. Exempted from head taxes and literacy requirements and in violation of Mexican law requiring contracts and the issuing of visas by U.S. consuls in Mexico, seventy thousand to eighty-three thousand temporary Mexican workers are brought into the United States.

The Jones–Shafroth Act grants U.S. citizenship to all citizens of Puerto Rico.

Article 123 of Mexico's new constitution asserts that municipalities must ensure that workers emigrating abroad have signed contracts detailing wages, hours, and repatriation costs borne by the employer. Additionally, the new constitution states the holders of public office must be Mexican citizens through natural birth.

1918

Concerned about the possibility of the United States conscripting Mexican nationals during World War I, Mexican President Carranza accelerates an ongoing campaign aimed at persuading potential migrants that strong measures will be taken to prevent the exiting of workers with no contracts. In one example, the state of Tamaulipas increases its international bridge fees to discourage emigration to the United States.

The United States passes the Passport Act, requiring official documentation for entry into the United States. Canadians and Mexicans are issued border crossing cards.

In Los Angeles, two hundred Mexican employees of the Pacific Sewer Pipe Company go on strike.

1919

In his study Essentials of Americanization, prominent sociologist Emory Bogardus observes, "In the Southwestern states the Mexican Problem has developed rapidly since 1900."

1921

At a cost of $1 million, the Carranza administration sponsors the repatriation of fifty thousand Mexican migrants through 1922. The government suspends the program in 1923 because of the cost and instead relies on periodic public warnings and other methods, such as the 1925 ban on selling railway tickets in the interior to laborers heading to the United States.

The United States passes the Emergency Quota Act, limiting the annual number of European immigrants to 3 percent of the number of each European nationality present in the United States according to the 1910 Census figures. Additionally, European immigrants must obtain visas prior to arriving in the United States.

1922

In the southwestern United States, 75 percent of fruit and vegetable workers and 50 percent of cotton workers are Mexicans. In Michigan, Ohio, Iowa, Kansas, and Minnesota, Mexicans make up 24 percent of sugar beet contract labor.

1924

The United States passes the Immigration Act of 1924, placing restrictions on Middle Eastern, Asian, African, and Eastern European immigration. Additionally, the National Origins Quota Act limits the annual number of European immigrants to 2 percent of the number of each European nationality present in the United States according to the 1890 Census figures.

The U.S. Border Patrol is created.

1926

The Office of the Governor of California releases a report claiming that the six major southwestern railroads employ at least fifty thousand Mexicans, comprising approximately 75 percent of all track workers.

The Mexican Congress passes legislation requiring that the labor rights of and benefits accrued by Mexican migrant workers be stipulated in written contracts. Additionally, the legislation seeks to alleviate the repatriation costs assumed by the Mexican government and Mexican workers upon their return to Mexico from the United States. Control over the enforcement of this law is shared by the Secretariat of Foreign Relations as well as by the Secretariat of the Interior.

Threatened by attempts to diminish the Catholic Church as an institutional competitor and expand the purview of Mexico City over peripheral areas, supporters of the Catholic Church rise up against the Mexican government in the Cristero War. The fighting begins in the city of Guadalajara, expanding throughout the Mexican state of Jalisco and eventually spilling over into the Mexican State of Guanajuato. The conflict is brought to a diplomatic conclusion in 1929. A smaller second war foments from disagreements over federal agrarian and educational reforms, lasting into the mid-1930s.

Mexican anthropologist Manuel Gamio undertakes a survey of Mexican immigrants in the United States, eventually publishing two books based on his findings: *Mexican Immigration to the United States* (1930) and *The Mexican Immigrant: His Life Story* (1931).

1928

The period known as El Maximato begins, lasting until 1934. It is composed of the presidencies of Emilio Portes Gil, Pascual Ortiz Rubio, and Abelardo Rodríguez, although true power was maintained by former President Calles, self-appointment as the Jefe Máximo.

1929

The Great Depression begins following the U.S. stock market crash of October 29, 1929. The Mexican-born population in the United States stands at approximately 740,000, up from just 100,000 in 1900.

1930

The United States begins the deportation of millions of Mexicans and Mexican Americans, some of whom are U.S. citizens. The Mexican Department of Migrations estimates that 70,127 migrant workers returned to Mexico from the United States during 1930; this number increased to 138,519 the following year.

Nueces County, the leading cotton-producing county in Texas, has a Mexican labor force reaching 97 percent.

Mexico passes the Law of Migration, setting up the Advisory Council of Migration to be led by the chief of the Secretariat of the Interior's Department of Migration as well as representatives from seven other federal secretariats.

1931

The Mexican Department of Migrations estimates that 138,519 migrant workers returned to Mexico from the United States; this number decreased by 44 percent the following year to 77,453.

Following decades of intimidation, violence, and repression, the Mexican government forcibly expels Mexico's small but well-established Chinese population.

The Mexican National Commission for Irrigation begins building settlements throughout northern Mexico to facilitate the repatriation of Mexican migrant workers.

1932

The Mexican government creates the Committee for National Repatriation to facilitate the reincorporation of repatriated Mexicans. The first of two settlements for repatriated

Mexicans is created in El Coloso, near Acapulco, to house twenty Mexicans repatriated from Detroit, Michigan. Mexican Secretary of the Interior Eduardo Vasconcelos initiates the "Campania de medio millon," raising 500,000 pesos for the purpose of repatriating Mexicans.

1933

The Committee for National Repatriation creates the second of two colonies in Pinotepa Nacional, Oaxaca, accommodating 362 Mexican repatriates. In 1934 the second colony fails, causing a controversy when news of its demise is picked up by the national media.

1934

Lázaro Cardenas becomes President of Mexico.

1936

President Cárdenas pronounces the General Population Law (*Ley General de Población*), which contains conditions concerning the growth and movement of Mexican and non-Mexican populations. Focusing on the dynamics of migration, internal growth, and naturalization, the law mandates the "fusion of all the nation's ethnic groups" and "the general protection, conservation, and improvement of the species, within the limits and through the procedures laid out in this law."

1939

With Germany's invasion of Poland, World War II begins. Over the past ten years, approximately 469,000 Mexicans have been forcibly expelled from the United States owing to the pressures on labor in the United States resultant from the Great Depression.

1940

The United States passes the Alien Registration Act, among other elements requiring all noncitizen residents of the United States to register with the government.

1941

Following the attack on Pearl Harbor, the United States officially enters World War II on December 8, 1941. As a member of the Allies, Mexico is minimally involved in military matters but becomes a significant supplier of oil and other raw materials to the United States.

1942

Responding to the demand for manual labor in the United States, the United States and Mexico initiate the Bracero Program, allowing for Mexican guest workers to legally enter the United States on limited-term contracts. The program is renewed continuously until 1964.

1943

Fearing the loss of their local work forces, governors from the Mexican states of Jalisco, Guanajuato, and Michoacán ban the contracting of braceros until 1944.

1946

No longer fearing the mass departure of local workers, officials from the Mexican state of Guanajuato petition the government for bracero permits for their unemployed workers.

1947

Twenty-three countries including the United States, Canada, the United Kingdom, France, and China, sign the General Agreement on Tariffs and Trade (GATT). GATT is meant to liberalize world trade through the dismantling of economic barriers such as import tariffs, subsidies for national businesses, and other restrictive trade policies. Mexico does not participate in GATT until 1986, when negotiations begin to expand GATT into what will be known as the World Trade Organization (WTO).

Mexico's 1947 Law of Population directs government policies toward population growth through natural increase, immigration, and repatriation.

Operation Bootstrap is the name given to the set of programs aimed toward the industrialization of Puerto Rico, which lay the groundwork for the "great migration" of the 1950s.

1948

Hoping to force the United States to agree to some concessions on the Bracero Program, the Mexican government refuses to allow workers to cross into the United States. In response and under pressure from U.S. employers, the U.S. government opens the border at El Paso, Texas, allowing approximately four thousand workers to enter undocumented. The Mexican government responds by suspending the program, which is not renegotiated until August 1949.

1951

Responding to an increase in undocumented migrants leaving for the United States and aggressive U.S. officials, the Mexican government negotiates what formally becomes a second Migratory Labor Agreement (Public Law 78, 1951–1964).

1952

The United States passes the Immigration and Nationality Act. In abolishing the Asiatic barred zone, it set Japan's quota to 185 annually, with China's quota set to 105 and the rest of Asia given 100 slots. Additionally, the national origins quota system established in 1924 is upheld. Colonial subjects from those European nations are not eligible under the quota system.

The H2 temporary visa establishes a large but generally ignored guest-worker program.

1953

The Mexican government creates the Labor Exchange Office to facilitate the matching of bracero jobs with pockets of unemployment in Mexico.

1954

A program of the U.S. Immigration and Naturalization Service (INS), Operation Wetback, deports approximately 1 million undocumented Mexicans. One year prior to

Operation Wetback, the rate of braceros entering the United States stood at 200,000 per year. Following Operation Wetback, that rate increases to 450,000 per year.

In response to the U.S. government adopting a policy of unilateral contracts with Mexican workers, the governor of the Mexican state of Jalisco warns municipalities that force will be used to prevent workers contracted as such from leaving. In January, Mexican troops are employed to quell rioting workers trying to cross over into the United States.

1959

Fourteen percent of Mexico's male population has departed for the United States at one point or another as braceros.

Following the Cuban Revolution and Fidel Castro's ascension to power, the Attorney General of the United States allows Cuban immigrants to enter the United States as refugees.

1961

The U.S. Department of Labor almost concedes to demands of labor leaders from El Paso, Texas, to ban green-card holders. The Mexican government poses strong diplomatic opposition to the idea and it is eventually dropped.

1964

Despite opposition from the Mexican government, the United States ends the Bracero Program. In total more than 4.6 million bracero contracts have been issued to at least 1 million individuals.

1965

The United States passes the Voting Rights Act, outlawing practices that discriminate against voters in the United States.

The Immigration and Nationality Act (Hart–Cellar Act) is passed, provisions of which do not go into effect until 1968. The act sets immigration quotas for countries in the western hemisphere at 20,000 per country with a cap of 120,000. Immediate family members are excluded from the quotas. Family reunifications, skilled labor, and up to 17,400 refugee cases are given special attention. Also, a Select Commission on Western Hemisphere Immigration is established to report back to Congress in 1968.

1967

The U.S. Immigration and Naturalization Service apprehends 161,608 undocumented immigrants. That number increases to 484,824 in 1972 and to over 1 million in 1977 and 1983, topping off at 1,348,749 in 1985. Approximately 60 to 75 percent of those apprehended are Mexicans.

1968

Mexico City hosts the Summer Olympic Games. Government troop massacre hundreds of student protestors in Tlatelolco Plaza, Mexico City.

Following the Hart–Cellar Act, which imposed numerical caps on Mexican immigration to the United States, the INS detains and deports approximately 151,000 Mexican migrants. That number increases to 781,000 in 1976.

1969

The INS estimates that forty-eight thousand workers commute legally along the border annually, up from thirty-four thousand workers in 1963 and forty-four thousand in 1966. The number decreases to forty thousand in 1973. These are Mexicans with green cards who work in the United States but choose to reside in Mexico. These "green-card commuters" are paid an average of $1.55 per hour, five cents below the United States' minimum wage. Twenty-seven percent of males and 42 percent of females earned below $1.46 per hour.

1970

The state of California is home to 53 percent of all foreign-born Mexican immigrants.

In the border regions of Mexico, 120 factories known as maquiladoras, where products destined for the United States are assembled with reduced taxation, employ approximately 20,327 people. Those numbers increase to 585 maquiladoras employing 184,400 people by 1984. In 1975, 78 percent of those workers are women, with the percentage dropping to 70 percent by 1985.

Agricultural production in Mexico exceeds national levels of consumption, allowing for increased exports in cotton, coffee, fruits, vegetables, and livestock. Mexico's population reaches 48 million, up from 19.7 million in 1948.

1972

Mexico's National Center for Labor Information and Statistics estimates that only 436,000 undocumented Mexicans are in the United States. That number increases to 606,000 in 1974 and 1.2 million in 1977.

1974

The Supreme Court of the United States upholds the constitutionality of the green-card commuting system.

Attorney General William Saxbe asserts that as many as 7 million undocumented people live in the United States, whereas United States Commissioner of Immigration Leonard F. Chapman, Jr., claims that the number could be higher than 12 million.

In a reversal of the 1947 Law of Population, Mexican President Echeverria informs the Ford Administration of the United States that Mexico is no longer interested in renewing the Bracero Program. Furthermore, family planning aimed at population control will replace earlier legislation seeking to increase the population.

1975

Mexican imports from the United States total $5.1 billion, whereas Mexican exports to the United States total $1.7 billion. Those numbers increase to $15.4 billion and $10 billion, respectively, by 1980.

1976

The United States applies a uniform quota of twenty thousand immigrants to all western hemisphere countries. Cuban refugees are not included in the quota system. Legal Mexican immigration falls by 40 percent.

1977

U.S. President Carter proposes the Carter Plan, in which he calls for "a set of actions to help markedly reduce the increasing flow of undocumented aliens in this country and to regulate the presence of the millions of undocumented aliens already here."

1978

President Carter and the Congress establish the Select Commission on Immigration and Refugee Policy. The Commission is tasked with evaluating current immigration policy and recommending future legislation.

Separate Eastern and Western Hemisphere quota systems for immigration into the United States are eliminated and replaced by a new worldwide quote of 290,000.

In El Paso, Texas, the Coalition against the Fence holds a demonstration protesting the "Tortilla Curtain" and the possible militarization of the border.

1979

The City of Los Angeles implements "Special Order 40," which minimizes the amount of cooperation city agencies are allowed to supply to the enforcement of federal immigration laws. Other American cities such as New York, Chicago, and Houston implement similar policies.

U.S. President Carter and Mexican President Jose Lopez Portillo discuss the Tortilla Curtain controversy during broad bilateral talks in Mexico.

1980

Mexicans constitute just 0.7 to 5.9 percent of all foreign-born immigrants in the traditional southern United States (i.e., not including Florida and Texas). The large majority of Hispanics in the traditional southern United States are born in the United States, ranging from 66.4 percent in Virginia to 89.8 percent in Alabama. Florida's Hispanic population is 871,640, whereas Texas' is 4,304,325. Fifty-seven percent of foreign-born Mexicans call California home, with Mexican immigration to the forty-five nongateway states at 8.5 percent. Meanwhile, the U.S. Census estimates the undocumented population in the United States at 6 million.

The United States passes the Refugee Act, which allows the President, in consultation with Congress, to set refugee quotas each year. The act revamps systems of admissions of refugees and adjudications of asylum cases at the border. Additionally, immigration quotas are adjusted from 290,000 to 270,000.

1981

The U.S. Select Commission on Immigration and Refugee Policy issues its final report. Recommendations include sanctioning employers who knowingly hire undocumented workers and the legalization of persons who have been in the United States illegally since before January 1, 1980. The Commission also recommends that the annual immigration quota be increased from 270,000 to 350,000, with additional increases over the subsequent five years. Allowances are suggested for the parents of permanent residents and the grandparents and children of citizens to come to the United States outside of the quota system. These recommendations form the basis of what will become the 1986 Immigration Reform and Control Act (IRCA).

1982

The INS conducts Operation Jobs, raiding workplaces and arresting five thousand undocumented migrants.

1986

The Uruguay round of GATT negotiations begins, culminating in 1994 in the creation of the WTO. The WTO provides a framework within which participating nations can negotiate trade agreements and resolve disputes, for the purpose of greatly facilitating the liberalization of world trade. Although greatly beneficial to wealthy and industrialized nations, further rounds of WTO negotiations stall in 2001 as less developed nations demand a greater consideration of their needs.

The United States passes IRCA, which legalizes all undocumented immigrants who can demonstrate continued residence in the United States since 1982. Approximately 1.7 million immigrants apply. The Special Agricultural Workers provision of the act legalizes those engaged in temporary agricultural work in 1985 and 1986. Approximately 1.3 million are approved. Employer sanctions are instituted that require employers to verify the immigration status of their workers. Additionally, the H2 temporary worker program is divided between agricultural (H2A) and nonagricultural (H2B) workers. Although the IRCA is applicable to all immigrants, Mexicans make up 75 percent of those legalized.

In Mexico, traditional patterns of migration involving mostly men moving back and forth across the border are replaced with unidirectional ones, in which newly legalized Mexicans in the United States begin to sponsor the immigration of their families to the United States. In response to the prospect of legalization, there is an influx of illegal migration into the United States.

The Border Patrol apprehends almost 1 million Mexican migrants, up from eighty thousand in 1970.

1988

Hoping the opinions of Mexican migrants will influence the vote back home, Mexican Presidential Candidate Cuauhtémoc Cárdenas campaigns in the United States, attracting large crowds of Mexican migrants with promises of dual nationality and the right to vote from abroad. In response, the ruling Institutional Revolutionary Party begins to accept an expanded conception of the Mexican nation inclusive of Mexicans living abroad.

Marking a growing recognition of "Hispanics" in the United States, President Ronald Reagan changes National Hispanic week into National Hispanic Month.

1990

In Tijuana, Mexico, the Grupo Beta migrant protection police is formed. The force is then expanded across the northern and southern borders. In 2000, seventy-five Grupo Beta agents are positioned along the border with the United States. They arrest approximately one hundred coyotes per month. In 2001, the Mexican government decides that Grupo Beta cannot forcibly prevent migrants from crossing into the United States illegally. Grupo Beta stops policing the border, instead focusing on the protection and rescuing of undocumented immigrants.

In the United States, 20.6 percent of all immigrants are Mexican. Although 28 percent of all immigrants in traditional gateway states are Mexicans, they make up just 1.8 to 9.4 percent of immigrants in traditional southern states. In California, Mexican immigrant populations peak at 58 percent. That percentage drops to 48 percent by 2000. The midwestern United States replaces the southern United States as the least common region for immigrant settlement.

As a result of IRCA, approximately 2.3 million Mexicans have become legal residents of the United States.

The United States passes the Immigration Act of 1990, which among other provisions sets the worldwide quota to 700,000. Visas are reserved for cases of family reunifications and employment-based migrations. Visas are also set aside for a lottery.

The Mexican government establishes the Program for Mexican Communities Abroad, which works toward formalizing ties between hometown associations of Mexican migrants in the United States and their communities of origin in Mexico. With the program Tres por Uno (Three for One), the Mexican government matches funds supplied migrants in the United States toward infrastructure programs in the communities of origin. By 2008, the project is spending approximately $125 million on projects throughout Mexico, with 25 percent of that money originating in the United States.

1993

President Clinton begins a program of intensifying border security through the buildup of border agents and control infrastructure. Operation Hold the Line is initiated in El Paso, with operation Gatekeeper in San Diego the following year. A total of 820,000 Mexican migrants crossing the border illegally are apprehended. Prior to these buildups, the number of migrants dying during the border crossing stands roughly at 3 per 100,000. Within four years of these buildups, the death rate doubles.

1994

The North American Free Trade Agreement (NAFTA) is established, removing trade barriers among Canada, the United States, and Mexico. Although contentious within the United States, the passage of NAFTA is seen as a great achievement by the Mexican government, which actively lobbied in the United States for its passage. NAFTA is considered to have had positive and negative effects. Businesses have experienced the added benefit of expanded manufacturing options and markets, whereas the wages of workers suffered at the hands of increased competition. Additionally, although food prices have generally dropped, low-yield agriculture in Mexico has suffered greatly because of the lower prices offered by agrobusiness in the United States and Canada.

The United States announces Operation Gatekeeper, which aims to strengthen the San Diego border crossing with an increase in manpower and physical deterrents such as fencing and lights.

California voters pass Proposition 187, which would have greatly limited access to social services by undocumented immigrants. In an example of Mexican foreign policy advocating for the rights of Mexican migrants in the United States, Mexican consulates coordinate with Mexican American politicians against the proposition. In the end, Proposition 187 is found to be unconstitutional. In reaction to Proposition 187, however, naturalization of Mexicans legally in the United States begins to skyrocket, from 23,000 in 1993 to over 255,000 in 1996.

1996

The United States passes the Personal Responsibility and Work Opportunity Reconciliation Act, which restricts legal permanent residents from accessing many federal aid programs unless they have lived in the United States for five years.

The Illegal Immigration Reform and Immigrant Responsibility Act is passed, which among other provisions strengthens border controls, legal mechanisms, and information-gathering capacities. The act triples the number of immigrant detentions in the 1990s. It is now also a federal crime for noncitizens to vote in federal elections.

1997

The Mexican government passes a law no longer requiring Mexican citizens to forfeit other nationalities they might have, effectively sanctioning dual citizenship. The law goes into effect in 1998.

The United States passes the Nicaraguan Adjustment and Central American Relief Act, which adjusts the status of Nicaraguans and Cubans who have resided in the United States since 1995.

1998

Under U.S. President Bill Clinton, the INS's budget reaches $4.2 billion, up from $1.5 billion in 1993 and approximately eight times the number set with the IRCA in 1986. Of that, over $1 billion is allocated to the Border Patrol, up from $151 million in 1986, making it the nation's largest civilian police force.

California voters pass Proposition 227 outlawing bilingual education in the state.

2000

Vicente Fox Quesada is elected President of Mexico and serves until 2006. His views on Mexican immigration are in keeping with those of President George W. Bush in that he advocates for the controlled and legal migrations of Mexican workers to the United States through programs such as the Guest Worker Plan.

The United States passes the Legal Immigration Family Equity Act, which established the nonimmigrant V visa for the immediate family members of permanent residents who have had to wait more than four year for visas because of quota backlogs.

2001

On September 7, 2001, President Vicente Fox meets with President George W. Bush in Washington, D.C., to discuss immigration-related issues such as a temporary-worker program, the number of visas issued to Mexicans, and the possibility of normalizing the status of undocumented Mexican immigrants in the United States.

On September 11, 2001, terrorists affiliated with Al-Qaeda hijack four commercial airliners, successfully attacking the Pentagon and destroying the World Trade Center in New York City. Reactions to the 9/11 attacks consume the administration of George W. Bush, most notably involving wars in Afghanistan and Iraq.

The United States passes the Uniting and Strengthening America by Providing Appropriate Tools Required to Intercept and Obstruct Terrorism Act (USA Patriot Act). The act implements a host of antiterrorism-directed measures including the increase of border patrol agents and immigration inspectors.

A Mexican businessman living in Sacramento, California, is elected as mayor of his home town of Jerez, in the Mexican state of Zacatecas, only to have his election overturned because he is not a local resident. In 2003, the state of Zacatecas passes legislation allowing binational residents of Zacatecas to run for local and state offices. The Sacramento businessman runs again and is subsequently elected. The same legislation also creates an extraterritorial electoral district in the United States for the state congress of Zacatecas that seats two senators.

The Mexican state of Jalisco begins to coordinate with United States consulates to facilitate the legal and orderly recruitment of workers and to help them fill out H2B visa applications. The Mexican state of Zacatecas begins a similar program with the U.S. consulate in Monterrey for the recruitment of temporary workers.

2002

The U.S. Supreme Court rules in *Hoffman Plastic Compounds v. National Labor Relations Board* that employers cannot be held liable for unlawfully firing illegal immigrants whose status was found out after the firing. The decision gives immigration law precedence over labor law and renders unauthorized workers more vulnerable to exploitation.

Over the past four years over 5.8 million border crossing cards have been issued to Mexicans residing in border cities. These cards allow for travel within twenty-five miles of the border for a period of up to one month.

The United States passes the Homeland Security Act. The INS is replaced by the U.S. Citizenship and Immigration Services under the control of the Department of Homeland Security. Also, the Enhanced Border Security and Visa Entry Reform Act aimed at improving the visa-issuing and inspection process.

2003

The Program for Mexican Communities Abroad is rebranded as the Institute for Mexicans Abroad, which includes an advisory council composed of representatives from all levels of Mexican government as well as ten Latino organizations in the United States. In 2009, the Institute's advisory council calls for the creation of a cabinet-level position to oversee Mexican emigration policy.

Remittances from Mexican immigrants in the United States reach $13.8 billion, making up approximately 2.16 percent of the Mexican gross domestic product. By 2008, that number increases to $25 billion, making up approximately 2.8 percent of Mexican gross domestic product.

The INS conducts fewer than 2,200 audits of employers in the United States suspected of hiring undocumented workers. This number is down from almost 10,000 in 1990. Warnings to employers decline from 1,300 to 500 over the same period. The number of fines issued decline from almost 1,000 in 1991 to 124 in 2003.

2004

Chris Simcox founds the Minutemen Civil Defense Corps, a vigilante organization tasking itself with the defense of the U.S. border with Mexico against what it deems an unprecedented influx of illegal immigration.

2006

Felipe Calderón is elected President of Mexico in a contentious election. President Calderón continues the immigration politics of Vicente Fox, openly disapproving of proposals in the United States to build a wall between the two nations and advocating for the passage of comprehensive immigration legislation by the U.S. Congress. Additionally, this is the first election in which Mexicans living abroad are allowed to vote via mail. Approximately 30 percent of Mexicans living in the United States are eligible to vote, yet only 57,000 register and fewer than 33,000 ballots are considered valid.

In reaction to an increase in anti-immigrant sentiment throughout the United States, local legislative initiatives trying to further criminalize undocumented immigrants, and the debates in the U.S. Congress over comprehensive immigration reform, proimmigrant groups organize a series of conspicuous proimmigration rallies. The largest of these takes place on April 10, 2006, in which millions of immigrants and their supporters stage rallies throughout the United States in cities such as Los Angeles, Dallas, Chicago, and New York.

The U.S. Congress passes the Secure Fence Act authorizing the construction of hundreds of miles of new fence and the reinforcement of existing fence along the U.S.–Mexico border.

The mayor of Hazleton, Pennsylvania, introduces a city ordinance that would make it illegal for landlords to rent accommodations to undocumented immigrants and for businesses to hire them. Several towns throughout the United States adopt similar policies before a federal judge finds Hazleton's ordinance illegal.

2007

A total of 7.4 million entries are made into the United States by Mexicans with non-immigrant, short-term stay visas. A total of 891,000 undocumented migrants are detained and agree to return to Mexico voluntarily.

Of the 462,000 H1B visas issued by the United States, only 3.9 percent are issued to Mexicans. Mexicans receive 91 percent of the more than 87,000 H2A temporary agricultural visas and 68 percent of the 155,000 H2B and H2R seasonal nonagricultural worker visas. Additionally, almost 150,000 Mexicans make up 14 percent of new green-card holders, twice as many as any other group.

Since 2000, the number of apprehensions of Mexican migrants illegally crossing the border has decreased from 1.6 million to 858,000. The Department of Homeland Security credits this drop to increased enforcement efforts. Others point out that the decline in construction jobs in the United States, especially after 2005, is also a result of a decline in the U.S. economy.

A total of 1,059 immigration-related bills are taken up by local and state authorities in the United States. Of the 167 bills that pass, 60 expand migrant rights, 26 contract them, 24 regulate their employment, 30 regulate law enforcement and criminal justice, and 64 serve other functions. The top five states that pass immigration-related bills are Hawaii, Texas, Arizona, California, and Colorado.

A pilot program initiated with the IRCA evolves into the E-Verify program, in which employers can verify with a centralized database the status of their migrant workers. In 2008, the state of Arizona passes legislation requiring all businesses in the state to use the E-Verify system to vet their employees. By 2009, only 113,000 businesses nationwide use the system, representing only 2 percent of businesses in the United States.

The Development, Relief, and Education for Alien Minors Act (DREAM Act) fails to move beyond a filibuster in the U.S. Senate. The act would have provided provisional legal residency to undocumented migrants who entered the United States as children and graduate from U.S. high schools, thus making them eligible for in-state tuition rates and federal student loans. Efforts to pass new versions of the DREAM Act continue through 2010.

The U.S. Congress fails to pass the Comprehensive Immigration Reform Act of 2007, wrapping up over two years of legislative efforts and a vigorous and contentious public debate over the matter. The act would have provided a path to legalization of most undocumented immigrants in the United States, increased border enforcement and spending, made mandatory usage of the E-Verify system, and created a point system for selecting immigrants.

2008

The number of legal temporary workers entering the United States from Mexico exceeds 360,000, up from 17,000 in 1990.

There are 17,819 Border Patrol Agents along the Mexico–U.S. border, up from 5,878 agents in 1996. Additionally, the proposed 2009 Department of Homeland Security Budget for Customs and Border Protection is $10.94 billion, with an additional $5.68 billion for Immigration and Customs Enforcement.

Immigration and Customs Enforcement raids result in 1,103 criminal arrests of employers, mostly for harboring and knowingly hiring undocumented workers. A total of 5,184 undocumented immigrants are also arrested, constituting a nearly insignificant percentage of the 8.3 million undocumented immigrants working in the United States.

According to the Department of Homeland Security, 7 million Mexicans live in the United States illegally, up from 4.7 million in 2000. They make up approximately 61 percent of the total number of undocumented immigrants living in the United States. At 12.7 million, Mexican migrants and their descendants make up nearly 65 percent of that Latino population and account for 32 percent of all immigrants in the United States. Additionally, 11 percent of everyone born in Mexico now lives in the United States, a percentage that has skyrocketed since 1970, when it equaled only 1.4 percent of the Mexican population.

2009

As the first stop in a trip to Latin America, U.S. President Obama meets with Mexican President Calderon on April 16, 2009, to discuss issues including documented and undocumented Mexican migration to the United States.

2010

People of Latin America and Caribbean origin and heritage in the United States number approximately 50 million, or 16 percent of the population.

The Obama administration deports a record number of Mexicans and other immigrants back to their home countries, a 10 percent increase over similar efforts by the George W. Bush administration.

The Arizona Legislature passes the immigration law, Support Our Law Enforcement and Safe Neighborhood or SB 1070, legalizing racial profiling. The law ignites a heated debate and nationwide protests. A federal judge blocks the most controversial elements of SB 1070 before it could take effect on July 29.

President Obama signs into law the Southwest Border Security Bill—supported by a bipartisan majority—which increases funds for the militarization of the U.S.–Mexico border by $600 million. The bill includes funds to deploy 1,500 new Border Patrol agents as well as two aerial surveillance drones.

Contributors

Robert Buffington is an Associate Professor of Women and Gender Studies at the University of Colorado at Boulder. He has done extensive work on the histories of crime and sexuality in Mexico and Latin America. His books include *Criminal and Citizen in Modern Mexico* (University of Nebraska Press, 2000), *Reconstructing Criminality in Modern Latin America* (coedited with Carlos Aguirre, Scholarly Resources, 2000), and *True Stories of Crime in Modern Mexico* (coedited with Pablo Piccato, University of New Mexico Press, 2009). He is currently working on a book, *A Sentimental Education for the Working Man: Mexico City 1900–1910*, which will analyze the impact of modernity on working-class masculinities.

Alanis Enciso Fernando Saúl received his Ph.D. in history from the Colegio de México, A.C. México, D.F., and is a Level II researcher in the Sistema Nacional de Investigadores. He was awarded the Premio Nacional de Historia de México, Francisco del Paso y Troncoso Premios Veracruz, in 2001. He has been research profesor in the Colegio de la Frontera Norte, A.C., El Colegio de Michoacán. Currently he is a professor at the El Colegio de San Luis. He is the author of the book *Que se queden allá. El gobierno de México y la repatriación de mexicanos de Estados Unidos 1934–1940*, Tijuana, Baja California, México, El Colegio de la Frontera Norte/El Colegio de San Luis, 2007.

David Scott FitzGerald (Ph.D., UCLA, 2005) is Associate Professor of Sociology and Associate Director of the Center for Comparative Immigration Studies at the University of California, San Diego. He is the author of *A Nation of Emigrants: How Mexico Manages its Migration* (University of California Press, 2009) and *Negotiating Extraterritorial Citizenship* (CCIS, 2000) and coeditor of four volumes on contemporary Mexican migration published by CCIS and Lynne Rienner. His work on international migration has been published in the *American Journal of Sociology, International Migration Review, Comparative Studies in Society and History, Ethnic and Racial Studies, Qualitative Sociology, Du Bois Review, New York University Law Review, Journal of Interdisciplinary History* and *Journal of Ethnic and Migration Studies*. His major current project examines relationships between liberalism and racism in the immigration and nationality laws of twenty-two countries in the Americas from 1850 to 2000.

Jonathan Fox is a professor in the Latin American and Latino Studies Department at the University of California, Santa Cruz. His recent books and reports include *Subsidizing Inequality: Mexican Corn Policy Since NAFTA* (coeditor, Woodrow Wilson Center/CIDE, 2010), *Context Matters: Latino Immigrant Civic Engagement in Nine US Cities* (Woodrow Wilson Center, 2010), *Confronting the Coffee Crisis: Fair Trade, Sustainable Livelihoods and Ecosystems in Mexico and Central America* (coeditor, MIT Press, 2008), *Accountability Politics: Power and Voice in Rural Mexico* (Oxford University Press, 2007), *Mexico's Right-to-Know Reforms: Civil Society Perspectives* (coeditor, FUNDAR/Woodrow Wilson Center, 2007), and *Invisible No More: Mexican Migrant Civic Participation in the United States* (coeditor, Woodrow Wilson Center, 2006). In 2004, he was awarded the Latin American Studies Association/OXFAM Martin Diskin Memorial Lectureship in recognition of his contribution to research in the public interest. He currently serves on the boards of Fundar: Center for Analysis and Research (Mexico City), Oxfam-America (Boston), and the Community Agro-Ecology Network (Santa Cruz) and is an advisor to the Frente Indígena de Organizaciones Binacionales.

Gilbert G. Gonzalez is Professor Emeritus in Chicano Latino Studies at the University of California, Irvine. His research centers on the United States as an imperial economic power dominating much of Latin America, which has resulted in one hundred years of legal, undocumented, and temporary contract labor migration from Latin America. His publications include *Chicano Education in the Era of Segregation* (1990), *A Century of Chicano History: Empire, Nations and Migration* (coauthored with Raul Fernandez, 2004), and *Guest Workers or Colonized Labor? Mexican Labor Migration to the United States* (2006). He is currently producing and codirecting a documentary examining the Bracero Program, a temporary contract labor program with Mexico from 1942 to 1964. Completion is set for 2010.

Eithne Luibhéid is Director of the Institute for LGBT Studies and Associate Professor of Women's Studies at the University of Arizona in the United States. She is the author of *Entry Denied: Controlling Sexuality at the Border* (University of Minnesota Press, 2002), coeditor of a special issue of *Women's Studies International Forum* on "Representing Migrant Women in Ireland and the E.U." (2004), coeditor of *Queer Migration: Sexuality, U.S. Citizenship, and Border Crossings* (University of Minnesota Press, 2005), editor of a special issue of *GLQ* on "Queer/Migration" (2008), and the author of various articles and book chapters that explore intersections among sexuality, migration, and inequality.

Helen B. Marrow is Assistant Professor of Sociology at Tufts University. She received her Ph.D. in Sociology and Social Policy from Harvard University in 2007 and is the recipient of the 2008 Best Dissertation Award from the American Sociological Association. She is broadly interested in immigration, race and ethnicity, social class, and inequality and social policy. With Mary C. Waters and Reed Ueda, she is coeditor of *The New Americans: A Guide to Immigration since 1965* (Harvard University Press, 2007). She has also published on second-generation Brazilians in the United States, the dispersion of contemporary U.S. immigration streams into "new destinations," and Latin American immigrants in Ireland (forthcoming). As an RWJ Scholar in Health Policy, she is conducting research on the responses of health care institutions and workers to undocumented immigration.

Oscar J. Martínez is Regents' Professor of History at the University of Arizona. He has authored and edited eight books and many articles, book chapters, and reviews. His most recent works include *Troublesome Border* (2nd edition, University of Arizona Press, 2006) and *Mexican Origin People in the United States* (University of Arizona Press, 2001). His current book project seeks to explain why Mexico is poorer than the United States. Martínez has served on the boards of several journals and professional associations. He is a former president of the Association of Borderlands Scholars and a founder of the *Journal of Borderlands Studies*.

Douglas S. Massey is the Henry G. Bryant Professor of Sociology and Public Affairs at Princeton University. He currently serves as President of the American Academy of Political and Social Science and Past President of the American Sociological Association and the Population Association of America. He is a member of the National Academy of Sciences and the American Academy of Arts and Sciences.

Juan Mora-Torres is Associate Professor of Latin American History at DePaul University. His research focuses on the history of the U.S.-Mexican borderlands, Mexican migration, popular culture, working class formations, and Mexicans in Chicago. The author of *The Making of the Mexican Border: The State, Capitalism, and Society in Nuevo León, 1848–1910* (Texas, 2001). He is currently working on *"Me voy pa'l norte (I' m Going North)": The First Great Mexican Migration, 1900–1930*.

Mark Overmyer-Velázquez is the Director of the Center for Latin Amerian and Caribbean Studies and Associate Professor of History at the University of Connecticut. His first book, *Visions of the Emerald City: Modernity, Tradition, and the Formation of Porfirian Oaxaca, Mexico* (Duke, 2006) won the 2007 Best Book Prize from the New England Council on Latin American Studies. He is working on a new book project entitled *"Bleeding Mexico White": Race, Nation and the History of Mexico–US Migration* and is also editor of the two-volume series *Latino America: State by State* (Greenwood, 2008).

Alex Saragoza is Associate Professor of History in the Department of Ethnic Studies at U.C. Berkeley. His publications include *The Monterrey Elite and the Mexican State, 1880–1940* (Texas 1988), "Golfing in the Desert: Los Cabos and Post-PRI Tourism," in *Holiday in Mexico: Essays on Tourism and Tourist Encounters* (edited by Dina Berger and Andrew Wood, Duke, forthcoming), and "The Selling of Mexico: Tourism and the State, 1929–1952," in *Fragments of a Golden Age: The Politics of Culture in Mexico since 1940* (edited by Gilbert M. Joseph, Anne Rubenstein, and Eric Zolov, Duke, 2001). His current research investigates the privatization of the Mexican economy in general and the tourism industry in particular.

Saskia Sassen is the Robert S. Lynd Professor of Sociology and Member, The Committee on Global Thought, Columbia University (http://www.saskiasassen.com). Her new books are *Territory, Authority, Rights: From Medieval to Global Assemblages* (Princeton University Press, 2008) and *A Sociology of Globalization* (W. W. Norton, 2007).

Michael Snodgrass is an Associate Professor of Latin American History and International Studies at Indiana University Purdue University–Indianapolis. He received his doctorate from The University of Texas–Austin. He is the author of *Deference and Defiance in Monterrey: Workers, Paternalism, and Revolution in Mexico, 1890–1950* (Cambridge University Press, 2003; Fondo Editorial Nuevo León, 2009). His articles and essays appear in *Labor: Working-Class History of the Americas*, *Latin American Research Review*, *International Labor and Working-Class History*, as well as in edited volumes on postrevolutionary Mexico, the press and democratization, Latin American labor history, and Mexican immigration. His current research examines emigration policy and the effects of return migration in twentieth century Mexico.

Bibliography

Aboites Aguilar, Luis. *La irrigación revolucionaria. Historia del Sistema Nacional de riego de río Conchos, Chihuahua, 1927–1938*. Mexico: Secretaría de Educación Pública, CIESAS, 1987.

———. *Norte precario. Poblamiento y colonización en México (1760–1940)*. Mexico: El Colegio de México, Centro de Investigaciones y Estudios Superiores en Antropología Social, 1995.

Acome, Tiburcio. "Bacoachi." *Boletín de la Sociedad Mexicana de Geografía y Estadistica*, vol. 2. Mexico: Imprenta de Vicente G. Torres, 1850.

Acuña, Rodolfo. *Occupied America: The Chicano's Struggle toward Liberation*. San Francisco: Canfield Press, 1972.

———. *Occupied America: A History of Chicanos*. 2nd ed. New York: Harper & Row, 1981.

———. *Corridors of Migration: The Odyssey of Mexican Laborers, 1600–1933*. Tucson, AZ: University of Arizona Press, 2008.

———. *Occupied America: A History of Chicanos*. 7th ed. New York: Prentice Hall, 2010.

Adler, Rachel. *Yucatecans in Dallas, Texas: Breaching the Border, Bridging the Distance*. Boston: Pearson, 2004.

Aguila, Jaime R. "Protecting 'México de Afuera': Mexican Emigration Policy, 1876–1928." PhD diss., Arizona State University, 2000.

Aguirre Beltrán, Gonzalo. *La población negra de México: Estudio etnohistórico*. Mexico City: Flodo de Cultura Económica, 1989.

Alanís Enciso, Fernando Saúl. *El Primer Programa Bracero y el Gobierno de México, 1917–1918*. San Luis Potosí: Colegio de San Luis, 1999.

———. "No cuenten conmigo: La política de repatriación del gobierno mexicano y sus nacionales en Estados Unidos, 1910–1928." *Estudios Mexicanos* 19 (2003a): 401–61.

———. "Manuel Gamio: El inicio de las investigaciones sobre la inmigración mexicana a Estados Unidos." *Historia Mexicana* 52 (April–June 2003b): 979–1020.

———. "De factores de inestabilidad nacional a elementos de consolidación del Estado posrevolucionario: Los exiliados mexicanos en Estados Unidos 1929–1933," *Historia Mexicana*, LIV (April–June, 2005): 1155–205.

———. *Que se queden allá. El gobierno de México y la repatriación de mexicanos de Estados Unidos 1934–1940*. México: El Colegio de la Frontera Norte, El Colegio de San Luis, 2007a.

Alanís Enciso, Fernando Saúl. "Cuántos fueron? La repatriación de mexicanos de Estados Unidos durante la Gran Depresión. Una interpretación cuantitativa, 1930–1934." *Aztlán: A Journal of Chicano Studies* 32 (Fall 2007b): 65–91.

Alba, Francisco, and Joseph E. Potter. "Population and Development in Mexico since 1940: An Interpretation." *Population and Development Review* 12 (March 1986): 47–75.

Alba, Richard. "Looking beyond the Moment: American Immigration Seen from Historically and Internationally Comparative Perspectives." In *Border Battles: U.S. Immigration Debates.* Social Science Research Council. http://borderbattles.ssrc.org/Alba/, n.d. (accessed October 10, 2009).

Aleinikoff, Alexander T. *International Legal Norms and Migration: An Analysis.* Geneva: International Organization for Migration, 2002.

Almaguer, Tomas. *Racial Fault Lines: The Historical Origins of White Supremacy in California.* Berkeley: University of California Press, 1994.

Altamirano, Teófilo, and Lane Ryo Hirabayashi, eds. *Migrants, Regional Identities and Latin American Cities.* Washington, D.C.: Society for Latin American Anthropology, American Anthropology Association, 1997.

Alvarez, Robert. "The Mexican–US Border: The Making of an Anthropology of Borderlands." *Annual Review of Anthropology* 24 (1995): 447–70.

Anderson, Henry. *The Bracero Program in California.* Reprint. New York: Arno, 1976a.

———. *Harvest of Loneliness: An Inquiry into a Social Problem,* Berkeley: Citizens for Farm Labor, 1976b.

Anderson, Warren. "P'urépecha Migration into the U.S. Rural Midwest: History and Current Trends," In Jonathan Fox and Gaspar Rivera-Salgado, eds., *Indigenous Mexican Migrants in the United States,* La Jolla: University of California, San Diego, Center for Comparative Immigration Studies/Center for US-Mexican Studies, 2004.

Andreas, Peter. *Border Games: Policing the US–Mexico Divide.* Ithaca, NY: Cornell University Press, 2000.

Ansley, Fran, and Jon Shefner, eds. *Global Connections & Local Receptions: New Latino Immigration to the Southeastern United States.* Knoxville, TN: University of Tennessee Press, 2009.

Anuales del Ministerio de Fomento de la República Mexicana, tomo V. México: Imprenta de Francisco Díaz de León, 1881.

Anzaldúa, Gloria. *Borderlands/La Frontera: The New Mestiza.* San Francisco: Spinsters/Aunt Lute, 1987.

Aparicio, Frances R. *Musical Migrations: Transnationalism and Cultural Hybridity in Latin/o America.* New York: Palgrave Macmillan, 2003.

Appadurai, Arjun. *Modernity at Large: Cultural Dimensions of Globalization.* Minneapolis, MN: University of Minnesota Press, 1996.

Aquino Moreschi, Alejandra. "XXXX *École des hautes études en sciences sociales,"* Sociology Dept. Ph.D. dissertation, 2010.

Arredondo, Gabriela. *Mexican Chicago: Race, Identity and Nation, 1916–1939.* Chicago: University of Illinois Press, 2008.

Astor, Avi. "Unauthorized Immigration, Securitization, and the Making of Operation Wetback." *Latino Studies* 7, no. 2 (2009): 5–29.

Ayon, David. *Mobilizing Latino Immigrant Integration: From IRCA to the Ya es la hora Citizenship Campaign, 1987–2007.* Washington, D.C.: Mexico Institute, Woodrow Wilson Center for Scholars, 2009.

Bacon, David. *Communities without Borders: Images and Voices from the World of Migration.* Ithaca, NY: Cornell University Press, 2006.

————. *Illegal People: How Globalization Creates Migration and Criminalizes Immigrants.* Boston: Beacon Press, 2008.

Baca Zinn, Maxine. "Chicano Family Research: Conceptual Distortions and Alternative Directions." *Journal of Ethnic Studies* 7 (Fall 1979): 59–71.

Bada, Xóchitl. "Clubes de michoacanos oriundos: Desarrollo y membresía social comunitarios." *Migración y Desarrollo* 2 (April 2004): 82–103.

————. "Transnational and Trans-local Sociopolitical Remittances of Mexican Hometown Associations in Michoacán and Illinois." PhD diss., University of Notre Dame, 2008.

Bada, Xóchitl, Jonathan Fox, and Andrew Selee, eds. *Invisible No More: Mexican Migrant Civic Participation in the United States.* Washington, D.C., Mexico: Woodrow Wilson Center, Mexico Institute/University of California, Santa Cruz, Latin American and Latino Studies, 2006.

Baker-Cristales, Beth. "Mediated Resistance: The Construction of Neoliberal Citizenship in the Immigrant Rights Movement." *Latino Studies* 7 (2009): 60–82.

Balderrama, Francisco E., *In Defense of La Raza. The Los Angeles Mexican Consulate and the Mexican Community, 1929–1936,* Tucson, Arizona, The University of Arizona Press, 1982.

Balderrama, Francisco E., and Raymond Rodríguez. *Decade of Betrayal. Mexicans Repatriated in the 1930s.* Albuquerque, NM: University of New Mexico Press, 1995.

Balistreri, Kelly Stamper, and Jennifer Van Hook. "The More Things Change the More They Stay the Same: Mexican Naturalization before and after Welfare Reform." *International Migration Review* 38 (2004): 113–30.

Bailey, Raleigh. "New Immigrant Communities in the North Carolina Piedmont Triad: Integration Issues and Challenges." In *Beyond the Gateway: Immigrants in a Changing America,* edited by Elzbieta Gozdziak and Susan F. Martin, 57–86. Lanham, MD: Lexington Books, 2005.

Bancroft, Hubert H. *The Works of Hubert Howe Bancroft,* vols. 1–39. San Francisco: The History Company, 1886–1890.

————. *Resources and Development of Mexico.* San Francisco: The Bancroft Company, 1893.

Bankston, Carl L. "New People in the New South: An Overview of Southern Immigration." *Southern Cultures* 13, no. 4 (2007): 24–44.

Barcus, Holly R. "New Destinations for Hispanic Migrants: An Analysis of Rural Kentucky." In *Latinos in the South: Transformations of Place,* edited by Owen J. Furuseth and Heather A. Smith, 89–110. Aldershot, UK: Ashgate Press, 2006.

Barkan, E. R. "Return of the Nativists?" *Social Science History* 27 (2003): 229–83.

Barlow, Andrew. *Barlow's Report.* Mexico City, November, 1903.

————. "Emigration to the United States." In *Department of Commerce and Labor, Bureau of Statistics,* vol. 30. Washington, D.C.: Government Printing Office, 1904.

Barrera, Mario. *Race and Class in the Southwest.* Notre Dame, IN: University of Notre Dame Press, 1979.

Barrera Bassols, Dalia, and Cristina Oehmichen Bazán, eds. *Migración y relaciones de género en México.* Mexico City: Gimtrap, A.C.; IIA/UNAM, 2000.

Barron, Clarence. *The Mexican Problem.* Boston: Houghton Mifflin Co., 1917.

Bartra, Roger. "La crisis del nacionalismo en México." *Revista Mexicana de Sociología* 51 (July–September 1989): 191–220.

Batalova, Jeanne. "Mexican Immigrants in the United States." Washington, D.C.: Migration Policy Institute, 2008.

Bean, Frank D., R. Corona, R. Tuiran, K. A. Woodrow-Lafield, and J. Van Hook. "Circular, Invisible, and Ambiguous Migrants: Components of Difference in Estimates of the Number of Unauthorized Mexican Migrants in the United States." *Demography* 38 (2001): 411–22.

Behad, Ali. *A Forgetful Nation: On Immigration and Cultural Identity in the United States.* Durham, NC: Duke University Press, 2005.

Beirich, Heidi. *The Nativist Lobby: Three Faces of Intolerance*, edited by Mark Potok. Montgomery, AL: Southern Poverty Law Center, February 2009.

Belshaw, Michael. *A Village Economy: Land and People of Huecorio.* New York: Columbia University Press, 1967.

Bender, Thomas. *A Nation among Nations: America's Place in World History.* New York: Hill & Wang, 2006.

Benhabib, Seyla. *The Rights of Others: Aliens, Residents and Citizens.* Cambridge, NY: Cambridge University Press, 2004.

Bennett, Herman. *Colonial Blackness: A History of Afro-Mexico.* Bloomington, IN: University of Indiana Press, 2009.

Bensel, Richard Franklin. *The Political Economy of American Industrialization, 1877–1900.* Cambridge: Cambridge University Press, 2000.

Berthoff, Rowland T. "Southern Attitudes toward Immigration, 1865–1914." *The Journal of Southern History* 17 (1951): 328–60.

Besserer, Federico. *Moisés Cruz: Historia de un Transmigrante.* Culiacán: Universidad Autónoma de Sinaloa/Universidad Autónoma Metropolitana, Iztapalapa, 1999a.

———. "Estudios transnacionales y ciudadanía transnacional." In *Fronteras Fragmentadas*, edited by Gail Mummert, 215–38. Zamora, Mexico: Colegio de Michoacán/CIDEM, 1999b.

———. *Topografías transnacionales: Hacia una geografía de las comunidades transnacionales de origen mixteco.* Mexico, Iztapalapa: Universidad Autónoma Metropolitana, Plaza y Valdés, 2004.

———. "Luchas transculturales y conocimiento práctico." In *El país transnacional: Migración mexicana y cambio social a través de la frontera*, edited by Marina Ariza and Alejandro Portes, 323–48. México: UNAM/IIS, 2007.

Besserer, Federico, and Michael Kearney, eds. *San Juan Mixtepec: Una comunidad transnacional ante el poder clasificador y filtrador de las fronteras.* Mexico City: Juan Pablos, Universidad Autónoma Metropolitana, Iztapalapa, University of California at Riverside, 2006.

Bhabha, Homi K., ed. *Nation and Narration.* London: Routledge, 1990.

"Billions for a US–Mexico border fence, but is it doing any good?" *Christian Science Monitor.* September 19, 2009. http://www.csmonitor.com/2009/0919/p02s09-usgn.html (accessed November 10, 2009).

Birns, Larry. "Mexico's Calderón: 'I Did It My Way.'" *Council on Hemispheric Affairs*, May 21, 2010.

Biso, J. Lúcas. "Resumen y explicatorio de los pueblos del partido de Arispe." In *Boletín de la Sociedad Mexicana de Geografía y Estadistica*, vol. 2. México: Imprenta de Vicente G. Torres, 1864.

Blaine to Morgan, *Papers Related to the Foreign Relations of the United States*, 1881.

Blichfelt, E. H. *A Mexican Journey.* New York: Thomas Y. Crowell, 1912.

Boehm, Deborah A. "'Now I Am a Man *and* a Woman!' Gendered Moves and Migrations in a Transnational Mexican Community." *Latin American Perspectives* 35 (2008): 16–30.

Bogardus, Emory. *Essentials of Americanization*. Los Angeles: University of Southern California, 1919.

——. *The Mexican in the United States*. Los Angeles: University of Southern California Press, 1934.

Bolton, Herbert E. *The Spanish Borderlands: A Chronicle of Old Florida and the Southwest*. New Haven, CT: Yale University Press, 1921.

"Bonanzas en la Alta California." In *Boletin de la Sociedad Mexicana de Geografia y Estadistica*, vol. 11. México: Imprenta de A. Boix, 1865.

Boruchoff, Judith. *The Road to Transnationalism: Reconfiguring the Spaces of Community and State in Guerrero, Mexico and Chicago*. Chicago: University of Chicago, Center for Latin American Studies, Working Papers Series, 1999.

The Bracero Archive, http://braceroarchive.org/

Branton, Regina, and Johanna Dunaway. "Spatial Proximity to the U.S.–Mexico Border and Newspaper Coverage of Immigration Issues." *Political Research Quarterly* 62 (June 2009): 289–302.

Brettell, Caroline. *Anthropology and Migration: Essays on Transnationalism, Ethnicity, and Identity*. Walnut Creek, CA: AltaMira Press, 2003.

Brewer, Cynthia A. and Trudy A. Suchan. 2001. "Mapping Census 2000: The Geography of U.S. Diversity." *Census 2000 Special Reports* (CENSR/01–1). Washington, DC: U.S. Department of Commerce, Economics and Statistics Administration, U.S. Census Bureau (June). http://www.census.gov/population/www/cen2000/atlas/pdf/censr01–1.pdf (accessed December 17, 2009).

Bronfenbrenner, Kate. "Uneasy Terrain: The Impact of Capital Mobility on Workers, Wages, and Union Organizing." Washington, D.C.: U.S. Trade Deficit Review Commission, 2000.

Brookings Institution. *A Report on the Media and the Immigration Debate*. Washington, D.C.: Brookings Institution, 2008.

Brownell, Peter. "The Declining Enforcement of Employer Sanctions." Washington, D.C.: Migration Policy Institute, 2005.

——. "Low Pay for Unauthorized Immigrants: 'Superexploitation' or Employers' Risk of Sanctions?" Annual Meeting of the American Sociological Association, Boston, 2008.

Bryan, Samuel. "Mexican Immigrants to the United States." *The Survey* 28, no. 23 (September 7, 1912), 726, 730.

Buchanan, Patrick J. *State of Emergency: The Third World Invasion and Conquest of America*. New York: Thomas Dunne Books, 2006.

Buffington, Robert M. "Subjectivity, Agency, and the New Latin American History of Gender and Sexuality." *History Compass* 5 (July 2007): 1640–660.

Bump, Micah. "From Temporary Picking to Permanent Plucking: Hispanic Newcomers, Integration, and Change in the Shenandoah Valley." In *Beyond the Gateway: Immigrants in a Changing America*, edited by Elzbieta Gozdziak and Susan F. Martin, 137–76. Lanham, MD: Lexington Books, 2005.

Bump, Micah, B. Lindsay Lowell, and Silje Pettersen. "The Growth and Population Characteristics of Immigrants and Minorities in America's New Settlement States." In *Beyond the Gateway: Immigrants in a Changing America*, edited by Elzbieta Gozdziak and Susan F. Martin, 19–53. Lanham, MD: Lexington Books, 2005.

Burke, Garance. "Yucatecos and Chiapanecos in San Francisco: Mayan Immigrants Form New Communities." In *Indigenous Mexican Migrants in the United States*, edited by Jonathan

Fox and Gaspar Rivera-Salgado, 243–54. La Jolla, CA: University of California, San Diego, Center for Comparative Immigration Studies/Center for U.S.–Mexican Studies, 2004.

Bustamante, Jorge A. *Espaldas mojadas: Materia prima para la expansión del capital norteamericano.* México: Centro de Estudios Sociológicos, Colegio de México, 1983.

———. *Cruzar la línea. La migración de México a los Estados Unidos.* México: Fondo de Cultura Económica, 1997.

———. *Migración internacional y derechos humanos.* México, D.F.: Universidad Nacional Autónoma de México, 2002.

———. *Report of the Special Rapporteur on the Human Rights of Migrants, Jorge Bustamante: Addendum.* Geneva: United Nations, March 2, 2007.

———. *Report of the Special Rapporteur on the Human Rights of Migrants: Mission to the United States of America.* Geneva: United Nations, March 5, 2008.

Bustos, Emilo. *Estadística de la república mexicana,* vol. 1. México: Imprenta de Ignacio Cumplido, 1889.

Calavita, Kitty. *Inside the State: The Bracero Program, Immigration, and the I.N.S.* New York: Routledge, 1992.

Callcott, Frank. "The Mexican Peon in Texas." *The Survey* 44 (June 26, 1920): 437.

Camargo Martínez, Abbdel. "Hermanos, paisanos y camaradas: Redes y vínculos social en la migración interna e internacional de los indígenas asentados en el Valle de San Quintín B.C." Master's thesis, Colegio de la Frontera Norte, 2004.

Camarillo, Albert. *Chicanos in a Changing Society: From Mexican Pueblos to American Barrios in Santa Barbara and Southern California, 1848–1930.* Cambridge, MA: Harvard University Press, 1980.

Cano, Arturo. "Los indios sin fronteras." *La Jornada, Masiosare* 380 (April 3, 2005).

Cano, Gustavo, and Alexandra Délano. "The Mexican Government and Organized Mexican Immigrants in the United States: A Historical Analysis of Political Transnationalism (1848–2005)." *Journal of Ethnic and Migration Studies* 33 (2007): 695–725.

Cantú, Lionel. *The Sexuality of Migration,* edited by Nancy Naples and Salvador Vidal-Ortiz. New York: New York University Press, 2009.

Capps, Randy, Everett Henderson, John D. Kasarda, James H. Johnson, Stephen J. Appold, Derrek L. Croney, Donald J. Hernandez, and Michael Fix. "A Profile of Immigrants in Arkansas: Executive Summary." Washington, D.C.: The Winthrop Rockefeller Foundation, 2007.

Cardoso, Lawrence A. "La repatriación de braceros en la época de Obregón 1920–1923." *Historia Mexicana* 26 (April–June 1977): 576–95.

———. *Mexican Emigration to the United States, 1897–1931.* Tucson, AZ: University of Arizona Press, 1980.

Carr, Harry. *Old Mother Mexico.* Boston: Houghton Mifflin, 1931.

Carreras de Velasco, Mercedes. *Los Mexicanos que Devolvió la Crisis 1929–1932.* Tlatelolco, Mexico: Secretaría de Relaciones Exteriores, 1974.

Carrigan, William D., and Clive Webb. "The Lynching of People of Mexican Origin or Descent in the United States, 1848–1928." *Journal of Social History* 37 (2003): 411–38.

Carrillo, Héctor, Jorge Fontdevila, Jaweer Brown, and Walter Gómez. "Risk across Borders: Sexual Contexts and HIV Prevention Challenges among Mexican Gay and Bisexual Immigrant Men. Findings and Recommendations from the Trayectos Study", 2008. http://www.caps.ucsf.edu/projects/Trayectos (accessed June 1, 2009).

Castañeda, Alejandra. *The Politics of Citizenship of Mexican Migrants.* New York: LFB Scholarly Publishing, 2006.

Castañeda, Jorge. *Ex Mex: From Migrants to Immigrants*. New York: The New Press, 2007.

Castañeda, Xóchitl, and Patricia Zavella. "Changing Constructions of Sexuality and Risk: Migrant Mexican Farmworkers in California." In *Women and Migration in the U.S.-Mexico Borderlands: A Reader*, edited by Denise Segura and Patricia Zavella, 249–68. Durham, NC: Duke University Press, 2007.

Castles, Stephen and Mark J. Miller. *The Age of Migration: International Population Movements in the Modern World*. 4th ed. London: Palgrave Macmillan, 2009.

Castellanos, M. Bianet, and Deborah Boehm. "Introduction. Engendering Mexican Migration." *Latin American Perspectives* 35 (2008): 5–15.

Castillo, Manuel Ángel. "Mexico–Guatemala Border: New Controls on Transborder Migration in View of Recent Integration Schemes? *Frontera Norte* 15 (January–June 2003): 35–65.

Cazneau, Jane Maria McManus, and Cora Montgomery. *Eagle Pass or Life on the Border*. Austin, TX: The Pemberton Press, 1966.

Ceballos Ramírez, Manuel, ed. *Encuentro en la frontera: mexicanos y norteamericanos en un espacio común*. Mexico: El Colegio de México, 2001.

Chamberlain, George Agnew. *Is Mexico Worth Saving?* Indianapolis, IN: Bobbs Merrill Co., 1920.

Chau Romero, Robert. *The Dragon in Big Lusong: Chinese Immigration and Settlement in Mexico, 1882–1940*. Tucson, AZ: University of Arizona Press, 2010.

Chavez, Leo R. *Covering Immigration: Popular Images and the Politics of the Nation*. Berkeley: University of California Press, 2001.

——. "A Glass Half Empty: Latina Reproduction and Public Discourse." In *Women and Migration in the U.S.-Mexico Borderlands: A Reader*, edited by Denise A. Segura and Patricia Zavella, 67–91. Durham, NC: Duke University Press, 2007.

——. *The Latino Threat: Constructing Immigrants, Citizens, and the Nation*. Stanford, CA: Stanford University Press, 2008.

Chavez, Xochitl. "Reinventions: Transmigratory Flows of Performative Traditions, the Guelaguetza Festival and the Diosa Centeotl." Presented at the American Anthropological Association, 2007.

Chevalier, M. M. *France, Mexico and the Confederate States*. New York: C. B. Richardson, 1863.

Chicago Daily Tribune, 1894 and 1896.Chishti, Muzaffar, and Claire Bergeron. "Arizona Employer Sanctions Law Takes Effect." Washington, D.C.: Migration Policy Institute, 2008a.

——. "Unauthorized Immigration Declining, But Experts Disagree on Why." Washington, D.C.: Migration Policy Institute, 2008b.

Chinni, Dante. "Is the Fairness Doctrine Fair Game?," http://pewresearch.org/pubs/546/fairness-doctrine, July 19, 2007.

Chomsky, Aviva. *"They Are Taking Our Jobs!": And 20 Other Myths about Immigration*. Boston: Beacon Books, 2007.

Chu, Jeff. 2008. "10 Questions for Pat Buchanan." *Time Magazine*, August 28, p. 6.

Clark, Victor S. "Mexican Labor in the United States." *Bulletin of the Bureau of Labor* 78 (September 1908): 466–522. Reprinted as *Mexican Labor in the United States*. New York: Arno Press, 1974.

Cline, Howard F. *Mexico: Revolution to Evolution, 1940–1960*. New York: Oxford University Press, 1962.

——. *The United States and Mexico*. New York: Atheneum, 1971.

Coatsworth, John H. "Railroads, Landholding, and Rural Protest in the Early Porfiriato." *Hispanic American Historical Review* 54 (February 1974): 48–71.

———. "Obstacles to Economic Growth in Nineteenth-Century Mexico." *American Historical Review* 83 (February 1978): 80–83.

———. *Growth against Development: The Economic Impact of Railroads on Porfirian Mexico*, DeKalb, IL: Northern Illinois University Press, 1981.

Cobb, James C. *The Selling of the South: The Southern Crusade for Industrial Development, 1936–1990*. Baton Rouge, LA: Louisiana State University Press, 1982.

Cobb, James C., and William Stueck, eds. *Globalization and the American South*. Athens, GA: University of Georgia Press, 2005.

Cobb, Wilbur K. "Retardation in Elementary Schools of Children of Migratory Laborers in Ventura County, California." Master's thesis, University of Southern California, 1932.

Cohen, Deborah J. "Caught in the Middle: the Mexican State's Relationship with the United States and Its Own Citizen-Workers, 1942–1954." *Journal of American Ethnic History* 20 (2001): 110–132.

———. "From Peasant to Worker: Migration, Masculinity, and the Making of Mexican Workers in the US." *International Labor and Working-Class History* 69 (2006): 81–103.

Cohen, Jeffrey. *The Culture of Migration in Southern Mexico*. Austin, TX: University of Texas, 2004.

CONAPO (National Population Council of Mexico) http://www.conapo.gob.mx/index. php?option=com_content&view=article&id=323&Itemid=251 (accessed September 24, 2009).

Conley, Edward. "The Americanization of Mexico." *American Monthly Review of Reviews* 32 (1907).

Constantakis-Valdes, Patricia. "Univision and Telemundo on the Campaign Trail: 1988." In *The Mass Media and Latino Politics: Studies of U.S. Media Content, Campaign Strategies and Survey Research, 1984–2004*, edited by Federico A. Subervi-Velez. New York: Routledge, 2008.

Coonan, Terry. "Dolphins Caught in Congressional Fishnets—Immigration Law's New Aggravated Felons." *Georgetown Immigration Law Journal* 12 (1998): 589–619.

Córdova Plaza, Rosío. "Sexuality and Gender in Transnational Spaces: Realignments in Rural Veracruz Families due to International Migration." *Social Text* 25 (Fall 2007a): 38–55.

———. "Vicisitudes de la intimidad: Familia y relaciones de género en un contexto de migración acelerada en una comunidad rural de Veracruz." In *In God We Trust: del campo mexicano al sueño americano*, edited by Córdova Plaza, Rosío, María Cristina Núñez Madrazo, and David Skerritt Gardner, 219–38. Veracruz: Universidad de Veracruz, Plaza y Valdés, 2007b.

Cornelius, Wayne A. "Death at the Border: Efficacy and Unintended Consequences of US Immigration Control Policy." *Population and Development Review* 27 (2001): 661–85.

———. "Evaluating Enhanced US Border Enforcement." May 2004. http://www.migrationinformation.org/feature/display.cfm?ID=223 (accessed July 13, 2009a).

———. "Billions for a U.S.–Mexico Border Fence, but Is It Doing Any Good?" *Christian Science Monitor*, September 19, 2009b.

Cornelius, Wayne A., and Jorge A. Bustamante. *Mexican Migration to the United States: Origins, Consequences, and Policy Options*. San Diego, CA: Center for U.S.–Mexican Studies, University of California, San Diego, 1989.

Cornelius, Wayne, David FitzGerald and Pedro Lewin Fischer, eds. *Mayan Journeys: the New Migration from Yucatan to the United States*, La Jolla: UC San Diego, Center for US-Mexican Studies, 2007.

Cornelius, Wayne A., David FitzGerald, and Scott Borger, eds. *Four Generations of Norteños: New Research from the Cradle of Mexican Migration.* La Jolla, CA, and Boulder, CO: CCIS and Lynne Rienner Publishers, 2009.

Cornelius, Wayne A., David FitzGerald, Jorge Hernández Díaz, and Scott Borger, eds. *Migration from the Mexican Mixteca.* La Jolla, CA, and Boulder, CO: CCIS and Lynne Rienner Publishers, 2009.

Cornelius, Wayne A., David FitzGerald, and Pedro Lewin Fischer, eds. *Mayan Journeys: The New Migration from Yucatán to the United States.* La Jolla, CA, and Boulder, CO: CCIS and Lynne Rienner Publishers, 2007.

Cornelius, Wayne A., and Jessa M. Lewis, eds. *Impacts of Border Enforcement on Mexican Migration: The View from Sending Communities.* La Jolla, CA: Center for Comparative Immigration Studies, University of California at San Diego, 2007.

Cornelius, Wayne A., David FitzGerald, Jorge Hernández Díaz, and Scott Borger, eds. *Migration from the Mexican Mixteca.* La Jolla, CA and Boulder, CO: CCIS and Lynne Rienner Publishers, 2010.

Corwin, Arthur F. "Mexican Emigration History, 1900–1970: Literature and Research." *Latin American Research Review* 8 (Summer 1973): 3–24.

——. "Mexican Policy and Ambivalence toward Labor Emigration to the United States." In *Immigrants and Immigrants: Perspectives on Mexican Labor Migration to the United States,* edited by Arthur F. Corwin, 176–219. Westport, CT: Greenwood Press, 1978.

——. "The Numbers Game: Estimates of Illegal Aliens in the United States, 1970–1981." *Law and Contemporary Problems* 45 (Spring 1982): 223–97.

Cotter, Joseph. *Troubled Harvest: Agronomy and Revolution in Mexico, 1880–2002.* Westport, CT: Praeger, 2003.

Coutin, Susan Bibler. "From Refugees to Immigrants: The Legalization Strategies of Salvadoran Immigrants and Activists." *International Migration Review* 32 (1998): 901–25.

Craib, Raymond, and Mark Overmyer-Velázquez. "Migration and Labor in the Americas: Praxis, Knowledge, and Nations." *Hispanic American Historical Review,* forthcoming.

Craig, Richard. *The Bracero Program: Interest Groups and Foreign Policy.* Austin, TX: University of Texas Press, 1971.

Cravey, Altha J. "The Changing South: Latino Labor and Poultry Production in Rural North Carolina." *Southeastern Geographer* 37 (1997): 295–300.

Creagan, James. "Public Law 78: A Tangle of Domestic and International Relations." *Journal of Inter-American Studies* 7 (1965): 541–56.

Creelman, James. *Diaz, Master of Mexico.* New York: D. Appleton and Co., 1911.

Cross, Harry E., and James A. Sandos. *Across the Border; Rural Development in Mexico and Recent Migration to the United States.* Berkeley: Institute of Governmental Studies, 1981.

Cruz, Rodrigo Alonso. "Lamentan el mínimo impacto que tendrá el voto foráneo." *Cambio de Michoacán,* November 9, 2007.

Dale, Jack G., Susan Andreatta, and Elizabeth Freeman. "Language and the Migrant Worker Experience in Rural North Carolina Communities." In *Latino Workers in the Contemporary South,* edited by Arthur D. Murphy, Colleen Blanchard, and Jennifer A. Hill, 93–104. Athens, GA: University of Georgia Press, 2001.

Daniel, Cletus E. *Bitter Harvest: A History of California Farmworkers, 1870–1941.* Berkeley: University of California Press, 1982.

Dauvergne, Catherine. *Making People Illegal. What Globalization Means for Migration and Law.* Cambridge, NY: Cambridge University Press, 2008.

Davila, Arlene. *Latinos, Inc.: The Marketing and Making of a People.* Berkeley: University of California Press, 2001.

———. *Latino Spin: Public Image and the Whitewashing of Race.* New York: New York University Press, 2008.

Davíla, F. T. *Sonora histórico y descriptivo, reseña histórica de los sucesos muy importantes acaecidos en Sonora desde la llegada de los españoles hasta nuestros días.* Nogales, AZ: Tipografía de R. Bernal, 1894.

De Armond, Michelle. "Tribe: Some 400 Members Are Trying to Stop an Effort to Remove Them from the Group." *Bay Area Indian Calendar, February 25, 2003.*

Decena, Carlos Ulises, Michele S. Sheridan, and Angela Martínez. "'Los hombres no mandan aquí': Narrating Immigrant Genders and Sexualities in New York." *Social Text 24 (Fall 2006): 35–54.*

De Genova, Nicolas. "Migrant 'Illegality' and Deportability in Everyday Life." *Annual Review of Anthropology 31 (2002): 419–47.*

———. "The Legal Production of Mexican/Migrant 'Illegality.'" *Latino Studies* 2 (2004): 160–85.

———. *Working the Boundaries: Race, Space and "Illegality" in Mexican Chicago.* Durham, NC: Duke University, 2005.

———. "Introduction: Latino and Asian Racial Formations at the Frontiers of U.S. Nationalism." In *Racial Transformations: Latinos and Asians Remaking the United States,* edited by Nicholas De Genova, 1–20. Durham, NC: Duke University Press, 2006.

De Genova, Nicolas, and Ana Y. Ramos-Zayas. *Latino Crossings: Mexicans, Puerto Ricans and the Politics of Race and Citizenship.* New York: Routledge, 2003.

De Grazia, Victoria. *Irresistible Empire: America's Advance through 20th Century Europe.* Cambridge, MA: Belknap Press, 2005.

De la Garza, Rodolfo O., Harry Pachon, Manuel Orozco, and Adrián D. Pantoja. "Family Ties and Ethnic Lobbies." In *Latinos and U.S. Foreign Policy: Representing the "Homeland,"* edited by Rodolfo O. de la Garza and Harry Pachon, 43–101. Lanham, MD: Rowman & Littlefield, 2000.

De la Garza, Rodolfo O., and Gabriel Szekely. "Policy, Politics and Emigration." In At the *Crossroads: Mexican Migration and U.S. Policy,* edited by Frank D. Bean, Rodolfo O. de la Garza, Bryan R. Roberts, and Sidney Weintraub, 201–25. Lanham, MD: Rowman & Littlefield, 1997.

De León, Arnoldo. *The Tejano Community, 1836–1900.* Albuquerque, NM: University of New Mexico Press, 1982.

De León, Arnoldo, and Kenneth L. Stewart. *Not Room Enough: Mexicans, Anglos, and Socio-Economic Change in Texas, 1850–1900.* Albuquerque, NM: University of New Mexico Press, 1993.

Department of Economic and Social Affairs. World Economic and Social Survey 2004: International Migration. New York: United Nations Publication, 2004.

Department of Homeland Security. "Annual Report: Immigration Enforcement Actions: 2007." Washington, D.C.: Department of Homeland Security, 2008a.

———. "Yearbook of Immigration Statistics: 2007." Washington, D.C.: Department of Homeland Security, Office of Immigration Statistics, 2008b.

———. "Annual Flow Report: U.S. Legal Permanent Residents: 2007." Washington, D.C.: Department of Homeland Security, Office of Immigration Statistics, 2008c.

———. "Budget-in-Brief: Fiscal Year 2009." Washington, D.C.: Department of Homeland Security, 2009a.

———. "Population Estimates: Estimates of the Unauthorized Immigration Population Residing in the United States: January 2008." Washington, D.C.: Department of Homeland Security, Office of Immigration Statistics, 2009b.

———. "Supplemental Brief, in the Matter of [redacted and unreadable]." http://graphics8.nytimes.com/packages/pdf/us/20090716-asylum-brief.pdf, n.d. (accessed August 1, 2009).

Department of Homeland Security/Immigration and Naturalization Services Annual Yearbooks, 1980–2007.

Department of State (2006). "Visa Bulletin for April 2006." No. 92: vol. viii. Washington, DC.

Deutsch, Sarah. *No Separate Refugee: Culture, Class, and Gender on an Anglo-Hispanic Frontier, 1880–1940.* New York: Oxford University Press, 1987.

De Zavala, Lorenzo. *Ensayo histórico de las revoluciones de méxico: Desde 1808 Hasta 1830.* Paris: Imprenta de P. Dupont et G.-Laguionie, 1831.

Diaz, May. *Tonalá: Conservatism, Responsibility, and Authority in a Mexican Town.* Berkeley: University of California Press, 1966.

Dickinson, Tim. "Blame Pedro," http://www.rollingstone.com/politics/story/18072935/blame_pedro, February 7, 2008.

Diplomatic and Consular Reports. *Mexico: Report on the Trade and Agriculture of the State of Sonora.* London: Harrison and Sons, 1900.

"Dispoción del 13 de Febrero de 1856" in *Código de colonización y terrenos baldíos de la república mexicana, formulado por Francisco F. de la Maza.* México: Oficina Tip. De la Secretaría de Fomento, 1893.

Dobbs, Lou. *War on the Middle Class: How the Government, Big Business, and Special Interest Groups Are Waging War on the American Dream and How to Fight Back.* New York: Viking, 2006.

Docquier, Frédéric, and Abdeslam Marfouk. "International Migration by Education Attainment, 1990–2005." In *Migration, Remittances and the Brain Drain,* edited by C. Ozden and M. Schiff. Washington, D.C.: World Bank, 2005.

Dolny, Michael. "What's in a Label?" *Fairness & Accuracy in Reporting.* May/June 1998.

Domínguez Santos, Rufino. "The FIOB Experience, Internal Crisis and Future Challenges. In *Indigenous Mexican Migrants in the United States,* edited by Jonathan Fox and Gaspar Rivera-Salgado, 69–80. La Jolla, CA: University of California, San Diego, Center for Comparative Immigration Studies/Center for U.S.–Mexican Studies, 2004a.

———. "Migración y organización de los indígenas oaxaquenos." In *La Ruta Mixteca,* edited by Sylvia Escárcega and Stefano Varese, 77–94. Mexico City: Universidad Nacional Autónoma de México, 2004b.

———. "Los primeros Ñuu Savi en los Estados Unidos." *El Tequio: Nueva época* 4 (2008): 16–17.

Donato, Katharine M., Carl L. Bankston, and Dawn T. Robinson. "Immigration and the Organization of the Onshore Oil Industry: Southern Louisiana in the Late 1990s." In *Latino Workers in the Contemporary South,* edited by Arthur D. Murphy, Colleen Blanchard, and Jennifer A. Hill, 105–13. Athens, GA: University of Georgia Press, 2001.

Donato, Katharine, Donna Gabaccia, Jennifer Holdaway, Martin Manalansan IV, and Patricia Pessar, "A Glass Half Full? Gender in Migration Studies," *International Migration Review* 40:1, 3–26, 2006.

Donato, Katharine M., Melissa Stainback, and Carl L. Bankston. "The Economic Incorporation of Mexican Immigrants in Southern Louisiana: A Tale of Two Cities." In *New Destinations: Mexican Immigration to the United States,* edited by Victor Zúñiga and Rubén Hernández-León, 76–100. New York: Russell Sage, 2005.

Donato, Katharine M., Charles M. Tolbert, Alfred Nucci, and Yukio Kawano. "Changing Faces/ Changing Places: The Emergence of Non-Metropolitan Immigrant Gateways." In *New Faces in New Places: The Changing Geography of American Immigration*, edited by Douglas S. Massey, 75–98. New York: Russell Sage, 2008.

Dreby, Joanna, *Divided by Borders: Mexican Migrants and Their Children*. Berkeley: University of California Press, 2010.

Driscoll, Barbara. *The Tracks North: The Railroad Bracero Program of World War II*. Austin, TX: Center for Mexican American Studies, 1999.

Duggan, Lisa. *The Twilight of Equality? Neoliberalism, Cultural Politics, and the Attack on Democracy*. Boston: Beacon Press, 2003.

Dunn, Timothy J. *The Militarization of the U.S.–Mexico Border, 1978–1992: Low-Intensity Conflict Doctrine Comes Home*. Austin, TX: Center for Mexican American Studies, University of Texas at Austin, 1996.

Dunn, Timothy J., Ana María Aragonés, and George Shivers. "Recent Mexican Immigration in the Rural Delmarva Peninsula: Human Rights versus Citizenship Rights in a Local Context." In *New Destinations: Mexican Immigration to the United States*, edited by Victor Zúñiga and Rubén Hernández-León, 155–83. New York: Russell Sage, 2005.

Durand, Jorge. "Los migradólares: Cien años de inversión en el medio rural." *Argumentos: Estudios Críticos de la Sociedad* 5 (1988): 7–21.

——, ed. *Migración México–Estados Unidos. Años veinte*. México, D.F.: Consejo Nacional para la Cultura y las Artes, 1991.

——. "Los Migradolares: Cien años de inversión en el medio rural." In *Estados Unidos y el occidente de México. Estudios sobre su interacción*, edited by Adrián León Arias, 55–72. Guadalajara: Universidad de Guadalajara, 1992.

——. "From Traitors to Heroes: 100 Years of Mexican Migration Policies." *Migration Information Source*, March 1, 2004. http://www.migrationinformation.org/Feature/display.cfm?ID=203 (accessed June 1, 2009).

——. "De traidores a héroes." In *Contribuciones al análisis de la migración internacional y el desarrollo regional en México*, edited by Raúl Delgado Wise and Beatrice Knerr, 15–38. México: Universidad Autónoma de Zacatecas-Miguel Ángel Porrúa, 2005.

——. "Un acuerdo bilateral o un convenio obrero patronal?" In *Braceros: Las miradas mexicana y estadounidense*, edited by Jorge Durand, 11–29. México: Universidad Autónoma de Zacatecas, 2007.

Durand, Jorge, and Paricia Arias. *La Experiencia Migrante: Iconografía de la Migración México–Estados Unidos*. México, D.F.: Altexto, 2000.

Durand, Jorge, and Douglas S. Massey. "Mexican Migration to the United States: A Critical Review." *Latin American Research Review* 27, no. 2 (1992): 3–42.

——. "The Costs of Contradiction: US Border Policy 1986–2000." *Latino Studies* 1 (2003): 233–52.

Durand, Jorge, Douglas S. Massey, and Chiara Capoferro. "The New Geography of Mexican Immigration." In *New Destinations: Mexican Immigration to the United States*, edited by Victor Zúñiga and Rubén Hernández-León, 1–20. New York: Russell Sage, 2005.

Durand, Jorge, Douglas S. Massey, and Fernando Charvet. "The Changing Geography of Mexican Immigration to the United States: 1910–1996." *Social Science Quarterly* 81 (March 2000): 1–15.

Durand, Jorge, Emilio Parrado, William Kandel, and Douglas S. Massey. "International Migration and Development in Mexican Sending Communities." *Demography* 33 (1996): 249–64.

Durón González, Gustavo. *Problemas migratorios de Mexico: Apuntamientos para su resolución.* México: Talleres de la Cámara de Diputados, 1925.

Eckes, Alfred E. "The South and Economic Globalization, 1950 to the Future." In *Globalization and the American South,* edited by James C. Cobb and William Stueck, 36–55. Athens, GA: University of Georgia Press, 2005.

Edinger, Steven T. *The Road from Mixtepec: A Southern Mexican Town and the United States Economy.* Fresno, CA: Asociación Cívica Benito Juárez, 1985.

Ejército Zapatista de Liberación Nacional. *La marcha del color de la tierra: Comunicados, carts y mensaje del Ejército Zapatista de Liberación Nacional, del 2 de diciembre del 200 al 2 de abril, del 2001.* Mexico City: Rizoma, 2001.

El Nuevo Mundo, October 10, 1907.

El Trueno, October 23, 1904.

Elliott, James R., and Marcel Ionescu. "Postwar Immigration to the Deep South Triad: What Can a Peripheral Region Tell Us About Immigrant Settlement and Employment?" *Sociological Spectrum* 23, no. 2 (2003): 159–80.

Ellis, Andrew, ed. *Voting from Abroad: The International IDEA Handbook.* Stockholm: International Institute for Democracy and Electoral Assistance, 2007.

Emery, Marla R., Clare Ginger, and Jim Chamberlain. "Migrants, Markets, and the Transformation of Natural Resources Management: Galax Harvesting in Western North Carolina." In *Latinos in the South: Transformations of Place,* edited by Heather A. Smith and Owen J. Furuseth, 69–88. Aldershot, UK: Ashgate Press, 2006.

Engstrom, James. "Industry and Immigration in Dalton, Georgia." In *Latino Workers in the Contemporary South,* edited by Arthur D. Murphy, Colleen Blanchard, and Jennifer A. Hill, 44–56. Athens, GA: University of Georgia Press, 2001.

Escárcega, Sylvia. "Las políticas de identidad entre migrantes jovenes mexicanos en California." In *La Ruta Mixteca: El impacto etnopolítico de la migración transnacional en los pueblos indígenas de México,* edited by Sylvia Escárcega and Stefano Varese, 315–47. Mexico City: UNAM, 2004.

———. "Indigenous Migration from Oaxaca: New Conceptual and Methodological Contributions." *Latin American and Caribbean Ethnic Studies* 4 (2008): 93–100.

Escárcega, Sylvia, and Stefano Varese, eds. *La Ruta Mixteca.* Mexico City: Universidad Nacional Autónoma de México, 2004.

Escobar Latapí, Agustín, and Susan Forbes Martin, *Mexico–U.S. Migration Management: A Binational Approach,* Lanham: Lexington Books, 2008.

Fábila, Alfonso. *El problema de la emigración de obreros y campesinos mexicanos.* México: Talleres Gráficos de la Nación, 1929.

Fagen, W. Patricia. *Transterrados y ciudadanos. Los republicanos españoles en México.* México, Fondo de Cultura Económica, 1973.

Falcón, Sylvanna. "Rape as a Weapon of War: Militarized Rape in the U.S.-Mexico Border," in Denise Segura and Patricia Zavella, eds., *Women and Migration in the U.S.-Mexico Borderlands.* Durham: Duke University Press, 203–223, 2007.

Fanella, Antonella. *With Heart and Soul: Calgary's Italian Community.* Calgary: University of Calgary Press, 1999.

Farr, Marcia. *Rancheros in Chicagoacán: Language and Identity in a Transnational Community.* Austin, TX: University of Texas Press, 2006.

Federal Bureau of Investigation. "Uniform Crime Reports, Hate Crime Statistics." http://www.fbi.gov/ucr/ucr.htm#hate (accessed August 1, 2009).

Federation for American Immigration Reform. *Anchor Babies: Part of the Immigration-related American Lexicon.* April 2008.

Felix, Adrian, Carmen Gonzalez, and Ricardo Ramirez. "Political Protest, Ethnic Media, and Latino Naturalization." *American Behavioral Scientist* 52 (2008): 618–34.

Fennelly, Katherine. "Prejudice Toward Immigrants in the Midwest." Pp. 151–78 in *New Faces in New Places: The Changing Geography of American Immigration,* edited by Douglas S. Massey. New York: Russell Sage, 2008.

Ferguson, Niall. *Colossus: The Rise and Fall of the American Empire.* New York: Penguin, 2004.

Fernandes, Deepa. *Targeted: Homeland Security and the Business of Immigration.* New York: Seven Stories Press, 2007.

Fernández-Kelly, María Patricia. *For We Are Sold, I and My People: Women and Industry in Mexico's Frontier.* Albany, NY: State University of New York Press, 1983.

Fink, Leon. *The Maya of Morganon: Work and Community in the Nuevo New South.* Chapel Hill, NC: University of North Carolina Press, 2003.

Fischer, Mary J., and Marta Tienda. "Redrawing Spatial Color Lines: Hispanic Metropolitan Dispersal, Segregation, and Economic Opportunity." In *Hispanics and the Future of America,* 100–37. Washington, D.C.: National Academies Press, 2006.

FitzGerald, David. *Negotiating Extra-Territorial Citizenship: Mexican Migration and the Transnational Politics of Community.* La Jolla, CA: University of California at San Diego, Center for Comparative Immigration Studies, 2000.

———. "Beyond 'Transnationalism': Mexican Hometown Politics at an American Labor Union." *Ethnic and Racial Studies* 27 (March 2004): 228–47.

———. "Nationality and Migration in Modern Mexico." *Journal of Ethnic and Migration Studies* 31 (2005): 171–91.

———. "Inside the Sending State: The Politics of Mexican Emigration Control." *International Migration Review* 40 (Summer 2006a): 259–93.

———. "Rethinking Emigrant Citizenship." *New York University Law Review* 81 (2006b): 90–116.

———. *A Nation of Emigrants: How Mexico Manages Its Migration.* Berkeley: University of California Press, 2009.

FitzGerald, David Scott, Rafael Alarcón Acosta, and Leah Muse-Orlinoff, eds. *Recession without Borders: Mexican Migrants Confront the Economic Downturn.* La Jolla, CA, and Boulder, CO: CCIS and Lynne Rienner Publishers, forthcoming.

Fix, Jeffrey and Wendy Zimmerman. "All Under One Roof: Mixed Status Families in an Era of Reform," *IMR* 34:2 (Summer), 397–419, 2001.

Flores, William V., and Rina Benmayor. "Constructing Cultural Citizenship." In *Latino Cultural Citizenship: Claiming Identity, Space, and Rights,* edited by William V. Flores and Rina Benmayor, 1–23. Boston: Beacon Press, 1997.

Florescano, Enrique. *Etnía, estado y nación: Ensayo sobre las identidades colectivas en México.* Mexico: Taurus, 1996.

———. *Historia de las historias de la nación mexicana.* Mexico City: Taurus, 2002.

———. *National Narratives in Mexico: A History.* Norman, OK: University of Oklahoma Press, 2006.

Foley, Neil. *White Scourge: Mexicans, Blacks and Poor Whites in Texas Cotton Culture.* Berkeley: University of California Press, 1997.

Foster, George. *Tzintzuntzan: Mexican Peasants in a Changing World.* Boston: Little, Brown, 1967.

Foucault, Michel, "Governmentality," in Graham Burchell, Colin Gordon, and Peter Miller, eds., *The Foucault Effect*. Chicago: University of Chicago Press, 87–104, 1991.

Fox, Claire. *The Fence and the River: Culture and Politics at the US–Mexico Border*. Minneapolis, MN: University of Minnesota Press, 1999.

Fox, Jonathan. "The Difficult Transition from Clientelism to Citizenship: Lessons from Mexico." *World Politics* 46 (January 1994): 151–84.

———. "How Does Civil Society Thicken? The Political Construction of Social Capital in Rural Mexico." *World Development* 24 (June 24, 1996): 1089–104.

———. "Indigenous Mexican Civil Society in the United States." Presented at Latin American Studies Association, Las Vegas, Nevada, October 2004.

———. "Unpacking 'Transnational Citizenship.'" *Annual Review of Political Science* 8 (June 2005): 171–201.

———. "Reframing Mexican Migration as a Multi-Ethnic Process." *Latino Studies* 4 (2006): 39–61.

———. *Accountability Politics: Power and Voice in Rural Mexico*. Oxford, UK: Oxford University Press, 2007.

Fox, Jonathan, and Xóchitl Bada. "Migrant Organization and Hometown Impacts in Rural Mexico." *Journal of Agrarian Change* 8 (April and July 2008): 435–61.

———. "Migrant Civic Engagement," in Irene Bloomraad and Kim Voss, eds., *Rallying for Immigrant Rights*, Berkeley: University of California Press, 2009.

———. "Migrant Civic Engagement." In *Rallying for Immigrant Rights,* edited by Irene Bloomraad and Kim Voss. Berkeley: University of California Press, 2011.

Fox, Jonathan, and Gaspar Rivera-Salgado. "Building Civil Society among Indigenous Migrants." In *Indigenous Mexican Migrants in the United States*, edited by Jonathan Fox and Gaspar Rivera-Salgado, 1–65. La Jolla, CA: University of California at San Diego, Center for Comparative Immigration Studies/Center for U.S.–Mexican Studies, 2004.

Fregoso, Rosa Linda. "Toward A Planetary Civil Society." In *Women and Migration in the U.S.–Mexico Borderlands: A Reader*, edited by Denise Segura and Patricia Zavella, 35–66. Durham, NC: Duke University Press, 2007.

Freithaler, William O. *Mexico's Foreign Trade and Economic Development*. New York: Praeger, 1968.

Frey, William H. "Census 2000 Shows Large Black Return to the South, Reinforcing the Region's 'White–Black' Demographic Profile." In *Population Studies Center Research Report*, no. 01–473. Ann Arbor, MI: Institute for Social Research, University of Michigan, May 2001.

———. "The New Great Migration: Black Americans' Return to the South, 1965–2000." Living Cities Census Series. Washington, D.C.: Brookings Institution, Center on Urban and Metropolitan Policy, May 2004.

Friedrich, Paul. *Agrarian Rebellion in a Mexican Village*. Chicago: University of Chicago Press, 1977.

Gabaccia, Donna R. "Is Everywhere Nowhere? Nomads, Nations, and the Immigrant Paradigm of United States History." *The Journal of American History* 86 (December 1999): 1115–34.

Gabbard, Susan, Edward Kissam, James Glasnapp, Jorge Nakamoto, Russell Saltz, and Daniel Carroll. "Identifying Indigenous Mexican and Central American Immigrants in Survey Research." Presented at the American Association for Public Opinion Research, May 2008.

Galarza, Ernesto. *Merchants of Labor: The Mexican Bracero Story, an Account of the Managed Migration of Mexican Farm Workers in California, 1942–1960*. Charlotte, NC: McNally and Loftin, 1964.

Galvez, Alyshia. *Guadalupe in New York: Devotion and the Struggle for Citizenship Rights among Mexican Immigrants*, New York, NYU Press, 2009.

Gamboa, Erasmo. *Mexican Labor and World War II: Braceros in the Pacific Northwest, 1942–1947*. Austin, TX: University of Texas Press, 1990.

Gamio, Manuel. *Mexican Immigration to the United States: A Study of Human Migration and Adjustment*. Chicago: University of Chicago Press, 1930.

Gans, Herbert. "The Possibility of a New Racial Hierarchy in the Twenty-First-Century United States." In *The Cultural Territories of Race: Black and White Boundaries*, edited by Michéle Lamont, 371–89. Chicago and New York: University of Chicago Press and Russell Sage, 1999.

García, Crescendio. "Producciones utilísimas en los confines de los estados de Michoacán y Jalisco, que pueden ser fácilmente explotados." *Boletín de la Sociedad de Geografía y Estadística de la República Mexicana*, 2nd ed., vol. 4. México: Imprenta de Gobierno en Palacio, 1872.

Garcia, Mario T. *Desert Immigrants: The Mexicans of El Paso, 1880–1920*. New Haven, CT: Yale University Press, 1981.

Garcia, Matthew. *A World of Its Own: Race, Labor, and Citrus in the Making of Greater Los Angeles, 1900–1970*. Chapel Hill, NC: University of North Carolina Press, 2002.

García Leyva, Jaime. "Por los caminos del sur indígena." *Ojarasca (La Jornada)*, 79 (November 2003).

García Ortega, Martha. "Nómadas, viajeros y migrantes: La comunidad sin límites de la región Nahua del Alto Balsas, Guerrero." Master's thesis, Escuela Nacional de Antropología e Historia, 2002.

———. "Rituales de paso y categorías sociales en la migración internacional nahua del Alto Balsas, Guerrero." *Cuicuilco* 15 (January–April 2008a): 77–96.

———. "Nahuas en Estados Unidos. Capitales migratorias de una región indígena del sur de México." In *La migración y los latinos en Estados Unidos: Visiones y conexiones*, edited by Elaine Levine, 75–91. Mexico, CISAN/UNAM, 2008b.

García y Griego, Manuel. "The Importation of Mexican Contract Laborers to the United States, 1942–1964: Antecedents, Operation, and Legacy." In *The Border That Joins: Mexican Migrants and U.S. Responsibility*, edited by Peter G. Brown and Henry Shue, 49–98. Totowa, NJ: Rowman & Littlefield, 1983.

Garcilazo, Jeffrey. "Traqueros: Mexican Railroad Workers in the United States, 1871 to 1930," PhD diss., University of California, Santa Barbara, 1995.

Garroutte. Eva Marie. *Real Indians: Identity and the Survival of Native America*. Berkeley: University of California, 2003.

"Gen. Foster on Mexico," *National Geographic* 12 (1901): 159.

Gil Martínez de Escobar, Rocío. *Fronteras de Pertenencia. Hacia la construcción del bienestar y el desarrollo comunitario transnacional de Santa María Tindú, Oaxaca*. Mexico: UAM, Juan Pablos, 2006.

Gilbert, James A. *A Field Study in Mexico of Mexican Repatriation Movement*. Unpublished Master's thesis, University of Southern California, 1934.

Gilboy, Janet. "Deciding Who Gets In: Decisionmaking by Immigration Inspectors." *Law and Society Review* 25 (1991): 571–99.

Glaberson, William. "Who Is a Seminole, and Who Gets to Decide?" *New York Times*, January 29, 2001.

Glenn, Evelyn Nakano. *Unequal Freedom: How Race and Gender Shaped American Citizenship and Labor*. Cambridge, MA: Harvard University Press, 2002.

Godoy, S. Mara Pérez. "Social Movements and International Migration: The Mexican Diaspora Seeks Inclusion in Mexico's Political Affairs, 1968–1998." PhD diss., University of Chicago, 1998.

Gómez Izquierdo, José Jorge. *El movimiento antichino en México, 1871–1934. Problemas del racismo y del nacionalismo durante la Revolución Mexicana.* Mexico: Consejo Nacional para la Cultura y la Artes, Instituto Nacional de Antropología e Historia, 1991.

Gómez-Quiñones, Juan. "Notes on an Interpretation of the Relations between the Mexican Community in the United States and Mexico." In *Mexican–U.S. Relations: Conflict and Convergence*, edited by Carlos Vásquez and Manuel García y Greigo, 417–39. Los Angeles: UCLA Chicano Studies Research Center Publications, 1983.

Gonzales, Alfonso. "The 2006 Mega Marchas in Greater Los Angeles: Counter-Hegemonic Moment and the Future of El Migrante Struggle." *Latino Studies* 7 (2009): 30–59.

González, Gilbert G. *Mexican Consuls and Labor Organizing: Imperial Politics in the American Southwest.* Austin, TX: University of Texas Press, 1999.

———. *Culture of Empire: American Writers, Mexico, and Mexican Immigrants, 1880–1930.* Austin, TX: University of Texas Press, 2004a.

———. "El amigo ambivalente de los trabajadores?: Los cónsules mexicanos y las huelgas agrícolas californianas de 1933 y 1934" in Alanís Enciso, Fernando Saúl (coord.), *Labor consular mexicana en Estados Unidos. Siglos XIX y XX. Cinco ensayos históricos*, 173–6. México, Senado de la República, 2004b.

———. *Guest Workers or Colonized Labor? Mexican Labor Migration to the United States.* New York: Paradigm, 2005.

González, Gilbert G., and Raúl A. Fernández. *A Century of Chicano History: Empire, Nations, and Migration.* New York: Routledge, 2003.

González, Juan. *Harvest of Empire: A History of Latinos in America.* New York: Penguin, 2001.

González, Luis. *San Jose de Gracia: Mexican Village in Transition.* Austin, TX: University of Texas Press, 1974.

González-López, Gloria. *Erotic Journeys. Mexican Immigrants and Their Sex Lives.* Berkeley: University of California, 2005.

González-López, Gloria, and Salvador Vidal Ortiz. "Latinas and Latinos, Sexuality, and Society: A Critical Sociological Perspective." In *Latinos/as in the United States: Changing the Face of América*, edited by Havidán Rodríguez, Rogelio Sáenz, and Cecilia Menjívar, 308–22. New York: Springer, 2008.

González Navarro, Moisés. "Los braceros en el porfiriato." *Estudios sociológicos* 5 (1954): 261–80.

———. *Historia Moderna de Mexico, El Porfiriato*, vol. 4. Mexico City: Editorial Hermes, 1957.

———. *La colonización en México.* Mexico: Talleres de Impresión de Estampillas y Valores, 1960.

———. "Los efectos de la crisis de 1929, en *Historia Mexicana*, México, El Colegio de México, vol. XIX, núm., 4, 1970, pp. 536–558.

———. *Población y sociedad en México, 1900–1970.* México: El Colegio de México, 1974.

———. *Los Extranjeros en México y los Mexicanos en el Extranjero, 1821–1970*, vol. 3. Mexico City: Colegio de México, 1994.

———. "No vayáis al norte." In *El México olvidado: La Historia del Pueblo Chicano*, edited by David R. Maciel, 235–55. El Paso, TX: University of Texas Press, 1996.

González Quiroga, Miguel A. "Los trabajadores mexicanos en Texas." In *El norte de México y Texas, 1848–1880: Comercio, capitales y trabajadores en una economía de frontera*, edited by Mario Cerutti and Miguel Angel González Quiroga, 115–73. México: Instituto de Investigaciones Dr. José María Luis Mora, 1999.

Gónzalez Roa, Fernando. *El aspecto agrario de la Revolucíon Mexicana*. Mexico: Departamento de Aprovisionamiento Generales, Dirección de Talleres Gráficos, 1919.

Good, Catherine. "'Making the Struggle, One Big One': Nahuatl Resistance to the San Juan Dam, Mexico." Presented to the Agrarian Studies Colloquium, Yale University, October 30, 1992.

Gordon, Jennifer. "Transnational Labor Citizenship." *Southern California Law Review* 80 (2007): 503.

Gordon, Linda. *The Great Arizona Orphan Abduction*. Cambridge: Harvard University Press, 1999.

Gould, Betty. "Methods of Teaching Mexicans," Master's Thesis, University of Southern California, 1932.

Government Accountability Office. "Employment Verification: Challenges Exist in Implementing a Mandatory Electronic Verification System." Washington, D.C.: Government Accountability Office, 2007.

———. "Border Security: State Department Is Taking Steps to Meet Projected Surge in Demand for Visas and Passports in Mexico." Washington, D.C.: Government Accountability Office, 2008.

———. "Immigration Enforcement: Better Controls Needed over Program Authorizing State and Local Enforcement of Federal Immigration Laws." Washington, D.C.: Government Accountability Office, 2009.

Gozdziak, Elzbieta, and Micah N. Bump. "Poultry, Apples, and New Immigrants in the Rural Communities of the Shenandoah Valley: An Ethnographic Case Study." *International Migration* 42 (2004): 149–64.

Graizbord, Boris, and Adrián Guillermo Aguilar. "Regional Differences and the Economic and Social Geography of Mexico at the Beginning of the Twenty-first Century." In *Changing Structure of Mexico: Political, Social, and Economic Prospects*, 2nd ed., edited by Laura Randall, 91–118. Armonk, NY: M. E. Sharpe, 2006.

Grandin, Greg. *Empire's Workshop: Latin America, the United States, and the Rise of the New Imperialism*. New York: Holt, 2007.

Gratton, Brian, and Myron P. Gutmann. "Hispanics in the United States, 1850–1990: Estimates of Population Size and National Origins." *Historical Methods* 33 (Summer 2000): 137–53.

Graves, Rachel. "Ignored by Society, Black Mexicans Deny their History." *Houston Chronicle*. July 3, 2004.

Grebler, Leo. *Mexican Immigration to the United States: The Record and Its Implications*. Los Angeles: University of California, 1966.

Greenbaum, Susan. "Urban Immigrants in the South: Recent Data and a Historical Case Study." In *Cultural Diversity in the U.S. South: Anthropological Contributions to a Region in Transition*, edited by Carole E. Hill and Patricia D. Beaver, 144–63. Athens, GA: University of Georgia Press, 1998.

Griffen, Solomon Bulkey. *Mexico of Today*. New York: Harper and Brothers, Franklin Square, 1886.

Griffin, Larry J., and Katherine McFarland. "'In My Heart I'm an American': Regional Attitudes and American Identity." *Southern Cultures* 13, no. 4 (2007): 119–37.

Griffith, David. *Jones's Minimal: Low-Wage Labor in the United States*. Albany, NY: State University of New York Press, 1993.

———. "New Immigrants in an Old Industry: Blue Crab Processing in Pamlico County, North Carolina." In *Any Way You Cut It: Meat Processing and Small Town America*, edited by Donald D. Stull, Michael J. Broadway, and David Griffith, 153–86. Lawrence, KS: University of Kansas Press, 1995a.

———. "*Hay Trabajo*: Poultry Processing, Rural Industrialization, and the Latinization of Low-Wage Labor." In *Any Way You Cut It: Meat Processing and Small Town America*, edited by Donald D. Stull, Michael J. Broadway, and David Griffith, 129–51. Lawrence, KS: University of Kansas Press, 1995b.

———. "Rural Industry and Mexican Immigration and Settlement in North Carolina." In *New Destinations: Mexican Immigration to the United States*, edited by Victor Zúñiga and Rubén Hernández-León, 50–75. New York: Russell Sage, 2005.

———. *American Guestworkers: Jamaicans and Mexicans in the U.S. Labor Market*. University Park, PA: Pennsylvania State University Press, 2006.

Griffith, David, Ed Kissam, Jeronimo Camposeco, Anna Garcia, Max Pfeffer, David Runsten, and Manuel Valdés Pizzini. *Working Poor: Farmworkers in the United States*. Philadelphia: Temple University Press, 1995.

Grillo, Ralph. "Betwixt and Between: Trajectories and Projects of Transmigration." *Journal of Ethnic and Migration Studies* 33, no. 3 (2007): 199–217.

Griswold del Castillo, Richard. *The Treaty of Guadalupe Hidalgo: A Legacy of Conflict*. Norman, OK: University of Oklahoma Press, 1990.

Guajardo, Lázaro. *Testimony, Apodaca* (Nuevo León, Mexico), July 30, 1874, in Papers Related to the Foreign Relation of the United States, 1875.

Guérin-Gonzales, Camille. *Mexican Workers and American Dreams: Immigration, Repatriation, and California Farm Labor, 1900–1939*. New Brunswick, NJ: Rutgers University Press, 1994.

Guidi, Marta. *Estigma y Prestigio: La tradición de migrar en San Juan Mixtepec (Oaxaca, Mexico)*. Bonn, Germany: Holos Publishing, 1992.

———. "La construcción de la subalternidad: Un ejemplo de Oaxaca." In *Interculturalidad e identidad indígena: Preguntas abiertas a la globalización en Mexico*, edited by Andreas Koechert and Barbara Pfeiler. Hannover, Germany: Universitat Bremen, 1999.

Guinn, J. M. "The Sonoran Migration." *Historical Society of Southern California* 8 (1909–1911): 31–6.

Guthey, Greig. "Mexican Places in Southern Spaces: Globalization, Work, and Daily Life in and Around the North Georgia Poultry Industry." Pp. 57–67 in *Latino Workers in the Contemporary South*, edited by Arthur D. Murphy, Colleen Blanchard, and Jennifer A. Hill. Athens: University of Georgia Press, 2001.

Gutiérrez, David G. *Walls and Mirrors: Mexican Americans, Mexican Immigrants, and the Politics of Identity*. Berkeley: University of California Press, 1995.

———, ed. *Between Two Worlds: Mexican Immigrants in the United States*. Wilmington, DE: Scholarly Resources, 1996.

———. "Migration, Emergent Ethnicity, and the 'Third Space': The Shifting Politics of Nationalism in Greater Mexico." *Journal of American History* 86 (September 1999): 481–517.

———. *The Columbia History of Latinos in the United States since 1960*. New York: Columbia University Press, 2004.

Gutiérrez, David, and Pierrette Hondagneu-Sotelo, "Introduction: Nation and Migration." *American Quarterly* 60 (2008): 503–21.

Gutiérrez, Elena R. *Fertile Matters: The Politics of Mexican-Origin Women's Reproduction.* Austin, TX: University of Texas Press, 2008.

Gutiérrez Nájera, Lourdes. "Yalálag Is No Longer Just Yalálag: Circulating Conflict and Contesting Community in a Zapotec Transnational Circuit." PhD diss., University of Michigan, 2007.

Gutiérrez, Natividad. *Nationalist Myths and Ethnic Identities: Indigenous Intellectuals and the Mexican State.* Lincoln, NE: University of Nebraska, 1999.

Gutiérrez, Ramón. "The Erotic Zone: Sexual Transgressions on the U.S.–Mexican Border." In *Mapping Multiculturalism*, edited by Avery Gordon and Christopher Newfield, 253–62. Minneapolis, MN: University of Minnesota Press, 1996.

Gutmann, Matthew C. *The Meanings of Macho: Being a Man in Mexico City.* Berkeley: University of California Press, 1996.

Haber, Stephen H. *Industry and Development: The Industrialization of Mexico, 1890–1940*, Stanford, CA: Stanford University Press, 1989.

Hahamovitch, Cindy. *The Fruits of Their Labor: Atlantic Coast Farmworkers and the Making of Migrant Poverty.* Chapel Hill, NC: University of North Carolina Press, 1997.

Hancock, Richard. *The Role of the Bracero in the Economic and Cultural Dynamics of Mexico: A Case Study of Chihuahua.* Stanford, CA: Hispanic American Society, 1958.

Handlin, Oscar. *The Uprooted.* Boston: Little, Brown and Company, 1951.

Hanna, Alfred J., and Kathryn Abbey Hanna. "The Immigration Movement of the Intervention and Empire as Seen through the Mexican Press." *Hispanic American Historical Review* 27 (May 1947): 220–46.

Hansen, Roger D. *The Politics of Mexican Development* . Baltimore: The Johns Hopkins University Press, 1971.

Harper's New Monthly Magazine, 1882.

Hart, John Mason, ed. *Border Crossings: Mexican and Mexican-American Workers.* Wilmington, DE: Scholarly Resources, 1998.

———. *Empire and Revolution: The Americans in Mexico since the Civil War*, Berkeley: University of California Press, 2002.

Harvey, David. *A Brief History of Neoliberalism.* Oxford, UK: Oxford University Press, 2007.

Hawley, Ellis. "The Politics of the Mexican Labor Issue, 1950–1966." *Agricultural History* 40 (July 1966): 157–76.

Hayduk, Ronald. *Democracy for All: Restoring Immigrant Voting Rights in the United States.* New York: Routledge, 2006.

Henderson, Timothy J. Beyond Borders: *A History of Mexican Migration to the United States.* Malden, MA: Wiley-Blackwell, 2011.

Hendricks, Tyche. "Immigrant Sanctuary Laws Seen as Practical." *San Francisco Chronicle*, July 6, 2008.

Hernández, Daniel Manuel. "Pursuant to Deportation: Latinos and Immigrant Detention." *Latino Studies* 6 (2008): 35–63.

Hernández, José Angel "El Mexico Perdido, El Mexico Olvidado, y El Mexico de Afuera: A History of Mexican American Colonization, 1836–1892," PhD diss., University of Chicago, 2008.

"From Conquest to Colonization: Indios and Colonization Policies after Mexican Independence." *Mexican Studies/Estudios Mexicanos* 26 (Summer 2010a): 285–315.

———. "Contemporary Deportation Raids and Historical Memory: Mexican Expulsions in the Nineteenth Century."*Aztlán: A Journal of Chicano Studies* 35 (Fall 2010b): 115–42.

———. Hernández, Kelly Lytle. "The Crimes and Consequences of Illegal Immigration: A Cross-Border Examination of Operation Wetback, 1943 to 1954." *Western Historical Quarterly* 37 (Winter 2006): 421–44.

Hernández Díaz, Jorge. "Representaciones híbridas: La participación de los mixtecos migrantes en el proceso electoral." In *Dilemas de la democracia en México: Los actores sociales ante la representación política*, edited by Aline Hemond and David Recondo, 273–89. Mexico: Instituto Federal Electoral/Centro Francés de Estudios Mexicanos y Centroamericanos, 2002.

Hernández-León, Rubén. *Metropolitan Migrants: The Migration of Urban Mexicans to the United States*. Berkeley: University of California Press, 2008.

Hernández-León, Rubén, and Victor Zúñiga. "'Making Carpet by the Mile': The Emergence of a Mexican Immigrant Community in an Industrial Region of the U.S. Historic South." *Social Science Quarterly* 81 (2000): 49–65.

———. "Appalachia Meets Aztlán: Mexican Immigration and Inter-Group Relations in Dalton, Georgia." In *New Destinations: Mexican Immigration in the United States*, edited by Victor Zúñiga and Rubén Hernández-León, 244–73. New York: Russell Sage, 2005.

Hernández Sánchez, Ernesto. "Género, poder y trabajo en la comunidad transnacional." In *San Juan Mixtepec: Una comunidad transnacional ante el poder clasificador y filtrador de las fronteras*, edited by Federico Besserer and Michael Kearney. Mexico City: Juan Pablos/Universidad Autónoma Metropolitana, Iztapalapa /University of California at Riverside, 2006.

Herrera-Sobek, Maria. *Northward Bound: The Mexican Immigrant Experience in Ballad and Song*. Bloomington, IN: University of Indiana Press, 1993.

Heyman, Josiah M. *Life and Labor on the Border: Working People of the Northeastern Sonora, Mexico, 1886–1986*. Tucson, AZ: University of Arizona Press, 1991.

———. "Putting Power in the Anthropology of Bureaucracy: The Immigration and Naturalization Service at the Mexico–United States Border." *Current Anthropology* 36 (1995): 261–87.

Himes, Joseph S. "Introduction: Background of Recent Changes in the South." In *The South Moves into the Future: Studies in the Analysis and Prediction of Social Change*, edited by Joseph S. Himes, 1–10. Tuscaloosa, AL: University of Alabama Press, 1991.

———. *Cultural Capital: Mountain Zapotec Migrant Associations in Mexico City*. Tucson, AZ: University of Arizona, 1993.

———. "The Politicization of Regional Identity among Mountain Zapotec Migrants in Mexico City." In *Migrants, Regional Identities and Latin American Cities*, edited by Teófilo Altamirano and Lane Ryo Hirabayashi, 9–66. Washington, D.C.: Society for Latin American Anthropology, American Anthropology Association, 1997.

Hirabayashi, Lane Ryo. *Cultural Capital: Mountain Zapotec Migrant Associations in Mexico City*, Tucson: University of Arizona, 1993.

———. "The Politicization of Regional Identity among Mountain Zapotec Migrants in Mexico City," in Teófilo Altamirano and Lane Ryo Hirabayashi, eds., *Migrants, Regional Identities and Latin American Cities*, 49–66. Washington, D.C: Society for Latin American Anthropology, American Anthropology Association, 1997.

Hirsh, Jennifer. *A Courtship after Marriage: Sexuality and Love in Mexican Transnational Families*. Berkeley: University of California Press, 2003.

Hirschman, Charles, and Douglas S. Massey. "Places and Peoples: The New American Mosaic." In *New Faces in New Places: The Changing Geography of American Immigration*, edited by Douglas S. Massey, 1–21. New York: Russell Sage, 2008.

Hodges, R. E. "Imperial Valley, Active and Very Promising." *Pacific Rural Press*, November 25, 1933.

Hoerder, Dirk. *Cultures in Contact: World Migrations in the Second Millennium*. Durham, NC: Duke University Press, 2002.

Hoerder, Dick. "Transnational States, Nations, and People" in *The Historical Practice of Diversity: Transcultural Interactions from the Early Modern Mediterranean to the Postcolonial World*, edited by Dirk Hoerder, 13–32, New York: Berghahn Books, 2003.

Hoffman, Abraham. *Unwanted Mexican Americans in the Great Depression. Repatriation Pressures, 1929–1939*. Tucson, AZ: University of Arizona Press, 1974.

Hollar, Julie. "CNN's Immigration Problem: Is Dobbs the Exception—Or the Rule?" *Fairness & Accuracy in Reporting*, May/June 2006.

Holmes, Seth. "An Ethnographic Study of the Social Context of Migrant Health in the United States," *PLoS Med*, October, 3(10): e448, www.plosmedicine.org 1776–1793, 2006.

——. "Oaxacans Like to Work Bent Over": The Naturalization of Social Suffering among Berry Farm Workers," *International Migration*, 45(3), 2007.

Hondagneu-Sotelo, Pierrette. *Gendered Transitions: Mexican Experiences of Immigration*. Berkeley: University of California, 1994.

——. "Gender and Immigration: A Retrospective and an Introduction," in Pierrette Hondagneu-Sotelo, ed., *Gender and US Immigration: Contemporary Trends*. Berkeley: University of California Press, 3–20, 1999.

Hondagneu-Sotelo, Pierrette, and Ernestine Avila. "'I'm Here But I'm There': The Meanings of Latina Transnational Motherhood." In *Gender and US Immigration: Contemporary Trends*, edited by Pierrette Hondagneu-Sotelo, 317–40. Berkeley: University of California Press, 1999.

Hooker, Juliet. "Indigenous Inclusion/Black Exclusion: Race, Ethnicity and Multicultural Citizenship in Latin America." *Journal of Latin American Studies* 37 (2005): 285–310.

"How Changes to Family Immigration Could Affect Source Countries' Sending Patterns." http://www.migrationpolicy.org/pubs/FS18_FamilyImmigration_062007.pdf (accessed July 3, 2009).

Howe, Cymene, Susana Zaraysky, and Lois Lorentzen. "Transgender Sex Workers and Sexual Transmigration between Guadalajara and San Francisco." *Latin American Perspectives* 35 (2008): 31–50.

Hu-DeHart, Evelyn. "Immigrants to a Developing Society: The Chinese in Northern Mexico, 1875–1932." *Journal of Arizona History* 21 (Autumn 1980): 275–312.

Huizar, Javier, and Isidro Cerda. "Indigenous Mexican Migrants in the 2000 US Census: Hispanic American Indians." In *Indigenous Mexican Migrants in the United States*, edited by Jonathan Fox and Gaspar Rivera-Salgado, 279–302. La Jolla, CA: University of California, San Diego, Center for Comparative Immigration Studies/Center for U.S.-Mexican Studies, 2004.

Hull, Elizabeth. *Without Justice for All: The Constitutional Rights of Aliens*. Westport, CT: Greenwood, 1985.

Hulshof, Marije. *Zapotec Moves, Networks and Remittances of U.S.-Bound Migrants from Oaxaca, Mexico*. Amsterdam: Koninklijk Nederlands Aardrijkskundig Genootschap, 1991.

Human Rights Watch, and Immigration Equality. "Family, Unvalued. Discrimination, Denial, and the Fate of Same-Sex Binational Couples under US Law." New York: Immigration Equality and Human Rights Watch, 2006.

Immigration Equality. "LGBT/HIV Asylum Manual, 1. Asylum Law Basics." http://www.immigrationequality.org/manual_template.php?id=1064 (accessed July 13, 2009).

Inda, Jonathan Xavier. *Targeting Immigrants. Government, Technology, and Ethics*. Malden, MA: Blackwell Publishing, 2006.

"Increase of Mexican Labor in Certain Industries in the United States," *Monthly Labor Review* 37 (July 1933).

Informe de la Comisión Pesquesidora de la frontera norte al ejecutivo de la Unión. Monterrey: Archivo General del Estado de Nuevo León, 1984.

Ingersoll, Ralph M. *In and Under Mexico*. New York: Century Co., 1924.

"Jesus M. Ainza contra México." In *Boletín oficial se la Secretaría de Relaciones Exteriores*, vol. 14. Mexico: Imprenta de Francisco Díaz de León, 1902.

Jiménez, Tomás R. "Mexican-Immigrant Replenishment and the Continuing Significance of Ethnicity and Race." *American Journal of Sociology* 113 (2008): 1527–67.

———. *Replenished Ethnicity: Mexican Americans, Mexican Immigrants, and Identity*. Berkeley: University of California Press, 2010.

Johns, Michael. *The City of Mexico in the Age of Diaz*. Austin, TX: University of Texas Press, 1997.

Johnson, Frank W. *A History of Texas and Texans*, vol. 1. Chicago: The American Historical Society, 1914.

Johnson-Webb, Karen D. *Recruiting Hispanic Labor: Immigrants in Non-Traditional Areas*. New York: LFB Scholarly Publishing, LLC, 2003.

Jonas, Susanne, and Susie Tod Thomas, eds. *Immigration: A Civil Rights Issue for the Americas*. Wilmington, DE: Scholarly Resources, 1999.

Joseph, Gilbert M., and Daniel Nugent, eds. *Everyday Forms of State Formation: Revolution and the Negotiation of Rule in Modern Mexico*. Durham, NC: Duke University Press, 1994.

Joseph, Gilbert M., Anne Rubenstein, and Eric Zolov, eds. *Fragments of a Golden Age: The Politics of Culture in Mexico since 1940*. Durham, NC: Duke University Press, 2001.

Kandel, William A., and John Cromartie. "New Patterns of Hispanic Settlement in Rural America." Rural Development Research Report, no. 99. Washington, D.C.: United States Department of Agriculture, 2004.

Kandel, William A., and Emilio A. Parrado. "Industrial Transformation and Hispanic Migration to the American South: The Case of the Poultry Industry." In *Hispanic Spaces, Latino Places: Community and Cultural Diversity in Contemporary America*, edited by Daniel D. Arreola, 266–76. Austin, TX: University of Texas Press, 2004.

Kanstroom, Daniel. *Deportation Nation: Outsiders in American History*. Cambridge, MA: Harvard University Press, 2007.

Kasarda, John D., Holly L. Hughes, and Michael D. Irwin. "Demographic and Economic Restructuring in the South." In *The South Moves into Its Future: Studies in the Analysis and Prediction of Social Change*, edited by Joseph S. Himes, 13–31. Tuscaloosa, AL: University of Alabama Press, 1991.

Kasarda, John D., and James H. Johnson. "The Economic Impact of the Hispanic Population on the State of North Carolina." Chapel Hill, NC: Frank Hawkins Kenan Institute of Private Enterprise, January 2006.

Kasinitz, Philip, John H. Mollenkopf, Mary C. Waters, and Jennifer Holdaway. *Inheriting the City: The Second Generation Comes of Age*. Cambridge and New York: Harvard University Press and Russell Sage, 2008.

Katz, Friedrich. "Labor Conditions on Haciendas in Mexico: Some Trends and Tendencies." *Hispanic American Historical Review* 54 (February 1974): 1–47.

Kaushal, Neeraj. "In-state Tuition for the Undocumented: Education Effects on Mexican Young Adults." *Journal of Policy Analysis and Management* 27 (2008): 771–92.

Kearney, Michael. "Mixtec Political Consciousness: From Passive to Active Resistance." In *Rural Revolt in Mexico and U.S. Intervention,* edited by Daniel Nugent, 113–24. La Jolla, CA: University of California, San Diego, Center for U.S.–Mexican Studies, 1988.

Kearney, Michael. "The Effects of Transnational Culture, Economy, and Migration on Mixtec Identity in Oaxacalifornia." In *The Bubbling Cauldron: Race, Ethnicity, and the Urban Crisis,* edited by Michael Peter Smith and Joe R. Feagin, 226–43. Minneapolis, MN: University of Minnesota Press, 1995.

——. "Transnational Oaxacan Indigenous Identity: The Case of Mixtecs and Zapotecs." *Identities* 7 (2000): 173–95.

Kearney, Michael, and Federico Besserer. "Oaxacan Municipal Governance in Transnational Context." In *Indigenous Mexican Migrants in the United States,* edited by Jonathan Fox and Gaspar Rivera-Salgado, 449–66. La Jolla, CA: University of California, San Diego, Center for Comparative Immigration Studies/Center for U.S.–Mexican Studies, 2004.

Keegan, Rebecca Winters. "A Hispanic Hit at the Cineplex." *Time.* March 28, 2008.

Kelley, Sean. "'Mexico in His Head': Slavery and the Texas–Mexican Border, 1810–1860." *Journal of Social History* 37 (2004): 709–23.

Kerber, Linda K. "Toward a History of Statelessness in America." *American Quarterly* 57 (2005) 727–749.

Kersey, Vierling. *Your Children and Their Schools.* Los Angeles: Los Angeles Board of Education, 1937.

Kim, Claire Jean. "The Racial Triangulation of Asian Americans." *Politics and Society* 27 (1999): 105–38.

Kissam, Ed. "Trends in the Ethnic Composition of the California Farm Labor Force." Memo to the Agricultural Worker Health Initiative Policy Advisory Group, July 1, 2003.

Kissam, Ed, et al. "No Longer Children: Case Studies of the Living and Working Conditions of the Youth Who Harvest America's Crops." San Mateo, CA: Aguirre International, 2001.

Kissam, Ed, and Ilene Jacobs. "Practical Research Strategies for Mexican Indigenous Communities in California Seeking to Assert Their Own Identity." In *Indigenous Mexican Migrants in the United States,* edited by Jonathan Fox and Gaspar Rivera-Salgado, 303–42. La Jolla, CA: University of California, San Diego, Center for Comparative Immigration Studies/Center for U.S.–Mexican Studies, 2004.

Klaver, Jeanine. *From the Land of the Sun to the City of Angeles: The Migration Process of Zapotec Indians from Oaxaca, Mexico to Los Angeles, California.* Utrecht: Netherlands Geographical Studies, 1997.

Knight, Alan. "Cardenismo: Juggernaut or Jalopy?" *Latin American Studies* 26 (February 1994a): 73–107.

——. "Peasants into Patriots: Thoughts on the Making of the Mexican Nation." *Mexican Studies/Estudios Mexicanos* 10 (Winter 1994b): 135–61.

Kochhar, Rakesh, Roberto Suro, and Sonya Tafoya. "The New Latino South: The Context and Consequences of Rapid Population Growth." Washington, D.C.: Pew Hispanic Center, July 26, 2005.

Kohut, Andrew, and Roberto Suro. "No Consensus on Immigration Quandary or Proposed Fixes." Washington, D.C.: Pew Research Center for the People and the Press and Pew Hispanic Center, 2006.

Konet, Dawn. "Unauthorized Youths and Higher Education: The Ongoing Debate." Washington, D.C.: Migration Policy Institute, 2007.

Krissman, Fred. "Californian Agribusiness and Mexican Farm Workers, 1942–1992: A Bi-National System of Production/Reproduction." PhD diss., University of California, Santa Barbara, 1996.

———. "Apples and Oranges? Recruiting Indigenous Mexicans to Divide Farm Labor Markets in the Western U.S." Presented at "Mexican Indigenous Migrants in the US: Building Bridges between Researchers and Community Leaders," University of California, Santa Cruz, October 2002.

Kun, Josh. "What Is an MC if He Can't Rap to Banda? Making Music in Nuevo L.A." *American Quarterly* 56 (2004): 741–58.

———. "The Twiins: Mexican Music, Made in America." *New York Times*. May 14, 2006.

———. "Mexican Bands Hear Success Calling." *New York Times*. April 5, 2009.

Lacy, Elaine C. "Mexican Immigrants in South Carolina: A Profile." Columbia: Consortium for Latino Immigration Studies, University of South Carolina at Columbia, January, 2007.

Laglagaron, Laureen, Cristina Rodríguez, Alexa Silver, and Sirithon Thanasombat. "Regulating Immigration at the State Level: Highlights from the Database of 2007 State Immigration Legislation and the Methodology." Washington, D.C.: Migration Policy Institute, 2008.

Lamb, Mark R. "On Horseback in Chihuahua." *Engineering and Mining Journal* 86, no. 4 (July 25, 1908).

———. *Política demográfica estatuida en el plan sexenal*. México, June 21, 1935 (no publisher).

Landa y Piña, Andrés. *El Servicio de Migración en México*. México, DF: Talleres Gráficas de la Nación, 1930.

La voz de Nuevo León, February 23, 1889.

Lázaro Salinas, José. *La Emigración de Braceros: Visión Objetiva de un Problema Mexicano*. León: Imprenta Cuauhtémoc, 1955.

Leach, Mark. "Linking the Past to the Present: Mexican Migration to New Destination States." Unpublished Manuscript, University of California at Irvine, 2004.

Leco Tomás, Casimiro. "De una Montaña a Otra: Movilidad y Socialización de los Migrantes Purhépechas de Cherán a Burnsville, Norte Carolina," Universidad Michoacana de San Nicolás de Hidalgo, Instituto de Investigaciones Económicas y Empresariales, Ph.D Dissertation, 2005.

LeDuff, Charlie. "At a Slaughterhouse, Some Things Never Die: Who Kills, Who Cuts, Who Bosses Can Depend on Race (Sixth in the Series on "How Race Is Lived in America")." *New York Times*. June 16, 2000.

Lee, Erika. *At America's Gates: Chinese Immigration during the Exclusion Era, 1882–1943*. Chapel Hill, NC: University of North Carolina Press, 2003.

Lee, Jennifer, and Frank D. Bean. "Reinventing the Color Line: Immigration and America's New Racial/Ethnic Divide." *Social Forces* 86, no. 2 (2007): 1–26.

Lentnek, Barry. "Economic Transition from Traditional to Commercial Agriculture: The Case of El Llano, Mexico." *Annals of the Association of American Geographers* 59 (1969): 65–84.

León Portilla, Miguel. *Historia documental de México*. Mexico: Universidad Nacional Autónoma de México, Instituto de Investigaciones Históricas, 1964.

Levenstein, Harvey A. *Labor Organizations in the United States and Mexico: A History of Their Relations*. Westport, CT: Greenwood Publishing, 1971.

Leyva Solano, Xochitl, and Gabriel Ascencio Franco. *Lacandonia el fila del agua*. Mexico City: CIESAS/UNAM/UCAEC/FCE, 1996.

Licea de Arenas, Judith, Emma Santillán-Rivero, Miguel Arenas, and Javier Valles. "Desempeño de becarios mexicanos en la producción de conocimiento científico ¿De la bibliometría a la política científica?" *Information Research* 8, no. 2 (2003). Available at http://informationR.net/ir/8-2/paper147.html (accessed July 1, 2009).

Lida, Clara E., *Inmigración y exilio. Reflexiones sobre el caso español*, México, siglo xxi editores, 1997.

Limón, José E. *American Encounters: Greater Mexico and the United States and the Erotics of Culture.* Boston: Beacon Press, 1998.

Lippard, Cameron D., and Charles A. Gallagher, eds. *Being Brown in Dixie: Race, Ethnicity, and Latino Immigration in the New South.* Boulder, CO: First Forum Press, 2011.

Liss, Sheldon. *A Century of Disagreement: The Chamizal Conflict, 1864–1964.* Washington, D.C.: University Press of Washington, D.C., 1965.

Loewen, James W. *The Mississippi Chinese: Between Black and White*, 2nd ed. Long Grove, IL: Waveland Press, 1988.

López, Felipe, and David Runsten. "Mixtecs and Zapotecs Working in California. Rural and Urban Experiences." In *Indigenous Mexican Migrants in the United States*, edited by Jonathan Fox and Gaspar Rivera-Salgado, 249–78. La Jolla, CA: University of California, San Diego, Center for Comparative Immigration Studies/Center for U.S.–Mexican Studies, 2004.

López Castro, Gustavo, ed., *Diáspora Michoacana.* Zamora, Mexico: Colegio de Michoacán/ Gobierno de Michoacán, 2003.

López, Felipe and David Runsten. 2004. "Mixtecs and Zapotecs Working in California. Rural and Urban Experiences," In *Indigenous Mexican Migrants in the United States*, edited by Jonathan Fox and Gaspar Rivera-Salgado, 249–278. La Jolla: UC San Diego, Center for Comparative Immigration Studies & Center for US-Mexican Studies, 2004.

López Monjardín, Adriana. "Organization and Struggle among Agricultural Workers in Mexico," In *Unions, Workers and the State in Mexico*, edited by Kevin Middlebrook, 185–212. La Jolla: University of California, San Diego, Center for US-Mexican Studies, 1991.

Los Angeles City Schools, Department of Psychology and Educational Research, *Los Angeles Educational Research Bulletin* 6 (14 June 1926).

Los Angeles School District Journal 16 (February 1923).

Los Angeles School District Journal 11 (May 14, 1928).

Los Angeles School District Publication, no. 185, 1929.

Lowell, B. Linday, and Allan M. Findlay. "Migration of Highly Skilled Persons From Developing Countries: Impact and Policy Responses." Report prepared for the International Labour Office, Geneva, 2001.

Loyo, Gilberto. *La emigración de Mexicanos a los Estados Unidos.* Rome: Instituto Poligrafico dello Stato, 1931.

———. *La Política Demográfica de México.* Mexico City: La Impresora, 1935.

———. "Interrelación Entre la Migración Internacional y la Migración Interna en México." *Papeles de Población* 8 (July–September 2002): 81–100.

Lucassen, Leo. *The Immigrant Threat: The Integration of Old and New Migrants in Western Europe since 1850.* Chicago: University of Illinois Press, 2005.

Lugo, Alejandro. "Theorizing Border Inspections." *Cultural Dynamics* 12 (2000): 353–73.

Luibhéid, Eithne. "Heteronormativity and Immigration Scholarship: A Call for Change." *GLQ* 10 2 (2004): 227–35.

———. "Heteronormativity, Responsibility, and Neo-liberal Governance in U.S. Immigration Control." In *Passing Lines: Sexuality and Immigration*, edited by Brad Epps, Keja Valens, and Bill Johnon Gonzalez, 69–101. Cambridge, MA: Harvard University David Rockefeller Center for Latin American Studies, 2005.

——. " 'Looking Like a Lesbian': The Organization of Sexual Monitoring at the United States–Mexico Border." In *Women and Migration in the U.S.–Mexico Borderlands: A Reader*, edited by Denise Segura and Patricia Zavella, 106–33. Durham, NC: Duke University Press, 2007.

——. "Sexuality, Migration, and the Shifting Line Between Legal and Illegal Status." *GLQ* 14, (2008): 289–315.

Maciel, David R. "Pochos and Other Extremes in Mexican Cinema; or El cine mexicano se va de bracer." In *Chicanos and Film: Representation and Resistance*, edited by Chon A. Noriega, 94–113. Minneapolis, MN: University of Minnesota Press, 1992.

Maciel, David R., and Maria Rosa Garcia-Acevedo. "Celluloid Immigrant: The Narrative Films of Mexican Immigration." In *Cultures across Borders: Mexican Immigration and Popular Culture*, edited by David R. Maciel and Maria Herrera-Sobek, 149–202. Tucson, AZ: University of Arizona Press, 1998.

Maciel, David R., and María Herrera-Sobek. "Introduction: Culture across Borders." In *Culture across Borders: Mexican Immigration and Popular Culture*, edited by David R. Maciel and María Herrera-Sobek, 3–25. Tucson, AZ: University of Arizona Press, 1998.

Maciel, David R., Isidro Ortiz, and Maria Herrera-Sobek, eds. *Chicano Renaissance: Contemporary Cultural Trends.* Tucson, AZ: University Arizona Press, 2000.

Mahler, Sarah J., and Patricia R. Pessar. "Gendered Geographies of Power: Analyzing Gender across Transnational Spaces." *Identities: Global Studies in Power and Culture* 7 (2001): 441–59.

Majka, Linda, and Theo Majka. *Farm Workers, Agribusiness, and the State.* Philadelphia: Temple University Press, 1982.

Maldonado, Centolia, and Patricia Artía. " 'Now We Are Awake': Women's Political Participation in the Oaxacan Indigenous Binational Front." In *Indigenous Mexican Migrants in the United States*, edited by Jonathan Fox and Gaspar Rivera-Salgado, 495–510. La Jolla, CA: University of California, San Diego, Center for Comparative Immigration Studies/Center for U.S.–Mexican Studies, 2004.

Manalansan, Martin. "Queer Intersections: Sexuality and Gender in Migration Studies." *International Migration Review* 40 (Spring 2006): 224–49.

Mapes, Kathleen. " 'A Special Class of Labor': Mexican (Im)Migrants, Immigration Debate, and Industrial Agriculture in the Rural Midwest." *Labor: Studies in Working-Class History of the Americas* 1, no. 2 (2004): 65–88.

Marcosson, Isacc. "Our Financial Stake in Mexico." *Collier's* 57 (July 1, 1916): 22–23.

Mariscal, George. "Can Cultural Studies Speak Spanish?" In *The Chicana/o Cultural Studies Reader*, edited by Angie Chabram-Dernersesian, 61–80. New York: Routledge, 2006.

Marroni, María da Gloria. "¿Insensibilidad al génaro? Debates, constrastes y experiencias migratorias femininas." In *In God We Trust: Del campo mexicano al sueño americano*, edited by Córdova Plaza, Rosío, María Cristina Núñez Madrazo, and David Skerritt Gardner, 187–218. Veracruz: Universidad de Veracruz, Plaza y Valdés, 2007.

Marrow, Helen B. "Hispanic Immigration, Black Population Size, and Intergroup Relations in the Rural and Small-Town U.S. South." In *New Faces in New Places: The Changing Geography of American Immigration*, edited by Douglas S. Massey, 211–48. New York: Russell Sage Foundation, 2008.

——. "New Immigrant Destinations and the American Colour Line." *Ethnic and Racial Studies* 32, no. 6 (2009): 137–57.

Marrow, Helen B. *New Destination Dreaming: Immigration, Race, and Legal Status in the Rural American South.* Stanford, CA: Stanford University Press, 2011.

Martin, David A., and Peter H. Schuck. *Immigration Stories.* New York: Foundation Press, 2005.

Martin, Percy F. *Mexico's Treasure-House (Guanajuato): An Illustrated and Descriptive Account of the Mines and Their Operations in 1906.* New York: Cheltenham Press, 1906.

Martin, Philip. "NAFTA and Mexico–US Migration: Policy Options in 2004." *Law and Business Review of the Americas* 11 (2005): 361–85.

——. "The Effects of Migration on Sending Countries: A Comparison of Mexico and Turkey." *Well-Being and Social Policy* 2 (May 2006): 89–101.

Martínez, John. *Mexican Emigration to the U.S. 1910–1930.* Berkeley: R. and E. Research Associates, 1972.

Martinez, Konane, David Runsten, and Alejandria Ricardez. "The Mexican Migrant Community in San Diego County." In *The Times That Bind Us,* edited by Richard Kly and Christopher Woodruff, 100–25. Boulder, CO: Lynne Rienner, 2005.

Martínez, Oscar J. "La frontera vista por René Mascareñas Miranda: Entrevista de historia oral." Unpublished manuscript on file at the Institute of Oral History at the University of Texas at El Paso, 1976.

——. *Border Boom Town: Ciudad Juárez since 1848.* Austin, TX: University of Texas Press, 1978.

——. *Troublesome Border,* 1st ed. Tucson: University of Arizona Press, 1988.

Martínez, Oscar J., Miguel Angel Martínez Lasso, and Ellwyn R. Stoddard. *El Paso-Ciudad Juárez Relations and the "Tortilla Curtain": A Study of Local Adaptation to Federal Border Policies.* El Paso, TX: El Paso Council on the Arts & Humanities, 1979.

Martínez, Ruben. *Crossing Over: A Mexican Family on the Migrant Trail.* New York: Picador, 2002.

Martinez Novo, Carmen. *Who Defines Indigenous? Identities, Development, Intellectuals and the State in Northern Mexico.* New Brunswick, NJ: Rutgers University Press, 2006.

Martínez Saldaña, Jesús. "At the Periphery of Democracy: The Binational Politics of Mexican Immigrants in Silicon Valley." PhD diss., University of California, Berkeley, 1993.

——. "Building the Future: The FIOB and Civic Participation of Mexican Immigrants in Fresno, California." In *Indigenous Mexican Migrants in the United States,* edited by Jonathan Fox and Gaspar Rivera-Salgado, 125–44. La Jolla, CA: University of California, San Diego, Center for Comparative Immigration Studies/Center for U.S.–Mexican Studies, 2004.

Martínez Saldaña, Jesús, and Raúl Ross Pineda. "Suffrage for Mexicans Residing Abroad." In *Cross-Border Dialogues: US–Mexico Social Movement Networking,* edited by David Brooks and Jonathan Fox, 275–92. La Jolla, CA: University of California, San Diego, Center for U.S.-Mexican Studies, 2002.

Massey, Douglas S. "Understanding Mexican Migration to the United States." *The American Journal of Sociology* 92 (May 1987): 1372–403.

——. *Categorically Unequal: The American Stratification System.* New York: Russell Sage Foundation, 2007.

——. *New Faces in New Places: The Changing Geography of American Immigration.* New York: Russell Sage Foundation, 2008.

——. "Battlefield: El Paso." *The National Interest,* July/August (2009): 44–51.

Massey, Douglas S., Rafael Alarcón, Jorge Durand, and Humberto González. *Return to Aztlán: The Social Process of International Migration from Western Mexico.* Berkley: University of California Press, 1987.

Massey, Douglas S., Joaquín Arango, Graeme Hugo, Ali Kouaouci, Adela Pellegrino, and J. Edward Taylor. *Worlds in Motion: Understanding International Migration at the End of the Millennium*. Oxford, UK: Clarendon Press, 1998.

Massey, Douglas S., and Chiara Capoferro. "The Geographic Diversification of American Immigration." In *New Faces in New Places: The Changing Geography of American Immigration*, edited by Douglas S. Massey, 25–50. New York: Russell Sage, 2008.

Massey, Douglas S., Jorge Durand, and Nolan J. Malone. *Beyond Smoke and Mirrors: Mexican Immigration in an Era of Economic Integration*. New York: Russell Sage, 2002.

Massey, Douglas S., and Nolan J. Malone. "Pathways to Legalization." *Population Research and Policy Review* 21 (2003): 473–504.

Massey, Douglas S., Karen A. Pren, and Jorge Durand. "Nuevos Escenarios de la Migración México-Estados Unidos. Las Consecuencias de la Guerra Antiinmigrante." Papeles de Población 15(61) (2009): 101–128.

Massey, Douglas S., and Audrey Singer. "New Estimates of Undocumented Mexican Migration and the Probability of Apprehension." *Demography* 32 (1995): 20 3–13.

Matesanz, José Antonio, *México ante la guerra civil española 1936–1939*. PhD thesis, El Colegio de México, Centro de Estudios Históricos, 1995.

Mautner, Bertram, and W. Lewis Abbot. *Child Labor in Agriculture and Farm Life in the Arkansas Valley of Colorado*. Colorado College General Series, no. 164, Studies Series no. 2. Colorado Springs, CO: Colorado College, 1929.

McAnulty, Ellen Alice. "Distribution of Intelligence in the Los Angeles Elementary Schools." *Los Angeles Educational Research Bulletin* 8 (March 1929): 6–7.

McClain, Paula D., Niambi M. Carter, Victoria M. DeFrancesco Soto, Monique L. Lyle, Jeffrey D. Grynasviski, Shayla C. Nunnally, Thomas C. Scotto, J. Alan Kendrick, Gerald F. Lackey, and Kendra Davenport Cotton. "Racial Distancing in a Southern City: Latino Immigrants' Views of Black Americans." *The Journal of Politics* 68 (2006): 571–84.

McClain, Paula D., Monique L. Lyle, Niambi M. Carter, Victoria M. DeFrancesco Soto, Gerald F. Lackey, Kendra Davenport Cotton, Shayla C. Nunnally, Thomas C. Scotto, Jeffrey D. Grynasviski, and J. Alan Kendrick. "Black Americans and Latino Immigrants in a Southern City: Friendly Neighbors or Economic Competitors?" *Du Bois Review* 4 (2007): 97–117.

McClintock, Anne. "Family Feuds: Gender, Nationalism, and the Family." *Feminist Review* 44 (Summer 1993): 61–80.

McCullough, Kenneth Bruce. "America's Back Door: Indirect International Immigration via Mexico to the United States from 1875 to 1940." PhD diss., Texas A & M University, 1992.

McDaniel, Josh, and Vanessa Casanova. "Pines in Lines: Tree Planting, H2B Guest Workers, and Rural Poverty in Alabama." *Southern Rural Sociology* 19 (2003): 73–96.

McKay, Reynolds. *Texas Mexican Repatriation during the Great Depression*. PhD diss., The University of Oklahoma at Norman, 1982.

McLean, Robert N. *That Mexican as He Really Is, North and South of the Rio Grande*. New York: Home Missions Council, 1930.

McWilliams, Carey. *Factories in the Fields: The Story of Migratory Farm Labor in California*. Boston: Little, Brown, 1939.

———. *Ill Fares the Land*. New York: Barnes and Noble, 1942.

———. *North from Mexico: The Spanish-Speaking People of the United States*. Philadelphia: J. B. Lippincott, 1949.

Medina, Luis. *Historia de la Revolución Mexicana 1940–1952. Del cardenismo al avilacamachismo*, no. 18. Mexico: El Colegio de México, 1978.

Melero Malpica, Daniel. "Indigenous Mexican Migrants in the City of Los Angeles: Social Networks and Social Capital among Zapotec Workers." PhD diss., University of California, Los Angeles, 2008.

Memoria de la Secretaría de Hacienda y Crédito Público, 1892.

Menchaca, Martha. *Recovering History, Constructing Race: The Indian, Black and White Roots of Mexican-Americans.* Austin, TX: University of Texas Press, 2001.

Mendelson, Margot, Shayna Strom, and Michael Wishnie. "Collateral Damage: An Examination of ICE's Fugitive Operations Program." Washington, D.C.: Migration Policy Institute, 2009.

Mexicans in California, Report of C. C. Young's Mexican Fact Finding Committee [1930] Sacramento, State of California.

"Mexican Labor and Foreign Capital," *The Independent* (May 24, 1924).

Mignolo, Walter D. *Local Histories/Global Designs: Coloniality, Subaltern Knowledges, and Border Thinking.* Princeton, NJ: Princeton University Press, 2000.

———. *The Idea of Latin America.* Oxford, UK: Blackwell Publishing, 2005.

"Migrantes presionan en México." *La Opinión.* April 24, 2009.

Migration Policy Institute Data Hub. http://www.migrationinformation.org/DataHub (accessed December 17, 2009).

Mindiola, Tatcho, Yolanda Flores Niemann, and Nestor Rodríguez. *Black–Brown Relations and Stereotypes.* Austin, TX: University of Texas Press, 2002.

Mines, Richard, Sandra Nichols, and David Runsten. *California's Indigenous Farmworkers.* Final Report of the Indigenous Farmworker Study (IFS) to the California Endowment, California Rural Legal Assistance, 2010.

Mitchell, Don. *The Lie of the Land: Migrant Workers and the California Landscape.* Minneapolis, MN: University of Minnesota Press, 1996.

Moctezuma Langoria, Miguel. "La voz de los actores sobre la ley migrante y Zacatecas." *Migración y Desarrollo* 1 (October 2003): 100–3.

Mohl, Raymond A. "Latinization in the Heart of Dixie: Hispanics in Late-Twentieth-Century Alabama." *Alabama Review* 55, no. 4 (2002): 243–74.

Monroy, Douglas. *Rebirth: Mexican Los Angeles From the Great Migration to the Great Depression.* Berkeley: University of California Press, 1999.

Montejano, David. *Anglos and Mexicans in the Making of Texas, 1836–1986.* Austin, TX: University of Texas Press, 1987.

Montoya, Ramon Alejandro. "El cura y los braceros: la administración de la fe y la migración de mano de obra en Cerritos, San Luis Potosí, durante el programa bracero." In *Emigración de San Luis Potosí a Estados Unidos: Pasado y presente,* edited by Fernando Alanís Enciso, 77–94. Monterrey: El Colegio de San Luis, 2001.

Moore, Jean. *Mexican Americans.* New York: Prentice Hall College Division, 1976.

Moore, Joan W., with Alfredo Cuéllar. *Mexican Americans.* Englewood Cliffs: Prentice-Hall, Inc., 1970.

Mora-Torres, Juan. *The Making of the Mexican Border.* Austin, TX: University of Texas Press, 2001.

Morawska, Ewa. "Disciplinary Agendas and Analytic Strategies of Research on Immigrant Transnationalism: Challenges of Interdisciplinary Knowledge." *International Migration Review* 37 (Fall 2003): 611–40.

Moreno, Antonio. *Papers Related to the Foreign Relations of the U.S. 1879,* pp. 831–833.

Moscoso Paniagua, Pepe. "Reviviendo mis recuerdos." *El Oaxaqueño,* June 26, 2004.

Mowry, Sylvester. *Arizona and Sonora: The Geography, History and Resources of the Silver Region of North America.* New York: Harper & Brothers, Publishers, 1866.

Moya, José C. *Cousins and Strangers: Spanish Immigration in Buenos Aires, 1850–1930.* Berkeley: University of California Press, 1998.

———. "A Continent of Immigrants: Post-Colonial Shifts in the Western Hemisphere." *Hispanic American Historical Review* 86 (February 2006): 1–28.

Mutersbaugh, Ted. "Migration. "Common Property and Communal Labor: Cultural Politics and Agency in a Mexican Village." *Political Geography,* June 21, 2002.

Nagengast, Carole, and Michael Kearney. "Mixtec Ethnicity: Social Identity, Political Consciousness and Political Activism." *Latin American Research Review* 25, no. 2 (1990): 61–91.

Nagengast, Carole, Rodolfo Stavenhagen, and Michael Kearney. *Human Rights and Indigenous Workers: The Mixtecs in Mexico and the United States.* La Jolla, CA: University of California, San Diego, Center for U.S.–Mexican Studies, 1992.

National Archives, *Through Oil Fields of Mexico,* n.d.

National Center for Lesbian Rights. "The Challenges of Successful Lesbian Asylum Claims." http://www.nclrights.org/site/DocServer/challenges_lesbian_asylum_cases. pdf?docID=1142 (accessed August 1, 2009).

National Council of La Raza. "Out of the Picture: Hispanics in the Media." In *Latin Looks: Images of Latinas and Latinos in the U.S. Media,* edited by Clara E. Rodriguez, 21–35. Boulder, CO: Westview Press, 1997.

National Council of State Legislatures. "Immigrant Policy Project: 2009 Immigration-Related Bills and Resolutions." Washington, D.C.: National Council of State Legislatures, 2009. http://www.ncsl.org/documents/immig/2009ImmigFinalApril222009.pdf (accessed June 24, 2009).

National Immigration Law Center. "Overview of State's Driver's License Requirements." Washington, D.C.: National Immigration Law Center, 2008.

National Immigration Project. "HIV/AIDS and Immigrants, A Manual For Service Providers." http://www.nationalimmigrationproject.org/hiv/2004hivmanual (accessed August 1, 2009).

Neal, Micki, and Stephanie A. Bohon. "The Dixie Diaspora: Attitudes Toward Immigrants in Georgia." *Sociological Spectrum* 23 (2003): 181–212.

Nelson, Cynthia. *The Waiting Village: Social Change in Rural Mexico.* Boston: Brown Books, 1971.

"The New Nativism," *The Nation,* August 10, 2006.

Nevins, Joseph. *Operation Gatekeeper. The Rise of the 'Illegal Alien' and the Making of the U.S.– Mexico Boundary.* New York: Routledge, 2002.

———. "A Beating Worse Than Death: Imagining and Contesting Violence in the U.S.–Mexico Borderlands." *Ameriquests* 2 (2005). http://ejournals.library.vanderbilt.edu/ameriquests (accessed September 23, 2009).

Ngai, Mae. *Impossible Subjects: Illegal Aliens and the Making of Modern America.* Princeton, NJ: Princeton University Press, 2004.

Nodin Valdes, Dionicio. *Al Norte: Agricultural Workers in the Great Lakes Region, 1917–1970.* Austin, TX: University of Texas Press, 1991.

Noel, Linda Carol. "'The Swinging Door': U.S. National Identity and the Making of the Mexican Guestworker, 1900–1935." PhD Diss., University of Maryland, 2006.

North, David. *The Mexican Border Crossers: People Who Live in Mexico and Work in the United States.* Washington, D.C.: Department of Labor, 1970.

Novo, Salvador. *La vida en México en el periodo presidencial de Lázaro Cárdenas.* Mexico: Empresas Editoriales, S.A., 1964.

"Obama: Immigration Reform?" *Migration News* 15, no. 3 (July 2009). http://migration.ucda-vis.edu/mn/more.php?id=3522_0_2_0 (accessed September 23, 2009).

Oboler, Suzanne. *Ethnic Labels, Latino Lives: Identity and the Politics of (Re)Presentation in the United States.* Minneapolis, MN: University of Minnesota Press, 1995.

Obregón, Esquivel. *Influencia de España y los Estados Unidos sobre México.* Madrid: Casa Editorial Calleja, 1918.

Ocampo, Melchor. *Obras completas de Melchor Ocampo: Escritos políticos*, vol. 2, edited by F. Vasquez. Mexico, 1901.

———. "Unsettled in the Suburbs: Latino Immigration and Ethnic Diversity in Metro Atlanta." In *Twenty-First Century Gateways: Immigrant Integration in Suburban America*, edited by Audrey Singer, Susan W. Hardwick, and Caroline B. Brettell, 105–36. Washington, D.C.: Brookings Institution Press, 2008.

Odem, Mary E. "Unsettled in the Suburbs: Latino Immigration and Ethnic Diversity in Metro Atlanta." In *Twenty-First Century Gateways: Immigrant Integration in Suburban America*, edited by Audrey Singer, Susan W. Hardwick, and Caroline B. Brettell, 105–36. Washington, DC: Brookings Institution Press, 2008.

Odem, Mary, and Elaine Lacy, eds. *Latino Immigrants and the Transformation of the U.S. South.* Athens, GA: University of Georgia Press, 2009.

O'Leary, Anna Ochoa. "Close Encounters of the Deadly Kind: Gender, Migration, and Border (In)security." *Migration Letters* 5, no. 2 (October 2008): 111–21.

Ong, Aihwa. *Flexible Citizenship: The Cultural Logics of Transnationality.* Durham, NC: Duke University Press, 1999.

Oppenheimer, Rubén. "The Deportation Terror." *New Republic*, no. 69, January 13, 1932.

Organista, Kurt C., Héctor Carrillo, and George Ayala. "HIV Prevention with Mexican Migrants. Review, Critique, and Recommendations." *Journal of Acquired Immune Deficiency Syndrome* 37, suppl. 4 (November 1, 2004): 227–39.

Overmyer-Velázquez, Mark. "Traspasando las fronteras: Pasado y futuro de los estudios de migración México–Estados Unidos." In *Voces de la historiografía para una traza de América*, edited by Boris Berenzon and Georgina Calderón, 105–40. Morelia, Michoacán, México: Instituto de Investigaciones Históricas, Universidad Michoacana de San Nicolás de Hidalgo, 2007.

———, ed. *Latino America: State-by-State* (2 vols.) Westport, CT: Greenwood Press, 2008a.

———. "Transforming Race and Nation: New Trends in Latin(o) American Migration." *Latin American Perspectives* 35, no. 6 (2008b): 196–205.

Pachon, Harry P., et al. "Missing in Action: Latinos in and out of Hollywood." In *The Future of Latino Independent Media: A NALIP Sourcebook*, edited by Chon A. Noriega, 15–55. Los Angeles: University of California, Los Angeles, CSRC, 2000.

Padgett, Tim and Dolly Mascarenas. "Can a Mother Lose Her Child Because She Doesn't Speak English?," *Time*, August 27, 2009.

"Paranoia Pandemic: Conservative Media Baselessly Blame Swine Flu Outbreak on Immigrants." *Media Matters for America*, April 27, 2009.

Paredes, Américo. *Folklore and Culture on the Texas–Mexican Border.* Austin, TX: University of Texas Press, 1993.

Park, Edward J. W., and John S. W. Park. *Probationary Americans.* New York: Routledge, 2005.

Parker, Kunal M. "Thinking Space, Thinking Community: Lessons from Early American 'Immigrant' History." In *Repositioning North American Migration History: New Directions in Modern Continental Migration, Citizenship and Community*, edited by Marc S. Rodriguez, 284–301. Rochester, NY: University of Rochester Press, 2004.

Park, Michael Y. "Speedy Gonzales Caged by Cartoon Network," http://www.foxnews.com/story/03566,48872,00.html. March 28, 2002.

Parker, Morris B. *Mules, Mines, and Me in Mexico: 1895–1932.* Tucson, AZ: University of Arizona Press, 1979.

Parrado, Emilio A., and William A. Kandel. "New Hispanic Migrant Destinations: A Tale of Two Industries." In *New Faces in New Places: The Changing Geography of American Immigration,* edited by Douglas S. Massey, 99–123. New York: Russell Sage, 2008.

Passel, Jeffrey S. "Further Demographic Information Relating to the DREAM Act." Washington, D.C.: The Urban Institute, 2003.

——. "Naturalization Trends and Opportunities: A Focus on Mexicans." Washington, D.C.: Pew Hispanic Center, 2005a.

——. "Unauthorized Migrants: Numbers and Characteristics." Washington, D.C.: Pew Hispanic Center, 2005b.

Passel, Jeffrey S., and Cohn, D'Vera. "A Portrait of the Unauthorized Immigrants in the United States." Washington, D.C.: Pew Hispanic Center, 2009.

Pastor, Robert A., and Jorge G. Castañeda. *Limits to Friendship: The United States and Mexico.* New York: Vintage Books, 1988.

Paz, Ireno and Manuel Tornel. *Guía de México.* México: Imprenta de Ireneo Paz, 1882.

Paz, Octavio. *El Laberinto de la soledad.* Mexico City: Fondo de Cultura Económica, 1959.

Peacock, James L., Harry L. Watson, and Carrie R. Matthews, eds. *The American South in a Global World.* Chapel Hill, NC: University of North Carolina Press, 2005.

Peck, Gunther. *Reinventing Free Labor: Padrones and Immigrant Workers in the North American West, 1880–1930.* Cambridge, UK: Cambridge University Press, 2000.

Pennybacker, Anna J. Hardwicke. *A History of Texas.* Austin, TX: Mrs. Percy Pennybacker Publishers, 1912.

Peña Delgado, Grace. "At Exclusion's Southern Gate: Changing Categories of Race and Class among Chinese Fronterizos." In *Continental Crossroads: Remapping U.S.–Mexico Borderlands History,* edited by Samuel Truett and Elliot Young, 183–207. Durham, NC: Duke University Press, 2004.

Pérez, Emma. "Queering the Borderlands. The Challenge of Excavating the Invisible and the Unheard." *Frontier* 24, no. 2–3 (2003): 122–31.

Pérez Montfort, Ricardo. *Hispanismo y falange. Los sueños imperiales de la derecha española y México,* México: Fondo de Cultura Económica, 1992.

——. *Estampas de nacionalismo popular mexicano. Ensayos sobre cultura popular y nacionalismo.* México: CIESAS, Ediciones de la Casa Chata, 1994a.

——. "Los estereotipos nacionales y la educación posrevolucionaria en México, (1920–1930)", en Pérez Montfort, *Estampas de nacionalismo popular mexicano.* México, CIESAS, Ediciones de la Casa Chata, 1994b.

——. *Estampas de nacionalismo popular mexicano. Ensayos sobre cultura popular y nacionalismo,* México, CIESAS, Ediciones de la Casa Chata, 1994c.

Pérez Rendon, Alberto. "The Mental Health Status of the Yucatec Maya in San Francisco: A Community Health Needs Assessment." San Francisco: San Francisco State University Department of Health Education, August 2005.

Perucho, Javier. *Migrantes, pachucos y chicanos en la literatura mexicana.* México: Conaculta, 2000.

Pessar, Patricia R., and Sarah J. Mahler. "Transnational Migration: Bringing Gender In." *International Migration Review* 37 (Fall 2003): 812–46.

Pew Hispanic Center. "Who's Hispanic?" May 28, 2009. http://pewhispanic.org/reports/report.php?ReportID=111 (accessed September 24, 2009a).

Pew Hispanic Center. "Hispanics of Mexican Origin in the United States, 2007." September 16, 2009b. http://pewhispanic.org/files/factsheets/49.pdf (accessed September 24, 2009).

——. "Troubled by Crime, the Economy, Drugs and Corruption: Most Mexicans See Better Life in U.S.—One-in-Three Would Migrate." September 23, 2009c. http://pewglobal.org/reports/pdf/266.pdf (accessed September 23, 2009).

——. "Unemployment Rose Sharply Among Latino Immigrants in 2008." Washington, D.C.: Pew Hispanic Center, 2009d.

Pew Hispanic Center. "Mexican Immigrants in the United States, 2008." Washington, D.C.: Pew Hispanic Center, 2009e.

Pew Hispanic Center/Kaiser Family Foundation. "National Survey of Latinos." Washington, D.C.: Pew Hispanic Center, December 17, 2002.

Pham, Huyen. "The Inherent Flaws in the Inherent Authority Position: Why Inviting Local Enforcement of Immigration Laws Violates the Constitution." *Florida State University Law Review* 31 (2004): 965–1003.

——. "The Private Enforcement of Immigration Laws." *Georgetown Law Journal* 96 (2008): 1–50.

Pimentel, Francisco. *Obras completas de D. Francisco Pimentel*. México: Tipografía Económica, 1903.

Pitt, Leonard. *The Decline of the Californios: A Social History of the Spanish-Speaking Californians 1846–1890*. Berkeley: University of California Press, 1966.

Pitti, Stephen. *The Devil in Silicon Valley: Northern California, Race, and Mexican Americans*. Princeton, NJ: Princeton University Press, 2003.

Pla Brugat, Dolores, "Características del exilio en México en 1939", en Lida, Clara E., *Una inmigración privilegiada. Comerciantes, empresarios y profesionales españoles en México en los siglos XIX y XX*, Madrid: Alianza Editorial, 1994.

Planchet, Regis. *La cuestión religiosa en México ó sea vida de Benito Juárez*. Rome: Librería Pontificia de Desclée, LeFebvre y Cia, 1906.

Pletcher, David. *Rails, Mines and Progress: Seven American Promoters in Mexico, 1867–1911*. Ithaca, NY: Cornell University Press, 1958.

Pletcher, David M. "The Fall of Silver in Mexico, 1870–1910, and Its Effects on American Investments." *Journal of Economic History* 18 (March 1958): 33–55.

Poblete, Juan, ed. *Critical Latin American and Latino Studies*. Minneapolis, MN: University of Minnesota Press, 2003.

Portes, Alejandro. "Global Villagers: The Rise of Transnational Communities." *The American Prospect*. March 1, 1996.

Portes, Alejandro, and Robert L. Bach. *Latin Journey: Cuban and Mexican Immigrants in the United States*. Berkeley: University of California Press, 1985.

Portes, Alejandro, and Rubén G. Rumbaut. *Legacies: The Story of the Immigrant Second Generation*. Berkeley: University of California Press, 2001.

Posadas Segura, Florencio. *Movimientos sociales de los trabajadores agrícolas asalariados en el noroeste de México, 1970–1995*, Culiacán, Sinaloa: Universidad Autónoma de Sinaloa, 2005.

Povinelli, Elizabeth A., and George Chanucey. "Thinking Sexuality Transnationally. An Introduction." *GLQ* 5 (1997): 439–50.

Preston, Julia. "Survey Shows Pull of the U.S. Is Still Strong Inside Mexico." *New York Times*. September 24, 2009a.

——. "U.S. Opens Path to Asylum for Victims of Sexual Abuse." *New York Times*. July 16, 2009b.

Prieto, Guillermo. "Crónicas de Viaje a los Estados Unidos." In *Obras Completas de Guillermo Prieto*, vol 6. Mexico: Consejo Nacional para la Cultura y el Arte, 1993.

Project on Excellence in Journalism, *PEJ Talk Show Index:* June 3–8, 2007.

Quan, Robert Seto. *Lotus among the Magnolias: The Mississippi Chinese.* Jackson, MS: University Press of Mississippi, 1982.

Quijada Hernández, Armando, and Juan Antonio Ruibal Covella, eds. *Historia General de Sonora, 1831–1883*, vol. 3. Hermosillo: Gobierno del Estado de Sonora, 1985.

Raat, W. Dirk, and Michael Brescia, *Mexico and the United States: Ambivalent Vistas*, 4th ed. Athens, GA: University of Georgia Press, 2010.

Ramirez Berg, Charles. *Latino Images in Film: Stereotypes, Subversion & Resistance.* Austin, TX: University of Texas Press, 2002.

Ramírez Romero, Silvia J. *La reconstrucción de la identidad política del Frente Indígena Oaxaqueño Binacional.* México: Comisión Nacional para el Desarrollo de los Pueblos Indígenas, 2003.

Ramón Garcia, Juan. *Operation Wetback: The Mass Deportation of Mexican Undocumented Workers in 1954.* Westport, CT: Greenwood Press, 1980.

"REAL ID, States and Cities." *Migration News* 14, no. 2 (2008).

Reddy, Chandan. "Asian Diasporas, Neoliberalism, and Family: Reviewing the Case for Homosexual Asylum in the Context of Family Rights." *Social Text* 84–85 (Winter 2005): 101–19.

Reichert, Joshua. "A Town Divided: Economic Stratification and Social Relations in a Mexican Migrant Community." *Social Problems* 29 (1982): 411–23.

Reimers, David M. "Asian Immigrants in the South." In *Globalization and the American South*, edited by James C. Cobb and William Stueck, 100–34. Athens, GA: University of Georgia Press, 2005.

Reinemeyer, Gretchen, and Jeanne Batalova. "Spotlight on Legal Immigration to the United States." Washington, D.C.: Migration Policy Institute, 2007.

Reisler, Mark. *By the Sweat of Their Brow: Mexican Immigrant Labor in the United States, 1900–1940.* Westport, CT: Greenwood Press, 1976.

Rénique, Gerardo. "Race, Region, and Nation: Sonora's Anti-Chinese Racism and Mexico's Postrevolutionary Nationalism, 1920s–1930s." In *Race and Nation in Modern Latin America*, edited by Nancy P. Appelbaum, Anne S. Macpherson, Karin Alejandra Rosemblatt, 211–36. Chapel Hill, NC: University of North Carolina Press, 2003.

Report of the Industrial Commission of Immigration, 1901.

Reports of the Committee of Investigations Sent in 1873 by the Mexican Government to the Frontier of Texas. New York: Baker & Goodwin Printers, 1875.

Reséndez, Andrés. *Changing National Identities at the Frontier: Texas and New Mexico, 1800–1850.* Cambridge, UK: Cambridge University Press. 2005.

"Restauración del regimen federativo" in *Boletín de la Sociedad de Geografía y Estadística de la República Mexicana*, 1894.

Reynolds, Clark W. *The Mexican Economy: Twentieth Century Structure and Growth.* New Haven: Yale University Press, 1970.

Rice, Claude T. "Mines of Penoles Company, Mapimi, Mex.—I." *Engineering and Mining Journal* 86 (August 15, 1908).

Rich, Brian L., and Marta Miranda. "The Sociopolitical Dynamics of Mexican Immigration in Lexington, Kentucky, 1977 to 2002: An Ambivalent Community Responds." In *New Destinations: Mexican Immigration to the United States*, edited by Victor Zúñiga and Rubén Hernández-León, 187–219. New York: Russell Sage, 2005.

Richardson, Albert D. *Beyond the Mississippi.* Hartford, CT: American Publishing Company, 1869.

Rico, Carlos. "Migration and U.S.–Mexican Relations, 1966–1986." In *Western Hemisphere Immigration and United States Foreign Policy,* edited by Christopher Mitchell, 221–83. University Park, PA: Pennsylvania State University Press, 1992.

Rivera-Salgado, Gaspar. "Mixtec Activism in Oaxacalifornia." *American Behavioral Scientist* 42 (1999): 1439–58.

Rivera-Salgado, Gaspar. "Binational Grass-Roots Organizations and the Experience of Indigenous Migrants." In *Cross-Border Dialogues: U.S.–Mexico Social Movement Networking,* edited by David Brooks and Jonathan Fox, 259–74. La Jolla, CA: University of California, San Diego, Center for U.S.–Mexican Studies, 2002.

Rivera-Salgado, Gaspar, and Luis Escala Rabadán. "Collective Identity and Organizational Strategies among Indigenous and Mestizo Mexican Migrants." In *Indigenous Mexican Migrants in the United States,* edited by Jonathan Fox and Gaspar Rivera-Salgado, 145–178. La Jolla, CA: University of California, San Diego, Center for Comparative Immigration Studies & Center for U.S.–Mexican Studies, 2004.

Rivera-Salgado, Gaspar, and Veronica Wilson. *Today We March, Tomorrow We Vote: Latino Migrant Civic Engagement in L.A.* Washington, D.C.: Woodrow Wilson Center for Scholars, June 2009.

Robles, Sergio. "Migration and Return in the *Sierra Juárez.*" In *Indigenous Mexican Migrants in the United States,* edited by Jonathan Fox and Gaspar Rivera-Salgado, 467–82. La Jolla, CA: University of California, San Diego, Center for Comparative Immigration Studies/Center for U.S.–Mexican Studies, 2004.

Robinson, William I. "Why the Immigrant Rights Struggle Compels Us to Reconceptualize Both Latin American and Latino/a Studies." *Forum, Latin American Studies Association* 38, no. 2.

Rocco, Raymond. "Transforming Citizenship: Membership, Strategies of Containment and the Public Sphere in Latino Communities." *Latino Studies* 2, no. 4–5 (2004): 4–25.

Rockquemore, Kerry Ann. "Negotiating the Color Line: The Gendered Process of Racial Identity Construction among Black/White Biracial Women." *Gender & Society* 16 (2002): 485–503.

Rodríguez, Cristina, Muzaffar Chisti, and Kimberly Nortman. "Testing the Limits: A Framework for Assessing the Legality of State and Local Immigration Measures." Washington, D.C.: Migration Policy Institute, 2007.

Rogers, Allen H. "Character and Habits of Mexican Miners." *Engineering and Mining Journal* 85 (April 6, 1908): 700.

Romero, Matias. "The Free Zone in Mexico." *North American Review,* no. 322 (1892): 459.

———. Mexico and the United States (New York: G.P. Putnam's Sons, 1898.

Romero, Matías, ed. *Reciprocidad comercial entre México y los Estados Unidos (el Tratado Comercial de 1883.* México: Colección de documentos para la historia del comercio exterior de México; Publicaciones del Banco Nacional de Comercio Exterior, S.A., 1971.

Romo, Richard. *East Los Angeles: History of a Barrio.* Austin, TX: University of Texas Press, 1983.

Rosaldo, Renato. "Cultural Citizenship, Inequality, and Multiculturalism." In *Latino Cultural Citizenship: Claiming Identity, Space, and Rights,* edited by William V. Flores and Rina Benmayor, 27–38. Boston: Beacon Press, 1997.

Rose, Nikolas. *Powers of Freedom: Reframing Political Thought.* Cambridge, UK: Cambridge University Press, 1999.

Rosenblum, Marc R. "Moving Beyond the Policy of No Policy: Emigration from Mexico and Central America." *Latin American Politics and Society* 46(4) (2004): 91–126.

Ross, Edward Alsworth. *The Social Revolution in Mexico.* New York: Century, 1923.

Rouse, Roger. "Mexican Migration and the Social Space of Postmodernism." In *Between Two Worlds: Mexican Immigrants in the United States,* edited by David G. Gutierrez, 247–64. Wilmington, DE: Scholarly Resources, 1977.

Rudolph, James D. *Mexico: A Country Study.* Washington, D.C.: Foreign Area Studies, The American University, 1985.

Ruggles, Steven, Matthew Sobek, Trent Alexander, Catherine A. Fitch, Ronald Goeken, Patricia Kelly Hall, Miriam King, and Chad Ronnander. *Integrated Public Use Microdata Series: Version 3.0 [Machine-readable database].* Minneapolis, MN: Minnesota Population Center, 2004. http://www.ipums.org (accessed June 1, 2009).

Ruíz, Vicki L. *Cannery Women/Cannery Lives: Mexican Women, Unionization and the California Food Industry, 1930–1950.* Albuquerque, NM: University of New Mexico Press, 1987.

———. "Nuestra América: Latino History as United States History." *Journal of American History* 93 (December 2006): 655–72.

Rus, Diane, and Jan Rus. "La migracion de los trabajadores indigenas de Los Altos de Chiapas a Estados Unidos, 2001–2005: El caso de San Juan Chamula." In *Migraciones en el sur de Mexico y Centroamerica,* edited by Daniel Villafuerte Solís and Maria del Carmen Garcia Aguilar. Mexico City: UNICACh/Porrúa, 2008.

Rus, Jan. "The 'Comunidad Revolucionaria Internacional:' The Subversion of Native Government in Highland Chiapas, 1936–1968." In *Everyday Forms of State Formation: Revolution and the Negotiation of Rule in Modern Mexico,* edited by Gilbert Joseph and Daniel Nugent, 265–300. Durham, NC: Duke University Press, 1994.

Sacchetti, Maria. "Nervous Employers Turn to ID Check for Workers." *Boston Globe,* March 6, 2009.

Saenz, Rogelio. "Earnings Patterns of Mexican Workers in the Southern Region: A Focus on Nonmetro/Metro Distinctions." *Southern Rural Sociology* 16 (2000): 60–95.

Saenz, Rogelio, Katharine M. Donato, Lourdes Gouveia, and Cruz C. Torres. 2003. "Latinos in the South: A Glimpse of Ongoing Trends and Research." *Southern Rural Sociology* 19(1): 1–19.

Saldívar, José David. *Border Matters: Remapping American Cultural Studies.* Berkeley: University of California Press, 1997.

Salinas Alvarez, Samuel. *Demanda educativa de la población jornalera agrícola migrante,* Mexico City: Secretaría de Educación Pública, 2006.

Samora, Julian. *Los Mojados: The Wetback Story.* Notre Dame, IN: University of Notre Dame Press, 1971.

Sanchez, George J. "'Go after the Women': Americanization and the Mexican Immigrant Woman 1915–1929." In *Unequal Sisters: A Multicultural Reader in U.S. Women's History,* edited by Ellen Carol DuBois and Vicki L. Ruiz, 250–63. New York: Routledge, 1990.

———. *Becoming Mexican American: Ethnicity, Culture, and Identity in Chicano Los Angeles, 1900–1945.* Oxford, UK: Oxford University Press, 1993.

———. "Face the Nation: Race, Immigration and the Rise of Nativism in Late Twentieth Century America." *International Migration Review* 31 (Winter 1997): 1009–30.

Sánchez Gómez, Martha Judith. "Algunos aportes de la literatura sobre migración indígena y la importancia de la comunidad." *Center for Migration and Development Working Paper Series,* no. 5 (January 2005). http://econpapers.repec.org/paper/pricmgdev/372.htm (accessed June 1, 2009).

Sánchez Gómez, Martha Judith. "La importancia del sistema de cargos en el entendimiento de los flujos migratorios indigenas." In *El país transnacional: Migración mexicana y cambio social a través de la frontera*, edited by Marina Ariza and Alejandro Portes, 349–90. Mexico: UNAM/IIS, 2007.

Sánchez Mejorada, Javier. *Obra social de la Comisión Nacional de Irrigación*. Mexico: CNI, 1928.

Santa Ana (California) Board of Education. Minutes. June 5, 1919.

Santa Ana, Otto. *Brown Tide Rising: Metaphors of Latinos in Contemporary American Public Discourse*. Austin, TX: University of Texas Press, 2002.

Santibáñez, Enrique. *Ensayo acerca de la inmigración mexicana en los Estados Unidos*. San Antonio, TX: Clegg, 1930.

Saragoza, Alex M. "Recent Chicano Historiography: An Interpretive Essay." *Aztlán* 19 (Spring 1988–1990): 1–77.

Sassen, Saskia. *Globalization and Its Discontents*. New York: New Press, 1998.

Saxbe v. Bustos, 419 U.S. 65 (1974).

Schaeffer-Grabiel, Felicity. "Cyberbrides and Global Imaginaries: Mexican Women's Turn from the National to the Foreign." In *Women and Migration in the U.S.-Mexico Borderlands: A Reader*, edited by Denise Segura and Patricia Zavella, 503–20. Durham, NC: Duke University Press, 2007.

Schiller, Nina Glick, ed. *Towards a Transnational Perspective on Migration: Race, Class, Ethnicity, and Nationalism Reconsidered*. New York: New York Academy of Sciences, 1992.

——. "Transmigrants and Nation-States: Something Old and Something New in the U.S. Immigrant Experience." In *The Handbook of International Migration: The American Experience*, edited by Charles Hirschman, Philip Kasinitz, and Josh DeWind, 94–119. New York: Russell Sage Foundation, 1999.

Schiller, Nina Glick, Linda Basch, and Cristina Blanc-Szanton. "Towards a Definition of Transnationalism: Introductory Remarks and Research Questions." In *Towards a Transnational Perspective on Migration*, edited by Nica Glick Schiller, Linda Basch, and Cristina Blanc-Szanton, vol. 645, ix–xiv. New York: The New York Academy of Sciences, 1993.

Schmid, Carol. "Immigration and Asian and Hispanic Minorities in the New South: An Exploration of History, Attitudes, and Demographic Trends." *Sociological Spectrum* 23, no. 2 (2003): 129–57.

Schmidt, Ella and María Crummett. "Heritage Recreated: Hidalguenses in the U.S. and Mexico," In Jonathan Fox and Gaspar Rivera-Salgado, eds., *Indigenous Mexican Migrants in the United States*, 401–418. La Jolla: UC San Diego, Center for Comparative Immigration Studies/Center for US-Mexican Studies, 2004.

Schmidt Camacho, Alicia. *Migrant Imaginaries: Latino Cultural Politics in the U.S.-Mexico Borderlands*. New York: New York University Press, 2008.

Schoenholtz, Andrew I. "Newcomers in Rural Arkansas: Hispanic Immigrants in Rogers, Arkansas." In *Beyond the Gateway: Immigrants in a Changing America*, edited by Elzbieta Gozdziak and Susan F. Martin, 213–38. Lanham, MD: Lexington Books, 2005.

Schuck, Peter H., and Rogers M. Smith. *Citizenship without Consent: Illegal Aliens in the American Polity*. New Haven, CT: Yale University Press, 1985.

Secretaría de Fomento, Colonización e Industria y Comercio, *La crisis monetaria: estudios sobre la crisis mercantil y la depresión de la plata*. México: Oficina tipográfica de la Secretaría de Fomento, 1886.

Secretaría de Gobernación. 1996. *Compilación Histórica de la Legislación Migratoria en México, 1909–1996*. México, D.F.: Secretaría de Gobernación.

Secretaría de Relaciones Exteriores de México. "Migrantes mexicanos fallecidos en la frontera sur de EUA en su intento por internarse sin documentos, 2004–2010." Mexico: SRE, 2010.

Segunda parte del expediente formado en la Secretaría de Hacienda y Crédito Público sobre el proyecto de arancel. México: Imprenta de Gobierno en Palacio, 1869.

Segura, Denise A., and Patricia Zavella. "Introduction" In *Women and Migration in the U.S.–Mexico Borderlands: A Reader*, edited by Denise Segura and Patricia Zavella, 1–32. Durham, NC: Duke University Press, 2007.

———. "Introduction: Gendered Borderlands." *Gender and Society* 22 (October 2008): 537–44.

Seis años de gobierno 1934–1940. México, Talleres Tipográficos de la Nación, 1940.

"Senate: Immigration Reform Stalls." *Migration News* 13, no. 3 (2007).

Senate Reports of the Immigration Commission, Abstracts of Reports of the Immigration Commission (1912).

Serrano Carreto, Enrique, Arnulfo Embriz Osorio and Patricia Fernandez Ham, eds. *Indicadores socioeconomicos de los pueblos indigenas, 2002*, Mexico: Instituto Nacional Indigenista/Programa de las Nacionaes Undias para el Desarrollo, 2003.

Sheahan, John. *Patterns of Development in Latin America*. Princeton, NJ: Princeton University Press, 1987.

Shepherd, Grant. *The Silver Magnet: Fifty Years in Mexican Silver Mine*. New York: E. P. Dutton and Co., 1938.

Shukla, Sandhya, and Heidi Tinsman. "Editors' Introduction." *Radical History Review* 89 (Spring 2004): 1–10.

———, eds. *Imagining Our Americas: Toward a Transnational Frame*. Durham, NC: Duke University Press, 2007.

Simpich, Frederick. "A Mexican Land of Canaan," *The National Geographic*, July 1919.

Simpson, Leslie Byrd. *Many Mexicos*, 4th ed. Revised. Berkeley: University of California Press, 1966.

Singer, Audrey, and Douglas S. Massey. "The Social Process of Undocumented Border Crossing." *International Migration Review* 32 (1997): 561–92.

Sklair, Leslie. *Assembling for Development: The Maquila Industry in Mexico and the United States*. San Diego, CA: University of California, San Diego, Center for U.S.–Mexican Studies, 1993.

Smith, Anna Marie. *Welfare Reform and Sexual Regulation*. New York: Cambridge University Press, 2007.

Smith, Barbara Ellen. "Across Races and Nations: Toward Worker Justice in the U.S. South." Paper presented at the *Color Lines Conference*, Harvard Law School, Cambridge, MA (August 29–September 1, 2003).

Smith, Barbara Ellen, Marcela Mendoza, and David H. Ciscel. "The World on Time: Flexible Labor, New Immigrants, and Global Logistics." In *The American South in a Global World*, edited by James L. Peacock, Harry L. Watson, and Carrie R. Matthews, 23–38. Chapel Hill, NC: University of North Carolina Press, 2005.

Smith, Heather A., and Owen J. Furuseth, eds.*The New South: Latinos and the Transformation of Place*. Aldershot, UK: Ashgate Press, 2006.

———. "The 'Nuevo South': Latino Place Making and Community Building in the Middle-Ring Suburbs of Charlotte." In *Twenty-First Century Gateways: Immigrant Incorporation in*

Suburban America, edited by Audrey Singer, Susan W. Hardwick, and Caroline B. Brettell, 281–307. Washington, D.C.: Brookings Institution Press, 2008.

Smith, Michael M., "The Mexican Secret Service in the United States, 1910–1920", in *The Americas*, vol. 59, no. 1, July 2002.

Smith, Michael P., and Matt Bakker. *Citizenship across Borders: The Political Transnationalism of El Migrante*. Cornell, NY: Cornell University Press, 2007.

Smith, Robert C. *Mexican New York: The Transnational Lives of New Immigrants*. Berkeley: University of California Press, 2006.

Smith, Rogers. *Stories of Peoplehood: The Politics and Morals of Political Membership*. Cambridge, UK: Cambridge University Press, 2003.

Smith-Nonini, Sandy. "Federally Sponsored Mexican Migrants in the Transnational South." *The American South in a Global World*, edited by James L. Peacock, Harry L. Watson, and Carrie R. Matthews, 59–79. Chapel Hill, NC: University of North Carolina Press, 2005.

———. "H2A Guest Workers and the State in North Carolina: From Transnational Production to Transnational Organizing." In *Global Connections & Local Receptions: New Latino Immigration to the Southeastern United States*, edited by Fran Ansley and Jon Shefner, 249–78. Knoxville, TN: University of Tennessee Press, 2009.

Snodgrass, Michael. "Patronage and Progress: The Bracero Program from the Perspective of Mexico." In *Workers across the Americas: The Transnational Turn in Labor History*, edited by Leon Fink. New York: Oxford University Press, 2011, 245–66.

Sohoni, Deenesh. "The 'Immigrant Problem': Modern-Day Nativism on the Web." *Current Sociology* 54 (2006): 827–50.

Somerville, Siobhan. *Queering the Color Line*. Durham, NC: Duke University Press, 2000.

Sridharan, Swetha. "The Difficulties of US Asylum Claims Based on Sexual Orientation." Council on Foreign Relations, 2008. http://www.migrationinformation.org/Feature/print. cfm?ID=700 (accessed August 1, 2009).

Stack, Carol. *Call to Home: African Americans Reclaim the Rural South*. New York: Basic Books, 1996.

Standart, Mary Colette. "The Sonoran Migration to California, 1848–1856: A Study in Prejudice." In *Between Two Worlds: Mexican Immigration in the United States*, edited by David G. Gutiérrez, 3–22. Wilmington, MD: Scholarly Resources, 1996.

Stephen, Lynn. *¡Zapata Lives! Histories and Cultural Politics in Southern Mexico*. Berkeley: University of California Press, 2002.

———. "Mixtec Farmworkers in Oregon: Linking Labor and Ethnicity through Farmworker Unions and Hometown Associations," In *Indigenous Mexican Migrants in the United States*, edited by Jonathan Fox and Gaspar Rivera-Salgado, 179–202. La Jolla, CA: University of California, San Diego, Center for Comparative Immigration Studies & Center for U.S.-Mexican Studies, 2004.

———. *Transborder Lives: Indigenous Oaxacan Migrants in the U.S. and Mexico*. Durham, NC: Duke University Press, 2007.

Stoddard, Ellwyn R. *Maquila: Assembly Plants in Northern Mexico*. El Paso: Texas Western Press, 1987.

Stoddard, Ellwyn R., Oscar J. Martínez, and Miguel Angel Martínez Lasso. *Maquila: Assembly Plants in Northern Mexico*. El Paso, TX: Texas Western Press, 1987.

Striffler, Steven. "Inside a Poultry Processing Plant: An Ethnographic Portrait." *Labor History* 43 (2002): 305–13.

———. *Chicken: The Dangerous Transformation of America's Favorite Food*. New Haven, CT: Yale University Press, 2005.

———. "Immigration Anxieties: Policing and Regulating Workers and Employers in the Poultry Industry." In *Global Connections & Local Receptions: New Latino Immigration to the Southeastern United States*, edited by Fran Ansley and Jon Shefner, pp 129–54. Knoxville, TN: University of Tennessee Press, 2009.

Studstill, John D., and Laura Neito-Studstill. "Hospitality and Hostility: Latin Immigrants in Southern Georgia." Pp. 68–81 in *Latino Workers in the Contemporary South*, edited by Arthur D. Murphy, Colleen Blanchard, and Jennifer A. Hill. Athens: University of Georgia Press, 2001.

Stuesse, Angela C. "Race, Migration, and Labor Control: Neoliberal Challenges to Organizing Mississippi's Poultry Workers." In *Latino Immigrants and the Transformation of the U.S. South*, edited by Mary E. Odem and Elaine Lacy, 91–111. Athens, GA: University of Georgia Press, 2009.

Stull, Donald D., and Michael J. Broadway. *Slaughterhouse Blues: The Meat and Poultry Industry in North America*. Belmont, CA: Wadsworth, a division of Thomson Learning, 2004.

Suárez-Orozco, Marcelo. "Mexican Immigration…and the Latinization of the United States." *ReVista: Harvard Review of Latin America*. Fall 2001.

Suárez, Marcelo M., and Mariela M. Páez, *Latinos: Remaking America*. Berkeley: University of California Press, 2009.

Suro, Roberto, and Audrey Singer. "Latino Growth in Metropolitan America: Changing Patterns, New Locations." Survey Series, Census 2000. Washington, D.C.: The Brookings Institution, 2002.

Suro, Roberto, and Gabriel Escobar. "*Survey of Mexicans Living in the U.S. on Absentee Voting in Mexican Elections*." Washington, D.C.: Pew Hispanic Center, 2006.

Swanson, Barbara, Katharine Ballash, and Michelle Kost. "No Culture Left Behind: Reaching the Purepecha Indigenous People." *ORTESOL Journal*, 2006. www.ortesol.org/journal/08/no_culture_left_behind.pdf.

Swarns, Rachel L. "A Racial Rift That Isn't Black and White." *New York Times*, October 3, 2006a.

———. "In Georgia, Immigrants Unsettle Old Sense of Place." *New York Times*, August 4, 2006b.

Szasz, Ivonne. "La perspectiva de género en el estudio de la migración femenina en México." In *Mujer, género y población en México*, edited by Brígada García, 167–210. Mexico City: El Colegio de México/Sociedad Mexicana de Demografía, 1999.

Taylor, Paul S. *Mexican Labor in the United States*, 12 vols. Berkley: University of California Press, 1928–1934.

———. *An American–Mexican Frontier: Nueces County, Texas*. Chapel Hill, NC: University of North Carolina Press, 1934.

Teague, Charles C. *Fifty Years as a Rancher*. Los Angeles: Ward Ritchie Press, 1944.

Telles, Edward, and Vilma Ortiz. *Generations of Exclusion: Mexican Americans, Assimilation, and Race*. New York: Russell Sage Foundation, 2008.

Thompson, Jerry. *Cortina: Defending the Mexican Name in Texas*. College Station, TX: Texas A & M University Press, 2007.

Thrall, Homer S. *A Pictorial History of Texas, from the Earliest Visits of European Adventurers, to A.D. 1879*. St. Louis, MO: N. D. Thompson, 1879.

Torres, Rebecca, Jeff Popke, Holly Hapke, Matilde Elisa Suarez, Heidi Serrano, Brian Chambers, and Paola Castaño. "Transnational Communities in Eastern North Carolina: Results from a Survey of Latino Families in Greene County." *The North Carolina Geographer* 11 (2003): 88–107.

Torres, Rebecca, E. Jeffrey Popke, and Holly M. Hapke. "The South's Silent Bargain: Rural Restructuring, Latino Labor and the Ambiguities of Migrant Experience." In *The New South: Latinos and the Transformation of Place*, edited by Heather A. Smith and Owen J. Furuseth, 37–68. Aldershot, UK: Ashgate Press, 2006.

Torres Bodet, Jaime. *La victoria sin alas... Memorias*. México: Porrúa, 1970.

Treff, Simon Ludwig. "The Education of Mexican Children in Orange County, California." Master's Thesis, University of Southern California, 1934.

Truett, Samuel, and Elliott Young, eds. *Continental Crossroads: Remapping U.S.-Mexico Borderlands History*. Durham, NC: Duke University Press, 2004.

Tumlin, Karen, Linton Joaquin, and Ranjana Natarajan. "A Broken System: Confidential Reports Reveal Failures in U.S. Immigrant Detention Centers." Washington, D.C.: National Immigration Law Center, 2009.

Turner, Frederick J. *The Frontier in American History*. New York: Henry Holt, 1920.

Tutino, John. "The Revolutionary Capacity of Rural Communities." In *Cycles of Conflict, Centuries of Change: Crisis, Reform and Revolution in Mexico*, edited by Elisa Servín, Leticia Reina, and John Tutino, 211–61. Durham, NC: Duke University Press, 2007.

Tweedie, Mrs. Alec. *Mexico as I Saw It*. London: Hurst and Blackett, 1901.

United Nations. *Trend in Total Migrant Stock: The 2008 Revision*. New York: UN Population Division, Department of Economic and Social Affairs, 2009.

United Nations Population Division. http://www.un.org/esa/population/unpop.htm (accessed September 24, 2009).

United States Court of Appeals For the Ninth Circuit, no. 04–70868, Jorge Soto Vega, Petitioner, v. John Ashcroft, Attorney General, Respondent, On Appeal from the United States Board of Immigration Appeals, Opening Brief of the Petitioner, by Jon W. Davidson, Lambda Legal Defense and Education Fund, Inc., 2006.

Urías Horcaditas, Beatriz, "Eugenesia e ideas sobre las razas en México, 1930–1950." In *Historia y Grafía*, vol. 17, 172–201. México: Universidad Iberoamericana, 2001.

Uribe Salas, José A., and Álvaro Ochoa Serrano. *Emigrantes del Oeste*. Mexico City: Consejo Nacional para la Cultura y las Artes, 1990.

U.S. Bureau of Foreign Commerce, 1896.

U.S. Census Bureau http://www.census.gov/newsroom/releases/archives/facts_for_features_special_editions/cb10-ff17.html, July 15, 2010 (accessed July 30, 2010).

U.S. Immigration and Naturalization Service. *Statistical Yearbooks of the Immigration and Naturalization Service*, 1978, 1985, 2003.

U.S. Select Commission on Immigration and Refugee Policy, *U.S. Immigration Policy and the National Interest*. Washington, D.C.: Government Printing Office, 1981.

U.S. Select Commission on Western Hemisphere Immigration, *The Impact of Commuter Aliens along the Mexican and Canadian Borders*, 1970.

Vaca, Nick C. "The Mexican-American in the Social Sciences, 1912–1935, Part I." *El Grito* 3, no. 3 (1970): 3–24.

Vallas, Steven P. and Emily Zimmerman. "Sources of Variation in Attitudes Toward Illegal Immigration." Fairfax, VA: Center for Social Science Research, George Mason University, 2007.

Vargas, Zaragoza. *Labor Rights Are Civil Rights: Mexican American Workers in Twentieth Century America*. Princeton, NJ: Princeton University Press, 2005.

Vargas y Campos, Gloria. *El problema del bracero mexicano*. Mexico: Universidad Nacional Autonoma de México, 1964.

Varsanyi, Monica. "Interrogating 'Urban Citizenship' vis-à-vis Undocumented Migration." *Citizenship Studies* 10 (2006): 229–49.

Vásquez, Manuel A., Chad E. Seales, and Marie Friedmann Marquardt. "New Latino Destinations." In *Latinas/os in the United States: Changing the Face of America*, edited by Hávidan Rodríguez, Rogelio Saenz, and Cecília Menjívar, 19–35. New York: Springer, 2008.

Vaughn, Bobby, and Ben Vinson III. "Unfinished Migrations: From the Mexican South to the American South: Impressions on Afro-Mexican Migration to North Carolina." In *Beyond Slavery: The Multilayered Legacy of Africans in Latin America and the Caribbean*, edited by Darién J. Davis, 223–45. New York: Rowman & Littlefield Publishers, 2007.

Vaughan, Mary Kay. "Ideological Changes in Mexican Educational Policy, Programs, and Texts (1920–1940)." In *Los intelectuales y el poder en México. Memoria de la VI Reunión de Historiadores Mexicanos y Estadounidenses*, 507–26. Mexico: El Colegio de México, University of California, Los Ángeles, UCLA Latin American Center Publications, 1991.

Velasco Grajales, Jesús. "Acuerdo migratorio: la debilidad de la esperanza." Documento de Trabajo, no. 168, CIDE, January 2008.

Velasco Ortiz, Laura. *El regreso de la comunidad: migración indígena y agentes étnicos (Los mixtecos en la frontera Mexico–Estados Unidos)*. Mexico: El Colegio de México/El Colegio de la Frontera Norte, 2002.

———. "Organizational Experiences and Female Participation among Indigenous Oaxaqueños in Baja California," In Jonathan Fox and Gaspar Rivera-Salgado, eds., *Indigenous Mexican Migrants in the United States*, 101–124. La Jolla: UC San Diego, Center for Comparative Immigration Studies & Center for US-Mexican Studies, 2004.

———. *Mixtec Transnational Identity*. Tucson, AZ: University of Arizona Press, 2005a.

———. *Desde que tengo memoria: Narrativas de identidad en indigenas migrantes*. Tijuana: Colegio de la Frontera Norte, 2005b.

Velásquez, María Cristina. "Migrant Communities, Gender, and Political Power in Oaxaca." In *Indigenous Mexican Migrants in the United States*, edited by Jonathan Fox and Gaspar Rivera-Salgado, 483–94. La Jolla, CA: University of California, San Diego, Center for Comparative Immigration Studies & Center for U.S.–Mexican Studies, 2004.

Vila, Pablo. *Border Identifications: Narratives of Religion, Gender, and Class on the U.S.–Mexico Border*. Austin, TX: University of Texas Press, 2005.

Villafuerte Solís, Daniel and María del Carmen García Aguilar. "Crisis Rural y Migraciones en Chiapas," *Migración y Desarrollo*, no. 6, pp. 102–130, 2006.

Vizcaíno, Fernando. "Los cambios recientes del nacionalismo mexicano." In *La identidad nacional mexicana como problema político y cultural. Los desafíos de la pluralidad*, edited by Béjar, Raúl and Héctor Rosales. Mexico: Universidad Nacional Autónoma de México, Centro Regional de Investigaciones Multidisciplinarias, 2002.

"Vocational Education." Texas Educational Survey Commission Report 7. Austin, TX: Texas Educational Survey Commission, 1924.

Wade, Peter. *Race and Ethnicity in Latin America*. London: Pluto Press, 1997.

Waldinger, Roger D. "Immigrant 'Transnationalism' and the Presence of the Past." In *From Arrival to Incorporation: Migrants to the U.S. in a Global Era*, edited by Elliott R. Barkan, Hasia Diner, and Alan M. Kraut, 267–285. New York: New York University Press, 2008.

Waldinger, Roger D., Porzecanski, Rafael, and Thomas Soehl. "Caged: Expatriate Voting and Its Limits." Manuscript. University of California, Los Angeles, 2009.

Walsh, Casey."Región, raza y riego: el desarrollo del norte mexicano, 1910–1940" en *Nueva Antropología*, México, INAH, vol. XIX, núm. 64, enero-abril, 2005, pp. 53–73.

———. *Building the Borderlands: A Transnational History of Irrigated Cotton along the Mexico-Texas Border*. College Station, TX: Texas A&M University Press, 2009.

Warner, Michael. "Introduction." In *Fear of a Queer Planet. Queer Politics and Social Theory*, vii–xxxi. Minneapolis, MN: University of Minnesota Press, 1993.

Wasserman, Mark. *Capitalists, Caciques, and Revolution: The Native Elite and Foreign Enterprise in Chihuahua, Mexico, 1854–1911*. Chapel Hill, NC: University of North Carolina Press, 1984.

Waters, Mary C., Reed Ueda, and Helen B. Marrow, *The New Americans: A Guide to Immigration since 1965*. Cambridge, MA: Harvard University Press, 2007.

Weber, David. *Foreigners in Their Native Land: Historical Roots of the Mexican Americans*. Albuquerque, NM: University of New Mexico Press, 1973.

Weber, Devra. *Dark Sweat, White Gold: California Farm Workers, Cotton and the New Deal*. Berkeley: University of California Press, 1994.

———. "Un pasado no visto: perspectivas históricas sobre la migración binacional en pueblos indígenas." In *Migración, fronteras e identidades étnicas transnacionales*, edited by Laura Velasco Ortiz. Tijuana: Colegio de la Frontera Norte/Ed. Miguel Angel Porrúa, 2008.

Weil, Patrick. "Access to Citizenship: A Comparison of Twenty-Five Nationality Laws." In *Citizenship Today: Global Perspectives and Practices*, edited by Thomas Alexander Aleinikoff and Douglas B. Klusmeyer, 17–35. Washington, DC: Carnegie Endowment for International Peace, 2001.

Weintraub, Sidney. *A Marriage of Convenience: Relations between Mexico and the United States*. New York: Oxford University Press, 1990.

———. *Unequal Partners: The United States and Mexico*. Pittsburgh, PA: University of Pittsburgh Press, 2010.

Weise, Julie M. "Mexican Nationalisms, Southern Racisms: Mexicans and Mexican Americans in the U.S. South, 1908–1939." *American Quarterly* 60 (2008): 749–77.

Werner, Alejandro M., Rodrigo Barros, and Jose F. Ursúa. "The Mexican Economy: Transformation and Challenges." In *Changing Structure of Mexico: Political, Social, and Economic Prospects*. 2nd ed., edited by Laura Randall, 67–90. Armonk, NY: M. E. Sharpe, 2006.

Weyl, Walter E. "Labor Conditions in Mexico." *U.S. Department of Labor Bulletin*, no. 38. Washington, D.C.: Government Printing Office, 1902.

Whetten, Nathan L. *Rural Mexico*. Chicago: University of Chicago Press, 1948.

White, Hayden. "Interpretation in History" *New Literary History* 4 (Winter 1973), 281–314.

———. "The Question of Narrative in Contemporary Historical Theory." *History and Theory* 23 (February 1984), 1–33.

Whiteside, Ann. ""We Are the Explorers": Transnational Yucatec Maya-speakers Negotiating Multilingual California," University of California, Berkeley, Linguistics Dept., PhD Dissertation, 2006.

Willen, Sarah S. "Toward a Critical Phenomenology of 'Illegality': State Power, Criminalization, and Abjectivity among Undocumented Workers in Tel Aviv, Israel." *International Migration* 45, no. 3 (2007): 8–36.

Williams, Edward J. and Mitchell A. Seligson. *Maquiladoras and Migration: Workers in the Mexico–United States Border Industrialization Program*. Austin, TX: Mexico–U.S. Border Research Program, 1981.

Williams, Philip, Timothy Steigenga and Manuel Vásquez, eds. *A Place to Be: Brazilian, Guatemalan, and Mexican Immigrants in Florida's New Destinations*, New Brunswick: Rutgers University Press, 2009.

Willis, Rachel A. "Voices of Southern Mill Workers: Responses to Border Crossers in American Factories and Jobs Crossing Borders." In *The American South in a Global World*, edited by James L. Peacock, Harry L. Watson, and Carrie R. Matthews, 138–51. Chapel Hill, NC: University of North Carolina Press, 2005.

Wilson, Patricia M. *Exports and Local Development: Mexico's New Maquiladoras.* Austin, TX: University of Texas Press, 1992.

Wilson, Tamar Diana. *Women's Migration Networks in Mexico and Beyond.* Albuquerque, NM: University of New Mexico Press, 2009.

Wimberley, Ronald C., and Libby V. Morris. "The Regionalization of Poverty: Assistance for the Black Belt South?" *Southern Rural Sociology* 18 (2002): 294–306.

Winders, Jamie. "Nashville's New 'Sonido': Latino Migration and the Changing Politics of Race." In *New Faces in New Places: The Changing Geography of American Immigration*, edited by Douglas S. Massey, 249–73. New York: Russell Sage, 2008.

Winter, Nevin O. *Mexico and Her People of Today.* Boston: L. S. Page and Company, 1907.

Winton, George B. *Mexico Today: Social, Political and Religious Conditions.* New York: Missionary Education Movement, 1913.

Wishnie, M.J. "The Border Crossed Us: Current Issues in Immigrant Labor." *New York University Review of Law & Social Change* 28 (2004): 389–95.

Woodbridge, Dwight E. "La Cananea Mining Camp." *Engineering and Mining Journal* 82 (October 6, 1906): 623.

The World Almanac and Book of Facts. New York: Newspaper Enterprise Association, 1902.

World Bank. *Migration and Remittances Factbook.* http://econ.worldbank.org/WBSITE/ EXTERNAL/EXTDEC/EXTDECPROSPECTS/0,contentMDK:21352016~pagePK:64165 401~piPK:64165026~theSitePK:476883,00.html (accessed October 28, 2009).

Wozniacka, Gosia. "P'urhepecha Indians in Portland Hold Fast to Their Identity with a Trance like Dance." *The Oregonian*, December 29, 2008.

Wright, Gavin. *Old South, New South: Revolutions in the Southern Economy.* New York: Basic Books, 1986.

Wyman, Mark. *Round-Trip to America: The Immigrants Return to Europe, 1880–1930.* Cornell, NY: Cornell University Press, 1996.

Yancey, George A. *Who Is White? Latinos, Asians, and the New Black/Nonblack Divide.* Boulder, CO: Lynne Rienner, 2003.

Yanes, Rizo, Pablo, Virginia Molina, and Oscar González, eds. *Ciudad, Pubelos Indígenas y Etnicidad.* Mexico City: Universidad de la Ciudad de México/Dirección General de Equidad y Desarrollo Social, Gobierno del Distrito Federal, 2004.

Yañez, Augustín. *The Edge of the Storm (Al filo del agua).* Austin, TX: University of Texas Press, 1971.

Yu, Henry. "Los Angeles and American Studies in a Pacific World of Migrations." *American Quarterly* 56 (September 2004): 531–43.

Zabin, Carol, ed. "Mixtec Migrant Farm Workers in California Agriculture." *Working Paper,* no. 9. Davis, CA: California Institute of Rural Studies, 1992a.

——, ed. *Migración oaxaqueña e los campos agrícolas de California.* La Jolla, CA: University of California, San Diego, Center for U.S.–Mexican Studies, 1992b.

——. "U.S.–Mexico Economic Integration: Labor Relations and the Organization of Work in California and Baja California Agriculture." *Economic Geography* 73 (July 1997): 337–55.

Zabin, Carol, Michael Kearney, Anna García, David Runsten, and Carole Nagengast. *Mixtec Migrants in California Agriculture: A New Cycle of Poverty*. Davis, CA: California Institute of Rural Studies, 1993.

Zavella, Patricia. *Women's Work and Chicano Families: Cannery Workers of the Santa Clara Valley*. Ithaca, NY: Cornell University Press, 1987.

Zeskind, Leonard. "The New Nativism," *The American Prospect*, http://www.prospect.org/cs/articles?articleId=10485, October 23, 2005.

Zolberg, Aristide R. "The Archaeology of 'Remote Control.'" In *Migration Control in the North Atlantic World: The Evolution of State Practices in Europe and the United States from the French Revolution to the Inter-War Period*, edited by Andreas Fahrmeir, Olivier Faron, and Patrick Weil, 195–222. New York: Berghahn Books, 2003.

———. *A Nation by Design: Immigration Policy in the Fashioning of America*. Cambridge, MA, and New York: Harvard University Press and Russell Sage Foundation, 2006.

Zuñiga, Victor, and Rubén Hernández-León, eds. *New Destinations*. New York: Russell Sage, 2005a.

———. "Introduction." In *New Destinations: Mexican Immigration to the United States*, edited by Victor Zúñiga and Rubén Hernández-León, xi–xxix. New York: Russell Sage, 2005b.

Zuñiga Herrera et Al., eds., *Migración México–Estados Unidos: Implicaciones y retos para ambos países*. Mexico City: CIESAS, 2006.

Index

CPSIA information can be obtained
at www.ICGtesting.com
Printed in the USA
BVOW06s1927290917

496275BV00004B/13/P

9 780195 382228